HISTORY OF RELIGION

Myth and Religion of the North

Myth and Religion of the North

The Religion of Ancient Scandinavia

E. O. G. TURVILLE-PETRE

GREENWOOD PRESS, PUBLISHERS
WESTPORT, CONNECTICUT

Library of Congress Cataloging in Publication Data

Turville-Petre, Edward Oswald Gabriel.
  Myth and religion of the North.

  Reprint of the ed. published by Holt, Rinehart and
Winston, New York.
  Bibliography: p.
  Includes index.
  1. Mythology, Norse. 2. Scandinavia--Religion.
I. Title.
 [BL860.T8 1975]   293'.0948   75-5003
 ISBN 0-8371-7420-1

Originally published in 1964 by Holt, Rinehart and Winston, New York

Copyright © 1964 by E.O.G. Turville-Petre

Reprinted with the permission of Holt, Rinehart and Winston, Inc.

Reprinted in 1975 by Greenwood Press
A division of Congressional Information Service, Inc.,
88 Post Road West, Westport, Connecticut 06881

Printed in the United States of America

10 9 8 7 6 5

CONTENTS

PREFACE   ix

I   THE SOURCES   1
Introductory—Old Norse Poetry—Histories and Sagas—
Snorri Sturluson—Saxo Grammaticus

II   ÓÐINN   35
God of Poetry—Lord of the Gallows—God of War—Father of
Gods and Men—Óðinn and his Animals—Óðinn's Names—
Óðinn's Eye—The Cult of Óðinn—Woden-Wotan

III   THÓR   75
Thór and the Serpent—Thór and the Giants—Thór's Ham-
mer and his Goats—The Worship of Thór—Thór in the
Viking Colonies—Thór-Thunor—Conclusion

IV   BALDR   106
The West Norse Sources—Saxo—The Character of Baldr and
his Cult—Continental and English Tradition

V   LOKI   126

VI   HEIMDALL   147

VII   THE VANIR   156
The War of the Æsir and Vanir—Njörð—Freyr-Fróði-Nerthus-Ing—Freyja

VIII   LESSER-KNOWN DEITIES   180
Týr—Ull—Bragi—Iðunn—Gefjun—Frigg and others

IX   THE DIVINE KINGS   190

X   THE DIVINE HEROES   196
Ermanaric, Sigurð and the Burgundians—Starkað—Harald
Wartooth—Hadding

XI   GUARDIAN SPIRITS   221
The Dísir—Fylgja and Hamingja—Elves, Earth-Spirits,
Dwarfs

CONTENTS

XII   TEMPLES AND OBJECTS OF WORSHIP   236

XIII SACRIFICE   251

XIV   GODLESS MEN   263

XV   DEATH   269

XVI   THE BEGINNING OF THE WORLD AND ITS END 275

      ABBREVIATIONS   286

      NOTES   287

      BIBLIOGRAPHY   321

      INDEX   331

AUTHOR'S NOTE

In Old Norse þ has the value of *th* unvoiced; ð has that of *th* voiced. Q expresses a sound between *a* and *o*.

The asterisk is used to show that the form of the word is hypothetical or reconstructed.

vi

LIST OF ILLUSTRATIONS

1 Scene from Rogaland *Photo: University Museum, Oslo*

2 Helgafell *Photo: Guðmund Hannesson, Iceland*

3 Thórsmörk *Photo: Guðmund Hannesson, Iceland*

4 Thingvellir *Photo: Guðmund Hannesson, Iceland*

5 Burial mounds at Uppsala *Photo: ATA*

6 Church of Borgund *Photo: University Museum, Oslo*

7 Carved head of man *Photo: University Museum, Oslo*

8–11 Animal heads from the Oseberg ship-burial *Photos: University Museum, Oslo*

12 Image of female figure *Photo: National Museum, Denmark*

13 Image of a man from Rällinge *Photo: ATA*

14 Miniature figure from Iceland *Photo: National Museum, Iceland*

15 Bronze image probably of Thór *Photo: National Museum, Iceland*

16 Image, supposedly of Thór's hammer *Photo: National Museum, Iceland*

17 Thór's hammer *Photo: ATA*

18 Crucifix from Birka *Photo: ATA*

19 Bedpost from ship-grave of Gokstad *Photo: University Museum, Oslo*

20 Animal head from the Scheldt *Photo: British Museum*

21 Rune stone from Altuna *Photo: ATA*

22 Carved stone from Hunnestad *Photo: ATA*

23 Rune stone from Sønder-Kirkeby *Photo: National Museum, Denmark*

24–7 Picture stones from Gotland *Photos: ATA*

28 Rune stone from Eggjum *Photo: University Museum, Bergen*

29 Rune stone from Ledberg *Photo: ATA*

30 Rune stone from Rök *Photo: ATA*

31 Tapestry from the Oseberg grave *Photo: University Museum, Oslo*

32 Rune stone from Ramsundsberget *Photo: ATA*

33–4 Wood-carvings from church of Hylestad *Photos: University Museum, Oslo*

35 Wood-carving from Austad *Photo: University Museum, Oslo*

36 Panel or cart from Oseberg grave *Photo: University Museum, Oslo*

37 Panel on cart from Oseberg grave *Photo: University Museum, Oslo*

38 Cross slab from Isle of Man *Photo: Manx Museum and National Trust*

39 Wood-carving from churches of Urnes *Photo: University Museum, Oslo*

40 Reconstructed grave *Photo: National Museum, Iceland*

41 Grave objects from Ketilsstaðir *Photo: National Museum, Iceland*

42 Handle-seating of bucket from Oseberg grave *Photo: University Museum Oslo*

43 Gold foil from Rogaland *Photo: University Museum, Bergen*

44 Gundestrup bowl *Photo: National Museum, Denmark*

45 The Oseberg ship *Photo: University Museum, Oslo*

46 Gokstad burial chamber *Photo: University Museum, Oslo*

47 The Oseberg cart *Photo: University Museum, Oslo*

48 The Dejbjerg cart *Photo: National Museum, Denmark*

49 Bucket from the Oseberg grave *Photo: University Museum, Oslo*

PREFACE

Many years of experience as a teacher have shown me how strong is the interest in the pagan religion of the north, although no survey of it has been published in English for many years. The literature of this subject in other languages is enormous and consists, for the most part, of monographs, often published in learned journals. I have had to content myself with mentioning only a small part of this literature, and that to which I am especially indebted. Outstanding modern works are those of J de Vries and of G. Dumézil, to which reference will frequently be made in the following pages. Many have disputed the revolutionary conclusions of Dumézil, but the significance of his keen observations cannot be questioned. It is not too much to say that this scholar has restored our confidence in the validity of Norse tradition as it is expressed in the literary records of Iceland. In quite another way the studies of the late Magnus Olsen, who has investigated Scandinavian place-names in the light of ancient literature, have been no less important.

I am indebted to scholars, not only for their published works, but also for advice and for the long discussions which I have had with them. Among many, I would particularly like to name Einar Ól. Sveinsson, of Reykjavík and Dag Strömbäck of Uppsala, both of whom have listened patiently and criticised my views.

Joan Turville-Petre has helped me untiringly and made many suggestions which have influenced my work, and David Wilson of the British Museum has helped me with the illustrations, and so has my friend Dr. Kristján Eldjárn. I can hardly say how much I owe to Professor E. O. James, General Editor of this Series, for his encouragement and criticism. I am indebted also to Miss G. Feith for the care with which she has made the index. I would like finally to thank the Publishers and Printers for the work which they have done on a book which is in many ways difficult.

Oxford   E. O. G. Turville-Petre

CHAPTER ONE

THE SOURCES

Introductory—Old Norse Poetry—Histories and Sagas—Snorri Sturlason—Saxo Grammaticus

Introductory

THE RELIGION of the ancient Norsemen is one of the most difficult to describe, indeed far more so than are the older religions of Rome, Greece, Egypt, Israel, Persia or India. Reasons for this are not hard to appreciate. The followers of these southern religions could express their own thoughts in writing, and left hymns, myths and legends, but the pagan Norsemen knew little of writing.

In its obscurity, the Norse religion has much in common with that of the neighbouring Celts. Both of them have to be studied chiefly from poems and traditions written down generations after the pagan religion had been abandoned. The Celtic traditions were enshrined largely in the literature of medieval Ireland, and the Norse ones mainly in texts written in Iceland in the twelfth and especially in the thirteenth century. As Ireland was the storehouse of Celtic tradition, Iceland preserved that of the north. In other words, tradition survived longest on the periphery.

The history of Iceland is thus of some importance for the present study, and an extraordinary history it is. The first permanent settlement on that barren island was made late in the ninth century. The settlers came partly from the mixed Norse-Celtic colonies in Ireland and the western isles, but mainly from western Norway. Their chieftains left their homes, not for conquest, but rather, as medieval writers persistently tell, for political reasons. They wished to preserve their traditional, patriarchal way of life, rather than submit to the centralized form of government introduced by Harald Finehair (*c.* 885), for this was alien to them.[1] This may partly explain why the Icelanders preserved northern tradition as no other nation did.

The Icelanders adopted Christianity in the year 1000, so that paganism flourished among them for little more than a century. They began to write history early in the twelfth century and, in the course of the Middle Ages, they put down in writing, not only the traditions of their own people, but also those of other Scandinavian lands. The provenance and reliability of their work will be the subject of the following sections. For the present it must suffice to say that without the Icelandic texts, our knowledge of Norse heathendom would be but a fragment of what it is, and the myths, which will fill so large a part of this work would be practically unknown.

I remarked that the pagan Norsemen knew little of writing. Nevertheless, they possessed an alphabet which could well have been used for writing texts on parchment. In fact, the runic alphabet, as it is called, was used only for carving inscriptions on stone, metal and wood. The origin of this alphabet has not yet been decided, but it shows affinities with Latin, Greek and other European alphabets.[2] It was used throughout the Germanic world, and the oldest inscriptions found in Scandinavia are thought to date from the beginning of the third century AD. These early inscriptions are generally short, consisting of a word or two, or a name, or sometimes of groups of letters which defy interpretation, although they must have had a meaning for the masters who painstakingly carved them.

The runes were said to be divine (*reginkuðr*)[3]; Óðinn had acquired them, as it seems, from the world of death, and they had a mystical force. Their significance becomes plainer as time draws on. The inscription of some 200 runes found at Eggjum, in western Norway, and said to be written early in the eighth century, is plainly magical in content. A recent scholar claims to find a direct allusion to Óðinn in it.[4] The stone from Rök in Östergötland (Sweden) belongs to the early Viking Age and contains some 700 runic symbols.[5] It was set up by a father in memory of his son. It is partially in verse, and is thus a rare record of pre-Christian Swedish poetry and, indeed, of heroic tradition. Towards the end of the pagan period, we find inscriptions over graves in which a pagan deity is invoked directly in such terms as *Þórr vigi* (may Thór hallow, protect).[6]

The place-names of Scandinavia, studied in conjunction with the literature, are especially informative. From the point of view of religious history, those of Norway have been sifted most carefully, and particularly by M. Olsen,[7] to whose books and papers I shall frequently refer. Swedish place-names of religious interest have also been studied in some detail,[8] and provide much evidence of heathen cults, while those of Denmark are also valuable.[9] The place-names of Iceland, none older than the late ninth century, tell much about the distribution of temples and the worship of certain gods, of whom Thór was the foremost.[10]

Philologically many of the place-names are difficult to interpret, but one of their chief values is that they show something about gods and their cults before the Viking Age, when Iceland was peopled and our oldest poetic records took shape. They also show how eminent were some of the gods and goddesses, such as Ull (Ullinn),[11] Hörn (identified by Snorri with Freyja) who, for us, are only shadowy figures. Occasionally they preserve names of gods and goddesses of whose existence we should otherwise hardly know. Place-names also show how one god might be worshipped with another, or perhaps a god next to a goddess, and how some gods were favoured in one region and others elswhere. Much can also be learnt from place-names about the distribution of temples and more primitive places of worship at various ages.[12]

No branch of Norse study has made greater advances in the last century than the archaeology of prehistoric times, and the findings are proving of ever-growing value for the study of social conditions, art and religious history.

Interpretation of the various objects discovered must be left to specialists, but so many useful handbooks are available[13] that even a layman can form some ideas about their meaning.

Undoubtedly the finds give some insight into religious concepts of prehistoric periods which fall outside the scope of this book. J. Maringer,[14] in the present series, has described the rock-carvings and paintings of the so-called Arctic Stone Age and considered their relations with the older, naturalistic art of palæolithic Europe. The objects so naturalistically depicted by Stone Age artists are chiefly animals, especially reindeer and elk, occasionally bears and sometimes whales and fishes.

This is the art of a hunting people, and it is agreed that its purpose is either religious, magical or both. By naturalistic drawing man could gain power over his quarry; he might also invoke the deities who ruled the animal world.

Some believe that this arctic art derived from the palæolithic art of western Europe. Comparison with the art and practices of modern arctic and other primitive peoples may gradually explain its meaning. In short, it must be said that it is not yet possible to trace any link between it and the Old Norse religion with which we are now concerned.

The gradual introduction of agriculture, say 3000 BC, inevitably led to a more settled form of life, and a changed religious outlook. Gods of the hunt must give way to gods of the soil. The Megalith graves, evidently introduced from abroad in the third millennium BC, probably implied changed views about life after death. Whole families were interred together, generation after generation. Probably they were thought to live on in their dead bodies, much as they had done in this life.

A conception of this kind, of the living corpse, was widespread in Scandinavia in the Viking Age, but it cannot be known whether the beliefs of the Megalith people had any historical relations with those of the classical Norsemen. They could well have developed independently.

The so-called Battle-axe people invaded Scandinavia from the south and south-east, probably early in the second millennium BC. They were so-named from their characteristic weapon, and changed the civilization of Scandinavia radically. Megaliths gave way to single graves, again implying changed beliefs about death. The invaders blended with the Megalith people, until a unified culture was established.

Whatever their predecessors may have been, many specialists believe that the Battle-axe people were Indo-Europeans.[15] This means that they spoke an Indo-European language and had adopted something of the culture which has come to be called Indo-European.

Even if this is doubted, it is plain that an Indo-European people overran Scandinavia in prehistoric times. The original home of the Indo-Europeans is still disputed, but we may well believe that, before their language split up into its divergent groups, they had certain religious concepts which developed differently among different peoples. This may have some importance for the study of Norse religion.

J. Grimm[16] and many succeeding scholars have been astonished by certain similarities between myths of the Indo-European world from India to Iceland, and some of the religious practices resemble each other too closely to be explained by chance. Scholars have thus been led to think of a common Indo-European inheritance. It must, however, be allowed that the religious conceptions of the different groups of Indo-Europeans were influenced by those of other cultures with which they came into contact.

It is not known that Scandinavia suffered any major invasion after that of the Battle-axe people, and it may be supposed that there has been a certain cultural continuity since that time, although trade and travel kept the way open to foreign influences.

Such influences led to the Bronze Age, covering the period from about 1500 to 500 BC. This age was one of great wealth, especially in Denmark, as is shown by the priceless treasures which survive. For the study of religion, the rock-carvings are of greatest interest.[17] They are found over a wide area, particularly in Skåne and coastal districts. They are in many ways unlike the beautiful pictures of the Arctic Stone Age. Little attempt is made to reproduce nature, and there is little art. The figures are drawn schematically and the motives are very varied.

4

It would be rash for any but the specialized archaeologist to attempt to interpret these stylized pictures, but the absence of artistic endeavour may, in itself, give evidence of religious purpose. The most common of the figures depicted are ships, which are often surmounted with trees, and especially discs. Sometimes groups of men are seen together with one several times their size. Men are depicted swinging axes, fighting and shooting bows. Some men support circular objects. Marriage scenes are depicted and ithyphallic figures are common. The impression of footprints is also much favoured, while ploughs and ploughmen provide common motives.

If, as is now generally supposed, the pictures are religious symbols, they must belong to a people who lived largely by agriculture. The discs and concentric circles, whether supported by men, ships or standing alone, are thought to represent the sun. The ship, sometimes carrying a disc, could be carrying the sun over the sky, but it may also turn our thoughts to the numerous ships buried in howes and the descriptions of ship funerals from later ages. It could be bearing the dead to the Other World. In fact, there is little contradiction in this, for as I shall attempt to explain in later chapters, death and fertility are hardly separable.

The pictures of the Stone Age did not provide clear evidence of belief in personal gods, although this is not to deny that they were worshipped. There is greater reason to believe that the pictures of the Bronze Age reflect such beliefs. We see little men, sometimes accompanying a big man, generally ithyphallic, and sometimes carrying an axe. The big man may represent a god, and the tool may be a symbol of his divine power, even the forerunner of Thór's hammer, bringing thunder and rain. The footprints may be those of a god, believed to have been present on one or another occasion. The sun-discs and other objects depicted on the rocks may thus be symbols of the sun-god and of other divinities.

There are many other finds dating from the Bronze Age which must have a religious meaning. These are commonly precious objects planted in bogs or pools, as if as votive offerings. Among the most remarkable is the famous disc from Trundholm, in Zealand, dating from the early Bronze Age.[18] This consists of a richly decorated disc, standing on six wheels and drawn by a horse. The disc is, on one side, gilded. It may represent the sun and, if so, it represents a conception like that known from the *Vafþrúðnismál* (strs. 12–14) and from later sources. The horse, *Skinfaxi* (Shining maned) is said to draw the sun, or day, over men, while another horse, *Hrímfaxi* (Frost-maned), is said to draw the night. Perhaps the gilded side of the disc represents day, and the other night.

Heathen burial customs can be followed in detail to the end of the pagan period. These customs were undoubtedly founded on beliefs in the after-life, although the meaning may have been forgotten by many who practised them. In some cases they may even have been adopted as fashions from foreign lands, having little significance for the Scandinavians. As Snorri[19] was well aware, inhumation alternated with cremation and, in some regions, the two went on together. The Viking Age was the richest in grave-goods and the most splendid of all graves was that found at Oseberg in S.E. Norway, dating from the ninth century. Besides the ordinary necessities of life, this grave contained a magnificent yacht, a decorated chariot, a bucket adorned with a figure like Buddha, elaborate tapestries and the bones of about sixteen horses. This woman, who was perhaps a queen, was well provided for her journey to the Other World.[20] The grave-goods of Iceland have lately been studied in close detail.[21] Poor as they are these throw considerable light on conceptions of the after-life.

The Indo-European language split up into its different dialects, and with these went divergent cultures. The Germanic dialect is thought to have developed during the first millennium BC, and its home is sought in northern Germany or perhaps in Denmark. We can now speak, although with certain reservations, of a Germanic culture and religion, practised by all peoples who spoke the Germanic dialect until their religion gave way to Christianity. The Goths who, according to their own traditions, had emigrated from Scandinavia and settled in south Russia, followed some of the same religious practices which we know from Scandinavian records of the Middle Ages. Sparse as the literary records are, we know that some of the deities worshipped were called by the same names in all Germanic lands.

Among the closest neighbours of the Germanic peoples were, for a long time, the Celts, with whom their traditions had much in common. We may even suppose that some of the Celtic and Germanic traditions, such as those of Sigurð and Finn, developed in close proximity to each other.[22]

It was remarked that the Bronze Age was one of riches. The use of iron first became known in Scandinavia about 500 BC, and this was an age of poverty and deteriorating climate; it is likely that some of the northern regions of Scandinavia now became uninhabitable. There were probably political reasons for the decline in economy as well. The Celts had come to dominate the trade-routes of central Europe, thus isolating Scandinavia from the rich markets of the Mediterranean. Economic recovery hardly set in before the last centuries BC.

It was during this time that classical authorities first showed an interest in the north. In the fourth century BC Pytheas of Marseilles had sailed round Britain and from Shetland he had reached 'Thule', probably meaning Norway. Although Pytheas's work survives only in the excerpts of later writers, it contains a number of observations on the geography of the north and the life of the inhabitants. Pytheas did not, as far as is known, describe the religious practices of the northerners.

Cæsar[23] made some general statements about the social organization and religion of Germans, but he was struck chiefly by the differences between them and the Gauls. The Germans had no druids and no interest in sacrifice, worshipping only gods whom they could see, the sun, Vulcan and the moon. Such remarks probably apply to Germans on the Rhine, and certainly present a one-sided picture of religious practice and organization.

Tacitus in his *Germania*, written *c.* AD 98, presented a lucid picture of the civilization of continental Germans and threw some light on that of Scandinavia. It is now generally believed that he worked chiefly from older books, and especially from a lost *Bella Germaniae* of the Elder Pliny (*c.* AD 23–79), although he must also have gained information from merchants, soldiers and others who had penetrated Germany.[24]

Many of Tacitus's observations on the religion of the Germans help to explain those of Scandinavia as they are described in later times. His description of the cult of the goddess Nerthus on an island in the north is of especial importance (see Ch. VII, Njörð and Freyr-Froði-Nerthus-Ing).

As we approach the Middle Ages, the writings of the foreign observers grow richer. The Gothic historian, Jordanes (*c.* 550),[25] wrote of the history and traditions of his own people who, as he asserts, had come from Scandinavia. This slight history is an excerpt of a larger one written by Cassiodorus (*c.* 490–580), which is now lost. Cassiodorus, in his turn, followed older historians, most of whose work has perished.

Rimbert (died 888), priest and afterwards bishop, described the journeys of the missionary Anskar (died 865) among Danes and especially Swedes, first in 829 and again about the middle of the ninth century.[26] Although hagiographic in tone, the *Vita Anskarii* contains valuable observations on Scandinavian heathendom. In his *History of the Bishops of Hamburg* (*c.* 1070), Adam of Bremen wrote especially of Swedish paganism, giving detailed accounts of festivals, sacrifice and of the glorious temple of Uppsala.[27]

Vernacular writers of the Viking Age told of Norse heathens who had invaded their lands. Foremost of these are the English and Irish chroniclers. The Nestorian Chronicle throws some light on the practices of Norsemen settled in Russia. Arab travellers of the tenth century also left interesting descriptions of Norsemen whom they had met in Russia in the tenth century. The most remarkable of these Arab writers was Ibn Fadlán, who gave an unusually detailed account of a ship burial among Norsemen in Russia and of the beliefs which it expressed.[28]

The works of the foreign chroniclers are valuable because they described contemporaries, some of whom they had seen with their own eyes. But, in general, it must be admitted that few medieval foreigners took an objective interest in Norse heathendom. They regarded it as diabolical superstitition to be eradicated.

Scandinavian scholars of the present century frequently allude to the practices of Finns and especially of Lapps, believing that these may throw light on those of their Scandinavian neighbours. The Lappish and Finnish practices have been recorded only in recent centuries, but some specialists believe that Lapps and Finns were influenced by the religion of the Scandinavians as early as the Bronze Age.[29] They could thus preserve features of Norse religion in a form older than we would otherwise know them.

Popular practices, sayings and superstitions, which survive today, have been used by some scholars as sources of Old Norse religious history. They may sometimes confirm the conclusions which we draw from older records, and I shall refer to them here and there. It is, however, doubtful whether such sources have great independent value. Scandinavians, like other European peoples, suffered waves of foreign influences after they adopted Christianity. They were in contact with foreigners and they read books.

Old Norse Poetry

Among the richest sources for the study of northern heathendom are the poetic ones, many of which will be mentioned and some described in the following chapters, although a few introductory words should be said now.

The Old Norse poetry is of various ages, but hardly any of it is preserved except in manuscripts written in Iceland in the thirteenth and later centuries. It falls broadly into two classes, called the 'Eddaic' and the 'scaldic'. Inappropriate as these terms are,[1] the differences between the two kinds of poetry will be discussed below.

The Eddaic poetry owes its name to a small, unpretentious manuscript, commonly known as the 'Elder' or 'Poetic Edda',[2] in which most of the poems of this class are preserved. This manuscript was written in Iceland in the later decades of the thirteenth century, or about 1170, but it derives from one or more lost manuscripts written early in that century.[3] In fact the name 'Edda' did not originally belong to this book, but to Snorri's Edda, which will be discussed later. It was first applied to the 'Elder Edda' in the seventeenth century.

The Eddaic poetry is distinguished from the scaldic largely in its form. It is composed in three distinct measures, of which there are minor variants,[4] but all of them are rhythmical and alliterative, and the syllables are not strictly counted. The Eddaic poetry is thus of the same type as Old English and German poetry, as exemplified in the 'Fight at Finnsburh' and the 'Lay of Hildebrand'.

In substance, and it is this alone which concerns us now, the Eddaic poetry is chiefly of two kinds, mythical and heroic. The one kind describes the world of gods, and the other that of such legendary heroes as Sigurð, Helgi and Ermanaric. The distinction, mythical and heroic, may be found unwarrantably sharp. It will be seen in later chapters that some of the earthly heroes were originally divine, or lived against a background of myth.

The poems about gods are, in their turn, of several kinds. Some of them are narrative, telling of the gods' fates and adventures, and these may be compared with the heroic lays. Others are didactic and, in them, mysteries of the universe, of gods and men, their origins and end are disclosed.

The most renowned of the divine poems is the *Vǫluspá* (Sibyl's Prophecy). There is no poem in early Germanic literature of such scope. As presented, it is spoken by a sibyl (*vǫlva*) born before the world began. She addresses men and gods, and particularly Óðinn. The sibyl tells about primeval chaos and its giants, the beginning of the world and of men. She describes the age of the youthful, innocent gods, their trials and corruption and finally the impending doom in the Ragnarök (Doom of the gods).

Although the subject of the *Vǫluspá* is pagan, few would now deny that it is coloured by Christian symbols, and particularly in the description of the Ragnarök.[5] This had led to the conclusion that it was composed about the beginning of the eleventh century, when men were turning from the old religion to the new.

While the *Vǫluspá* stands supreme as a literary monument, it must be treated with reserve as a source of mythology. It has a logical unity lacking in many poems of the Edda. It must be judged as the work of a mystic, an individual who did not necessarily express views on the fates of gods and men which were popular in his time.[6]

Among the narrative poems, the *Skírnismál* (Words of Skírnir), telling of Freyr's courtship of his bride from the giant world, will be much quoted in the body of this book. The *Þrymskviða* will also be cited several times. This is a burlesque, telling how Thór's hammer had fallen into the hands of giants. The giant (Thrym) would restore it only if he could have Freyja as his bride. Therefore the virile Thór must go to the giant-land disguised as the goddess Freyja. There he recovered his hammer and overcame the giants.

Two of the didactic poems, the *Grímnismál* (Words of Grímnir) and the *Vafþrúðnismál* (Words of Vafthrúðnir) are especially valuable as sources of myth. Both of them are presented in frames, and Óðinn appears in disguise. In the *Grímnismál*, using the name Grímnir (Masked), he comes to an earthly king Geirröð. The King, believing that Grímnir was a wizard, had him seized and tortured between two fires, where he thirsted for eight days until the King's son took pity on him and brought him drink. In this state, the god spoke as if he saw visions. He described dwellings of many gods. Óðinn's own home, Valhöll, is described in two passages of the *Grímnismál*, and these are the only detailed accounts of it which survive in early poetry. Óðinn later spoke of rivers flowing through the worlds of gods, men and the dead, and of the world tree, Yggdrasill, its roots and torments. He spoke again of the formation of the world out of the flesh, blood and bones of the giant Ymir. Finally the accursed King Geirröð fell on his sword and died.

The *Grímnismál* includes many beautiful strophes. In parts it may seem disjointed, and the text may contain some interpolations, but, in a perceptive study, M. Olsen[7] showed that it has a fundamental artistic unity.

The *Vafþrúðnismál* is equally valuable as a work of art and as a source. The disguised Óðinn visits the aged giant, Vafthrúðnir, wishing to test his wisdom. First the giant asks Óðinn a few questions about the cosmos, and then god and giant settle down to a contest of wits, on which each wagers his head.

It is Óðinn's turn to ask questions, and the giant answers seventeen of them correctly. He tells of the origin of earth, of heaven, moon, sun, of worlds of the dead, of life in Valhöll, of the Ragnarök and its sequel. Óðinn's eighteenth question defeats him. He discloses his own identity by asking what Óðinn had whispered into Baldr's ear before he went to the funeral pyre. None but Óðinn can answer this, and so the giant's head was forfeit.[8]

Whatever its age, there is no reason to doubt the unity of the *Vafþrúðnismál*. Whether the work of a devout pagan or of a Christian antiquarian, it is a short handbook of myth.

In the *Lokasenna* (Flyting of Loki), gods and goddesses are assembled at a feast in the hall of the sea-god, Ægir, and Loki arrives uninvited. He hurls abuse at one after another; he boasts of his own evil deeds and reminds goddesses of their illicit love-affairs, even with himself. While

Loki's abuse is often crude, it generally has a sound basis in myth. It was not without reason that he accused Freyja of incest (see Ch. VII, Njörð and Freyja), and probably not when he boasted that Óðinn has once been his foster-brother.

Another flyting poem is the *Hárbarðsljóð*, in which Thór and Óðinn confront each other. Óðinn, this time under the name Hárbarð (Grey-beard), appears as a ferryman, while Thór, on his way from the giant world in the east, asked for a passage over the water. The ferryman was stubborn and abusive, and the two gods began to boast, each of his own achievements. Hárbarð boasted chiefly of his amorous successes, of his magical powers and of how he incited princes to fight. It was he who took the fallen princes, while the thralls were left for Thór. Thór, in his turn, told how he had beaten the giants. The whole world would be peopled by them were it not for him.

The particular interest of the *Hárbarðsljóð* is that it emphasizes the differences between the two foremost gods of the hierarchy. On the one side stands the cunning trickster, Óðinn, promoter of war; on the other the valiant Thór, who protects our world from the giants.

In the Codex Regius, the chief manuscript of the Edda, the title *Hávamál* is applied to a collection of about 164 strophes. In applying this title, the redactor showed that he regarded all of these strophes as the words of Óðinn, the High One (Hávi). Whether he was right or wrong, it is plain that the collection includes some six poems, or frag-ments, about various subjects and of devious origin.

The first eighty strophes of the *Hávamál* are not strictly mythical, but rather gnomic. They embody cynical rules of conduct such as we might expect in the Viking Age of a society in the throes of social and political upheaval (see Ch. XIV). In other sections Óðinn tells of his amorous experiences; how one woman had fooled him, and how he had fooled another, robbing her of the precious mead of poetry (see Ch. II). In another section (Strs 138–145), Óðinn tells how he hung for nine nights on the windswept tree, and thus acquired runes and poetry and much of his occult wisdom. Obscure as these strophes are, they give some in-sight into the mystical aspects of the pagan religion.

The last section of the *Hávamál* (Strs. 146–63), the so-called *Ljóðatal* (list of songs) consists of a list of magic songs of which the speaker is master. He can blunt the weapons of his enemies, break his bonds, turn a javelin in flight, get the better of witches and make the hanged man talk. In the final strophe the title *Hávamál* is used in verse, suggest-ing that it is correctly applied at least to this last section.

As already said, the heroic lays of the Edda also contain much mythi-cal matter. This applies especially to the lays of the two Helgis, in which

Óðinn and his valkyries play a decisive part.[9] The so-called *Sigrdrífu-mál* (Words of Sigrdrífa), in which Sigurð awakens the sleeping valkyrie, contains gnomic utterances like those in the first section of the *Hávamál*, as well as a list of the magical uses of runes. Poems about the young Sigurð also present the hero as the favourite of Óðinn (see Ch. X).

If we could know the ages of the mythical lays and where they originated, we should be better able to evaluate them as sources of religious history. As I have said, such lays are scarcely to be found except in Icelandic manuscripts. Most of them are preserved in the Codex Regius of the later thirteenth century, and some in the related fragment (commonly called 'A') of the beginning of the fourteenth century.[10]

These manuscripts are commonly agreed to derive from one or more written in Iceland early in the thirteeth century.

In recent years, the Norwegian scholar, D. A. Seip, has attempted to show that the manuscript sources, at least of many of the Eddaic lays, were Norwegian, and were written in the twelfth century.[11] Such a conclusion, if accepted, would revolutionize our conceptions of the development of Norwegian and Icelandic literatures. Seip's arguments are brilliant and persuasive, but few scholars have been able to agree with his conclusions.[12]

Probably the lays were first written in Iceland early in the thirteenth century, and the redactors were guided by the antiquarian interests of their age. But this does not show that all the lays originated in Iceland. The *Vǫluspá*, as stated above, seems to date from the beginning of the eleventh century. The symbolism in it is coloured, not only by Christian legend, but also by the scenery of Iceland, its volcanoes, sandy beaches, even its midnight sun. It expresses the religious conceptions, not of a people, but of one Icelander.

The *Hávamál* was mentioned, and parts of it will be discussed in later chapters.[13] The first eighty strophes, if they are to be assigned to an age and a country, should probably be assigned to viking Norway. One of the strophes is quoted by the Norwegian Eyvind the Plagiarist in his memorial lay on Hákon the Good, composed about 960.[14] The mystical passages of the *Hávamál* (Strs. 138–164) must also belong to the Heathen Age, and their home is likely to be Norway, where the cult of runes was old and deep.

There may be little dispute about the ages and origins of the *Vǫluspá* and of various sections of the *Hávamál*, but there is little agreement about other lays. The prototypes of some of the heroic lays, such as the *Hamð-ismál* are believed to be continental, and, in some cases, to go back to the Dark Ages,[15] but this cannot be said of the extant mythical lays. Although the continental Germans certainly had myths, and probably incorporated them in lays,[16] the mythical lays found in the Icelandic manuscripts can hardly derive from these ancient Germanic ones. It might well be argued that some of them originated in Sweden, Denmark, and in the viking colonies of the British Isles.[17]

A number of the mythical lays were quoted by Snorri in the *Gylfaginning*. These include the *Vǫluspá*, *Grímnismál*, *Vafþrúðnismál* and, to a lesser extent, *Skírnismál*, *Lokasenna* and *Hávamál*. Whether or not Snorri had such lays in written form, it is plain that he believed them to be very old. This suggests that even the latest of them were composed some generations before Snorri's time.

In general, it must be admitted that critics fall back on subjective arguments in dating the mythological lays. While the one says that *Þrymskviða* was composed in the tenth century, others argue that it dates from the twelfth century or the thirteenth, or even that it is the work of Snorri Sturluson.[18] *Rígsþula* is said by some to belong to the tenth century, while others assign it to the late thirteenth.[19] It may be hoped that detailed analysis of the language, metres and syntax will give us clearer ideas about the ages and homes of the mythical lays than we have now.[20]

When we study the myths, the ages of the poems may be of less importance than might appear at first sight. The survival of pagan tradition as late as the thirteenth century is well proved by the works of Snorri. Even if Snorri were the author of the *Þrymskviða*, its value as a source would not be altogether vitiated.

The surviving mythical lays are only a fraction of those which once existed. The extant lays contain material of many different kinds, whose authors had different aims. While some of the lays are didactic, and some may contain relics of ritual poetry, others, like the *Þrymskviða*, are designed for entertainment. In many, the author's object is primarily artistic. The lays are not hymns, and the Edda is not a sacred book.

The Eddaic lays reflect the myths in which their authors believed, or else treasured as hereditary tradition. But the sharp contrast between the lays and the historical records suggests that the lays give a one-sided picture of religious life. In the lays, Thór, the bold defender of Miðgarð, is put in the background, and even laughed at, while Óðinn reigns supreme. This may help to show the social conditions under which poetry of this kind developed. Óðinn is not only the god of poetry; he is also god of princes and warriors.

As noted above, the term 'scaldic', as used today, has no basis in Old Norse, but derives only from the word *skáld* (*skald*), meaning 'poet'.[21]

The modern usage is a loose one and a precise definition of scaldic poetry is hardly to be found. We think commonly of the difference between the scaldic and the Eddaic as one of form. While the Eddaic lays are in free, rhythmical metres, in the scaldic poetry every syllable is counted and measured. Not everyone would accept this definition, for the Eddaic and the scaldic differ also in substance.

The Eddaic poetry is all anonymous, telling of gods and of heroes who lived in a distant past. Most of the scaldic poetry is ascribed to named authors. Its subject is not, in the first place, myth or legend, but rather contemporary history. The scalds praise a chieftain for his valour and generosity, either during his lifetime or in a memorial lay made after his death. They commemorate a battle between princes of Scandinavia or the British Isles, or even a scrap between Icelandic farmers.

The measures used by the scalds do not always differ from those of the Eddaic poets. One of the better-known scalds was Thorbjörn Hornklofi, a favourite of Harald Finehair (died c. 945). His most famous work is the *Haraldskvæði* (Lay of Harald) or *Hrafnsmál* (Words of the Raven), of which a considerable part survives.[22] This lay is presented in a frame, like some of the Eddaic ones. It consists of a dialogue between a valkyrie and a raven. The bird, ever since he was hatched, had followed the young king, rejoicing in the carrion left on the battlefield. This may be called a scaldic poem, but Thorbjörn uses, not the syllabic measures typical of scaldic poetry, but the simpler measures of the Edda. At the same time, he uses some abstruse imagery generally associated with scaldic poetry.[23] The same could be said of the *Eiríksmál*, a lay made in memory of Eirík Bloodaxe, killed in England about the middle of the tenth century, as well as of the *Hákonarmál*, composed by Eyvind the Plagiarist in memory of Hákon the Good, who died in Norway a few years later. These two lays are especially interesting in the pictures which they give of the reception of dead chiefs in Valhöll.[24]

The poems so far mentioned could be called 'half-scaldic', and the same could be said of the *Ynglingatal* (List of the Ynglingar), in which Thjóðólf of Hvin, another contemporary of Harald Finehair, traced the descent of Norwegian princes to the illustrious Ynglingar, kings of the Swedes.[25]

The Eddaic poetry, the half-scaldic and the strictly scaldic went on together. Thjóðólf of Hvin, Thorbjörn Hornklofi and Eyvind the Plagiarist also left poetry in strict scaldic form.

We must consider briefly what this form is. As already said, this is a syllabic poetry. There are many different measures, but the one most widely used was the Court Measure (*Dróttkvætt*). The lines consisted of six syllables, of which three were stressed. Each line ended in a trochee, and the lines were bound by alliteration in pairs. The measure was strophic, and the strophe consisted of eight lines, divided by a deep cæsura into half-strophes of four lines. The scaldic verses are often transmitted in half-strophes, and it is likely that the half-strophe of four lines was the original unit. Internal rime and consonance are employed, generally according to strict rules.[26]

Syllable-counting was not characteristic of Germanic poetry, and its introduction was a break with the Germanic tradition. For this and other reasons, some have believed that the scaldic technique was an innovation devised in the ninth century under foreign influences, notably medieval Latin and Irish.[27]

The first to whom poetry in scaldic form is ascribed was Bragi Boddason, the Old. Bragi's chief surviving poem is the *Ragnarsdrápa* (Lay of Ragnar) of which twenty strophes and half-strophes are preserved in Snorri's *Edda*. The poet describes the pictures painted on a shield said to be given to him by Ragnar Loðbrók. These pictures were scenes from legend and myth; they included Gefjun's plough[28] and Thór's struggle with the World Serpent.[29]

We read in several sources of a god of poetry, called Bragi. It will be suggested in a later chapter that the historical Bragi devised the scaldic form of poetry, and that he was promoted to godhead after death.[30]

Several later scalds followed Bragi's tradition in describing pictures of mythical scenes. In the *Haustlǫng*, which is also a 'shield' poem, Thjóðolf of Hvin described the rape of Iðunn[31] and Thór's battle with the giant Hrungnir.[32] In the elaborate *Þórsdrápa* (Lay of Thór), of the late tenth century, Eilíf Guðrúnarson described Thór's visit to the giant Geirrøð.[33] This lay may also be based on pictures. Úlf Uggason in his *Húsdrápa* (House Lay), composed late in the tenth century, described panels carved on the inner timbers of a house in Iceland. The scenes depicted included the cremation of Baldr[34] and the fight between Loki and Heimdall for possession of the Brísing necklace.[35]

Egill Skalla-Grímsson (c. 910–990) was, without doubt, the greatest master of the scaldic art. He was one of those tenth-century Icelanders who had travelled far and seen much. He had lived as a viking, fighting battles in England and other lands. His verses are not generally about religious subjects, but they are rich in allusion to myth, and especially to Óðinn, god of poetry.

The earliest scalds, or court poets, of whom we read, were Norwegians, although their work is preserved chiefly in Icelandic manuscripts. It is strange that after Eyvind the Plagiarist (died c. 990) we hear little more of Norwegian scalds, and their successors were nearly all Icelanders.[36] One of the foremost of these was Einar Skálaglamm, a younger friend of Egill Skalla-Grímsson. His chief work is the *Vellekla* (Gold-dearth), made in praise of Hákon the Great (died 995). Hákon, who was an ardent pagan, had expelled the half-Christian sons of Eirík Bloodaxe, and Einar, in magnificent language, celebrates the restoration of temples and sacrifice.

Hallfreð, nicknamed the troublesome poet, was the particular favourite of the Christian king, Ólaf Tryggvason (died AD 1000), who, with difficulty, converted him to the new religion. In some of his verses, Hallfreð expresses his regret at deserting the heathen gods of his ancestors.[37]

The Icelandic Family Sagas contain numerous scaldic verses, made for one occasion or another. In their kennings these are often valuable as sources of mythology. Some of those dating from the period of the Conversion have religious themes. A woman poet, Steinunn, praised the god Thór for wrecking the ship of the missionary, Thangbrand (c. 999).[38]

From the present point of view the interest of the scaldic poetry is largely in its diction. All poets use periphrases, but the scalds developed these periphrases, or kennings as they are called, in ways of which other Germanic poets had not dreamed. Any poet might call the sea the 'land of waves', but when a poet calls it the 'blood of Ymir', the 'wounds of the giant's neck', it is plain that he is addressing hearers to whom myth was familiar.

The kenning, as has sometimes been said, may present a myth in miniature. Many of the kennings for poetry are based upon the myth of its origin, or of Óðinn's theft of it.[39] It may be called the 'blood of Kvasir', 'rain of dwarfs', 'theft of Óðinn', the 'hallowed cup of the raven-god'.

Scaldic poetry dates from the ninth century to the thirteenth (and even later). Most of it is assigned to named poets, whose dates are approximately known. It has been said that the mythological kennings declined early in the eleventh century with the introduction of Christianity, to revive as meaningless phrases about the middle of the twelfth century.[40] Such a conclusion should be accepted with reserve. Much of the surviving poetry dating from 995–1030 was dedicated to the fanatical Christian kings, Ólaf Tryggvason and Ólaf the Saint, who understandably disliked pagan imagery.[41] The fragments left by humbler Icelandic poets of the period, e.g. Gizur Gullbrárskald and Hofgarða-Ref,[42] suggest that pagan tradition was cherished and that it was not broken.[43] This may partly explain how the pagan myths survived in Iceland until the thirteenth century.[44]

Much of the scaldic poetry is preserved in the works of Snorri and in the sagas of kings and of Icelanders. Every reader must wonder whether the ascription to this or that poet is correct. In some cases it is clearly not. Few would believe that all the verses ascribed to Grettir Ásmundarson (died c. 1031) were really his work, and many have questioned the authenticity of the verses ascribed to Gísli Súrsson (died *c.* 978).[45] But few have doubted that many verses are correctly ascribed to the Norwegian and Icelandic scalds of the ninth and tenth centuries. Even if some of the verses are spurious, they can, in many cases, be proved by linguistic argument to be much older than the prose texts in which they are embedded. Without explanation, many of the scaldic verses would be meaningless, and could not live. It follows that many of the explanations of these verses, found in prose sources, whether correct or not, date from an early period. The scaldic poetry is one of the most valuable sources of myth.

Histories and Sagas

Comparatively little history was written in medieval Scandinavia, except in Iceland. History was first written in that country about the end of the eleventh century, and the first work of which we hear was a history of the kings of Norway, written by the aristocratic priest, Sæmund Sigfússon (1056–1133). We read that Sæmund had studied in France, most probably in Paris, and it is likely that continental models prompted him to undertake this work. It is nearly certain that Sæmund wrote in Latin. His history is lost, but references to it in later works, and occasional quotations from it, show that it was a concise history, and suggest that Sæmund laid great emphasis on the chronology of the kings' lives.[1]

Sæmund's younger contemporary, Ari Thorgilsson (1067–1148) is of far greater significance. He too was a priest and was the first to write history in Icelandic or any Scandinavian language. Ari's surviving *Libellus Islandorum* (*Íslendingabók*) is a summary history of Iceland from the settlement in the late ninth century to his own time. He wrote, in the first place, for the bishops of Iceland, and shows especial interest in the Conversion of the Icelanders (AD 1000) and in the history of the early Church. In fact the extant version of this book is a second one, but some later historians, and especially Snorri, show that they knew the book in its original form. Ari is not a romancer, but writes as a scientific historian, stating and weighing his evidence.[2]

The 'Book of Settlements' (*Landnámabók*)[3] is a much more detailed history of Iceland, district by district and family by family. There are good reasons to believe that this was largely Ari's work, although it survives today only in versions of the thirteenth and later centuries, notably those of Sturla Thórðarson (died 1284), of Hauk Erlendsson (died 1334), in the fragmentary *Melabók* and in derivatives of these.[4] The *Landnámabók* is of immense value as a source of social and religious history. In one version (that of Hauk), it includes the opening clauses of the heathen law, introduced in Iceland about AD 930. These clauses provide for the administration of temples, for the position of the *goði* (priest and chieftain), for sacrifice and for the form of the oath sworn in the names of Freyr, Njörð and the all-powerful god. It is also laid down that none may approach the shores of Iceland with a dragon-head on his ship, lest the guardian-spirits should take fright.[5]

The *Landnámabók* must have taken many years to compile and much painstaking research, and it is likely that Ari had collaborators. A certain Kolskegg, probably an older contemporary of Ari, is named in the text as if he were author or source of some chapters about the east and south-east of the country.[6]

There are some other scraps or *schedae* which may also be ascribed to Ari. One of these is a summary life of the chieftain Snorri Goði (died 1031), which was an important source for the *Eyrbyggja Saga.*[7] The *Droplaugar Sona Saga* and the *Bjarnar Saga Hítdœlakappa*[8] are also believed to be based partly on summary lives written in the twelfth century, and there were perhaps many more of these than we know of now. If so, they may give us confidence in the historicity of Family Sagas of the thirteenth century.

Certain histories in Latin and in the vernacular are also ascribed to Norwegians of the twelfth century. One of them, the *Historia de anti- quitate regum norwagensium* was written by a monk, Theodricus (Theodo- ricus).[9] It is a synoptic history of the kings from the ninth century to the twelfth, and is dedicated to Eysteinn, Archbishop of Niðaróss (died 1188). It is of no great importance for the present study, but it is interest- ing to notice how Theodricus pays tribute to Icelanders, who had pre- served memories of antiquity in ancient verses. He can only refer to scaldic verses about the kings of Norway.

The Icelandic sagas, to which we must now turn, fall into several groups. The oldest of them, written about 1170–90 treat chiefly of the two Christian kings of Norway, Ólaf the Saint (died 1030), and Ólaf Tryggvason (died 1000). These are markedly clerical works. Their form is modelled partly on that of medieval lives of saints, of which a number were known in Iceland at that time. The material, on the other hand, is drawn much from scaldic poetry and other traditional sources.

These early biographies of kings are of less interest from the present point of view than are some of the later ones, and particularly those of Snorri, who made copious use, not only of older histories, but also of scaldic poetry and tradition (see Snorri Sturluson, below).

The Icelandic Family Sagas are among the most important of our sources and, at the same time, the most difficult to evaluate. They were mostly written in the thirteenth century,[10] and tell of the lives of Ice- landers who lived in the tenth and early in the eleventh century. It used to be said that many of them were composed almost at the time when the events described took place, and were transmitted orally, and nearly without change, until they were written down. If this were so these sagas could be trusted implicitly as records of history, but few believe it now. The Family Sagas must be studied as the product of a literary movement of the thirteenth century, perhaps the most astonishing in medieval Europe. They are often realistic, and this has led many to believe that they are historically exact.

In recent years, reaction against such views has gone far. We read sometimes that these sagas are fiction and no more, and that their authors' concepts of pagan religion were based only on Christian outlook and prejudice.[11]

D. Strömbäck[12] has shown with telling examples how deeply the descriptions of pagan belief found in the sagas could be influenced by Christian legend. Nevertheless, the survival of scaldic poetry with its allusive diction implied a survival of pagan tradition. Moreover, some sagas, at least, drew on summary histories written early in the twelfth century, when memories of the Heathen Age still lived.

The Icelanders were converted to Christianity on one day in the year AD 1000, although pagan practices were permitted for some time afterwards.[13] It is not extravagant to suppose that memories of heathendom lived on until, with the remarkable learning of the twelfth and thirteenth centuries, they acquired an antiquarian value.[14]

We should not speak of Family Sagas in any general way. Each one is governed by the aims, methods and sources of its author. Some authors, relying on the written and oral sources which they knew, aimed to write history, and this may more often be true of the older than of the later ones. For some the object was to entertain or to compose a work of art.

Few of the Family Sagas describe religious beliefs and practices in close detail. An exception is the *Eyrbyggja Saga*, whose author gave an account of the worship of Thór among the settlers of Iceland. He also left a detailed description of a temple and of the sacrifices conducted in it, as well as narratives illustrating conceptions of death which, as he believed, were current in the Heathen Age. As already remarked, this author used older histories, when these were available, as well as numerous scaldic poems and local traditions. His history may not be exact, but he may yet draw a fair picture of life and religion in pagan Iceland.

Some sagas, and especially the later ones, have been proved to be mainly, or even wholly fictitious. An example is the famous *Hrafnkels Saga*, one of the most realistic and convincing of the whole group.[15] It has been shown that some of the leading characters in this saga never existed. In outline the story must be fiction, but this need not imply that the author created it out of nothing. The *Hrafnkels Saga* includes an exceptionally interesting account of the worship of the god, Freyr, and of that god's relations with a dedicated stallion. Comparative study shows that the author based this on reliable sources, whether written works now lost, poetry or amorphous tradition. For the study of religious history it is not important whether Hrafnkell, the hero of the saga, worshipped Freyr in the manner described, or whether others did so.[16]

Although most of the Family Sagas contain few details of religious life, they allude to many pagan practices. They tell of such practices as sprinkling the new-born child with water, naming him, and occasionally dedicating him to a god. They tell of temples, their administration and of dues payable for their upkeep. In contrast to the Eddas, they suggest that Thór was the favourite god of the Icelanders, and next to him came the fertility god, Freyr. Presiding over all is an impersonal, unapproachable fate.

Besides Family Sagas, we have to consider another group of sagas as religious sources. These are sometimes called in English 'Heroic Sagas' and, in Icelandic, *Fornaldar Sögur*.[17] They are of many different kinds but, to define them in the simplest words, they are tales about heroes who were supposed to have lived before Iceland was peopled in the ninth century. They contain little history, but much tradition, some of it ancient. Some of them tell of heroes of the Dark Ages, such as Ermanaric, Hrólf Kraki, and others of viking heroes, such as Ragnar Loðbrók and his notorious sons. Others are based chiefly on medieval folklore and, in many, these three kinds of material are combined.

In their extant form, few Heroic Sagas can be older than the second half of the thirteenth century, and many date from the fourteenth century. There are some exceptions. The *Skjǫldunga Saga*, a history of the mythical and legendary kings of the Danes, was known to Snorri, and Snorri himself compiled the *Ynglinga Saga* (see Snorri Sturluson, below).

In some cases it is possible to see how Heroic Sagas were compiled. The *Vǫlsunga Saga* is based largely on lays about Sigurð and his kinsmen preserved in the Poetic Edda, and on some which have fallen from that book.[18] Its introductory chapters contain much mythological matter drawn from unknown sources. The *Heiðreks Saga*, which also has much mythological interest, is based largely on verses, many of which are quoted in its text. Some of these verses are believed to be among the oldest preserved in Norse, while others probably date from the twelfth-century.[19]

Although most Heroic Sagas are written in a late form and style, some have a preliterary history which can be followed comparatively closely. It is related in the *Þorgils Saga ok Hafliða* how two stories were told at a wedding feast held in western Iceland in AD 1119. In one of these there was a viking, Hröngvið, and a warrior king, Óláf. It was told how the cairn of a berserk had been plundered. A certain Hrómund Gripsson also appeared in the story, and many verses went with it. The man who told this story is named as Hrólf of Skálmarnes, and it is said in the text that he had composed it (*saman setta*) himself. Since Hrólf is remembered as a poet, we may believe that he had composed the verses as well.

This passage in the *Þorgils Saga* is difficult to interpret. Its age and veracity have been questioned, but recent commentators have regarded it as a genuine record.[20] The story told by Hrólf may have some slight basis in history, for Hrómund appears in genealogies as if he had lived in Telemark in the eighth century. But, although there can have been little history in it, Hrólf's story survived orally for some two centuries. It appears in a sequence of verses (*Griplur*), probably of the fifteenth century, which are believed to be based on a saga of the fourteenth century.

The especial interest of this passage from the *Þorgils Saga* is that it shows something about a Heroic Saga in preliterary form. Much of it was in verse, and in subject it was plainly related to some of the lays of the Edda, notably those of Helgi and the lost *Káruljóð*.[21]

Saxo, writing early in the thirteenth century (see Saxo, below) also retold much that he had heard about gods and heroes of old, and much of this was in verse. The myths and legends were, in many cases, exceedingly ancient, but Saxo treated his sources freely and put his own interpretation upon them. The form in which the stories are presented in Heroic Sagas is a late, romantic one. These sagas were written chiefly for entertainment. In so far as they represent pagan myth and tradition, they bring us back to the world of the Eddaic lays. Óðinn, appearing one-eyed, or disguised, is often the decisive figure.

Snorri Sturluson

The works of Snorri Sturluson (*c.* 1179–1241) have unique importance for the study of Norse heathendom, or rather Norse myths. They will often be quoted in the following pages, but have been discussed so fully in many books which are easily available[1] that little need be said of them here.

Snorri came of a powerful family of northern Iceland, but at the age of two he was taken to Oddi, where he was brought up by Jón Loptsson

(1124–97), the most eminent chieftain of his age. Jón and his family, the Oddaverjar, as they were called, dominated the cultural and political scenes of Iceland throughout the twelfth century, and Snorri's profound learning and interest in antiquity must be traced largely to his early years in their charge.

Snorri's foster-father, Jón, was described by contemporary writers. He was not only a secular chieftain, but was also a deacon in orders and, despite his loose morals, a pious man. He was accomplished in the clerical arts, which he had learnt from his parents. His father, Lopt, was a priest and was himself the son of Sæmund (1056–1133), who had established not only the fortunes of the family but also the practice of writing history in Iceland.

Many of Sæmund's descendants took holy orders and were noted for their learning. They were also proud of their family traditions, claiming to descend not only from the Skjöldungar, the ancient kings of Denmark, but also from the kings of Norway. It was acknowledged that the mother of Jón Loptsson was a natural daughter of King Magnús Bareleg (died 1103). To commemorate this, an anonymous poet composed a *Nóregs Konunga Tal* (List of the Kings of Norway), tracing the decent of Jón to the ninth century. This poem, in an antiquated style, was based partly on the Chronicle of Sæmund.[2]

Some important historical works appear to have been written by the Oddaverjar or under their guidance.[3] These include the *Skjǫldunga Saga* and the *Orkneyinga Saga*, both of which Snorri used as sources.

Undoubtedly a large library was kept at Oddi, and we may suppose that Snorri acquired his taste for learning there. He did not take orders, which were now withheld from chieftains,[4] and his education was rather that of a layman. While it cannot be shown that he studied Latin, as many of the Oddaverjar had done, he seems to have read all the historical, or quasi-historical literature written in Icelandic before his day. In his writing he made copious use of earlier works, sometimes alluding to them by name, and sometimes copying word-for-word.

But Snorri did not use written sources alone; he also used oral ones, and this greatly adds to the value of his work for the study of mythology.

The first of Snorri's major works was his *Edda*,[5] written about 1220, which, to this day, remains the most valuable summary of Norse myths. It was not, in the first place, designed as a treatise on this subject, but rather on prosody. As it seems, Snorri was aware that the scaldic art was dying out, and believed that it should be revived and explained.[6] His *Edda* consists of a Prologue and four sections. The last section, which is called the *Háttatal* (List of Verse-forms), was perhaps written first.[7] It consists of 102 strophes exemplifying 100 different forms of verse. These verses are addressed to Hákon Hákonarson, the young King of Norway, and his uncle, Jarl Skúli. Snorri has added a detailed commentary on each form of verse which he uses, and this remains the basis of our knowledge of the metrical variations used by the scalds. It is the second and first sections of the book which chiefly concern us here. The second is called the *Skáldskaparmál* (Speech of Poetry). Snorri's aim in writing this section was to explain kennings and other poetical expressions used by the scalds. He illustrated their usage with lavish quotations from early poetry, and thus saved much from oblivion.

While explaining the kennings, Snorri often tells at length the myths or legends upon which they are based. He thus tells why poetry is denoted by such kennings as 'Kvasir's blood', 'the ship of the dwarfs', 'Óðinn's mead', and why gold is 'the speech of the giants', 'the payment for the otter', and battle 'the storm of the Hjaðnings'.

Since the scaldic kennings were based to a great extent on myths, it was necessary to give a description of the Norse Olympus. Therefore Snorri wrote the first section of his *Edda*, the *Gylfaginning* (Deceiving of Gylfi), which is the section most widely read today, both for its literary and mythological interest. It is set in a kind of frame: Gylfi, a king of the Swedes, goes to Ásgarð, the citadel of the supposed gods, who deceived his eyes by the force of their wizardry. He asked them question after question about the origins of the earth, of the giants, gods and men. He heard of the feats, failures and tragedies of the gods, and finally of the terrible *Ragnarǫk*, which is yet to come.

Snorri used many sources for the *Gylfaginning*, but a great part of it came from Eddaic poetry. It is likely that Snorri had received this poetry orally, although some believe that he had written versions of it.[8] The outline of the story told to Gylfi was supplied by the *Vǫluspá*, from which Snorri quotes many strophes. Like the author of the *Vǫluspá*, Snorri traces the history of the gods from the beginning to the *Ragnarǫk*, but he has added much from other sources, quoting both from Eddaic poems known to us, and from others which are forgotten. He quoted no scaldic poetry except at the beginning, although he drew from it, and based some of his stories largely upon it.

Although educated as a layman, Snorri derived his literary education from men of clerical training. Consequently his views about heathen gods were coloured by Christian teaching. In the *Gylfaginning* he expresses a kind of euhemerism, but it is mixed with other views. The Æsir, who deceived Gylfi, were not really gods; they were wizards. They had evidently come to the north from Asia. Their original home, the ancient Ásgarð (*Ásgarðr hinn forni*) was identified with Troy.[9] But euhemerism did not carry Snorri all the way. The gods, of whom his hosts told Gylfi, were those whom they worshipped themselves (*goð-mǫgn þau, er þeir blótuðu*). They deceived Gylfi by pretending that they were the same as those gods (*allir váru einir þeir æsir, er nú var frá sagt, ok þessir er þá váru þau sǫmu nǫfn gefin*).[10]

Snorri's *Edda* is preceded by a Prologue, which need hardly concern us here. This is so different from the rest of the book that some have doubted whether it is really Snorri's work,[11] although manuscript evidence suggests that it is. The purpose of the Prologue is plain; it brings Norse mythology into line with the European learning of the age. It begins with the creation of the world, passes on to the flood, and tells how the name of God was forgotten, although people observed the wonders of nature and concluded that there must be some ruler over the elements. The geography of the world is then described, as well as the Trojan heroes, who were ancestors of the Norse gods. This story is filled in with genealogies of English origin,[12] and it is told finally how the Æsir, the men of Asia, migrated to Sweden.

The reliability of Snorri's *Edda* as a source of mythology has been judged very variously. Snorri was writing more than two centuries after Iceland had adopted Christianity, and a Christian spirit runs through his work. He sometimes misunderstood the sources which he quoted, and tended to systematize and rationalize. Some critics have suspected that nearly everything which Snorri adds to known sources was invented, either by him or by his contemporaries. Thus the story which Snorri tells in the *Gylfaginning* (Ch. 6) of the drowning of the giants in the blood of one of their own race is merely an adaptation of the story of the biblical flood, far removed as it is.[13] Similarly, it has been said, Loki had no place in the story of Baldr's death,[14] because this is not plainly stated in the extant poetic sources, even if it is implied.

Such views have been found hypercritical, and a sharp reaction has set in in recent years. Using the comparative method, G. Dumézil[15] has shown that Snorri's evidence cannot be so lightly dismissed. Many examples illustrating this will be quoted in the body of this work, but to take one of them, the story of the origin of poetry, 'the blood of Kvasir', finds a very close parallel in an Indian myth.

If we admit that Snorri had a deep knowledge of Norse myths, we may wonder how he acquired it. It is clear that the *Skjǫldunga Saga* and some 'mythography' had been written before Snorri's time, but it is doubtful whether this was much. Although Snorri's sources appear to be largely oral, it is difficult to understand how myths could have lived orally through two centuries of ardent Christianity. A partial answer may be given. Scaldic poetry had lived orally from the tenth century until Snorri's time, and new poetry, often about Christian subjects, was composed in the same vein throughout the period. Poetry of this kind is rarely self-explanatory; in other words commentators were needed to explain the kennings and sophisticated diction.[16] We may believe that many of the stories which Snorri told in the *Skáldskaparmál* were based on the verbal commentaries of those who had instructed him in the scaldic art. Although they had originated in the scaldic period, these stories must have been modified, partly by successive narrators, and partly by Snorri himself.

It is another question how far Snorri gives a true picture of the pagan hierarchy. It seems one-sided. Óðinn, All-father, is presented under his many names as chief of all the gods, and once equated with God Almighty, while Thór is benevolent and, on occasion, fooled. The historical sources, on the other hand, show that, in Western Scandinavia at least, Thór enjoyed the widest respect and trust (see previous section). The reasons for this discrepancy are not difficult to see. Snorri was following the tradition of the poets. While the peasants placed their faith in Thór, Óðinn was the favourite god of the poets and of the princes who supported them. Poetry was Óðinn's mead, his theft, his burden.

In later life, Snorri turned more to history. The historical works commonly ascribed to him are the Saga of St. Ólaf and the *Heimskringla*, a history of the Kings of Norway from the earliest times to the late twelfth century. There are also good reasons to believe that Snorri was the author of the *Egils Saga*.[17] It may be supposed that these works were written between *c.* 1223 and 1235.

Snorri had travelled in Norway and S.W. Sweden (Gautland) in the years 1218–20, and his historical works may be regarded partly as the outcome of this visit. He shows a more detailed knowledge of the geography and traditions, both of Norway and Sweden, than he could be expected to acquire in Iceland alone.

It was suggested that Snorri had based much of his *Edda* on oral sources. But his historical works, treating largely of the Kings of Norway, depend largely on older sagas about these Kings, for many had been written before Snorri's time. Nevertheless, Snorri added much, partly from his own deductions and observations, and from stories which he had heard on his travels. As he says himself in his Prologue to the *Heimskringla*,[18] he had a strong faith in the scaldic poetry made in honour of the kings whom he described, although he realized that it might be corrupt or misunderstood.

Snorri's histories contain numerous allusions to pagan practices, particularly those which cover the period of the Conversion, in the late tenth and early eleventh centuries.

But for the study of myths, the most valuable of Snorri's historical, or quasi-historical works is the *Ynglinga Saga*, the first section of the *Heims-kringla*. Here Snorri tells of the mythical and legendary ancestors of the Ynglingar, the Kings of the Swedes.

Like many others, these Kings were believed to descend from the gods, and Snorri traces their mythical ancestry in some detail. He expresses the same euhemeristic views as he did in his *Edda*, but carries them further. He tells of the two tribes of gods, Æsir and Vanir, of the war between them and subsequent treaty. He tells how the gods, under the leadership of Óðinn, had come from Asia to Scandinavia, where Óðinn had distributed dominions among his sons and followers.

After Óðinn had died in Sweden, Njörð was ruler of the Swedes, and after him his son Freyr. Freyr was also known by another name, Yngvi, and it was after him that the Kings were called Ynglingar.

In this part of the *Heimskringla*, Snorri has used many sources of devious kinds, which could not profitably be discussed in this space.[19] His chief source was the poem *Ynglinga Tal* (List of the Ynglingar), which was composed in the ninth century by the Norwegian Thjóðólf of Hvin.[20] The poet's aim was to glorify the petty kings of south-eastern Norway, demonstrating their descent from the splendid house of the Ynglingar.

The poem, of which some thirty-seven strophes survive, is a strange mixture of myth and history, and it is difficult to know whether some of those named as kings of the Swedes had ever lived or not. But the *Ynglinga Tal* corresponds in many things closely with the Old English *Beowulf*, showing that the Swedish traditions embodied in this Nor-wegian poem go back to the sixth century at least.[21]

In its present form, the *Ynglinga Tal* tells little about the Kings of the Swedes, except how they died and where they were buried. The be-ginning, which must have told of Óðinn, Njörð, Freyr, is lost.[22] It is not improbable that Snorri received this poem in written form; it seems to have been known to Ari Thorgilsson and to have influenced some other medieval writers, if indirectly.[23]

Whether or not it was written down before the time of Snorri, the *Ynglinga Tal* must certainly have been accompanied by explanatory stories, in which something more was told about the kings than their death and burial. It is also likely that, while he was in Sweden, Snorri heard some traditions which he incorporated in the *Ynglinga Saga*. He seems to know of the three great burial mounds at Uppsala, and to believe that three kings were buried in them.[24]

Since the traditions upon which the *Ynglinga Tal* is based reach so far back into antiquity, it is likely that it was itself based on poetry

26

older than the ninth century. If so, much of this poetry was probably Swedish. It would be in the same tradition as the genealogical poetry mentioned by Tacitus (*Germ.* II), in which Germans celebrated their descent from Tuisto. Jordanes also alluded to poetry in which the Goths commemorated their ancestors, and he seemed to know records which told of the deaths of the Gothic princes and their burial.[25]

Historical or not, the early kings of the Swedes were the kinsmen of the gods; they presided over the sacrifices and, on occasion, they were the victims of sacrifice (see Ch. IX). If only in death, cremation and inhumation, they reflect ancient religious beliefs and practices.

Saxo

The *Gesta Danorum* of the Danish historian Saxo, nicknamed Grammaticus, will be mentioned frequently in this book.[1] The work consists of sixteen books in Latin, and is a comprehensive history of the Danes from prehistoric times to the late twelfth century.

Saxo's aim and the conditions under which he worked may be considered briefly. He was probably born about 1150, and little is known of his life, except that he was secretary of Absalon, Bishop of Roskilde 1158 and Archbishop of Lund 1178–1201.

As Saxo himself tells,[2] it was at the instigation of Absalon that he undertook his stupendous task. Its object was, in the first place, the glorification of the Danes which, in Saxo's mind, combined with a hatred of Germans. It is supposed that he began his work about 1185 and finished it long after Absalon's death. It is dedicated to Andreas (died 1228), who succeeded Absalon, and to King Valdemar II (1202–42). The strictly historical section, covering Books X–XVI, from Harald Bluetooth (936–86) to Saxo's own time, was evidently written first, and was based on Danish sources.[3]

The first nine Books, and it is these alone which concern us here, were probably written as an afterthought, forming an introduction to the whole.

These Books were completed about 1215, or a little later, and they are an invaluable source, not so much of early history as of legend, mythology and religious tradition.

The stories which Saxo tells are often chaotic and difficult to follow, and his sources and methods of work must be considered if his status as an authority is to be judged.

It is plain that, while Saxo used Danish folktales and oral traditions, these provided only a part of his material. The bulk of it was made up by West Norse tradition. A. Olrik, in his monumental work, *Kilderne til Sakses Oldhistorie* (I–II, 1892–94), attempted to distinguish the Danish from the West Norse elements and, in general, his conclusions must be accepted.

It is more difficult to discover how Saxo came to know these West Norse traditions. He provides a partial answer himself. In his Prologue (p. 3), he lavishes praise on the *Tylenses*, the men of Iceland (Thule). He praises them, not only for their sobriety and wisdom, but especially for their profound knowledge of the ancient history of lands other than their own. He adds that he has composed 'no small part' (*haut paruam . . . partem*) of his work by weaving together their narratives.

In his Prologue (p. 6), Saxo also gives a detailed and remarkably exact description of the island of Iceland, although there is nothing to suggest that he had ever been there himself. We may then wonder who were the Icelandic informants who told Saxo about their legends and their country. Olrik[4] inclined to believe that there was only one of them, and this was Arnoldus Tylensis, who is identified with Arnhall Thorvaldsson, said in an Icelandic source to have composed poetry for the King of Denmark, Valdemar the Great (1157–82).[5] Only one story is told of Arnoldus, and that by Saxo in Book XIV (594); he was said to be in the company of Bishop Absalon about the year 1167, and was praised for his sagacity, knowledge of history and power of recounting.

It is not known whether Saxo had met Arnoldus, but if he was born about the middle of the twelfth century, he would have been only seventeen years old in 1167. Olrik therefore suggested[6] that the stories which Arnoldus told were transmitted to Saxo by Danish middlemen, and this would account for certain misunderstandings found in his narrative.

This theory had appeared to many as unnecessarily elaborate, and it seems to conflict with the words used by Saxo in his Prologue, for he praises the Icelanders as a people and as the repository of ancient tradition.

Several Icelandic poets other than Arnoldus are known to have worked for kings of Denmark in Saxo's time,[7] and many Icelanders must have passed through Denmark on their way to the south.

One of the most eminent and learned Icelanders of this period was Gizur Hallsson. Gizur travelled widely and frequently.[8] He had lived in Norway and been to Rome, and was the author of a *Flos Peregrinationis*, now lost. He is named as an authority on German emperors,[9] on Ólaf Tryggvason[10] and, strangely enough, on the kings of Denmark.[11] Gizur was an older man than Saxo, dying in 1206 about the age of eighty. The course of his life, since he was Law-speaker from 1181 to 1200, may make it improbable that he and Saxo had met. Nevertheless, we could suppose that he was the kind of scholarly Icelander, of whom there were many in those days, with whom Saxo exchanged learning. It could be added that Gizur's son, Magnús, afterwards Bishop of Skálaholt (1216–37), was in Denmark in 1188 and probably again on his way to and from Rome in 1202 and 1203.[12]

Olrik's brilliant exposition has sometimes been criticized in another point, although less generally. As he believed, the West Norse stories were told by an Icelander, but they were based, to a great extent, on a Norwegian, and not on an Icelandic tradition. Saxo's narrative is particularly rich in place-names of Western Norway. The traditions were, therefore, gathered by an Icelander who had travelled the Norwegian coast.[13] Elsewhere,[14] Olrik thought also of Norwegian prelates, exiled from Norway in the reign of King Sverrir (died 1202), as the transmitters of Norwegian tradition. It should, however, be remarked that the Icelanders of the twelfth century were great travellers, and they knew no foreign part so well as Western Norway. It is believed also that Saxo had himself visited Norway in the year 1168,[15] but his contempt for the drunken Norwegians makes it improbable that he owed any great debt to them.

The source of one of Saxo's sections has aroused particular interest and controversy among scholars. This is the so-called *Brávallaþula*, in which Saxo enumerates the champions on either side in the legendary battle of Brávellir, where Harald Wartooth lost his life (see Ch. X, Harald Wartooth). Saxo claims to be following the words of the hero Starkað, and some 160 champions are named. They come from all the known world, and their nicknames and places of origin are often added.

It was noticed long ago that, in this imposing list of champions, Saxo was reproducing a metrical list of the kind called in Icelandic *þulur*. This same list is given, although in shorter form, in the so-called 'Fragmentary History (of Kings of Denmark)' (*Sǫgubrot*),[16] preserved in an Icelandic manuscript of *c.* 1300.

The origin of this list, or *þula*, is disputed, and many have argued that it is Norwegian, claiming to find a Norwegian, or Telemarkian patriotism in its lines, besides certain historical anachronisms, of which an Icelander of the twelfth century would not be guilty.[17] Others, using close linguistic arguments, claim more precisely that it originated in south-eastern Norway, and even that manuscripts written in that region provided the model, both for Saxo and for the 'Fragmentary History'.[18] These conclusions have been accepted widely,[19] but the most recent investigator[20] shows that the arguments on which they are based are unreliable, partly because of our defective knowledge of Norwegian dialects at so early a period.

If it is studied from the point of view of literary history, the *Brávalla-*

þula fits more easily into an Icelandic setting. Metrical name-lists (*þulur*) flourished in Iceland, where many are preserved. It is believed that these lists date mainly from the twelfth century, and to this period the *Brávallaþula* most probably belonged.

It is is agreed that Saxo received a great part of the traditions incorporated in his first nine books from Icelanders, it is still difficult to know in what form these traditions reached him, and what was their ultimate origin.

Again, we may find a partial answer to the first question in Saxo's own words. His sources were partly in verse and, as he says himself, he took care to render verse by verse (*metra metris reddenda curaui*).[21] The verse, which Saxo wrote in Latin, was in flowery language and elaborate measures, altogether obscuring the form of his originals. Nevertheless, Icelandic vernacular sources sometimes show what these were like. As Saxo tells the story of Hadding's disagreement with his wife (see Ch. X, Hadding), the couple address each other in more than thirty lines. When the god Njörð and his giant wife, Skaði, addressed each other in words which must be close to the source of Saxo's Latin, they used twelve short alliterating lines of *Ljóðaháttr*, in which they expressed nearly as much.

In Book II Saxo tells the famous story of Hrólf Kraki and his last battle at Hleiðra (Lejre), when the castle was set alight, apparently by its own defenders. Saxo (II, 67) gives the latter scene in lengthy hexameters, purporting to reproduce a 'Danish' poem (*danici . . . carminis*), known to many antiquarians. The term 'Danish' (*dǫnsk tunga*) was often applied, in the Middle Ages, to Scandinavian languages in general, and therefore this does not show that Saxo received the poem from a Dane. He could equally well have heard it from an Icelander, and there are some reasons to think that he did. Not only the underlying legends, but the poem itself was known to Icelanders of Saxo's time, and was called the *Bjarkamál*. In his account of the battle of Stiklastaðir (AD 1030), where St Ólaf laid down his life, Snorri tells that, on the morning before the battle, the Saint called his Icelandic poet, Thormóð, to awaken his men with a stirring, martial song. He chanted the *Bjarkamál*, which was also called *Húskarlahvǫt* (Incitement of Housecarles)[22] and by Saxo *Exortationum Series*.[23] The first two strophes of the poem are quoted by Snorri in the *Heimskringla*, and Snorri quotes three other strophes, which he assigns to it, in his *Edda*.[24]

The *Bjarkamál*, as Saxo retells it, is a trialogue, spoken chiefly by the champion, Hjalti, to awaken the sleeping warriors, calling them to lay down their lives for their generous lord, as the enemy approach. On the basis of Saxo's version, A. Olrik[25] was able to reconstruct a convincing version of this poem in modern Danish, which was subsequently adapted in English by L. M. Hollander.[26]

Good reasons have been given for believing that the *Bjarkamál* was, in fact, a Danish poem of the tenth century.[27] It cannot, however, be used as evidence that alliterative verse survived in Denmark in Saxo's time. The Icelanders, as Saxo makes plain, stored and developed the traditions of lands other than their own.

The *Bjarkamál* and the legends of Hrólf Kraki are mentioned here because they provide an exceptionally good example of the preservation and growth of tradition. The basis is partly historical, and founded on events which took place in Denmark in the sixth century. Allusion is made to them, not only in the rich Icelandic sources, but also in the Old English *Beowulf* and *Widsith*.

But in the Norse tradition, the Danish prince has adopted some of the qualities of an Óðinn hero. Saxo may not fully have realized this. In his version of the *Bjarkamál*, Óðinn appears suddenly on the battlefield among the assailants of Hrólf. Arngrímr Jónsson, in his excerpt from the *Skjǫldunga Saga*,[28] makes this incident plain. When Hrólf was returning from a successful raid on Uppsala, Óðinn disguised as a farmer had offered him a corselet and a cloak (*loricam et clamydem*), but the hero had offended him by refusing the gifts. When he realized who the farmer was, Hrólf knew that he could expect no more victory. The late Icelandic *Hrólfs Saga*[29] says that neither Hrólf nor his chosen companions ever sacrificed to the gods,[30] but it preserves the same motive about Hrólf's refusal of the god's gifts, and enlarges upon it, telling how the disguised Óðinn had twice come to the aid of Hrólf with his advice. It seems to be implied that Hrólf was under the protection of Óðinn but, when time was ripe, the war-god turned against him, and took him to himself, just as he took Harald Wartooth, Eirík Bloodaxe and many another (see Chs. II, X).

By no means all that Saxo heard from the Icelanders was told to him in verse. In Chs. III and V, two stories will be cited from Saxo about the journeys of a certain Thurkillus. It is the first of these stories which concerns us here, and Saxo makes it plain that it had come from the men of Thule.[31] In outline it closely resembles the story of Thorsteinn Bœjarmagn (*Þorsteins Þáttr*) found in an Icelandic manuscript of the late fifteenth century. Both of these stories describe the visit of a hero, Thurkillus or Thorsteinn, to the terrible and revolting giant Geirröð (Geruthus). They derive ultimately from an ancient myth, recorded in the *Þórsdrápa* of the late tenth century, and again by Snorri in his *Edda*, of the perilous journey of the god Thór to the house of the giant Geirröð. Saxo, in fact, makes a direct allusion to the myth.[32]

31

But the god has been dropped, both from the Icelandic and from Saxo's version. The reasons are not difficult to see. Both of them are placed in a Christian or half-Christian setting. Thorsteinn is an attendant of the Christian King Óláf Tryggvason, and it is upon his kingly force (*hamingja*) that he relies in his perils. Thurkillus is not a Christian to begin with, but he is a model pagan. When his companions invoked their gods, Thurkillus called only on the Lord of the Universe. Before the end of his life, Thurkillus went to Germany and adopted the Christian religion.[33]

Saxo has enriched his version of this story from wide reading in European letters. Some sections of the story of the journey of Thurkillus in the frozen north read like the Navigation of Brendan and other Irish *imramma*. He seems also to make use of Adam of Bremen's account of a Friesian expedition to the North Pole.[34] Influences of other European literature have also been detected.[35]

Mixed, and confused as it is, Saxo's story of Thurkillus throws much light on the development of mythical tradition in Iceland. He combines the visit to Geirröð with that to Guðmund, said to be the brother of the giant, ruling a neighbouring territory. This is, of course, Guðmund of Glæsisvellir (the Shining Fields), who is famous in late Icelandic sagas, although never named in early texts. In his glorious kingdom, it was said, lay the Ódáinsakr, the field of eternal life.[36]

Both Thurkillus and Thorsteinn had to pass through the kingdom of Guðmund before they reached the giant world of Geirröð, divided from it by a river or torrent. Guðmund, according to the Iceland sources, is not the brother of Geirröð, but his unwilling vassal.

The Icelandic *Þorsteins Þáttr* has enriched the story with motives of its own, which are often hard to trace, but Saxo shows that, already in his day, the Icelanders had combined the myth of Thór and Geirröð with that of Guðmund in his Shining Fields. He thus shows that stories told in such late Icelandic texts as the *Þorsteins Þáttr* cannot be too lightly dismissed. He also shows something about the state of Icelandic tradition in the late twelfth century. That which Saxo shares with the *Þorsteins Þáttr* must have been in his oral Icelandic source. Saxo is thus one of our chief authorities for the state of Icelandic tradition in his age. This tradition had grown from exceedingly ancient roots.

We may doubt whether alliterative poetry in the style of the *Edda* survived in Denmark in the time of Saxo,[37] but we should not belittle the importance of Danish folktale and tradition as sources for his history. His version of the myth of Baldr and Höð will be mentioned in Ch. IV below. So great are the differences between Saxo's version and those given in the Icelandic records that it is hard, in spite of the arguments of Heusler and others,[38] to believe that Saxo was here following an Icelandic, or even a Norwegian source. Indeed, in this section, Saxo quotes several folktales based on place-names of Denmark. Much as he has added to it, we may believe that the picture which Saxo drew of Baldr and Höð was largely a Danish one.

In general, Saxo's descriptions of the gods resemble those left by Icelandic writers of his age. Óðinn was the chief of them, and was credited with the false honour of godhead throughout Europe, while commonly residing in Uppsala.[39] He appears under many names, as he does in Iceland, and in the disguises typical of Icelandic tradition. He is an old man with one eye, appearing at a critical moment.[40] He calls from the shore to a favourite hero; boards his ship and teaches him how to deploy his army.[41] Óðinn calls his chosen warriors to himself when their time has come, although Valhöll is nowhere named in Saxo's work.[42] On one occasion, Óðinn rides through the air and over the sea on his magical charger.[43] The charger, Sleipnir, was well known to the Icelanders, but Óðinn more often appeared on foot. To judge by the folktales, collected in modern times, Óðinn, the wild rider, was better known in Danish than in Icelandic tradition.[44]

Thór is distinguished for his might and armed, if not with a hammer, with a club.[45] Freyr residing in Uppsala with his sons, is the patron of orgies and revolting sacrifices.[46] He is once presented as King of the Swedes.[47]

Although he did not express it so clearly, Saxo shared the belief of his Icelandic contemporaries that the gods had come from the near East, and their original home was Byzantium.[48]

For Saxo, as for the medieval Icelanders, the gods were not gods, but crafty men of old. With superior cunning they had overcome the primeval giants; they had deluded men into believing that they were divine.[49]

But Saxo carried euhemerism further than the Icelanders did. Saxo's gods play a more intimate part in the affairs of men. They beget children with earthly women. Baldr, according to Icelandic sources, was son of Óðinn and Frigg. Saxo also says that he was son of Óðinn, but he was only a demigod, secretly begotten on an earthly woman.[50] In the same way, Óðinn in disguise begat Bous on the Ruthenian princess, Rinda.[51]

The gods fight with men, and their superior magic does not always bring them victory. When they fought for Baldr against his rival, Höð, who for Saxo was not a god, they were ignominiously put to flight.[52]

Saxo differs from the Icelandic writers chiefly in his bitter contempt of the gods and all they stood for. Snorri sometimes poked fun at them, but it was a good-humoured fun, of a kind which had no place in Saxo's mind.

Saxo tells much about the substance of Icelandic traditions living in the late twelfth and early thirteenth centuries, but his education was in European letters and his literary models were medieval and post-classical. He tells little about the forms, whether in prose or in verse, in which he received the Icelandic myths.

CHAPTER TWO

ÓÐINN

God of Poetry—Lord of the Gallows—God of War—Father of Gods and Men—Óðinn and his Animals—Óðinn's Names—Óðinn's Eye—The Cult of Óðinn—Woden-Wotan

THE NORWEGIAN and Icelandic poets, as well as Snorri, whose work derives from theirs, present Óðinn as the foremost and chief of all the gods. In Snorri's eyes, Óðinn excelled the other gods so far that, in one passage (*Gylf.* 4), he endows Óðinn with immortality and other qualities of the Christian God:

He will live throughout all ages, ruling his whole kingdom and governing all things great and small. He fashioned the earth and the sky and all that is in them . . . But the greatest is this, that he created man and gave him the spirit which shall live and never perish, even though the body rot to soil or burn to ashes.

God of Poetry

The immediate reason for the poets' regard for Óðinn is not far to seek. Óðinn is the god of poetry. He himself was said to speak only in poetry (*Yngl. S.* VI); one of his gifts to his favourite Starkað was that of making poetry as fast as he could talk (see Ch. X).

Óðinn was conceived as god of poetry, not in an abstract, but in a concrete sense. Poetry is the 'precious mead' (*hinn dýri mjǫðr*), and it was Óðinn who had brought it from the Other World and given it to gods and men. Several versions of this myth are preserved, and we may begin with the latest of them, that of Snorri (*Skáld.* 4–6), which is the most lucid and detailed. The chief points in Snorri's story may be summarized:

When peace was concluded between the two tribes of gods, the Æsir and the Vanir (see Ch. VII), the parties signified their friendship by spitting into a jar. Not wishing to let this symbol of their union perish, the gods fashioned a human figure of their spittle. He was called Kvasir, and he was so wise that there was no question which he could not answer. Wandering throughout the world, imparting his wisdom to others, Kvasir came to the house of two

35

dwarfs, Fjalar and Galar. They killed him secretly, telling the gods that he had suffocated in his own wisdom, but they ran off his blood into three vessels, whose names were *Óðrœrir* (heart-stirrer), *Són* and *Boðn*.[1] Mixing the blood with honey, the dwarfs brewed such a mead, that everyone who drinks it becomes a poet or man of learning.

When the dwarfs were later entertaining a giant, Gilling, they murdered him by capsizing the boat in which they were rowing. When they told his wife, she wept bitterly and, annoyed by her howling, they dropped a mill-stone on her head. When Gilling's son (or nephew), Suttung, heard this, he paid a visit to the dwarfs; he carried them out to a skerry submerged at high tide. They saved themselves by giving the mead to Suttung as weregild for his father. He took it to his mountain dwelling Hnitbjörg, where he placed it in charge of his daughter, Gunnlöð.

The story now turns to Óðinn. He was travelling under the name Bölverk (Evil-doer) and, after some strange adventures (see Óðinn's Names, below), he took service with the giant Baugi, brother of Suttung. As his wages, Bölverk demanded a drink of Suttung's mead, but Suttung refused to give it. Using his gimlet, Rati, Bölverk bored a hole in the rock of Suttung's castle. He then changed, as he must often have done, into the form of a ser-pent, and crawled through the hole. He found the giantess Gunnlöð and slept with her for three nights. In the end she granted him three sups of the mead. In the first he emptied Óðrœrir, in the second Boðn, and in the third Són.

Then Oðinn changed into the form of an eagle and flew off, while Suttung took the same form and pursued him. When the gods saw Óðinn approach-ing they placed jars by the wall of Ásgarð. Óðinn regurgitated the mead into these jars but, since Suttung was close on his tail, some of it spilt outside the wall. Anyone can drink this, and it is called 'the fool-poet's portion' (*skáld-fíflahlutr*).

When we consider older versions of this myth, we may learn some-thing about Snorri's methods and his use of sources. The closest parallel is to be found in Strs. 104–10 of the *Hávamál*, which are allusive and sometimes difficult to interpret. The sequence in these strophes differs in some way from that of Snorri's story:

Óðinn had visited the aged giant Suttung, and his eloquence brought him much success (104). Gunnlöð gave him a drink of the precious mead, but he ill-repaid her generosity (105). With the point of Rati (the gimlet?), he bored a hole through the rock (apparently to escape), thus risking his own head (106). Now Óðrœrir (i.e. the mead) has come to the dwelling of the gods (107). Óðinn could not have escaped without the help of Gunnlöð (108). On the next day, frost-giants came to the hall of Hávi (*Hávahǫll*, i.e. Ásgarð) to ask news of Bölverk. Was he among the gods, or had Suttung killed him (109)? Óðinn had sworn an oath on the holy ring, but he had not kept it. He had cheated Suttung of his mead and left Gunnlöð in tears (110).

The most noticeable difference between this account of the theft of the mead and that given by Snorri is that according to the *Hávamál* Óðinn used Rati, whether a gimlet or not, to escape from the giant's stronghold, whereas, in Snorri's story, he used it to get in.[2] In the *Hávamál* (107), Óðrœrir appears to be the name of the mead, but according to Snorri it was the name of a cauldron in which it was brewed or stored.

In a later section, the so-called *Rúnatals þáttr*, the *Hávamál* (140) alludes to another version of the story of the acquisition of the mead. According to this, it was one of the results of Óðinn's suffering as he hung on the windswept tree (see Lord of the Gallows, below).

The *Hávamál* (13–14) contains an allusion to yet a third version of this myth. The lines may be quoted in full:

Óminnis hegri heitir,	He is called the heron of oblivion,
sá er yfir ǫlðrum þrumir:	who hovers over drinking bouts;
hann stelr geði guma;	he steals the wits of men.
þess fugls fjǫðrum	I was entangled
ek fjǫtraðr vark	in the feathers of that bird
í garði Gunnlaðar.	in the house of Gunnlöð.
Qlr ek varð,	I was drunk,
varð ofrǫlvi	I was exceedingly drunk
at ins fróða Fjalars . . .	in the house of the wise Fjalar . . .[2a]

It is not told elsewhere that Óðinn lost his wits when he drank the precious liquor, nor that he drank it in the house of the wise Fjalar. The name Fjalar is occasionally applied to giants, but since, according to Snorri, it was also the name of a dwarf who brewed the mead, we may suppose that the author of these lines knew a version of the myth in which Óðinn had won the mead from the dwarfs.

Snorri's ostensible reason for writing his elaborate account of the theft of the mead was to explain certain poetic expressions, which would otherwise be obscure. Why do the scalds call poetry 'Kvasir's blood', 'the water of the dwarfs or of Óðrœrir of Hnitbjörg', or why 'the mead of Suttung' and 'the prize of Óðinn'?

The story of Óðinn's conquest of the mead is not told in any of the scaldic poems, but many of the scalds allude to poetry as the god's possession, theft, or gift. In the *Hǫfuðlausn* (Head-Ransom, str. 2), which he composed in York about the middle of the tenth century, Egill said:

37

berk Óðins mjǫð   I bring Óðinn's mead
á Engla bjǫð   to the land of the English.

In the same poem (str. 19), Egill called poetry 'the sea of Óðinn' (*Óðins ægir*).

Óðinn has many names (see below); the name 'Óðinn' is often replaced by another. Poetry is 'the cup of Ygg' (*Yggs full*),[3] 'the mead of Ygg' (*Yggs mjǫðr*);[4] it is 'Viður's theft' (*Viðurs þýfi*),[5] 'the feast of Gauti' (*Gauta gildi*),[6] and again 'the holy cup of the Raven-god'[7] (*helga full Hrafnásar*), 'the gift of Grímnir' (*Grímnis gjǫf*).[8]

Sometimes the kennings in which such allusions are made are more complicated. Óðinn's mother was Bestla, and poetry was 'the waterfall of Bestla's son' (*forsar Bestlu niðs*)[9] and even 'the waterfall of the burden of Gunnlǫð's arms' (*horna fors farms Gunnlaðar arma*),[10] and the 'rain of the servants of Háar', i.e. 'rain of the poets, Óðinn's servants'.[11]

Óðinn delivered the mead to the gods in the form of an eagle, carrying it in his crop, and the scalds sometimes allude in their imagery to this incident in its history. Poetry is 'the sea of Óðinn's breast' (*Viðris munstrandar marr*).[12] In Egill's words, poetry is 'the seed of the eagle's bill' (*arnar kjapta ǫrð*).[13] A poet of the early twelfth century refers to the poor verses of his antagonist as 'the mud of the old eagle' (*leirr hins gamla ara*),[14] evidently alluding to the 'fool-poet's portion', which fell outside the wall of Ásgarð.

Before Óðinn seized it, the mead had been in the hands of dwarfs and giants; it was brought ages before from the world of giants.[15] But since the mead was of no use to gods or men until Óðinn stole it, it is not surprising that scalds should refer less commonly to these stages in its history. Indeed, when they do, it is often difficult to know whether they allude to poetry as the property of giants or dwarfs.

Surt was the name of a vicious fire-giant, and Hallfreð, in his lay in memory of Ólaf Tryggvason (died AD 1000) called poetry 'the drink of Surt's tribe' (*Surts ættar sylgr*).[16] Narfi was the name of another giant, probably the son of Loki and, in an obscure strophe, Egill called poetry 'the inheritance of the sons of Narfi' (*niðjerfi Narfa*).[17] A poet of uncertain age calls his poetry after a frost-giant 'the river of Hrímnir's horn' (*Hrímnis hornstraumr*).[18] In the kenning 'the cup of Billing's son' (*Billings burar full*),[19] the allusion may be either to a giant or a dwarf.

Poetry is the drink or water of dwarfs. A poet of the twelfth century called it 'the rain of dwarfs' (*dvergregn*),[20] and in a verse ascribed, perhaps wrongly, to Gísli Súrsson (died *c.* 977), it is 'the drink of dwarfs (*dverga drykkja*).[21] The names of Fjalar and Galar, the dwarfs who brewed the sacred mead, are not found in kennings but, following scaldic practice, names of other dwarfs are sometimes used instead. Poetry is 'the cup of Dvalinn' (*Dvalins full*),[22] 'the mead of Suðri' (*Suðra mjǫðr*).[23]

If kennings of this type are somewhat colourless, there are others alluding in closer detail to the mead as the possession of the dwarfs. A Norwegian of the tenth century called poetry 'the weregild for Gilling' (*Gillings gjǫld*),[24] and an Icelander of the eleventh century, remembering that Ám (*Ámr*) was the name of a giant and Austri that of a dwarf, called it 'the treaty of Ám and Austri' (*sættir Áms ok Austra*).[25]

Occasionally poetry is called 'the ship of dwarfs' (*skip dverga*).[26] In more sophisticated language, Hallfreð called it 'the boat of Austri's son' (*Austra burar nǫkkvi*).[27] The allusion appears to be to an incident included in Snorri's account of the myth: the giant Suttung carried the murderous dwarfs to a rock submerged at high tide. They saved their lives by surrendering the precious mead. The mead was therefore the ship which carried them away (*farskostr dverga*).[28] As Snorri tells, the mead was brewed from the blood of the sage, Kvasir. Scaldic poetry contains only one allusion to this; Einar Skálaglamm, an Icelander of the late tenth century, called his poetry 'the blood of Kvasir' (*Kvasis dreyri*).[29]

If we examine Snorri's story in the light of the *Hávamál* and the surviving scaldic kennings, it is plain that Snorri did not get all his details from them, and many have doubted whether any faith should be placed in his account of the myth.[30] Some have supposed that Snorri or his 'school' invented the story to explain the kennings. This is not probable. We may be satisfied that verses containing such kennings as 'the seed of Óðinn's breast', 'the seed of the eagle's bill', 'the mud of the old eagle', 'Gilling's weregild', 'Kvasir's blood', had lived orally for two centuries and more before Snorri wrote them down. But poetry of this kind could not be understood unless the imagery were explained. The explanations must, in this case, have been transmitted orally. Inevitably changes would be made in transmission and variant versions of the the myth would develop. It has been suggested that Snorri attempted to combine two main versions of the myth. In the first, Óðinn had stolen the mead from the giant Baugi, nowhere named in early poetry as its owner. In the second version, which has a sounder basis in surviving poetry, the mead was stolen from Suttung, whom Snorri calls the brother of Baugi.[31] Already the *Hávamál* implies that there were two, if not three versions of this myth. It cannot be said which of them is the original, but it can be said that they were current already in the tenth century.

Particular interest has been shown in the brewing of the mead from the blood of the murdered Kvasir. Snorri once names Kvasir in the

Ynglinga Saga (Ch. IV) as the wisest of the Vanir, and one of those whom the Vanir sent to the Æsir as a hostage when peace was concluded between the two tribes. The story that the mead was brewed from his blood is supported only by Einar Skálaglamm's allusion to poetry as 'Kvasir's blood'. It contains elements known from the folklore of many countries, probably present in it long before Snorri's time. The god, or sage, Kvasir was created from the spittle of the Æsir and Vanir, and his blood was afterwards to provide the basis of the precious mead.

The use of spittle both as a symbol of friendship and as an agent of fermentation is recorded widely.[32] In the Icelandic *Hálfs Saga ok Hálfs-rekka*,[33] probably of the fourteenth century, it is told how two women competed to brew the best beer. One of them invoked Freyja, but the other Óðinn who, claiming her unborn son as his price, spat in her beer to promote its fermentation.[34] The magical properties of spittle, as of blood, are recorded among many peoples.[35]

The name *Kvasir* has often been associated with Danish *kvase* (to squeeze to extract juice), with English *quash* and with other Germanic words of suchlike meaning.[36] However that may be, the god Kvasir is the personification of the divine spittle, and his blood the foundation of the divine mead.

Until recently this incident in the myth was thought to be unique. It was G. Dumézil[37] who first noticed a strange parallel in an Indian myth. Indra and the other gods had refused the two Nāsatya, seen as counterparts of the Vanir, entry into their society. An ascetic friend of the Nāsatya has then created a monster who threatened to swallow the world, and Indra gave way. The name of the monster was Mada, interpreted as 'drunkenness'. After he had fulfilled his purpose, the dangerous monster was cut into four parts, which today form the drunkenness of alcohol, of womanizing, gaming and hunting. In India, drunkenness, unless the result of soma, may be considered evil, but in Scandinavia the ecstatic states produced by alcohol and poetry are holy, taking their place in ritual and even bringing men into communion with the gods.[38] If it is difficult to say what are the relations between Snorri's story and the Indian one, it is even more difficult, in spite of obvious differences, to believe that their similarities are fortuitous.

Myths and tales comparable with this one have been told in many lands.[39]

The object of the theft of the god or hero is often the water of wisdom, and Irish legend contains versions of it which resemble the Norse myth of the sacred mead in several details. In one of these it is told how Finn got a drink from the well of Bec mac Buain of the Tuatha Dé

Danann.[40] Finn, hunting with two companions, found the door of a fairy-mount (*síd*) open. The three heroes quickly approached, while the three daughters of Bec, who guarded the well of wisdom, strove to shut the door. The eldest was carrying a bowl of the precious water and, in the struggle, some of it spilt into the mouths of Finn and his companions.

The stories of Sigurð who gained wisdom from the dying dragon and of Finn who won it from the salmon (see Ch. X, first section), although remote from those of Óðinn's acquisition of the mead, and Finn's of the water of wisdom, contain some of the same elements. In all of them the god or hero wrests his wisdom from a god or demon of the Other World.

But once again, the closest parallel to the story of Óðinn is to be found in Indian myths about the rape of soma, the half-personified, intoxicating sacrificial liquor. It would be rash, in a book of this kind, to venture into so specialized and exotic a field, of which I have no first-hand knowledge, but I shall rely on such established authorities as A. Hillebrandt[41] and A. A. Macdonell.[42] Soma is said to stimulate the voice, and to be the leader of poets. Those who drink it become immortal and know the gods.

Soma gives strength to gods and men, but especially to Indra. Indra, filled with soma, conquered the monster Vritra, and fortified with it he performed many a mighty feat. The soma was brought from heaven to Indra; as is frequently told in the *Rigveda*, it was brought by an eagle. The eagle, according to one passage, broke into a fortress of iron to seize the soma. Although Indra is occasionally called, or likened to an eagle, he does not, in the *Rigveda*, appear to be identified with the eagle who raped the soma. It has, however, been remarked that, in one later passage, it is Indra himself, in the form of an eagle, who carried off the soma.[43] It is said widely today that Óðinn, the priest magician, is a god of the first class, corresponding with the Indian Varuna, while Thór, the warrior god, belongs to the second class, and corresponds with Indra.

As noticed by Olrik,[44] the myths of the soma and the mead must derive from a common source, and be part of Indo-European heritage. Are we, therefore, to suppose that Óðinn, in this myth, has usurped the place of Thór, as he has sometimes usurped the places of other gods? Perhaps we should rather doubt the stability of the tripartite system (see Conclusion Ch. III). It was appropriate that Óðinn, god of magic and wisdom, should master the sacred mead.

Lord of the Gallows

No more mysterious myth is recorded in Norse literature than that in which it is told how Óðinn hung for nine nights on a windswept tree. This is found in a section of the *Hávamál* (strs. 138–45), the so-called *Rúnatals Þáttr*, in words said to be spoken by the god himself. The first four strophes, to which I add a tentative translation, read as follows:

138. Veit ek at ek hekk
    vindga meiði á
    nætr allar níu,
    geiri undaðr
    ok gefinn Óðni,
    sjálfr sjálfum mér,
    á þeim meiði,
    er manngi veit,
    hvers hann af rótum renn.

    I know that I hung
    on the windswept tree
    for nine full nights,
    wounded with a spear
    and given to Óðinn,
    myself to myself;
    on that tree
    of which none know
    from what roots it rises.

139. Við hleifi mik sældu[1]
    né við hornigi,
    nysta ek niðr,
    nam ek upp rúnar,[2]
    œpandi nam,
    fell ek aptr þaðan.[3]

    They did not comfort me with bread,
    and not with the drinking horn;
    I peered downward,
    I grasped the 'runes',[2]
    screeching I grasped them;
    I fell back from there.

140. Fimbulljóð níu
    nam ek af enum frægja syni
    Bǫlþórs, Bestlu fǫður,
    ok ek drykk of gat
    ens dýra mjaðar,
    ausinn Óðreri.

    I learned nine mighty songs
    from the famous son
    of Bölthór, father of Bestla,
    and I got a drink
    of the precious mead,
    I was sprinkled with Óðrerir.

141. Þá nam ek frævask
    ok fróðr vera
    ok vaxa ok vel hafask;
    orð mér af orði
    orðs leitaði,
    verk mér af verki
    verks leitaði.

    Then I began to be fruitful
    and to be fertile,
    to grow and to prosper;
    one word sought
    another word from me;
    one deed sought
    another deed from me.

These lines have been interpreted in many different ways, which cannot all be discussed here, and it will be long before agreement can be reached on every detail.

S. Bugge[4] and his followers have seen the hanging Óðinn as a pagan reflexion of Christ on the Cross. The similarities between the scene described here and that on Calvary are undeniable. Christ hung on the rood-tree, as an English poet of the Middle Ages said, 'in the wylde wynde';[5] he thirsted and they gave Him vinegar; like Óðinn, Christ was pierced with a spear. Before His death Christ cried out in a loud voice, just as Óðinn cried out as he grasped the 'runes'. The similarity does not end there. The rood-tree, on which Christ died had no roots; the tree on which Óðinn hung rose from unknown roots. If the myth of the hanging Óðinn did not derive from the legend of the dying Christ, the two scenes resembled each other so closely that they came to be confused in popular tradition.

A folksong recorded in Unst (Shetland) in the last century[6] includes the following lines:

Nine days he hang	pa de rütless tree;
for ill was da folk,	in' güd wis he.
A blüdy mael[7]	wis in his side—
made wi' a lance—	'at wid na hide.
Nine lang nichts,	i' da nippin rime,
hang he dare	wi' his naeked limb.

Some, dey leuch;
but idders gret.

The subject of these lines is Christ, but the nine days, and perhaps the nipping rime accord better with the myth of Óðinn than with the legend of Calvary.

While we cannot preclude the possibility of Christian influence on the scene described in the *Hávamál*, when we analyse the lines, we realize that nearly every element in the Norse myth can be explained as a part of pagan tradition, and even of the cult of Óðinn.

The spear was Óðinn's favourite weapon, and already the poet Egill called him 'Lord of the spear' (*geirs dróttinn*).[8] He was owner of the spear Gungnir, which according to Snorri,[9] was forged by dwarfs. In a verse ascribed to Bragi, Óðinn was called 'Gungnir's shaker' (*Gungnis váfaðr*).[10] In the *Ynglinga Saga* (Ch. IX), where Óðinn is described as a mortal king of the Swedes, it is said that before he died in his bed, Óðinn had himself marked with a spear-point believing that he would go to the world of gods (*Goðheimr*). Njörð, who followed Óðinn, evidently did the same for, on his death-bed, he had himself 'marked for Óðinn'. It was appropriate that Óðinn, as he hung on the tree, should be stabbed with his own weapon.

Óðinn is also the god of the dead and particularly of the hanged. A poet of the mid-tenth century called him 'lord of the gallows' (*gálga valdr*),[11] while others called him 'god of the hanged' (*hangatýr, hangagoð*).[12]

But the scalds saw Óðinn not only as the lord of the gallows and the hanged; they saw him also as the victim of the gallows. One of the names by which he was known was *Hangi* (the hanged).[13] Even more graphically, Eyvind the Plagiarist called Óðinn 'the load of the gallows' (*gálga farmr*).[14]

Óðinn's relations with the gallows and the hanged are explained more fully in a later section of the *Hávamál* (str. 157). If he saw a gallows-bird swinging on a tree above him, he could carve and paint such runes that the dead man would walk and talk to him. Again in the *Ynglinga Saga* (Ch. VII), Snorri tells that Óðinn would awaken the dead and sit down beneath hanged men. It was perhaps for this reason that a poet of the eleventh century called him 'visitor of the hanged' (*hanga heimþingaðr*).[15]

Óðinn is among other things, the recipient of human sacrifice, as may be illustrated by a story of the hero Starkað, incorporated in the longer version of the *Gautreks Saga* (Ch. VII), and told in a slightly different form by Saxo. (See Ch. X, Starkað.)

The famous champion, Starkað, was one of Óðinn's favourites. Together with his foster-brother, King Víkar of Agðir (S.W. Norway), and a number of other champions, he engaged in warlike ventures in coastal districts. The King esteemed none of his champions so highly as Starkað, and they fought together for fifteen years. It happened once that the party lay becalmed off an island and, casting sacrificial chips to find out how to get a favourable wind, they learned that it was Óðinn's will that one of their number, chosen by lot, should be hanged as a sacrifice to him. When the lots were cast, the name of King Víkar came up, and the champions were dumbfounded. They resolved to meet on the following day, and discuss what steps should be taken.

During the night, Starkað was awakened by his old foster-father, who, assuming the name Hrosshársgrani (Horse-hair-bearded), ordered the hero to follow him. They took a boat and rowed to a neighbouring island, where they came to a clearing in the forest. There they found eleven men sitting on chairs, while a twelfth chair stood empty. As Hrosshárs-Grani sat down in the empty chair, the others greeted him by the name of Óðinn. Óðinn told his companions that the time had now come to determine the destiny of Starkað.

The first to speak was no other than the god Thór. As the enemy of the giants, Thór had a grudge against Starkað. Starkað descended from giants, for his grandmother had given her favours to a very wise giant (*hundvíss jǫtunn*) instead of to Thór himself. Thór's first judgment was that Starkað should beget neither son nor daughter, and his race should die with him. But Óðinn gave it as his judgment that Starkað should have three spans of life, to which Thór replied that he would commit a dastardly act during each one of these three spans. Óðinn said that Starkað should have splendid weapons

44

and treasures in plenty, but Thór said that he would never own land and never be satisfied with what he had. Óðinn gave Starkað the gift of poetry, saying that he would make verse as fast as he could talk, but Thór said that he would never remember a line of his verse. Óðinn said that Starkað would be prized by the highest and noblest men, but Thór laid down that he would be loathed by all the commonalty.

Then Óðinn conducted Starkað back to his party, and as he left him, Óðinn said that he would expect some payment for the great gifts which he had bestowed upon him: Starkað must send King Víkar to him. As he said this, Óðinn handed the hero a spear, which looked like nothing other than a harmless reed.

When the champions met on the following morning, they resolved to make a token sacrifice of their king. Beside them stood a fir-tree, from which a slender twig drooped, and below it was a stump. The cooks were busy slaughtering a calf, and when the gut was drawn, Starkað tied a noose in it, and hung it on the drooping twig. The king now stepped on to the tree-stump; the noose was placed round his neck, and Starkað struck him with a reed, saying: 'Now I give you to Óðinn'. At that moment, the reed turned into a bitter spear, the stump fell from beneath the king's feet, and the calf's gut became a tough rope. The slender twig was now a stout branch, and it sprang aloft, raising the king to the upper limbs of the tree, where he gave up his life. Starkað had accomplished the first of his dastardly acts.

The similarities between this story and that of Óðinn on the tree are evident. In both of them the victim is at once hanged and gashed with a spear. In both cases he is 'given' to Óðinn, and similar phrases are used. While Óðinn says that he was 'given to Óðinn, myself to myself' (*gefinn Óðni, sjálfr sjálfum mer*), Starkað says, as he lunges at his king with Óðinn's spear: 'now I give you to Óðinn' (*nú gef ek þik Óðni*).[16]

Óðinn's relations with the gallows and their victims are complicated. When he made the hanged men talk, or sat down beneath them, he was clearly in quest of occult wisdom, which belongs only to the dead, just as he was when he woke up dead men,[17] and rode to the gates of Hel, calling a sibyl, long dead, from her grave, to ask her what fate held in store for Baldr.[18] The sibyl, born long ago, who told of the past and the future in the *Vǫluspá*, may well have been called by Óðinn from her grave, to sink back when the prophecy was finished.[19]

We may wonder what kind of wisdom it was that Óðinn acquired from the dead, and especially from the hanged. The sibyl in the *Baldrs Draumar* told reluctantly of Baldr's fate, and the one in the *Vǫluspá* told of the origin of the world, of men and gods and especially of the Ragnarök.

Óðinn, as it is said, acquired the mead, the art of poetry, from giants and perhaps, according to another version of the myth, from dwarfs.

45

But according to a cryptic allusion made by the Orkney poet, Bishop Bjarni Kolbeinsson, early in the thirteenth century, he seems to have learned the art from the hanged. Bjarni said:

Varkak fróðr und forsum,	I did not grow wise under waterfalls,[20]
fórk aldrigi at gǫldrum	I never dabbled in magic;
. . .	
ǫllungis namk eigi	by no means did I learn
Yggjar feng und hanga	the prize of Ygg (i.e. the art of poetry) under the hanged.[21]

In the Norse tradition, Óðinn is the chief, although not the only recipient of human sacrifice. In the one detailed account of a sacrifice to Óðinn, that of King Víkar, the victim was hanged on a tree. The Greek historian, Procopius, writing about the middle of the sixth century about the customs of the men of Thule (Thulites) said that they would offer their first prisoner of war to the god Ares, deeming this the highest form of sacrifice. They would hang the victim on a tree, or throw him among thorns.[22] Jordanes,[23] writing about the same period, spoke of similar practices among the Goths. They sacrificed their prisoners to Mars, believing that the lord of war would be placated by human blood, and they hung the captured war-trappings on trees. Whether or not Ares and Mars should be identified with Óðinn, both of them, like Óðinn, must be regarded as gods of war.

It does not follow that all of Óðinn's victims were hanged, nor even that all sacrificial hangings were dedicated to Óðinn. Snorri[24] tells that, in time of famine, the Swedes 'gave their king', Ólaf Woodcutter, to Óðinn, burning him in his house. This story seems to be supported by the *Ynglinga Tal* (str. 21), although it is possible that Snorri misunderstood his source, and that the poet alluded rather to cremation of the king after he was dead.[25]

In another passage, Snorri[26] tells how the Swedes suffered famine in the reign of King Dómaldi. In the first autumn they sacrificed oxen, but the harvests were no better; in the second autumn they sacrificed men, and in the third they fell upon their king and reddened the altars with his blood. In the *Ynglinga Tal* (str. 5), which Snorri quotes, it is said that the Swedes reddened the earth with the blood of their lord. The Norwegian *Historia Norvegiae*,[27] probably written rather earlier than Snorri's work, gives a different version of this story. The Swedes hanged their king for the fertility of the crops. The victim was not, in this case, dedicated to Óðinn, but to Ceres, by whom the historian probably meant Freyja. It is possible that, in the original story, from which the *Ynglinga Saga*, the *Ynglinga Tal* and the *Historia Norvegiae* derive, the king's blood was shed while he hung on a gibbet or a tree.

Óðinn, as the sources suggest, was most readily placated with royal or princely victims, whether hanged or not. It was told of another king of the Swedes, Aun the Old, that he struck a bargain with the god. Óðinn granted the king ten years of life for every one of his sons that he sacrificed (*gaf*). He had sacrificed nine of them and grown so old that he had to lie in bed and drink out of a horn like a baby. But when it came to the tenth son, the king's subjects put a stop to the sacrifice, and he died a natural death.[28]

In the *Gautreks Saga* it was said that the king was not only hanged, but also pierced with a spear. As already remarked, the spear was Óðinn's favourite weapon, as shown by many allusions both in older and later literature.[29] It was, thus, natural that a victim sacrificed, or 'given' to Óðinn should be transfixed with a spear. According to a prose passage in the Second Lay of Helgi Hundingsbani (24 ff) a certain Dag offered sacrifice to Óðinn, so that he might avenge his father on his brother-in-law, Helgi, who had killed him. Óðinn lent Dag his spear (*geirs sins*), and Dag ran it through his brother-in-law by Fjöturland (Fetter-grove).

Those who fell in battle might be regarded as gifts to Óðinn, but particularly, it seems, victims of the spear or javelin. The *Styrbjarnar Þáttr*[30] contains an incident in one way reminiscent of the story of Víkar. On the night before he joined battle with his nephew Styrbjörn, Eirík the Victorious, King of the Swedes (died *c.* 993) went into the temple and 'gave himself' (*gafsk*) to the god for victory, stipulating that he should have ten more years to live. Soon afterwards a big man appeared in a broad-brimmed hat. He gave Eirík a reed (*reyrsproti*), telling him to hurl it over his nephew's army, saying: 'you all belong to Óðinn' (*Óðinn á yðr alla*). As the reed flew through the air, it appeared to be a javelin (*gaflak*). Styrbjörn's men were struck blind and a mountain fell on them. Allusion is made to a practice of this kind in the more realistic *Eyrbyggja Saga* (Ch. XLIV). Before a battle started, one of the chiefs hurled a spear over the enemy, 'following an ancient custom' (*at fornum sið*), as if to dedicate them to the battle-god. Even Óðinn himself was said to observe this custom, for, at the opening of the first war in the world, when the Æsir fought the Vanir (see Ch. VII), he hurled a spear, or javelin into the enemy host.[31]

We have seen Óðinn as the lord of the gallows, the god of the hanged, the god of the spear and the chief recipient of human sacrifice. It might be expected that his victims should be hanged or gashed with a spear, but if they were hanged and gashed at once, the ritual would be more nearly complete.

A number of Óðinn's legendary victims have been named, and they were mostly kings or princes, and not the 'worst men', criminals hurled over cliffs or crushed against rocks, such as pagans of the last period were said to sacrifice.[32]

The highest sacrifice to Óðinn of which we have read in this world was that of King Víkar, for not only was he hanged and pierced, but he was also a king. But a still higher sacrifice must be that of the king of the gods, swinging in the wind from a tree and gashed with a spear.

Like King Víkar, Óðinn hung on a tree, and not on a hand-made gibbet, as many unfortunate men were said to do.[33] But the tree from which Óðinn swung was no ordinary tree. It can hardly be other than the World Tree, the holy Yggdrasill. *Yggr* (the terrifier, awe-inspirer) is one of Óðinn's names, and *drasill* is a common word in poetry for a 'horse'. In spite of arguments to the contrary,[34] the compound *Yggdrasill* can hardly mean other than 'Óðinn's horse'.

Scalds frequently refer to the gallows or gallows-tree as a horse. The basic word is either *Sleipnir*, the name of Óðinn's mythical horse,[35] or else the allusion is to the legend told by Saxo[36] of Sigar, who hanged his daughter's lover, Hagbarð, giving the gallows the name 'Sigar's horse' (*Sigars jór*)[37] The metaphor is carried further. Men swing on the gallows, and the verb *ríða* means both 'to swing' and 'to ride'. Therefore, Sigvat said in his lay in memory of St Ólaf, 'men ride to the world of death on Sigar's horse' (*ríða . . . til Heljar Sigars hesti*).[38] We may also remember that the horse was a symbol of death, carrying men to another world, a concept which may have influenced the diction of the scalds.[39]

The sacrifice of Óðinn to himself may thus be seen as the highest conceivable form of sacrifice, in fact so high that, like many a religious mystery, it surpasses our comprehension. It is the sacrifice, not of king to god, but of god to god, of such a kind as is related in Scripture of the sacrifice of Christ.

Every gift, every sacrifice looks for its reward,[40] and we may wonder what Óðinn achieved by his supreme sacrifice. The answer is given in the verses. Óðinn won the 'runes' and the secrets which go with them; he learned nine mighty magic songs, and got a drink of the precious mead of poetry. He grew and he prospered and became fruitful so that one word brought forth another, one deed gave rise to another. In other words, Óðinn became the master of magic and of secret wisdom.

In str. 139 of the *Hávamál*, which was lately quoted, there was some doubt whether *rúnar* should be interpreted as 'runes', the magic symbols, or as 'secret wisdom'. However that may be, it is shown in str. 144 that, by his sacrifice, Óðinn learnt the arts of carving runes, painting them, of invocation and of sacrifice.

From whom did Óðinn wrench such wisdom? Again the answer is partly given. Óðinn learned the mighty songs from the son of Bölthór (*Bǫlþórr*). Bölthór, whom Snorri calls Bölthorn (*Bǫlþorn*)[41], was a giant, and was father of Bestla, Óðinn's giantess mother. The famous son of Bölthorn must, in this case, be a giant and Óðinn's maternal uncle. It was appropriate that Óðinn should learn the mighty songs from a maternal uncle, for a man has no closer ties.[42] Óðinn's uncle, like his mother and grandfather, must have belonged to the giant tribe.

Giants are said to be exceedingly wise (*hundvíss, alsvinnr, fróðr*). Many of them are also said to be very old (*aldinn*), as Óðinn, their descendant, is said to be.[43] The giants were born an immeasurable time ago,[44] and this must contribute to their wisdom. Like the dead, they live in hills and rocks. They may be seen as the devouring demons of death, and even as the dead themselves.

Óðinn, god of poetry, runes and magic, acquired much of his wisdom from his giant relatives, and particularly from the wise giant Vafthrúðnir. Vafthrúdnir could tell the secrets of the giants and of all the gods for he had travelled through all the nine worlds; he had even penetrated Niflhel, into which men pass from the world of death (Hel), as if dying for a second time.[45]

On these lines we can partly interpret the strange strophes of the *Hávamál*. Óðinn, swinging on the tree of the world, was in the company of the dead, sharing the wisdom which only they possess. But this is nearly the same as to say that the god was himself dead. If wisdom could be won from a dead delinquent swinging on the gallows, how much more could be gained from Óðinn after he had passed through the world of death.

Like Christ, Óðinn rose from death, now fortified with the occult wisdom which he communicated to gods and men. This thought is conveyed in the last lines of the *Rúnatal* (str. 145) where it says: this is what Thund (*Þundr*, Óðinn) wrote (*reist*) before men's fates were laid down, where he rose up when he came back.

Óðinn hung on the tree for nine nights. This might at first sight seem to reflect the legend of Christ who rose from the dead on the third day. But the significance of the number nine in Norse heathendom must be deeper than this.[46] We read in the *Vǫluspá* (stra. 2) and the *Vafþrúðnismál* (str. 43) of nine worlds, and it was said of Heimdall that he was the son of nine mothers.[47] In fact, this number seems to be associated especially with Óðinn and with sacrifice. Óðinn learnt nine mighty songs from the son of Bölthór.

According to Adam of Bremen, the notorious festival at Uppsala was held every nine years, and continued for nine days. Nine head of every living thing was sacrificed, and the bodies were hung on trees surrounding the temple (See Ch. XII below.). We could believe that the hanged victims were dedicated to Óðinn, whose image stood with those of Thór and Fricco in the temple of Uppsala.

As was said at the beginning of this chapter, it is not impossible that the myth of Óðinn was influenced by that of Christ on the Cross. But if so, the Christian motives have been made to accord thoroughly with traditional pagan ones. We could believe that a viking in the British Isles had seen an image of the dying Christ, whom he identified with the dying Óðinn. This might give rise to the poetic expression of the myth and the combination of motives such as hanging as a sacrifice of god to god, thirst, piercing with a spear and rising again, although every one of these had its roots in pagan tradition.[48]

Óðinn did not only thirst, he also fasted. A. G. van Hamel[49] has drawn attention to many instances in Irish legend in which men fast, and thus gain mystical power over their antagonists.

The views expressed in this section may appear different from those generally current today, although the differences are not fundamental. The sacrifice of Óðinn has been seen widely as an initiation ceremony, and practices of shamans of Finno-Ugric culture have been compared.[50] Initiation is regarded largely as a symbolic death, often followed by the rebirth of the initiate under another name. It is well possible that such ceremonial practices were known to the Norsemen in very early times, but the literary sources give scant evidence of them.[51]

The myth of Óðinn seems to represent a real rather than a symbolic death. There is no way to master all the wisdom of the dead but to die. Óðinn died, and like Christ he rose up and came back. We may remember a story quoted by J. G. Frazer[52] about an Eskimo shaman of the Bering Strait, who burned himself alive, expecting to return with greater wisdom.

God of War

Snorri's story of Óðinn's journey to rob the mead of poetry includes a grotesque and apparently irrelevant episode. The god came to a meadow, where nine thralls were mowing. Drawing a whetstone from his belt, he sharpened their scythes, and when they found the blades so much sharper than before, the thralls asked to buy the stone. Óðinn said that the purchaser would have to pay a fair price, but since they all wanted it, he hurled the stone into the air. The nine thralls struggled for it, and ended by slashing each other's heads with their scythes.[1]

Óðinn then went his way, calling himself Bölverk, and came to the giant Baugi, for whom the thralls had been working. He took their place and did the work of nine men.

The origins of this peculiar story had been discussed widely. It bears some resemblance to the story of Lityerses, said to be of Asiatic origin. Lityerses would induce travellers to work for him and, when they failed to keep up with him in reaping, he would chop off their heads and wrap their bodies in sheaves. Stories of Cadmus, Jason and the dragon's teeth have also been compared. When the hero sowed the teeth, armed men sprang from the soil, and the hero provoked them to fight each other, in one case by hurling a stone into their midst.[2]

Whatever its origins, Snorri's story serves as a caricature of Óðinn, and explains his name Bölverk or 'Evil-doer'. Óðinn was god of war, and it was in his interest to promote strife. For this reason, poets called him *Hnikarr, Hnikuðr*, names which probably imply 'the one who incites to battle'.[3] In the *Hárbarðsljóð* (str. 24), Óðinn is made to boast that he had always incited princes against each other, and never made peace between them.[4]

We might expect the northern god of war to be noble, valiant, and an example to every soldier, but Óðinn was far from that. According to the sources in which he is most fully described, he was evil and sinister. He delighted especially in fratricidal strife and in conflict between kinsmen. It is told in the *Helgakviða Hundingsbana* II[5] how Dag sacrificed to Óðinn, who lent him a spear, with which to kill his sister's husband, Helgi.

It is thus that Óðinn is depicted in the *Gesta Danorum* of Saxo and in some of the Heroic Sagas. Saxo told how Óðinn, as usual in disguise, promoted dissension between Harald Wartooth and his nephew Hring, culminating in the battle of Brávellir.[6] The *Heiðreks Saga* of the late thirteenth century contains the story of a certain Gizur, nicknamed Grýtingaliði.[7] Gizur's function in the saga was to provoke war between Angantýr, King of the Goths, and his half-brother, Hlöð, King of the Huns. Some have seen Gizur as an emanation of Óðinn, or even as Óðinn himself. It would be difficult to know whether Gizur was conceived as Óðinn already in the tradition upon which the *Heiðreks Saga* was based, but there can be little doubt that those who compiled and listened to the saga in the thirteenth century saw him as such. Gizur was a common personal name in Iceland, but in the *Þulur* (name-lists)[8] it was also applied to Óðinn. It is still more telling that in the *Málsháttakvæði*, probably of the early thirteenth century, Óðinn was called Gizur and was described almost in the same words as he was in the *Hárbarðsljóð*, as the promoter of strife:

Gizur varð at rógi saðr	Gizur was guilty of slander
etja vildi jǫfrum saman	he would incite princes against
	each other.[9]

It is hardly less remarkable that, in a verse composed in 1261, Sturla Thórðarson replaced the name of Gizur Jarl, who had cheated him, with those of Óðinn and Gaut, another Óðinn name.[10]

We may wonder how old and how fundamental is the conception of Óðinn as the promoter of strife and the source of evil. When Óðinn stole the mead, as is described in the *Hávamál*,[11] his motives may have been virtuous, but his methods were reprehensible, and he had broken his most sacred oath. Even in these lines he bore the name Bölverk (Evil-doer), a name by which he was also said to call himself in the *Grímnismál* (str. 47).

The ages of the poems and legends just quoted may be questioned, but something more may be learnt about Óðinn's place in Norse heathendom from the histories of the kings and the poems about them. In the *Hákonarmál*, composed in memory of Hákon the Good (*c.* 961–3), Óðinn was described as malicious (*illúðigr*).[12] The story of Eirík Blood-axe is more illustrative and more complicated. After Eirík was killed in England in 954, his widow, Gunnhild, ordered a poet to compose a lay in his memory. The subject, as will be explained in a later chapter,[13] was the reception of Eirík by the fallen heroes, Sigmund and Sinfjötli, and by Óðinn in Valhöll. Óðinn had called Eirík because he needed his support, and Eirík, who had brought five kings with him, is presented as Óðinn's particular favourite. The reasons are not difficult to see. No king of Norway was better fitted to be the chosen hero of Óðinn, and none had held the bonds of kindred in deeper contempt. Eirík had ruthlessly slaughtered his brothers and, in the words of one saga, had hurled his kinsmen against the wall.[14]

Adam of Bremen (IV, xxvii) tells how, in case of war, the Swedes would sacrifice to Óðinn, and Snorri, in his life of Hákon the Good,[15] tells that the men of Thrándheim drank the toasts of Njörð and Freyr for fruitful harvests and peace, but of Óðinn for victory and the success of their king.

As the god of war, Óðinn apportions victory, as is plainly stated in the *Hyndluljóð* (str. 3). Among his many names were *Sigfaðir* (father of victory) and *Sigrhǫfundr* (judge or author of victory).

As will be explained in closer detail in Ch. X, Óðinn is often described as the patron and protector of legendary heroes. He teaches them strategy, or makes them invulnerable to steel. Such heroes may, in some cases, be seen as earthly representatives of the god himself, as

Gizur, who was described in the *Heiðreks Saga*, appeared to be. Óðinn was also the guardian, and even the ancestor of illustrious families. The Völsungar stood under his protection and the name of one of them, Sigmund, was also applied to Óðinn.[16]

It was said that Óðinn often awarded victory unjustly[17], and it is a standard motive that, in the end, the god turns against his own favourites. In Sigmund's last battle a one-eyed man came against him wearing a black cloak and wielding a spear. When the hero's sword struck the spear, the sword broke; the battle turned against him, and Sigmund lost his life.[18] Several stories illustrating this aspect of Óðinn's character will be quoted in Ch. X, below. These will be drawn mostly from Saxo and from Heroic Sagas, but it is plain that the motive is an old one. It is present in the Lay of Hákon and is expressed even more plainly in the Lay of Eirík. Óðinn needed his favourites to support him in Valhöll, for he apprehended that the Ragnarök might come at any minute.

Earlier in this chapter a few passages were quoted showing that those who fell in battle were taken into Óðinn's band. It was suggested that victims of the spear were especially welcome to the war-god. But it was a widespread belief, or at least a poetic conceit, that every fallen warrior went to Óðinn. Consequently, those who slew their enemies in battle could regard the act as a sacrifice to the war-god. This thought is occasionally expressed by Saxo and in the Heroic Sagas. Harald Wartooth, in exchange for the invulnerability which Óðinn granted him, promised the souls of all he killed to Óðinn.[19] In the battle of Brávellir, the same hero dedicated (*gaf*) all who fell to the god.[20] According to the *Orkneyinga Saga* (Ch. VIII) Torf-Einar, Jarl of Orkney, captured a rebellious son of Harald Finehair, cut his ribs from the back, symbolizing the blood-eagle (see Ch. XIII) and 'gave' him to Óðinn.

We may place little faith in the prose sources just quoted, but the same thought is expressed time after time by poets of the heathen age. An Icelander of the mid-tenth century, objecting to his widowed mother's suitor, met him at the cross-roads and killed him. He commemorated the deed in a verse: he had given his enemy to Óðinn; he had paid the sacrifice (*tafn*) of Gaut (i.e. Óðinn) to the lord of the gallows and fed a corpse to the raven.[21]

Hákon the Great (died 995) was remembered as the most ardent pagan among Norway's rulers, and several poets said, in praise of him, that he had given his enemies to Óðinn. Thorleif said that Hákon had sent nine princes to Óðinn and the raven was eating their flesh,[22] and Einar, in the *Vellekla*,[23] that the warlike Hákon had swelled the following of Thund (i.e. Óðinn). Already one of Harald Finehair's poets said that slaughtered men lying on the sand were dedicated to the one-eyed consort of Frigg.[24]

The dead warriors go to Óðinn's palace, Valhöll, as is stated in the *Eiríksmál* and the *Hákonarmál*. There they join the ranks of Óðinn's glorious band, awaiting the Ragnarök.

The scaldic poets have little to say of Valhöll, and their allusions to it are generally obscure. The only detailed descriptions of it are found in the *Grímnismál* (strs, 8–10, 23–26) and in Snorri's *Gylfaginning* (Chs. 24–5), based mainly on this poem.

Valhöll stands in *Glaðsheimr*, the World of Joy; its rafters are spear-shafts and the tiles are shields, as was known already by Harald Fine-hair's poet, *Þorbjörn Hornklofi*.[25] A wolf lurked to the west of the entrance and an eagle hovered over the building. There Óðinn dwelt with his wolves, Geri and Freki, and his ravens, Huginn and Muninn, who fly over the world every day. Óðinn lives on wine alone, but the fallen warriors feast on the flesh of the boar Sæhrímnir which, according to Snorri,[26] is stewed every day and arises whole in the evening. The warriors drink the liquor which flows from the udders of the goat, Heiðrún, nourished by the foliage of the tree *Læraðr*. These warriors fight each other in the courts every day, but in the evening they sit together at peace.[27]

The gate, through which the fallen warriors probably enter, is called *Valgrind* (Grill of the Fallen), and the palace has no less than five hundred and forty (i.e. 640) doorways. Eight hundred (i.e. 960) warriors will march abreast through each doorway, when they go to fight the wolf in the Ragnarök.[28]

The description of Valhöll has more to do with art than with popular belief. The splendid picture is not free from foreign influences. The glorious hall is modelled on a royal palace, but such palaces were not to be found in Scandinavia in the heathen age. J. Grimm[29] observed that, according to a chronicler of the tenth century, Charles the Great had set up a flying eagle of bronze on the roof of his palace. Later scholars have carried the comparison with European architecture further, and M. Olsen sees the Valhöll described in the *Edda* as the reflexion of a Roman amphitheatre, or even of the Colosseum, which a Scandinavian traveller had seen. There the warriors fight, day in day out. The building has many doors, and the Emperor, presiding in the high seat, might correspond with Óðinn, presiding in Valhöll.[30]

Olsen's arguments should not be rejected as lightly as they have been,[31] but they apply to the picture of Valhöll drawn by the poets of the Edda, and not to the fundamental conceptions underlying the belief.

Formally, the name Valhöll could mean 'the foreign hall', and it has sometimes been interpreted in this way,[32] although it more probably means the 'castle of the slain'. The word *valr* is applied collectively to corpses slain in battle.[33] It has been noticed that the name *Valhall* is applied to certain rocks in southern Sweden, and these were believed to be dwelling-places of the dead.[34] It is, therefore, likely that the second element in the name *Valhǫll* was not originally *hǫll* (hall), but rather *hallr* (rock). In this case, it was the imagination of the poets which turned the rock of the dead into a noble, glorious palace.

If this is so, Valhöll represents little more than a refinement of the common belief that the dead dwell in a rock, or that men die into a rock, as they died into the Helgafell in western Iceland.[35] Óðinn presides over them, originally perhaps as god of death rather than as god of war.

Father of Gods and Men

In one of his less consistent passages Snorri[1] says that Óðinn is called *Alfǫðr* (*Alfaðir*, 'Father of All') because he is father of all gods and men. He is father, not only of Thór, but also of Thór's mother, Jörð (Earth).

Many myths of the northern gods are difficult to reconcile with this statement. Óðinn can hardly, in pagan tradition, have been father of the Vanir, Njörð, Freyr, Freyja, with whom he went to war (see Ch. VII, first section). Loki, who was included among the gods (Æsir), was said to be son of the giant Fárbauti. According to one tradition, Heimdall was the father of men,[2] and it is improbable that this son of nine mothers had Óðinn for his father.

Nevertheless, Óðinn was father of a number of gods. His legitimate wife was Frigg, with whom he sometimes sat on his throne at Hliðskjálf looking over all the worlds.[3] By Frigg, Óðinn was father of the ill-fated Baldr, and he begat Váli on Rind so that he might take vengeance for Baldr.

The ancestry of Óðinn and of his two brothers, Vili and Vé, is itself puzzling. Their mother was Bestla, daughter of the giant Bölthór (Bölthorn),[4] and their father was Bur (Bor), son of Buri (Búri). Buri, in Snorri's well-known story of creation,[5] had neither father nor mother, but was made by the primeval cow, Auðumla, as she licked the salty rocks into the shape of a man.

If Óðinn was not the father of men, he played sufficient part in their creation to be called *Aldafǫðr* (Father of men). As Snorri tells,[6] Óðinn and his brothers, walking by the seashore, came upon two tree-trunks, which they shaped into the man and woman, *Askr* and *Embla*,[7] from whom the human race is descended. The *Vǫluspá* (strs. 17–18) contains a different version of this myth; Óðinn was accompanied, not by Vili and Vé, but by Hœnir and Lóður.[8] Each of these contributed his own gift to the animated figures, and Óðinn's gift was *ǫnd* (breath, life, spirit).

Óðinn was not only patron and protector of famous heroes; he was also seen as the ancestor of princely families. He was said to be the father of Sigi, ancestor of the Völsungar,[9] and of Skjöld, the eponymous father of the Skjöldungar, the kings of the Danes.[10] He was even called the father of Yngvi,[11] who is identified with Freyr, and said to be ancestor of the Ynglingar, the kings of the Swedes.

These relationships are probably based upon learned conjecture, and influenced by foreign models. The royal houses of England were commonly said to descend from Óðinn (Woden), and English genealogies were known in Iceland in the twelfth century.[12] A more ancient tradition may be preserved in the story that the Jarls of Hlaðir (*Hlaða Jarlar*), rulers of northern Norway, descended from Óðinn. Their ancestor, Sæming, was said by Eyvind the Plagiarist in the *Háleygjatal* (*c.* 985) to be a son of Óðinn and of Skaði, formerly wife of Njörð.[3]

Óðinn's Animals

Óðinn was accompanied by certain animals, and among them was the horse, Sleipnir. Allusions to this horse in early poetry are comparatively few; he was described in the *Grímnismál* (str. 44) as the finest of horses, runes were carved on his teeth (*Sigrdrífumál* 15), and in the *Hyndluljóð* (str. 40) it was said that he was born of Loki and Svaðilfari. This incident is not easy to understand, but Snorri[1] explains it in curious detail. Loki had taken the form of a mare and, after copulating with the giant's horse, Savðilfari, he bore the grey foal, Sleipnir. Sleipnir, as is told both by Snorri and in one of Gestumblindi's riddles,[2] had eight legs.

The horse and his phallus are well-known symbols of fertility, and are associated especially with the god Freyr.[3] It could, therefore, be supposed that, as god of the horse, Óðinn was beginning to usurp the place of Freyr, as he usurped that of many another god.[4] But another explanation is more probable. Fertility cults and symbols were closely linked with those of death. In the *Ynglinga Tal* (str. 14) the gallows are the 'high-chested rope-Sleipnir' (*hábrjóstr hǫrva Sleipnir*), and in the same poem (str. 7) the goddess of death was called *Glitnis Gná*, which probably means 'goddess (valkyrie of the horse', i.e. goddess in horse form). This may possibly be the meaning of the word *jódís* applied to the death-goddess in the same strophe.[5]

The hundreds of horses found buried in graves throughout Scandinavia, about sixteen in the Oseberg grave alone, suggest close association between horses and death.[6] The stately horses depicted on the Oseberg tapestries,[7] some mounted and others drawing chariots, may well be carrying their charges to the other world. Hákon the Good, according to the lay composed in his memory, seems to ride to Valhöll.[8] Both Óðinn and his son Hermóð rode on Sleipnir to the World of Death.[9]

Sleipnir was a grey. Apparitions portending death often appear mounted on greys. The good dream-woman, calling Gísli 'home' was riding a grey,[10] as was Guðrún Gjúkadóttir, when she came, in the year 1255, from the World of Death (*Násheimr*) to appear in a dream foretelling disaster.[11] In a later tale,[12] the impending Black Death appeared as a man and woman riding greys, and many stories of this kind have been recorded in Iceland in recent times. We may also remember the *helhäst* (death-horse), of which numerous tales have been told in Scandinavia.[13] Misshapen horses with varying numbers of legs have been widely recorded as portents of evil.[14]

We may wonder whether Óðinn himself took the form of a horse, as he took the forms of serpents and eagles. The nicknames *Hrosshársgrani* (horse-hair bearded) and *Jálkr* (probably 'gelding') may well suggest that this was one of the forms in which he appeared, and further evidence of this might be cited.[15]

Sleipnir was the swiftest of horses, galloping through the air and over sea. The stone of Tjängvide (Gotland), probably of the eighth century, shows a mounted horse, which appears to have eight legs. This may well be an image of Óðinn riding Sleipnir, but it is no less likely that the eight legs were intended to give an impression of the horse's speed.[16] In this case, the tradition that Sleipnir, the swiftest horse, had eight legs may derive from pictorial representations of this kind.

Some of the other pictorial objects found in Sweden and Gottland may help to show the age of Óðinn's association with the horse. A figured helmet-plate, found at Vendel in Swedish Uppland, shows a rider armed with a spear and accompanied by two birds, which could be ravens. This plate, probably made in the late seventh century, may represent Óðinn riding on Sleipnir, even though the horse has only four legs. There are other pictures of mounted men carrying spears, but it would be rash to say that every one of these represents Óðinn riding Sleipnir.

While describing Valhöll,[17] Snorri called Óðinn the 'god of ravens' (*hrafnaguð*), and told how two ravens, Huginn and Muninn, perched on his shoulders, reporting all that they had seen and heard. Óðinn sent the ravens every day over the whole world, and they returned at dinner-time.

Snorri's chief source for this latter statement was the *Grímnismál* (str. 20), which he quotes:

Huginn ok Muninn.	Huginn and Muninn
fljúga hverjan dag	fly every day
jǫrmungrund yfir;	over the wide earth;
óumk ek of Hugin,	I am afraid for Huginn
at hann aptr ne komit;	that he will not come back;
þó sjámk meirr um Munin.	but yet I fear more for Muninn.

The names of these ravens are especially interesting. The first derives from *hugr* and the second from *munr*. These have been interpreted respectively as *animus, cogitatio*, and *mens*,[18] but they were perhaps too nearly synonymous to be sharply distinguished. The ravens, Huginn and Muninn, must be seen as Óðinn's spiritual qualities in concrete form.[19] A man's fetch, appearing in the guise of an animal, is sometimes called *hugr*.[20]

Since Huginn was the name of one raven, it could, in poetic language, be applied to every raven, and examples of this usage are found in early poetry. Egill[21] called blood 'Huginn's sea' (*Hugins vǫrr*) and another poet called it 'the raven's drink' (*Hugins drekka*).[22] The warrior was called 'the reddener of Huginn's claws' (*fetrjóðr Hugins*),[23] or 'of his bill' (*munnrjóðr Hugins*).[24] A simple kenning for battle was 'Huginn's feast' (*Hugins jól*).[25] The name of Muninn is used in the same way, although rather less commonly.[26]

The relationship between Óðinn and the raven is old and deep, as is shown by numerous kennings both for Óðinn and for raven. Óðinn is the 'raven-god' (*Hrafnáss*),[27] the 'raven-tempter' (*hrafnfreistuðr*)[28] and, more strangely, 'the priest of the raven-sacrifice' (*hrafnblóts goði*).[29] In the *Helga Kviða Hundingsbana* II (str. 43), the ravens are 'Óðinn's greedy hawks' (*átfrekir Óðins haukar*). In the scaldic language it was more usual to substitute one of Óðinn's other names, so that the raven was 'Ygg's seagull' (*Yggjar már*),[30] his 'swan' (*Yggs svanr*),[31] or even his 'cuckoo' (*Gauts gaukr*).[32]

Many have wondered what is the foundation of Óðinn's relationship with the raven. No single answer can be given. The raven is the bird of death, for he feeds on corpses. Poets called him the 'corpse-goose' (*nágagl*),[33] and the 'corpse-cuckoo' (*hræva gaukr*),[34] and by many other kennings which have similar meaning.

Since the raven's most ready prey were corpses left on the battlefield, denied of proper burial or cremation, he is above all the bird of battle.

The raven haunts the battlefield, where the warrior feeds him on carrion. This thought was expressed plainly by Harald Finehair's poet, Thorbjörn Hornklofi, in the lay 'Words of the Raven' (*Hrafnsmál*).[35]

For such reasons the raven was the 'blood-swan' (*sveita svanr*),[36] 'blood-goose' (*blóðgagl*)[37] and the 'wound-grouse' (*benþiðurr*).[38] He was also the 'osprey of the spear-storm' (*geira hríðar gjóðr*),[39] the 'battle-swallow' (*dolgsvala*),[40] the 'battle-crane' (*hjaldrs trani*).[41]

Since Óðinn was god of death and of war, men slaying their enemies in battle could see the deed as a gift to Óðinn. But the fallen warrior was also a gift for the raven. In a poem already quoted (see p. 53 above), an Icelander said that he had given sacrifice to Óðinn and fed a corpse to the raven. Among the hundreds of kennings for men and warriors are many which imply 'feeder of ravens'.[42] The warrior is 'feeder of battle-hawks' (*gunnvala brœðir*),[43] 'raven-feeder' (*hrafngrennir*)[44] and 'fattener of the battle-starling' (*folkstara feitir*).[45] As shown in several texts,[46] it was a good omen for a warrior going to battle to be followed by a raven; the bird could expect a feast.

If he could predict victory, the raven could also assure it, and this may explain why figures of ravens were so frequently depicted on battle-standards. In the year 878, as is told in the Old English Chronicle (manuscripts BCDE),[47] King Alfred captured from the Danes in Devonshire a banner called *Ræfen* or *Hræfn*. This banner, according to the twelfth-century *Annals of St Neots*,[48] had been woven by three daughters of Ragnar Loðbrók in a single midday hour. If those before whom it was borne were to be victorious, the raven embroidered on it would appear flying, but otherwise it would droop.

Again, according to the *Encomium Emmae Reginae*,[49] a magical banner was borne in the battle of Ashingdon (1016) by the Danes under Canute. This banner was woven of white silk without image, but, in time of war, a raven would appear on it. He would flap his wings and open his bill if the owners were to be victorious, but if they were to be defeated he would droop.

Yet a third raven-banner is mentioned in an English source, and again it belonged to a Dane. This was called *Ravenlandeye*, which is glossed as *corvus terrae terror*, and has been compared with the banner *Landeyða* (land-waster)of Harald Harðráði.[50] According to the *Passio et Vita Waldevi*, of the twelfth or thirteenth century, the *Ravenlandeye* was given to Siward of Northumbria (died 1055), when he was hoping to fight a dragon, by a nameless old man sitting on a steep hill. The similarity between this story and that of the old man on the rock (*karl af bergi*),[51] who gave advice to Sigurð, who was on his way to avenge his father, is too close to be accidental. In both stories the old man must be

59

Óðinn, and we may suspect that a story of the legendary Sigurð has been transferred to his namesake, Siward of Northumbria.

Icelandic sources also mention a magical raven-banner. This was called *Hrafnsmerki*, and is described in the *Orkneyinga Saga*,[52] *Þorsteins Saga Síðu-Hallssonar*,[53] and in *Njáls Saga*.[54] Allusion was made to it also in the lost *Brjáns Saga*.[55] The *Hrafnsmerki* was woven for the Orkney Earl, Sigurð Hlöðvésson, by his mother Auðna (Eðna). When the wind blew, the raven embroidered on it would seem to flap his wings. This banner had the property that it always brought victory to the man before whom it was borne, but death to the man who bore it. It was borne before Sigurð in the battle of Clontarf (1014), but after he had lost three standard-bearers, he was obliged to carry it himself, and so lost his life.

Ravens were not only Óðinn's intellectual attributes, his thought or memory; they also came to be identified with the god himself. This is well illustrated by a story of Hákon the Great (died 995),[56] based partly on the *Vellekla*. Hákon had been forcibly baptized in Denmark; he sailed to Sweden, where he held a sacrifice. Two ravens, croaking loudly, flew over him, and then he knew that Óðinn had accepted his sacrifice. The story of Flóki, who sacrificed to three ravens before exploring Iceland,[57] may also suggest that the bird was one of the forms taken by the god.

Besides his ravens, Óðinn kept two wolves, whose names, *Geri* and *Freki* mean 'the greedy one'. Snorri[58] tells that Óðinn fed his wolves from his own table, for he himself lived on wine alone. In this statement, Snorri echoes the *Grímnismál* (str. 19).

The poets have less to tell of Óðinn's wolves than of his ravens, but their significance is similar. Like the raven, the wolf haunts the battlefield, devouring corpses. For this reason he is 'Óðinn's dog' (*Viðris grey*),[59] the 'bitch of wounds' (*benja tík*),[60] and the warrior is the 'man who reddens the wolf's teeth' *ulfs tannlituðr*)[61] and 'dispels his hunger' (*eyðir ulfa gráðar*).[62]

In Norse tradition, as in that of many other peoples,[63] the wolf, and sometimes the dog, are the most cruel demons of death and destruction. Such beliefs could well arise independently among peoples who had experience of wolves. The most vicious of all wolves described in Norse sources is Fenrir, the chained wolf, who lies ready to spring on the dwellings of gods and men, destroying all before him,[64] and in the Ragnarök is destined to devour Óðinn himself.[65] Fenrir is the child of Loki and the giantess *Angrboða* (Presager of Evil), and he is thus a brother of the World Serpent and of the death-goddess, Hel.[66] Two other wolves pursue the sun and the moon and, it is said, are destined to swallow them.[67]

Since the wolf is a beast of death and of war, Óðinn probably appeared in this guise, representing his most evil and sinister aspect.

From the foregoing pages it appears that Óðinn might take the form of a serpent, a raven, an eagle, a horse and a wolf. He probably assumed other forms besides these. According to the *Ynglinga Saga* (Ch. VII), Óðinn had power to change his shape; his body would lie as if asleep or dead and, in the twinkling of an eye, he would be away in a distant land.

It is hard to know how far the myths about Óðinn's shape-changing reflect cult-practices, and how far such practices reflect myth.[68] It is easy to believe that in ritual drama, Óðinn would appear as a horse, wolf, or even as a bird. But unless we suppose that anthropomorphic gods developed from those in animal form, we can hardly doubt that such cults derived from myth.

Óðinn's assumption of wolf-shape may lead us to think of were-wolves, about which legends are preserved over so great a part of Europe. In fact, the man who put on a wolf-skin probably felt himself a wolf, and a berserk, clothed in a bear-skin, thought he was a bear. Berserks were sometimes called *ulfheðnar* (wolf-skinned),[69] and they howled like wolves.

The Völsungar, Sigmund and Sinfjötli, typical Óðinn-heroes, lived in the forest as wolves.[70] A bronze plate found at Torslunda (Öland, Sweden), and probably dating from the sixth century, shows a figure with a wolf's head, skin and tail, but human feet. The figure carries a spear.[71]

O. Höfler,[72] among many valuable observations, quotes a remarkable passage from the work of the Swedish scholar, Olaus Magnus, published in 1555.[73] Men of that time, both in Scandinavia and in neighbouring lands, used to turn into wolves, especially on Christmas Eve. They would roam and plunder in bands, and do far more damage than ordinary wolves, even breaking into beer-cellars. They could assume or throw off the wolf-shape at will, and were a presage of death.

The wolves here described are not associated with Óðinn, but Óðinn lived in popular tradition more vigorously than any other pagan god. He led the wild hunt, the troop of the dead, with their horses and dogs. They were active, especially at the Christmas season.[74]

Óðinn was the god of Yule (*Jól*), and one of the older scalds called him *Jólnir*,[75] while an early historian said, perversely, that *Jól* (Yule) was named after *Jólnir*, another name for Óðinn.[76]

Óðinn's names

Snorri,[1] quoting the *Grímnismál* (strs. 46–50), gives a long list of names for Óðinn. Gangleri observes that it would take deep learning to explain the events which gave rise to all of these names, but Hár answers that the chief reason why they are so many is that so many different peoples wished to invoke Óðinn, each in their own language. The remarks ascribed to Gangleri and Hár both contain elements of truth, and there are various reasons why Óðinn should be called by about 170 names, besides numerous kennings, some of which might almost be regarded as names.[2]

Some of Óðinn's names reflect his practices or incidents in his career. To this class belong *Bǫlverkr* (Evil-doer), *Gangráðr*, *Vegtamr* (Road-practised), *Hangaguð* (God of the Hanged), *Hangi* (Hanged), *Sigfaðir* (Father of Victory).

Examples have already been given of names for Óðinn which have to do with the animal shapes which he took. To this class belong *Arnhǫfði* (Eagle-headed), and perhaps *Bjarki*, *Bjǫrn* (Bear).

Whether in cult or myth, Óðinn also appeared in many human guises. He is *Grímnir* (Masked), *Blindr* (Blind), *Tvíblindi* (Double-blind) and, at the same time, *Báleygr* (Fire-eyed). Óðinn appears commonly with one eye, and this may be implied in his nickname *Hárr*, said to derive from **Haiha-hariR* (the One-eyed Hero) and to be related to Gothic *haihs* (one-eyed) and ultimately to Latin *caecus*.[3]

Óðinn is an old man, and so he is called *Karl*; he is tall and called *Hávi*; he has a long, grey beard and is, therefore *Síðskeggr* (Long-, broad-bearded) and *Hárbarðr* (Grey-bearded). He wears a broad hat, and so he is *Síðhǫttr* (Broad hat), or simply *Hǫttr*.

Óðinn, as already explained, had a number of favourite heroes. Some of these were perhaps conceived as the god on earth, and their names could be applied to him; he is *Sigmundr* and *Gizurr* (see God of War, above).

Óðinn bore yet other names which suggest that his cult was extending in the Viking Age and before, and that many peoples were coming to regard him as the highest of the gods. He is called *Gautr*, which may originally have been the name of the eponymous father of the Gautar (people of Gautland), and hence of the Goths.[4] He is also called *Skilfingr*, and this was perhaps the name of the first ancestor of the *Ynglingar*, the kings of the Swedes who, in *Beowulf*, are called *Scylfingas*.

Óðinn took over the names and functions of other gods. He is often called *Fjǫlnir*, but Fjǫlnir who, in the *Ynglinga Saga* (Ch. X) is called the son of Freyr, must originally have been a fertility-god, hardly distinct from Freyr himself.[5] Óðinn is, in one text, called *Jǫrmunr*. If the reading is correct, it probably implies that he has usurped the place of another god, identical with the *Irmin* of the Saxons and the ancestor of the *Erminiones*, the great Germanic tribe.[6]

Some of Óðinn's names are even more puzzling. He is called *Njótr*, a name which might be borrowed from that of the Saxons and Anglo-Saxons, *Sahsnot, Saxneat*.[7]

This perhaps implies that, by those who considered Óðinn the highest of the gods, the chief god or eponymous father of other peoples came to be identified with Óðinn. It is also possible that various peoples whose chief god was originally other than Óðinn had come to believe that he was the same. Such suggestions may be supported by two other names. Óðinn is called *Sváfnir*, which is also the name of one of the serpents gnawing the roots of the World Tree, Yggdrasill.[8] It could well mean 'the one who puts to sleep, kills', but when we read of a Sváfnir, King of Sváfaland,[9] we may wonder whether Óðinn was not identified with the eponymous father of the Suebi.[10] Óðinn was also called *Langbarðr*, which means 'Long-bearded', but may also be influenced by the tribal name of the Lombards.[11]

Óðinn's Eye

Thorbjörn Hornklofi in his 'Words of the Raven' referred to Óðinn as 'the one-eyed consort of Frigg' (*enum eineygja Friggjar faðmbyggvi*),[1] showing that the myth of the one-eyed god was well known and comparatively old. The *Vǫluspá* (str. 28) also contains an allusion to the loss of one of Óðinn's eyes. The sibyl, as if to prove her wisdom, tells Óðinn that she knows well enough where he hid (*falt*) his eye; it was in the glorious Well of Mímir.[2] This well, according to Snorri,[3] stood beneath one of the roots of the tree Yggdrasill, and all wisdom was stored in it. Snorri goes on to say how Óðinn's eye came to be there. The god had begged for one draught from the well, but it was not granted until he placed his eye as a pledge.

This story may be an attempt to rationalize the myth but, whatever its age, it is not difficult to understand. Óðinn's sight was his most precious possession, and for this reason he must sacrifice a part of it. In the same way, Týr must sacrifice his arm before the wolf Fenrir could be bound[4] and, as some believe, Heimdall, whose hearing was the keenest, sacrificed one of his ears.[5]

Several tales are told of Óðinn's remarkable vision. It is told in the prose introduction to the *Grímnismál* how Óðinn and his wife, Frigg, were sitting in *Hliðskjálf*, looking over all the worlds. Snorri[6] has more to tell of Hliðskjálf, evidently thinking of it as a kind of throne (*hásæti*) in Ásgarð. When Óðinn sat there, he could see everything, and even saw where the fugitive Loki had hidden after the death of Baldr. Scalds must also allude to a myth of this kind when they call Óðinn *Hliðskjálfar harri, gramr* (lord, prince of Hliðsjalf).[7]

The name *Hliðskjálf* is of some interest. Its second element, *skjálf* (*skjalf*) has been interpreted as 'a steep slope', 'a cutting off of a high plateau',[8] while usages of the corresponding *scelf, scylf* in Old English might suggest a meaning such as 'crag, rock', 'turret, pinnacle'.[9]

The first element in the name, *hlið-*, most probably means 'opening, gap'. The whole may then mean approximately 'the hill, rock with an opening in it'. Perhaps the god looked through this opening over all the worlds.[10]

But why should the place where Óðinn sits be called a *skjálf*? An interesting, if speculative explanation was offered by M. Olsen.[11] He noticed that, in the *Grímnismál* (str. 6), a *Válaskjálf* was mentioned; it was built in days of old and roofed with silver. We could suppose that this was the home of Óðinn's son, Váli, who was born to avenge Baldr (see Ch. IV below).[12] It is still more interesting, as Olsen points out, that the place-name *Válaskjálf* (*Valaskioll*) was found in south-eastern Norway, and in the same region there was probably a *Viðarskjálf* (*Viskjøl*).

Viðar was another son of Óðinn, and he was 'the silent god' (*hinn þǫgli áss*),[13] whose function was to avenge his father on the wolf Fenrir in the Ragnarök.[14]

The place-names, as Olsen suggests, may derive from myth and ritual. Óðinn and his two avenging sons, Váli and Viðar, seem to sit, reside in a *skjálf*. Óðinn was called *Skilfingr* and his sons might be **Skilfingar*, which formally could mean 'men of the *skjálf*', and thus be equivalent to the name *Scylfingas*, given in *Beowulf* to the royal dynasty of the Swedes.[15] This, it is now generally believed, derived from one of the place-names in *skjálf* (*skälf*) of which a number are found in Swedish Uppland.[16] Since Óðinn was king of the gods, he and his sons might be expected to have a *skjálf* as well.

Alternatively, the names *Hliðskjálf, Válaskjálf* and *Skilfingr* might imply little more than that Óðinn and his sons were lords of the rock.

The Cult of Óðinn

Óðinn has already been seen as a complicated figure. He descended on the one side from giants and on the other from the primeval Buri. He was of great age (*aldinn*) and had immense wisdom. He played a part in the creation of men, giving them *ǫnd* (breath, life, spirit), and brought other gifts, both to men and to gods, among them poetry and runes.

Óðinn was also master of magic (*galdr*) and was called *galdrsfaðir* (father of magic). Chanting his corpse-charms he called the dead from their graves, wrenching their secret wisdom.[1] He had learnt nine mighty magic songs from the son of the giant Bölthór, and he mastered eighteen spells, known neither to man nor woman.[2] With these he could blunt swords, turn a javelin in flight, quell fire and calm the sea; he could carve such runes that a gallow's bird would walk and talk to him.

It was also said that Óðinn could blind, deafen and strike panic into his enemies, making their weapons as blunt as sticks. He could inspire the berserk rage, and his own men, invulnerable to steel, would fight without corselets, savage as wolves and strong as bulls.[3]

Óðinn was master, not only of the kind of magic called *galdr*, but also of a baser kind known as *seiðr*,[4] which had first been taught to the Æsir by the goddess Freyja. By means of it, Óðinn could see into the future, cause death, misfortune and sickness, and deprive men of their wits. This form of magic was accompanied by such depraved practices (*ergi*)[5] that it was held to be dishonourable for the male sex, and generally reserved for the goddesses.[6] It is even implied that Óðinn changed his sex, as he often changed his form.[7]

Óðinn is god of war and dissension, delighting not least in fratricidal strife. He is lord of the slain (*Valfǫðr*) and of the dead (*drauga dróttinn*). He is presented as the lord of gods and men, and no god is described in closer detail in the literary sources. These sources were largely the work of Icelanders and, with few exceptions, were preserved in Iceland alone. It is, therefore, surprising that medieval authors rarely allude to the worship of Óðinn in Iceland itself, richly as they describe it in other lands.

It has been argued from such negative evidence that the cult of Óðinn had scarcely reached Iceland by the end of the Heathen Age.[8] This difficult problem may be approached by various ways.

Place-names and personal names often preserve memories of heathen cult. While Iceland has many place-names compounded with *Þór-* (Thór-)[9] and some compounded with the names of Njörð and Freyr, it has none compounded with Óðinn's name. The same must be said of names for men and women, for while there are a great many which have *Þór-* as their first element, and some whose first element is *Frey-*, none begin with Óðinn's name. Some personal names which are really names of animals suggest that Óðinn was worshipped by those who bore them, or by their ancestors. Not a few Icelanders were called *Hrafn* (Raven), *Úlfr* (Wolf), and by names compounded with these elements. Although the raven and the wolf were associated with Óðinn, it would be rash to say that men called by such names came of families which had Óðinn for their favourite god. It is told of Hrafnkell, the son of Hrafn, that he was 'priest of Freyr' (*Freysgoði*).[10]

If Óðinn enjoyed comparatively little worship in Iceland, we may wonder how the Icelandic authors came to know so many myths about him. A partial answer has already been given; Óðinn was the god of poetry, and our records of Óðinn derive chiefly from poets, whether directly or indirectly.

Place-names and personal names on the mainland of Scandinavia may tell something about the cult of Óðinn. A casual glance at sketch-maps marking place-names compounded with *Óðin-* shows that these are fairly common in Denmark [11] and southern Sweden, especially in east and west Gautland. But when we turn to Norway, the picture changes. M. Olsen,[12] the chief living expert on theophoric place-names in that country, counts no more than twelve which contain the element *Óðin-*, while 33 appear to preserve the name *Ullr*, 27 have the element *Þór-*, 26 *Njǫrð-* (*Njarð-*), and about 48 the names of the god and goddess Freyr and Freyja.

The Norwegian *Óðin-* names are most numerous in the south-east. There are perhaps four in Tröndelag, one in Sogn and one in Fjordane but, as far as is known, none in south-western Norway. In other words, this region, in which a great proportion of her settlers originated, pro-vides the same picture as Iceland herself.

The distribution of *Óðin-* names has been explained variously. Many have seen in it evidence that Óðinn was not indigenous to Scandinavia, and that his cult had spread from the south. According to some, this cult reached the north *c.* 200–400 AD, and others have given it a later date, while some have believed that Óðinn was little known in Scan-dinavia before the Viking Age.[13]

It may be questioned whether it would be right to draw such far-reaching conclusions from the absence of personal names and the rarity of place-names compounded with *Óðin-* in the western districts.

It was seen that a small group of place-names containing this ele-ment has been identified in Tröndelag. One of these, *Onsöien*, was re-corded earlier as *Odinsyn*, said to be from *Óðinsvin* (Óðinn's meadow),[14] and -*vin*, denoting a sacred meadow, or place of worship is said, as a place-name element, to belong to a very early period, even to the Bronze Age.[15]

It must, however, be admitted that an isolated place-name can tell little. It could be transferred from one place to another, as the names *Uppsalir* and *Sigtúnir*, applied to two neighbouring farms in the Ice-landic Eyjafjörður, were probably influenced by those of the two glorious cities of Sweden.[16]

While there is no compelling evidence that the cult of Óðinn was practised widely in the west before the Viking Age, there are reasons to believe that it spread and developed during that age.

Historical sources may throw some light. It is plain that Norway suffered a social revolution in the ninth and tenth centuries. It was in this period that Harald Finehair unified Norway, making it a single kingdom. His achievement was not altogether lasting, for we read as late as the twelfth century of petty kings and of a divided Norway.

Harald's work was continued for a few years by his favourite son, Eirík Bloodaxe, until he was driven from Norway.

We may wonder what kind of a social system Harald introduced, and what were the results of his work. He was judged varyingly by medieval historians. According to the *Fagrskinna*,[17] compiled in Norway early in the thirteenth century, he brought peace and good government (*friðaði ok siðaði*). But the settlers of Iceland saw Harald in a different light. He put down rebellious spirits without mercy; he took to himself all the hereditary estates (*óðul*), and all the land, inhabited or not, even the sea and the lakes, and all farmers were obliged to be his tenants.[18]

This tyrannical rule, according to Icelandic sources, drove many from their homes, and was the reason for the settlement of Iceland. If there were, in fact, other reasons, this was certainly a major one.

It has been said already that few of the settlers appear to have venerated Óðinn. They were a conservative people, who emigrated largely to preserve their traditional way of life, rule by farmers of leading families, independent of kings and central government.[19] Their social units and loyalties were based upon blood-relationship.

These settlers were mostly men of western, and particularly of south-western Norway.[20] They venerated Thór, Njörð and Freyr, but seem to pay little heed to Óðinn. There is, however, much to suggest that Harald was Óðinn's man. In the *Haraldskvæði* (Words of the Raven), one of the oldest poems about Harald, Thorbjörn Hornklofi tells how the raven followed the young king, hungry for the corpses which he left on the battlefield. These corpses were dedicated to Frigg's one-eyed husband (see previous section).

We cannot overlook a strange story preserved in the *Flateyjarbók*[21] of the fourteenth century, which appears to have ancient origins. This story is not altogether clear, but it seems that, in his childhood, Harald had been the guest of Óðinn.

Three years before his death, Harald conducted his son Eirík to the high seat, proclaiming him sovereign over the whole land. If there should be any doubts about Harald's allegiance to Óðinn, there can be none about Eirík's. In his contempt for the bonds of kindred and his unscrupulous slaughter of his brothers, he showed himself a typical Óðinn hero. It was said that he was baptized in England a few years before his death but, in the end, Óðinn accorded him a splendid welcome in Valhöll.[22]

A contemporary poet called Harald 'the young Yngling' (*ungum Ynglingi*)[23] and Thjóðolf Hvin traced his descent, or rather that of his cousin, Rögnvald, through doubtful stages to the famous house of the Ynglingar, kings of the Swedes. Eirík Bloodaxe was also called 'son of the Yngling' (*Ynglings burr*).[24]

Whether or not Harald's family descended from the Ynglingar, and thus from the gods, it seems clear that the centre of their power was Vestfold, in the neighbourhood of the Vík. This was the region most strongly influenced by Danes and Jutes, who repeatedly claimed over-lordship.[25] It was also in this part of Norway that the place-names con-taining the element *Óðin-* were most common, and some of them, such as *Óðinsakr* (Óðinn's cornfield), of which there are several examples, were probably age-old.[26]

Although Harald's family claimed to descend from the Swedish dynasty, some of them bore names resembling those of Danish princes. The name Harald was itself common among them, as was Hálfdan (Half-Dane?), the name of Harald's father. Harald Finehair had more to do with Danes than with Swedes. His favourite wife, the mother of Eirík Bloodaxe, was daughter of a king of Jutland and, as Hornklofi said, he rejected Norwegian women in her favour.[27] Eirík, in his turn, married the Danish princess, daughter of King Gorm.[28]

If we see Harald and Eirík as followers of Óðinn, we can better understand one side of Óðinn's character. His is not the cult of land-owners, the hereditary aristocracy bound by ties of blood. It is the cult of landless men and those without family ties, of men like Starkað[29] and soldiers of fortune, even of berserks, who join the king's court in hope of gain.

We may wonder whether the social system, which Harald was said to favour, had affinities with any practised in other lands. It closely resembles a system which, according to Cæsar,[30] was practised among Germans of his day.

They had little interest in agriculture, living chiefly on meat and milk. No one was allowed to own land, but the land was parcelled out every year by the chieftains among tribes and families. At the end of the year they must move elsewhere.

Cæsar was probably describing tribes in western Germany, or-ganized for war. Their system was not, in our sense, an aristocratic one; it left no room for hereditary landowners or established families, but placed all power in the hands of military chiefs. It is the antithesis of the system based on family units which the settlers introduced into Iceland, but yet it has close affinities with the social system described in *Beowulf*, as prevailing among the Geatas (Gautar) and especially the Danes.

This may partly explain the rarity of the cult of Óðinn in Iceland and the strange distribution of place-names containing the element *Óðin-*, which should be considered more closely. It was seen that they are rare in a great part of Scandinavia, but common in Denmark and Gautland, extending sporadically into south-eastern Norway and Swedish Uppland. Some of them denote places of public worship and temples of various forms and ages. Among these may be counted *Óðinsvé*, which is fairly widespread in Jutland and eastern Sweden,[31] *Óðinshǫrgr* (*-hargher*)in Swedish Uppland,[32] *Óðinssalr* (Tröndelag, S.E. Norway and S.W. Sweden), *Óðinshof* (S.E. Norway). Others, such as *Óðinsakr* (chiefly Gautland and S.E. Norway) and *Óðinsvin*, suggest that, for some, Óðinn was partly a fertility god. *Óðinslundr*, of which there are several examples in Sweden, may show that, like several other gods, Óðinn was worshipped in sacred groves. The name *Odinsberg*, fairly widespread in Sweden and Denmark,[33] leads us again to think of Óðinn as the *Karl af bergi*[34] (Man of the rock).

It could be said that the name Óðinn was purposely avoided in some districts because the god was revered so deeply as to be unmentionable. But there is a more natural explanation. If those of the western districts knew Óðinn, they had neither respect for him as a god nor love for all he stood for.

I have suggested that the cult of Óðinn spread widely and rapidly in the ninth and tenth centuries. This may be illustrated from the careers of certain Icelanders. S. Nordal[35] made some especially interesting observations on the religious life of Egill Skalla-Grímsson (died *c.* 990). Egill had grown up, the son of an industrious farmer, in the worship of Thór. When he left Iceland at the age of seventeen, Egill came into touch with the cult of Óðinn, associating with princes and living as a viking and a poet. Another Icelandic poet, although a lesser one, has been seen as a 'convert' to the cult of Óðinn.[36] This was Víga-Glúm (died *c.* 1003). Like Egill, Glúm grew up on a farm. Beside this farm, at Thverá in northern Iceland stood the temple of Freyr, and close by the ever-fertile cornfield *Vitazgjafi* (the Certain Giver),[37] probably under the protection of the god. On his father's side, Glúm came of a family evidently devoted to Freyr but, as a young man, he visited his mother's father, the old viking, Vigfúss of Vörs in Norway, and proved his prowess before him. As he left, Vigfúss gave his grandson a cloak, sword and spear, saying that he would maintain his authority so long as he kept them. When Vigfúss died, his guardian spirit (*hamingja*), seen in a dream as a gigantic woman, came to Iceland and joined Glúm. The spear, as already seen, was Óðinn's favourite weapon, the cloak his favourite garb.

Throughout his adult career Glúm was on bad terms with the god Freyr. To begin with, he slew an enemy on the cornfield, Vitazgjafi, and thus defiled it. The father of this man had no legal case, and was expelled from the district. But before he left, he brought an ox to Freyr's temple. The beast bellowed and fell dead, showing that the god had accepted the sacrifice and would repay it.

Glúm's relations with Freyr grew worse as time wore on. He concealed his outlaw son, Vigfúss, within the sacred precincts of the temple. He emulated Óðinn in swearing an ambiguous oath in three temples, one of which was the temple of Freyr. Afterwards he had a strange dream. He saw Freyr sitting on a chair on the bank of the river, where many had come to visit him. These were his dead kinsmen, who had come to intercede with the god on his behalf. But Freyr answered abruptly and angrily, remembering the ox which Glúm's enemy had given him.

Freyr, as it seems, could do little harm to Glúm, so long as he kept the cloak and spear given to him by his viking grandfather. But after swearing the ambiguous oath, he gave them away. He could no longer withstand his enemies, and was driven from his lands in disgrace.

Woden-Wotan

It is not easy to describe Woden (Óðinn) as continental and English heathens saw him, but it is plain that, in the eyes of the English, he had some of the characteristics so vividly described in the Norse sources.

Woden appears as the god of chieftains, and thus the highest god. Hengist and Horsa, the legendary founders of the English nation, were said to descend from him and, as Bede said,[1] many, indeed nearly all of the provincial kings traced their descent from Woden.[2] In certain royal genealogies, Woden appears with a son Bældæg, whom some identify with Baldr.[3] Woden himself is said to descend from Geat (Geata), whose name corresponds with *Gautr*, applied in Norse literary sources to Óðinn.[4]

As the ancestor of princes, Woden was worshipped as a god and, according to the tenth-century chronicler Æthelweard,[5] sacrifice was brought to him for victory and bravery.

In England, as in Scandinavia, Woden was master of magic, as is illustrated by the so-called *Nine Herbs Charm* against poison. In the text and translation of G. Storms[6] this reads:

> Wyrm com snican, toslat he nan.
> Þa genam Woden VIIII wuldortanas,
> sloh ða þa næddran þæt heo on VIIII tofleah.

A worm came crawling, it killed nothing.
For Woden took nine glory-twigs,
he smote then the adder that it flew apart in nine parts.

The nine *wuldortanas* could well imply rune-staves, or staves with runes cut on them.[7] The repetition of the number nine may also be significant. After hanging for nine nights on the tree, Óðinn learned nine magic songs, and he boasted, in the *Hávamál,* that he mastered eighteen charms.

It is possible that the English heathens had regarded Woden as the discoverer of runes but, if so, memories of this had faded by the time the records were written. In England, as elsewhere, Woden was commonly identified with Mercury, and in the prose fragment *Salomon and Saturn,*[8] Mercury the giant (*Mercurius se gygand*) is said to be the founder of letters.

Again in the Old English *Runic Poem* it is said of the rune *Os*:

Os byþ ordfruma   ælcre spræce . . .
Os (?) is the source of all language . . .

It would be natural to suppose that the name *Os* was Latin, and meant 'mouth', as it may well have done for the man who gave the poem its present shape, But the corresponding lines of the late Icelandic Runic Poem[10] read:

Óss er aldinn Gautr   Óss is the ancient Gautr,
ok Ásgarðs jǫfurr,   prince of Ásgarð,
ok valhallar vísi.   lord of Valhöll.

In the latter case, *óss* was equivalent to *áss* (god), and designated Óðinn.

Memories of Woden's cult are also preserved in some English place-names. If not many, these names are comparatively widespread.[11] Among them may be mentioned *Wodnes beorh* (Woden's barrow), probably applied to a burial mound in Wiltshire, later called Adam's Grave.[12] The half-hundred name Wenslow, in Bedfordshire, is recorded earlier as *Wodenslawe* (1169) and as *Weneslai* (1086),[13] and derives ultimately from **Wodnes hlæw*, also meaning 'Woden's barrow'. These names, corresponding with the Scandinavian **Óðinsberg* and **Óðinshaugr*,[14] suggest that Woden was seen as god of the dead. The name Wednesfield (Staffs) is recorded earlier as *Wodnesfeld*,[15] and might be compared with **Óðinsakr*, whereas Wensley (Derbyshire, older *Wodnesleie*) is reminiscent of the Swedish **Óðinslundr*. The name of

Woden is also preserved in Wansdyke (*Wodnes dic*, 903)[16] and *Wodnes-dene* (939). Óðinn's nickname, *Grímr* (masked), is also supposed to be present in Grim's Ditch or Dyke.[17]

Under influence of the invaders, the English homilists commonly used the Norse form *Óðinn* (*Óðon*, etc.) instead of the English *Woden*.[18] This usage shows how vigorously the traditions of Óðinn lived among the invaders, but tells little about his place in English heathendom.

In short, the English records suggest that, among the pagan English, Woden had filled a place similar to that which he filled in Scandinavia as late as the tenth century. This implies that already the north German ancestors of the English, *Saxones*, *Angli* and *Iutae*, has seen him in a similar light; he was god of princes, victory, death and magic, perhaps also of runes, speech, poetry. It is not insignificant that the English came chiefly from north Germany and Denmark, where the cult of Óðinn seems to be old and particularly firmly established.

Poor as the records are, it is evident that Woden (Wotan) was worshipped widely in continental Germany. He is named in the second place, between Thunaer and Saxnot, in the Saxon baptismal vow,[19] probably of the late eighth century. He is also named, together with other gods on the Nordendorf clasp of about AD 600.[20]

A remarkable tale of Wotan was told in the *Origo gentis Langobardorum* of the seventh century and again by Paulus Diaconus (died *c.* 795) in his *Historia Langobardorum* (I,7–8), whose version will be followed here.

The Lombards, then called *Winnili*, were said to have come from Scandinavia under the leadership of two brothers, Ibor and Aio (Agio). When the Vandals demanded tribute of them, they were persuaded by their mother, Gambara, to take up arms.

Before joining battle, the Vandals called on Godan (Wotan) to award them victory, but he said that he would give victory to those whom he saw first at sunrise. Gambara, in her turn, invoked Frea (Frigg), the wife of Godan. She commanded that the Winnil women should spread their hair over their faces in the shape of beards. They should assemble with their men in view of a window, from which Wotan used to look at the rising sun. When he saw them, the god exclaimed: 'qui sunt isti longibarbi?' Having given the Lombards their name, the god must add a gift, and the gift was victory. Godan, according to Paulus, was only another name for Wotan, formed by adding one letter, and perhaps implying that there was a form *Gwotan*. Wotan, Paulus adds, was worshipped by all Germanic peoples, and the Romans called him Mercury.

This *ridiculosa fabula*, as Paulus calls it, is interesting in many ways.[21] Wotan looking down on the earth through a window (*per fenestram*) recalls Óðinn, sometimes accompanied by his wife, Frigg, gazing over all the worlds from Hliðskjálf. In the Lombard tale, Wotan is seen already to be married to Frea (i.e. Frigg), and he dispenses victory, as he does in the Norse sources.

The god Wotan (Wuoden) is also named in the Second Merseburg Charm, together with other gods and goddesses, as the one whose magic heals sprains.[22]

It was seen that Paulus identified Woden with Mercury, and this was a commonplace in the Germanic world. It was expressed in the name for the week-day, *Dies Mercurii*, called in Old English *Wodnesdæg*, in Old High German *Wuotanestac* and in Old Norse *Óðinsdagr*.

In a number of votive inscriptions of the second and third centuries, found chiefly in western and Lower Germany, a *Mercurius* is named, and various nicknames are given to him.[23] It is probable that some of these are dedicated to Wotan, but the chief god of the neighbouring Celts was, according to Cæsar,[24] also called Mercurius. It is therefore difficult to know whether the inscriptions are dedicated to a Germanic or Celtic Mercurius.

Looking further back into antiquity, we find that already Tacitus (*Germania* IX) named Mercury as foremost of Germanic gods, but it does not follow that *Mercurius* was the only Latin name given to Wotan-Óðinn. Adam of Bremen identified him with Mars. The Goths used to sacrifice their prisoners to a god whom Jordanes[25] called Mars, hanging captured war-gear on trees. The Mars of the Goths may well have been Wotan.

Writing of the Semnones, said to be the noblest of the Suebi, Tacitus (*Germania* XXXIX) remarked that at a given time they would assemble in a sacred forest. A man was slaughtered and gruesome rites performed. The participants believed that in this forest their tribe had its origin, and it was so holy that none might enter it unless bound with a chain. If he were to fall, he must not get up, but roll himself out. This forest was the abode of the *regnator omnium deus*.

Many have identified the *regnator* with Týr, but it is more probable that this terrifying god was Wotan, or Mercury. According to an earlier passage in the *Germania* (IX), Mercury received human sacrifice, whereas other gods, Hercules and Mars (Thór and Týr) were placated with animals.

There is another reason to identify the *regnator omnium deus* with Wotan. It was mentioned that no one might enter the sacred forest unless bound with a chain. A prose passage in the *Helga kviða Hundingsbana* II (str. 24, cf str. 30) was quoted above. It tells how Dag, wishing to take vengeance on his brother-in-law, Helgi, sacrificed to Óðinn,

73

who lent him his spear. Dag met Helgi in or by *Fjǫturlundr* (Fetter-grove), and there killed him with the spear.

Many have seen Dag's act as a sacrifice to Óðinn,[26] and have associated the Helgi cycle of legends particularly with the Suebi and Semnones. Evidence of this association has been seen in the name of the heroine *Sváva* and in *Sváraland*, said to be related to *Suebi*. The place-name *Sefa-fjǫll*, found in the *Helga kviða Hundingsbana* II, is also associated by some with the tribal name *Semnones*.[27]

However that may be, Óðinn claimed in the *Hávamál* (str. 149) that he was the master of fetters; he could also make his enemies impotent in battle, so that they were struck blind and deaf, and their weapons cut no more than sticks.[28] It is not extravagant to suppose that Óðinn could also inflict the *herfjǫturr* (battle-fetter), a kind of panic which struck men in battle and made them powerless.[29]

CHAPTER THREE

THÓR

Thór and the Serpent—Thór and the Giants—Thór's Hammer and his Goats—
The worship of Thór—Thór in the Viking Colonies—Thór-Thunor—Conclusion

IN THE EYES of many Norsemen, particularly in western regions, Thór, the thunderer, was the noblest and most powerful of gods, and he seems to grow in stature as the Heathen Age comes to its close.

Thór lived in Thrúðheim (the World of Might) or Thrúðvangar (Fields of Might), where his house, Bilskírnir, was as splendid as Valhöll. Every day, Thór waded rivers to sit in judgment beneath the World Tree, Yggdrasill.[1] He maintained the order of the universe, defending our world (Miðgarð)[2] and the world of gods (Ásgarð).[3] His weapon was the hammer, Mjöllnir, with which he held the forces of chaos in check. These forces were represented chiefly by giants and giantesses, dwelling in Jötunheimar, in the east.

Before considering Thór's place in the divine hierarchy and in the minds of his worshippers, we may recall some of the myths in which he figures, obscure as they may be.

Thór and the Serpent
The most formidable of Thór's enemies was the serpent, Miðgarðsorm or Jörmungand, who lay coiled around the earth.[4] Thór's struggle against this symbol of evil provided motives, not only for poets, but also for pictorial artists. It is believed to be represented on carved stones of the eleventh century, found at Altuna in Sweden and Gosforth in Cumberland.[5] In his *Ragnarsdrápa*, the ninth-century scald, Bragi,[6] inspired by a picture painted on a shield, described Thór's battle with the serpent. The god was seen pitting his strength against the monster out at sea. Accompanied by a giant, the god had cast his line, and the 'hideous thong of the sea' was hooked, glaring from the deep at the enemy of giants. Thór would have crashed his hammer on the serpent's skull, had not his giant companion taken fright and cut the line.

In pagan times there was another version of this myth of Thór and the serpent and, according to it, the god killed his enemy. This version underlies the work of Úlf Uggason[7] who, in the late tenth century, described a pictorial panel in a house in Iceland (see Ch. I, second section) : Thór was seen striking off the serpent's head on the waves. The *Hymiskviða* (22–4), one of the later poems of the *Edda*,[8] drew on this same version of the story, but the text is defective. It is also told in the *Hymiskviða* that Thór baited his hook with the head of an ox. This detail, repeated by Snorri, seems also to be represented on the Gosforth slab.

Snorri[9] retold the story of Thór and the serpent at length. As he, or rather his speaker (Hárr) believed, the god had failed to destroy the serpent, who still lives in the encircling sea. Although this version agrees with Bragi's *Ragnarsdrápa*, which Snorri knew well, we may suppose that in the original myth, Thór had conquered his enemy. Gods and heroes who did battle with such monsters generally overcame them, as did Indra, Marduk, Sigurð, Finn. Dualistic conceptions, creeping into Norse heathendom from Christian and near-eastern eschatology, perhaps demanded that the symbol of evil should survive until the Ragnarök.

In the Ragnarök, according to Snorri,[10] Thór and the serpent will kill each other. Snorri seems here to be following cryptic lines of the *Vǫluspá* (56), which he probably interprets correctly. This story of the primeval serpent may be influenced by those of Leviathan and the old dragon of Revelation (20), who shall be loosed at the end of the world.

Thór and the giants

Giants and giantesses were Thór's natural enemies. If all of them had escaped the force of his hammer, there would be no life left in this world, and Ásgarð would be peopled by giants.[1] The poets Vetrliði[2] and Thorbjörn Dísarskáld[3] gave lists of giants and giantesses whom Thór had destroyed. Numerous kennings, which poets used to denote Thór, contained allusion to his enmity with giants and his victories over them.[4] It was a standard motive for poets and medieval writers that Thór was away in the east, fighting the giants.

Among the giant enemies of Thór, two were particularly vehement, Hrungnir and Geirröð. A picture representing the god's battle with Hrungnir was painted on a shield. This shield was given to Thjóðólf of Hvin, who described the scene magnificently, though obscurely, in his poem *Haustlǫng* (see Ch. I, Old Norse Poetry).

The god was seen on his way to the giant world; his temper rose and the sky (*mánavegr*, 'path of the moon') rumbled beneath him. The heavens glowed with fire and the earth was pelted with hail, as Thór's chariot, drawn by goats, sped to the meeting with Hrungnir. Rocks shivered and broke and, when he prepared to meet the god, the giant stood on his shield (*randar íss*). He was crushed by the hammer but, as he fell, the giant's whetstone, evidently the counter-part of Thór's hammer, crashed into Thór's skull, where it lodged until a woman loosened it with a magic song.

The sequence of the *Haustlǫng* is by no means easy to follow, but other poets showed by their allusions that the story of Thór and Hrungnir was known widely. Bragi described Thór as 'Hrungnir's skull-splitter',[5] and his hammer was called 'Hrungnir's bane'.[6] The scald, Kormák, in the late tenth century, called a shield 'the platform of Hrungnir's feet',[7] and Bragi[8] called it by the double kenning 'the leaf of the feet of the thief of Thrúð'. The thief of Thrúð must be Hrungnir and, since Thrúð was a daughter of Thór, we may suppose that there was a version of the myth in which the giant had provoked the god's anger by raping her.[9]

Snorri,[10] who preserved the lines quoted from the *Haustlǫng*, told an elaborate tale of Thór and Hrungnir, showing that he had access to other sources besides this poem. Because of Óðinn's indiscretion, the giant had been invited into Ásgarð while Thór was away in the east. As he got drunk, Hrungnir began to use boastful, threatening words; he would take the whole of Valhöll to the world of giants; he would sink Ásgarð and kill all the gods and goddesses, except Freyja and Thór's wife, Sif, whom he would keep for himself. In their distress, the gods named Thór, who appeared brandishing his hammer. He accepted Hrungnir's challenge to a duel, and the giant now set off to prepare for it. Meanwhile, Hrungnir's brother-giants were apprehensive. How would they fare at the hands of Thór, if Hrungnir, strongest of their race were killed? They resorted to a ruse; they built a gigantic figure of clay, called him *Mǫkkurkálfi*, and put a mare's heart into him, the only heart big enough.

The clay giant stood terrified beside Hrungnir on the appointed field, waiting for Thór. Thór drew near accompanied by his follower, Thjálfi, who ran forward and deceitfully told Hrungnir that he did unwisely in holding his shield before his body, for Thór would attack him from underground. It was because of this that the giant stood on his shield.

At the next moment, amid thunder and lightning, Thór appeared. The god hurled his hammer and the giant his whetstone, and the weapons met in mid-air. The hammer completed its course and smashed the giant's skull, but the whetstone split in two, and one half lodged in Thór's head. When the giant fell, his leg was over Thór's neck, holding him to the ground. No one could move it but Magni, the infant son of Thór and the giantess Járnsaxa.

77

Thór then returned to his home, Thrúðvangar, with the stone in his skull. It was deduced from the *Haustlǫng* that the witch had drawn out the stone by magic, but Snorri tells a more elaborate story and, as he had it, the operation was not successful. The witch Gróa arrived and began her chant; the stone was loosened, but before she had finished, Gróa forgot her words, and so the stone remains fast in Thór's skull.

Snorri's explanation why Thor's skull was not relieved of the stone is yet more puzzling. Gróa, the witch, was the wife of Aurvandill (v.l. *Ǫrvandill*), nicknamed the Bold. As she began to loosen the stone in his head, Thór wished to please her; he told her how he had carried her husband from the distant north in a basket, and it would not be long before he arrived home. As a proof, Thór said that one of Aurvandill's toes, sticking out of the basket, had frozen. Thór had broken it off and hurled it into the sky, where it became a star called 'Aurvandill's toe'. The witch was so pleased with this news that she forgot her charms.

It is likely that 'Aurvandill's toe' was the name given to a star in the Middle Ages, whether to the morning-star or another. This is supported by the use of the word *earendel* in Old English, which is glossed as *jubar* and *aurora*. In a Blickling Homily, St John the Baptist is called: *se niwa eorendel* and, in a hymn in the Exeter Book[11], Christ is addressed:

Eala Earendel,   engla beorhtast

translating:

O jubar angelorum, angelorum splendissime.

In his account of Thór and Aurvandill, Snorri was probably retelling a folk-story, which had arisen to explain the name of a star called 'Aurvandill's toe'. Saxo tells also of a hero called Horvendillus, father of Hamlet, and a Middle High German epic names an Orendel. Attempts have been made to identify these figures with Snorri's Aurvandill, but they have nothing but names in common.[12] It should be added that, in the *Hárbarðsljóð* (19), Thór boasted that he had hurled the eyes of the giant Thjazi (see Ch. VII, Njörð) into the sky, where they shone as a perpetual mark of his glory. According to Snorri, on the other hand, it was Óðinn who made stars of Thjazi's eyes.

The tale of Thór's visit to the giant Geirröð was hardly less famous than that of his duel with Hrungnir. It was described in the *Þórsdrápa*[13] of Eilíf Goðrúnarson, a scald of the late tenth century (see Ch. I, second section) and again by Snorri.

The *Þórsdrápa* is the most intricate of all scaldic lays, and it will be long before agreement is reached on details of its interpretation. The poet begins by describing how his faithless friend, Loki, had urged the thunder-god (*Herþrumu Gautr*) to visit the house of Geirröð, telling him that green paths lay all the way. Thór set off for the giant world, evidently accompanied by the runner, Thjálfi. The journey was beset with danger. A raging torrent had to be crossed; it was not a natural torrent, but one swollen with the urine or menstrual blood of giantesses. The waters reached to Thór's shoulders (str. 8), and Thjálfi would have succumbed, had he not clung to his master's belt or shield-strap (str. 9). The god and his companion were driven by the stream, perhaps to a rowan-tree (*esja vón* or *vǫn*).[14] After they arrived at the house of the giant, some obscure incidents followed. Thór, it seems, broke the backs of the two daughters of the giant, and the giant hurled a pole of red-hot iron at the god's mouth (str. 15). When Thór caught the glowing iron in mid-air, the giant took refuge behind a pillar, but Thór drove the pole into his belt and crashed his hammer upon him (str. 19). Meanwhile, Thjálfi helped his master, and fell upon the giant, evidently in the form of a falcon (strs. 19, 20).

Many phrases in the *Þórsdrápa* are obscure to us because our knowledge of the underlying myth is less than the poet expected.[15] It has been said that Snorri, who alone preserved the lay, has misinterpreted it, and thus made it more difficult for us. In reality, Snorri's account of Thór's journey provides an interesting example of his method; he combined Eilíf's version of the story with those which he knew from other sources. He quotes two strophes from a poem in Eddaic and not scaldic form, and it is probable that he knew more of this poem, and perhaps more of the *Þórsdrápa* that he quoted.

Snorri leads in with an introduction, explaining how it was that Loki undertook to get Thór into the house of the giant (see Ch. V). This introduction is humorous in tone, and we may suspect that it was devised by mythologists of the twelfth century to answer the question left obscure in older sources, why Thór had been persuaded to undertake the perilous journey.

According to Snorri, Thór set off without his belt of strength (*megingjarðar*) and without his hammer. This seems to contradict the *Þórsdrápa* (str. 19) where, according to the most natural interpretation, the god was equipped with Mjöllnir, the symbol of his power.

Another difference between Snorri's story and that of the *Þórsdrápa* is that Snorri makes Loki the companion of Thór, and says nothing of Thjálfi. On his way to the house of the giant, Thór came to a giantess, Gríð, one of Óðinn's mistresses. She warned Thór of the giant's unfathomable cunning, and lent him a girdle of strength, a pair of iron gloves and a staff. The god reached the torrent, here called Vimur, and pressed upstream, while the river was made to swell up to his shoulders by Gjálp, one of the daughters of Geirröð, who was straddling it. Thór hurled a rock at the giantess, saying in an alliterating phrase: 'a river must be damned at the source' (*at ósi skal á stemma*). Thór struggled to shore, where he grasped a rowan (*reynir*), and it afterwards became a proverb: 'the rowan is the salvation of Thór' (see Thór in the Viking Colonies, below).

When Thór and his companion came to the house of the giant, they were conducted to a goat shed. The god sat on a chair, and it began to rise to the rafters; he struck the rafters with the stick lent him by Gríð, and the chair sank rapidly. Beneath it were Gjálp and Greip, the two daughters of Geirröð, whose backs were broken.

After this, the giant summoned Thór to his hall to join him in sports. The giant seized some glowing iron and hurled it at Thór with his tongs, but the god caught it in his iron gloves. The giant took refuge behind a pillar, but Thór threw the glowing iron through the pillar, the giant, the wall of the house, and out into the earth.

The tale of Thór and Geirröð remained popular in the Middle Ages (see Ch. I, Saxo Grammaticus). In Saxo's version (Book VIII) the place of the god is taken by Thurkillus, who died a Christian, and, in the Icelandic *Þorsteins Þáttr Bæjarmagns* by Thorsteinn, a servant of Ólaf Tryggvason. The giant, in Saxo's version, was brother of Guð-mund of Glasisvellir,[16] a half-earthly king. The lands of these brothers were separated by a river spanned with a bridge of gold. The residence of the giant was foul, gloomy and neglected and in it was an old man whose body had been pierced with red-hot irons. With him were three diseased women with broken backbones. At this point Saxo distin-guished his hero from Thór, for he made Thurkillus say that years ago the god Thór, provoked by the giants' insolence, had driven red-hot irons through the vitals of Geirröð (Geruthus), and the backs of his women had been smashed by thunderbolts (*fulminum*).

The *Þorsteins Þáttr* is, in some details, closer to Snorri's version of the story of Thór than to Saxo's of Thurkillus, although it contains some strange motives not to be found in any of the others. In spite of great differences, several motives in these four versions of the story remain constant. The most significant is that of the torrential river, whether called Vimur or Hemra, which divides the world of men from that of giants. It is like the river Gjöll, spanned with a gold-thatched bridge, over which Hermóð passed on his way to the world of death. The giants are the devouring demons of death; they may even be the dead, and it is Thór who defends us from their greed.

Thór's hammer and goats

In some of the myths just quoted, Thór was seen swinging or hurling a hammer. The hammer is occasionally replaced by a club,[1] and it is hard to think of the mighty god without such a symbol of power.

The hammer was called *Mjǫllnir* and, although the origin of this name is not known, etymological speculation has not been unfruitful, *Mjǫllnir* has been compared with the Icelandic verbs *mala* (to grind) and *mølva* (crush), but some have associated it rather with Russian *mólnija* and Welsh *mellt* (lightning).[2] The suggestion that the name of Mjöllnir is ultimately related to these words is particularly attractive. Since Thór was the god of thunder, we may suppose that his weapon was originally the lightning, or like Indra's, the thunderbolt. In Saxo's version of the story of Geirröð, Thór seems to crush the giantesses with the force of thunderbolts.

Allusions to Thór's hammer were made by heathen poets, Bragi[3] and Eilíf,[4] but for detailed accounts of its force and functions we must look to Snorri's *Edda* and particularly to the poem *Þrymskviða* (see Ch. I, Old Norse Poetry). This poem, as already remarked, is a joke, presenting a caricature of the noble Thór. The poet has drawn on several older lays which we know, and it is not venturesome to suggest that he also drew on ancient lays now lost.

Parts of the story told in the *Þrymskviða* will be given in a later chapter. In brief, it tells how Thór's hammer was stolen by the giant Thrym, whose tribe would conquer Ásgarð unless it were recovered. But the giant refused to restore it unless the gods gave him Freyja as his bride. The goddess angrily refused to go to the world of the giants, but the poet describes Thór, most masculine of gods, travelling to the giant world wearing the dress and jewels of Freyja, and pretending to be the giant's bride. Even in this disguise Thór could not restrain his enormous appetite. In the *Hymiskviða* (str. 15) he had devoured two oxen while visiting a giant, and in the *Þrymskviða* (str. 24) he made supper of an ox, eight salmon and all the dainties reserved for the ladies, washed down with three gigantic measures of mead.

In the end, the hammer was brought forth and placed on the knees of the supposed bride, in order to hallow her (*brúði at vígja*, str. 30), but the god now disclosed his identity; he grasped the hammer and crashed it on the skulls of giants.

Ironical as it is, this story explains one of the functions of Mjöllnir. It was not merely an offensive weapon. In hallowing the bride, it probably brought her fertility, and it has sometimes been regarded as a phallic symbol.[5]

According to the *Haustlǫng* (str. 15) Thór rode in a chariot drawn by goats. In the *Húsdrápa* (str. 3) he was called *hafra njótr* (user of goats), and in the *Hymiskviða* (str. 31) he is the *hafra dróttinn* (lord of goats). A story in clerical tone, probably dating from the late twelfth or early thirteenth century is preserved in the great codex *Flateyjarbók*.[6] It is told there how the Christian King Ólaf Tryggvason entered a temple at Mærin, in Thrándheim. He saw many idols, and Thór, who was worshipped most of all, was in the middle of them: 'he was of enormous size, and worked all over in gold and silver. This is how Thór was arranged: he was sitting in a chariot, a very splendid one, and two wooden goats, finely carved, were harnessed before it . . .'

As the boar was held sacred to Freyr, and the ram to Heimdall, the goat was sacred to Thór.[7] The *Hymiskviða* (str. 37) alludes obscurely to a story that Loki had half-killed one of Thór's goats. This must be a variant of Snorri's famous story about Thór's journey to the giant Útgarðaloki.[8] According to Snorri, it was the youth Thjálfi who damaged the goat and, in recompense, Thjálfi and his sister Röskva were made Thór's bounden followers. Snorri's story of the wounded goat is exceptionally interesting. Thór had slaughtered both his goats and eaten them for supper. In the morning he hallowed (*vígði*) them with his hammer. They stood up, but one of them was lame in the hind leg because Thjálfi had split the thigh-bone to get at the marrow. Comparable stories have been recorded in Ireland and in many other lands,[9] but the closest parallels, applied to calves rather than to goats, are found in Armenian apocrypha. Stories are told there of a calf, the gift of God or an angel, which was slaughtered, and one leg thrown away. It was afterwards revived, but one leg was missing.[10]

The use of the verb *vígja* (to hallow, consecrate)[11] suggests that in Thór's revival of his goats we have to do with something deeper than folktale. It is, indeed, remarkable how often this verb is used to denote the activities of Thór and his hammer. As the funeral pyre of Baldr was set alight, Snorri says: *Þórr vígði bálit með Mjǫllni* (Thór hallowed the pyre with Mjöllnir).[12] Thór's object may have been, as it was when he hallowed his goats, to restore the god to life, or it may have been to preserve him from danger on his journey to the world of death.

Until the end of the pagan period, Thór was remembered as the protector and hallower of the dead. His name had been read in a cipher found on the great memorial stone of Rök in East Götland, commonly assigned to the mid-ninth century.[13] The god's protection is also invoked in plainer language in a number of memorial inscriptions of the tenth and eleven centuries and in these the characteristic verb *vígja* is sometimes used. An inscription on a stone, found at Glavendrup in Fyn and carved about 900–925, contains the words *þur uiki þasi runar* (may Thór hallow these runes). The stone of Virring in Denmark, carved about the end of the tenth century, reads: *þur uiki þisi kuml* (may Thór hallow this memorial). Sometimes a shorter formula *þur uiki* (may Thór hallow) is found, and sometimes, as on the stone of Læborg in Jutland (*c.* 925–50), the god's protection is invoked by the picture of a hammer carved on the stone. It will be noticed that stones which bear such inscriptions are found in Denmark and in southern Sweden. They were perhaps inspired by the example of Christians, who carved such inscriptions as: 'may God help his soul'.[14]

While some invoked Thór's protection of their dead in runes and carved pictures, others placed miniature hammers of silver or other metal in graves. More than forty of these amulets have been found, and some of them measure little more than 2 cms in length. They are often furnished with a loop, so that they might be attached to clothing, These hammers date mostly from the latter years of the tenth century, or early eleventh, and are found in greatest numbers in Denmark, southern Norway and south-eastern Sweden,[15] where the influence of Christianity was strongest. They may perhaps be regarded as the pagan answer to the miniature cross, worn on clothing or placed in graves. One example, now in the British Museum, was found at Cuerdale, in Lancashire.[16] In quality and workmanship, the hammers vary greatly. Some of them are beautifully worked in silver, ending in fantastic eagle-heads with piercing eyes, reminiscent of the piercing eyes of Thór as they are described in the *Þrymskviða* (*ǫndótt augu,* str. 27). Others are roughly and simply worked in iron, and can have nothing more than a symbolic value.

A particularly interesting find was made at Foss in Hrunaman-nahreppur, in S.W. Iceland.[17] This is believed to date from the tenth century. It is very different from the typical images of hammers found in Scandinavia, and looks as if it were a compound of a hammer and a cross, even the work of a man of mixed religion. A miniature silver axe is also reported to have been found in the same place.

Another interesting find was made in the north of Iceland. This is a bronze statuette, 6.7 cms tall, of a sitting man with a long beard, said to date from about AD 1000.[18] With his two hands, the man grasps an object which closely resembles the Foss 'hammer' just mentioned. Such objects were probably made to be carried in the purse or pocket, en-suring the protection of the god. It may be remembered how the Ice-landic poet, Hallfreð, by that time a Christian, was charged before Ólaf Tryggvason with keeping an ivory image of Thór in his purse, and worshipping it secretly.[19]

D. Strömbäck[20] has made some observations on the significance of the hammer in Iceland. In a list of churches and notable places in the diocese of Skálaholt, it is said that Helkunduheiðr, in the extreme north-east, divides the Eastern Quarter from the Northern, and there, on the moor, Thór's hammer (*hamarr Þórs*) is erected, and this is the dividing mark. Although preserved only in manuscripts of the seventeenth and eighteenth centuries, this document was probably drawn up about 1200.[21]

The axe, in form, resembles the hammer and it seems also to be associated with Thór. Strömbäck, in the paper just mentioned, quotes a passage from the *Landnámabók*,[22] illustrating its sacral significance. A certain Einar Thorgeirsson sailed from Orkney with a party of others to settle in north-eastern Iceland. They landed in a fjord, since called *Øxarfjǫrðr* (Axe-fjord). They set up an axe at a place called *Reistargnúpr*, an eagle at another point, and a cross at the third, and thus they took possession of the whole of the Axe-fjord.

The axe and the cross suggest that Einar and his companions were of mixed belief, like Helgi the Lean, and those in whose graves miniature crosses and hammers have been found side by side.[23] The significance of the eagle is more difficult to determine, and it is not said whether it was a dead eagle, a live one, or an image. But the eagle, like his sworn brother (*eiðbróðir*), the raven, is Óðinn's bird; an eagle, probably in effigy, hovers over the door of Valhöll;[24] cutting the blood-eagle (*blóðǫrn*) was a form of sacrifice to Óðinn.[25] It seems, therefore, that these settlers placed their new lands under the protection of three gods, Thór, Óðinn and Christ.

The goat, the hammer and the axe were, as it seems, the oldest attributes of Thór, and as symbols of divinity were perhaps older than Thór himself. Scandinavian rock-carvers of the Bronze Age depicted human figures, often ithyphallic, swinging an axe and sometimes a hammer, showing that the axe was a fertility symbol. At least one of these figures, grasping two hammers, has a head horned like that of a goat. Gold bracteats of the Iron Age show distorted human figures mounted on horned and bearded beasts.

The swastika, which is of eastern origin, must have been introduced into the north at a very early time, since it is found on rock-carvings and other objects of the Bronze Age.[26] It must also have been used as a symbol of Thór's hammer at a comparatively early time. The Lappish god Horagalles (*Þórr Karl*), who was adapted from Thór, perhaps in the early Iron Age, is depicted, not only with a hammer, or two hammers, but also with a swastika.[27] In Iceland a form of swastika was used until recently as a charm to detect thieves, and was called *Þórshammar*.[28] According to Snorri,[29] King Hákon the Good, a Christian at heart, made the sign of the Cross over his cup when he drank the libation, but his heathen friends said that he was making the sign of the hammer and dedicating his drink to Thór. The Christian sign might well be mistaken for that of the hooked cross, and the Christian custom of making the sign of the Cross over a drink or meal, could have led pagans to hallow their food and drink with a comparable symbol.

The images of Thór's hammer are often short in the shaft. Whatever its meaning, this fashion appears to be based on an old tradition. Snorri gives an explanation: the hammer was forged by a dwarf, but he was interrupted in his work by a gnat biting his eyelids.[30]

Snorri[31] tells of two other treasures possessed by Thór. He had a belt (*megingjarðar*) and when he girded himself with it his divine strength (*ásmegin*) was doubled. An allusion to this belt was made already by Eilíf in his *Þórsdrápa* (7).[32] He also had a pair of iron gloves with which he wielded his hammer. The giantess Gríð lent Thór a girdle of strength and iron gloves when he was on his way to the house of Geirröð, but these are distinguished from his own treasures.

The Worship of Thór

Snorri[1] tells how, when the gods were in distress, they called out the name of Thór, and he would come to their aid at once, even though he might be far away. Rune-masters of the tenth century inscribed Thór's name on stone, asking his protection, and Icelandic poets of the end of the pagan period composed hymns of praise, which can be addressed only to Thór. These hymns were preserved by Snorri,[2] and they are unlike the scaldic and Eddaic poetry quoted so far in this chapter. In them the god is addressed directly in the second person. He is praised for his victories over giants and giantesses, for defending our world against the forces of chaos.

Vetrliði Sumarliðason, murdered by Christian missionaries in AD 999, made a poem in the simple form *Málaháttr*, commending Thór for destroying two giants and two giantesses, including Gjálp (*Gjǫlp*), probably the daughter of Geirröð:

Leggi brauzt Leiknar,	You smashed the limbs of Leikn,
lamðir Þrívalda,	you bashed Thrívaldi,
steypðir Starkeði,	you knocked down Starkað,
stétt of Gjǫlp dauða.	you trod Gjálp dead under foot.[3]

Thorbjörn Dísarskáld (Poet of the Dís), probably of the same period, praised Thór in the scaldic measure, *Dróttkvætt*, for despatching two giants and six giantesses:

Ball í Keilu kolli,	(Your hammer) rang on Keila's skull,
Kjallandi brauzt alla,	you crushed the body of Kjallandi—
áðr drapt Lút ok Leiða,	you had killed Lút and Leiði—
lézt dreyra Búseyru,	you made blood flow from Búseyra,
heptuð Hengjankjǫptu,	you finished Hengjankjapta,
Hyrrokin dó fyrri,	Hyrrokin died before that,
þó vas snemr en sáma	earlier the dusky Svívör
Svívǫr numin lífi.	was robbed of her life. [4]

These fragments are slight, but they represent a long and rich tradition of religious poetry. [5] No sentiments could be more abhorrent to early Christians than those expressed here. The fragments were preserved until Snorri's time because of the names of giants and giantesses which they contain. Such things were the stock-in-trade of poets.

Much can be learnt about the worship of Thór and his place in the minds of men of the late Viking Age from Icelandic historical writings. In these sources Thór appears not only as the chief god of the settlers but also as patron and guardian of the settlement itself, of its stability and law.

The opening clauses of the heathen law of the settlement have been quoted. [6] Everyone who had business to perform at a public assembly, prosecuting, defending or giving evidence, must swear an oath, and call to witness Freyr, Njörð and the all-powerful god (*hinn almáttki áss*). Attempts have been made to interpret the unnamed and all-powerful one as Ull, [7] and as Óðinn, [8] but he can scarcely be other than Thór. [9] Thór stands in contrast to Óðinn, a chaotic, amoral figure, as the upholder of order; he is the chief god of our world.

Evidence of the regard in which the settlers held Thór may be seen in the names which they bore. More than a quarter of some 260 settlers named in the *Landnámabók* bore names of which the first element was *Þór-* and, of about 4,000 people named in the whole book, nearly 1,000 bore names beginning with *Þór-*. Such names were often inherited from Norwegian ancestors, but even if they do not show a personal relationship between the god and the men who bore them, they suggest that there was a strong tradition of Thór-worship in the families of those who settled Iceland. Few names of other gods appear in Iceland as elements in personal names. [10]

Frequently we read of men whose names were changed, either because of their own devotion to Thór or because their parents 'dedicated' them to this god. Thus *Grímr* came to be called *Þórgrímr*, *Steinn* became *Þorsteinn*, *Oddr* became *Þóroddr*. [11]

The predominance of the worship of Thór among the settlers of Iceland may also be seen in the place-names. Some twenty place-names, excluding secondary ones, distributed throughout the island have *Þór-* as their first element.[12] No less than five of these are *Þórshofn* (Thór's Haven), and another five *Þórsnes* (Thór's Headland), confirming the impression gained from historical literature that Thór was, at this time, a god of seafarers.

Place-names, like personal names, may be transferred from one to another, and their value as evidence of the religious outlook of immigrants may be limited. But, devotion to Thór is expressed plainly in the story of one of the settlers, Ásbjörn Reyrketilsson. According to the *Landnámabók,*[18] Ásbjörn took possession of a wooded region in the south of Iceland: 'he dedicated his settlement to Thór and called it Thór's Forest (*Þórsmörk*)'.

The richest and probably the most reliable of the historical sources for the study of Thór is the *Eyrbyggja Saga.*[14] This saga tells of Hrólf, a chieftain of south-western Norway. He kept a temple, *Þórshof,* dedicated to Thór, and he was so devoted to his patron and beloved friend (*ástvinr*), that his name was changed to Thórólf. When, about the year 884, Thórólf emigrated to Iceland, he took the timbers of the temple with him. As will be mentioned in a later chapter, the image of Thór was carved on one of the main supporting pillars. Thórólf threw these pillars overboard when he drew near the coast of Iceland, and he made his home at the place where they drifted ashore. He believed, not only that Thór guided the drift of the pillars, but he was himself in them: 'Thór had landed!' (*Þórr hafði á land komit!*). As Thór upheld the world, he upheld the temple and many another building.

Thórólf built a temple near the spot where the pillars had come to shore,[15] establishing an assembly and proclaiming the surrounding field a holy place (*helgistaðr*), to be soiled neither with excrement nor with the blood of vengeance.

After the death of Thórólf, this field was soiled with blood and then deemed no holier than any other. Therefore the assembly place was moved, and, we may assume, the temple with it. The new field, a few miles further inland, was hardly less holy than the old. It contained a *dómhringr,* or circle of stones within which judgment was delivered. In, or beside this circle was a stone called Thór's Stone (*Þórs steinn*), upon which the bones of men sentenced to be sacrificed were broken.

The *Eyrbyggja Saga* was probably written about the middle of the thirteenth century,[16] but it contains material of much greater age, because its author made use of much older works, some of which dated from the early twelfth century.[17] The passages quoted are also found, in reduced form, in the *Landnámabók,*[18] which seems here to derive from the *Eyrbyggja.*

The *Landnámabók* contains several other tales illustrating the veneration and affection with which early Icelanders regarded Thór. He was the god of pillars which upheld their houses, and he was their guide in voyages at sea, and he came to their aid in distress.

Hallsteinn, the son of Thórólf who was lately mentioned, took possession of land in Thorskafjörð, to the north of his father's settlement. After he had offered sacrifice, asking Thór to send him some supporting pillars, an enormous tree was washed ashore. Pillars were made of it, not only for Hallsteinn's house, but for nearly all the houses in the neighbourhood.[19]

One of the settlers of northern Iceland, when he first sighted land, refused to jettison his pillars, saying that he preferred to invoke Thór directly, asking him to show him where to make land. If the land were already settled, he would fight for it.[20]

Thór was the chief patron of the settlement but, in the minds of the settlers, Thór and Christ were not yet the deadly enemies which they were later to become. Several settlers came of the mixed Gaelic-Norse families of Ireland and the Hebrides. One of the best-known of these was Helgi the Lean, who grew up in Ireland. He believed in Christ, but would call on Thór to guide him at sea, and when great decisions had to be made. When he drew near to the coast of Iceland, he called on Thór to show him where to land, and the answer came that he must go to the north. But when he had established his new home, Helgi called it Kristnes (Christ's Headland), as it is called to this day.[21]

Since these tales were recorded by Christians at a time when memories of heathendom had faded, they often bear a strong Christian colouring. One of them tells of a man called Örlyg, brought up in the Hebrides by 'the holy Bishop Patrick'. Before he sailed for Iceland, the Bishop gave him some sacred objects, a bell and timbers to build a church, which was to be dedicated to St Columba (Kolumkilli). Örlyg made the voyage with his foster-brother, Koll, who commanded another ship. They held the two ships together until they ran into a storm and lost their way. Örlyg called on Patrick to help him, and made land safely in a bay since called Patrick's Fjord (*Patreksfjörðr*), but his foster-brother invoked Thór, and his ship was wrecked.[22]

This story is rather confused, but it looks as if 'the holy Bishop Patrick' was, originally, the patron of Ireland, who is set up as a successful rival to Thór.

Some of the more romantic sagas contain interesting tales about the worship of Thór among Icelanders and Greenlanders. Many of these bear a clerical stamp, but they may still show what heathens of the latest period expected of their favourite, or at least what early Christians thought they expected. When Thorfinn Karlsefni and his followers were exploring the New World, soon after the end of the tenth century, they ran short of food. Christian as they were, these men called on God to help them, except for one of their number, Thórhall, who was a bad Christian (*illa kristinn*). He lay on a rock, gazing into the air and muttering verses about his patron, Thór. Soon afterwards a whale drifted ashore and Thórhall could boast that he had got something for his poetry; the red-bearded Thór had proved stronger than Christ. But when the explorers tasted the meat they fell ill because it was poisoned.[23]

Stories like these, to which more could be added,[24] give an impression of the growing rivalry between Thór and Christ. Signs of this might also be seen in the miniature hammers found in graves, and the inscribed prayers for his protection. To the end, Thór was the defender of the pagan world, the world of gods (Ásgarð). Thorbjörn Dísarskáld, already mentioned, said:

Þórr hefr Yggs með árum   Thór has nobly defended Ásgarð
Ásgarð of þrek varðan   with the help of Ygg's (Óðinn's) servants

It was not only the monsters of chaos whom Thór must ward off. In earlier times, heathens had looked on the White Christ tolerantly, and even with indulgence,[25] but when they knew that Christianity threatened the existence of their world, Christ and his agents assumed the position of chaotic demons. It is to the credit of early Christian apologists that they allow us to appreciate the sentiments of their antagonists.

When the German missionary Thangbrand was in Iceland (997–999), he found some powerful supporters, but also many opponents, especially among the poets. Some of these made verses deriding and slandering him, and among them was Vetrliði, whom the missionaries murdered while he was cutting peat. Another poet, also murdered by the Christians, had described Thangbrand as the 'effeminate enemy of gods' (*argan goðvarg*).[26] Most remarkable of all Thangbrand's opponents was the poetess, Steinunn, whose lines clearly show Thór as the champion of heathendom.

When Thangbrand's ship was driven on to a rock and badly damaged, Steinunn claimed a victory for Thór. Triumphantly she declared in two verses that Thór, slayer of the son of the giantess (*mǫgfellandi mellu*) had wrecked the ship of the keeper of the bell (priest); the gods (*bǫnd*) had driven the horse of the sea (ship), and Christ had not protected it.

This story is told in the *Kristni Saga* (IX), where the verses are preserved, and in slightly different form in the *Njáls Saga*,[27] which adds something to it. The poetess met the missionary and tried to convert him to the heathen religion. She asked him whether he had heard that Thór had challenged Christ to a duel, but Christ had not dared to fight. Thangbrand said only that he had heard that Thór would be nothing but dust and ashes, were it not God's will that he should live. The source and age of this story cannot be determined, but it typifies the rivalry, perceptible already in earlier sources, between Christ and Thór, the noble defender of Ásgarð. It shows also how Christians regarded Thór; he might sink to the level of a demon, but no one could say he did not exist.

I have delayed long over the worship of Thór in Iceland because the picture is here uniform and comparatively clear. The history of Iceland covers little more than the last century of heathendom. At that time Thór was worshipped more widely than any other god, although Freyr and Njörð, perhaps also Óðinn and Baldr were worshipped as well.

Runes, archaeological finds, and some of the poems quoted have shown that Thór was well known on the mainland of Scandinavia in the late pagan period. At this time, his cult was perhaps strongest in Norway.

Such an impression is confirmed by the historical sources, although these are neither so rich nor so trustworthy as those in which the worship of Thór in Iceland was described. For the most part these historical sources are the work of Icelanders, and many of them may be traced to Christian apologists, and especially to Benedictine monks of the late twelfth century, to Odd Snorrason and to Gunnlaug Leifsson (died 1218) who could see little in Thór but a demon, arch-enemy of the Christian religion. The first aim of such writers was to praise the victories of the Christian kings, Ólaf Tryggvason (died AD 1000) and Ólaf the Saint (died AD 1030) over the agents of Satan. They had read widely in European hagiography, and the stories which they tell are often coloured by this reading. But yet, in their descriptions, the god Thór preserved many of the characteristics and attributes which he had shown in other sources. He was wise, and he came to the aid of those who invoked him. He was the enemy of the giant race, carrying his hammer and riding in his chariot.

It is frequently said that Óðinn awards victory, and his toast is drunk for victory and the prosperity of kings,[28] but it is often emphasized that Thór was the god held in greatest veneration, and he is mentioned first when sacrifice to the gods is described.[29]

Odd,[30] followed by several later historians, told a characteristic story of a meeting between Thór and Ólaf Tryggvason. As the King was sailing off the coast of Norway in his magnificent Long Serpent, a man called from a headland, asking for passage. This was granted, and the stranger came aboard, a fine-looking man with a red beard. He made much of himself, and poked fun at the King's men. When they asked him to tell them some ancient history, he answered that there would be no questions which he could not answer. The stranger was brought before the King, and he told him the history of the land which they were passing. In the old days it had been peopled by giants, but all of them had died except for two women. Then men had come from the east to people this region, but they were so cruelly persecuted by the two surviving giantesses that they called 'Red-beard' to their aid. He appeared without delay, drew his hammer from his shirt and crushed the giantesses. When he had finished his tale, Thór dived into the sea and vanished.

Odd[31] had also described the famous temple of Mærin in Trondheim, where Thór was the God most worshipped. When Ólaf Tryggvason visited this temple, the squires were preparing a human sacrifice. Pretending to take part in this sacrifice, Ólaf stepped before the idol and smashed it with his axe.

Ólaf Tryggvason did not put an end to the worship of Thór. Sagas about Ólaf the Saint tell of the temple of Guðbrand í Dölum, in central Norway. The chief idol was made in the image of Thór, but, unlike the idol at Mærin, this one was tall and stout and stood on a platform holding a huge hammer. Thór was hollow inside, and so was the platform underneath him. Every day he was fed with great quantities of bread and meat. When the idol was brought to the assembly-field at daybreak, all the heathens bowed down before him. St Ólaf told them to look to the east and behold his own god riding in glorious light. At that moment one of the King's men struck the idol with a club and he fell in fragments. Out of him jumped rats as big as cats and all sorts of crawling monsters, well nourished on bread and meat.[32]

This story bears the stamp of hagiographic symbolism. The Christian god is the sun, and St Ólaf is, almost as a medieval poet saw him, the ray (*geisli*) of the sun. The chief interest of this story from the present point of view is that the God of the Christians is pitted against Thór.

Another story was told, first by Odd,[33] and again by later writers, which plainly illustrates this. Jarl Eirík, son of the pagan champion, Hákon the Great, was among the chiefs who defeated Ólaf Tryggvason in the battle of Svölð. Eirík had vowed that he would submit to baptism if he defeated the King. Until that time he had worn the image of Thór on his ship's prow, but now he broke it and replaced it with a Cross.

There are other stories which illustrate the veneration in which Thór was held by the last heathens of Norway.[34] On the whole the medieval sources suggest that Thór was admired most by those among whom tradition was strongest, especially by the landowners of Trondheim and of central Norway. He was wise, mighty and brave, incorporating the ideals of his worshippers and, as Christian propagandists fail to conceal, he was the enemy of evil, chaotic giants.

This impression of late Norwegian heathendom is gleaned chiefly from Icelandic histories, but when we turn to other sources of knowledge the picture changes. M. Olsen's studies of Norwegian place-names[35] have thrown inestimable light on the development of Thór's cult and on his status at earlier periods. The place-names of Norway seem to show that Thor's popularity grew as Christianity drew nearer.

Although the name of the god is often difficult to detect, since it may be confused with such derivative personal names as Þórir, it seems that memories of the god Thór are preserved in the names of some thirty places in Norway. Thór's name is sometimes combined with words denoting natural objects, as it often was in Iceland. Norway provides such examples, as Þórsnes (Thor's Headland), Þórsberg (Thor's Rock), Þórsey (Thor's Island), But, unlike Iceland, Norway has a number of places in which the name of the god is combined with that of a temple or sanctuary. The name Þórshof is applied to some ten places, grouped closely together in the south-east of the country.

As will be explained in another chapter (Ch. XII), the word hof, if not borrowed from continental German, probably developed the meaning 'temple' under continental influence. This might lead us to think that the cult of Thór developed in Norway in the Viking Age, and even that it was introduced from the Continent. In fact, the total absence of place-names compounded with Þór- in Trondheim, where the historical sources give strong evidence of the cult, might suggest that the god was not known there before the last years of the pagan period.

Such conclusions could not be justified in the present state of our knowledge, although the evidence of the place-names does suggest that the public cult of Thór increased greatly in Norway during the ninth and tenth centuries. Thór's name is also combined with some other elements, less pronouncedly sacral. Eight or nine places bore the name Þórsland. Since -land is often combined with names of other deities, we may suspect that, like -akr, it developed a sacral meaning. Land was often applied to small, dependent farms, and if they give evidence of the cult of one god or another, it might be of a private, rather than of a public kind. Nevertheless, some of the land-names appear to date from well before the Viking Age. The name Þórsland is found chiefly in western Norway, and may suggest that Thor's cult was established there before the Viking Age. It was from this region that many emigrated to Iceland in the late ninth century. This may explain why the god Thór enjoyed a higher status than any other in the new settlement.

Conditions in Sweden and Denmark are yet more obscure. In Uppsala and Svealand, as Icelandic and other sources show, Freyr must for long have been foremost of the gods, but at the end of the pagan period he seems to be overshadowed by Thór. Describing the temple of Uppsala about the year 1070, Adam of Bremen (IV, 26) mentions idols of three gods, Wodan, Thór and Fricco. As in some of the Norwegian and Icelandic temples, Thór had his place in the middle, the others standing on either side. Thór was the most powerful of the gods; he ruled in the sky and governed thunder, lightning and produce of the soil. If there is danger of pestilence, sacrifice is offered to him. Holding his sceptre he resembled Jove. Adam's observer probably mistook Thór's hammer for a sceptre, and the idol perhaps resembled the one holding an enormous hammer in the temple of Guðbrandsdal.

Public veneration of an idol of Thór in Sweden is also mentioned in a second passage by Adam (II, 62). About the year 1030, Wilfred, an English missionary, insulted and publicly smashed this idol with a double-headed axe (*bipennis*). He won the martyr's crown and the heathens sank his body in a marsh.

In his description, Adam showed that, in the eyes of the Swedes of his age, it was largely Thór who brought fertility to the crops. Whatever his origin, Thór was at this time a fertility god. This is also suggested by the occasional occurrence of the place-name *Þórsakr* (Thor's Cornfield), particularly in central Sweden. The name of the god is often combined with other elements in place-names, especially in those of the eastern regions of Sweden. The second element has sometimes a sacral force, e.g. *lundr* (grove), *vé* (sacred place), *hǫrgr* (mound, shrine). Names like these suggest that Thór was publicly worshipped in the places to which they were applied. More often the name of Thór is combined with that of a natural object, such as *sær* (lake), *berg* (rock), *áss* (ridge).[36]

Thór was not among the first gods to enjoy public worship in Sweden, but he rose to eminence in the last period of heathendom. In the end, it was not Óðinn, and no longer Freyr, but Thór who was mightiest of gods (*potentissimus eorum*), and took the central place.

The religious history of Denmark is yet more obscure than that of Sweden, but the inscriptions and miniature hammers of the late Viking period show that Thór was rising in eminence there as elsewhere. Innumerable place-names which may contain the name *Þór-* are found throughout Denmark, although doubts have been cast on the origin of many of them. Among the names believed to preserve reliable memories of Thór's cult are no less than seven of the type *Þórslundr* (Thór's Grove) and two *Þórsakr* (Thor's Cornfield), showing that here, as in Sweden, Thór was one of those gods who brought fertility to the fields. Thór's name appears in many instances to be combined with designations of natural objects, e.g. *haugr* (mound), *berg* (rock), *ey* (island).[37]

Consideration of the worship of Thór in various parts of Scandinavia had led to the conclusion that he grew more and more eminent in the evening of heathendom. He defended men against monsters, and the gods relied on him to save Ásgarð from the giants. In the same way, Thór was thought best fitted to defend heathendom against the aggression of Christ. But the evidence of Iceland, and to a lesser extent of the West Norwegian place-names shows that Thór's cult was firmly established in western districts in the latter part of the ninth century. The settlement of Iceland, as is emphasized in historical sources, was prompted largely by conservative interests. Thór maintained order and security. It was to him that men turned, not only for protection against Christ and giants, but also against the landgrabbing, upstart kings of Norway.

Thór in the Viking Colonies

Vikings of the ninth and tenth centuries carried their religion to colonies in the west, where it thrived and even spread. In Ireland, Thór was the chief god of the invaders. The Norse rulers of Dublin were called 'the tribe of Tomar' (*muinter Tomair*), and *Tomar* is an Irish adaptation of the name *Þórr*.[1] In the neighbourhood of Dublin there was a ring or bracelet (*fail no fáine*) belonging to Tomar, and probably kept in a temple dedicated to him. This ring may correspond with those holy rings, kept in temples of Iceland, on which oaths were sworn. It was seized by an Irish chieftain in the year 994.

In the same region there was a *Coill Tomair* or 'Grove of Thór'. It consisted of stately trees and huge oaks and was burnt down by Brian about the year 1000.[2] The Grove of Thór in Ireland may be associated with the *Þórslundar* of eastern Scandinavia, as well as with other sacred groves in Iceland, Sweden and Germany.

The vikings of Normandy also worshipped Thór and, according to Dudo of St Quentin,[3] they offered him human sacrifice, the most precious of all, expecting to assure favourable winds at sea and good fortune in war.

The Norse god Thór was also well known in England in Viking times. Whether the work of a Scandinavian or British artist, the 'Fishing Stone' of Gosforth suggests that the pagan myth of Thór, the giant Hymir and the World Serpent had infiltrated the Christian legend of Leviathan.

In the year 876, Scandinavian invaders undertook to leave the kingdom, swearing an oath before Alfred on the 'holy ring', an oath so holy that they had consented to swear it before no people before.[4] It might be supposed that these vikings were swearing in the name of Thór, the all-powerful god. But since they broke their oath the same night, it is more probable that they called on Óðinn, the oath-breaker, to witness it.

Thór had, of course, been known to English pagans under the name Þunor. But English homilists who wrote of him in the late tenth and eleventh centuries consistently called him by his Scandinavian name Þur, Þor. They thus showed that they were facing, not a revival of English heathendom, but an alien religion introduced by Vikings, and, as Wulfstan showed in his famous address to the English (c. 1014),[5] gaining ground at his period.

Ælfric, in his Life of St Martin[6] tells how the Devil used to appear before that Saint in the form of heathen gods, sometimes in the form of Jove, who is Þor, sometimes in the form of Mercury, whom people called Oþon, and sometimes in the form of that foul goddess Venus, who is called Fricg.

The homily De falsis deis is commonly assigned to Ælfric,[7] and it is included with slight modification among Wulfstan's homilies.[8] Thór is there identified with Jove, most venerable of gods (arwurðost), and he is the one whom the Danes love most. But the homilist returns to the identification of Thór with Jove, for it causes him some difficulty. It is true that the Danes, in their ignorance, said that Thór was the same as Jove, but they were wrong; the god whom the Danes called Þor was son of Mercury, whom they call Oþon, but it was known from books that Jove was the son of Saturn.

These rather dialectical remarks show that Scandinavians in England knew the tradition that Thór was son of Óðinn, and this must have been more than a poetic conceit. It is interesting also to learn that Thór was the god whom the invaders of England loved most.

The cult of the Scandinavian Thór has certainly left traces in English place-names, but the god's name is difficult to distinguish, both because of confusion with personal names of the type Þórir and because of confusion with names derived from the original English Þunor.[9] Future studies will certainly throw light on such problems, but English scholars who have studied place-names of religious significance have generally excluded those which may be of Scandinavian origin.[10]

Scandinavian or Varangian merchants and settlers of the ninth and tenth centuries probably carried the worship of Thór to their colonies in the east although the cult there is less easy to trace. A chronicler mentions a *Turova božnica* in Kiev in the year 1046, and this may originally have been a temple of Thór.[11] But, in Russia, the god whom Norsemen worshipped most was generally called *Perun*, and he is mentioned some five times in the Chronicle between 907 and 988. In 907, Oleg concluded a treaty with the Christian Greeks, who kissed the Cross. The heathen 'Russians', in their turn, swore according to 'Russian' custom, by their weapons and by their god Perun, as well as by Volos, god of cattle and wealth.

Again in 945, Christians swore by Almighty God, but the pagans called down the wrath of Perun on their own heads; may their shields give them no protection, may they fall by their own weapons, and be slaves in this world and the next if they break their oath. The 'Russians', under Svyatoslav, swore a similar oath in the year 971, and again invoked Volos as well as Perun.

It has been noticed that the oath on weapons is typically Scandinavian in form,[12] and this is one of the reasons which have led many to agree that Perun, whom the Varangians called 'their god', was in fact Thór, the god most widely worshipped by viking settlers.

With less reason, Volos has been identified with the Norse fertility symbol Völsi (see Ch. XIII), and therefore with the fertility god Freyr,[13] but he seems rather to be a Slav god than a god of the Varangians. Unlike Perun, he is not 'their god'.[14]

In 980, Vladimir, who was still a heathen, set up an idol of Perun in Kiev. It stood, together with idols of other gods, on a mound; it was made of wood with a head of silver and a moustache of gold. Men used to bring their sons and daughters to these idols, and the ground was soiled with blood.[15] We may suppose that Varangians and Slavs used to sacrifice their sons and daughters to Perun, just as heathens in the island of Gotland sacrificed their sons and daughters (*synum oc dydrum sinum*).[16] This human sacrifice was perhaps dedicated in the first place to Perun, just as human sacrifice was offered to Thór in western Iceland[17] and by vikings in Normandy.[18]

Perun appears to be the chief god of the Varangians and it would be natural to suppose that, if he was really Thór, he was given the name of a corresponding Slav god. But Perun is scarcely mentioned except in connexion with the Varangians, and it has been denied that there ever was a Slav god of that name. It has been suggested rather that *perun* is a *nom agentis*, meaning 'striker', and this would be an apt name for the thunder-god, Thór.[19] But, in spite of certain philological difficulties, it is hard to dissociate Perun from the Lithuanian thunder-god Perkunas.[20] The name Perkunas is comparable with that of the Old Norse god *Fjǫrgynn* (see Ch. VIII, Frigg and others, below), although relationship between the two has been questioned.[21] Ultimately, the names Perun and Perkunas are perhaps related with that of the Indian storm-god Parjanya, but the etymology is altogether obscure.[22]

Perkunas was known among Old Prussians as *Percuno*(s). Mrs Chadwick[23] remarks on a practice recorded among this people in the sixteenth century. A sacrifice held in honour of Percuno(s) included the slaughter of a goat.[24] The goat was the beast sacred to Thór, and perhaps to Percuno(s) as well.

I have just mentioned a Norse god Fjörgynn, about whom very little is known. According to the *Lokasenna* (str. 26), Frigg, wife of Óðinn, was *Fjǫrgyns mær*. This could be interpreted 'Fjörgynn's mistress', which would seem the most likely meaning in the context, but Snorri[25] said that Frigg was daughter of Fjörgynn.

Beside the male god Fjörgynn, there was a goddess Fjörgyn, of whom rather more is told. In the *Vǫluspá* (str. 26) and in the *Hárbarðsljóð* (str. 56), Fjörgyn is said to be the mother of Thór, and she may therefore be identified with Jörð (Earth), who is said in other texts to be Thór's mother. In poetry, Eddaic as well as scaldic, the word *fjǫrgyn* is used for 'earth'. It is said to be related to Old English *furh*, Old High German *furuh*, and Latin *porca*, meaning either 'ridge' or 'furrow'.[26] It has been further argued that the male god Fjörgynn had no ancient roots, and that he was invented arbitrarily to form a male counterpart of the goddess Fjörgyn.

There are some reasons to doubt this conclusion. Fjörgyn herself is so shadowy a figure, and so rarely mentioned, that it is hard to see why poets of a late period should feel the need of creating a male counterpart for her. The name Fjörgynn appears in various forms, but only in the genitive. In the Codex Regius of the Poetic Edda, it is *Fjǫrgyns*; in Snorri's *Edda* it appears in different manuscripts as *Fjǫrgvins*, *Fjǫrgyns* and *Fjǫrgvns*. A nom. form such as *Fjǫrgunn* would correspond more closely with the Lithuanian *Perkunas*, and would allow us to suppose that Fjörgunn was an ancient storm-god or thunder-god. This could explain why his female counterpart was identified with the earth-goddess, Jörð, mother of Thór. Thór might, then, have been thought of, at one time, as son of the goddess Fjörgyn and the god Fjörgynn, whose position he later usurped. Without further argument, this could explain why the eastern Scandinavians, always archaic in their religious practices, identified their thunder-god with the Balto-Slav Perkunas or the Slav Perun.

It is not surprising that the Lapps adopted the cult of Thór from their southern neighbours, just as they adopted many other figures of Norse mythology, and developed them in their own way.

The practices of the heathen Lapps have been recorded only since the seventeenth century, but they express beliefs many centuries old.

The Lappish thunder-god was known by various names. In some regions he was *Diermes* or *Tiermes*, the sky-man, and in others he was *Hora galles* which is a loan from the Norse *Þórr Karl* (the Old Man Thór), a name occasionally given to the Norse thunder-god.[27] He was also known to the Lapps under the name *Tor*.

It may not be necessary to believe with Olrik,[28] that the Lapps borrowed Thór with other members of the Norse pantheon so early as the Bronze Age or early Iron Age, but the Lappish thunder-god preserves archaic features which have been obscured in the Norse literary records. While Snorri and the Norse poets give Thór a wife, Sif, the Lapps gave Hora galles a wife, *Ravdna*. This, it seems, is no other than the Norwegian *raun*, Swedish *rönn* and Icelandic *reynir*, 'rowan, mountain ash'. It was said that the red berries of this tree were sacred to Ravdna.[29]

In the myth of Thór and the giant Geirröð, as it was told by Snorri, and perhaps also in the obscure lines of the *Þórsdrápa*, Thór saved himself in the torrent by clinging to a rowan, and thus arose the proverb, 'the rowan is the salvation of Thór' (*reynir er bjǫrg Þórs*). Probably the wife of Thór was once conceived in the form of a rowan, to which the god clung. The rowan was a holy tree in many lands, but nowhere more than in Iceland, where it has been revered from the settlement to the present day.[30]

The Lapp thunder-god was depicted on the shamans' drums with a hammer in each hand, or with a hammer in one hand and an axe in the other. He was a terrible, dangerous god, but if proper sacrifice were offered, he would drive the thunder and lightning away with one hand and hurl it with the other on the enemies of his worshippers. According to an authority of the seventeenth century,[31] one of the god's functions was to kill the trolls, who dwelt in every mountain, rock and lake. He also governed health, life and death.

The Finns called their thunder-god *Ukko*, the 'old man'. He had a wife called *Rauni*, which is the same word as the Lappish *Ravdna*, but in other ways Ukko differs greatly from the Lappish god.[32] He is less to be feared, and in him the fertilizing results of the thunder and the rain which follows it are more strongly emphasized.

Thór-Thunor

The heathen English had worshipped a god Thunor (*Þunor*), but when

I mentioned the introduction of the Scandinavian Thór into England during the Viking Age, I purposely excluded the corresponding native deity. By the ninth century, when the Viking invasions began, English heathendom had long been dead, at least as an organized religion, and the god Thunor can have been remembered by few. The English forms Þunor, Þuner are occasionally used to gloss Jupiter, although the Norse forms Þur, Þor are not less common in such texts.

In a study of heathendom and Old English place-names, F. M. Stenton[1] reached some remarkable conclusions about the cult of Thunor in pre-Christian England. Þunor- is by no means uncommon as an element in place-names, but it is strangely limited in distribution. In the territories of the Saxons and perhaps of the Jutes, the element Þunor is common enough, but there are no certain examples of it in Anglian territory, which may imply that the god was hardly known among the Angles.

The second element of the Þunor- names is also of much interest. The hundred-name Thurstable in Essex originally meant Thunor's Pillar.[2] Names of the type Þunores hlæw or Thunor's Mound are recorded more than once, and seem to preserve memories of public worship. Stenton also mentions no less than six examples in which the god's name is compounded with leah, which is interpreted 'sacred grove'. These names therefore correspond with Þórslundr (Thor's grove), which is common in eastern Sweden and is also found in Denmark. The English god's name is also compounded with feld (field) in examples such as Þunresfeld. These are reminiscent of Þórsakr and Þórsvin, which again are characteristic of eastern rather than of western Scandinavia, and suggest that English worshippers emphasized the fertilizing power of Thunor and his rain-bringing thunder.

In Old English thunder is called ðunorrad and ðunorradstefn, compounds in which the second element rad probably means 'moving, travelling'. This is reminiscent of Icelandic words for thunder, such as reiðarþruma, reiðarduna, or simply reið (f., generally plural), which seem to imply that thunder is believed to be the noise which Thór makes travelling in his chariot. This conception was probably present already in the Haustlǫng (str. 14), which was quoted above.

In the Old English dialogue Salomon and Saturn,[3] the thunder is said to strike the devil with a fiery axe (þære fyrenan æcxe). Perhaps this reflects a conception that the thunder-god was armed with an axe.

For the rest, the literary sources have next to nothing to tell of Thunor. Unlike other gods, he does not figure in the genealogies of royal houses. His name is, however, applied in an apocryphal story, probably written in the eleventh century, to a wicked man of Kent.[4]

99

The story appears to be invented to explain a place-name *Þunores hlæw*. Its chief interest lies in the fact that a man, said in some sources to be a King's counsellor, is called by the name of the god. This suggests that the author had forgotten that there ever was a god Thunor, for men do not usually bear the names of gods.

It will be noticed that in the later compound names there is some alternation between the forms *Þunres-* and *Þures-*, as in *Þunresdæg* and *Þuresdæg* (Thursday). The forms without -*n*- might be influenced by Scandinavian ones, but this is not certain because *n* was regularly lost before *r* in later West Saxon.[5]

It is not doubted that the thunder-god was also worshipped in Germany, although the evidence there is even poorer than it is in England. In a manuscript of the ninth century in the Old Saxon dialect a baptismal vow is preserved.[6] It wàs plainly drawn up, probably in the eighth century, for men newly converted from heathendom; the postulant is made to name his favourite gods and renounce them. He says:

end ec forsacho allum dioboles uuercum and uuordum, Thunaer ende UUoden ende Saxnote ende allum them unholdum the hira genotas sint.	I renounce all the words and works of the devil, Thunaer, Woden and Saxnot, and all those demons who are their companions

Since Thunaer is here named first of the gods, it is likely that the Saxons of this age regarded him as the foremost. Saxnot remains a riddle. Since he is named together with Thunaer and Woden, he must have been an important god. He must also have been known in England for the genealogies of the East Saxon kings are traced to a *Seaxnet*.[7] Seaxnet does not appear in the other royal genealogies, which shows that the kings of Essex were believed to descend from a divine ancestor who was not the parent of other dynasties.[8] Saxnot has often been identified with Týr, but chiefly because he is named together with two other great Germanic gods. Probably he was conceived originally as the eponymous god of the Saxons, whether his name meant 'companion of the sword' or 'friend of the Saxons'.[9] If Saxnot is to be fitted into the Indo-European tripartite system, he is better associated with Njörð, or with Freyr who, under the name Yngvi-Freyr, was the ancestor of the Ynglingar, the ruling house of the Swedes.

A clasp found at Nordendorf in Bavaria, and said to date from the seventh century, bears a cryptic inscription in runes. Among the forms read on it are *Logapore, Wodan, Wigiþonar* (or *Wiguþonar*).[10] The first of these will be mentioned in a later chapter (see Ch. V); in the second we may see the name of Woden (Óðinn), and in the third that of Thunar

(Thór) combined with another word or compound element. The reading of the fourth rune in this last group has been disputed, but most have read it as *i* rather than *u*.[11] If the form *Wigiþonar* is correct, it naturally leads us to think of the formula in the Danish inscriptions of the tenth century *þur uiki* . . . (may Thór hallow). *Wigi* has been regarded as an imp. 2 sg. of the verb which appears in Gothic as *weihan* and in O.H.G. as *wihen*, related (by Verner's Law) with O.N. *vígja*. The meaning of *wigi þonar* would in this case be 'hallow, Thór', and the god would be called upon to hallow the clasp, or the runes, imparting his divine force.[12] But even if this reading is adopted, *Wigiþonar* is still open to other interpretations. It has been read as a compound and associated with names for Thór recorded in Norse literary sources. In the *Hymiskviða*, Thór is three times called *Véurr*, and the expression *Miðgarðs véur(r)* in the *Völuspá* (str. 56) most probably applies to him.

Formerly *véurr* was thought to be a contracted form of *vé-vǫrðr* (guardian of the holy place), or of *vé-árr* (servant of the holy place). Whatever the second element in *véurr* may be, the first can be no other than *vé* (holy or sanctified place), and it is thus related to the verb *vígja* (to hallow). This element appears also in other names for Thór, e.g. *Harðvéurr* and perhaps *Véþormr*.

Wigiþonar of the Nordendorf inscription has also been associated with another group of names applied to Thór, *Vingnir* and *Vingþórr*.[13] If this is correct, the first element in all of these names would seem to mean 'hallowing-'. It must, however, be admitted that the philological arguments which have led to the close association of the elements *wigi-* (or *wigu-*), *vé-* and *ving-* are hypothetical and tenuous. It remains probable that in the expressions *Wigiþonar* and *véurr*, Thór is thought of as the hallower. The compound element *ving-* cannot yet be explained.[14]

In many parts of Germany, place-names containing the element *Donner-* have been recorded, and those in the form *Donnersberg* (older *Thoneresberg*, *Thuneresberg*, etc) are particularly widespread.[15] Most of these are probably named after the god, rather than after thunder, and they so closely resemble Scandinavian place-names of the type *Þórsberg*, *Þórsáss* that they suggest that Thór, like some other gods, was worshipped on hills and rocks.

English and Norse writers of the Middle Ages commonly identified Thór with Jupiter,[16] and the similarity between the two was emphasized by Adam of Bremen (see above p. 93), who saw Thór's hammer, or perhaps his club, as Jupiter's sceptre.

The identification of Jupiter with Thór is older and deeper than this. When Germanic names were given to days of the week, probably in the third century, *Dies Jovis* became 'Thór's Day' (O.E. *Þunresdæg*, O.N.

Þórsdagr). The question remains why, in pre-Christian as well as in Christian times, Thór and Jupiter were thought to be the same.

The answer is probably to be found in the Celtic world. As remarked, there was perhaps a Celtic god of lightning called **Meldos*. There are also records of another god worshipped in Gaul, whose name is given as *Taranis* and, apparently, in various forms such as *Taranucus*, *Taranucnus*.[17]

The name *Taranis* can hardly be dissociated from the Welsh word *taran* (*f.* thunder) and the Irish *torann* (*m.* loud noise, thunder). Taranis is named together with two other Gallic gods by Lucan, by whom he is compared with Diana, and perhaps thought of as female. Later writers occasionally identified Taranis with Dis Pater, but more regularly with Jupiter. The reason can only be that Jupiter, the sky-god, was also god of thunder and lightning; he was *fulgur, fulmen, tonans, tonitrator*.

A votive stone of the mid-second century, found at Chester, contains the interesting inscription *I O M* (*Jovi optimo maximo*) *Tanaro*. *Tanarus* is presumably the same as *Taranis*, but the variation is difficult to explain.[18] While *Taranis* is to be associated with words for thunder, *Tanarus* corresponds philologically remarkably closely with Germanic names for the thunder-god: *Þórr, Þunor*. It can only be because of their association with thunder and lightning that Taranis (Tanarus) and Thór were both identified with Jupiter.

It has been suggested that the Germanic thunder-god, Thór, was, in fact borrowed from the Celtic figure.[19] This would be easier to believe if there were evidence that Taranis was an important god, enjoying widespread worship among the Celts. There is no evidence of this.[20]

Although Thór was identified with Jupiter, it is possible that some thought of him rather as Hercules. Tacitus (*Germ.* III) said that the Germans believed that Hercules had once been among them and, advancing into battle, they sang his praises as the first of strong men (*primumque omnium virorum fortium*). Phrases like these do not prove that Hercules was a Germanic god; he might equally well have been a traditional hero of the type of Sigurð, or even Arminius. But in another passage (*Annals* II, 12), Tacitus shows that there was, indeed, a Germanic god whom the Romans called Hercules. He mentions a 'sacred forest of Hercules' (*silva Herculi sacra*) in the region of the Weser, a meeting place of various tribes. This forest of Hercules calls to mind the Old English *Þunresleah*, the Old Norse *Þórslundr* as well as the Irish *coill Tomair*, all of which mean 'grove of Thór'.

In yet another passage (*Germ.* XXXIV), Tacitus mentioned some 'pillars of Hercules' (*Herculis columnas*). This has led many to suppose that Hercules was the same as Irmin, god of the Saxon pillar *Irminsul*, which seemed to uphold the world.[21] But the name Thurstable in Essex seems originally to have meant 'Thór's Pillar' (see above p. 99), and, as was shown above, Thór was the god of the *ǫndvegissúlur*, the main supporting pillars of the house.

From this it seems likely that Hercules, with his supernatural strength and his club, was sometimes identified with Thór.

The name *Hercules* appears many times in inscriptions found in Germanic areas, mostly of the third century. These include *Hercules Barbatus*, *Hercules Saxanus* and *Hercules Magusanus*. There is no strong reason to identify the bearded Hercules with Thór, because many gods must have had beards. Hercules Saxanus, whose name appears in a great number of inscriptions, appears to be the protector of the quarrymen. Hercules Magasanus, whose votive-stones are concentrated on the Lower Rhine, has stronger claims to Germanic godhead, although all attempts to explain his nickname have been unconvincing.[22]

Conclusion

In the preface to the second edition of his *Teutonic Mythology*, written in 1844, J. Grimm said: 'Indra is akin to Donar (Thór), being the wielder of lightning, and the ruler of air and winds, so that as god of the sky he can be compared with Zio'.[1]

The similarity between Thór and Indra is so remarkable that many have gone further than Grimm did, believing that, in origin, the two gods were one and the same. This opinion was carried far by V. Rydberg,[2] whose views were extreme and, therefore, won less recognition than they deserved. The theory has been developed subtly by F. R. Schroeder[3] in a particularly informative paper.

G. Dumézil has emphasized the similarities between Thór and Indra in many works.[4] His analysis accords with his general conceptions of a common Indo-European religion. In his view, the Indo-European gods fall into three classes. The first class is represented by two aspects. On the one hand stands the furious, magical sovereign, represented by Óðinn and Varuna. On the other hand stand the more congenial gods of law and justice, Týr and Mitra. The third class is represented by gods of riches and fertility, the Vanir[5] in the north, and the Asvin (Nasatya) in India.

The second class is composed of warrior-gods, such as Thór and Indra. I have not the equipment to criticize this theory of a tripartite Indo-European religion. Comparative scholars will discuss it for many generations to come. But even if we do not accept it, and doubt the stability of the tripartite system, we cannot fail to remark on some of the details in which Thór and Indra resemble each other. Whatever the explanation, it is hardly possible to believe that the resemblances are accidental. Reading a description of Indra, such as the recent one given by J. Gonda,[6] we could believe that we were reading a description of Thór.

In the first place, Indra was the slayer of the dragon Vritra, at whose death the waters were released. Dragon-slayers are, of course, common enough both in legend and myth. It is they who overcome evil forces, and especially the forces of primeval chaos.[7]

Like Thór, Indra is a warrior-god; he defends others, slaying demons of drought and darkness. Indra is also god of thunder, and his weapon, *vajra* is interpreted as the lightning or thunderbolt.[8]

According to Snorri,[9] Thór's hammer, Mjöllnir, was forged by a dwarf, or dark elf, Sindri, who also made other treasures for the gods. Indra's *vajra* was fashioned by Tvastr. Tvastr is an obscure figure, but he is remembered as a craftsman who made treasures for gods.

Thór is the son of Óðinn and of the earth-goddess, Jörð. Strange stories are told of Indra's birth, but he is said to be the son of Dyaus, the sky-god, and apparently of his consort, the earth. He is created by heaven and earth.[10]

The Norse god, like the Indian, was an enormous eater and drinker. On one occasion Thór devoured two oxen and, on another, a whole ox, eight salmon and enormous measures of mead.[11] When he was fooled in the house of Útgarðaloki, Thór drank the seas shallow.[12] Indra had an even greater appetite; he ate three hundred buffaloes and drank three lakes of *soma*.[13]

Indra and Thór are bold and brave, but they also have cunning, and certain affinities with Óðinn. Indra takes many forms; he turns into a horse-hair, a bird of prey,[14] and even a woman. Thór was the deep thinker (*djúphugaðr*), and he also took the form of a woman when he went to the Giant World to recover his hammer. The manly qualities of these two gods are not inconsistent with those of the hermaphrodite.

Indra and Thór go on long journeys in pursuit of demons; both of them cross mighty torrents and are battered by storms and hail. They travel mostly in chariots; Indra's chariot is drawn by horses, generally two.[15] Thór's chariot was drawn by two goats, beasts hardly suitable for carrying a warrior-god. It is remarkable that the Indian Pusan also rode in a chariot drawn by goats, and the goat was especially sacred to him, as it was, apparently, to Thór. Pusan's origin is obscure, but he hardly appears except as the companion, almost the doublet of Indra.[16]

There are as many differences between Indra and Thór as there are between India and Iceland, but more points of similarity could be mentioned.

The major correspondences may count for little, but the minor details are more telling. If it is hard to believe that the two figures developed independently, it is almost to admit that they descend from a common original and they must, in this case, be part of an Indo-European heritage.

CHAPTER FOUR

BALDR

*The West Norse Sources—Saxo—The Character of Baldr and his Cult—
Continental and English Tradition*

The West Norse Sources

THE GOD BALDR takes a prominent place in the literary sources, but their inconsistency is so great that we are left, not with one, but with differing pictures of this god. He is the son of Óðinn and Frigg,[1] and the most detailed account of him is that given by Snorri, who has nothing but good to say of him. Baldr is beautiful to look at, and so bright that light shines from him. There is a flower so white, the ox-eye daisy, or matricary, that its petals are likened to Baldr's eyelashes (or eyelids) and it is called *Baldrsbrá*.[2] Baldr is the wisest of the *Æsir*, fairest of speech and most gentle, but yet his judgment never holds. His home is *Breiðablik* (Broad Splendour) in the sky and nothing unclean may be there. He has a wife Nanna Nepsdóttir, and a son Forseti.[3]

This description of Baldr's appearance and character would have little interest were it not for the story of his death, to which allusion is made frequently by northern writers. When he related it in close detail, Snorri wrote one of his finest passages.[4] His story may be summarized:

Baldr had dreams in which his life was threatened. When he told the other gods about them, they resolved that oaths should be demanded of all objects to spare their favourite. Baldr's mother, Frigg, received these oaths, sworn by fire and water, metals, stones, trees, sicknesses, beasts, birds, serpents.

After this, Baldr used to entertain the gods by standing in the meeting places, while the others shot shafts, pelted him with stones and struck at him, knowing that no harm would come to him.

But when the evil Loki saw this, he was filled with spite. He took the form of a woman and went to Frigg, who unsuspectingly told him that there was a slender shoot, called Mistletoe (*Mistilteinn*), growing to the west of Valhöll, from which she had demanded no oath, thinking that it was too young.

Loki tore up the mistletoe and carried it to the meeting place, where he found the god Höð standing outside the ring and taking no part in the sport because he was blind and had no missile. Loki put the mistletoe into the hands of Höð and directed his aim, and the shaft pierced the body of Baldr, who fell dead to the ground. This, it was said, was the greatest tragedy which had ever befallen gods or men. No vengeance could be taken on the spot, for the place was a sacred one (*griðastaðr*), and so shocked were the gods that they could not speak.

When the gods recovered their senses, Frigg promised her love to anyone who would undertake a journey to the world of the dead, and offer the death-goddess, Hel, a ransom if she would release Baldr. Hermóð the Valiant, a little-known son of Óðinn, responded. He mounted Óðinn's horse and galloped away.

Meanwhile the gods took the body of Baldr to the seashore, intending to place it on his mighty ship, Hringhorni, and to cremate it on board. But since the gods could not launch the ship they sent to the Giant World (*Jǫtunheimar*) for the giantess, Hyrrokin, who came riding a wolf, using a serpent for reins. The giantess launched the ship at the first push; flames shot from the rollers and all the world trembled. Thór, seeing his old enemy, the giantess, was so enraged that he gripped his hammer and would have crushed her skull, had not the gods interceded.

When the body of Baldr was carried on board, his wife, Nanna, died of grief and she was laid beside him. Thór, meanwhile, hallowed the pyre with his hammer and, still enraged, he kicked a little dwarf, Litr, into the fire.

Snorri describes those who attended the funeral of Baldr. Óðinn was there with Frigg and his valkyries and ravens. Freyr drove in a chariot drawn by his boar, *Gullinbursti* or *Slíðrugtanni*; Heimdall rode his horse, *Gulltopr*; Freyja drove her cats and a great crowd of frost-giants and rock-giants was present. As a parting gift, Óðinn placed on the pyre the sacred arm-ring, Draupnir, from which eight rings of equal weight dripped every ninth night. Finally, Baldr's horse was led to the pyre with all his harness.

Snorri then returns to the story of Hermóð, who rode for nine nights through dark, deep dales, until he reached the resounding river, Gjöll. The maiden, *Móðguðr*, guarding the bridge over this river, questioned him, remarking that he had not the look of a dead man. She told him that Baldr had passed that way, and that the road to the world of death lay downward and northward.

Hermóð rode on until he came to the gates of Hel; he pricked his horse and cleared it. He entered the hall of death, where he found his brother, Baldr, in the seat of honour.

Next morning Hermóð asked Hel to allow Baldr to ride home with him, and told her of the grief of the gods. Hel laid down her terms. If everything, animate and inanimate, would weep for Baldr, then he might go back to the gods, but if anyone refused to weep, then Baldr must stay with Hel.

Hermóð left the house of the dead, bearing gifts which Baldr and Nanna sent to the gods and goddesses. When he returned to Ásgarð, Hermóð told all that he had seen and heard. The gods sent messengers to demand of all things, even trees and metals, that they should 'weep Baldr from Hel'.

When they thought that that had completed their errand, the messengers came upon an old giantess (*gýgr*) in a cave. She called herself Thökk, and when they asked her to weep, she answered:

Þǫkk mun gráta	Thökk will weep
þurrum tárum	with dry tears
Baldrs bálfarar;	for the funeral of Baldr;
kyks né dauðs	alive or dead
nautkak Karls sonar,	I cared nothing for the Old Man's son,
haldi Hel því er hefr.	May Hel keep what she has.

Snorri adds a detailed story of the punishment of Loki, although he says nothing of vengeance taken against Höð.

While all have admired the structure and the style in which Snorri tells this story, its origins, provenance, and even its authenticity have been hotly disputed. Problems of this kind may gradually become clearer when we consider other vernacular sources in which Baldr is mentioned. Those in prose, with one exception, are of little importance, but Baldr is also mentioned in Eddaic lays and in some of the works of scalds.

We may consider first extant poetic works which Snorri must have known. After he had described Baldr's character, Snorri quoted the *Grímnismál* (str. 12), which probably dates from the tenth century. Here it was told that *Breiðablik* was the name of the place where Baldr had built his hall, standing in a land where evil (*feiknstafir*)[5] was hardly known. At least, this shows that Snorri followed an established tradition, when he described Baldr's spotless character, although the *Grímnismál* does not account for Snorri's comparison of Baldr with the ox-eye daisy or some similar flower.

As already remarked, Snorri drew the outline of the *Gylfaginning* largely from the *Vǫluspá*. In that poem (strs. 31–5), the slaughter of Baldr was described, although somewhat allusively. The sibyl said that she had seen the fate in store for Baldr, the blood-stained god (*blóðgum tívur*)[6]. She had seen a mistletoe, slender and very beautiful, towering above the plains. From this slender shoot, a vicious shaft had been made, and shot by Höð. Very soon afterwards a son was born to Óðinn, who neither washed his hands nor combed his hair until he had brought Baldr's enemy (i.e. Höð) to the funeral pyre. Frigg wept for the sorrows of Valhöll. The sibyl had also seen a form, like to that of Loki, in the grove of springs and Sigyn, wife of Loki, sorrowing over him.

The lines last quoted show that Snorri was following an established tradition when he said that Baldr was slain by the mistletoe and, strangely enough, that according to this tradition, the mistletoe was a slender shrub. As Snorri said, Loki tore it up (*sleit upp*). This implies that the tradition reached its final form in a land where the mistletoe was not known, in Iceland or perhaps in western Norway. The allusion to the punishment of Loki in the *Vǫluspá* (35) shows that, in spite of the arguments of E. Mogk,[7] not only Snorri, but also the author of the *Vǫluspá* believed that Loki took some part in the murder of Baldr, although the shaft was shot by Hǫð. This tradition is confirmed by the words which Loki is said, in the *Lokasenna* (str. 28), to have spoken to Frigg:

ek því réð,	I was the cause
er þú ríða sérat	that never again
síðan Baldr at sǫlum.	will you see Baldr ride to your hall.

In another passage[8] Snorri mentions a kenning for Loki: *ráðbani Baldrs* (contriver of Baldr's death).

Among the most interesting poetic records of Baldr is the *Húsdrápa* (House-Lay), composed by the Icelandic poet Úlf Uggason about 983. The verses are recorded by Snorri in the *Skáldskaparmál*,[9] and the circumstances under which they were composed are described in the *Laxdæla Saga* (Ch. XXIX). Ólaf the Peacock had built a splendid house in western Iceland, and scenes from the lives of the gods were carved on the timbers with such skill that the hall looked better when the tapestries were down than when they were up. After the work was finished, Úlf made a poem about the mythical scenes carved in relief. On one panel the funeral of Baldr could be seen. Freyr was mounted on his golden-bristled boar, and Óðinn was riding to the pyre accompanied by his ravens and valkyries. Heimdall was also mounted, and the mighty goddess of the mountains (i.e. giantess) could be seen launching the sea-horse (ship), while Óðinn's warriors felled her mount.

In spite of minor differences, the *Húsdrápa* must have provided Snorri with much of the material for the scene which he describes so vividly. His description is richer than that preserved in the *Húsdrápa* but he probably knew more strophes of the poem than the few recorded.

The anonymous poem *Baldrs Draumar* (The Dreams of Baldr),[10] preserved only in a manuscript of the fourteenth century, may also have been known to Snorri, but he makes little use of it. The *Baldrs Draumar* is closely related to the *Vǫluspá*, and, whichever influenced the other, the two poems are probably of comparable age. The *Baldrs Draumar* tells how the gods and goddesses met in council after Baldr had dreamed his foreboding dreams. Óðinn saddled his horse and rode down to the gates of the Misty Hel (*Niflheimr*). Using his powers of necromancy, he dragged a sibyl, dead for centuries, from her grave. Under the false name *Vegtamr* (Travel-tame), he forced the sibyl to answer his questions. Why were the benches in the hall of death strewn with rings and gold? It was for Baldr that the mead had been brewed and the feast prepared. It was Hǫð who would bring Baldr to his death, and he would be avenged by Váli,[11] to be born to Óðinn by Rind. Váli would fight when one day old, and would never wash his hands nor comb his hair until he had brought Baldr's enemy to the pyre.

Finally, on this as on other occasions, Óðinn asked an unanswerable, as indeed incomprehensible question, and thus disclosed his identity. The sibyl told him to make off, saying that Loki had broken his chains and the Ragnarök was at hand.

In the *Baldrs Draumar* it is not told that Loki contrived Baldr's death, although the last strophe has been taken to imply that the thought was not far from the poet's mind. If so, this poet's thoughts were ill consistent with those expressed by Snorri and in the *Voluspá* for, according to these, it was not until after the death of Baldr that Loki was bound in chains. It is possible that the poet of the *Baldrs Draumar* was following another tradition, according to which Höð alone caused the death of Baldr.

Not everything which Snorri tells about Baldr's death can be traced to extant poetry, nor can the remainder be traced only to vague 'tradition'. Snorri also drew on poems unknown to us. Among these was a lay in which the descent of Hermóð to the world of death and his attempts to ransom Baldr were described. The poetic form shines through Snorri's prose, and the alliteration is apparent in phrase after phrase, to quote but one:

> han reið niu nætr døkkva dali ok djúpa
> (he rode for nine nights through dark dales and deep).

There was perhaps another lay, which told in closer detail than the *Voluspá*, how the shaft was hurled at Baldr and the gods dumbfounded at his death.[12]

Several poets, other than those mentioned, allude to the myth of Baldr and his death. They may not add much to the traditions already cited, but they help to show how old these traditions were. The *Skírnismál* (21-2), which incorporates material of some antiquity, mentions the ring (*Draupnir*), which was burned on the pyre of Baldr. In the *Vafþrúðnismál* (54), Óðinn, pitting his wits against those of the giant, Vafthrúðnir, finally discloses his identity with the unanswerable question:

> hvat mælti Óðinn   what did Óðinn whisper
> áðr á bál stigi   before he climbed on the pyre
> sjálfr í eyra syni?   into the ear of his son?[13]

It was said in the *Baldrs Draumar* (str. 11) that a woman called Rind (*Rindr*) would bear Váli, the son of Óðinn, who would take vengeance on Höð. This does not appear in Snorri's chapter on Baldr's death, and Snorri tells of no vengeance taken on Höð. But the tradition embodied in the *Baldrs Draumar* was old and widespread and was known to Snorri. He gives several scaldic kennings in which it is implied, and he quotes the words of the poet Kormák (died *c.* 970): *seið Yggr til Rindar* (Óðinn won Rind by magic).

So far, Baldr has appeared as the perfect, spotless god, an ethereal, if less active Sigurð, suffering for the sins of others. Interest is chiefly in the story of his death, but it would be too much to believe that Baldr had gone for ever. If Hermóð had failed to bring Baldr back from the world of the dead, he would come back in the end. In the *Vǫluspá* (str. 62), it is said that after the fire and floods of Ragnarök Baldr will return. He and his innocent slayer, Höð, will dwell together, all evil will pass and unsown cornfields will bear fruit.

This section of the *Vǫluspá* is strongly influenced by Christian eschatology and symbolism, but the dim hope that the beloved god would one day return did not derive from Christianity alone. After the death of Eirík Blood-axe, about the middle of the tenth century, his widow commissioned a memorial lay, in which the poet described how Óðinn and his warriors welcomed Eirík in Valhöll. As the dead king approached, the benches creaked, as they would if Baldr were returning.[14]

According to Snorri, all things, animate and inanimate, wept for Baldr except the giantess Thökk (Loki), and he quoted a strophe which confirms the ogress's recalcitrance. The early sources known to us have little to say about the weeping of nature for the beloved god. The *Vǫluspá* (33) mentions only the weeping of Baldr's mother, Frigg, and some have seen an allusion to the weeping waves of the sea, the 'daughters of Ægir' in the obscure strophe of the *Baldrs Draumar* (12).[15] But the story of the weeping nature was well known before Snorri wrote of it, and was popular enough to be the subject of a cruel joke.

In the year 1196, Thormóð, a delinquent guilty of trickery in the sheepfolds, 'offered his head'[16] to the chieftain whom he had offended. The chieftain told him to do what he liked with his head, but an observer made the following verse:

Hvatvetna grét	All things wept
—hefk þat fregit;	Baldr out of Hel
býsn þótti þat—	—I've heard of that
Baldr ór helju.	and a wonder it was.
þó hefr hæra,	But yet Thormóð,
þás hǫfuð fœrði,	bringing his head,
Þórmóðr þotit.	howled louder still.
þat's ólogit.	There's no lie in that.[17]

Saxo

Vernacular sources have little more to tell of Baldr, but when we turn to the Danish historian, Saxo Grammaticus, who wrote his *Gesta Danorum* about 1200, we find a very different Baldr, and read a very different story about him.[1]

Saxo has euphemerized the story more thoroughly than Snorri did, and it takes place, not in Ásgarð, but on earth, chiefly in Denmark and Sweden.

For Saxo Höð (Hotherus) has no claims to godhead, and Baldr (Balderus), although son of Óðinn, was described as a demigod (semideus). In no section of his work does Saxo express his contempt for heathen gods with greater virulence than he does in this one. In fact, they are not gods: *deos autem pocius opinatiue, quam naturaliter dicimus. Talibus namque non natura, sed gencium more, diuinitatis uocabulum damus* (III, 73–4).

While lacking the tragic dignity of Snorri's story, Saxo's is sensational and blood-curdling, and sometimes fails in consistency.

Höð was the son of Hodbrodd, a King of Sweden, and brother of Athisl (ON. *Aðils*, OE. *Eadgils*). After the death of his father Höð was brought up by Gevar in Norway. He was early distinguished for his skill in sports, and especially on the harp. By the power of his music he could turn men's minds and, with it, he quickened love in the heart of Nanna, the daughter of Gevar.

Nanna was beautiful, and when Baldr saw her bathing, he was inflamed with lust, and resolved to kill his rival Höð.

One day when Höð was hunting, he lost his way in a fog, and came to a hut in which he found some forest maidens. They declared that it was chiefly they who decided the fortunes of war, and that they took part unseen in battle. They told Höð of the intentions of Baldr, but warned him not to attack, hateful though Baldr was, since he was a demigod. The house and the maids vanished, and Höð was left alone on an open field.

When Höð returned to his foster-father, Gevar, he sued for the hand of Nanna, but Gevar dare not give her for fear of Baldr. Instead he told Höð of a sword, capable of killing Baldr, and of an arm-ring, which would bring wealth to its owner. These treasures were in the hands of Miming, a satyr dwelling in a distant, frozen region.

Höð set off on the long journey and, by a ruse, he got the satyr in his power and seized the treasures from him.

Some adventures followed, which have little to do with the main theme. For a second time Höð went to the far north and, while he was away, Baldr came and demanded Nanna from Gevar. The decision was left to the girl, and she subtly refused Baldr on the grounds that he was a god, and their natures would be incompatible.

112

Enraged by Baldr's insolence, Höð and his allies joined battle with him, evidently in Denmark. Óðinn and all the gods fought on the side of Baldr, and Thór was in the forefront, striking with his club. Victory would have gone to the gods, had not Höð struck off the head of Thór's club. Then all the gods took to an ignoble flight, and Höð was free to marry Nanna. He took her to Sweden, where the people honoured him, while Baldr was held up to ridicule.

Soon afterwards, fortunes changed and Baldr won a victory over Höð in Denmark. His victory did Baldr little good, for now he began to be troubled by nightly visions of Nanna. His health declined, and he grew so weak that he had to be carried in a chariot.

For a time, the fortunes of war alternated, until Baldr won another victory over Höð, who left the field as a fugitive. Wandering alone through forests of Sweden, he came upon the same maidens whom he had met before. This time they told him that he would overcome his enemy if only he would taste of the magic food which sustained the strength of Baldr. Again the two parties joined battle and, after great slaughter on both sides, they retired for the night.

At the dead of night, Höð spied three maidens carrying the magical food. He pursued them to their dwelling and, making out that he was a minstrel, entertained them with his music. They were preparing the food of Baldr with the venom of three serpents. In spite of textual difficulties, it seems that Höð induced them to let him taste it, and they gave him a girdle of victory.

On his way back, Höð met his old enemy, and pierced him with his sword. Baldr fell to the ground mortally wounded, but was able to renew the battle next day, carried on a litter. On the following night he had a vision, or a dream, in which the goddess Proserpine promised her embraces. After three days Baldr was dead, and after a royal funeral, his body was laid in a barrow.

Óðinn now plotted revenge. He sought the help of a Lappish wizard Rostiophus (ON. *Hrossþjófr*?), who told him that the avenger must be born to him by Rinda (ON. *Rindr*) daughter of the King of the Ruthenians (Russians). Óðinn, assuming various disguises, took service with that King. The maid rejected his advances, until disguised as a woman, Óðinn became her servant and raped her.[3]

Bous, the son of Rinda and Óðinn, met Höð in battle and slew him, while receiving a mortal wound himself.

In outline, Saxo's story resembles that told by Snorri and alluded to by the West Norse poets. According to Saxo, as in Snorri's story, Baldr was struck down by Höð. As mentioned in the *Húsdrápa* and again in Snorri's story, Baldr was given a splendid funeral. Saxo agrees with the *Baldrs Draumar* that Óðinn begat a son by Rindr, who avenged Baldr.

But the differences between Saxo's account, and that given in the

West Norse sources leap to the eye, and it is not necessary to consider all of them in detail.

In the first place, it is noticeable that, according to Saxo, Höð alone was the slayer of Baldr, and no room was left for Loki.[4] This may have been what the author of the *Baldrs Draumar* thought, but Saxo's differences from the West Norse sources are deeper than this. The positions of Höð and Baldr are nearly reversed, for Nanna, according to Saxo, is the devoted wife of Höð, not of Baldr.

For Saxo Baldr is not the passive, suffering god; he is a lustful bully, and only Höð displays any moral virtues. Baldr is the son of Óðinn and a demigod, but Höð is not his brother; he is the brother of Aðils of Sweden, and is thus drawn into a genealogy which is largely historical.[5]

Baldr was not, according to Saxo, killed by the mistletoe, but by a magic sword, seized from a satyr in the frozen north.

West Norse poets say that Óðinn's son, who avenged Baldr, was called Váli, but Saxo calls him Bous, and Saxo adds a wealth of detail about his conception not given by the West Norse poets.

In Saxo's account there is a mystico-magical element not to be found in the Icelandic sources. Höð owes his victory much to the forest maidens, who must be valkyries, since they take part unseen in battle.

Every reader must wonder what were the sources of Saxo's story, and whether he presents the Baldr myth in a more or less archaic form than the West Norse authorities.

It has often been said that Saxo followed an Icelandic tradition, an oral *Haðar Saga* (Saga of Höð).[6] Although, as he says himself, Saxo used Icelandic sources, it is difficult to believe that he could have derived the picture which he draws of Baldr from them. Baldr could not have lived in such different guises in the small Icelandic community. It is more likely that Saxo was largely following Danish or eastern traditions about Baldr, while Snorri derived his version of the myth from the Icelandic and West Norwegian poets. Saxo repeatedly refers to places in Denmark, and once in Norway, with which traditions about Baldr were associated. He tells how, after a victory over Höð, Baldr drove his sword into the earth and uncovered a fresh spring for his thirsty soldiers. He adds that these springs had not yet dried up, and that the story was preserved in the name of the place (*Eorundem uestigia sempiterno firmata uocabulo*). Saxo was probably referring to Baldersbrønde, near to Roskilde. This name, from an earlier *Baldorpsbrønde*[7] is unlikely to contain the name of the god, but Saxo must have followed a folk-etymology, showing that Baldr lived in the Danish traditions of his time. Saxo also mentions a village in Jutland in which Höð stayed, and gave his name to it. He may mean Horsens, or more probably Højer (earlier *Høthær*). Saxo also tells of men of his own day who had raided a burial mound, believed to be that of Baldr, in the hope of finding treasure.

Whatever his ultimate sources, Saxo does not present the story of Baldr in archaic form. It is enriched with many wandering medieval motives, such as the bewitching harp and the druidical mist.

In spite of this, Saxo may well preserve ancient elements not to be found in the western sources. It may well be that Baldr was not, in the beginning, the passive, suffering god, but was a doughty warrior. This is perhaps implied in the kennings for 'warrior' such as West Norse poets frequently use, e.g. *sárlinns Baldr* (Baldr of the wound-snake, sword), *skjaldar Baldr* (Baldr of the shield), *atgeirs Baldr* (Baldr of the spear), although the names of most gods, even if they are not especially war-like, can be combined by poets with those of weapons to mean 'warrior', 'man'.[8] Höð need not, in the first place, have been the pathetic, blind instrument of evil. His name means 'warlike', and appears also to be used in kennings for 'warrior'.[9] In fact, it may be suggested that Höð was not, in the first place, a separate god, but that his name was one of the many used for Óðinn. From this could arise the myth that he was blind. One of Óðinn's names was *Tvíblindi* (Blind in Both Eyes).

Saxo mentions meetings between Höð and the maidens of the forest, who must be valkyries. They gave him a corselet, a girdle, and told him how to win his ultimate victory. The valkyries are the warrior maidens of Óðinn. Besides this, *Nanna*, the name of Höð's (or Baldr's) wife, is a valkyrie name,[10] and it probably had a similar meaning to that of Höð, 'warlike'.[11]

It may not be extravagant to suppose that there was yet another version of the story, in which the blind or half-blind Óðinn contrived the death of his own son. If so, Óðinn was inspired by the same motive which guided him on many other occasions. He needed his son Baldr to join him in his Kingdom, just as he needed his favourites Sigmund, Harald Wartooth, Eirík Bloodaxe and others.[12]

Loki is excluded from Saxo's story of Baldr's death. It is not possible to decide whether he figured in the myth in its original form,[13] although West Norse poets also suggested that there was an early version of the story in which he took no part.

Contradicting Snorri and the *Völuspá*, Saxo says that Baldr was killed by a magic sword, and not by a mistletoe. In this, priority must be given to the West Norse tradition. The sword with which, according to Saxo, Baldr was killed, was found far away in the north, while the mistletoe grew to the west of Valhöll, beyond the world known to gods or men.[14] It is not necessary to emphasize the veneration in which the mistletoe was held among many peoples, and not least among the Gauls and others of western Europe.[15] The reasons for such veneration could not profitably be discussed in a book of this kind, but like the Yggdrasill and the tree venerated in Uppsala (see Ch. XII), the mistletoe is evergreen. Like the Yggdrasill, it grows from unknown roots, and seems to triumph over death and even over life. The Icelanders did not know this plant, and they could believe that a deadly shaft was made of it, but when the story was rationalized by Saxo or his authorities, the mistletoe had to be replaced by a sword. In certain romantic sagas, *Mistilteinn* (Mistletoe) is the name given to a sword, and it is listed in an early source as a poetic word for 'sword'.[16] In such cases, also, we may suspect that a myth has been rationalized.

The Character of Baldr and his Cult

Literary sources preserve myths of Baldr in a wealth of detail, but their authors have left no clear picture of him, or rather they have left two pictures hard to reconcile with each other. On the one hand stands Baldr, the passive, innocent martyr, but on the other he is a vigorous warrior, even though his motives may, on occasion, have been lustful rather than heroic.

These sources tell little about a cult of Baldr. Only the *Friðþjófs Saga* (Ch. I) tells of a *Baldrshagi* (Baldr's Meadow) in Sogn (Western Norway). This was a sanctuary and the site of a splendid temple, in which there were idols of many gods, although Baldr was venerated most of them all. The *Friðþjófs Saga*, probably written in the fourteenth century, is romantic and fictitious, and its description of the temple and sanctuary was perhaps influenced by some of those quoted in Ch. XII below. The story told in the saga may be based partly on place-names which, rightly or wrongly, were thought to contain the name of Baldr. *Baldersgroi*, *Baldersvold* and *Baldershagi* are said to be recorded in the region of Sogn,[1] although their age and authenticity are questionable.

Evidence of the cult of Baldr has been sought in place-names. In the districts of Eyjafjörðr and Þingeyjarsýsla, in northern Iceland, there are two places called *Baldrsheimr* (Baldr's Home), and there is another place of the same name in Nordhordland, in Norway. This name may reflect *Breiðablik* which, in the myth, was the home of Baldr. Such a name shows that the myth of Baldr was remembered, but it does not show that the places to which it was applied were centres of his cult.

M. Olsen,[2] who has carefully studied place-names in which the element Baldr may be contained, attaches particular significance to *Baldrshóll* (*Balleshol*) in Hedemarken and *Baldrsberg* (*Basberg*) in Vestfold. A *Baldrsberg* is also recorded in southern Sweden.[3] A few names,

THE NORTHERN LANDSCAPE

1. Scene from Rogaland in south-western Norway. In the foreground stands a memorial stone of the early eleventh century about two metres high. Many examples are found of memorial stones of this type.

2. Helgafell (the Holy Hill) in western Iceland. It was revered as the dwelling place of departed ancestors. See Ch. XV.

3. Thórsmörk (Thór's Forest), a valley in the south of Iceland. According to an early source, this valley was dedicated by its first settler to the god Thór.

4. Thingvellir in south-western Iceland. The priest-chieftains would meet here every summer. Laws were made and judgments delivered. This view is taken from the meeting place.

5. The great mounds at Uppsala, Sweden, in which kings were buried. They measure about 65 metres across. Uppsala was for long the chief city of Sweden and the site of the glorious temple described in Ch. XII.

6. The church of Borgund in Sogn (western Norway). This is the most splendid of the stave-churches preserved, and dates from the twelfth century. The stave-churches are widely believed to be modelled on pagan temples.

7. Head of man carved on the cart found in the famous Norwegian grave of Oseberg, of the ninth century.

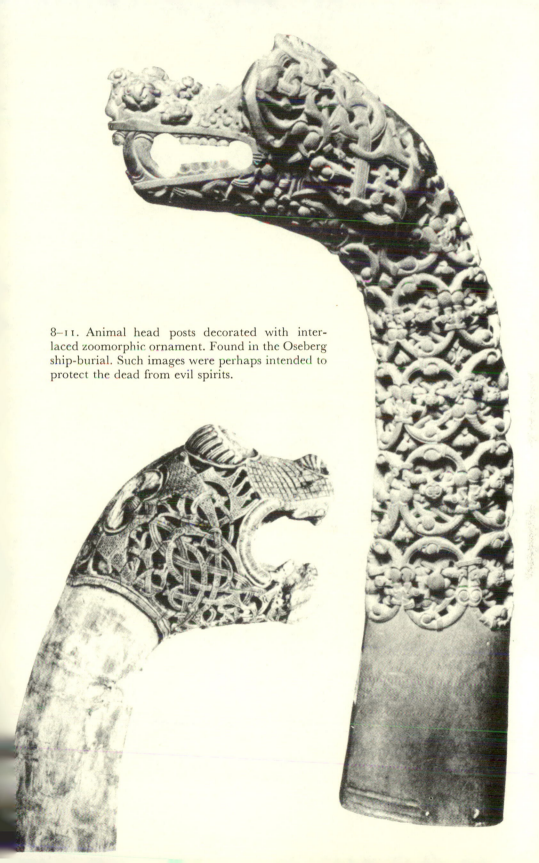

8–11. Animal head posts decorated with inter-laced zoomorphic ornament. Found in the Oseberg ship-burial. Such images were perhaps intended to protect the dead from evil spirits.

12. (top left) Image, probably of goddess, found in Jutland. Middle Bronze Age. Height 6·5 cm.

13. (top right) This image, found at Rällinge, Södermanland (Sweden), represents Freyr or another fertility god. It is reminiscent of the idol of Fricco (Freyr) in the temple of Uppsala, as described by Adam of Bremen. See Ch. XII.

14. (bottom left) Miniature figure found at Baldrsheimr in northern Iceland. This has commonly been regarded as the image of a god, but may be the "king" in the board-game *Hneftafl*. Height *c*. 4 cm.

15. (bottom right) Bronze image found in northern Iceland, about actual size. The image probably represents Thór clasping his hammer. Cf Plate 17.

16. (above) Silver image, probably of Thór's hammer, found in southern Iceland. It appears to be influenced by images of the Cross. Length about 5 cm.

17. (left) Image of Thór's hammer in silver from Skåne (Sweden). It is decorated with filigree ornament and embellished with a beaked head at the loop. The head bears the piercing eyes attributed to the god Thór (see Ch. III, Thór's Hammer). The image dates from about AD 1000.

18. (right) Silver image of the tenth century found in a grave at Birka (Sweden). Although a crucifix, this image bears some resemblance to those of Thór's hammer. Height c. 4·7 cm.

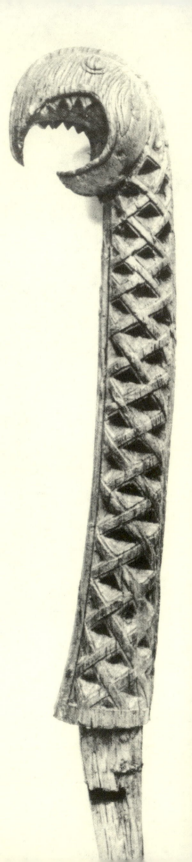

19. Animal head carved on bed-post in the ship-grave of Gokstad, Norway.

20. (right) Animal head found in the mouth of the Scheldt. It bears some resemblance to the animal heads found at Oseberg (see Plates 8–11), but Dr. D. M. Wilson of the British Museum kindly suggests that it belongs to an earlier period, perhaps the Migration Period.

RUNE STONES AND MEMORIALS

22. Carved stone from Hunnestad, Skåne (Sweden). At the cremation of Baldr, as Snorri relates, a giantess arrived mounted on a wolf, using serpents for reins. A scene like this is depicted on the stone. See Ch. IV.

23. Memorial stone of the late pagan period from Sønder-Kirkeby, Denmark. It contains the words: 'may Thór hallow these runes'. Above is seen a ship equipped with shields.

21. (left) Rune-stone from Altuna, Uppland, Sweden. The lower part seems to show Thór with his hammer fishing for the World Serpent (see Ch. III, Thór and the Serpent). As in Snorri's story, the bait is an ox-head and, when he got angry and exerted his strength, the god's legs went through the bottom of the boat.

24–27. These plates show a selection of pictorial stones from the island of Gotland. It is agreed that the pictures represent scenes from myth and legend, although they are difficult to interpret. The motives have been most thoroughly analysed by S. Lindquist, *Gotlands Bildsteine*, I–II, 1941–2.

Ships and mounted warriors predominate. The mounted figure armed with a spear (Plate 25) might be Óðinn with his spear Gungnir. The mounted figure on Plate 27 may again be Óðinn on the eight-legged Sleipnir, unless the eight legs are intended to give the impression of speed. The ships may be bearing the dead to the Other World. The finest examples of Gotland picture stones date from the ninth century.

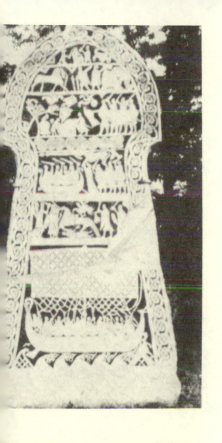

28. This stone, inscribed with some 200 runes, was found over a grave at Eggjum (Sogn W. Norway) in 1917. It is believed to date from the seventh century, and the inscriptio is of mystical or magical content. A recent scholar has read a name for Óðinn (*Heráss* in its text. The horse may be seen as the symbol of death. See Gerd Høst in *Norks Tids skrift for Sprogvidenskap*, XIX, 1960, 489 ff.

29. (below left) Rune-stone from Ledberg, Östergötland (Sweden), probably showing scene from the Ragnarök (see Ch. XVI). The wolf, Fenrir, attacks the helmeted warrio perhaps Óðinn. Another warrior restrains the wolf.

30. (below right) The stone found at Rök, Östergötland (Sweden), dates from the nin century and contains the richest of all runic inscriptions. It is partly in verse, and is th an important record of pre-Christian literature. Some of the runes are in cipher. S Ch. I, Introductory.

1. The tapestry here shown was reconstructed by Mary Storm from fragments found
 the Oseberg grave. The horses and chariots, both symbols of death and rebirth, will
 e noticed, as well as swastikas and other mystic signs. The breadth is about 23 cms. See
 jørn Hougen in *Viking*, 1940, 85 ff.

2. Rune stone from Ramsundberget, Södermanland (Sweden), of the eleventh century.
 cenes from the life of Sigurð are depicted. He is killing the dragon, roasting his heart
 d listening to the speech of birds. See Ch. X, Ermanaric, etc.

35. The heart of Högni is cut from his breast, as described in the Old
Norse poem *Atlakviða*. The picture is carved in wood in the church of
Austad (Setesdal), Norway. See Ch. X, Ermanaric, etc.

33–4. (left) Wood-carvings from church of Hylestad, Setesdal (Norway),
dating from the twelfth century. These show scenes from the life of Sigurð.
See Ch. X, Ermanaric, etc.

36. Panel from the cart in the Oseberg grave. Believed to represent Gunnar in the serpent pit, as described at the *Atlakviða*. Ninth century.

37. Another panel from the Oseberg cart. A man is seen on horseback, as if received at the end of a journey. He is possibly riding to the world of the dead.

38. Cross slab from Kirk Andreas, Isle of Man. Óðinn is believed to be struggling with the wolf Fenrir, as his will in the Ragnarök (see Ch. XVI). The Cross dates from the tenth century. *c.* 14 × 7½ in.

39. Portal of door of the church of Urnes, Sogn (Norway). The deer is perhaps biting the leaves of the world tree, Yggdrasill. See Ch. XVI.

40. (top) Reconstructed grave of tenth century in National Museum of Iceland.

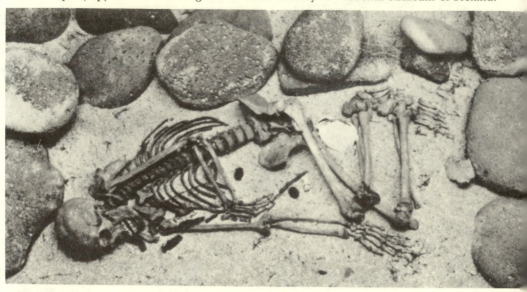

41. Various objects found in grave at Ketilsstaðir, Eastern Iceland.

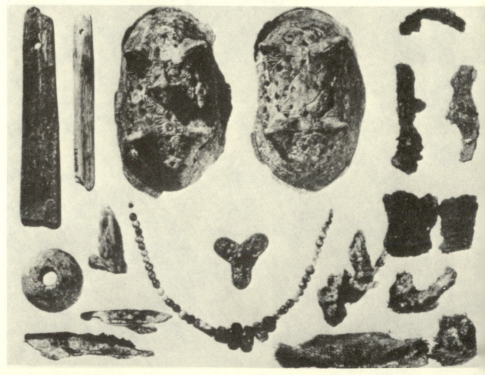

42. (below left) Figure like Buddha of Hiberno-Saxon origin. It forms the handle-seating of a bucket found in the Oseberg grave.

43. (below right). Miniature gold foil from Rogaland (Norway), showing a man and a woman. Such foils, of which a number survive, have often been taken to represent the god Freyr and his wife Gerð (see Ch. VII, Freyr). For another interpretation see W. Holmquist, *Acta Archaeologica*, 1960, 101 ff.

44. Magnificent silver bowl found at Gundestrup, Jutland. It measures about 70 cms. in diameter, and is commonly believed to be Celtic work of the early Iron Age. Mounted warriors and infantry are seen, as well as human sacrifice. See Ch. XIII.

45. The ship found in the grave at Oseberg, S.E. Norway, dates from the ninth century, and is one of the most beautiful preserved in Scandinavia. On the significance of ship burials see Ch. XV.

46. Burial chamber found in the ship-grave of Gokstad, Norway. It was placed on board the ship.

47. Cart found in the Oseberg grave. On all sides it is covered with elaborate carving, no doubt representing scenes from myth and legend. It appears to be designed for ceremonial rather than practical purposes. See Ch. VII Njörð.

48. This cart, dating from the early Iron Age, was found at Dejbjerg in Jutland. Like the one illustrated in Plate 47, it must have been designed for ceremonial purposes.

49. Hooped bucket, one of several found in the Oseberg grave. Several of these contained wild apples, which we may be tempted to associate with the magical apples kept by the goddess Iðunn. See Ch. VIII, Iðunn.

which may preserve memories of the cult of Baldr have also been re-corded in Denmark, and they include a *Bollesager* which may mean 'Baldr's Cornfield', although the origins and authenticity of these Danish names have been questioned.[4]

In fact, little can be learnt about the cult of Baldr from place names. They suggest that it was not practised widely, and was connected with rocks and hills and, perhaps, that Baldr, like many another god, brought fertility to the crops.

Baldr has the attribute 'the good' (*hinn góði*) and he is the good ruler, in whose land evil was unknown. A good ruler is always *ársæll*, i.e. the crops flourish and the people prosper under his rule.[5] In that sense, at least, Baldr was a fertility god, but, like other good rulers, he had war-like qualities as well.

G. Neckel[6] emphasized certain similarities between Baldr and Freyr. Both of them are 'bright' (*bjartr*), and Neckel thought of them both as gods of sun and fertility, believing that the cult of Freyr had over-shadowed that of Baldr. The meaning of the name of Baldr, like that of Freyr, has generally been taken to be 'the Lord', on the analogy of the Old English *bealdor*, but H. Kuhn has shown that there are reasons to doubt whether there really was a word *baldr/bealdor* meaning 'Lord' in any Germanic dialect.[7] The name *Baldr* has been associated by some with *baldinn* (bold, defiant), and by others with *bál* (fire, etc), and various Indo-European words meaning 'shining' or 'white'.[8] Since Baldr is the whitest of the gods, the latter suggestion is attractive, but scholars tend to base their conclusions about the origin of the name on their views of the fundamental character of the god.

The ultimate origins of the god Baldr have been much discussed. G. Neckel[9] believed that he derived from gods of the near east, of the type Tammuz, Attis, Adonis, Baal and even Orpheus, who went down to Hades in the hope of recovering his dead wife. Gods of this kind often died in youth and violently. In some societies their deaths were pub-licly lamented at festivals held in autumn, as if the participants would weep them from the Underworld. Their return, sometimes celebrated in spring, was the occasion of jubilation.

Tammuz, Attis and Adonis are pronouncedly fertility and seasonal gods;[10] they die with the winter and revive with the spring. But the Norse sources do not depict Baldr as a specialized fertility god, as they do Freyr. As already mentioned, the fertility of the crops may well have been one of the blessings which Baldr brought to his followers, but he brought peace and good government as well.

F. R. Schröder[11] has further emphasized the role of Baldr as a fer-tility god by drawing attention, as many had done before him, to the similarity between Baldr and the Finnish hero, Lemminkäinen. Lemminkäinen was beautiful, vigorous and a great lover. In quest of a maiden in the hostile north, he drove off all the men by the force of his magic songs, sparing only one, a miserable, blind herdsman. He won the maiden he desired, but on the condition of performing three perilous tasks. He succeeded in the first two, but the third was more difficult. He must procure the swan from the underground river of Tuonela. Lemminkäinen reached the river, but the blind herdsman shot him, as it seems, with a reed, or shaft of cowbane. The herdsman chopped his victim up and hurled the pieces into the river. After a long search and many trials, his mother fished the members out of the river with a magic rake and joined them together, and Lemminkäinen was restored to life.[12]

Few would deny that the story of Lemminkäinen owes a good deal to that of Baldr. Lemminkäinen's assailant, if not innocent as Höð was in Snorri's story, was blind and crippled, and his weapon was a seemingly harmless plant. But the story of Lemminkäinen contains many elements which do not appear in any Norse version of that of Baldr, and are hardly to be traced to it. Most striking of these is the dismemberment of Lemminkäinen's body and his revival. This may well represent a seasonal ritual, the death and revival of the fertility god. The dismemberment and re-assembly of the god also have parallels, e.g. in the story of Orpheus. Rituals of this kind were common in many parts of Asia and Europe, and it would not be difficult to believe that the Finns derived this element in their story of Lemminkäinen from a Germanic or Indo-European source. But it would be difficult to accept Schröder's suggestion that the story of Lemminkäinen, in motives like these, represents the myth of Baldr in a form older than we otherwise know it. There is nothing to suggest that Baldr will ever be restored to life until the Ragnarök, nor that his body was dismembered. Baldr shows some features of a fertility god, but less than many others. The myths of Baldr appear to be much more closely related to those of Óðinn than to those of the specialized fertility-gods.[13] He was the son of Óðinn and Frigg, and he was killed by a blind god with a seemingly harmless plant. Víkarr, a legendary king of Norway, was similarly pierced with a reed (reyrsproti),[14] which mysteriously turned into a spear, by one of Óðinn's agents. Eirík the Victorious, King of the Swedes, destroyed his enemies by hurling a reed (reyrsproti) over their heads, saying: 'you all belong to Óðinn'. The reed had been given to Eirík by Óðinn, and it turned into a javelin in flight.[15]

On occasion, Óðinn would take his own victims. In his broad-brimmed hat and blue cloak, the one-eyed Óðinn caused the death of Sigmund the Völsung[16] and, in the disguise of a charioteer, he battered his favourite Harald Wartooth to death with a club.[17] It will be noticed that those whose death is caused by Óðinn are commonly his favourites.

On such lines, we may suppose that, in an earlier version of the story of Baldr's death, the blind Óðinn killed his favourite son and took him to his own home. If this is true, the story of Baldr's death, as we read it in the *Vǫluspá*, *Baldrs Draumar* and in Snorri's *Edda* has been modified and humanized. Óðinn, earlier disguised as Hǫð, has been distinguished from him.

Some scholars, and especially S. Bugge,[18] have been struck by the similarity between Baldr and Christ. Apart from general characteristics, Bugge notices remarkable details in which legends of Christ and Baldr resembled each other. Even the story that everything, including all trees except the mistletoe, had taken an oath not to injure Baldr found a parallel in a medieval Jewish tale.[19] Every tree had sworn that it would not bear Christ's body, except for a cabbage stalk on which he was crucified. Bugge also mentioned later English traditions, according to which Christ was crucified on a mistletoe. According to the apocryphal *Vindicta Salvatoris*, he was crucified on a green tree (*in ligno viridi*).[20]

The most striking correspondence of legends of Christ with those of Baldr is to be found in the Old English *Dream of the Rood*.[21] A great part of this poem was inscribed in runes on the Ruthwell Cross in the late seventh or early eighth century, but the lines here quoted, although they may have been carved, cannot now be read on the stone, except for the last. They are read in the Vercelli Codex of the late tenth century.

Just as Snorri and another authority said that all things wept for the beloved Baldr, the shining god, so the Old English poet described the scene on Calvary in magnificent words:

> Þystro hæfdon
>
> bewrigen mid wolcnum   Wealdenes hræw,
> scirne sciman;   sceadu forðeode,
> wann under wolcnum.   Weop eal gesceaft,
> cwiðdon cyninges fyll;   Crist wæs on rode.

> Darkness had enveloped in clouds the corpse of the Lord, the shining splendour. The shadow came forth, dark beneath the clouds; all creation wept, lamented the death of the King; Christ was on the Cross.

As remarked by B. Dickins and A. S. C. Ross,[22] the similarity between this story and that of Baldr's death cannot be due to chance. It would be hard to believe that the myth of Baldr had influenced that of Christ, and it has often been said that the weeping of nature for the dead god is a motive strange to Norse, in which inanimate objects rarely display emotion.[23] For this reason, foreign influences upon the story of Baldr have been sought, and especially those of the fertility gods of the near east, whose deaths were followed by copious weeping.[24] The ultimate source of this weeping may well be oriental, but it is probable that nature wept for Baldr because, in the legend recorded by the English poet, she had wept for Christ. We might even go further, and suggest that the dry-eyed Thökk was introduced into the story of Baldr to explain why he did not rise from Hel as Christ did.

We need not go so far as M. Olsen[25] did, and describe the cult of Baldr as Christianity in pagan clothing, but it may well be allowed that Baldr's character in the original Norse myth laid him open to Christian influences. Like Christ, Baldr died, and like Christ he will return at the end of the world.

According to West Norse sources, Baldr was just, innocent and a martyr. He was bright and shining like the White Christ (Hvíta-Kristr). It is not, therefore, surprising that some Christian or half-Christian Norsemen came to regard him as a model of pagan justice, just as they regarded some of their early heroes, e.g. Thórhall the Prophet (see Ch. XIV) and Gunnarr of Hlíðarendi, to say nothing of Sigurð. But Saxo shows that there were contrary traditions about Baldr, and he sees him from another point of view.

Continental and English Tradition

It would be interesting to know whether the cult and myth of Baldr were known on the Continent, or in England.

Attention was early drawn[1] to the legend about the Gautish princes, Hæðcyn and Herebeald, sons of Hreðel, which was told cursorily in *Beowulf* (2434 ff). The younger brother, missing his target, accidentally shot his brother with an arrow:

Wæs þam yldestan	ungedelflice
mæges dædum	morþorbed stred,
syððan hyne Hæðcyn	of hornbogan,
his freawine,	flane geswencte,
miste mercelses	ond his mæg ofscet.

For the eldest a premature death by violence was brought about by a kinsman's deed: since Hæðcyn assailed him, his dear comrade, with an arrow from the curve-tipped bow; he missed the mark and killed his kin, with blood-stained shaft one brother shot another.

Many commentators have supposed that this legend is in some way related to the myth of Baldr's death; one brother shoots the other, perhaps by accident. In the northern story the brothers are called *Baldr* and *Hǫðr*; in *Beowulf* they are *Herebeald* and *Hæðcyn*. *Herebeald* resembles *Baldr* in its second element; *Hæðcyn* resembles *Hǫðr* in its first. These correspondences have been explained in various ways. The myth of Baldr, as some suggest, influenced the story of Herebeald. This influence was, therefore, present already in the south-Scandinavian lay, which was one of the sources of *Beowulf*. If the story was based on history, as many suppose it was, a poet had raised it into the divine world, making the names of the protagonists accord with those of Baldr and Höð, which he knew from myth.[2]

There is an alternative explanation. The incident mentioned in Beowulf was historical, and the myth was based on history or, at least, history supplied the names of the mythical figures.[3]

If the first explanation were correct, it would at least prove that the myth of Baldr and Höð was current in Scandinavia before the heroic poem used in this part of *Beowulf* took shape, shall we say, before the seventh century. If the second explanation were correct, the myth could not have existed in such a form as we know it until after that period.

But the similarities between the two stories are too superficial to force the conclusion that there was any relationship between them. The story of Herebeald could well be based on history for, as F. Klæber remarks,[4] accidents of this kind must often have happened. We are left with the correspondence, not of personal names, but of name-elements. The first elements *her-* (*hari-*) and *hǫð-* (*haþu*) are common enough in Old Norse.[5] The element *bald-* is rare in Old Norse personal names,[6] but is common in Old English, and the compound *Herebeald* is not rare.

Even if it is allowed that the story of Herebeald is related ultimately to that of Baldr, this does not show that the English poet knew of the relationship, or that he had ever heard of the god.

Some versions of the Old English royal genealogies, which embody traditions of great antiquity,[7] include a *Bældæg Wodening*, or Bældæg son of Woden. Æthelweard, in his Chronicle[8] written in the late tenth century, replaces Bældæg with Balder. In the same way, Snorri, who used a version of the Old English genealogies in the Prologue to his Edda, included as son of Óðinn, *Beldegg, er vér kǫllum Baldr* (Beldeg, whom we call Baldr).

The fact that Bældæg is said to be the son of Woden (Óðinn) has prompted many scholars to follow Æthelweard and Snorri in identifying him with Baldr.[9] But Æthelweard, when he made the identification was probably influenced by Norse traditions and, although this tells nothing about the traditions of the English, it does show that Norsemen in England in the tenth century remembered that Baldr was son of Óðinn.

For the rest, it is difficult to equate the name *Bældæg* with *Baldr*. The English name is, in fact, a compound containing the element *-dæg*, occasionally found in other English and Norse names, such as *Swipdæg* (O.N. *Svipdagr*), *Wægdæg*, *Leofdæg*.

Place-names provide no better evidence that Baldr was known or worshipped among the English. Those, such as *Baldersby* in Yorkshire, and *Balderston* in Lancashire, as well as *Bealdersleah* and *Bealderesbeorg*, recorded in Old English,[10] are thought to be compounded with the personal name *Baldhere*.

A few plant-names, which like the Old Norse *Baldrsbrá*, probably contain the name of the god, have been recorded in English. Examples include *Balder-herb*, *Balder Brae* and *Baldeyebrow*,[11] but it is believed that they are all of Norse origin.

It seems, therefore, that there is nothing to show that the ancient English knew the god Baldr, and English sources provide no evidence of the age or extent of his cult.

Although no positive evidence of a cult of Baldr can be found in Anglo-Saxon England, there are stronger reasons to believe that he was known in continental Germany. S. Gutenbrunner[12] and F. R. Schröder[13] called attention to a form *Baldruo* found on a votive stone at Utrecht, and said to date from the third or fourth century. But this may not necessarily be the name of the god.

The so-called Second Merseburg Charm is of greater interest, and is preserved in a manuscript of the ninth or tenth century. It is a charm to heal sprains, written in alliterative form and probably in the middle German dialect. I quote the text in the form given by J. K. Bostock[14] together with his rendering:

> Phol ende Uuodan uuorun zi holza.
> du uuart demo balderes uolon sin uuoz birenkit.
> thu biguolen Sinthgunt, Sunna era suister,
> thu beguolen Friia, Uolla era suister,
> thu beguolen Uuodan so he uuola conda:
> sose benrenki, sose bluotrenki, sose lidirenki—
> ben zi bena, bluot zi bluoda,
> lid zi geliden, sose gelimida sin.

Phol and Wodan went to the forest. Then Balder's horse sprained its foot. Then Sinthgunt the sister of Sunna

charmed it, then Frija the sister of Volla charmed it,
then Wodan charmed it, as he was well able to do. Be it
sprain of the bone, be it sprain of the blood, be it sprain
of the limb: Bone to bone, blood to blood, limb to limb,
thus be they fitted together.

It would not be suitable here to enter into the intricate problems
which these lines raise. It was noticed many years ago that there were
numerous charms like this one.[15] They are found throughout the Germanic world, and often contain an allusion to a horse with a broken
leg. In modern versions, it is commonly Christ's horse whose leg is
broken and healed, but similar phrases occur almost monotonously, e.g.

bone to bone,
sinew to sinew,
blood to blood,
flesh to flesh . . .

It seems also to be clear that a charm of this kind was known in Ireland
in early times. It is told that after Nuadu had lost his hand the physician
Dian Cecht fixed a silver one to him, and hence he was called Nuadu
of the Silver Hand. But there is an addition, or another version of this
story. Miach, the son of the physician, took away the silver hand, and
instead he fixed: 'joint to joint and vein to vein of his own hand upon
him, and in thrice nine days it was healed'.[16]

F. R. Schröder[17] plainly demonstrated the use of similar formulae in
the Finnish story of Lemminkäinen, when his mother joined his severed
limbs together and restored him to life. According to W. F. Kirby's
free rendering:

Then the flesh to flesh she fitted,
and the bones together fitted,
and the joints together jointed,
and the veins she pressed together.
Then she bound the veins together,
all their ends she knit together,
and with care the threads she counted . . .[18]

The Finns, as is generally supposed, derived these formulae from
their Germanic neighbours.

It has also been recognized that the tradition expressed in the Germanic, Celtic and Finnish phrases is a part of Indo-European inheritance, since similar thoughts, even similar phrases, are found in a charm
in the Indian *Atharva-Veda* (iv, 12).[19]

In the Merseburg Charm, as it seems, magical phrases of great antiquity have been embedded in a myth, just as they were later to be in the *Kalevala*. The Merseburg text is especially interesting because it is one of the few literary sources in German in which heathen deities are named, and because so many of them are named together.

The identity of these gods and goddesses and the underlying myth have been the subject of rich and productive discussion, but it will be long before any final solution is found. One of the goddesses, Sinthgunt, eludes every reasonable explanation. Most probably Phol, in spite of the irregular spelling of his name[20], is a male counterpart of Volla (Folla), here said to be the sister of Frija (Frigg). A goddess Fulla (Fyllr, Fylla) is known from the scaldic kennings and, according to Snorri, she was the handmaid and confidante of Frigg.[21] Her name (the filler, lifegiver)[22] and her flowing hair give her away as a fertility goddess, and she carried Frigg's basket, as if she were one of the matronae.[23] We can, therefore, suppose that Phol and Volla were a divine pair comparable with Freyr and Freyja.

Baldr's position in the Merseburg myth is no less difficult to determine. Some commentators have doubted whether it is right to render *balderes* as 'Baldr's', and have preferred to interpret it as an appellative meaning 'the lord', and referring back to Phol. This is improbable because there is no evidence of a word *balder* meaning 'lord' in continental German, and there are reasons to doubt whether there was such a word in other Germanic dialects.[24]

On such grounds we may conclude that the Merseburg Charm provides the only weighty evidence of a cult of Baldr outside Scandinavia and her colonies. We are left to wonder what the god Baldr had to do with sprains and injured horses.

No doubt this was told in the forgotten myth upon which the Merseburg Charm was based, but neither the German nor the Norse sources provide any story which explains it.

It has been said that the gods and goddesses were all riding to the sacred grove, or to the Yggdrasill, where they sat in judgment every day, and when Baldr's horse stumbled it was a presage of his doom, as it was when Gunnar's horse stumbled on his way to board ship.[25] This suggestion is, to say the least, fanciful.

It is more interesting to notice that Norse tradition of a horse called *Blóðughófi* (Bloody-hoofed). It is said in the *Kálfsvísa*,[26] a mnemonic poem containing a list of mythical and legendary horses:

> Reið bani Belja   Blóðughófa
> The slayer of Beli rode the Bloody-hoofed.

and in the *Þorgrímsþula*,[27] another mnemonic poem:

Blóðughófi hét hestr   er bera kóðu
  ǫflgan Atriða

Bloody-hoofed was the name of the horse whom
they said would carry the mighty Atriði.

The slayer of Beli is Freyr (see Ch. VII). It is, therefore, supposed
that 'Bloody-hoofed' was Freyr's horse, and that *Atriði* must be a name
for Freyr. This deduction is probably correct, although this same
name in its strong form (*Atriðr*, the up-rider) is applied to Óðinn in the
Grímnismál (str. 48). Freyr is the chief god of fertility in the literary
sources, but Baldr also shows some marks of a fertility god. It would not
be surprising if myths at one time applied to Baldr were later transferred to Freyr.

It has frequently been objected, on stylistic grounds, that there is no
room for three gods in the first two lines of the Merseburg Charm. For
this reason, *Balder*, if it does not mean 'the lord', must be another name
for Phol.[28] This objection should not be over-stressed. The Charm, for
all its historical interest, is without context and is poetry of a low class,
in which literary discipline is hardly to be expected.

In short, the Charm tells no details about the cult or character of
Baldr, but it shows that he was known on the Continent.

CHAPTER FIVE

LOKI

In the last chapter Loki appeared as the instigator of Baldr's murder; he was the *ráðbani*, while Höð, his blind instrument, was the *handbani*. There was an alternative version of this story, best represented by Saxo, in which Höð struck down Baldr without prompting. In this case Höð was not blind.

While both versions of the story appeared to be old, at least as old as the tenth century, it could not be decided which was the older. It is not likely that this question will ever be answered, but if we examine the character of Loki, as it is described in the Old Norse sources, we may learn something of his place in mythology, and see whether he was likely to be guilty of all the wickedness with which he was charged. The modern literature on this subject is immense. Nearly all of the critics have contributed something useful, but it is hard for the layman to find his way through the labyrinth of conflicting theory. It is, therefore, best to begin by considering the primary sources, and to see what can be learnt from them.

When other gods were discussed, it was generally possible to speak of a cult. These gods were worshipped at one time or another by a social or geographical group. Evidence of this was found partly in early poetry and partly in place-names, and sometimes in the later prose sources.

There is nothing to suggest that Loki was ever worshipped, and it would be hard to believe that he was ever the object of a cult. We can learn little of Loki except from the literary sources of the Middle Ages, but these are sufficient to show that he filled an important place in the Norse hierarchy, and was not merely the figment of later romancers.

The scalds of the tenth century tell something about Loki's origins and about his relations with other mythical beings. They also show how many divergent myths about this puzzling deity were current in early times.

The oldest scald to mention Loki was Thjóðólf of Hvin, the friend and contemporary of Harald Finehair (died *c.* 945).[1] In some twelve strophes of his *Haustlǫng*,[2] Thjóðólf told a story of Loki. The poem, as already remarked, is a 'shield' poem, in which the poet describes figures painted on a shield. On one of the panels the chief figures were the giant Thjazi, Loki and two other gods, Hœnir and evidently Óðinn.

Many phrases in the *Haustlǫng* are obscure but, with the help of Snorri, who retold the story in simple prose, it is possible to follow the story which passed through the poet's mind as he described the pictures on the shield. He beheld three mighty gods travelling together; they were stewing an ox for dinner. The meat was slow to cook and Óðinn knew that there was some reason for this. The giant Thjazi had flown down in the form of an eagle and had settled on a tree above the gods. The eagle, demanding his share of the feast, flew down from the tree, seized the four legs of the ox and devoured the meat greedily at the base of the tree, until Loki struck him with a pole. The pole stuck to the eagle and Loki stuck to the pole, and thus the eagle flew off, carrying the frightened god. In his distress, Loki begged for quarter. The giant laid down his terms, demanding that Loki should bring him Iðunn, the goddess who alone knew the remedy which saved the gods from growing old (see Ch. VIII, Iðunn). Loki fulfilled his promise and the gods, now old, hoary and ugly, met in conclave. They threatened to punish Loki unless he brought back their beloved Iðunn. Loki then changed into the form of a falcon; he recovered Iðunn and flew back carrying her to Ásgarð, while the giant pursued him, again in eagle form. Meanwhile the gods kindled a fire and the giant plunged into it and was burned.

Snorri added a number of interesting details to the allusive story of Thjóðólf, but already Thjóðólf had given a fairly clear picture of Loki. The kennings and other expressions by which he designates the god are of particular interest. Loki is called *Loptr*, probably meaning 'sky-traveller'. In the *Haustlǫng* (str. 5), as well as in a later poem, Loki is said to be the son of Fárbauti, According to Snorri, Fárbauti was a giant, as his name (perhaps the Cruel Striker) would suggest. Therefore, although he appears among the gods, Loki is not of divine origin.

According to the *Haustlǫng* (str. 7), Loki is *farmr Sigynjar arma*, 'the burden of Sigyn's arms', i.e. lover or husband of Sigyn. Little is known of Sigyn, but her relations with Loki are mentioned in several later sources. Loki is also said to be the father of the wolf (str. 8), i.e. of the monster Fenrir, who will break loose in the Ragnarök.

Thjóðólf alludes to several of Loki's evil deeds besides the rape of Iðunn. He was the thief of the Brísing belt, or perhaps necklace (*Brísings girðiþjófr* str. 9); he was often afterwards to cheat the gods (str. 12), and he is the one whom the gods watch bound in chains (str. 7).

But in the *Haustlǫng*, Loki does not appear only as the enemy of the gods. It was he who betrayed Iðunn, but also he who brought her back, albeit under compulsion, and it was Loki who caused the destruction of the giant. He is the companion of Óðinn and friend of Hœnir (str. 3) and, strangely enough, he is the friend of Thór (*Þórs of rúni* str. 8).

Thjóðólf's other great poem, the *Ynglinga Tal*, also contains allusions to Loki. He is the father of the death-goddess, Hel, who is, therefore called *Loka mær* (Loki's daughter, str. 7),[3] and he must be the brother of Býleist (str. 31). He is given the name *Hveðrungr* (str. 32), which probably means 'the roarer'.

I have delayed over the work of Thjóðólf because his description of Loki is by far the oldest preserved. It transpires from it that the character of Loki, as we know it from later sources, was largely formed by the early tenth century. He was son of a giant and parent of demons of death and destruction; he was a shape-changer and could travel through the air. His courage failed in his encounter with the giant; he cheated the gods and was bound in chains, but yet he was the friend and companion of Óðinn, Hœnir and Thór.

Later scalds also made occasional reference to Loki and added some features to the picture given by Thjóðólf. Among these was Eilíf Goðrúnarson, probably an Icelander, who lived at the end of the tenth century. He composed a lay about Hákon the Great (died 995) and another in honour of Christ, of which slight fragments survive.

The only considerable poem ascribed to Eilíf is the 'Lay of Thór' (*Þórsdrápa*).[4] The subject is the journey of Thór to the house of the giant Geirröð (see Ch. III, Thór's Hammer and his Goats), but it is doubtful how much of it could be understood had not Snorri[5] retold the story in prose and supplemented the account given in the *Þórsdrápa* from other sources.

According to the lay, it was Loki who tricked Thór into undertaking the perilous journey to the house of the giant: Loki was a great liar, a perjurer and a faithless friend of Thór. The two, as it seems, set out together, eager to assault the giant tribe. As in the *Haustlǫng*, Loki is called *Loptr* (Sky-traveller) and, in a transferred kenning (*ofljóst*) he is *Gammleið* (=path of a mythical bird=sky=Lopt(r)).[6] The poem contains an obscure allusion to Loki's marriage with Sigyn,[7] and he is said to be 'father of the rope of the ocean' (*lǫgseims faðir*), i.e. father of the Miðgarðsorm, the evil world-serpent.

Loki also figured in one of the carved panels described by Úlf Uggason in the *Húsdrápa* (see Ch. I, Old Norse Poetry). The strophe in which Loki is mentioned is open to every kind of interpretation, and many of those offered start with the assumption that Snorri, who transmitted the strophe, misunderstood it fundamentally. This is improbable because, according to Snorri, the poet made a long passage about this scene (*kvað langa stund eptir þeiri frásǫgn*), and we may be satisfied that he knew more of it than the single strophe which he quoted, and therefore understood it better than we do.

As Snorri interpreted the strophe in the *Húsdrápa*, it described a struggle between Loki (the sly son of Fárbáuti) and the god Heimdall (son of nine mothers, guardian of the land of the gods?) at a place called *Singasteinn* for possession of the beautiful *hafnýra* (literally 'sea-kidney'), which Snorri believed to be the Brísing necklace.[9] Singasteinn was evidently a rock far out at sea,[10] for Snorri says that the two gods had taken the form of seals.

Some Eddaic lays have far more to tell of Loki, but most of these are of uncertain age, and it is difficult to know to what period the conceptions implied in them belong. We may begin with one of the latest, the *Vǫluspá en skamma* (Short Völuspá), since it ties up closely with scaldic lays, and was no doubt influenced by them, although not necessarily by those known to us. The Short Völuspá is preserved only in the *Flateyjarbók* of the late fourteenth century. The few strophes which belong to it are incorporated in the *Hyndluljóð*, a lay of a very different kind.[11] The Short Völuspá is quoted by name by Snorri in his *Edda*,[12] and it appears to be an imitation of the great Völuspá, made by a Christian poet of the eleventh or twelfth century.

Just as Thjóðólf said, so this poet says that Loki was father of the 'wolf', but the author of the Short Völuspá is more precise. Loki begat the wolf on Angrboða, whose name (Distress-bringer) suggests that she was a giantess. Angrboða is named in no other source except by Snorri, who was probably influenced by the Short Völuspá.

In the Short Völuspá we also hear for the first time the astonishing story that Loki was not the father, but the mother of Óðinn's horse Sleipnir:

> en Sleipni gat   and begat Sleipnir
> við Svaðilfara   by Svaðilfari

This myth may become plainer when we pass on to other sources.

In another strophe (41) the Short Völuspá tells how Loki (again called *Loptr*) found the half-roasted heart of an evil woman and ate it, and from this became pregnant. Tales like this are common enough, but the poet probably expresses an ancient tradition when he says that every female monster (*flagð hvert*) on earth comes from Loki's brood.

The older poets already mentioned had seen Loki as the parent of monsters, but they had not shown that he was bisexual, and could bear as well as beget his foul progeny.

Assertions that Loki was bisexual, or homosexual appear again in the *Lokasenna* (The Flyting of Loki). This poem, found in the Codex Regius of the Poetic Edda, is of vital importance for the study of Loki as, indeed, of other deities, and it must be considered fairly closely.

The scene is described in a prose introduction. A feast was held in the house of the sea-god, Ægir. All the gods and goddesses were present, except for Thór, who was away on one of his journeys in the east, the world of giants. The place was a sanctuary, in which no violence might be done, but when the gods praised the excellence of Ægir's servants, Loki was so enraged that he killed one of them. The gods drove Loki out, but he made his way back, and with this the poem opens.

In crisp, succinct phrases Loki hurls abuse at one of the gods after another, and he finds the weak spot in everyone's conduct. Óðinn had often given victory to cowards instead of to the brave (str. 22), and he had dabbled in sorcery like a witch (str. 24); Freyja had been the mistress of all the gods and elves, even of her own brother (strs. 30–32). Thus the wrangling goes on until Thór appears and drives Loki out under the threat of his hammer. In a prose colophon, which may not originally have belonged to this context, it is told how Loki hid in a waterfall in the form of a salmon until the gods seized and bound him, as is told in detail by Snorri.

Much can be learnt about the gods from this poem, but some of its most interesting passages are about Loki himself. He is said to have borne children, and Óðinn says to him (str. 23):

átta vetr vartu fyr jǫrð neðan	You were seven years below the earth,
kýr mólkandi ok kona,	milking cows as a woman;
ok hefir þú *bǫrn* borit,	you have borne children
ok hugða ek þat args aðal.	and I thought that the way of a 'paederast'.

Óðinn also calls Loki the father of the wolf (str. 10), and there is an allusion to the day when Loki, the smith of all evil, will be bound in chains (str. 41). Loki is a cowardly, effeminate wretch (*rǫg vættr*, strs. 57 ff).

Loki, in his turn, boasts of the misfortunes he has brought upon the gods. It is because of him that Frigg will never again see her beloved son, Baldr, riding to the hall (str. 28); it was the crafty Loki who seduced Thór's wife (str. 54). He boasts before Skaði that it was he who had caused the death of her father, *Thjazi* (str. 50), and yet she had invited him to her bed (str. 52).

Loki's strangest boast is that, in the days of old, he and Óðinn had 'mixed their blood', i.e. sworn oaths of foster-brotherhood, and Óðinn had vowed that he would never taste beer but in the company of Loki (str. 9).

There has been some dispute about the age of the *Lokasenna*, but it probably belongs to the same period as the *Vǫluspá*, that of the Conversion, or rather to the age when the heathen religion was falling into disrepute. All the gods are shown in a bad light, with the sole exception of Thór.

There is nothing to suggest that the poet was a Christian. Apart from the slight respect which he shows for Thór, he despises all gods, and he might well be one of those irreligious men, who believed in their 'might and main', such as will be described in Ch. XIV.

This need not imply that the author of the *Lokasenna* disbelieved in the existence of gods, although he placed so little faith in them. If he had reacted against the pagan tradition, he was brought up in it, and the abuse of the gods which he puts into the mouth of Loki is soundly based. The same may be said of the accusations made against Loki. It transpires from these that Loki was not only a shape-changer, but also a sex-changer. This theme is further developed by Snorri.

Little as the author of the *Lokasenna* has in favour of the gods, Loki appears in his poem as the enemy of all of them. It is as if, evil as he was, he had drawn every kind of evil to himself.

Not the least surprising accusation brought against Loki is that he was bisexual, or sexually inverted, a fault which he shares with Óðinn. According to some Icelandic Family Sagas, there was no more despicable crime than passive homosexuality, or *ergi*, as it was called. Sometimes, as an insult, images of men in indecent postures would be erected[13] and, in one instance, the litigants were persuaded to settle the dispute out of court, rather than bring so unseemly a case before the Assembly[14]. In *Njáls Saga* (Ch. CXXIII), Skarpheðinn brought an accusation of this kind against Flosi, and Flosi brought a more subtle one against the beardless Njáll. According to Icelandic law, three insulting words (*ragr, stroðinn, sorðinn*),[15] all conveying the sense homosexual, or rather invert, were punishable by full outlawry. Similar provisions are made in early Swedish law.[16]

For all this, sagas[17] contain jolly jokes on this topic, which suggest that not everyone took it seriously, and it is difficult to know how deep was the horror of inversion sometimes expressed. As explained in another chapter, it had its place in Germanic ritual. Inversion was perhaps acceptable, or even demanded of priests of certain cults, *muliebri ornatu*,[18] and consequently it must, at least in early times, have been practised among the gods. But that which is permissible to gods and priests is not necessarily fitting for laymen. The author of the *Lokasenna*, certainly not a devout pagan, seems to dethrone the gods and to judge their conduct as he would that of an immoral neighbour, in whom inversion was unmanly.

As already remarked, Loki was not only the enemy of the gods, but he sometimes got them out of difficulties. According to the *Haustlǫng*, he rescued Iðunn from the clutches of the giants. Similarly the *Þrymskviða*, one of the best-known lays of the *Edda*, tells how Loki used his cunning to recover Thór's hammer.

The Eddaic lays contain few other references to Loki. According to the *Hymiskviða* (str. 37), it was the guileful Loki (*inn lævísi Loki*) who broke the leg of one of the goats who drew Thór's chariot. This appears to be a variant of the story of Thór and Thjálfi, told in detail by Snorri (see Ch. III, Thór's Hammer and his Goats).

The *Fjǫlsvinnsmál* (Words of Fjöllsvinn, str. 26), preserved only in late manuscripts, alludes to a magic sword, *Lævateinn*[19] (the guileful twig) forged with runes by Lopt (Loki) beneath the gates of death. Only this sword can slay the cock Víðófnir, who sits in the Mímameið (Tree of Mími, i.e. Yggdrasill).

The so-called *Reginsmál* (Words of Reginn) contains an introduction in prose, presumably the work of its thirteenth-century redactor, telling how the three gods, Óðinn, Hœnir and Loki, were travelling together, as they were in the story of the *Haustlǫng*. This story, which is given in closer detail by Snorri will be discussed below.

In the last chapter, Loki's part in the murder of Baldr, and his punishment for it, were considered in the light of the *Vǫluspá* and the *Baldrs Draumar*. The *Baldrs Draumar* contained an allusion to the bound Loki, who would break loose in the Ragnarök. The same apprehension is implied in the *Vǫluspá*. This poem (str. 51) also tells that, in the Ragnarök, Loki will be at the helm of the ship which carries the sons of Múspell, the demons of destruction, from the east.

Together the scalds and the Eddaic poets have left a fairly clear picture of Loki and his relations with other mythical beings. He is the friend of some of the gods, but a doubtful and untrustworthy friend. He is associated particularly with Hœnir, of whom next to nothing can be known, and with Óðinn, of whom in the days of old he was fosterbrother. Loki is wily and malicious (*lævíss*, *lægjarn*, *slægr*), and he forged the sword *Lævateinn*; he is the blood-relative of demons and monsters, although he often broke the bonds of kindred by contending with them in the interest of the gods. He is a shape- and sex-changer, and long before the Ragnarök he will be the arch-enemy of all gods, waiting until his chains break, when he will join the demons.

Loki thus appears in the poems as a complicated figure, who must have many generations of development behind him.

Little is told of Loki by the prose writers of the Middle Ages, except by Snorri, who repeats most of the stories which I have quoted, adds others to them, and supplies a wealth of detail. It is plain that Snorri had richer sources than those known to us.

When he introduces Loki, Snorri gives an impression of the complexity of his character:

There is yet another counted among the Æsir, whom some call the slander-bearer (*rógbera*) of the Æsir, the promoter of deceit, the stain of all gods and men. He is called Loki or Lopt, and is the son of the giant Fárbauti. His mother is called Laufey or Nál, and his brothers are Býleist and Helblindi (Death-blind). Loki is handsome and fine to look at, but evil in temper, and very variable in manner. He excels others in that form of wit which is called guile (*slægð*), and he resorts to wiles for everything. Time and again he has brought the gods into grave trouble, but often rescued them by his wiles.[20]

Snorri goes on to tell that Sigyn was the wife of Loki, and their son was Narfi or Nari. He tells of Loki's children by the giantess Angrboða, the wolf Fenrir, the World-serpent and the death-goddess, Hel.

In the *Skáldskaparmál* (XXIV) Snorri returns to Loki and gives a list of kennings and poetic expressions which may be used to designate him. Many of these are based on Loki's relations with other mythical creatures, with the giant, Fárbauti, the wolf, Fenrir, the world-serpent, with Hel, Óðinn and other gods. He is also the thief of Sif's hair, of the Brísing necklace and of Iðunn's apples. Loki is the sly god, the slanderer and the crafty one. He is the instigator of Baldr's murder (*ráðbani*), the bound god, the enemy of Heimdall and Skaði.

Some of these kennings were used in poems discussed above. Others may have been used in poems known to Snorri but not to us, and Snorri may have constructed some of them from the myths which he told. As already remarked the expression *ráðbani Baldrs* finds its counterpart in the Short Völuspá (str. 29), where Höð is called the *handbani* or physical slayer of Baldr.

It is not necessary to discuss the myths which Snorri repeats from the poems already quoted, but it may be helpful to mention some details which he adds to the existing poems.

Snorri[21] retells the story of Loki, the giant Thjazi and the goddess Iðunn, closely following the *Haustlǫng* but adds some details. The remedy against old age (*ellilyf*), which Iðunn alone controlled, consisted, according to Snorri, of sacred apples which the gods used to eat. Loki enticed the goddess into the forest saying that he had found some wonderful apples, and she must bring hers to compare with them. Loki, when he undertook to bring Iðunn back, flew to the Giant World in Freyja's falcon-skin (*valshamr*). The giant was away, and he found Iðunn alone. He changed her into the form of a nut and flew off bearing her in his claws. The giant pursued him in the form of an eagle and lost his life as is told in the *Haustlǫng*.

Snorri appends another story to this, and a peculiar one it is. Skaði, the daughter of Thjazi took up arms and made her way to Ásgarð, determined to avenge her father. To appease her anger, the gods said that she could choose any one of their number, but must choose him by his legs alone. She chose the sea-god Njörð thinking, evidently from his clean legs, that he was Baldr (see Ch. VII, Njörð). The gods did something else to please Skaði. She said that, after her father's death, they would never make her laugh, but the gods contrived to do so. Loki tied his testicles to the beard of a goat. As Loki pulled one way and the goat the other, they both squawked, and when Loki fell on Skaði's knee she laughed. It is also told that, to please Skaði, Óðinn took the eyes of Thjazi and hurled them into the sky where they became two stars. In another source, it was Thór who did this (see Ch. III, Thór and the Giants).

Since Snorri followed a known source closely in the greater part of this tale, we may suspect that he was following lost sources closely in his additions. The scene in which Loki struggles with the goat is complicated and primitive, and hardly of the kind which the sophisticated Snorri would invent.

Eilíf Goðrúnarson's *Þórsdrápa* was mentioned earlier (Ch. I, Old Norse Poetry). When Snorri retold the story to which Eilíf alludes,[22] he added many details. He derived some of these from another poetic source, which he quotes, and he may have supplied others to make the story more comprehensible.

According to the *Þórsdrápa*, it was Loki who induced Thór to make the journey to the house of the giant Geirrøð, but Snorri explains the circumstances under which Loki did this. Loki was disporting himself in Frigg's hawk-skin and, out of curiosity, he flew to the house of the giant and peered through the window. A serving man caught the hawk and showed him to the giant who could see that his eyes were not those of a bird. He shut him in his chest and starved him until Loki promised to bring Thór to the giant's house without his girdle of strength or his hammer. Loki, as it seems, accompanied Thór on the first part of his journey, but he disappears from the scene.

According to the Short Völuspá, as already mentioned, the shape-, sex-changing Loki bore the famous colt, Sleipnir, to Svaðilfari. Without the help of Snorri we could make little of this, but Snorri[23] tells a long and rather confused story to explain it.

The gods had just established Miðgarð and Valhöll when a builder arrived and offered to build a wall (*borg*) secure against the giant-race. His terms were hard. If he finished the work in one winter, he was to be rewarded with the goddess Freyja and to take the sun and the moon from the sky. He must be helped by no one, but Loki arranged that he might use his stallion, Svaðilfari. The stallion dragged great rocks, and the work went speedily and, with only three days left before the end of winter, the builder had completed the wall and nearly reached the gate. In dismay, the gods met in council to discover who had made the disastrous bargain, under which they would be deprived of Freyja as well as of the sun and the moon, and condemned to live in perpetual darkness. They threatened Loki with death unless he could find a way out of this contract. Loki was afraid, and he undertook to cheat the builder, but he did so in an unseemly manner. In the night, while the builder and his stallion were carting rocks, a mare galloped from the forest and whinnied, and the stallion pursued her, and so the work was stopped. The builder seeing that the task could not be finished, flew into a giant rage (*jǫtunmóðr*), and the gods knew now, if they had not known before, that their builder was a rock-giant. They called for Thór, who crashed his hammer on the monster's skull and sent him to Niflheim, the world of death. Soon afterwards, Loki bore the foal Sleipnir, grey and with eight legs.

Snorri supports his story with two strophes from the *Vǫluspá*:

25. þá gengu regin ǫll á rǫkstóla, ginnheilog goð, ok of þat gættusk, hverir hefði lopt alt lævi blandit eða ætt jǫtuns Óðs mey gefna.	Then all the powers went to their judgment seats, the most holy gods, and took council about this: who had filled the sky with guile and given the wife of Óð (Freyja) to the race of giants.
26. Á gengusk eiðar orð ok sœri mál ǫll meginlig, er á meðal fóru; Þórr einn þar vá þrunginn móði, hann sjaldan sitr, er hann slíkt of fregn.	Oaths were broken, bonds and covenants all mighty pacts sealed between them. Thór alone struck there, swollen with rage. He seldom stays still when he hears such things.

The context in which Snorri places these strophes differs so sharply from that of the *Vǫluspá* that Snorri has widely been accused of misunderstanding the poem, and even of falsifying his evidence. It is improbable that he did either.

According to the poem, the prelude to the strophes quoted was the war between the Æsir and the Vanir, in which the wall of Ásgarð had been destroyed (see Ch. VII, first section). Peace was evidently concluded between the warring parties, but extant texts of the *Vǫluspá* contain no allusion to the reconstruction of the wall. Possibly these texts are defective, but it is no less likely that the poet expected more knowledge of his hearers than we possess.

In either case, a considerable time must have elapsed between strophe 24, in which the Vanir broke down the wall of Ásgarð, and strophe 25, in which the Vanadís, Freyja, was dwelling among the Æsir and had been given, or promised, to the giant-race.

Loki is not mentioned at this point in the *Vǫluspá*, but this need not lead us to suppose that Snorri was wrong in charging him with the betrayal of Freyja. Nor need we conclude, as many critics have done, that Snorri misunderstood the lines

> hverr (v.l. *hverir*) hefði lopt alt
> lævi blandit.

The noun *læ* (neut.) sometimes means 'destruction'; in compounds such as adjectives *læviss*, *lægjarn*, and the noun *lævísi* (fem.), it means rather 'malice, guile'. It is interesting to notice that such compounds are most frequently associated with Loki, and that he, according to the *Fjǫlsvinnsmál* (str. 26), forged the magic sword *Lævateinn*. If anyone had infused the sky with 'guile' it was most likely to be Loki. His way of doing so could well be, as Snorri believed, by disposing of the sun and the moon, so that the sky would be dark, cold, dank and unpurged by the life-giving sun.

Snorri's story does not contradict the *Vǫluspá*, but he did not find all that he tells in its extant texts. Nor is it likely that such motives as those of the stallion and the god-mare would ever have been included in this serious, moral poem. If Snorri's story is not always consistent, it is probably because here, as in other passages, he was attempting to reconcile conflicting sources.

Snorri's story contains elements common in folk-tale. Everyone has heard stories about a master who bargains with a builder to complete a church or some other great work within a given time. The builder may be a giant or troll, or even the devil himself. As his reward, the builder may claim his master's soul, his son, even the sun and the moon. In the end the master uses some trick, and the builder is cheated.[24]

But Snorri's story is more elaborate than these are, and contains motives strange to the folktale. The strangest of all is that of the master, or his agent changing into a mare, and seducing the builder's stallion. Snorri could not have invented this, in all its complexity, on the basis of the Short Völuspá alone. We might rather suppose that he was combining the original *Vǫluspá* with a far more detailed source. This source, whatever its form, was based on the myth of the shape- and sex-changing Loki, and of his motherhood of the monstrous horse, but it was enriched with the motives of folktale. It could be an oral tale, even a tale written before Snorri's time. It could also be a light-hearted poem like the *Þrymskviða*.

Snorri tells a number of tales of Loki not found in the older sources. Some of these explain kennings and other poetical expressions. Gold, Snorri tells us, may be called the 'hair of Sif' (*haddr Sifjar*).[25] This kenning is not found elsewhere, but it may well be genuine.

Sif was the wife of Thór, and Loki, out of malice (*til lævísi*) cut off her hair. The enraged husband seized him and forced him to go to the black elves, or dwarfs, sons of Ívaldi, and to prevail on them to forge a golden head of hair, which would grow like any other hair. Not only did the dwarfs forge the golden hair, but by a ruse, Loki persuaded them to forge other treasures as well. These treasures were distributed among the gods, and seem to symbolize their divine functions. Óðinn received the spear, Gungnir, and the magic arm-ring, Draupnir; Thór, besides the golden hair, received the hammer, Mjöllnir, and Freyr received the ship, Skíðblaðnir, and the golden-bristled boar.

In this story, confused as it is, Loki preserves much of his traditional character; he is sly and rather cowardly and changes into the form of a fly. It is because of his mischief that the shaft of Thór's hammer is too short. In the end, Loki cheated the dwarfs, to whom he owed his head, and they had to be content with sewing up his lips.

We could suppose that stories like these had grown up to explain the scaldic kennings and the origin of the divine treasures, some of which figure so prominently in early poetry.

The famous, jovial story of Thór and his visit to the giant Útgarðaloki belongs to another chapter. On this, as on another occasion, Thór was accompanied by Loki, as well as by his servant, the runner Thjálfi. According to Snorri, it was Thjálfi who lamed one of Thór's goats but, as already remarked, the *Hymiskviða* (str. 37) says it was Loki who did this.

The *Hymiskviða* is, no doubt, older than Snorri, but Snorri probably represents the original tradition more faithfully on this point. Loki is the cause of most evil (*flestu illu ræðr*),[26] and so he could well be charged with crimes of which he was innocent.

In Snorri's story, Loki was on the side of Thór and competed, on Thór's behalf, against Logi (fire), the agent of Útgarðaloki, in eating meat. Snorri appears to be retelling a folktale, which has changed from the original myth in which Útgarðaloki must have been Loki himself.

Saxo (VIII) tells a story about *Utgardilocus* which plainly shows this, and he derived his story from Icelanders, or men of Thule (*a Tylensibus*). Saxo's story is overlaid, even more heavily than Snorri's, with international motives of folktale. The hero Thorkillus, whose name seems to replace that of Thór, sets out from Denmark on a perilous journey to seek the monster Utgardilocus in the hope of treasure. The repulsive giant was laden hand and foot with enormous chains. Utgardilocus appears to be Loki, expelled from Ásgarð into Útgarð, in the form which he took after he had caused the murder of Baldr. He was bound with fetters, and thus he will remain until the Ragnarök.

I mentioned the story told in the prose attached to the *Reginsmál* about the recurring trio Óðinn, Hœnir, Loki and the Niflung gold. This story is repeated with little difference in the *Vǫlsunga Saga* (XIV), and it is used by Snorri[27] to explain kennings for gold, such as *rógmálmr* (metal of dissension).

As Snorri tells the story, the three gods came upon an otter by a waterfall, eating a salmon. Loki picked up a stone, killed the otter, and prided himself with having won an otter and a salmon with one throw.

The gods took their bag and came to a farmer called Hreiðmar, who was filled with witchcraft. When Hreiðmar saw the otter, he said that it was his own son. He and the otter's brothers laid hands on the gods and demanded weregild. The gods must fill the hide with gold and cover it as well. Óðinn sent Loki to the world of the dark elves. There he found a dwarf, Andvari, who changed into a fish and swam in the water. Loki seized him and demanded all the gold which he kept in his rock. The dwarf attempted to conceal one golden ring, but Loki took it from him. The dwarf put a curse on the ring, saying that it would bring death to anyone who possessed it. Loki took the gold; the otter-skin was filled and covered, except for one whisker. Hreiðmar noticed this, and so Óðinn brought out the accursed ring. This gold, and in particularly the last ring, were to be the cause of the Niflung tragedy.

While it is plain from the *Reginsmál* that Snorri did not invent this story, and hardly likely that he combined it with the story of the Niflung hoard, it would be difficult to believe that the association between the myth and the legend was old or fundamental. Its chief interest lies in the reappearance of the trio, Óðinn, Hœnir, Loki, and in Loki's function as Óðinn's agent. It is, however, possible that this feature derives from the *Haustlǫng*.

Snorri gives another story about Loki, which has great interest for folklorists,[28] but has less to do with pagan conceptions of the god. After the murder of Baldr, Loki made off; he hid in a mountain, where he built a house with four doors, so that he could see in all directions. By day, he used to change into a salmon, swimming in a waterfall (Fránangrsfors). He made a fishing-net, evidently the first ever made, but when the gods approached he threw it into the fire and took his salmon form in the river. When the gods arrived at the house, Kvasir, the wisest of them, saw the pattern of the net in the ashes, and knew that it was a device for catching fish. The gods made another like it and, after a chase, Thór grasped the salmon as he leapt over the net. The salmon slipped through Thór's fingers, but Thór held him by the tail. That is why salmon are narrower at the tail. This same story is given in the prose colophon to the *Lokasenna*, although with few details.

I have mentioned the punishment inflicted on Loki after the murder of Baldr. In the *Lokasenna* (str. 49, cf str. 50) Skaði, daughter of Thjazi, whose death had been caused by Loki, threatens that he will be bound to a rock with the guts of his rime-cold son. An allusion to this may also be seen in the *Vǫluspá* (str. 35), although in obscure phrases. According to the oldest manuscript, the Codex Regius of the thirteenth century, the sibyl says:

Hapt sá hon liggja	She saw a captive lying
undir Hveralundi,	beneath Hveralund (the grove of hot springs?),
lægjarns (?) líki	like to the form
Loka áþekkjan;	of the guileful Loki.
þar sitr Sigyn,	There stays Sigyn,
þeygi um sínum	over her husband
ver vel glýjuð—	little rejoicing.
vituð ér enn, eða hvat?	Do you understand me yet, and what more?

Instead of the first half of this strophe, the fourteenth-century manuscript *Hauksbók* reads:

> þá kná Vála
> vígbǫnd snúa,
> heldr váru harðgǫr
> hǫpt, ór þǫrmum.

These lines are particularly difficult to interpret, but if we accept the emendation *Vála* >*Váli* (nom.), they give the meaning: 'then Váli twists the bonds of war; these chains of gut were firm enough . . .'[29] If correct this probably implies that Váli was born only to take vengeance for Baldr and, as it seems, on Höð alone.

This is not how Snorri understood the text and, presumably, not the form in which he received it, although the version of the *Vǫluspá* which he followed at this point was closer to the *Hauksbók* than the Codex Regius. According to Snorri, the gods seized Loki together with his. two sons Váli and Nari (or Narfi). They turned Váli into a wolf, and he tore his brother to pieces; they drew out his gut, which turned to iron, and with it they bound Loki to three rocks. The prose colophon to the *Lokasenna*, which must be related to Snorri's work, tells the story in slightly different form; Loki was bound with the guts of his son Nari (or the son of Nari), and Loki's son Narfi turned into a wolf. The penalty is not, in this passage, related immediately to the murder of Baldr.

In the passage just quoted from the *Vǫluspá*, Sigyn is said to stay sorrowful beside her husband. The scene is developed in the prose colophon mentioned and in closer detail by Snorri. Skaði fastened a poison serpent over Loki's head, and his wife stayed beside him, catching the drops of poison in a bowl. When the bowl is full, Sigyn goes to empty it, and a drop falls on Loki's head; he struggles and there is an earthquake. This scene is said to be depicted on the stone cross at Gosforth, Cumberland, although some would interpret this panel in terms of biblical, rather than of pagan legend.[30]

The apprehension that the chained Loki, like other wicked beings, would break loose when the time of Ragnarök drew near could be seen in the *Baldrs Draumar* (str. 14). The sibyl, whom Óðinn had called from her grave, had answered his questions reluctantly. When she perceived his identity, she told him to make off, saying that Loki had broken loose and the Ragnarök was at hand. This same thought was expressed in the *Vǫluspá* (str. 51), when, in her prophecy of the Ragnarök, the sibyl said that Loki would captain the ship which was to bring the sons of Múspell from the east.

Snorri also knew of the belief that Loki would break his bonds and fight on the side of the demons, and his account is, in some things, more precise than those of the *Baldrs Draumar* and *Vǫluspá*. Loki will be chained until the Ragnarök. He will arrive on the field of battle with the giant Hrym and all the frost-giants. All the followers of the death-goddess (Hel) will be with Loki. In the ensuing battle, Loki will meet his old enemy, Heimdall, and they will kill each other.

Loki has been named several times as the thief of the Brísing belt, or necklace. This motive recurs in the *Sǫrla Þáttr*, a fictitious tale found in the *Flateyjarbók*[31] of the late fourteenth century. Loki is presented as the son of Fárbauti, said to be an old man (*karl*). He was exceptionally cunning and malicious (*lœviss*), and so he joined Óðinn in Ásgarð, and became his man, performing many difficult tasks for his master.

Freyja was now living in Ásgarð, and was Óðinn's mistress, although not always faithful. She dwelt in her own house, which was so secure that none could enter it against her will. One day she came upon four dwarfs, who lived in a rock. They were forging a necklace, which the goddess coveted. She offered them money, but they had no need of that; they would surrender the treasure only if Freyja would agree to spend the night with each one of them in turn.

Loki got to know about this shameful bargain, and he told Óðinn, who said that Loki must steal the necklace and bring it to him. Loki could not get into Freyja's stronghold until he took the form of a fly. He spied Freyja asleep, wearing the necklace, but the clasp was below her. Loki turned into a flea, and bit the goddess on the cheek. She turned over, and then Loki was able to steal the jewel and take it to Óðinn.

This tale, made the prelude to that of the eternal battle of the Hjaðningar (*SnE. Sk.* LXIII), must have been told for entertainment rather than for instruction, but it still preserves some of the traditional characteristics of Loki: he is Óðinn's agent, and a sly shape-changer, flying and taking the form of an insect. The late medieval author of this tale probably drew on older written sources.

Scholars have given much attention to Scandinavian folk-tales, recorded in recent times, in which Loki is named.[32] These tales are laden with popular motives, such as are commonly applied to Lucifer and Beelzebub; Loki brings fleas and sows weeds. The tales contribute little to the pagan conceptions of Loki but, since they are found over so wide an area, they show how widely Loki was known and how long his name was remembered. They may also show that Loki was predisposed to the influences of the devils of Christian legend.

Some of the folktales were perhaps influenced by the texts mentioned in this chapter, particularly those recorded in Iceland and the Faroe Islands. The Faroe ballad, *Loka-táttur*, probably composed in the later Middle Ages, presents the familiar trio Óðinn, Hœnir, Loki.

These are the chief sources in which Loki appears, and it is time to think of his place in the Norse hierarchy. In the oldest literary source, as in the latest, he was closely associated with Óðinn; he was Óðinn's companion and friend and, in the days of old, they had been fosterbrothers. A third god, Hœnir, was seen in the *Haustlǫng*, and again in later sources, in the company of these two.

Next to nothing can be told of Hœnir. According to Snorri,[33] he was one of the two whom the Æsir sent to the Vanir at the end of the war between them. The other was Mímir, wisest of the Æsir. Hœnir was a noble figure, and the Vanir made him a chieftain. His weakness was in his wits; he could never reach a decision unless Mímir was beside him. If he attended council when Mímir was away, he could only say 'let others decide' (*ráði aðrir*). The Vanir thought they had been cheated and, in revenge, they chopped off Mímir's head and sent it to the Æsir. Óðinn pickled the head with herbs, and it talks to him, and he derives much of his occult wisdom from it. Although no such story is told elsewhere, allusion to the great wisdom of Mímir's head is made in two of the Eddaic poems, the *Vǫluspá* (str. 46) and *Sigrdrífumál* (str. 14).

As kennings for Loki, Thjóðólf used such expressions as 'Hœnir's friend'. Snorri[34] gives some other expressions by which Hœnir may be designated. He is the 'swift god', the 'long leg', and *aurkonungr*, which may mean 'mud- or marsh-king'.[35] According to the *Sǫgubrot*,[36] Hœnir was the most fearful of all the gods.

The only other source in which Hœnir figures prominently is the *Vǫluspá*. He will survive the Ragnarök (str. 63) and read the auguries (*hlautvið kjósa*). In an earlier passage of the same poem (str. 18), Hœnir appears with two others, Óðinn and Lóður, to give life to the inanimate tree-trunks and make them man and woman. Each of the three gods made his own contribution and Hœnir's was *óðr*, which Snorri[37] seems to interpret as *vit ok hræring* (wit and movement). This is surprising when we remember how witless Hœnir appeared to be when Snorri described him in the *Ynglinga Saga*.

Many explanations of Hœnir have been offered on the basis of his name, his long legs and his supposed association with mud or marsh, but it is doubtful whether their authors have meant all of them seriously. He is the barnyard cock, the swan, the white stork and, finally, the black stork (*ciconia nigra*), which is known in Swedish dialect as *odensvala* (Óðinn's swallow).[38]

Little more can be told of Hœnir, except that in the earlier sources he appears only beside Óðinn, and seems to usurp Óðinn's place when he endows mankind with *óðr*. If Hœnir's name is, in fact, that of a bird, or derived from a bird-name, he must be Óðinn's bird. In poetic language, Óðinn's bird, whether he is called a swan, falcon, seagull, blackcock, is a raven. Óðinn's ravens, Huginn and Muninn represent his intellectual qualities (thought and memory), and this perhaps explains why it is Hœnir who gaves *óðr* to men. When divorced from their master, Óðinn's ravens could have little wit, for it was his wit which they incorporated. When separated from Mímir, Hœnir had no wits, and was no better than a barnyard cock. But Mímir's wits were Óðinn's wits. Óðinn consulted the pickled head of Mímir in times of stress, and Hœnir depended on the living Mímir. In this case, Hœnir appears to be little more than an aspect of Óðinn.

In the *Vǫluspá* (str. 18), it was not Loki, but Lóður who appeared beside Óðinn and Hœnir. Even if it were not for the superficial similarity of their names, readers might think that Lóður was another name for Loki. Lóður, according to this text, gave the race of men *lá . . . ok litu góða*, which Snorri, who did not follow the *Vǫluspá* precisely, replaced with *ásjónu, mál ok heyrn ok sjón* (appearance, speech, hearing and vision). *Litu góða* may be interpreted as 'good countenance', but *lá* has puzzled all the commentators. According to some, it means 'warmth' and is related ultimately to the name of Vulcan, god of fire.[35] This interpretation is perhaps influenced by supposed etymologies of Lóður and Loki, for no ward *lá* meaning 'warmth' is recorded in other Norse or even Germanic texts. Snorri gave *lá* as a poetic word for 'hair', a meaning not altogether impossible in this context. The homonym *lá* is used for 'sea', 'water', and the kenning *oddlá* (spear-water) means 'blood'. The old interpretation of the word in the *Vǫluspá*, based on this usage, is perhaps nearest to the truth. It would then imply 'blood' and the other liquids of the body, corresponding with the sap of the trees from which men were made.[40]

To return to the etymologies of *Lóðurr* and *Loki*. The first has been equated with *logaþore*, which is read in the inscription on a clasp, dating from about AD 600, which was found at Nordendorf, near Augsburg.[41] Whether it is a name or not, *logaþore* is there combined with *Wodan* and *Wigiþonar* (?), perhaps equivalent to the Norse Óðinn and *Vingþórr*. It is sometimes said to mean 'fire-bringer', but others identify it with Old English *logðor, logeþer* (magician). Loki (also *Lokki*) is said to be a shortened, pet name for Lóður. If this is true, it provides evidence that Loki was known in continental Germany as early as the seventh century, but the arguments are tenuous.

J. Grimm,[42] and many later scholars, supposed that Loki was an alternative form of *logi* (flame), and found support for this in Snorri's story of the contest in which Loki was pitted against Logi, but the difficulties are manifold and obvious.

Lóður has also been seen as a god of a kind quite different from Loki, and as a fertility-god, whose name in earlier form would be *Loðverr*, the counterpart of *Loðkona*, a goddess whose name is deduced from Swedish place-names.[43] These names are related to Gothic *liudan* 'to grow', but if *Lóðurr* is related to them, we are faced with the difficulty that an Icelandic scald of the twelfth century rimes *Lóðurr* with *glóða*, showing that, for him, the root vowels were identical.[44]

Speculative suggestions like those last quoted have, at least, shown how little etymology can help in determining the significance of mythical figures of whom records are so poor.

In spite of such difficulties, Loki and Lóður may still be identical, rather because the one takes the place of the other in the trio than because their names sound somewhat alike. It is worth adding that Óðinn is called 'the friend of Lóður' (*Lóðurs vinr*) by the tenth century scald Eyvind the Plagiarist, and again by Hauk Valdísarson[45] in the twelfth century. Another early poet called Óðinn 'the friend of Lopt (Loki)' (*Lopts vinr*), and this may support the suggestion that Lóður and Loki were one and the same.

The sources have presented Loki as the companion and friend of Thór; in the tale of the *Þrymskviða* he helped Thór to recover his hammer, but he was a false friend (*vilgi tryggr*).[46]

Loki's relations with Óðinn were closer; he was Óðinn's companion friend and foster-brother. Both of them were shape-changers, sex-changers and deceivers.

It could be said that Loki was not a god, because he was son of the giant Fárbauti.[47] But the differences between gods and giants were not fundamental. Óðinn was son of a giantess, and even Thór, the arch-enemy of giants, must have had giant blood in his veins if he was son of Óðinn. Thór also had a giant mistress Járnsaxa. The giantess Skaði, after her father's death, was accepted as a goddess.

This implies that the dualist system, according to which gods were good and giants were bad, developed late in Norse heathendom. Óðinn was, in many things, bad, and Loki was generally bad, although he sometimes got the gods out of difficulties at the expense of giants.

Loki has been seen as a 'trickster',[48] even as the prototype of the joker in popular drama, wielding a stick instead of a spear or sword,[49] as the 'fool' in the Morris dances wields a harmless pig's bladder on the end of his whip. It is difficult to believe that the father of the death-goddess, of the World-serpent and of evil monsters of every kind could be so light-hearted.

Loki has been compared with many mythical and semi-mythical figures found throughout Europe and further afield. A. Olrik,[50] concentrating on the chained Loki and his part in the Ragnarök after he had broken his bonds, found closely similar figures in legends recently recorded in the Caucasus. Stories are told there of chained monsters, struggling and causing earthquakes, when they are tormented by eagles and serpents. One day, these monsters will break loose and destroy the world.

The bound Loki must be related to the bound monsters of the Caucasus, as well as to the bound Prometheus, but Olrik's interpretation of this relationship is difficult to accept. As he thought, the conception of the wicked Loki, bound and struggling until the Ragnarök, was borrowed by the Norsemen from the Caucasians. The intermediaries were the Goths, who were active in south Russia in the first centuries of our era.[51]

This hypothesis is too complicated to be readily acceptable, but Olrik was probably right in supposing that the bound Loki, one day to break loose, was foreign to Norse mythology. It is easier to believe that this chapter in Loki's history was derived from Christian legend, according to which Antichrist lies bound in Hell, and will break loose before the Day of Judgment. Just as Baldr, in his innocence, was predisposed to the influences of Christ, so Loki was predisposed to those of Satan. The Caucasians and the Icelanders could, independently, belive that the monster's struggle would cause an earthquake.

Loki has been compared with another legendary figure, Bricriu of the Evil Tongue, who plays so prominent a part in Irish legend of the Ulster cycle.[52] Bricriu is clever, and his wits may be useful to the heroes, but he is fundamentally malicious, provoking conflict 'between the kings, the leaders . . . till they slay one another, man for man', and 'enmity between father and son, so that it will come to mutual slaughter.' Bricriu will 'make a quarrel between mother and daughter', and he will 'set the two breasts of each Ulster woman at variance, so that they come to deadly blows . . .'[53]

Bricriu is a coward and keeps out of battle, and ends in a ridiculous death, when the bulls fighting in the *Táin*[54] trample him into the ground. He bears a distinct resemblance to Loki, but when he boasts of provoking such strife between the heroes that the dead will be more numerous than the living, he is more like Óðinn than Loki. Óðinn incited kinsman against kinsman:

| . . . með sifjungum | between kinsmen |
| sakrúnar bar | sowed dissension[55] |

or he says himself:

| atta ek jǫfrum | I incited the princes |
| en aldri sættak | never made peace between them[56] |

It may be added that Óðinn, god of war, will never join in battle himself until the Ragnarök.

G. Dumézil,[57] who studied the legends of the Ossetes and of other peoples of the Caucasus, drew attention to two figures in the heroic cycle of the Narts. The legends about the Narts were recorded in the nineteenth and twentieth centuries,[58] and it is believed that, although presented as supermen, they were originally gods. Among their number were two, Soslan (or Sosryko) and Syrdon. Soslan was fine and noble, and beloved as Baldr, but Syrdon resembled Loki. Other Narts treated Syrdon as a menial; he accompanied them as Loki accompanied greater gods. Like Loki, Syrdon sometimes got his masters out of difficulties, but he was cunning, treacherous and gifted, as Loki was, with power to change his shape. As Loki caused Baldr's death, Syrdon caused the death of Soslan, although he used very different means. Soslan's body was invulnerable except at one point, the legs or knees. Syrdon, in one of his disguises, discovered Soslan's weakness, just as Loki discovered that of Baldr and, by a series of ruses, caused a mysterious toothed wheel to cut off Soslan's legs. The wheel may symbolize the sun, and the story of Soslan's death may, in origin, be a nature myth, as that of the death of Baldr might be too.

In the first edition of his work on *Loki*, Dumézil called attention to the similarities between Loki and Syrdon, but drew no conclusion: 'annonçons-le tout net: nous ne sommes pas en état d'apporter une solution probable'.[59] He rejected the suggestion that the one figure was modelled on the other, and did not believe that similar social conditions could have evoked both of them independently. Nor, in view of the differences between Syrdon and Loki, was Dumézil satisfied that they descended from a common Indo-European prototype.

In the second edition of his *Loki*,[60] Dumézil was less confident in rejecting the Indo-European hypothesis. In another book,[61] he was more positive. He there compared a third story with those of Syrdon and Loki, found in the *Maharabhata*. He believed that Snorri and the *Maharabhata* showed the closest agreement, and that the Ossete story preserved: 'le dernier débris de la version scythique' of the same Indo-European myth, of which traces were found in India, Iceland and elsewhere.[62]

For the study of Norse mythology, the importance of Dumézil's work on Loki lies in his proof that it was not Snorri who made Loki the plotter of Baldr's death (*ráðbani*). This myth of Baldr's death was known in the tenth century and perhaps long before. There was also another version of the myth, according to which Höð killed Baldr unaided. It is not yet possible to say which is the older version, nor is it possible to dismiss the hypothesis that Loki, as well as Höð, were, in origin, aspects of Óðinn. Snorri[63] said it was Loki who caused most evil but, according to the *Helgakviða Hundingsbana* II (str. 34), Óðinn causes all evil.

CHAPTER SIX

HEIMDALL

It was noticed that Úlf Uggason, the Icelandic poet of the tenth century, described a struggle between Loki, cunning son of Fárbauti, and another figure, the son of nine mothers. The two had struggled for possession of the beautiful *hafnýra* or 'sea-kidney'. Snorri, when he quoted this verse, explained that the son of nine mothers was Heimdall, and he identified the 'sea-kidney' with the Brísing necklace (*Brísingamen*). He added that the gods had fought in the shape of seals, and said that Úlf had described the battle at length. In the *Gylfaginning* (XXXVIII), Snorri again presented Heimdall as the mortal enemy of Loki, and said that they would kill each other at the end of the Ragnarök.

Snorri had more than this to tell of Heimdall. Earlier in the *Gylfaginning* (XV), he quoted a poem called *Heimdalargaldr* (or *Heimdallargaldr*), the 'Magic Song of Heimdall', in which the god himself had exclaimed, as if in triumph:

níu emk meyja (*v.l.* mœðra) mǫgr,	I am son of nine maidens (or mothers),
níu emk systra sonr	I am son of nine sisters.

The mysterious birth of Heimdall by his nine mothers is related in much closer detail in the 'Short Völuspá':

35. Varð einn borinn	There was one born
í árdaga	in days of old,
rammaukinn mjǫk,	filled with strength,
ragna kindar;	of the race of gods;
níu báru þann	nine bore him,
naddgǫfgan (?) mann,	that weapon-glorious (?) man,
jǫtna meyjar	daughters of giants,
við jarðar þrǫm. . . .	on the edge of earth. . . .
37. Hann Gjálp um bar,	Gjálp bore him,
hann Greip um bar,	Greip bore him,
bar hann Eistla	Eistla bore him
ok Eyrgjafa	and Eyrgjafa;

hann bar Úlfrún	Úlfrún bore him
ok Angeyja,	and Angeyja,
Imðr ok Atla	Imðr and Atla
ok Járnsaxa.	and Járnsaxa.

38. Sá var aukinn	He was made strong
jarðar megni,	with the force of the earth,
svalkǫldum sæ	with the cold sea
ok sonar dreyra	and the blood of the sacrificial boar (?)

In another passage (*Skáldskaparmál* XVI), Snorri spoke again of Heimdall and the Magic Song. He said there: 'Heimdall's head is a name for "sword" '; this is related in the *Heimdalargaldr*, and because of it, the 'head' has been called the 'fate (death) of Heimdall'. Heimdall, as Snorri said, was struck to death with a man's head.

The kenning *Heimdalls hjǫrr* (Heimdall's sword) was used by a certain Bjarni[1] in the lines:

Varð, þats fylkis fœrðu,	It was a cruel deed
fárverk, bráa merki,	when the trees of gold (men)
gǫr varð heipt, ór hjǫrvi	dragged the stars of eyelashes (eyes)
Heimdalls viðir seima.	from the prince's 'sword of Heimdall' (head)
	an act of hatred was done

In these lines, the poet perhaps alluded to the cruel blinding of King Magnús by his rival Harald Gilli in 1135.[2] In another poem ascribed, although probably wrongly, to Grettir, the same kenning is used in the form *Heimdala hjǫrr*.[3]

These introductory sentences have already shown Heimdall as a complicated and enigmatical figure. He was born in days of old, the son of nine giantesses, he was killed by a man's head, he was the mortal enemy of Loki and, if Snorri is to be believed, he will face death again when he and Loki will kill each other at the end of the Ragnarök.

Difficult as it is to understand statements like these, it is evident that Heimdall filled a certain place in the Norse hierarchy in earlier times, although the memory of him was somewhat faded by the time the extant sources were composed.

Heimdall's position among the gods is shown partly in the *Grímnismál* (Words of Grímnir, Óðinn), where the poet lists the dwellings of the gods:

13. Himinbjǫrg eru in áttu,	Himinbjörg is the eighth
en þar Heimdall	and there Heimdall, it is said,
kveða valda véum;	rules his divine dwellings;

þar vǫrðr goða	the guardian of gods
drekkr í væru ranni,	drinks in his peaceful hall
glaðr, in góða mjǫð.	merrily the splendid mead.

Snorri (*Gylfaginning*, XV) quoted this strophe with slight variation. According to him, Heimdall was called 'the white god' (*hvíti áss*); he was great and 'holy', and was borne by nine maidens, all sisters. He dwelt in Himinbjörg, which stands by the bridge *Bifrǫst* (*Bilrǫst*), i.e. the quaking path, the rainbow. He stays at the edge of heaven to guard the bridge against the rock-giants. He needs less sleep than a bird, and can see a hundred leagues by night as by day. He can also hear grass growing on the fields and wool on the sheep. He has the trumpet Gjallarhorn (The ringing horn), and its note is heard throughout all worlds.

Heimdall appears in other sources as the 'guardian' or 'watchman' of the gods, and his wakefulness is emphasized.[4] The reasons for Heimdall's wakefulness are given in the *Vǫluspá* (str. 46). At the first signs of the Ragnarök, Heimdall will blow his horn, which is raised aloft. According to the dualistic conceptions of the author of the *Vǫluspá*, the god knew that evil monsters were approaching to do battle with gods and men.

Heimdall was mentioned in an earlier passage of the *Vǫluspá* (str. 27), which is less easy to understand. The sibyl says that she knows that the *hljóð* of Heimdall is hidden, or pledged beneath the ever-bright, holy tree, i.e. the Yggdrasill.

The first difficulty is in the meaning of the word *hljóð*. This has often been rendered 'trumpet'.[5] Snorri[6] may perhaps have understood the obscure lines in this way, when he wrote that the god Mímir was filled with wisdom because he drank from the well beneath the tree out of the Gjallarhorn, suggesting that the horn was made for drinking as well as for blowing.

It is possible that the Gjallarhorn, together with Óðinn's eye and all wit and wisdom, was stored beneath the Yggdrasill, or in the holy well, but improbable that the author of the *Vǫluspá* alluded to the horn with the word *hljóð*. Old Norse provides no other instance of the meaning 'trumpet' for *hljóð*. It sometimes means 'noise', even 'music', but also 'silence, listening, hearing'.

Since the hearing of Heimdall was so precious, we may suspect that this was the object hidden at the base of the holy tree. It may be conceived in concrete form, as one of Heimdall's ears. Óðinn was gifted with exceptional vision and, from his seat *Hliðskjálf*, he could see throughout all worlds. But Óðinn had only one eye; the other lay in the well of Mímir, beneath the World Tree, because, according to Snorri, he had pledged it in exchange for knowledge. Thus, the two gods, Óðinn and Heimdall, seem each to have pledged or pawned one of their most precious gifts.[7]

Heimdall was also named in the first strophe of the *Vǫluspá* where, according to the interpretation now generally accepted, men were addressed as 'sons of Heimdall' (*megir Heimdallar*).[8]

The conception of Heimdall as the father of mankind is developed in another text, the *Rígsþula*. In its present form this poem is introduced with a few words of prose. It is told there that, according to ancient tales, the god Heimdall walking by the seashore, came to a human dwelling and called himself *Rígr*. He found a couple there called *Ái* and *Edda* (great-grandfather and great-grandmother). They entertained the visitor with coarse bread and, when night fell, he lay down between them. After three nights, Ríg went on his way and, nine months later, Edda bore a son. He had dark skin, and they called him *Þræll* (Thrall). He grew up with an ugly face and gnarled hands. He did manual work and married an uncomely woman, *Þír* (Bondwoman). The race of thralls is descended from their children.

Ríg went on to another house, where he found *Afi* and *Amma* (grandfather and grandmother). He slept for three nights between them, and after nine months Amma bore a son called Karl (Freeman). The race of Freemen descended from Karl and his bride.

Ríg went on his way, until he came to a third couple, *Faðir* and *Móðir* (Father and Mother), living in luxury and engaged in aristocratic pursuits. Nine months afterwards, Móðir bore a son, called Jarl (Earl, Prince). His hair was blond, and his eyes glittered like those of a serpent. He grew up skilled with the bow, the spear and the horse. One day Ríg came to him from under a bush; he acknowledged his son, gave him his own name and taught him the runes.

When Jarl grew up, he had twelve noble sons, but Kon, the youngest, was noblest of all. Like Óðinn he understood the runes and could blunt weapons and, like Sigurð, he understood the speech of birds. The end of the poem is missing, but it breaks off when a crow is telling Jarl of two princes, *Danr* and *Danpr*, who live in even greater splendour than he does.

This poem is found only in one manuscript of Snorri's *Edda* (Wormianus), written about the middle of the fourteenth century, where it is commonly believed to be interpolated. There has been less agreement about the date of the poem itself. Some have assigned it to the tenth or eleventh century, or even to the ninth,[9] but others have argued that it dates from the twelfth or thirteenth century, and found signs of post-

classical taste in its metrical and linguistic forms.[10] It has been regarded as the product of learned speculation about the origins of the
three social classes. This suggestion would be more convincing if the
ancestor of these three classes were Noah or even Adam.[11]

Whatever may be the age of the *Rígspula*, it is hard to doubt that it
incorporates certain ancient traditions. The names *Rígr, Danr, Danpr*
recur in ancient genealogies of kings of Denmark, albeit in varying
order.[12] The name *Rígr* is now generally held to be borrowed from the
Irish word *rí* (gen. *ríg*, king),[13] and commentators have seen other
signs of Celtic influence in the poem, some believing that it originated
in the northern British Isles or in Ireland.[14]

The question why, in the prose introduction to the *Rígspula*, Ríg is
identified with Heimdall, is no easier to answer. This is perhaps because the redactor knew a tradition, according to which Heimdall was
the father of men. But if this tradition is an ancient one, the two gods
must have been identified in early times.

Heimdall has many names. Besides being the white or shining god,
he is called the 'Golden-toothed' (*Gullintanni*) and, according to
Snorri, he owned the horse *Gulltoppr* (Golden forelock). Another of his
names was *Hallinskíði*, probably meaning the one with the leaning
stick, or sticks.[15] A poet of the tenth century alluded to Heimdall's or
Hallinskíði's golden teeth, calling gold 'the teeth of Hallinskíði'.[16]

Strangely enough, Hallinskíði is also given as a poetic name for ram.
The identity of the two names might be regarded as accidental, were it
not that the ram is also called *Heimdali*.[17] This could mean 'the one in
the home-dale', but it is also the form of Heimdall's name used in the
poem assigned to Grettir and quoted above.

Although this has frequently been denied, it is difficult to escape the
conclusion that Heimdall, if he did not appear in the form of a ram, was
associated with the ram as Thór was with the goat, Freyr with the boar
and horse, Óðinn with wolves and ravens and a horse with eight legs.
He could, as has been suggested,[18] have developed the same significance
for sheep-breeders as Freyr evidently had for corn-growers and probably
pig-breeders.

There is some evidence that the ram was a sacral beast in the eyes of
Scandinavians and of other Germanic peoples.[19] While the Goths
called a sacrifice *saups*, Norsemen called a sheep *sauðr*, and both words
are related to *sjóða* (to cook). The *Ljósvetninga Saga* (IV) contains a
peculiar story of a man who planned to deprive another of his share of a
goðorð. He said: 'we must redden ourselves in sacrificial blood (*goðablóði*)
according to ancient custom, and he slaughtered a ram, claiming Arn-
steinn's *goðorð* for himself, and he reddened his hands in the blood of

the ram.' The use of the personal name *Hrútr* (ram), although less common than *Bjǫrn* (Bear), *Hrafn* (Raven), *Úlfr* (Wolf), *Galti* (Boar), etc, may also suggest that the ram was held sacred to one god or another.

Heimdall is said to be son of Óðinn and of nine mothers.[20] This mysterious story may imply that he was born and was to die nine times.[21] At least we know that he was once killed by a man's head, and will be killed again in the Ragnarök.

Scholars since the early nineteenth century have often seen Heimdall's mothers as the waves of the sea, who are called daughters of the sea-god, Ægir, and said to number nine.[22]

G. Dumézil[23] has lately found support for this view in an unexpected source. According to a Welsh antiquarian, who published his results in 1909, breaking waves used to be called the sheep of the mermaid, Gwenhidwy, but the ninth of them was called the ram! Interesting as it is, this story is not well authenticated, although in Icelandic, as well as in other traditions, the third wave, the sixth or the ninth, were particularly dangerous or portentous.[24]

There are some reasons to doubt that the mothers of Heimdall were the waves, daughters of Ægir. Ægir's nine daughters were twice named, by a poet, probably of the twelfth century and, with slight variation, by Snorri.[25] Their names are typical words for 'wave', e.g. *Bylgja*, *Hrǫnn*, *Uðr*. The mothers of Heimdall were plainly stated in the Short Völuspá to be giantesses, and the names there given to them are mostly recorded in other texts as names for giantesses.

Celtic sources have been invoked repeatedly to explain various features of Heimdall, his by-name *Rígr* and his strange parentage.[26] The story that he was killed with a man's head may also have affinities with Celtic tradition.

It is told in a version of 'The Death of Conchobar'[27] that the Ulster heroes used to drag the brain from the head of every warrior whom they slew, mix it with lime and make a hard ball of it. Conall the Victorious used to carry the heads of his victims as trophies.[28] It was he who slew Mes-Gegra, King of Leinster, in single combat, as is related in 'The Siege of Howth'.[29] Conall drew out the brain of his adversary, hardened it and boasted of it until it fell into the hands of the Connaught warrior, Cet. Cet carried the brain in his girdle in every battle against the Ultonians, hoping to slay one of them with it, for it had been foretold that Mes-Gegra would take vengeance after death. In one battle Cet employed a cunning ruse and got into range of the Ulster King Conchobar. He fixed the brain in his sling and drove it into the head of the King. The King survived as a cripple for a while, but when he heard of the death of Christ on the Cross, he was overcome by such emotion that Mes-Gegra's brain jumped out of his head, and this was his end.

In the 'Story of Mac Datho's Pig',[30] the same Conall boasted that he never slept a night without the head of a Connaught man under his head or knee. As he spoke, Conall took the head of a Connaught warrior from his belt and hurled it at Cet's chest with such force that blood spurted over his lips.

Stories of this kind may seem less strange in the Irish setting than in the Icelandic, but this need not imply that the Icelanders derived their story from the Irish. It might equally well derive from a Celto-German tradition, as some of the stories of Sigurð also seem to.[31] In either case, the fundamental significance of this story remains obscure.

Readers may have noticed some inconsistency in the form of the god's name. It appears in the forms *Heimdallr*, *Heimdalr* and probably *Heimdali*.[32] Many different explanations of these forms have been given, but few of them contribute to our understanding of the god's character. The most usual form, and that best authenticated is *Heimdallr*, and the other two might be explained on phonological or folk-etymological grounds.[33]

The masc. *Heindallr* naturally leads us to think of the goddess-name *Mardǫll*, which is used by scalds and is applied by Snorri[34] to Freyja, although Mardǫll may originally have been another goddess. This might imply that, while Mardǫll was a goddess of the sea (*marr*), Heimdall was a god of the world. We are left to decide the meaning of the masc. *dallr* and the fem. *dǫll*. The most satisfying suggestion so far offered is that of J. de Vries:[35] -*dallr*, according to this suggestion, would derive from a root *dal-* with a suffix -*þu*, accounting for the long -*ll*-. The root is associated with Greek θαλλω (to be luxuriant) and θαλερός (blooming) and again with Gothic *dulþs* (feast). The word may be seen again in the late Icelandic *dallur* glossed by Björn Hall-dórsson[36] as *arbor prolifera*. No instance of this later *dallur* is recorded, but if the gloss is genuine, it leads us back to the association, frequently remarked,[37] between Heimdall and the World Tree, at whose roots the god's hearing is hidden. Heimdall may thus be raised to the dignity of Óðinn, whose eye was hidden beneath the tree, and who himself hung upon it.

While Heimdall has certain affinities with Óðinn, he has others with Thór. Thór was accompanied by his goats and Heimdall, in a manner not clearly defined, was associated with a ram. Thór defends the world of gods and men against giants, and Heimdall is the watchman, able to apprehend the first signs of danger.

But Heimdall has affinities, not only with Óðinn and Thór; he is also said to see into the future 'like the other Vanir' (*sem Vanir aðrir*).[38] Attempts to interpret this line in other ways are forced and it is plain that, whatever his age, the author of the *Þrymskviða* thought that Heimdall belonged to the Vanir.

The watchman of the gods dwells in Himinbjörg (Rocks of Heaven),[39] beside the frail rainbow-bridge Bilröst (Bifröst), at the point where it reaches the sky. When the signs of doom appear, he will sound his ringing horn (Gjallarhorn),[40] and, according to Snorri, he will awaken all the gods to battle against Loki and the monsters.

Many readers have found the holy watchman, blowing his horn at the end of the world, alien to Norse heathendom. He is reminiscent of the Archangel Michael who, according to a Christian legend widespread in the early Middle Ages, will awaken the dead with the blast of his trumpet.[41] In the Norwegian visionary poem, *Draumkvæde*,[42] probably of the thirteenth century, St Michael appears mounted on a white horse, as Heimdall once appeared on his splendid *Gulltoppr* (Golden forelock).[43] Michael carried the horn under his arm and, when he blew it, the dead must come forth to judgment.

In the *Draumkvæde* Michael faces Grutte Grey-beard, who rides from the north, mounted on a black, wearing a black hat. Grutte is perhaps the diabolical Óðinn.[44] According to Snorri, the shining white Heimdall will face Loki, arch-enemy of gods and men.

It seems that Heimdall has suffered as Loki and perhaps Baldr did. They were not in origin Christian figures. Loki, in his evil was predisposed to the influence of Satan, and Heimdall, the watchman, was predisposed to the influence of Michael, foremost of guardian-angels (*fylgjuengill, varðhaldsengill*).[45]

As was said at the beginning of this chapter, Heimdall appears to be an ancient god, whose memory had faded by the time the extant sources were composed. He has some affinities with Óðinn and perhaps some with the Vanir, if rather more with Thór.

J. de Vries, in a recent paper,[46] strongly emphasized Heimdall's relations with Thór, and assigned him to the second class in Dumézil's tripartite hierarchy; while Thór was the warrior, Heimdall was the watchman or sentry, which is also a military function. Dumézil himself has developed rather different thoughts.[47] He has seen Heimdall as the 'first' god (*primus*), the god of the beginning, and has shown that, in several things, Heimdall resembles the Indian Vāyu and still more the Roman Janus. Pursuing these thoughts, Dumézil understands from str. 1 of the *Voluspá*[48] that Heimdall is ancestor of all the gods. If this is true, Snorri[42] must be mistaken when he says that Heimdall may be called 'son of Óðinn' (*sonr Óðins*). Dumézil[50] has shown how dangerous it is to under-estimate Snorri's knowledge of Norse myths, and it is perhaps arbitrary to reject this plain statement on the basis of a questionable interpretation of the *Vǫluspá*, which Snorri knew well.

CHAPTER SEVEN

THE VANIR

The War of the Æsir and Vanir—Njörð—Freyr-Fróði-Nerthus-Ing—Freyja

ALL THE GODS may be called *Æsir* (sing. *áss*; fem. pl. *ásynjur*), but dwelling in their midst were gods who came of a distinct tribe, the *Vanir*. The origins of these names have been discussed widely,[1] but so far the discussion has proved sterile, as have discussions of many mythological names.

The War of the Æsir and Vanir

Other gods might help to promote the fertility of crops and herds, but the Vanir were the more specialized gods of fertility. They live in peace and friendship among the Æsir, but myth tells us that this has not always been so. In primeval days there had been a bitter war between the two tribes, to which Snorri alludes twice in rather varying terms. His most coherent account of it is given in the *Ynglinga Saga* (IV). Here as elsewhere, Snorri has reduced the pagan gods to champions and military leaders.

The Æsir lived in Asia or *Ásaland* (*Ásaheimr*), where their chief city was *Ásgarðr*.[1] Their neighbours were the Vanir, living in *Vanaheimr* or *Vanaland*. This name is associated with *Tanais*, the classical name for the River Don.[2]

Óðinn, as Snorri says, led his army against the Vanir, but they resisted stoutly. First one side and then the other was successful. They plundered each other's territories until, growing tired of the struggle, they concluded peace on equal terms. Each party sent hostages to the other. The Æsir sent Hœnir and Mímir to the Vanir,[3] while the Vanir, in exchange, sent Njörð and his son Freyr. With these, according to the *Ynglinga Saga*, they sent Kvasir, the wisest of their race. In this last remark, Snorri contradicts himself, for he had said in the *Skáldskaparmál* (IV) that Kvasir, whose blood was to be the foundation of poetry, was created from the saliva of the Vanir and Æsir, as they spat into a communal cauldron while concluding peace. The kenning *Kvasis dreyri*

(Kvasir's blood, poetry) suggests that this form of the story is the closer to the original.[4]

Poets sometimes say that Njörð was reared in Vanaheim, and that he was sent to the Æsir as a hostage,[5] but they seldom allude to the war between the two tribes of gods. Only in the *Vǫluspá* (strs. 21–4) is this war described, and there in such allusive terms that some have denied that the strophes have to do with this primeval war at all.[6] They have preferred to see in them a battle between gods and giants, but difficulties become only greater if this interpretation is adopted. If, however, it is allowed that the war described in the *Vǫluspá* was fought between Æsir and Vanir, it must be admitted that the myth was a commonplace to the author's audience. His object was not to instruct, but to give life to a tale which his hearers knew.

I attempt to translate and explain the relevant strophes, realizing that every rendering and interpretation must be partly subjective.

21. Þat man hon folkvíg
    fyrst í heimi,
    er Gullveigu
    geirum studdu
    ok í hǫll Hárs
    hána brendu;
    þrysvar brendu
    þrysvar borna,
    opt, ósjaldan,
    þó hon enn lifir.

She remembers the war[7]
first in the world,
when they riddled
Gullveig with spears[8]
and burned her
in the hall of Hár (Óðinn);
thrice they burned her,
the thrice born,
often, time again;
but yet she lives.

22. Heiði hána hétu
    hvars til húsa kom,
    vǫlu vel spá,
    vitti hón ganda;
    seið hón hvars hon kunni,
    seið hón hugleikin,
    æ var hón angan
    illrar brúðar.

They called her Heið[9]
in every house where she came,
sibyl skilled in prophecy;
she enchanted magic wands,
she cast spells wherever she could,
she cast spells in a trance;[10]
she was ever the joy
of evil women.

23. Þá gengu regin ǫll
    á rǫkstóla,
    ginnheilug goð,
    ok um þat gættusk,
    hvárt skyldu æsir
    afráð gjalda,
    eða skyldu goðin ǫll
    gildi eiga.

Then all the gods
went to the chairs of fate,
the all-holy gods,
and deliberated this:
whether the Æsir
should pay the tribute,
or should all the gods
receive the tribute.[11]

24. Fleygði Óðinn	Óðinn cast his spear,
ok í folk um skaut,	hurled it into the host;
þat var enn folkvíg	this was still the war
fyrst í heimi;	first in the world;
brotinn var borðveggr	shattered was the plank-wall
borgar ása,	of the castle of the Æsir;
knáttu vanir vígspá	the Vanir with battle-magic[12]
vǫllu sporna.	held the field.[13]

Str. 24 can hardly be explained except as the account of a battle, perhaps one of a series, in the war between the Æsir and Vanir.[14] As the battle opened, Óðinn hurled his spear, his sacred weapon, into the enemy host. The act was a ritual; like some of the earthly heroes described elsewhere,[15] he dedicated his enemies to the war-god and to death. Armed with magic, rather than with military prowess, the Vanir shattered the wall of Ásgarð and held the field.

Strs. 21–22 seem to allude to the causes of the divine war. Gullveig, in the hall of Óðinn, had been riddled with spears and burnt three times, only to revive as the witch, Heið, who practised evil magic (seiðr) and rejoiced the hearts of wicked women.

Str. 23 has also to be explained. It tells how all the gods, Æsir and Vanir, sat in council. They had to decide whether the Æsir alone should bear the loss, paying tribute (afráð gjalda) to the Vanir, or whether all the gods should receive payment for the damage done. If this strophe belonged originally where it now stands, the negotiations did not succeed, and the battle described in Str. 24 began.

But if str. 24 is placed before str. 23, or even if its sense is understood as pluperfect, the sequence agrees closely with that given in the bare sentences of the Ynglinga Saga. The Æsir and Vanir had been at war with varying success. Tiring of hostilities they settled their differences, and each party received tribute, or payment in the form of hostages delivered by the other.

The cause of the war must be sought in strs. 21–2. Gullveig had been assaulted in the house of Óðin, tortured by the Æsir, and was reborn as Heið, the witch.

We must wonder who was Gullveig, whose name is found nowhere else. The first element in this name means 'gold', but the second element is hard to interpret because there are so many words and usages with which it might be associated. It may well be present in the women's names Sǫlveig, Þórveig, etc, but the significance of the second element in these is disputed.[16] A word veig meaning 'gold' is given by the Icelandic lexicographer, Björn Halldórsson (1724–94)[17] and has been seen in the past participle veigaðr (brocaded ?).[18] There is also a *veig* meaning 'strength, force'. But, as used in poetry, *veig* nearly always means 'strong drink' and, according to the *Alvíssmál* (str. 34), it was the name which the Æsir gave to beer. Gullveig's name could thus mean the 'power', the 'drink', even the 'drunkenness' of gold, and hence the madness and corruption caused by this precious metal.[19]

The name Heið (*Heiðr*), used in str. 22, is sometimes applied to witches in other and later texts.[20] It probably derives from the adjective *heiðr* (bright, shining). If Gullveig appears in one strophe as the 'power' or the 'drunkenness of gold', and in the next as the glittering, seductive witch, her place in the myth is less obscure. She is one of the Vanir, who were gods at once of riches and of that evil form of magic called *seiðr*.

If we may be more precise, Gullveig can hardly be other than Freyja, the *Vanadís* and foremost goddess of the Vanir. It is not told that Freyja was one of the hostages surrendered by the Vanir after the war, but it is plain that she was established in the realm of the Æsir. She was a goddess of gold for, as the scalds knew, she wept tears of gold.[21] Her daughters were Hnoss and Gersimi, both of whose names means 'jewel' and Freyja owned the famous Brísing necklace (*Brísinga men*).[22] She was remembered as an amorous, seductive figure. According to the *Lokasenna* (strs. 30 ff), she had slept with all the gods, and even with her brother Freyr.

But Freyja was not only a goddess of gold and jewels; she was also a witch (*fordæða*)[23] and mistress of that disreputable magic, *seiðr*. This was the practice of the Vanir, and Freyja taught it to the Æsir and especially to Óðinn.[24]

It is not told how Freyja came to Ásgarð or the hall of Óðinn, but if we can identify her with Gullveig, it was because of her that the war of the gods broke out. It could be suggested that Gullveig (Freyja) had been sent to Ásgarð by the Vanir in order to corrupt the Æsir with greed, lust and witchcraft. Attempts by the Æsir to destroy her were vain, and she still lives.

The significance of the divine war remains obscure. Many have seen in it the record of some incident in history, even as a religious war between worshippers of the fertility gods, the Vanir, and the more warlike Æsir. The Vanir have most often been regarded as the original Norse gods and the Æsir as the invaders, although the *Vǫluspá* gives an opposite impression. The historical events said to be reflected in the myth have been assigned to very different ages. While some have placed them in prehistoric times, others have placed them as late as the Viking Age, and others have found the basis in the Lombard tale of the war between the Vinnili (Lombards) and the Vandals.[25]

From such records as we possess, it does not appear that the poly-theistic pagans of Scandinavia and Germany were so dogmatic or fanatical in their religious beliefs that they would be likely to go to war for the worship of one tribe of gods or another. This first war in the world seems rather to be a part of the creation myth. It explains how gods who promoted such different interests as the Vanir and Æsir lived in friendship. More than this, it explains why the Æsir are gods, not only of chieftains and of war, but also of fertility and magic, even of *seiðr*. If we follow the few lines of the *Skáldskaparmál* (IV), the war ended in a fusion of cults, expressed in the mixed spittle and the creation of the sage, Kvasir.

Difficult as it is to understand, we could suppose that this myth is related ultimately to Irish tales of the two battles of Mag Tured.[26] These have been seen by some as a combination of myth and history. To an outsider, at least, the mythical element seems to predominate, but the stories are something of a hotchpotch.

In the first battle, the Tuatha Dé Danann, who are agreed to be gods, defeated the Fir Bolg, whom many consider historical.[27] In the second battle the Tuatha Dé Danann defeated the Formorians. This second battle has been seen as one between the Tuatha Dé Danann, gods of light, life, day, and the Fomorians, gods of death and darkness.[28]

In fact, the explanation is probably more complicated. Like the Æsir, the Tuatha Dé Danann appear to act rather as gods of war than of light and life. Some of them bear a close resemblance to certain of the Norse Æsir. In the first battle of Mag Tured, Nuadu, leader of the Tuatha Dé Danann lost his hand and, because of the blemish, was con-sidered unfit to rule until the lost hand had been replaced by a silver one. During the seven years which elapsed, Bress was king. His mother was of the Tuatha Dé Danann, but his father came of the Fomorians. He was avaricious, stingy and inhospitable; after his subjects had visited him, their breath did not even reek of beer. When the Tuatha Dé Danann rose against him, Bress fled to his Fomorian father, and Nuadu was king again.

The Fomorians planned to conquer Ireland, but the Tuatha Dé Danann resisted. One of their chief warriors was Lug, the master of many crafts. He was partly a Fomorian and was grandson of the Fomo-rian Balor, the evil-eyed.

In the ensuing battle Nuadu was killed by Balor. Balor had but one eye, and when it opened it brought destruction; the warriors upon whom its gaze fell lost the power to resist their enemies. As the eye opened, Lug hurled a stone through it, and the Fomorians were routed.

This latter story looks in many ways like one of a battle between gods and giants or demons.[29] There are, however, complications, which lead us to think of the war between the Æsir and the Vanir. Nuadu, it need hardly be said, is reminiscent of Týr, whose hand was bitten off by the monster Fenrir.[30] It is remarkable that Balor, a leader of the Fomorians, the demon tribe, bore a strange similarity to Óðinn. Like Óðinn, he had only one eye, and this eye paralysed those upon whom its glance fell in battle.[31] Óðinn could also paralyse his enemies and blunt their weapons.[32] Balor was grandfather of Lug, leader of the divine Tuatha Dé Danann; Óðinn was often friendly with giants and those of giant race, and was himself of giant ancestry.

Lug, apart from his ancestry, also bore a strong resemblance to Óðinn.[33] He possessed a magic spear; before the battle he encouraged the army of the Tuatha Dé Danann; he walked round them on one foot with one eye closed, chanting a poem. This was clearly a ritual or magical act, no less than that of Óðinn, who hurled his spear at the opening of battle.[34]

The second battle, like the first, ended in victory for the Tuatha Dé Danann and not, like the war of the Æsir and Vanir, in a pact between the hostile tribes. But the position of Bress at the end of the war is enigmatical. He had been king of the Tuatha Dé Danann, but had joined the Fomorians. At the end of the second battle he fell into the hands of the Tuatha Dé Danann. He asked his captors to spare his life; in return he would assure that the cows would never go dry and that there would be a harvest every season. All this was refused, but in the end Bress saved his life by telling his captors how to plough, sow and reap.

In other words, Bress made an agreement with the Tuatha Dé Danann and brought fertility to their soil.[35] Consequently he had been seen as a fertility god. Even his name, meaning 'Beautiful', associates him with the bright Freyr of the Vanir.[36]

I have spent some lines on the Irish legends because they resemble the Norse myth in many ways, but there are other legends and myths with which the story of the Æsir and the Vanir might be compared.

G. Dumézil has discussed the war of the Norse gods in many works,[37] and places it in a wider Indo-European setting, basing it on the same tradition as the war of the Sabines and Romans. Dumézil's comparison of the Norse tale with the Indian one of the entry of the Nāsatya (Aśvins), givers of riches and fertility, into the divine hierarchy is striking. The Nāsatya, according to the stories cited by Dumézil, were not admitted into the hierarchy until after a struggle.

Whether or not common origin is accepted, the Norse, Irish, Roman and Indian tales seem to serve the same purpose. They explain how gods and men, who have such different interests and ambitions, as the agriculturalist, the merchant, the warrior and the king, can live together in harmony.

In one civilization, and at one time, the specialized gods of fertility might predominate, and in another the warrior or the god-king. The highest god owes his position to those who worship him, and if they are farmers, he will be a god of fertility, or one of the Vanir.

Njörð

As already remarked, Njörð was father of Freyr and Freyja. In the *Lokasenna* (36), Loki insultingly told Njörð that he had begotten Freyr on his own sister. Loki's taunts were generally well grounded, and Snorri[1] gives more details of Njörð's sexual life. Freyr and Freyja were born to him by a nameless sister when he dwelt among his native tribe, the Vanir. Such incestuous unions were permitted among the Vanir, but were frowned upon by the more moral Æsir.[2]

Njörð filled a certain place in the religious cults of Iceland and western Norway in historic times. In the remnants of the pagan law of Iceland, it is laid down that one who had to perform legal business, pleading, bearing witness, or passing judgment, should swear an oath on the holy ring, saying: 'so help me Freyr and Njörð and the all-powerful god (áss) . . .'[3] Again, according to the *Heimskringla*,[4] when sacrifice was held in Thrándheim about the middle of the tenth century, the first toast was drunk to Óðinn for victory and the success of the king, and afterwards the toasts of Njörð and Freyr were drunk for fruitful harvests and peace. When Egill Skalla-Grímsson, in a magnificent verse, cursed the tyrant Eirík Bloodaxe, he called on Freyr and Njörð together to drive him from his lands.[5] In his lay in praise of his friend Arinbjörn (str. 17), Egill again named Freyr and Njörð together, saying that it was they who had blessed Arinbjörn with riches.

It seems thus, that by the end of the Heathen Age, Njörð had come nearly to be identified with his more famous son, Freyr, and overshadowed by him. But both place-names and the myths in which Njörð figures show that in earlier times he had played a more important part in religious life. It is said in one of the Eddaic poems[6] that Njörð presides over countless temples and shrines and, in another, that this blameless prince of men rules a high-timbered shrine.[7]

The place-names also show that Njörð was worshipped widely, particularly in eastern Sweden and western Norway. Nearly thirty names in which *Njörð-* (*Njarð-*) forms the first element have been counted in Norway,[8] and there are many in Sweden as well, although few, if any, in Denmark. These names are of many types. A number which go back to an original *Njarðarvé (Njörð's temple), found chiefly in Östergötland and eastern Sweden, show that Njörð was publicly worshipped at an early period. The same may be said of those of the type *Njarðarlundr (Njörð's grove), found in similar regions.[9] South-eastern Norway provides two examples of *Njarðarhof, also implying public worship, if at a rather later period. Njörð's association with the sea is also borne out by place-names. Iceland has two examples of Njarðvík (Njörð's creek) and western Norway provides at least four of these. *Njarðarey (Njörð's island) is also fairly common in western Norway.[10]

In the Ynglinga Saga (IV) Snorri gives further evidence of Njörð's importance in cult and sacrifice. After they had come to the world of the Æsir, Óðinn appointed Njörð and Freyr as sacrificial priests (blótgoðar), and they were díar among the Æsir. The precise meaning of díar (plural) is not known, but there is little doubt that it was borrowed from the Irish día (god).[11] As Snorri uses the word díar it probably implies priests of a particularly exalted kind.

Njörð, it is said, was created in the world of the Vanir and given to the Æsir (goðin) as a hostage, but at the end of the world (aldar rǫk) he will return to his own tribe.[12] His home is Nóatún (the place of ships, harbour).[13] He should be invoked by seamen and fishermen.[14] Njörð is so rich that men of exceptional wealth might be said to be 'rich as Njörð'.[15] The god's riches belonged especially to ships and to the sea, and we may believe that such qualities were emphasized by his seafaring worshippers in western Norway and Iceland.

In the traditions about Sweden, Njörð takes his place beside his son Freyr as king. Ari the Wise (died 1148) appended to his Libellus Islandorum a list of his own ancestors. The first was Yngvi, King of the Turks (Tyrkja konungr),[16] the second Njörð, King of the Swedes, and the third Freyr. It is said elsewhere[17] that Yngvi was first king of the Swedes; his son was Njörð who, with his son, Freyr, was worshipped by the Swedes as a god for many centuries. It was also said that Njörð was first king of the Swedes but, following the tradition that Óðinn had brought the gods from Asia, and established the northern kingdoms, some writers[18] concluded that Njörð was another name for Óðinn.

In the Ynglinga Saga, Snorri was more precise, and described Njörð as a typical divine king. When Óðinn came to Sweden, he established Njörð in Nóatún and Freyr in Uppsalir.[19]. Nóatún has not been identified, but it was clearly supposed to be in Sweden. When Óðinn died, Njörð became ruler of the Swedes. He maintained the sacrifices, and his reign was one of peace and plenty. The Swedes believed that Njörð controlled men's wealth. Before he died, Njörð had himself marked, evidently with Óðinn's sacred weapon, the spear, so that he might go to Óðinn. The Swedes burned him and wept bitterly over his grave.[20]

After Njörð came to the Æsir, leaving his sister-wife, he married again, and his new wife was Skaði, daughter of the giant Thjazi.

The story of this marriage was peculiar, and a closely similar one was told of the legendary hero Hadding (Hadingus), which will be described below.[21] The marriage of Njörð and Skaði was one of the results of the theft of Iðunn's apples.[22] After the gods had burnt the giant Thjazi to death, his daughter, Skaði, arrived in Ásgarð in full armour, bent on vengeance. The Æsir made peace with her, and allowed her to choose a husband from their number, seeing his legs (or feet) alone. Njörð had the most beautiful feet, and Skaði chose him, believing he was Baldr.[23]

The marriage was a failure, for Njörð wished to live in Nóatún, by the sea, while Skaði preferred her father's home, Thrymheim[24] in the mountains. The one objected to the howling wolves and the other to the mewing seagulls. The couple tried spending nine nights in each place, but the marriage broke up, and Skaði returned to her mountain fastness.[25] According to another tradition, Skaði afterwards married Óðinn, to whom she bore many sons, including Sæming, ancestor of the Jarls of Hlaðir.[26]

Skaði was mentioned by several poets and figured in myths, but her relations with the gods, and especially with Njörð, are difficult to understand. The failure of her marriage is mentioned by a poet of the eleventh century.[27]

Two of the oldest scalds refer to Skaði as goddess, or deity, of snow-shoes,[28] and Snorri tells how she travelled on snow-shoes, wielded the bow and shot wild animals.[29] She was accused of over-friendly relations with Loki,[30] but showed herself his sworn enemy.[31] It was chiefly Loki who had caused the death of Skaði's father,[32] and it was Skaði who hung a poison serpent over Loki's head, when he was punished after the death of Baldr.[33]

Skaði, with her armour and snowshoes and bow, has some of the features of a male god. If she may be compared with any, it is with the god Ull (*Ullr*), of whom we know even less. Ull was the god of snow-shoes (*ǫnduráss*), of the bow (*bogáss*) and the hunting god (*veiðiáss*).[34]

The origin of Skaði's name has not been found, although many suggestions have been offered. Some have identified it with the Old Norse noun *skaði* (harm, injury) while others have related it to Gothic *skadus* and Old English *sceadu* (shade, shadow).[35] In either case, it could be implied that Skaði was a goddess of destruction, or perhaps of darkness and death.

The form of Skaði's name is typically masculine, but it is doubtful whether great significance should be attached to this. The masculine names *Skúta*, *Sturla* decline as feminines, and were perhaps originally nicknames. It may be that Skaði was originally a god, while her consort, Njörð, was a goddess, whose sex changed because the name appeared to be masculine.[36] If so, much remains to be explained. Why should a god, Skaði, with masculine name, be allowed to turn into a goddess?

If Skaði, this 'shining bride of gods',[37] was of giant race, it is surprising that she would be worshipped. But yet Skaði is made to boast of her temples and sanctuaries.[38] A number of place-names, particularly in eastern Sweden, are believed to represent an original *Skaðavé* (Skaði's temple), *Skaðalundr* (Skaði's grove) and suchlike, but specialists do not agree on the origins of these names.[39]

With her snowshoes, her howling wolves, and in her mountain dwelling to which she returns from Nóatún, Skaði seems to be a goddess of winter, and thus of darkness and death.[40]

The marriage of Skaði to the fertility-god, Njörð, runs parallel with that of Njörð's son, Freyr, with Gerð. Gerð was also of giant race, and probably came of the frost-giants. The meaning of these two myths is fundamentally the same. A god of fertility is allied to a goddess of winter and death. In Norse myths, as in others, fertility and death are intimately related.

Freyr-Fróði-Nerthus-Ing

At the end of the Heathen Age, the chief representative of the Vanir was Freyr, whose worship in Iceland and other lands is described fully in historical and quasi-historical sources.

A detailed account of this cult is given in the *Víga-Glúms Saga*, probably written early in the thirteenth century[1] and based largely on older writings, on ancient scaldic poems and on the tales which went with them.

The story of Glúm's enmity with Freyr was noticed in another context,[2] and a few details may be recalled. A temple dedicated to Freyr stood at Hripkelsstaðir, close to Thverá in the Eyjafjörð. Beneath it stood the cornfield, Vitazgjafi (the certain giver).[3] This name was also applied to an island in Hornafjörð and, in a legendary source, to a fjord in northern Norway teeming with fish.[4] Like names were applied to places in Norway in historical documents.[5]

The field described in the *Víga-Glúms Saga* was plainly sacred to the god Freyr, and the same may be said of fields called *Freysakr* (Freyr's cornfield) of which there are a number of examples in Sweden and

Norway.[6] It was the god who assured the never-failing harvests of the Vitazgjafi, and Glúm's crimes against the god were firstly in shedding blood on the sacred field, secondly sheltering an outlaw son within the sacred precincts, and thirdly swearing an ambiguous oath in the temple.

I suggested above that Glúm derived the cult and morals of Óðinn from his mother's viking family. The cult of Freyr appears to be stronger in the family of his father, and traditional in the Eyjafjörð, a rich agricultural district.

The worship of Freyr was perhaps introduced into the Eyjafjörð by the settler, Helgi the Lean, grandfather of Glúm. Helgi, as already explained,[7] was a man of mixed beliefs, worshipping Thór and Christ at once. There are reasons to think that Freyr was another of his favourite gods. Helgi was brought up in Ireland, son of a Scandinavian father and an Irish mother. When he emigrated to Eyjafjörð, Helgi, like many another settler, called on Thór to show him where to land.

The first winter was severe, and Helgi was dissatisfied. After putting to sea again, he came to a place called *Galtarhamarr* (Boar's cliff), where he put ashore a boar and a sow. These beasts were recovered three years later, leading a herd of seventy.[8] This story may be compared with others, telling how settlers were guided by pillars on which the image of Thór might be carved, or even by the coffin of a dead father.[9] The boar was one of the beasts particularly sacred to Freyr, the god of fertility, and Helgi's prolific boar may be seen as a good omen for his settlement.

The ancestors and descendants of Helgi included a number whose names began with *Ing-* and, as will be explained below,[10] this element may be associated with Freyr and related to the god's other name *Yngvi*. Helgi's son, Ingjald, grandfather of Glúm, built a great temple, probably the temple of Freyr described in the *Víga-Glúms Saga*.[11]

On his father's side Helgi came of a family of Sweden or Gautland, and his father, Eyvind, was called 'the easterner' (*austmaðr*) because he had come from Sweden (*Svíaríki*).[12] The first of Eyvind's ancestors was a King Fróði.[13] The name Fróði was borne by several legendary kings of the Danes, and seems also to be applied to the god Freyr.

Several chiefs of Iceland were given the title *Freysgoði* or 'priest of Freyr'. One of these, Thórð, is named frequently in genealogies and lived in the south-east of the country. His descendants were the *Freysgyðlingar* or 'priestlings of Freyr'.[14] Another priest of Freyr was Thorgrím, living in the north-west. This man is given his title *Freysgoði* only in a somewhat untrustworthy text,[15] but much is told of his relations with the god. According to the *Gísla Saga* (XV and XVIII), it was

Thorgrím's custom to hold a festival at the 'winter-nights' (*at vetrnóttum*), early in October. He would welcome the winter and offer sacrifice to Freyr. After he had been laid in his cairn, snow would not lie on it, and shoots sprouted in mid-winter. People believed that this was because of the love which Freyr bore for Thorgrím; he would not allow frost to come between them.

The story of Hrafnkell Freysgoði, a chieftain of eastern Iceland, is so well known that only a few details need be mentioned. Although named in several sources, Hrafnkell is called Freysgoði only in the *Hrafnkels Saga*, which is now commonly regarded as one of the latest and most fictitious of its whole class.[16] We may doubt whether the historical Hrafnkell was really the ardent worshipper of Freyr which the saga makes him out to be, but the story includes some motives which are probably based on tradition.

It is said of Hrafnkell that he loved no god more than Freyr, with whom he shared all his best possessions. One of these was a stallion, Freyfaxi (Freyr's maned one), accompanied by a stud of twelve mares. Hrafnkell had such affection for his stallion, that he had sworn an oath that he would be the death of anyone who rode him against his will.

After Hrafnkell's shepherd had mounted the stallion, Hrafnkell plunged an axe into his skull without hesitation. The sequel tells how Hrafnkell's enemies temporarily overcame him. Having seized his property they burnt down the temple. captured the accursed horse, tied a bag over his head and destroyed him by pushing him over a cliff into a pool below. When Hrafnkell heard of this, he decided that it was humbug to believe in gods, and never offered sacrifice again.

The author did not make all this out of nothing, but he seems rather to apply traditional motives to Hrafnkell, in whose family the cult of Freyr was perhaps traditional.[17] In the first place we may wonder why the knackers took the trouble to tie a bag over the stallion's head. This was no ordinary horse, and the slaughterers acted as did many who executed witches and wizards possessed of the evil eye.[18]

We may also wonder how this author knew so much about veneration of horses and of their importance in fertility rites and the cult of Freyr. While he may derive some of his knowledge from existing books, a proportion of it must come directly from tradition, or indirectly from lost books.

Freyfaxi was not the only Icelandic horse dedicated to Freyr. Another, called *Freysfaxi*, is mentioned in the *Vatnsdæla Saga* (XXXIV), where it is said that his owner had 'faith' (*átrúnaðr*) in him. According to a story of Ólaf Tryggvason,[19] horses in Norway were dedicated to

Freyr. Óláf had set out to desecrate the idol of Freyr in Thrándheim. As he landed near the temple, he saw a stud of horses and was told that they belonged to Freyr. The King mounted the stallion as if to insult the god, while his men took the mares. They rode in triumph to the temple, where Óláf derisively seized the idol. There are many stories from other countries of sacred horses, which must not be ridden or put to work, or touched by any except a priest.[20] As will be seen in later chapters, the flesh of the horse was eaten in sacrificial feasts, and his phallus was held in particular veneration.

The boar was also sacred to Freyr and the Vanir. While Freyr's sister, Freyja, had the nickname *Sýr* (sow), the god owned the boar *Gullinbursti* (Golden-bristled) or *Slíðrugtanni* (Cutting-tusked), made by a dwarf.[21] This boar would gallop through the air and over the sea more swiftly than any horse, while his glowing bristles gave light in darkest night. Freyr rode on his boar to the cremation of Baldr.[22] According to one text, a magnificent boar (*sonargǫltr*) was offered to Freyr at Yule, and oaths were sworn on his bristles.[23]

An ox was also offered to Freyr in the story quoted from *Víga-Glúms Saga*, and a story like this one, and perhaps derived from it, is given in another text.[24] Further evidence of relations between the Vanir and horned cattle will be given below.

The worship of Freyr has left its mark in a few place-names of eastern and south-eastern Iceland. *Freyfaxahamarr* (Freyfaxi's cliff), in Hrafn-kelsdal, where the horse was said to be destroyed, may well owe its name to the saga. The name *Freysnes* is also recorded three times, and *Freys-hólar* (Freyr's hillocks) once.[25]

More than twenty names of which *Frey-* forms the first element, have been recorded in Norway.[26] Two of these, *Freyshof* (Freyr's temple) in the south-east of the country, suggest public worship of the god in the last centuries of heathendom.[27] There are many more in which the god's name is compounded with words for fields, meadows, etc, e.g. *Freysakr*, *Freysland*, *Freysvin*. The place-names containing the element *Frey-* are found chiefly in south-eastern Norway, perhaps because of the importance of agriculture in that region.

The *Frey-* names in Sweden are far more numerous, and include many of the type *Freysvé* (Freyr's temple), *Freyslundr* (Freyr's grove), besides agricultural names such as *Freysakr*. Such names are particularly common in eastern Sweden (Svealand),[28] and it seems that this agricultural district was for long the centre of Freyr's cult.

Literature supports the evidence of place-names. In a passage ascribed to Styrmir Kárason (died 1245), Freyr is named as god of the Swedes, while Thór is god of the English and Óðinn of the Germans

(*Saxar*).[29] The Icelandic poet, Hallfreð, while still a pagan, promised sacrifice to the gods if the winds drove his ship away from Norway and from Ólaf Tryggvason. The sacrifice would go to Thór or Óðinn if the ship drifted to Iceland, but to Freyr if it reached Sweden.[30]

Many tales are told about idols of Freyr in Sweden. The idol of Fricco, who can be no other than Freyr, took his place beside Wodan and Thór in the temple of Uppsalir.[31] A wooden idol of Freyr was said to have been brought from Sweden to Thrándheim, and a remarkable tale is told of an animated idol of Freyr in Sweden, who wrestled with the fugitive, Gunnar Helming.[32]

Freyr was the chief god of the Swedes, and they called him 'God of the World' (*Veraldar goð*). But not only was Freyr the chief god of the Swedes, he was also the divine ancestor of their kings. While the name *Freyr* means only 'the Lord', the god had another name, *Yngvi*, and the *Ynglingar* the ruling house of the Swedes, were believed to take their name from him. The elements *Ing-* and *Yngv-* in personal names may be associated with *Yngvi*.

Freyr, as the divine king of the Swedes, will be discussed in another chapter,[33] but his relations with Fróði, another divine king, should be mentioned now. While Freyr was king of the Swedes the so-called 'Peace of Fróði' (*Fróða friðr*) began. This was a golden age, when there was welfare throughout the world, and the Swedes ascribed it to Freyr.[34] In the *Skáldskaparmál* (LIII), Snorri gave a detailed and rather different account of the Peace of Fróði. At that time, Fróði, a great-grandson of Óðinn, was King of the Danes. This was in the days when Augustus made peace throughout the world (*pax romana*) and Christ was born. But since Fróði was the most powerful king in the north, the age of peace and plenty was ascribed to him, and therefore the Scandinavians called it the Peace of Fróði. It is said in another passage that, while the Danes ascribed this peace to Fróði, the Swedes ascribed it to Freyr.[35]

Fróði's peace was frequently mentioned by poets. Einar Skálaglamm (died *c.* 995) said in praise of Hákon the Great that no prince had brought such peace except Fróði.[36] The golden age and its end formed the subject of the powerful *Grottasǫngr*. Such was the peace that a man would not even strike his brother's slayer if he found him in chains.

Histories of Denmark include a series of kings called Fróði, but the most remarkable parallel is between Freyr and the king who appears in Saxo's work as Fróði III.

It is said of Freyr, the king of the Swedes, that when he died it was kept secret. He was laid in a cairn, where tribute was paid to him for three years, and plenty and peace were maintained.[37]

Saxo tells that, when Fróði was dead, the nobles kept him embalmed, fearing rebellion and invasion if the news of his death were published. They conveyed him in a chariot (*vehiculo*), as if he were an infirm old man not in full possession of his forces.[38]

In the manner of his death, Saxo's Fróði III shows further affinities with Freyr and the Vanir. He was gored to death by a sea-cow (*maritima bos*), or rather by a sorceress who had taken this shape. This same Fróði, according to Arngrímur Jónsson,[39] was pierced by the antlers of a hart. It is also told that Freyr killed the giant Beli with a hart's horn.[40]

Saxo's Fróði III was conveyed ceremoniously in a chariot, both while he was alive and when he was mummified after death. In the story of Gunnar Helming,[41] the idol of Freyr was similarly conveyed in Sweden, bringing fertility to the crops.

In one passage[42] Freyr is called *inn fróði*, which probably means 'the fruitful', and that is probably the meaning of the name *Fróði*.[43] This implies that neither *Freyr* nor *Fróði* are proper names, but rather a title and a nickname. But, as already observed, Freyr was also called *Yngvi* and *Yngvi-Freyr*, and his full name and title might thus be *Yngvi-Freyr-inn-Fróði*, or 'the Lord Yngvi the Fruitful'.

But, as will be seen in a later chapter,[44] all the descendants of Freyr, the Ynglingar, kings of the Swedes, could be called *Yngvi* (*Ynguni*). This suggests that *Yngvi* was also a title or descriptive term, meaning, perhaps, 'the Ingvæonian', or even 'the man of *Ingwaz*'.[45]

In the *Lokasenna* (str. 43), as in the Greater Saga of St Ólaf,[46] Freyr is called *Ingunar-Freyr*. The precise significance of this name is not certain,[47] but in *Beowulf* (1319) the king of the Danes is called *Frea Ingwina*. The similarity is too close to be fortuitous, and the latter title can only mean 'lord of the friends of Ing.'[48]

Ing, as is well known, is named in the Old English Runic Poem,[49] for his name is that of the rune *NG*. The verse runs:

Ing wæs ærest	Ing was first
mid East-Denum	among the East-Danes
gesewen secgun,	seen by men,
oþ he siððan est	until afterwards eastward
ofer wæg gewat;	over the wave he departed;
wæn æfter ran . . .	his chariot ran after him . . .

These lines may be analysed. Ing originated among the eastern or island Danes. He afterwards departed eastward over the waves and his chariot followed him. In plainer terms this could mean that the cult of Ing was practised first among the Danes of the islands, but later its centre was transferred eastward, and perhaps northward to Svealand.

The chief idol and the ceremonial chariot could both have been moved from Denmark to Mälaren, although this is perhaps too literal an interpretation.

The Old English verse just quoted ends with the sentence:

ðus Heardingas	thus the Heardingas
ðone hæle nemdun	called this hero.

The Heardingas, as will appear in a later chapter (Ch. X, Hadding), probably came of the Vandals, whether this tribe originated in the north Jutish Vendsyssel (O.N. Vendill) or in the Swedish Vendel.

Ing, whose original name was probably *Ingwaz,[50] can only be the eponymous father, the divine ancestor of the Ingvæones.

The Ingvæones, according to Tacitus (*Germania* III), were one of the three great peoples of Germania. They lived next to the ocean, which probably means in north Germany and in the Danish islands. If so, they must include those seven tribes who worshipped• the goddess Nerthus.

The origin of the name *Nerthus is* disputed. It may well be related to Irish *nert* (strength),[51] implying that the goddess embodied the strength and fertility of the earth. If so, it is probably this word which appears in the Old Norse compounds *njarðgjǫrð* (girdle of strength),[52] *njarðláss* (mighty lock).

Nerthus, whatever her sex, was one of the Vanir, and her name corresponds exactly with that of the god Njörð. The worship of Nerthus is described by Tacitus (*Germania* XL) with unusual precision, and the chief features may be summarized. Nerthus is *Terra Mater*, and she was believed to interest herself in the affairs of men. The centre of her worship was an island in the ocean, which may be one of the Danish islands. There was a holy grove (*castum nemus*) on this island, and in it a chariot covered with a cloth, which only one priest was permitted to touch. The priest knew when the goddess was present, and she would be carried in her chariot drawn by cows and accompanied by the priest. When the goddess was present all weapons were laid aside, and these were days of peace and quietude. When Nerthus tired of the company of men, the priest would take her back to her temple. Afterwards the chariot, the cloth, and even the goddess herself would be secretly washed in a lake. The task was allotted to slaves, who were afterwards drowned in the lake. Hence there was a holy terror of this goddess, seen only by those about to die.

A more pregnant passage is hardly to be found in the works of Tacitus. We need mention only a few of the practices which correspond with those ascribed to the cult of the Vanir in Norse and German sources written more than a thousand years later.

King Fróði was carried in a chariot alive and dead, and the chariot of Ing followed him. Freyr, according to the late Icelandic *Gunnars Þáttr*,[53] was similarly carried around the provinces of Sweden.

Freyr, in this Icelandic story, was attended in his chariot by a woman, believed to be his wife. Nerthus was attended by a priest, and it is likely that the fertility goddess with her male companion and the god with his female were thought of as husband and wife, forming divine pairs.

In sources of Icelandic history we read of several women who bore the title *gyðja* (priestess) or *hofgyðja* (temple-priestess). Some of these women were said to have charge of temples and to administer sacrifice.[54] We cannot say that all of them were priestesses of Freyr, but in one case, the conclusion is difficult to avoid. Thuríð, the temple-priestess, whose family belonged to the south-east of the country, was half-sister of Thórð, Freyr's priest (*Freysgoði*), whose descendants were the *Freys-gyðlingar* (Freyr's priestlings).[55]

The days when Nerthus was present on her island were days of peace (*pax et quies*). The days of Freyr, as of Fróði, were days of peace (*friðr*) and prosperity (*ár*).

The nine-yearly festival of Uppsala will be discussed in a later chapter (Ch. XII). Uppsala was for long the centre of Freyr's cult. There was a sacred grove there, as there was on the island of Nerthus. There was also a well (*fons*) at Uppsala, in which sacrificial victims were immersed, just as were the slaves who washed the goddess Nerthus.

We may see Nerthus and her priest, Freyr and his female companion, as divine pairs, even as the sky-god and earth goddess, bringing fertility and peace. We may be satisfied that the cult described by Tacitus was fundamentally the same as that mentioned in the late Norse sources. Whether this cult first developed in Sweden or, as is more probable, in north Germany,[56] it maintained its form for some ten centuries. But a serious difficulty remains.

Nerthus cannot be other than Njörð, but Norse authors tell us that Njörð was a god and not a goddess; he was father of Freyr and Freyja. This problem of the change of sex may never be solved finally, but we might suppose that Nerthus was originally hermaphrodite or that we have to do with a divine pair, brother and sister like Freyr and Freyja. Njörð had his sister to wife; Freyja had cohabited with Freyr, and incest was the practice of the Vanir. In this case, there may have been both a male and a female Nerthus. It has been suggested that the Njörð remembered in some of the place-names of Sweden was not a god but a goddess.[57]

The chariot, as already seen, recurs in the stories of Nerthus, Fróði, Freyr and Ing, and its place in the cult cannot be questioned. A highly ornamental chariot, besides fragments of another, was found at Dejbjerg, near Ringkjøbing in Jutland. This chariot is generally assigned to the early Iron Age,[58] and it is now agreed that it was built for ceremonial rather than practical purposes. There must also be a religious meaning in the image of a disk like the sun, drawn on wheels by a model horse. This find was made at Trundholm in North Zealand, and is assigned to the Bronze Age.[59] It is said in the *Grímnismál* (str. 37) that the sun was drawn across the sky by horses.

Coming later down the centuries, we may remember the splendid chariot found in the Oseberg grave of the ninth century, as well as the four-wheeled chariots drawn by stately steppers depicted on the tapestries of that grave.[60] The chariot, as it seems, symbolizes death, fertility and so rebirth.

While he drove in a chariot, Freyr was also the keenest of riders,[61] and his horse was called *Blóðughófi* (Bloody-hoofed). Because of this name, some have seen Freyr's horse as the one in the Second Merseburg Charm, who suffered a sprain.[62]

Freyr was also owner of Skíðblaðnir, the best of ships, which was made for him by the sons of a dwarf.[63] According to Snorri,[64] this ship was so big that all the Æsir could board her fully armed. She always had a following wind, and was built of so many pieces that she could be folded up and put in a purse. Since the Bronze Age, the ship had had its place in fertility rites,[65] and ships are found time and time again in graves and are depicted on monuments. We have not only to think of the ships of Gokstad and Oseberg, but also of the hundreds of boat-graves found in Norway and Sweden. Several descriptions of burial in a ship are preserved in the historical literature of Iceland.[66] Strangely enough, the ships are sometimes anchored or made immovable.[67] If not precisely intended to take the dead to the Other World, the ship, like the chariot, must be seen as a symbol of death and fertility.

Freyr was called *blótguð svía* or 'sacrificial god of the Swedes,[68] and some details of his place in Swedish ritual may be gleaned from Saxo. Freyr, the 'satrap' of the gods, settled close to Uppsala, where he introduced human sacrifice.[69]. Hading, Saxo told in an earlier passage, had established an annual festival, which the Swedes called *Frøblod* (Freyr's sacrifice), when 'swarthy' (*furvis*) victims were sacrificed to the god.[70]

The cult of Freyr, since he was god of fertility, was accompanied by sexual rites. His idol in the temple of Uppsala, as Adam described it was furnished with a gigantic phallus.[71] A little image or amulet, bearing this characteristic, was found at Rällinge in Södermanland.[72] Saxo[73] also tells of sacrifices conducted under the sons of Freyr, the Ynglingar, in Uppsala. These sacrifices were accompanied by an unmanly clatter of bells and effeminate gestures, by which the hero Starkað was so revolted that he left the country.

Just as his father, Njörð, married the giantess Skaði, so Freyr took his bride from the Giant World. Her name was Gerð, and she was daughter of the giant Gymir.[74] Allusion to this marriage is made in several sources, and it forms the whole subject of the poem *Skírnismál* (The Words of Skírnir). The poem may be summarized:

Freyr (according to the prose introduction) had sat in Óðinn's high seat, Hliðskjálf[75]. He looked over all the worlds and into the World of Giants. There, in the castle of Gymir, he saw a maid so beautiful that he was sick with the love of her. He sent his loyal servant, Skírnir, on the perilous journey to the enemy world to win Gerð on his behalf. Freyr lent his servant the horse, which could understand speech, and his splendid sword, which fought by itself. Skírnir rode to the land of giants over misty hills through a dark, flickering fire (*myrkvan vafrloga*). Reaching the castle of Gymir, he tried to bribe the maid, first with eleven gold apples (*epli ellifu ... algullin*), and then with the magic arm-ring, Draupnir. Gerð would have none of these, and Skírnir turned to threats. He would cut the girl's head from her neck and kill her father as well. When these threats were of no avail, the messenger turned to curses, using mysterious words hardly comprehensible to us. Gerð would wither like a dry thistle; she would be plagued with perversion and unbridled sexual desire. When this last curse was uttered, the maid changed her mind. She agreed to meet Freyr after nine nights in the windless grove, Barri.

Many years ago M. Olsen[76] gave an explanation of this story which, in broad outline, is still widely accepted. Freyr is god of sunshine and fertility; he is *skírr* or 'shining', and his messenger, Skírnir (the Bright) is only another form of the god himself. Freyr, as is told in the *Lokasenna*, had two other servants, Byggvir and the female Beyla. While the name of the first is probably derived from *bygg* (corn, barley), that of Beyla has been related to *baula* (cow).[77]

Gerð (*Gerðr*), whose name is related to *garðr* (field), personifies the cornfield, held fast in the clutches of winter, i.e. of the frost-giants, among whom is counted *Hrímgrímnir* (Frost-masked). The god and his bride are to meet in the grove Barri. This name, it is said, derives from *barr* (barley).[78]

Such an explanation of the *Skírnismál* implies that Gerð differs little from Nerthus, Terra Mater.

It may also be implied that the *Skírnismál* reflects a ritual act or drama, representing a marriage between the god of sunshine and fertility and his earthly bride.[79]

But the *Skírnismál* is designed as a poem and a love-story. It certainly contains phrases of great antiquity, probably inherited from ritual, while including elements which cannot be of great age.

Influence of Old English has been seen in a number of words used in the poem, including *(hrím)kalkr* (crystal cup) believed to derive from English *calic*.[80] More surprisingly, the influence of Old English poetic diction is said to be present in *vafrlogi* (flickering flame), which has been compared with the Old English *wæfran liges*, and with a number of similar expressions used in Old English poetry.[81]

The eleven golden apples offered by Skírnir to the maid are somewhat surprising in this context. They should probably be identified with the apples kept by Iðunn, which the gods ate to prevent old age creeping on. In this case, the *epli ellifu* (eleven apples) of the *Skírnismál* (19–20) might be emended to *epli ellilyfs* (apples of old-age medicine).[82]

If the story of Iðunn's apples is ultimately of classical origin, it has closest affinities with Celtic stories, and particularly with the story of the children of Tuirenn.[83] Celtic influences have also been suspected in the enchanted fire, which none but the magic horse can penetrate.[84]

Freyr appears chiefly as a god of fertility. For some peoples, for whom welfare depended on the fertility of the crops, he was most important of all gods; he was 'god of the World'.

Sowing, reaping and harvesting depended greatly on peace, and Freyr was god of peace. But, if he was the most worshipped, he must also have been a warrior and defender, and the sources make it plain that he was. He is 'protector of the gods' (*ása jaðarr*).[85] In the *Húsdrápa*,[86] he is said to rule the armies and, in the *Skírnismál* (str. 3) he is *folkvaldi goða* (ruler of the hosts of the gods). Another name for Freyr is *Atriði*,[87] probably implying 'one who rides to battle'. The kenning *Freys leikr*, used by Thorbjörn Hornklofi, has been interpreted as 'Freyr's sacrifice', but it more probably means 'the sport of Freyr, battle'.[88]

Freyja

Freyr was the chief god of the Vanir and of fertility in the late pagan period, and his female counterpart was his sister, Freyja, the *Vanadís* (goddess of the Vanir), *Vanabrúðr* (bride of the Vanir). Both Freyja and her brother were said to be children of Njörð and his sister-wife (see Njörð above). It is not told plainly how Freyja came to the world of the Æsir (see War of the Æsir, above), but it is told that she taught them witchcraft (*seiðr*), and frequently that she was greedy and lascivious. She should be invoked in love, and she delighted in love-poetry (*mansǫngr*), such as was severely prohibited under the common law of Iceland[1].

Freyja had much in common with her brother. Pigs were sacred to her no less than to Freyr. One of her nicknames, *Sýr*, can hardly mean other than 'sow', in spite of arguments to the contrary,[2] and she probably took the form of a sow. In the *Hyndluljóð* (strs. 5–7), a poem comprising ancient beside late or 'learned' elements,[3] Freyja is seen riding a boar to Valhöll. This boar was called *Hildisvíni* (battle-boar); he had been made for Freyja by two dwarfs, and his golden bristles glowed like those of Freyr's boar. A later passage in the same poem (str. 45)[4] probably implies that Freyja's lover had the form of a boar, although the lines are hard to interpret.

The goddess was also related to other animals. She ran after her lover at night, as the mythical goat, Heiðrún, ran after billy-goats.[5] An early Christian poetaster described Freyja as a bitch (*grey*).[6] This man was convicted of blasphemy, but he may not have spoken loosely. As goddess of fertility and sensuality, Freyja was naturally associated, even identified with prolific and sensual beasts.

This is probably the meaning of a strange story told by Snorri.[7] Freyja did not only ride on a boar, but also, like other Vanir, in a chariot. Freyja's chariot was drawn by cats, and for this reason she might be called 'owners of cats' (*eigandi fressa*). The motive has been compared with stories of oriental goddesses, and especially with that of Cybele, whose chariot was drawn by lions or panthers,[8] but it is not necessary to assume foreign origin. The cat, as the Norse pagans must have known, is the most lascivious of beasts.

Freyja was the wife of Óð (*Óðr*), as appears both in the *Voluspá* (str. 25) and in the *Hyndluljóð* (str. 47) and again in the works of Snorri.[9] Óð, to judge by his name, can be no other than a doublet of Óðinn,[10] just as Ullinn must be a doublet of Ull.[11] The only story told of Óð bears this out. As Óðinn went away on more than one occasion, so Óð went away, travelling long distances. Freyja went in search of him and, meanwhile, she wept tears of gold. For this reason poets would call gold 'Freyja's tears'.[12]

This last story shows that Freyja was a divinity, not only of fertility but, like her father, of riches as well.

Freyja owned the famous Brísing necklace, or belt (*Brísinga men*),[13] and a late story tells how she sold her chastity to some dwarfs in exchange for a precious necklace which is probably to be identified with this one.[14] Freyja was said to have two daughters, both of whose names mean 'jewel' (*Hnoss* and *Gersemi*). The kenning *Sýrar mær* (daughter of Sýr) is used by Hallfreð to mean 'treasure'.[15]

Some stories of Freyja's erotic life have already been given. It is told several times how giants lusted after her. The giant Hrungnir, who was entertained by the gods, threatened to destroy Ásgarð and all its inhabitants except Freyja and Sif, whom he would keep for himself.[16] It is told in the *Þrymskviða*, how the giant Thrym promised to return Thór's stolen hammer if he could have Freyja as his bride. Snorri also told, in his elaborate story of building the wall of the gods' citadel, how the giant mason stipulated that his wages should include Freyja. From the passage of the *Vǫluspá* (str. 25), upon which Snorri's story is chiefly founded, it seems that Freyja was already in the hands of giants.

As Snorri tells the story of the wall, the giant mason demanded not only Freyja, but also the sun and the moon. This may help to show the meaning of the strange myth. The giants would plunge the world into eternal cold and darkness and take away the chief goddess of fertility. In other words, this myth has something in common with that of Freyr and Gerð; it symbolizes the change of seasons. The frost-giants (*hrím-þursar*) threaten eternal winter, sterility and darkness, such as northern peoples have reason to fear.

Freyja, whom the giants wished to possess, bears a certain resemblance to Gerð, who was brought from the giant world. In the previous section, the story of Gerð was seen as a seasonal fertility myth, and Gerð was nearly identified with Nerthus and Terra Mater. But Gerð, whose home could be reached only through a magic fire by a rider mounted on a magic horse, had some of the qualities of a shield maid[17] and hence of a valkyrie. Her mother was called *Aurboða*, which some read as *Qrboða* (arrow-bidder),[18] a fitting name for a valkyrie, and hence for a demon of war and death.

Freyja had such qualities. She was not only a fertility goddess, but also one of war and death. It is told in the *Grímnismál* (str. 14) that she lives in *Folkvangr*, interpreted as 'battlefield'. Every day she chooses half of those who fall in battle, while Óðinn takes the other half. Snorri[19] tells how she rides to battle.

The last story relates Freyja with Óðinn. Their relationship is apparent in other myths. Óðinn was god of wizardry (*seiðr*), but it was Freyja who introduced these disreputable practices to the Æsir.[20] It is not surprising to read in a late source that Freyja was once the mistress of Óðinn.[21] As already suggested, Freyja's legitimate husband, Óð, can hardly be distinguished from Óðinn.

Freyja is thus goddess of fertility, birth and death, the ever-recurring cycle.

The name *Freyja* corresponds with *Freyr*, and means only 'Lady'. In other words it is a title and not a name. Freyja had many other names and Snorri[22] says that the reason for this is that she assumed different names on her journeys among various peoples, while she was looking for Óð . There is much truth in this, for it implies that Freyja had come to be identified with local fertility goddesses whom she resembled too closely to be clearly distinguished.

Freyja is called *Hǫrn* (Hörn). This name is frequently used by scalds in kennings for 'woman', and it is commonly related to the O.N. *hǫrr* and Swedish dialect *hör*,[23] meaning 'flax, linen'. This implies that Hörn was a goddess of flax and her cult appears, on the evidence of place-names, to be old and locally restricted. Forms such as *Härnevi*, probably corresponding to an O.N. **Hǫrnarvé* (Temple of Hörn) are recorded several times in Swedish Uppland, while *Järnevi*, said to be of the same origin, is found in Östergötland.[24] Some have seen the name of Hörn in Danish place-names, but the examples given are questionable.[25]

Freyja is also called *Mardǫll* (or *Marpǫll*), especially in kennings for gold of the type *Mardallar tár* (Mardöll's tears), *Mardallar hvarma fagrregn* (the fair rain of Mardöll's eyelids).[26] The first element in this name is probably *marr* (sea), and the second may be related to *Dellingr* and thus indicate light.[27]

Another name for Freyja is *Gefn*, which appears frequently in kennings for 'woman', such as *linnvengis Gefn* (Gefn of the serpent's field, gold).[28] It is commonly related to the verb *gefa* (to give), and thus implies that the goddess is the giver of riches, fertility, wellbeing.[29] This must also be the meaning of *Gefjun* (see VIII, Gefjun), but Gefjun appears in myth as a separate goddess, not identified with Freyja.[30]

Little is told of the worship of Freyja. In the *Hyndluljóð* (str. 10) the goddess is made to boast of her favourite, Óttar, who had set up an altar (*hǫrgr*) for her and reddened it with sacrificial blood. But the place-names of Scandinavia show that the cult of Freyja was widespread and comparatively old. In place-names it is often difficult to distinguish Freyja from her brother Freyr, but a general picture of the types and distribution of the names in which Freyja is remembered may be obtained.

M. Olsen[31] counts between twenty and thirty place-names compounded with Freyja in Norway alone. Three of these appear to go back to a **Freyjuhof* (Freyja's temple). In others the goddess's name is compounded with words for 'meadow' (*-þveit, -land*) and suchlike. These names are particularly common on the west coast, and a considerable number are also found in the south-east.

In Sweden, the place-names compounded with Freyja are even more numerous and varied. They are distributed over a wide area, although they are particularly common in Uppland. A number of them are of the types **Freyjuvé* (Freyja's sanctuary, temple) and **Freyjulundr* (Freyja's grove),[32] preserving memories of public worship. Specialists also see a word corresponding with Gothic *alhs*, Old English *ealh* (temple) in such names as *Frøal*, *Fröale*,[33] of which a number of examples are recorded in Sweden, although these are open to other interpretations. The name of Freyja is also found in many instances compounded with words for fields, meadows, besides rocks, lakes and other natural objects.[34]

CHAPTER EIGHT

LESSER-KNOWN DEITIES

Týr—Ull—Bragi—Iðunn—Gefjun—Frigg and others

WHEN WE talk of minor gods and goddesses, we mean those about whose cult and myths in the north we have little knowledge. It is not necessarily implied that they had always been of little importance but, in some instances, their cult was so old as to be obscured by the time our records took shape.

Týr

One of these faded gods was Týr, who was undoubtedly of great significance, if not in Scandinavia, at least in Germany and perhaps in England.

Týr plainly had much to do with runes and with runic magic. The rune *t* (↑) is called by his name both in the Norwegian and Icelandic runic poems, and the name *tir* given to it in the Old English Runic Poem, varying with *ti* in the Salzburg manuscript, must be of the same origin.[1]

In the *Sigrdrífumál* (Words of Sigrdrífa, str. 16), it is said that one who hopes for victory must carve runes on the hilt and other parts of his sword, and he must repeat the name of Týr three times.

Both the Norwegian and Icelandic runic poets said that Týr was one-handed and *hinn einhendi áss* (the one-handed god) was said to be a proper designation of him.[2] Several poets allude to the loss of Týr's right hand,[3] but the story how he lost it is told by Snorri alone.[4]

Among the children of Loki and the giantess, Angrboða,[5] was the wolf, Fenrir. He was reared by the Æsir, but only Týr had the courage to feed him. Knowing what damage was to be expected of this wolf, the gods resolved to chain him. He broke two chains, but the third was a magic one, worked by dwarfs. It was made of the noise of a cat, the beard of a woman, breath of fish and spittle of bird. It was smooth and soft as a silken thread, but the wolf would only allow himself to be bound with it so long as one of the gods placed his hand between his jaws as a pledge. Only Týr dared do this; he lost his hand, but the wolf was bound and will not break loose before the Ragnarök, when he will be the death of Óðinn.

This story reminds us immediately of that of Nuadu of the silver hand (see Ch. VII). Indeed Týr, with his one hand seems to be juxtaposed to Óðinn with his one eye, as Nuadu with his one hand stood beside Lug with his magic and his closed eye. Some have seen the story of Týr in a far wider perspective. They have regarded Týr, not only as a war-god, as he is often said to be, but also as a god of contract and justice. The cruel, magical Óðinn is thus contrasted with Týr, as Varuna, god of night, is contrasted with Mitra, god of day.[6]

Snorri[7] characterizes Týr in general terms. He is no peacemaker, and, to a great extent, he disposes of victory. He is bravest of gods, and bold men should invoke him. In the Ragnarök, Týr will meet the wolf Garm, and they will kill each other. Týr is said by Snorri to be son of Óðinn but, according to the *Hymiskviða* (str. 5), he was son of the giant, Hymir.

The place-names of Scandinavia tell something of Týr's cult, and suggest that it was practised chiefly in Denmark. A number of forms representing O.N. *Týslundr* (Týr's Grove) have been recorded, besides others applied to lakes sacred to the god.[8] Names of this type in Sweden are few, if any, while Norway provides the exceptionally interesting *Tysnesøen* (island of Týr's headland) in Sunnhordland. This lies in a district formerly called *Njarðarlǫg* or 'law-district of Njörð'.[9]

Týr, as is well known, was given the Latin name *Mars*, and hence most Germanic peoples rendered *Dies Martis* by *Tuesday* (O.N. *Týsdagr*) and suchlike. It is clear that the Romans saw him chiefly as a war-god.

This is borne out by other allusions in the works of classical authors to the Germanic Mars. The Goths sacrificed prisoners to him, believing that the war-god was best propitiated with human blood.[10] The Hermundurii also offered human sacrifice to him,[11] while others regarded him as the highest of the gods.[12]

The name *Mars* appears on a number of votive stones from Germanic areas. An especially interesting one was found at Housesteads, by Hadrian's Wall. It dates from the third century, and was evidently erected for Germanic soldiers in Roman service. It was dedicated to *Mars Thingsus (Deo Marti Tingso . . .)*. If, as is widely believed, *Mars Thingsus* is Týr, god of the *þing*, or judicial assembly, the argument that Týr was god of justice, as well as of war, gains much support.[13]

As the name of the rune (*Tir, Ti*) shows, the heathen English knew the god Týr. Old English writers occasionally glossed the Latin *Mars* by

Tiw (*Tig*).[14] The name of this god has also been seen in some of the place-names of southern England.[15]

The name *Týr* is generally said to derive from an older **Tiwaz*. It has been equated with Latin *deus*, Old Irish *día*, Sanscrit *deva-*, which is also seen in the O.N. plural *tívar* (gods). In this case *Týr* means no other than 'god'. Some, however, relate it more closely with names of gods deriving from the same root, Greek *Zeus*, Sanscrit *Dyaus*.[16] In this case, *Týr* is stamped as an exceedingly ancient god of the sky and the day. In either case he must once have occupied a high position in the hierarchy, although he is not clearly described in our records.

Ull

We know hardly more of the god Ull than of Týr. Saxo gives one story of him, and Snorri[1] tells that he was son of Thór's wife, Sif, and thus stepson of Thór. He was of splendid appearance, had the qualities of a warrior and should be invoked in single combat. He was so skilled on skis that none could compete with him, and besides this he was an archer. He could be called the ski-god (*ǫnduráss*), the bow-god (*bogáss*), the hunting-god (*veiðiáss*), as well as the shield-god (*skjaldar áss*).

In the *Grímnismál* (str. 5) it is told that Ull's home was in *Ýdalir* (Yew dales). In the same poem (str. 42) Óðinn placed between fires, promised the favours of Ull and of all the gods to the one who first relieved him.

A more striking allusion to Ull is made in the *Atlakviða* (str. 30). Guðrún, cursing her perjurious husband, Atli, reminded him how he had sworn oaths to her brother, whom he had now betrayed. The last of these oaths, and presumably the most solemn, was on the 'ring of Ull' (*at hringi Ullar*).

The name of Ull is used often enough in scaldic kennings, but they add little. A warrior may be called 'Ull of battle' or 'Ull of the battle-goddess', and a poet 'Ull of poetry'.[2] Thór is called 'Ull's stepfather' by one of the oldest scalds.[3] Kennings of the type 'Ull's ship' for 'shield' are more puzzling, and must represent a myth no longer clearly remembered.[4] They may remind us of the story of the giant Hrungnir, who stood on his shield.[5]

Little as Snorri and the poets have told, they show that Ull was not isolated in the Norse pantheon. He was not only son of Sif, but he also bore a remarkable resemblance to Skaði, the giantess wife of Njörð.[6] Both travelled on skis, hunted and wielded the bow. Ull must, therefore, be related to Njörð himself, although the two gods can hardly be identified.[7]

Ull, as was said, lives in Ýdalir (Yew-dales). There can be little doubt that the ever-green yew was held sacred, whether or not the

Yggdrasill and holiest tree at Uppsalir were yews.[8] The best bows were made of yew,[9] and it is not surprising that the archer-god should live where yews flourished.

Students of Scandinavian place-names have thrown remarkable light on Ull and his cult. Names of which *Ull-* forms the first element are found in great numbers in central and eastern Sweden, as well as in south-eastern and southern Norway, with several examples on the west coast. In Denmark, on the other hand, no certain examples of this element have been detected.[10]

The types of place-name vary, but in Sweden the god's name is most frequently combined with words often applied to sanctuaries and places of public worship, e.g. *vé, horgr, lundr, akr.* In Norway, on the other hand, the name *Ull-* is compounded rather with words applied to meadows, pastures, e.g. *engi, land, vin, þveit,* also with words applied to purely natural objects, e.g. *ey, hváll, nes, vík.*

But the Norwegian place-names show that there was also a god called *Ullinn*, whose name stands in the same relation to Ull (*Ullr*) as Óðinn to Óðr,[11] and they can be little more than variants. In Norway the name *Ullinn-* is three times combined with *-hof* (temple), as well as with *vangr* and *akr.*[12]

The distribution of place-names compounded with *Ull-, *Ullinn-* shows that the cult was once very widespread and of great importance, particularly in eastern Sweden. The findings of recent research also suggest that the cult of Ull was old, and was overshadowed by those of other gods, particularly Thór, Freyr, Freyja, before the time reflected in literary records.[13]

There are certain reasons, if not strong ones, to doubt whether the cult of Ull was really extinguished so early as is commonly supposed. If the word *hof* (temple) is not a loan-word, it is unlikely that it was applied to temples long before the Viking Age.[14] This suggests that the Ull(inn) commemorated in the Norwegian *Ullinshof* was still worshipped at that time. The late Ólafur Lárusson[15] remarked on a great number of Icelandic place-names in which the first element was *Ullar-.* This could well be the genitive of the word *ull* (wool), but when we find *Ullarfoss* standing next to *Goðafoss* (fall of gods), and *Ullarklettur* next to *Goðaklettur* (gods' cliff), we may wonder whether the name of the god Ull is not the first element in the compound.

It was noted that Óðinn, promising the blessings of all gods to the one who rescued him from the fires, named Ull alone. This, in itself, is a sign that Ull filled an important place. The impression is confirmed by the *Atlakviða,* in which the most solemn oath is sworn on the ring of Ull. This can be no other than the *baugeiðr,* the oath on the sacred arm-ring, which Icelandic heathens swore in the names of Freyr, Njörð and the all-powerful god.[16] It is implied that for some peoples and at some times Ull was, if not chief of the gods, at least god of security and law.

Ull's eminence is also suggested in the only surviving myth about him, which is told by Saxo.[17] Óðinn chief of the gods, had disgraced the name of godhead by disguising himself as a woman in order to beget an avenger for Baldr.[18] Therefore he was expelled and replaced by Ollerus (Ull), who reigned for ten years and even assumed Óðinn's name. In the end the gods took pity on Óðinn and restored him. Ollerus fled to Sweden, but was afterwards killed by Danes. It was also told of Ollerus that he was a magician, and used to cross the sea on a bone inscribed with spells. In this some have seen a basis for the shield-kenning 'ship of Ull'.[19]

The story of Ull's usurpation of Óðinn's throne places him on a par with certain other mythical figures. On an earlier occasion, Saxo[20] tells, Óðinn left his kingdom in disgust at the unchastity of his wife, Frigg. His place was taken by another magician, Mithotyn, who also fled when Óðinn returned, and was afterwards killed. The name *Mithotyn* defies interpretation,[21] but it is difficult to believe that its second element is other than the name of Óðinn himself. The tales both of Mithotyn and Ollerus imply that these impostors competed with Óðinn for sovereignty. A similar meaning may be found in a story told by Snorri.[22] When Óðinn was away, his brothers Vili and Vé[23] ruled the kingdom and shared Frigg.

The meaning of Ull's name has long been disputed.[24] Of all the interpretations offered, one of the oldest has won most approval. The name is equated with Gothic *wulþus* (glory, perhaps brilliance), and Old English *wuldor* (glory, splendour, honour). This name may perhaps be seen in older form in the inscription found on a chape from Thorsbjærg (Slesvig), of about AD 300. This reads (o)wlþuþewaR . . ., and some have interpreted it as 'servant of Ull'.[25]

If the name of Ull means 'glory or brilliance', it is not difficult to believe that he was a sky-god. On his snow-shoes, as de Vries suggests,[26] Ull may represent the brilliance of the winter sky.

It has been suggested that Týr was also a sky-god. With his one arm, he corresponds with the one-eyed Óðinn. While the cult of Týr seems to be little known north of Denmark, that of Ull seems hardly to be known in Denmark or south of it. It looks as if Ull in the north was what Týr was in the south.

We could believe that Ull and Týr had been, for many peoples, the chief gods, even the sky-gods. In the course of the Viking Age, they were overshadowed by the furious, rabid Óðinn.

Bragi

Óðinn was described as god of poetry, as well as of runes and secret wisdom.[1] Nevertheless, he had one competitor, Bragi. In the *Grímnismál* (str. 44), Bragi is named as the foremost of poets (*œztr . . . skálda*), and the *Sigrdrífumál* (str. 16) tells cryptically of runes or spells carved on Bragi's tongue. He takes part in bickering with Loki, as described in the *Lokasenna* (strs. 8 ff), and is said to be husband of Iðunn, who guarded the apples of eternal youth.[2]

Snorri tells little more about Bragi, and there is no evidence of any cult. But the position of this god is complicated.

The first man to whom credible tradition assigns poetry in scaldic form was Bragi Boddason the Old. This man, author of the *Ragnarsdrápa*, was probably a native of south-western Norway and, to judge by the genealogies in which he figures, was born about 830–40.[3]

In the *Eiríks Mál* (Lay of Eirík Bloodaxe),[4] composed about the middle of the tenth century, Óðinn calls his henchmen to welcome the dead monarch in Valhöll. These henchmen are the famous Völsung heroes, Sigmund and Sinfjötli, besides Bragi. This motive is repeated by Eyvind in the *Hákonar Mál* (Lay of Hákon),[5] in which Bragi is named among the welcomers of Hákon the Good together with Hermóð. Hermóð is generally said to be the son of Óðinn,[6] although the name is also applied to a legendary hero in the *Hyndluljóð* (str. 2), and a *Heremod* is named in *Beowulf* as a king of the Danes.

We must wonder whether the Bragi named in the Lays of Eirík and of Hákon is the god of poetry or the historical poet who, with other heroes, had joined Óðinn's chosen band. We may even wonder whether we should not identify the two. This would imply that the historical poet, like other great men, had been raised to the status of godhead after death.[7] The suspicion grows deeper when it is realized that the name Bragi was applied to certain other legendary and historical figures, and that gods' names are rarely applied to men.

Even this explanation leaves a difficulty. The word *bragr*[8] is occasionally used for 'poetry', and Snorri[9] says that it derives from the name of the god. This same word is used in later Icelandic for 'manner, way, form, etc',[10] and the semantic development may be comparable with that of *háttr*, which also means 'manner, way, form', but in a more specialized sense is used for 'poetic form'.

There is also another *bragr* which, as it is used, means 'chief or best'.[11] Whatever its ultimate origin,[12] this word must be related to the Old English *brego*, which is used in the same way.

Such evidence as we possess does not suggest that Bragi was an ancient god, but rather that he was an historical poet, whom mythological speculators had promoted to the rank of godhead.

Iðunn

I have several times touched on the story of Iðunn.[1] Only one myth is told of her. As Snorri has it,[2] she kept magic apples in a basket. When the gods began to grow old they would bite them and would be young again. Through the guile of Loki, Iðunn and her apples fell into the hands of giants, and the gods became old and hoary. They met in council and compelled Loki to recover Iðunn and the apples. Taking the form of a falcon, he flew into the Giant World, where he found the goddess. He changed her into the shape of a nut and flew off, while the giant pursued him in the form of an eagle.

Iðunn is said to be the wife of Bragi. As was noted above, some have doubted whether Bragi was really a god, partly because his name is also used as a personal name. Iðunn's name is also found several times in historical sources as a personal name,[3] and there is no strong evidence from place-names or other sources that she was the object of a cult.[4]

Nevertheless, the myth of Iðunn and her rape is not altogether a late invention. It is described by Thjóðólf of Hvin in the *Haustlǫng* of about AD 900.[5] If only because of their obscurity, Thjóðólf's lines show that Iðunn was well known in his day. Thjóðólf mentions no apples, but he alludes to Iðunn as the one who knew the old-age medicine of the gods (*þá er ellilyf ása . . . kunni*).

The story of the apples has been said to be of foreign origin. Cultivated apples were not known in Scandinavia until the late Middle Ages.[6] But the Norse word *epli*, which appears in various forms in all Germanic languages, does not only mean 'apple'. It is applied to other round fruits, and even to acorns.[7]

The story of Iðunn's apples has been compared with well-known Jewish and classical ones, but it most closely resembles the Irish tale of the sons of Tuirenn.[8] The three sons robbed apples from the garden of Hisberna. These apples had medicinal properties. If they were eaten by a wounded man, or one in mortal illness, he would be healed at once. However much the apples were eaten, they would never grow smaller. The resemblance between the Norse and Irish stories is particularly in the way in which the apples were seized. The sons of Tuirenn took the form of hawks and were pursued by three female guardians of the apples in the form of griffins.

It is not necessary to assume influence of one of these stories upon the other, although they must derive from a common stock. In this instance, as in many others, the myths of the two most westerly peoples resemble each other most closely. The seizure of the precious food by one in the form of a hawk or falcon, and his pursuit by its guardian in the form of an eagle remind us also of Óðinn and the theft of the mead of poetry.[9] We may think, more remotely, of Indra, who stole the soma in the form of an eagle.

The apple and other round fruits may be seen as symbols of fertility and death. This is brought out strongly in another Irish story, that of Conle (Connla),[10] who received a magic apple from the woman of the Other World, with whom he afterwards went to live. Whether or not the wild apples of Scandinavia had practical value, they probably had a similar significance. This is suggested by the large numbers of wild apples found in buckets and other containers in the Oseberg grave, in one case together with grain.[11]

The rape of Iðunn and her apples resembles several other Norse stories. Gerð was in the hands of giants, and was taken from them by Freyr's emissary, Skírnir, the bright one.[12] The giants often lusted after Freyja and, as well as her, they demanded the sun and the moon. These demons of death would plunge the world into sterility and darkness. Iðunn, in this case, can be little different from Gerð and Freyja. Like Freyja, she was called the most erotic of goddesses, and was said to have consorted with her brother's slayer.[13] It may be implied in an obscure strophe of the *Skírnismál* (str. 16) that Gerð did the same. In another strophe of the same poem (str. 19) it may even be implied that Gerð was to possess the sacred apples.[14]

Gefjun

Snorri twice tells a story of Gefjun, whose name may be compared with Freyja's nickname *Gefn*.[1]

As Snorri has it in his *Edda*,[2] Gylfi, mythical king of the Swedes, rewarded a vagrant woman, Gefjun, with a piece of land of the size which four oxen could plough up in a single day. Gefjun came of the race of the Æsir. She brought four oxen from the Giant World, but they were really her own sons by a giant. The plough cut wide and deep and the land was torn up from the Swedish *Lǫgrinn* (Mälaren), and dragged to the Danish Zealand, where it came to rest. That is why headlands in Zealand correspond with inlets in *Lǫgrinn* like a jigsaw.

In the *Ynglinga Saga* (V), Snorri tells the story differently. Óðinn, migrating from the east, came to Fyn in Denmark. He sent Gefjun north to look for land. Gylfi granted her a measure, and she went on to the Giant World, where she begat four sons by a giant. She turned them into oxen and yoked them to the plough, and so dragged the land to Zealand.

In both passages, Snorri quotes a verse by Bragi, the ninth-century scald. This is agreed to belong to the *Ragnarsdrápa*, and the poet describes one of the panels on the painted shield which Ragnar Loðbrók had given him.

Commentators do not agree about the interpretation of some details in these lines,[3] but the general picture is tolerably clear. Gefjun was seen dragging the addition to Denmark (*Danmarkar auka*) away from Gylfi, while the draught-beasts steamed with sweat. The oxen in the picture had four heads and eight moonlike eyes (*ennitungl*).

It is evident that Gefjun, like Freyja or Gefn, is a goddess of fertility and especially of the plough. This implies that we have to do with a myth based upon ritual ploughing, such as that described in the Old English charm addressed to *Erce, eorþan modor* (Erce, mother of earth). When the first furrow was cut, the mother of earth should be greeted, and milk, flour of every kind and holy water should be laid in it.[4]

Little more is told of Gefjun. In the *Lokasenna* (str. 20) she is accused of selling her chastity for a jewel (*sigli*), as Freyja was once said to do.[5] More surprisingly, Snorri[6] says that Gefjun was a virgin, and that virgins went to her when they died.

It cannot be told how far Gefjun was the object of a cult. The story about her must be of Danish origin, and some scholars claim to see her name in place-names of Denmark, such as *Gevnø* and *Gentofte*.[7] Fundamentally, Gefjun can differ little from Gefn and Freyja, although she appears to be a particularly Danish variation.

Frigg and some others

The goddess Frigg has been mentioned several times because of her relations with other gods. She was mother of Baldr,[1] and it was seen that very early continental sources knew her as wife of Óðinn.[2] In the Second Merseburg Charm, in which she appeared as Frija, she accompanied Óðinn (Wodan) and other deities.[3] Among these was Volla, called sister of Frija. Volla can hardly be other than Fulla, whom Snorri[4] presents as Frigg's confidential attendant.

These bare allusions to Frigg in the continental sources show that, since early times, Frigg had a place in the divine hierarchy comparable with that which she has in the Norse literature. Her age and eminence are shown in the name of the weekday, Friday (O.E. *Frigedæg*, O. Fris. *Fri(g)endei*) for *dies Veneris*, which was borrowed in Old Norse as *Frjádagr*.[5]

Several allusions are made to Frigg's loose morals. Loki[6] upbraids her for consorting with Óðinn's brothers, Vili and Vé,[7] while Saxo[8] speaks of her unchastity and rapacity.

Some of the myths, however, show Frigg in another light. She is the tragic, weeping, loving mother of Baldr. It was she who took oaths from all things to spare her son, and sent Hermóð to the Underworld to ransom him. Like her husband, Frigg knew the fates, and, on occasion, even outwitted him.[9] She lived in a palace called *Fensalir*, which perhaps means 'Water-halls' or 'Marsh-halls'.[10]

In the *Lokasenna* (str. 26) Frigg is called *Fjǫrgyns mær*, and Snorri[11] says that she was daughter of Fjörgynn.[12] Nothing more is known about Fjörgynn, and so scholars must be content to speculate on the origin of his name.[13]

Considering Frigg's antiquity and exalted position, it is surprising how little evidence there is of her worship. Some have claimed to find her name in place-names, for the most part in Sweden. Most of these are of doubtful origin, although two, which probably go back to *Frigg-jarakr* (Frigg's Cornfield) have been noticed in Västergötland.[14]

Although there is little evidence of the worship of Frigg, and few myths are told of her, she must have been well known to the viking invaders of England. When Old English writers glossed the name of Venus they did not use the English *Frige*, but rather an anglicized form of the Norse name, *Fricg (Frycg)*. One metrical homilist wrote:

ðone syxtan dæg hi gesetton	The sixth day they appointed
ðære sceamleasan gydenan	to the shameless goddess
Uenus gehaten	called Venus
ond Frycg on Denisc	and Fricg in Danish.[15]

Together with Frigg and Freyja, Snorri[16] names many other goddesses. These include Sága, Eir the doctor, Sjöfn a love goddess, Lofn, Vár who heard oaths passing between men and women, and Gná, Frigg's messenger, whose horse, Hófvarpnir (Hoof-thrower), gallops through the sky. The names of most of these goddesses are used as basic words in scaldic kennings,[17] but myths of them are hardly to be found. Some of them might be regarded as local variations of the better-known goddesses.

Jörð (Earth), the mother of Thór has been mentioned.[18] She was also called *Fjörgyn*, which must be a feminine form of the name *Fjǫrgynn*. In fact, poets use *fjǫrgyn* as a word for 'earth', and this may well have been its original meaning.

CHAPTER NINE

THE DIVINE KINGS

THE BELIEF in the divinity of kings is world-wide, and is among the oldest religious conceptions which can be traced. Kings are commonly thought to form a bridge between the worlds of gods and of men. Among some peoples they are thought to descend from the sky and return to it at the end of their reign.[1]

Scandinavians, like their relatives in Germany and England, as well as their Celtic neighbours, believed that their kings were divine, assuring victory, good weather and harvests. But when we come to consider Norse conceptions of divine kingship more closely, we face difficulties and much obscurity. In what sense were the northern kings divine? The king might be regarded as the incarnation of a god; he might be the god on earth. He might alternatively be the son of the god, or his physical descendant, or he might, in some less clearly defined way, be endowed with divine force, as if he were the emanation of the god. Probably all of these conceptions were current among Norsemen at various times and in different regions.

Since it is one of our oldest records, it is pertinent to consider the story told by the Gothic historian, Jordanes (c. 550)[2] about the origins of the Goths. The Goths, according to this historian, came from Scandinavia, most probably Gautland, or southern Sweden. They may have left Scandinavia before the beginning of our era, and they made their way to the region of the Black Sea. Jordanes tells that, after a memorable victory over the Romans in the reign of Domitian (AD 81–96), the Goths could no longer regard their princes (*proceres*), by whose fortune (*fortuna*) the battle had been won, as ordinary men (*puros homines*), but they saw them as demigods (*semideos*) or *Ansis*.

Philologists commonly agree that the name *Ansis* is equivalent to Old Norse *Æsir*, the name of the divine tribe to which Óðinn, Thór and Týr belonged.[3] These *Ansis* were the ancestors of the Amalani, the clan who ruled the Ostro-Goths down to the time of Theodoric (died 526). The first of them was called *Gapt* in texts of Jordanes's work. *Gapt*, as most would agree, is a scribal corruption of *Gaut-*. This name occurs in Old Norse texts as *Gautr*, and it is one of the many names applied to Óðinn (see Ch. II, Óðinn's Names). While it would be rash to conclude that Gaut and Óðinn were originally identical, Jordanes's story shows that the Ostro-Goths in south-eastern Europe held that their princes were of divine origin, and themselves semi-divine.

When we return to northern Europe, we find evidence of beliefs which are nearly the same. Tacitus provides some of this evidence, and it is supplemented by that of scaldic poets, Icelandic historians and the Dane, Saxo, writing about eleven centuries later than Tacitus. Tacitus (*Germania* II) relates that, in ancient songs, the Germans celebrated their descent from a god Tuisto and his son Mannus, to whom they assigned three sons. From these three, the three great tribes of Germany descended, viz. Ingævones (Ingvæones), Herminiones, Istævones (Istræones). These tribes, as has frequently been suggested, must descend from three divine brothers, whose names might be *Ingvaz, *Erminaz, *Istraz.

It was seen (Ch. VII) that this Ingvaz, who chiefly concerns us here, could be identified with Freyr, or Yngvi-Freyr, who was remembered as a divine king of the Swedes. Indeed, Freyr bore the marks typical of divine kingship. His reign was one of fruitful harvests and peace. He died like other kings, but his subjects continued to revere him after death. They brought offerings of gold, silver and copper to his tomb, and peace and plenty persisted. All kings of the Swedes took the title Yngvi, and their clan, the Ynglingar, were thought to descend from Freyr.

According to the Prologue to Snorri's *Edda*,[4] other ruling houses of Scandinavia were also of divine origin. Óðinn, on his way from Asia Minor, came to Reiðgotaland or Jutland, where he left his son Skjöld as ruler; from him the kings of Denmark, the Skjöldungar, are descended. Óðinn went later to Norway, where he placed his son Sæming in charge. Certain rulers of Norway descended from Sæming, as is celebrated in the poem *Háleygjatal* of the tenth century.

The earlier successors of Yngvi-Freyr were plainly mythical figures, and are depicted as king-gods, although they gradually developed human failings. Fjölnir, son of Yngvi-Freyr, brought fertility to the crops and peace as his father had done, but in the end he fell into a vat of mead and was drowned. A few generations later came Dómaldi.[5] In his reign the crops failed and there were years of famine. First of all the Swedes sacrificed oxen, but the seasons did not improve. In the next year they offered human sacrifice, but still the crops grew no better. In the third year the Swedes decided that their misfortunes must stem from the king himself; they fell upon him and slaughtered him as a sacrifice for better harvests. This was the first, but not the only king whom the Swedes were said to have sacrificed. Many other peoples are known to have slaughtered their kings, either because the crops failed, or because they did not succeed in war, or else because they were growing old and their divine force, which Norsemen might call *gæfa* or *heill*, had left them.[6]

As already said, these early Yngling kings are mythical figures. The stories about them were preserved largely in poetry of the ninth and tenth centuries and, although not historical, they give an idea of the way in which Scandinavians of that period thought of their kingship.

While the first Yngling kings were mythical, their supposed descendants were historical, or at least partly so. For Snorri, as for Thjóðólf, author of the *Ynglingatal*, their chief importance was that they were said to be ancestors of the kings of Norway. One of these later Ynglingar was Ólaf Trételgja (Wood-cutter). He had been driven from Uppsala and cleared the forests of Vermaland (S.W. Sweden). Great crowds of Swedes, exiled by a Danish conqueror, flocked to join him, but the newly tilled soil could not support them; crops failed and there was famine. As Snorri says, it was the practice to attribute both good and bad harvests to their king. Since Ólaf was an irreligious man, little given to sacrifice, his followers gathered arms, seized his house and burned him in it as a sacrifice to Óðinn, believing that harvests would improve. Other medieval historians give different accounts of Ólaf's fate, but Snorri's interpretation of an obscure verse, in which allusion is made to it, is probably correct.[7]

Tradition had it that Harald Finehair and the subsequent kings of Norway descended from the Ynglingar through Ólaf the Wood-cutter. Whatever the historical truth of this tradition, it is plain that the Norwegians, like the Swedes, believed that their kings were descended from gods and were imbued with divine force. The belief in divine kingship is closely associated with the fertility of the soil, and most Norwegians were less deeply concerned with this than were the people of central Sweden. Perhaps for this reason the belief in divine kingship seems to be less dominant among the Norwegians than among the Swedes, but it is plain that it was held in Norway as well as in Sweden. It is told of one of the minor kings of Norway, Hálfdan the Black (ninth century), that his dead body was taken to the province of Hringaríki for burial, but the inhabitants of the three neighbouring provinces objected, each thinking that the presence of the king's body in their own territory would bring good harvests. According to one text,[8] men had never known a king whose reign was blessed with better harvests. The dispute, according to Snorri,[9] was resolved in this way. The king's body was divided into four parts and a part was buried in each of four provinces.

There are variants of this story,[10] but the tradition which Snorri represents reflects the same tradition as that which appears in the legend of Yngvi-Freyr, to whose dead body the Swedes brought sacrifice, believing that peace and prosperity would persist, so long as it remained uncremated in Sweden.

Later kings of Norway were also held responsible for the prosperity of their subjects. The sons of Eirík Bloodaxe (died *c.* 954) had been brought up partly in the British Isles and were Christians, at least in name. Under the leadership of Harald Greycloak, they seized the kingdom of Norway. According to a contemporary poet, Einar Skálaglamm, they broke down the temples, and thus put down sacrifice. Their reign was cursed by failure of the crops, and the seasons went awry. Eyvind the Plagiarist, another contemporary poet, said that while these men ruled Norway, snow fell at midsummer, and farmers had to keep their stock under cover like the Lapps.

Hákon the Great (died 995) followed the sons of Eirík as ruler of Norway. Unlike them, Hákon was an ardent pagan, and when he gained power he restored the temples and the sacrifices, and prosperity returned. As Snorri said, the herring swam right up to the shore and the corn flourished wherever it was sown. Einar Skálaglamm, who was Hákon's favourite poet, celebrated the restored fertility in memorable lines, which William Morris and E. Magnússon translated:

> Now as afore earth groweth
> since once again gold-waster (generous prince)
> lets spear-bridge (shields) wielders (men) wend them
> gladheart to holy places.[11]

The stories cited so far—some of them true and others apocryphal—show that Swedes and Norwegians believed that the seasons and crops depended on the conduct of their king and his relations with the gods. They believed, as some people in England still do, in 'royal weather'. The kings, descended from gods, incorporated some of the attributes of godhead, although this is not to say that they were incarnate gods.

Medieval historians give some slight indication that the concept of the incarnate god was not unknown in heathen Scandinavia, although it was perhaps not widespread and not clearly formulated. An interesting story is told of St Ólaf (died 1030). In a mysterious way, this arch-enemy of heathendom was linked with a heathen Ólaf, a petty king of S.E. Norway, who lived in the ninth century. The earlier Ólaf had the nicknames *Geirstaðaálfr* (Elf of Geirstaðir) and *Digrbeinn* (Thick-leg). He was reputed to be the uncle of Harald Finehair, first king of all Norway, and son of Guðrøð the Hunting-king, and thus a descendant

of the Yngling kings of the Swedes. A short time before his death, Ólaf
the Elf had a dream. He saw a huge ox rising in Gautland. The ox
walked through Ólaf's dominions; he came to every farm and blew on
the inhabitants and they dropped dead, even the king himself. Ólaf took
this dream to mean that severe pestilence would afflict his kingdom, and
that he would die with many others. He ordered his subjects to build a
great burial mound when he was dead, and to put him in it in full
regalia in a chair, but he asked them not to bring sacrifice to him.

Thus, many years passed, and the king's last wish was ignored. When
the crops failed and famine succeeded pestilence, sacrifice was brought
to Ólaf for fruitful harvests, and that was why he came to be called the
Elf of Geirstaðir.

In the first year of Ólaf Tryggvason's reign (995), Hrani, a landholder
of this region had another dream. A man appeared to him in a cloak of
scarlet, wearing a gold bracelet and a sword. He announced himself as
Ólaf the Stout (Digri), and told the dreamer to break open the howe at
Geirstaðir. He must seize the cloak, bracelet and sword of the dead
man, cut off his head, and take his belt and knife.

Hrani must afterwards go to Upplönd, where he would find Ásta, the
wife of a regional king, stricken with the pangs of childbirth; he was to
place the dead man's belt around her, and he himself must name the
child. When Ásta gave birth, her child was called Ólaf and nicknamed
the Stout, and was later Ólaf the Saint.[12]

Ólaf the Elf appears once more in the life of his namesake, St Ólaf,
and the story is of such interest that it may be translated:

It is told that once when King Ólaf (the Saint) was riding with his body-
guard (*hirð*) past the howe of Ólaf the Elf of Geirstaðir, one of his followers
(*hirðmaðr*), who is not named, questioned him: 'tell me, Lord, were you
buried here?' The King answered: 'never did my soul have two bodies, and
it never will have, neither now nor on the day of resurrection, and if I say
anything else, then the common faith is not truly implanted in me.' Then the
courtier said: 'people have said that when you came to this place before you
exclaimed; "here we were, and here we go." ' The King answered: 'I never
said that and I never will.' The King was deeply disturbed at heart; he
pricked his horse and sped from the place as fast as he could. It was easy to
see that King Ólaf wished to uproot and blot out this heretical superstition.[13]

It can be shown that some of these stories of Ólaf the Elf and his
namesake were written not later than 1200, and are therefore among
the older stories of St Ólaf put on parchment. Although apocryphal,
they show that the belief in the reincarnation of kings was not far from
the minds of Icelanders and Norwegians, even if they were Christian.

A story like the one last quoted can hardly be a medieval, Christian invention. We can safely say that some people thought that St Ólaf was his older namesake reborn, but we cannot say whether he was seen as an incarnate god, or only the descendant of a god.

Rimbert, in his Life of St Anskar (Ch. XXVI) also gave a story showing how a king might be raised to godhead after death. When Anskar was on his second mission to Birka (Sweden), about the middle of the ninth century, the Swedes heard of his approach. One of them claimed to have been at a meeting of the gods of the land. They objected to the introduction of an alien god. But if the Swedes wished to have more gods, they were ready to accept the lately defunct King Eirík as a full member of their college. The Swedes raised a temple in honour of their late king and, when Anskar arrived, the sacrifice had started.

Not only kings, but also chieftains might be revered as gods after death. It is said of Grím Kamban, settler of the Faroe Islands, that sacrifice was brought to him when he was dead because of his popularity.[14]

CHAPTER TEN

THE DIVINE HEROES

Ermanaric, Sigurð and the Burgundians—Starkað—Harald Wartooth—Hadding

IT WAS seen in earlier chapters that Freyr, Njörð, and other gods were believed to have ruled as earthly kings. Conversely, early chieftains, such as Ólaf the Elf in Norway and Grím Kamban in the Faroe Islands, were raised to the rank of gods after death. This implies that the line which divided gods from chieftains was less clearly defined than it afterwards came to be.

A great part of the early Norse literature is heroic. It records incidents from the lives of heroes who were supposed to have lived in various lands and at various ages, although in every case before the settlement of Iceland in the ninth century. These legends are preserved in their purest, but not their most complete form, in the Eddaic poems. Many of them were related at greater length by the Danish historian, Saxo, early in the thirteenth century. They were also told in Heroic Sagas, mostly written in Iceland in the late thirteenth and fourteenth centuries.

The problems of heroic legend cannot be discussed in a book of this kind, but they have formed the subject of many weighty volumes.[1] For the present we must be content to consider only a few heroes in their relation to myth and religious belief.

As is well known, some of the more famous of the heroic legends arc not of Scandinavian, but of continental German origin. Nevertheless, most of these legends are preserved best in Norse literature. Some are based partly on events in history, although history has been so distorted that the Norse sources are without value for the historian.

Ermanaric, Sigurð and the Burgundians
The oldest dateable event mentioned in the Norse heroic literature is the death of Ermanaric, Emperor of the Goths, in south-eastern Europe in the year AD 375. Comparatively little is known about Ermanaric in history, but the development of the legend about him can be followed in some detail.[2]

According to a contemporary historian, Ammianus Marcellinus, the empire of Ermanaric was invaded by the Huns and, being so distressed at its plight, he committed suicide. Nothing more is heard of Ermanaric until the middle of the sixth century, when the Gothic historian, Jordanes, wrote of him. By that time the story had changed, and legend had been at work, and the circumstances of Ermanaric's end were different.

When the Huns invaded his empire, the Rosomoni, a subject tribe, deserted him. To punish them, Ermanaric seized Sunilda, the wife of one of their chieftains, and had her torn to pieces by wild horses. In revenge, two brothers of the slaughtered woman, Ammius and Sarus, attacked Ermanaric. They wounded him severely, but he lingered on for a time.

It may be supposed that the fate of Ermanaric had already become the subject of heroic lay, and it was upon this that Jordanes based his story. It was far removed from fact, and elements which had nothing to do with history had been introduced.

At a comparatively early period, lays and legends of Ermanaric were brought to Scandinavia, and some details of the story were changed, although its outline remained. One of the oldest records of it in Scandinavia is the *Ragnarsdrápa*[3] of the scald Bragi (see Ch. I, Old Norse Poetry). By this time, the legend of Ermanaric (Jörmunrekk) had been combined with another, for the avenging brothers, now called Hamðir and Sörli, are said to be descendants of the Burgundian Gjúki (Gibica), although in history, Gjúki must have lived later than Ermanaric.

Another, and more dramatic change had taken place. The murdered woman was no longer the wife of Jörmunrekk's enemy, but she was his own wife. Her name had also been changed and made more meaningful. She was no longer called Sunilda, but Svanhild (Swan-hild), or in the poetic language of Bragi *Foglhildr* (Bird-hild).

The story of Ermanaric is told in closer detail in the poems of the Edda, *Guðrúnarhvǫt* and *Hamðismál* and again by Snorri in his *Edda* and in the *Vǫlsunga Saga* of the late thirteenth century. In these sources the legend is inextricably bound up, not only with that of the Burgundians, but also with the legend of Sigurð.

Like the legend of Ermanaric, that of the Burgundians has some basis in history. In history, their king, Gundicarius, son of Gibica, was killed in the year 437 with his whole tribe by Hunnish troops acting in Roman interests.[4] Gundicarius lives in Norse legend as Gunnar, son of Gjúki, but the story of his death has departed from history. The war between his tribe and the Huns has become a family quarrel, and Gunnar's antagonist is Atli (Attila), said to be married to Gunnar's sister, Guðrún.

I have passed quickly over the legends of Ermanaric and the Burgundians. While based partly on history, they show how legend, and the poets who transmitted it, distorted history and introduced other elements. Without the help of chroniclers, we could not know that there was any history in these legends.

There is nothing mythical in the Norse legends of Ermanaric and the Burgundians as they have so far been told, but they were combined with a third legend, that of Sigurð (Sigfrid), most glorious of Germanic heroes.

We cannot say when the legend of the Burgundians was combined with that of Sigurð. Bragi, when he speaks of Svanhild as wife of Jörmunrekk (Ermanaric), seems to imply that she was related to the Burgundians, and perhaps she had already been made daughter of Guðrún and Sigurð. In a great part of the Norse poetry, as in the *Vǫlsunga Saga*, the *Þiðreks Saga* and the German *Nibelungenlied*, the legends of Sigurð and the Burgundians are bound up with each other. It is, therefore, plain that they were first combined in Germany, and not in Scandinavia.

But there is some Norse poetry in which the legends are nearly separate. In the *Atlakviða*, Sigurð is never named, and allusion to his legend is indistinct.

The earlier parts of the legend of Sigurð, the tales of his youth, have nothing to do with the Burgundian legend. These tales are told in coherent form in the *Vǫlsunga Saga* and partly by Snorri.[5] In the Poetic *Edda* the text is defective and the stories are told in verses of various poetic form and plainly of devious origin.

In one section of the *Edda*, the so-called *Sigrdrífumál* (Words of Sigrdrífa), it is told, partly in verse and partly in prose, how Sigurð rode up the mountain Hindarfjall (Hind-mountain), and awakened the valkyrie, Sigrdrífa (Victory-giver), surrounded by a wall of glowing shields. The valkyrie had been put to sleep by Óðinn, evidently with a 'sleep-thorn', because she had awarded victory to the wrong man. After she awoke, the valkyrie spoke many words of occult wisdom and she and Sigurð, if the *Vǫlsunga Saga*[6] is to be trusted, were solemnly betrothed.

This legend leaves no room for the story, told in many other sources, of Sigurð's subsequent betrothal to Brynhild and his marriage with the Burgundian Guðrún. Ever since the Middle Ages poets and commentators have sought ways of explaining the hero's apparent faithlessness.[7] These explanations have led to ever-greater confusion, and it is easier to believe that there were two stories of Sigurð. In the one, he was in the mythical world of Óðinn and his valkyries, and in the other he lived among earthly heroes.

It is not easy to say which is the older of these legends, i.e. whether an earthly hero was raised to the divine world, or whether a divine figure became an earthly hero.

Some of the heroes named in this chapter have been identified in history. It would be interesting to know whether Sigurð can also be identified. His name, which appears regularly in O.N. as Sigurð (Sigurðr), is found in continental sources as Sigfrid. He has frequently been identified with the Frankish king, Sigeberht II (murdered 575), whose wife was Brunehilda, a Visigoth from Spain (died 613).

Since the legend of Sigurð is set, partly at least, in Frankish territory, and seems largely to have developed in that neighbourhood, we may well suppose that Sigeberht and his wife, with her unusual name, contributed their names, or parts of them, to the legend, but it is doubtful whether they contributed anything more.

There is an older figure in history who has also been claimed as the prototype of Sigurð. This is the Cheruscan, Arminius, who may well have helped to form the legendary figure.[8] Arminius was born in the year 16 BC; he defeated the Romans under Varus in AD 9, and was murdered by his own kinsmen in AD 21. Nearly a century afterwards, as Tacitus wrote, songs or lays about Arminius were still being sung.

It has often been argued that Arminius was not the real name of this chieftain, but was a nickname used by Romans, whether, as formerly supposed, it represents Herrmann (Warrior) or not.[9] In fact the father of Arminius was called Segimerus (O.N. Sigmarr), and names of which the first element was Segi (O.N. Sig-) predominated in his clan. O. Höfler[10] has lately drawn attention to some remarkable points of correspondence between the legendary Sigurð and Arminius. Sigurð is, strangely enough, compared with the hart; he towered above the sons of Gjúki as the long-legged hart above other beasts (Guðrúnarkviða II, 2). As Romulus and Remus were fostered by a wolf, so the infant Sigurð was fed by a hind (Þiðreks Saga CCLXVII). The mountain on which Sigurð found the sleeping valkyrie was Hindarfjall (Hind-mountain), and he appeared in a dream as a hart. One of the hero's supposed descendants was called Sigurð Hjǫrtr (Hart), and the hero's tragic death in the forest was like that of a hunted stag. Another hero, Helgi Hundingsbani, was compared with the dýrkálfr (young hart or elk), and the occurrence of the elements hjǫrtr and elgr in personal and nicknames suggests that beasts of this kind were sacred, no less than the boar, horse, wolf and raven.

A particular reason to associate Arminius with the hart may be found in the name of his tribe, Cherusci. This has been explained in various ways, but it is now generally associated with Germanic herut and O.N. hjǫrtr (hart).[11]

But, even if the Cheruscan Arminius and the Frankish Sigeberht were combined in the legend of Sigurð, history leaves much to be explained. History does not provide the motive of the sleeping valkyrie awakened by the dauntless hero. The greatest moment in Sigurð's life was when he slew the dragon, Fáfnir. It would be difficult to accept the suggestion that this reflects a victory over Roman legions fighting under a dragon banner.[12] Like the waking of the valkyrie, it is more readily explained as a myth. Dragons in myth are symbols of chaos and evil, and it is commonly gods who contend with them, and especially those gods who are most friendly to man, and often young, e.g. Thór, Herakles, Marduk, Indra.

In the Norse sources, the slaughter of the dragon is placed in a mythical setting, and the gold which the hero seized from him was of mythical origin. The gods had taken it from a dwarf and surrendered it to Hreiðmar, father of the dragon.[13] According to one source, Óðinn showed Sigurð how to kill the dragon without danger to himself.[14] The hero was in quest, not only of the dragon's gold, but also of his wisdom, which he wrung from him as he lay dying. After he had stabbed Fáfnir, Sigurð asked him questions about the mythical world: who are the norns (fates), who attend the birth of men; what is the name of the island on which gods and demons will fight their last battle?[15] As soon as Sigurð had tasted the blood of the dragon's heart, he understood the speech of birds.[16]

Many other episodes in Sigurð's career suggest that he has as much to do with the mythical as he has to do with our world. According to the *Þiðreks Saga* (CCLXIX), he was a foundling, drifting in a glass vessel over the sea and, as already mentioned, he was fed by a hind. When the wounded dragon first asked Sigurð his name and origin, he said that his name was 'the splendid beast' (*gǫfukt dýr*);[17] he had neither father nor mother, and had gone his way alone. Later the hero said that his father was Sigmund, as is told in other sources.

Sigurð's genealogy, traced in detail only in the *Vǫlsunga Saga*,[18] has more to do with myth than with legend; he is said to descend directly from Óðinn. His great-grandmother grew pregnant after eating an apple sent by Óðinn. Her son was Völsung, after whom the clan was named. Völsung was the father of Sigmund, father of Sinfjötli and Sigurð.

It could be argued that the introductory chapters of the *Vǫlsunga Saga*, in which these stories are told, are a late invention, since it cannot be shown that they are based on poetry, as much of the saga is. But Óðinn appears as the guardian, even as the possessor of the Völsung clan, also in later parts of the story, whose antiquity there is less reason to doubt. It was Óðinn who broke Sigmund's sword in his last battle, for he must fight only so long as Óðinn wished.[19] It was a raven, Óðinn's bird, which brought a leaf to heal the wounds of Sinfjötli.[20] It must also have been Óðinn who received the dead body of Sinfjötli, placed it in a boat and vanished.[21]

A well-known passage in *Beowulf* (875 ff) contains an interesting allusion to the Völsung legend, which agrees, in some ways, closely with the *Vǫlsunga Saga*. In *Beowulf*, Sigmund, the son of Wæls, and his nephew, Fitela, were said to live by deeds of daring and violence, as Sigmund and Sinfjötli did, sometimes in the shape of wolves, in the *Vǫlsunga Saga* (VIII). According to Norse tradition, Sinfjötli (Fitela) was not only the nephew of Sigmund; he was also his son, begotten by an incestuous union with Signý, sister of Sigmund. In this we may suppose that the Norse tradition is the more complete, and that the incest did not interest the English poet. *Beowulf* differs also from the Norse tradition in making Sigemund slay the dragon and seize the hoard.[22] As H. M. Chadwick pointed out,[23] the English tradition probably derived from Denmark or Jutland. But the differences between this and the tradition known from the Icelandic sources are not fundamental. In *Beowulf* it was Sigemund (Sigmund) who killed the dragon; in the Norse sources it was Sigurð, said to be son of Sigmund (Sigemund). But in German, the hero is called Sigfrid. Whether or not this hero is related to the historical Sigeberht, the second element of his name is not fixed.[24] If he was known from one source as Sigmund and from another as Sigurð, it would not be surprising that two heroes should be made of him, and that they should be father and son. The unchanging element in the dragon-slayer's name is *Sig-* (victory). It is remarkable how often this occurs as an element in poetic names for Óðinn; the god is *Sigðir, Siggautr, Sigtryggr, Sig-Týr* and even *Sigmundr.*[25]

A minor difference between *Beowulf* and the Norse sources is that in *Beowulf* Sigemund is not only called *Wælsing (Vǫlsungr)*, but is expressly said to be son of Wæls (*Wælses eafera*). In the Norse sources Sigmund is son of Völsung. In this priority must be given to the English source, for while Wælsing means 'son of Wæls', Völsung must originally have meant 'son of Völsi'. Völsi was the name given to a horse's penis which was worshipped as a god (see Ch. XIII), whether or not it may, at one time, have been used as a name for Óðinn.

If the dragon-slayer had such close affinities with myth as is here suggested, it is difficult to see how he came to be associated with the Burgundians, who have some basis in history.

The Burgundians were commonly called *Niflungar*. It has been said that this name derives from the place, Nivelles (Nyvel), in Flanders, but it is more likely to be related to the German *Nebel* (fog, mist), O.H.G. *nebul*, *nebil*, O.Sax. *nebal* (mist, darkness), and to other words which have suchlike meaning.[26]

The Niflungar are said in Norse literature to be 'black as ravens' (*hrafnbláir*); the sons of Guðrún, Sörli, Hamðir, Erp, all had raven-black hair, just like Gunnar, Högni and the other Niflungar.[27]

This may lead to the suspicion, as it has led many before, that the Niflungar, who slew Sigurð, were demons of darkness. In this case, they have something in common with the blind Höð, who struck down the shining god, Baldr. Baldr could be killed by one weapon alone; Sigurð, as the German sources say, could not be wounded except on one spot of his body, which the dragon's blood had not reached. In each case, it was a woman, mother or wife, who innocently gave the secret away, and the god, or hero, fell at the hand of his brother, brother-in-law or foster-brother.

This may partly explain why the assailants of Sigurð were called Niflungar; it does not explain why the Niflungar were identified with the semi-historical Burgundians.

The explanation given by A. Heusler[28] may be near the truth, and differs but slightly from the one offered here. Sigurð conquered not one, but two hoards of treasure. He took the hoard of the dragon, Fáfnir, and, according to German sources,[29] he also took the hoard of the Nibelung brothers, Nibelunc and Schilbunc, who were quarrelling over it. This hoard came from underground, and its keeper was Albrich, an elfish figure.

We could suppose that there was a story in which Sigurð had seized a hoard of gold from the mythical dark-elves (*døkkálfar*), the master-craftsmen. If so, a curse was on it, as it was on other treasures seized from elves or dwarfs,[30] and in the end, the elves must get their revenge. But if, in legend or history, the Burgundians were owners of a treasure-hoard, and if this were the cause of their downfall, as it was said to be, then their treasure could well be identified with Sigurð's hoard, which included treasure taken from the dark elves. If the Burgundians were in possession of Sigurð's hoard, they must have killed him to get it, and they could thus fill the place of the avenging dark elves, or Niflungar.

A central place is taken by Högni (Hagen). Since his name does not alliterate with theirs, he cannot, originally, have been a brother of the Burgundians, Gunnar, Guttorm, Guðrún, although he was said to be by Norse poets. In Norse sources it was not Högni who struck down Sigurð; according to the *Vǫlsunga Saga* (XXXII), he tried to dissuade his brothers from this dastardly act. But in German sources, and especially in the *Þiðreks Saga*, Högni is shown in another light; he is not the full brother of the Burgundians, but their half-brother. An elf had slept with the Queen, their mother, when she was drunk. Högni looked more like a troll than a man and, in one passage, he was said to be pale as bast and grey as ash; in another, he was dusky all over, with black hair and a black beard and cruel looking. In the *Þiðreks Saga* (CCIXC), as in the *Nibelungenlied* (*Âv.* XVI), it was Högni who treacherously struck Sigurð between the shoulder-blades.

The legend could develop in this way. Sigurð had seized the accursed treasure from the dark elves, the Niflungar. Högni was one of them and therefore, in revenge, he killed Sigurð. The Burgundians also held an accursed hoard, which led to their death; they must, therefore, have taken it from Sigurð. In this case, they must have killed Sigurð, and so Högni must be among them, even their brother. If this were so, the Burgundians must be Niflungar, and black as the elves.

It has often been noticed that some of the Norse legends have affinities with Celtic ones, which are too close to be explained by chance or by common Indo-European inheritance. No Norse hero resembles the Celtic ones as closely as does Sigurð, and the Celtic legends may help us to understand him.

It will be recalled that, after he had killed the dragon, Sigurð roasted the heart, and touched it with his finger to see whether it was fully cooked. Scalding his finger, the hero put it in his mouth, and at once he understood the speech of the birds.[31]

There are several stories which tell how the Irish hero, Finn mac Cumhaill gained his unsurpassed wisdom. According to some, it was by drinking water from a magic or fairy well. But according to another, Finn was roasting the salmon of wisdom and, scalding his thumb, he put it in his mouth and thus acquired wisdom.

These stories of the origin of Finn's wisdom have been carefully sifted by T. F. O'Rahilly.[32] Some of the versions recorded in Ireland and Scotland in recent times resemble the story of Sigurð more closely than the medieval one in *Macgnimartha Finn*,[33] and in some things are perhaps closer to the original. Since dragons, or serpents, are not found in Ireland, a story-teller would naturally exclude them from an Irish setting, and introduce the salmon instead. When Finn placed the scalded thumb in his mouth, he knew that the owner of the salmon was his enemy, and therefore he killed him, just as Sigurð killed Reginn, the dragon's brother, after he had learnt from the birds of his treachery.

O'Rahilly, G. Murphy and other Celtic specialists agree that Finn was originally a god. If so, he was transformed into an earthly hero by Christian story-tellers.

The story of Sigurð has affinities with Celtic legends other than that of Finn. According to the *Þiðreks Saga* (CCLXXI) and to the *Nibelungen-lied* (Âv. III), Sigurð bathed, or smeared himself in the blood of the dragon, and his skin became as hard as horn, except on one spot be-tween the shoulder-blades, which the blood had not reached. It was on that spot alone that he could be wounded, and it was Sigurð's wife who innocently betrayed the secret to his murderer.[34] It is told of more than one Irish hero that he had a skin of horn. One of them, Conganchnes (Horny-skin), was vulnerable only on the soles of his feet, and the secret was betrayed by his wife.[35]

In the *Vǫlsunga Saga* (XV), and more briefly in the prose of the *Reginsmál* (str. 14) the story is told of how the smith Reginn forged the sword *Gramr* for Sigurð. This was not an ordinary sword, for it was made from the fragments of an older one, which Sigurð's father had received from Óðinn. To test its keenness, Sigurð placed it in the Rhine, and a flock of wool drifting downstream was cut in two.

This story may remind us of the one in which Wayland the Smith tested the sword Mímung, cutting a stout piece of cloth drifting down-stream.[36] Irish legend contains several stories of this kind; heroes have weapons, stout, but sharp enough to cut a hair as it drifts down the stream.[37]

To these parallels may be added the tradition that the mother of Oisín, son of Finn, was a deer.[38] This may remind us of the story told in the *Þiðreks Saga* (CCLXVII) that Sigurð was fostered by a doe. He was once compared with a hart and was symbolized by a hart in a dream.[39]

It is not easy to explain the relationship between Sigurð and the Irish figures. While some have believed that the Irish legends were influenced by Norse ones,[40] many more have held that the Norsemen and Ger-mans borrowed from the Irish.[41] It may not be necessary to assume borrowing on either side, especially since some of the parallels quoted are found only in Norse versions of the story of Sigurð, and others only in German. The story of Sigurð centres on the Rhine and the land of the Franks; in fact, it seems to belong to western areas of mixed Celto-Germanic culture and to have flourished near the territories of the Belgæ.[42] This may imply that a legend or myth comparable with that of Sigurð had been formed already by the first century BC, when the Belgæ invaded Britain. In other words, the hero Sigurð may owe some-thing to Arminius, and something to Sigeberht, but fundamentally he is not an historical figure, and is older than either of these. In this case, he is a mythical, more than a legendary hero. Like the gods, Thór and Indra he fights a dragon and gains wisdom from him, as Finn gains it from the salmon. Like Baldr, the son of Óðinn, Sigurð suffers an un-expected death at the hands of a relative. Baldr's assailant was blind;

Sigurð's assailants were black as ravens. The Völsungs were under Óðinn's protection, and were said to descend from that god.

In short, the evidence at our disposal suggests that Sigurð was originally a god, or at least a demi-god. If so, he may have been conceived at one time as the divine ancestor of the Cherusci. If the name *Cherusci* is correctly related to **herut* (hart), then the sacred beast of their divine ancestor must have been the hart, and the hart must be one of the forms which he took. Arminius, as leader of the Cherusci, could be regarded as the divine ancestor reborn, and his career might well contribute something to the figure of myth and legend, although that figure was fundamentally older than he was.

Starkað

One of the strangest figures in Norse legend is Starkað, of whom a little was said in Ch. II above. Many stories are told of him, and they take very different forms, although they have a certain consistency.

Starkað is described most fully by Saxo in the *Gesta Danorum*, written early in the thirteenth century, and again in the Icelandic *Gautreks Saga*. There are also allusions to him in many other sources of various ages.

The critical literature about Starkað is so great that I can refer only to a small part of it in this book; scholars are far from agreement about his significance in legend or myth, and I must content myself with some general observations.

Many have seen Starkað as a semi-mythical figure, but while some have regarded him as an Óðinn-hero, others have been no less firmly convinced of his relationship with Thór.[1]

According to the *Gautreks Saga* (III),[2] Starkað descended from giants; his grandfather was another Starkað, who had the nickname *Áludrengr* (or *Áladrengr*), and was an exceedingly wise giant (*hundvíss jǫtunn*), according to some sources with eight arms. This Starkað had raped Álfhild, the daughter of a king in Norway, and the King had invoked Thór, the eternal enemy of giants. The god responded, killed the giant and rescued the King's daughter. She was now pregnant and bore a son called *Stórvirkr* (the man of great deeds), who, in his turn, was father of our Starkað.

Many scholars have distinguished two original Starkaðs, who came to be confused in later tradition. The one was the hero, and the other, the giant (*Áludrengr*), was a troll or water-demon. He was said, in one source, to live at Álufossar (or Álupollar) which is equated with Ulefoss in Telemark.[3] This explanation of the giant-like nature of the hero has led only to greater confusion. It is more reasonable to suppose that the older Starkað had no real 'existence' in legend, and was created only to explain some of the peculiar characteristics of the hero.[4]

According to Saxo (vi, 182), the hero Starkað was said by some to be of giant origin; he came from a land east of Sweden, where the world of giants is sometimes located. Like his giant grandfather in the *Gautreks Saga*, Starkað was born with an extraordinary number of arms or hands. The god Thór had torn off these extra hands, so that he had but two left, and his body was then less uncomely.

This last motive is puzzling, but the six, or eight, hands seem to be of some antiquity in the story. The *Gautreks Saga* contains a poem, perhaps of the twelfth century, ascribed to the hero. In lines which are not altogether clear,[5] Starkað seems to say that scoffing berserks, who said he was a giant reborn, claimed to see on his body the marks of eight arms which Thór (Hlórriði) had torn from the body of his grandfather.

Both from Danish and Icelandic sources we learn that it was chiefly Óðinn who decreed the course of Starkað's life. According to Saxo (vi, 184), Óðinn endowed him with three spans of human life, so that he should commit three execrable crimes. Óðinn also gave Starkað bravery, enormous size and the gift of poetry. One of Starkað's dastardly crimes was to kill his master, the Norwegian King Víkar, because this was Óðinn's wish. This story, as it is told in the *Gautreks Saga* was summarized in Ch. II above. Saxo's version differs in some details. Again the sacrifice of the King was to be symbolic, and Starkað was to hang him in a noose of twigs. According to one version, which Saxo rejects, the twigs grew tough as iron when placed around the King's neck; according to another, which Saxo accepts, the twigs were knotted in such a way that the King was strangled and, while he was still struggling, Starkað cut out his breath with his sword (*ferro*).

The differences between Saxo's version of the slaughter of Víkar and that given in the *Gautreks Saga* are not deep. In both the dastardly crime is committed for Óðinn, and can be seen only as a sacrifice of the King.

Since Starkað commits this crime on Óðinn's behalf, he must stand in some relation with Óðinn. But if he is an Óðinn-hero, he differs from others, such as Sigurð, Harald Wartooth and, if we may count him, Helgi Hundingsbani.

Even after the extra arms had been torn off, Starkað was never comely, as these heroes were said to be. As he was made to say himself:

Hlæja rekkar,	Warriors laugh
er mik séa,	to look on me,
ljótan skolt,	ugly pated
langa trjónu,	and long snouted,
hár úflgrátt,	with wolf-grey hair

hangar tjálgur,	and drooping paws,
hrjúfan háls,	a crinkled neck
húð jótraða.	and wrinkled skin.[6]

Starkað is commonly presented as grey-haired and misshapen, and very old; in other words, he was more like Óðinn himself than the other heroes were.

We may consider Starkað's relations with Óðinn more closely. As already mentioned, Danish and Icelandic authors relate that Starkað received, not only three spans of life, but also the gift of poetry from Óðinn. The *Gautreks Saga* (VII) is more precise in enumerating Óðinn's gifts. Starkað would possess the finest weapons and clothes, and great quantities of treasure. He would win victory in every battle, and be held in highest esteem by all the noblest men.

From Saxo's pages (vi, 184), it seems that it was Óðinn who decreed that Starkað should commit three dastardly crimes, but the *Gautreks Saga* makes this part of a curse laid on him by Thór.

We read clearly only of two of Starkað's crimes. The first of them, the slaughter of Víkar was plainly an Óðinn-sacrifice. The last (*síðasta óskapaverk*)[7] was hardly less famous, although its motives are rather less clear. It is mentioned in many Icelandic sources,[8] and described most fully by Saxo (viii, 265 ff).

Starkað's life was drawing to its close, and a certain Olo, known in Icelandic sources as Áli inn frœkni (also *Ármóðr*), was ruling in Denmark. He was so harsh and unjust that nobles revolted. Not trusting their own ability they bribed Starkað to carry out their design. In exchange for a large sum of gold, he agreed to stab the unarmed King in his bath. At first he drew back before Olo's piercing eyes, but when the King's head was covered, he cut him in the throat.[9]

When the deed was done, Starkað was overcome with remorse as, in the *Gautreks Saga*, he had been after he killed Víkar.

He was now decrepit and nearly blind, walking with two sticks. He longed for death, but it must not be a 'straw-death'; he must die by the sword. He hung his gold around his neck, so that it might tempt an assassin. He slew Lenno (Hlenni), one of those who had bribed him to commit his crime. When he met Hatherus, the son of Lenno, he taunted him for not avenging his father, as though he were a shepherd or a kitchen-worker.

Hatherus had less interest in vengeance than he had in Starkað's gold, which the hero handed to him, together with his sword. Hatherus now did the work of executioner, severing the old man's head, which bit the ground as it fell. The Icelandic *Helga kviða Huningsbana* II (str. 27) goes back to a very different version of Starkað's death, which yet has something in common with that of Saxo. According to the *Helga kviða*, Starkað fell in battle against the Danish hero Helgi, but his body went on fighting after the head was cut off:

. . . þann sá ek gylfa	That was the prince
grimmúðgastan,	I saw most defiant;
er barðisk bolr,	his body fought on
var á brott hǫfuð.	when the head was off.

After this brief consideration of Starkað's career and of his relations with Óðinn, we should consider his relations with Thór. According to the *Gautreks Saga* (VII), it was Thór who counter-balanced every blessing which Óðinn conferred upon the hero with a curse. It was Thór who decreed that he should commit three dastardly crimes, and when Óðinn laid down that Starkað should have the best of weapons and clothes, Thór said that he would ever be a landless man. He would possess uncountable riches, but he would always think that he had not enough. He would win victory in every battle, but suffer a severe wound in each. He would have the gift of poetry, but never remember a line of his verse. Although he would win the favour of chieftains, he would be loathed by all the common people and, most grievous of all, he would have neither son nor daughter.

Starkað is presented in the *Gautreks Saga* as the favourite of Óðinn and the enemy of Thór. The reasons are made plain enough. His paternal grandmother (i.e. Álfhild) had taken a cunning giant (i.e. Starkað Áludreng) as the father of her son, instead of Thór himself. In other words, the hero was of giant origin, and that would be sufficient to account for Thór's enmity.

Nevertheless, some have seen Starkað rather as a Thór- than as an Óðinn-hero. This opinion is based partly upon Saxo's peculiar story, telling how Thór tore off the hero's extra arms, thus improving his appearance. It was noticed above that a story of this kind was also known to the author of the *Gautreks Saga*, but we may wonder, in tearing off these arms, whether Thór was really conferring so great a favour on the hero or the giant. Starkað Áludreng had eight arms, but they were no impediment, for he won a duel wielding four swords at once.[10]

There are other reasons to believe that Thór was the enemy of Starkað. In an earlier chapter I quoted the fragment of a hymn in praise of Thór.[11] This contained a list of giants whom Thór had overcome, and one of the lines read:

Steypðir Starkeði	You knocked down Starkað[12]

208

The poet does not tell how Thór overcame the giant Starkað, but this is told in the *Rerum Danicarum Fragmenta of* Arngímur Jónsson (VIII), who undoubtedly follows an ancient source.[13] After tearing off the giant's arms, Thór came upon him alone in a boat in the Gulf of Finland, and drowned him.

If Starkað was of giant origin, we may wonder why he is presented as the favourite of Óðinn, for giants were said to be enemies of all the gods. Thór, we are told, was the son of Óðinn and Frigg, but Óðinn was less unfriendly to the giants and more closely related to them than Thór was. Not only did he entertain a giant in Ásgarð,[14] and drink giants' mead in Jǫtunheimar,[15] but, according to Snorri,[16] Óðinn's mother was Bestla, daughter of the giant *Bǫlþorn* (Evil Thorn), and this story was not far from the mind of the author of str. 140 of the *Hávamál.*

It was laid down that Starkað must commit three wicked crimes in the span of three mortal lives. The first crime was the slaughter of his master Víkar, and the third the slaughter of the unarmed Olo, or Áli the Bold. The medieval authors do not say which was the second crime.

G. Dumézil,[17] with his usual brilliance, claims to find it. Starkað, in the service of a Swedish prince, Regnaldus, was engaged in battle against the Danes. When Regnaldus fell, the whole of his army, including Starkað, turned and fled.[18] It may be added that this was not the only occasion on which Starkað fled from a battlefield. According to the *Norna-Gests Þáttr* (Ch. VII), he fled before Sigurð and the sons of Gjúki.

Neither of these stories of Starkað's flight from battle is described as a crime. They may even bring the hero closer to Óðinn himself. Óðinn is often present on the battlefield, but he will not fight until the Ragnarök; he likes to see courage in others but, unlike Thór, he does not display it himself.

J. de Vries[19] has offered a better acceptable suggestion about Starkað's third, or rather second crime.

He was in the service of King Fróði IV of Denmark. When Fróði was treacherously killed by the German, Sverting, his son Ingjald (Ingellus) succeeded. Ingjald was degenerate and lived in luxury, attended by German cooks. He married the daughter of Sverting and entertained Sverting's sons at his own court. It was then that Starkað returned from Sweden, an old man, dressed as a beggar.

For Saxo, Starkað was the apotheosis of Danish valour, despising German luxury and effeminacy. He insulted the Queen and then, in verses reproduced by Saxo in pompous Latin, he urged Ingjald to take vengeance for his father. The young King, stirred by the old warrior's taunts, unsheathed his sword and cut down his guests and brothers-in-law.

Neither Starkað's nor Ingjald's act is presented as a crime. In Saxo's eyes it was perhaps a virtue because the victims were Germans. But yet, it was as much a breach of the rules of hospitality as it was when Atli killed his brothers-in-law and guests, Gunnar and Högni.

The part played by Starkað in this story is remarkably like that played by Óðinn in others. As Óðinn boasts himself in the *Hárbarðsljóð* (str. 24):

atta ek jǫfrum,   I incited princes,
en aldrei sættak.   and never made peace.

It is said of Óðinn that he sows dissension between kinsmen, as he did between Harald Wartooth and Ring (Saxo, vii, 255), or as it is expressed in the *Helga kviða Hundingsbana* II (str. 34):

Einn veldr Óðinn   Óðinn alone
ǫllu bǫlvi,   promotes all evil;
þvíat með sifjungum he stirred up enmity
sakrúnar bar.   between the kinsmen.

Few heroic legends can be traced further back than that of Starkað and Ingjald. Allusions to it were made already in *Beowulf* (2024 ff), in a way which shows that it was well known to the English audience of the eighth century. In this version, the place which Saxo gives to the Danes is taken by their enemies the Heaðobards; while the place of the Germans is taken by Danes. In order to allay a feud between the two peoples, a Danish princess was betrothed to the Heaðobard, Ingeld, whose father Froda had been killed by Danes. When the princess came with her Danish escort to the Heaðobard court, an old warrior (*æscwiga*) of the Heaðobards was enraged to see the treasures of his late master borne by a Danish prince. He stirred the heart of the young Ingeld; Danish blood was shed and the feud broke out again.

The old warrior is not named in the *Beowulf*; he plays the part of Starkað, but it cannot be told whether he already bore that name. It was said of him: *him bið grim sefa* (2043), almost as it was said of Starkað, in a much later Icelandic source, that he was *grimmúðgastr*.[20]

It could be supposed that the story told in *Beowulf* had some basis in the history of the Danes and Heaðobards of the fifth century or the sixth. From the present point of view, this is of little significance. Even if the *eald æscwiga* was himself an historical figure, he was well disposed to develop into an Óðinn-hero, and to adopt the qualities of Óðinn himself.

There are further reasons to associate Starkað with the cult of Óðinn, although they may not all be strong. The name *Starkaðr* (*Stǫrkuðr*) has been interpreted in various ways. Some have taken it to mean 'the strong Heaðobard',[21] and others 'the strong Warrior'. It occurred to S. Bugge[22] that it might mean 'the strong Höð (*Hǫðr*)', although he preferred another interpretation. In fact, this interpretation is less improbable than it might appear at first sight. Óðinn's blind son Höð killed Baldr with a seemingly harmless mistletoe (see Ch. IV); Starkað, the favourite of Óðinn, killed Víkar with a reed. It is also surprising that, in Saxo's story, the man who killed Starkað was called Hatherus (i.e. *Hǫðr*). He did not kill him in battle but, by the hero's own wish, with a sword. It was as if Starkað wished to make sure that he would go to Óðinn in Valhöll, as the god-king Njörð did, when he 'had himself marked for Óðinn' before he died.[23] It is perhaps implied that one who died with the marks of a weapon on his body would go to Valhöll, as if he had died in battle and not, like those who died in their beds, to Hel. Óðinn himself, represented as King of the Swedes, was marked with a spear-point (*geirsoddi*) when he drew near to death, and was to take to himself all who died by weapons.[24]

While Óðinn laid down that Starkað should win the favour of chieftains, it was part of Thór's curse that all the common people (*ǫll alþýða*) would loathe him. Starkað's contempt for the common people is often emphasized; he despised the goldsmith, the shepherd, the cook. In the boasting words attributed to the god himself, Óðinn took all the princes who fell in battle, but the race of thralls belonged to Thór.[25]

The *Hárbarðsljóð*, whatever its age, implies an antithesis, a traditional enmity between Óðinn and Thór, even though they were sometimes said to be father and son. Thór is the god of the peasant, and Óðinn the god of the king, the court and the landless warrior. It is not, therefore, surprising that, under Thór's curse, Starkað must ever be a landless man.

It could be supposed that, originally, Starkað was the favourite of Óðinn, and was therefore the enemy of Thór. The foremost of Thór's enemies were giants and therefore Starkað was conceived as a hero of giant origin, and even as a full-blooded giant. This was how the poet Vetrliði saw him about the year 1000. As a giant, or troll, Starkað acquired eight arms and other monstrous qualities.

Harald Wartooth
Starkað had received the gift of poetry from Óðinn. Although it was a part of Thór's curse that he should never remember a line of his verse, medieval writers of Iceland and Denmark claimed to know many of them.

The Icelandic *Skáldatal* (List of Poets), probably drawn up in the twelfth century, opens with the words: 'Starkað the Old was a poet; and his verses are the oldest known now. He made poetry about the kings of the Danes.'[1] As a warrior-poet, Starkað was brought into touch with another and less complicated Óðinn-figure, with whom he shared certain features. This was the legendary Harald Wartooth (*Hilditǫnn*), of whom a few words should be said here.

Harald's career is traced in some detail by Saxo in Books VII and VIII of his History and again in the so-called 'Fragmentary History of Ancient Kings',[2] whose text is defective. The 'Fragmentary History' is derived from the lost *Skjǫldunga Saga*, a history of kings of Denmark written in Iceland about the beginning of the thirteenth century.[3] Harald was also mentioned by several poets, beginning with Einar Skálaglamm of the late tenth century.[4]

Like Starkað, Harald lived the span of three lives, or a hundred and fifty years. Like Völsung, he was born of a barren woman through the intervention of Óðinn.[5] Óðinn granted him victory, and made his body proof against steel and, in return, Harald dedicated all who fell in his battles to the god.

Unlike Starkað, Harald was a splendid figure but, while he was still young, two of his teeth were knocked out and gigantic molars, like tusks, grew in their place. For this reason he was called 'Wartooth' or 'Wartoothed'.[6]

Óðinn, described by Saxo[7] as a tall, one-eyed man, taught the young warrior how to deploy his forces in the field. The deployment was evidently a kind of wedge, and was called *svínfylking* or 'pig-formation', while those in the forefront were called 'the snout' (*rani*).

This formation may be of continental origin, and an imitation of the classical *porcinum caput*,[8] but its association with the tusked Harald is remarkable and may suggest that, like the more mythical Hadding, who was also a favourite of Óðinn, Harald was in one way associated with Freyr, or another fertility-god, to whom the boar was sacred.

Harald died the death typical of an Óðinn-hero. He had conquered all Denmark, Sweden and other lands. When he grew old, he placed his nephew Hring in charge of Sweden. If we follow Saxo's story,[9] which differs slightly from that in the Icelandic 'Fragmentary History', Óðinn, who impersonated Brún (Brúni), servant of Harald, sowed strife between Harald and his nephew. Harald was now blind, but still able to fight, and the two armies met at Brávellir in East Gautland.[10] Starkað was now on the side of the Swedes, and it was said to be in his verses that the story of this battle, most famous in the legendary history of the north, was recorded.

Multitudes fell on either side and, in the end, Harald learned that the Swedish army was deployed in wedge-formation like his own. Only Óðinn could have taught them this, and Harald knew now that the god had turned against him. Óðinn, who was now acting as Harald's charioteer under the name of Brúni, battered the King to death with his own club.

His nephew gave him a magnificent funeral, which is fully described by Saxo and in the 'Fragmentary History'. A great burial mound was built, and Harald was drawn into it in a chariot. The horse was killed, so that the King might drive or ride to Valhöll as he wished.

It is difficult to place Harald in history; some have assigned him to the sixth century, and some to the eighth or ninth.[11] Whether or not Harald ever lived, the story of his death shows the same conception as that of the historical Eirík Blood-axe, who was killed in England about the year 954. After Eirík's death, his widow, Gunnhild, commissioned an unnamed poet to make a memorial lay.[12] The poet told how Óðinn and fallen heroes welcomed the dead King in Valhöll. Óðinn had bereft Eirík of victory because he needed his support in case the Ragnarök should come. Already the grey wolf was glaring greedily at the dwellings of the gods. Closely similar conceptions are expressed in the *Hákonarmál*,[13] composed in memory of Hákon the Good, King of Norway, who lost his life a few years later than Eirík.

Hadding

We may finally consider the puzzling figure of Hadding (Hadingus), who stands closer to the world of gods than to that of men. Hadding's career is traced in detail by Saxo in Book I of his History of the Danes, with lavish quotations from poetry which show that Saxo relied largely on ready-made sources, probably of Norwegian or Icelandic provenance.[1]

Hadding was the son of Gram, King of Denmark, and, after his father had been killed by Svipdag, King of Norway, he was sent to Sweden, where he was brought up by giants. Hadding brooded on vengeance for his father, but was early seduced from this noble purpose by his giant foster-mother, Harðgreip (Harthgrepa), who quickened lust in his heart. It was she who had given him the breast and, therefore, as she said, she had claim to his first embraces.

Harðgreip was not only lustful, but also skilled in magic and necromancy, and forced a dead man to talk by cutting spells on a chip of wood and placing it under his tongue. Before long, however, she was torn to pieces by her own race, and it was after this that Hadding's heroic qualities developed. Óðinn now appeared in his life as a huge man with one eye. He prevailed on Hadding to enter a covenant of foster-brotherhood with a viking Liser. The ceremony was performed in traditional form, and the blood of the foster-brothers was mixed in their footprints.[2]

When Hadding and Liser were defeated by Loker, tyrant of the Kurlanders (Cureti), Óðinn rescued his favourite, carrying him off on his magical charger. He restored him with a draught and gave him useful advice. He would be captured by Loker, but using Óðinn's ruses, he would break his bonds. The god Óðinn, as he boasted in the *Hávamál* (str. 149) was expert in the use of spells for breaking bonds. Óðinn also told Hadding that he must kill a lion and devour its flesh and blood, from which he would gain strength. The introduction of the lion in Saxo's verse is surprising, and may replace another beast in his source. The underlying belief is the same as that expressed in several other legends. Sigurð acquired wisdom and vigour from the blood and heart of the dragon; his murderer, Guttorm, had to devour wolf's flesh and serpent's flesh before he had the manliness and cunning to commit his crime.[3]

Hadding later defeated and killed his father's slayer, Svipdag, and thus won his hereditary kingdom. Subsequently he enjoyed many of the conventional experiences of a viking, warring in Sweden and more distant lands of the north and east, but some of his adventures were out of the ordinary.

When he had fled to Helsingjaland, by the Gulf of Bothnia, after a defeat in battle, he slaughtered a monster of unknown kind, perhaps a *finngálkn*,[4] half man, half beast. A strange woman then appeared and cursed Hadding, for he had slain a bountiful god (*numinis almi*). He must suffer for his crime, as indeed he did. His fortunes were not restored until he propitiated the gods, evidently with human sacrifice.[5] This sacrifice was dedicated to Freyr, and afterwards became an annual one, called by the Swedes *Frøblot* (Sacrifice of Freyr).

Hadding's relations with giants were not yet over. He had heard that one of their tribe had raped Ragnhild (Regnilda), daughter of a king in Norway, and so he went to Norway and rescued her. The girl, grateful for her delivery, ministered to his wounds and, so that she might recognize him again, sealed up a ring in his leg. When she was later allowed by her father to choose a husband for herself, Ragnhild examined the legs of her suitors and selected Hadding.

While he was living with Ragnhild, Hadding had another mysterious experience. A woman appeared bearing some herbs. Wishing to know where such herbs grew in winter, Hadding went with this woman under the earth. They passed through mists, and then through sunny, fertile regions, where the herbs had grown. Then they came to a raging torrent, flowing with weapons. Crossing by a bridge, they came upon armies of fallen warriors, locked in eternal battle. As they pressed forward, a wall stood in their way; they could go no further, but the woman tore off the head of a cock, which she happened to have with her, and flung it over the wall. Immediately the cock came to life and crowed.

This interlude about Hadding's visit to the underworld runs off at a tangent in his story, but it contains a surprising number of notices commonly associated in Norse myth with the World of Death, or Hel. When Hermóð journeyed to Hel to ransom Baldr,[6] he travelled through dark deep valleys where he could see nothing. Like Hadding, Hermóð crossed a torrent, Gjöll, by a bridge and, in his story, the world of death was surrounded by a fence (*grind*). Thór, too, when he goes to the world of giants, which may be seen as the world of death, crosses mighty rivers.[7] The ever-fighting warriors can be no other than Óðinn's *einherjar*, whose home, in this case, is between the river and the wall of Hel. The decapitated cock is puzzling, but no less interesting. It has been said to represent the triumph of life over death[8] but, however that may be, he is reminiscent of some other poultry recorded in northern myth and history. In the *Vǫluspá* (strs. 42–3), we read of three cocks crowing at the approach of the Ragnarök. The second of these is 'Golden-combed' (Gullinkambi), and he awakens Óðinn's warriors. This cock must be the same as Salgofnir, who awakens the victorious band in Valhöll.[9]

Whatever its significance, the decapitated fowl figured in ritual as well as in myth. The Arab traveller, Ibn Fodlan, who watched the ship-funeral of a Norse chief in Russia early in the tenth century, remarked that the woman, who was to join him in death, cut off the head of a hen and threw it into the ship (see Ch. XV).

Saxo goes on to tell how Hadding returned to the world of the living and, once more, engaged in war. As he sailed off the coast of Norway, Óðinn beckoned to him from the shore, and boarded his ship, as he had once boarded that of Sigurð.[10] Óðinn instructed Hadding in deployment of his forces, as he also instructed Harald Wartooth. He informed him that he would never fall before an enemy, but would die by his own hand.

The story now returns to Hadding's relations with his wife, Ragnhild. They were like those between Njörð, god of the sea, and his giant wife, Skaði.[11] Like Njörð, Hadding declared that the rugged hills and howling wolves were hateful to him, while he yearned for the sea. His wife, in her turn, expressed her loathing of the shrieking seagulls.

Hadding's life ended as Óðinn had told him it would, but the circumstances were complicated. His friend, Hunding, King of the Swedes, had heard false reports that he was dead. Wishing to honour him, Hunding prepared a feast, and filled an enormous jar with beer. During the feast, Hunding fell into the liquor and drowned, as did Fjölnir, another legendary king of the Swedes (see Ch. IX).

When he heard of his friend's death, Hadding hanged himself in public.

Even from a sketch so brief as this, it must be plain that Saxo's story of Hadding contains many elements. In the past, many scholars have claimed to find an historical basis for the legendary figure, and identified him with the famous viking Hasting (Hæsten),[12] who was active in France and partly in England from 866 to 894.[13] Except that both lived as vikings, there is little but the superficial similarity of names to suggest that the two should be associated.

Hadding bears many of the marks of an Óðinn hero. Óðinn brought him into foster-brotherhood with the viking Liser. Óðinn rescued him in defeat, carrying him off on his supernatural horse. He taught him how to deploy his forces and to break his fetters, and assured him that he would never fall at the hands of an enemy. In the end, Hadding died as was fitting for an Óðinn hero, hanging himself in public.

But Hadding also has characteristics of another group of gods, the Vanir. As Freyr married the giantess Gerð, and Njörð the giantess Skaði, so Hadding took his bride from the giant world. Skaði chose her husband by his legs alone, and Ragnhild recognized Hadding by the ring locked in his leg.

Hadding told in verses of his hatred of the hills and the wolves and his attachment to the sea; while Ragnhild complained of the shrieking gulls by the shore. The verses which Saxo reproduces must be of the same origin as those which Snorri quotes, in which Njörð and Skaði complain in turn of the mountains and the seashore.[14]

It is widely held that the marriage myth was transferred from Njörd to Hadding,[15] largely because it accords better with other events in the story of Njörð. If this is so, it can only be because Hadding resembled Njörð so closely as to be confused, or even identified with him.

Hadding did not die an heroic death, but hanging on the gallows, he seems to sacrifice himself to Óðinn. Njörð, as King of the Swedes, died in his bed, but had himself 'marked for Óðinn', evidently with a spear-point, which would assure his entry into Valhöll.[16]

Njörð, at any rate in later tradition, is god of the sea and its wealth. Hadding lived the greater part of his life as a sea-rover, gloating over 'sea-gotten gains';[17] an Icelandic poet of the twelfth century seems also to refer to a legendary or mythical sea-king, Haddingr.[18]

There are some other reasons to associate Hadding with Njörð and the Vanir. The Vanir were, among other things, gods of sensuality and magic, and incest was practised among them. Njörð, before he came to dwell among the Æsir, had his own sister to wife,[19] and a similar charge was made against Freyja and her brother Freyr.[20] It is not told that Hadding lived in incest, but it is stated that his giant foster-mother claimed his embraces because it was she who had given him the breast.

Unlike Njörð and Freyr, Hadding was not married to a giantess, but he took his wife from the giant-world.

If any doubt should remain about Hadding's relations with the Vanir, it is dispelled when we learn that it was Hadding who established the annual festival which the Swedes called *Frøblot*, or 'Sacrifice of Freyr'.

It is plain that Hadding, as he is described by Saxo, combines the standard qualities of an Óðinn hero with the rarer characteristics of the Vanir, gods of fertility and riches. It would be interesting to know to which class of gods he was related fundamentally.

Hadding's name may help us to understand him. In Saxo's text he is called *Hadingus* but, as many have agreed, this can be no other than the name *Haddingr*, already quoted.[21] In a later passage (v, 166), Saxo himself names *duo Haddingi*, sons of the viking Arngrím. These appear in Icelandic sources as 'two Haddingjar' (*tveir Haddingjar*).[22] As already noted, the singular form of the name appears generally as *Haddingr*[23] and not, as might be expected, *Haddingi*.[24]

In fact, this name appears surprisingly often in the plural or dual. Of the 'two Haddingjar', already named, it was said in one text[25] that they were twins and could only do the work of one man. In a legendary genealogy of rulers of Norway, preserved in the *Flateyjarbók*[26] it is said: 'Hadding, son of Raumi, owned Haddingjadal and Thelamörk; his son was Hadding, father of Hadding, father of Högni the Red. After him three Haddingjar assumed authority, one after another. Helgi, Prince of the Haddings (*Haddingjaskati*) was with one of them.'

This last passage suggests that *Haddingjar* was believed in the Middle Ages to be the name of a dynasty which had founded and ruled Haddingjadal (now *Hallingdal*). This is supported by the name *Vallis Haddingorum* applied to that district in Latin.[27]

I have already mentioned Helgi, Prince of the Haddings (*Haddingjaskati*). The legends about him reach far back into antiquity. In the prose colophon to the 'Second Lady of Helgi Hundingsbani' (Slayer of Hunding), it is told that Helgi and his mistress, Sigrún, were believed to have been reborn. In her new life, Sigrún was called Kára, and Helgi's nickname was 'Prince of the Haddingjar'.[28] This was related in the poem *Káruljóð*. This last poem is lost, but its content seems to be reproduced in the so-called *Griplur,* a poetic sequence of the late Middle Ages, probably based on a lost saga.[29] Helgi there appears in the service of two kings of the Swedes, both called Haddingr.[30] His mistress appears as Kára,[31] and protects him in battle in the form of a swan. It is remarkable that in this text, as in others quoted, the Haddingjar are two, although they are sometimes more than two.

Further light may be thrown on these intricate problems by brief consideration of external sources. The lines of the Old English *Runic Poem* applied to the rune *Ing* (*NG*) read:

Ing wæs ærest	mid East-Denum
gesewen secgun,	oþ he siððan est
ofer wæg gewat;	wæn æfter ran;
ðus Heardingas	ðone hæle nemdun.

Ing was first seen by men among the East-Danes, till, followed by his car, he departed eastwards over the waves. So the Heardingas named the hero.[32]

Philologically the name *Heardingas* corresponds closely with *Haddingjar* (or *Haddingar*) and must, in these lines, be used as the name of a tribe or a dynasty. It is particularly interesting to read that the Heardingas were worshippers of the charioted god Ing, who is hardly other than Freyr. This implies that they pursued the cult of the fertility gods, the Vanir, as Saxo's Hadding was said to do.

Dynastic and tribal names need not be confined to one dynasty, one tribe, but may be transferred from one to another. The Heardingas mentioned in the *Runic Poem* appear to have dwelt among the eastern Danes. Their name corresponds also with that of another tribe, or more likely a dynasty, mentioned in older continental sources. It is told that in the latter half of the second century, a people called *Asdingi* or *Hasdingi* appeared in the region of Hungary.[33] They were led by two chieftains, Raos and Raptos, and probably belonged to a branch of the Vandals.

The names of the Hasding leaders are certainly surprising, since they seem to mean 'Reed' (O.N. *reyrr*) and 'Rafter' (O.N. *raptr*), names which might better be applied to primitive idols than to men. We could, however, suppose that the names of the idols or gods were used as titles for the joint leaders of the Hasdingi, just as all members of the ruling house of the Swedes took the title *Yngvi* or *Ynguni*.[34]

It is not stated in our poor sources that Raos and Raptos were brothers, or twins like the Haddingjar, but if their names were originally those of gods, it would not be rash to suppose that they represented a divine pair. The worship of divine brothers is recorded among other eastern Germans. The Naharvali, of whose religious practices Tacitus wrote a few words,[35] maintained a holy grove. They had no images or idols, but they worshipped two gods, conceived as brothers and young men. These, according to Tacitus, corresponded with Castor and Pollux, but in the German language they were called *Alcis*. This last name is too obscure to form the basis of argument, but is perhaps related to Gothic *alhs* (temple) and Old English *ealgian* (to protect).

However that may be, the Alcis were, like the Haddingjar, brothers and perhaps, like Castor and Pollux, twins. The priests who ministered to the Alcis were *muliebri ornatu*, which probably implies that they wore some emblem, rather than the full dress of women.[36] Some of the Lappish priests, it is said, used to wear a woman's hat or headdress.[37]

We may return to the Haddingjar, brothers, even twins who could only do the work of one. Their name has been variously explained, but most have agreed that it is related to the O.N. *haddr*[38] which, in the contexts where it is used, rarely if ever means other than 'a woman's coiffure'.[39] In other words, the name *Haddingjar* means 'those with their hair dressed as women'. This suggests not only that they were thought of as priests, but as priests of a distinct rite, and as such they would be divine, even incarnate gods.

It has been seen that Hadding and the Heardingas practised the cult of the Vanir. If so, it is not surprising that they should have feminine characteristics, for the Vanir were gods of voluptuary rather than of war. We may remember how the warlike Starkað, residing in Uppsala among the sons of Freyr, was disgusted at the effeminate gestures and the unmanly jingling of bells which accompanied the sacrifices.[40] We may remember too, that the Vanir originated the practice of *seiðr*, a kind of witchcraft which was accompanied by gross *ergi*,[41] a term covering homosexuality and every kind of unmanly practice.[42]

It could be objected that we have no evidence that the Haddingjar wore women's clothes, or had their hair dressed as women. Dumézil[43] has pointed out that Helgi, the Slayer of Hunding, who was also Prince of the Haddingjar, once escaped his pursuers by putting on the clothes of a bondwoman and turning the mill. In the *Griplur*,[44] the same story is told of Helgi's antagonist, Hrómund.

It is a more weighty objection that the Hadding (Hadingus) whose story Saxo tells is only one. Indeed, he had a brother, Guthorm, but he quickly vanishes from the story. It is as if Saxo, or the source which he used, had dropped one of the Haddingjar brothers because the concept of dual chieftainship was a thing of the past and was no longer understood.

In general, it appears that the Haddingjar were twin gods or divine ancestors, comparable with the Alcis, and perhaps with Hengest and Horsa, founders of the English nation.[45] They may thus be related ultimately to other legendary and mythical pairs in the Germanic world and far beyond it. We may think, not only of Castor and Pollux, but also of Romulus and Remus and the Indian Asvins, who were also said to be twins.

In this chapter we have read a few stories of kings and heroes, who appear, in one way or another, to be dedicated to divinities and protected by them. Some of them, like the Haddingjar, should perhaps be seen as gods rather than as men. Of others, including Harald Wartooth, we may say, in the words of the *Hyndluljóð* (str. 28) :

þeir váru gumnar   These warriors
goðum signaðir   were dedicated to gods.

The stories quoted in this chapter may have little basis in history, but the practice of dedicating a child to a god is well attested in historical records. In the *Eyrbyggja Saga* (Ch. VII) it is told that a boy was born and called Steinn, but his father 'gave' him to Thór, and so he was called Thorsteinn. The father himself was called Hrólf, but he was such an ardent worshipper of Thór that he was known as Thórólf (see Ch. III).

Such practices as these, if we may judge by a 'learned' passage in the fourteenth-century *Hauksbók*[46] were common enough in pagan times, and those who had the names of gods compounded with their own names were assured of good fortune and long life.

CHAPTER ELEVEN

GUARDIAN SPIRITS

The Dísir—Fylgja and Hamingja—Elves, Earth-spirits

The Dísir

POETS AND SAGA-WRITERS frequently mention female deities of a kind called *dísir* (sing. *dís*), and although they never describe them clearly they give some idea of their place in religious life.

A festival called the *dísablót* (sacrifice to the *dísir*) was held in their honour in autumn, or at the beginning of winter, the 'winter-nights',[1] and it was the occasion of heavy drinking.[2]

The festival was sometimes held in a private house,[3] but more than once mention is made of a *dísarsalr*, 'hall of the *dís* (sing.)', in which the sacrifice was performed.[4] Little is told about the form of the sacrifice, but according to the romantic *Heiðreks Saga*,[5] a woman reddened, or smeared sacrificial blood on the altar (*hǫrgr*) late at night.

According to the *Víga-Glúms Saga* (Ch. V) many gathered in the same house to celebrate the festival of the *dísir*, but these were friends and relations of the master of the house, and the festival seems generally to be private rather than public, at least in western Scandinavia.[6]

This suggests that the *dísir* were tutelary goddesses attached to one neighbourhood, one family, perhaps even to one man. Texts in which they are mentioned lend some support to this suggestion. A hero speaks in verse of 'our *dísir*',[7] and a woman, interpreting a dream, speaks of the *dísir* of her husband as 'thy *dísir*'.[8]

In passages like these, the *dísir* are hardly to be distinguished from the *fylgjur*, attendant spirits who protect an individual or a clan. Indeed, medieval writers sometimes identified the two, as in the story of Thiðrandi, which will be quoted below, where the word *dísir* interchanges with *fylgjur*; by the time the literary sources took shape, the conception of the *dísir* had grown hazy. In poetry the word *dísir* is occasionally applied to valkyries, who are called *Herjans dísir* (Óðinn's *dísir*), and by similar epithets. Remorseful for having killed their brother, the heroes, Hamðir and Sörli, said: 'the *dísir* incited us to this'.[9] For them the *dísir* can be no other than valkyries.[10]

Elsewhere, poets use the word *dísir* as if it meant 'norns', or fate-goddesses who attend the birth of every child.[11] In scaldic kennings the word is used basically to mean 'goddess'.[12] In heroic and encomiastic poetry it is occasionally applied to earthly women, and especially to those of high rank. In this usage poets were probably influenced by the Old High German *itis* or Old English *ides* ('woman', also 'virgin').[13] This word was long regarded as the same as O.N. *dís* but, because of philological difficulties, later scholars have favoured another etymology.[14] Even if not related, the words *ides* and *dís* are sufficiently alike for the poetical usage of the first to influence that of the second.

An instructive account of the *dísir*, apocryphal as it is, is given in the story of Thiðrandi,[15] who, according to *Njáls Saga*[16] was killed by the *dísir*. The scene of this story is south-eastern Iceland, shortly before the country was converted to Christianity in the year AD 1000.

Thorhall the Prophet (*spámaðr*), a settler from Norway, was a friend of Hall of Síða, who was to be one of the first chieftains to adopt Christianity and one of its most fervent protagonists. Hall's eldest son, Thiðrandi, is presented as the noble pagan, and a man of stainless character, who lived as a merchant, travelling from land to land.

One summer, Thorhall the Prophet was staying with Hall, and Thiðrandi was also present. As the summer drew on, the prophet grew ever more downcast; he was apprehensive about the approaching autumn feast, which his host was to hold. He had a premonition that a prophet (*spámaðr*) would be killed, but his host reassured him, saying that he had selected an ox for slaughter, and the ox was called 'Prophet' (*Spámaðr*).[17] Thorhall did not fear for his own life, but he apprehended disaster.

The feast was held at the 'winter-nights', and few attended because the weather was boisterous. Thorhall warned the household not to go out during the night, nor open the door, even if anyone knocked.

After the feasters had gone to bed there was a knock at the door, and Thiðrandi, disregarding the warning, opened it and took his sword. He saw no one, and went out to look round; he heard the sound of horses galloping from the north, and beheld nine women, dressed in black with drawn swords riding towards him. Looking to the south, he saw another group of nine women; these were dressed in shining raiment, and mounted on white horses. Thiðrandi turned back to the house, but the black-dressed women caught him up. He defended himself manfully, but they gave him a mortal wound. He was carried home and died after telling his tale on the next morning.

It was left to Thorhall the Prophet to explain these marvels. 'It is my belief,' he said, 'that these were not women, but the attendant spirits of your family (*fylgjur yðrar frænda*). After this, as I believe, there will be a change of religion, and a better one will come to this land. I think that those *dísir* of yours, who have adhered to the old religion (*þessum átrúnaði*), knew of the change beforehand, and they took Thiðrandi as their portion. The better *disir* wished to help him, but they could not do so as things stood . . .'

This story is preserved in the conflated version of the Saga of Ólaf Tryggvason. It has been said that it was written by the Benedictine monk, Gunnlaug Leifsson (died 1218).[18] In any case, it is a clerical piece, stamped with missionary ardour. Its Christian elements have been carefully sifted by D. Strömbäck.[19] It is a story of conflict between the Christian and heathen religions, between good and evil. The *disir* have assumed the characters of good and evil angels, the divine and Satanic guardians of medieval legend. They are like the hosts of angels who proceed from Heaven and Hell, struggling for a man's soul at the time of death. The better *disir* resemble the armies of *Revelation* (XIX), mounted on horses, clothed in linen pure and white.

But for all the Christian colouring, the story contains elements which cannot be explained from Christian legend, and it gives an insight into the pagan conceptions of the *disir*.

We learn, in the first place, that the *disir* are attached to one family. It was seen already that they might attend on one man, and it is not difficult to understand why Christian apologists should equate them with guardian angels, good and bad, who accompany everyone. We learn also that Thiðrandi was taken at the 'winter-nights', a time when a feast was held and it was customary to offer sacrifice to the *disir*. Although few were present, the seasonal feast was held on this occasion, but it is not told that any tribute was paid to the *disir*. Although still pagans, those who take part in this story are all described as upright and good men, far in advance of their contemporaries in Iceland. Even before Christianity came to Iceland, Hall was the trusted friend of Ólaf Tryggvason.[20] Thiðrandi had lately travelled in foreign lands and the author of the story sees him as a man inspired by Christian charity, 'gentle with every child'. Thorhall the Prophet showed that he was waiting for a better religion, despising the one in which he had been brought up.

The troop of black-clad women thus represent traditional heathendom, and the author creates a counterpart, the white-clad *disir*, who had not power to rescue their favourite in a pagan land. The black-clad *disir* knew well that a new religion was on the way, but they were not prepared to be neglected or to forfeit the tribute, which they were accustomed to receive at the winter-nights. Defrauded of ox-blood, they seized as their portion the eldest and most promising son of the house.[21]

As I have remarked, the *disir* are once called *fylgjur* in the story of Thiðrandi. Both *disir* and *fylgjur* were often described as female tutelary spirits and, although they are sometimes difficult to distinguish, certain fundamental differences are apparent.

Unlike the *fylgjur*, the *dísir* were the object of a cult, receiving sacrifice at regular times. The season of their festival was the winter-nights, but they were not the only deities who accepted sacrifice at that time. It is said in the *Gísla Saga* (X):

> Now summer passed and the time of the winter-nights arrived. It was then the custom of many to greet the winter, holding feasts and a winter-night sacrifice. Gísli had given up sacrifice since he had been at Viborg in Denmark, but he kept up his feasts and all his munificence just as before.

In a later chapter of the same saga (XV), we learn something about the purpose of the winter-night feast:

> Thorgrím Freysgoði (Priest of Freyr) intended to hold an autumn feast, to greet the winter and to sacrifice to Freyr.[22]

It was the custom to offer sacrifice to Freyr for fruitful harvest and peace (*til árs ok friðar*) as well as on the occasion of marriage. It was the ithyphallic Freyr who governed peace and bestowed sensual pleasure.[23]

Such considerations lead us to suspect that the *dísir* were, from one aspect, goddesses of fertility. This suspicion grows stronger when we remember that the fertility goddess, Freyja, is called *Vanadís* (*dís* of the Vanir);[24] she is the supreme *dís*, whose help should be sought in love.

The *dísir* are sometimes closely associated with women. A woman, according to the *Heiðreks Saga*, took the leading part in their worship, smearing the altar with blood, and another woman named in the same saga, hanged herself in the hall of the *dís* (*dísarsalr*).[25] It is not extravagant to suppose that one of the functions of the *dísir* was to support the clan by promoting the fertility of its women.

As shown in the story of Thiðrandi, the *dísir* may turn against their ward and withdraw their support. Before King Geirrøð fell on his sword, Óðinn said to him: 'the *dísir* are angry'.[26]

Sometimes the *dísir* are said to be dead, and therefore powerless to help. When the Norwegian hero, Útsteinn, boasted that the *dísir* of his band had come to Denmark, his enemy answered: 'for you all the *dísir* are dead'.[27] A more illuminating passage is found in the Greenland 'Lay of Atli'. Before the hero Gunnar set out on his perilous journey to Atli, his wife told him of a foreboding dream:

Konur hugðak dauðar	I dreamed that dead women
koma í nótt hingat,	came here tonight;
væri vart búnar,	they were sadly clothed,
vildi þik kjósa,	and wished to take you;

bjóði þér brálliga	they bade you come quickly
til bekkja sinna:	to their own homes;
ek kveð aflima	I say that powerless
orðnar þér dísir.	are the *dísir* for you.[28]

In this last passage, the *dísir* are dead women, calling the hero to join them in the world of the dead; they are probably dead female ancestors. It is described in other texts how the dead call doomed men to join them,[29] and the poet, Björn Hítdœlakappi, seems to speak of a *dís* who calls him home.[30] As is shown in many other sources, fertility cults cannot always be dissociated from the cult of the dead.

The word *dís* is not an uncommon element in place-names. Here and there, in north-western Iceland, rocks are called *Landdísasteinar* (stones of the land-*dísir*). Until recently it was forbidden to mow, or for children to play around them.[31] In such cases it looks as if the *dísir* were identified with the *landvættir*, the protecting spirits of the land.

The name *Disahrøys* (*hrøys*, stone-pile) is also recorded in Norway.[32] Another name, *Disin*, probably from *Dísavin* (meadow of the *dísir*), is applied to no less than five places in the south-east of Norway. Some of these stand close to places whose names contain the element *Þór-*, *Ull-* (*Ullinn-*), gods with whom the *dísir* were perhaps associated. The element *vin*, in place-names, appears to date from the prehistoric period, and was often applied to places of public worship. This suggests that the cult of the *dísir* was of great age, at least in south-eastern Norway. Association with the god Ullr (or Ullinn), almost a prehistoric figure, supports this suggestion.[33] The names *Diseberg* (rock of the *dísir*) and *Disevi* (temple, sanctuary of the *dísir*) are also recorded in Östergötland (Sweden).[34]

The names last mentioned may imply that, in eastern regions, the cult of the *dísir* was more public than it was in the west. Literary sources give strong evidence of this. The *dísablót*, held in the house of the King, according to *Heiðreks Saga*,[35] was in Álfheimar, said to lie in the extreme east of Norway. The *disarsalr*, where, according to the same saga, the Queen hanged herself, stood in Reiðgotaland, which may be Jutland but is, in any case, in the east. The traditions underlying the *Heiðreks Saga* are vague and untrustworthy, but greater faith may be placed in those which underlie the *Ynglinga Tal*, *Ynglinga Saga* and *Historia Norvegiae* (see Ch. I).

According to the *Ynglinga Saga* (Ch. XXIX): 'Aðils (King of the Swedes) was present at a sacrifice to the *dísir* (*disablót*) and, as he rode his horse around the hall of the *dís* (*disarsalr*), the horse stumbled, and the King fell forward, striking his head on a stone. His skull was broken, and the King's brains were left on the stone'.

The same story is given, although with fewer details, in the *Historia Norvegiae*,[36] where the hall of the *dís* is called *Ædes Dianæ*.

As Snorri tells it in the *Ynglinga Saga*, the story is based largely on the poem *Ynglinga Tal* of the late ninth century. In the poem, the circumstances of the King's death are substantially the same as they are in the sagas, but it is caused by the 'witch' (*vitta véttr*), who must be identified with the *dís* or the goddess Diana of the *Historia*. Whether or not the sudden death of the King was a royal sacrifice,[37] it seems clear that the term *dís* is here applied to a single goddess. This goddess, like the dead *dísir* of the *Atlamál*, had called the King to join her. If she is not herself dead, she is the goddess of death. Since Uppsala was certainly the scene of King Aðils's death, and this was the centre of the cult of the Vanir, it is not rash to suppose that we have here to do with the *Vanadís*, Freyja, and that the sacrifice at which the King met his end was a fertility sacrifice.

Far-reaching conclusions have been drawn from an earlier passage in the *Ynglinga Tal* (str. 7) in which the poet, speaking of a mythical King Dyggvi, who died in his bed, says:

Kveðkat dul,	nema Dyggva hrør
Glitnis Gná	at gamni hefr;
þvít jódís	Ulfs ok Nara
konungmann	kjósa skyldi;
ok allvald	Yngva þjóðar
Loka mær	at leikum (?) hefr.

These lines could be rendered tentatively: 'I tell no secret, the horse-goddess has taken the corpse of Dyggvi for her delight; for the *jódís* of Ulf and Nari chose the king; and the daughter of Loki has the ruler of the people of Yngvi as her plaything.'

The *jódís* of Ulf and Nari is here identified with the 'goddess' of the horse' (*Glitnis Gná*), and with the daughter of Loki, i.e. the goddess of death, Hel. Formally, *jódís* could mean 'horse-*dís*' and this is how many commentators have interpreted it.[38]

Freyja is the supreme *dís*; she is goddess of fertility and sister of the chief fertility god, Freyr. The horse is a symbol of Freyr and his fertility and, at the same time, the symbol of death,[39] and this explains why Hel is the 'goddess of the horse'. In the story of Thiðrandi the *dísir* angels of death were seen mounted, as were many other apparitions foreboding death.

It would be interesting to know whether female deities comparable with the *dísir* were venerated in continental Germany and England. As remarked, philologists doubt whether the word *dís* should be equated with the Old English and Old High German words *ides* and *itis* (woman). Consequently the *itis*, the women, who, according to the first Merseburg Charm,[40] cast spells inhibiting warriors, need not be the same as the *dísir*.

There are, however, stronger reasons to associate the *dísir* with the *matres* and *matronae*, whose cult was practised widely in Celtic and Germanic areas. *Matres* and *matronae*, carved in relief, are depicted on votive stones in Roman style, some of them dated as early as the first century of our era. These stones are most numerous on the left bank of the Lower Rhine, but examples are also found in Gaul, northern Italy and England.[41] Commonly three female figures are shown, holding baskets of fruit and occasionally giving suck to children.

Some of the *matres* are denoted in the accompanying inscriptions by local or tribal names, e.g. *matres Suebiae*, *matres Frisiavae paternae*, and sometimes they have more functional names, such as *Alagabiae* (lavish giver?), *Afliae* (cf O.N. *afl*, power).

Bede,[42] in his list of names by which the ancient English called their months, mentions a festival which English heathens used to celebrate at the Christmas season. They called this festival *modranect*, i.e. *matrum noctem*. Bede was, no doubt, thinking of the festival of the *matres*, who may be thought of as departed ancestors, assuring the welfare and prosperity of their descendants. The *dísir* were also described as 'dead women'; the deities of death and fertility are often linked and even identified.

Fylgja and Hamingja

In the story of Thiðrandi, the *dísir* were once called *fylgjur* (sing. *fylgja*). In the mind of the author, the two words must have been synonyms, or nearly so, and there are several texts which show how the conceptions underlying them tended to converge, although they were originally distinct.

Dís and *fylgja* might both be translated loosely as 'guardian-spirit, attendant', but some of the texts in which they are mentioned reveal fundamental differences between them. It is also noteworthy that, while *dís-* is fairly commonly used as an element in place-names, *fylgja* does not appear in them. The *dísir* plainly filled a more important place in religious life than the *fylgjur* did.

The *dísir* were objects of a cult, and their festival, the *dísablót*, was held at regular times. They were superior beings, detached from man, although standing in close relationship to an individual, a family or a community. Men must revere them or else incur their wrath.

The *fylgjur*, on the other hand, do not appear as the objects of a cult, and we never read of a festival held in their honour. They stood in closer relation to man than the *dísir* and, in origin, they were part of him. The word *fylgja* could perhaps be translated more precisely as 'fetch'.[1]

The origin of the word *fylgja* has been disputed. Formally, it could be nom. agentis of the verb *fylgja* (to accompany), and that was how some medieval writers understood it. But whether this is correct or not, the word cannot be dissociated from its homonym *fylgja*, which means 'afterbirth, caul'. This noun could also be derived from the verb, but it is more likely to be related to Icelandic *fulga* (thin covering of hay) and Norwegian dialect *folga* (skin, covering), and with the verb *fela* (to hide).[2]

However that may be, the superstitious practices recorded in Iceland in recent times show how intimately the beliefs in the afterbirth were associated with those in the fetch. The afterbirth was believed to contain a part of the infant's 'soul', which was incomplete until it had been released. It must, therefore be tended carefully, and not thrown out into the open, where animals might devour it, for then the child will be deprived of its fetch.[3] Beliefs of this kind are not confined to Iceland, but have been noticed among many peoples. For some of them, the afterbirth is not merely associated with the fetch; it is the fetch, or a twin brother who accompanies a man throughout life and defends him against danger.[4]

In early Icelandic stories the fetch is rarely visible except to men gifted with second sight, at the moment of death, and especially in dreams.[5] It takes the form of a woman, or more often of an animal. Its introduction at times of stress and before inpending disaster was used in Icelandic literature as a standard literary motive.

The fetch is not necessarily the companion of one man. It may accompany a family, or pass from one member of it to another through succeeding generations. In such cases its most usual form is that of a woman.

The conception of the family fetch may be illustrated by a story told in the *Hallfreðar Saga* (XI). Hallfreð, the favourite poet of Ólaf Tryggvason, fell ill at sea, and just before he died he and his companions beheld a great, armoured woman walking on the waves, as if on land. Recognizing the woman as his fetch (*fylgjukona*), the poet exclaimed: 'I declare that all is now over between us.' The woman now turned to the poet's brother, asking her to receive him, but he rejected her curtly. She passed on to the poet's son, who shared his father's name, Hallfreð, and when he welcomed her she vanished.

In other cases, the family fetch may protect those to whom she is obliged. In the *Vatnsdæla Saga* (XXXVI), a hero had undertaken to attend a party at which a sorceress plotted his death. For three succeeding nights 'the woman who had accompanied his family' appeared to him in sleep, warning him of the danger. In the end she touched his eyes, causing an illness which prevented him from going to the party, thus saving his life.

There are many more stories in which the fetch takes the form of an animal, and to see one's fetch in animal form is an omen of death. Before he was killed, Thórð, fosterer of the sons of Njáll, saw a goat covered with blood, but there was no goat, and the wise Njáll knew that Thórð was doomed.[6]

It is more often others who see a man's fetch, and especially his relations or enemies. If they have second sight, they may see it in a waking state, but it generally appears in dreams.

The form which a man's animal fetch takes is determined by his character, or rather by the estimate which those who see it make of his character. Before Guðmund the Mighty, chieftain of Eyjafjörð, died in 1025, his brother dreamed of a huge ox walking up the fjord. The ox dropped dead when he reached the high seat on Guðmund's farm.[7]

Sometimes whole herds of cattle appear in dreams, and each one is the fetch of a man. An old woman once dreamed of a herd of cattle, all of different colours and sizes, goring each other to death. These cattle were all fetches of men who appear in the saga, and the dream was a portent of manslaughter and a feud which was to plague two families through succeeding generations.[8]

Fetches often appear as bears, especially those of brave and noble men, such as Gunnar of Hlíðarendi and Örvar-Odd.[9] Those plotting attack are seen by their enemies as wolves. If the assailants are particularly sly and vicious, they may take the form of foxes.[10] In one passage a doomed man dreams of his own fetch in the form of a chestnut, i.e. a blood-coloured horse.[11] Fetches appear also as birds, eagles, swans, hawks. In less realistic sagas a whole menagerie of animals appears as fetches of men, and they include such exotic beasts as lions, leopards, etc. The influence of French romances, in which such beasts also appear as men's fetches is apparent.[12]

The fetch (*fylgja*) may be comparable with the 'soul' (*sál*), a word used by Norse Christian writers, for which the pagans had no exact equivalent.[13] The 'soul' is personified, even materialized, and lives a life of its own. Another word, *hugr*, which is often translated by 'thought, mind' is occasionally used in a concrete sense, synonymous with *fylgja*. Wolves and other vicious beasts seen in dreams are said to be *manna hugir* ('minds' of men).[14] The god Óðinn has two ravens, Huginn and

Muninn, who fly over the world every day, and may be his 'thought' and 'memory' in concrete form.[15]

Although the word *fylgja* is generally used in such concrete senses as those quoted, it also developed a more abstract meaning, and thus became nearly synonymous with *gipta, gæfa*, words which are often translated by 'luck, fortune', but imply rather a kind of inherent, inborn force. When a man says of his enemies: *hafa þeir bræðr rammar fylgjur*,[16] he does not mean that they have 'strong fetches', but rather that they are gifted with a mighty, inborn force. When the Jarl Rögnvald said to his son: *liggja fylgjur þínar til Íslands*, he meant only that his son's destiny lay in Iceland. Similarly, the word *kynfylgja*, which formally could mean 'family fetch', is recorded only in abstract senses, such as 'inherited gift, characteristic or failing'.[17]

The use of the word *hamingja* is comparable with that of *fylgja*. It is compounded with *hamr* (skin, shape), which is occasionally used to mean 'fetch'.[18] *Hamingja* is generally used in abstract senses of 'inborn force, luck'. But when a man 'lends' his *hamingja* to another,[19] as kings often do, the sense is more nearly concrete. More rarely, the *hamingja* is personified, and the word is applied to a female fetch. The hero, Glúm, dreamed on his farm in Iceland of a gigantic woman, who walked up the fjord towards his house, her shoulders brushing the mountains on either side. He knew that his maternal grandfather must have died in Norway, and the woman was his *hamingja*, or fetch, who had come to join his descendant in Iceland.[20]

Elves, earth-spirits, dwarfs

As will be seen in Ch. XII, a chieftain living in Iceland brought sacrifice to a rock, believing that it was the home of his *ármaðr*, who assured his prosperity, or of his *spámaðr*, who told him of things to come.

The man in the rock has something in common with an elf (*álfr*). It is told in an early saga how a man wounded in a duel was healed by elves (*álfar*). On the advice of a wise woman he bought the carcase of an ox, which had been ceremonially slaughtered on the duelling field. He smeared the blood of the ox on a mound or hillock inhabited by elves, and gave them a feast of its meat.[1]

Turning from Iceland to south-western Sweden, we hear of another sacrifice to elves, or *álfablót*. St Ólaf's favourite poet, Sigvat, went on a mission through the forests in that region about the year 1019, and left a record of his adventures in a series of verses which still survive.[2]

The natives, unchristian and inhospitable, drove the poet from their homes. He came to one farm and the housewife was standing in the doorway; she told him to make off, for she feared the wrath of Óðinn.

Her household was heathen and she was holding a sacrifice to the elves. The expressions used by Sigvat lead us to think that the housewife herself was conducting the sacrifice, just as women were seen sometimes to conduct the sacrifice to the *dísir* and to the deified priapus, Völsi.[3] It appears to be a private festival, to which no strangers were admitted.

The *álfablót* took place at the beginning of winter, about the same time as the *dísablót*, the sacrifice to Freyr and to the Völsi. It appears thus to be a sacrifice for fertility. It was seen in Ch. IX how sacrifice was offered to a dead king, Ólaf, for fruitful harvest. This king came to be called 'the elf of Geirstaðir' (*Geirstaðaálfr*).

Other instances are recorded of sacrifice to dead kings and chieftains (cf Ch. IX), but the nickname 'elf' applied to Ólaf, suggests that elves, dwelling in mounds, had come to be identified with the dead. In this case they may be male counterparts of the *dísir*. In support of this last suggestion it may be added that the woman who reddened the altar during the *dísablót* was called *Álfhildr*; she was daughter of *Álfr*, King of *Álfheimar*, said to lie in the extreme east of Norway.[4]

Snorri,[5] perhaps over-schematically, distinguished two kinds of elves, light elves (*ljósálfar*) and dark elves (*døkkálfar*). The dark elves were black as pitch and lived underground, but the light elves were more beautiful than the sun, and lived in a splendid place called *Álfheimr* (Elf-world). Snorri seems to describe two aspects of the elves; they are the dead and, at the same time the promoters of fertility; they are beautiful and hideous at once.

This is supported by the *Grímnismál* (str. 5), where it is said that the gods (*tívar*) gave *Álfheimr* to Freyr when he cut his first tooth. It was seen in earlier chapters how intimately the Vanir, gods of fertility and riches, were associated with death. The life-giving, fertilizing sun was sometimes called *álfröðull* (ray of the elves), almost as if the elves had made it.

Elves are often named in poetry together with Æsir, and occasionally both with Æsir and Vanir. The elves (*ylfa*, gen. pl.) are also coupled with Æsir (*esa*) in an Old English charm. This suggests that, in early times, they had stood nearly on a par with these great tribes of gods.

The light elves were beautiful, and the dark elves were black. Álfhild of Álfheimar, who was raped by the giant, was the most beautiful of women, and all people of that region were more beautiful than others.

These two aspects of the elves, the beautiful and the hideous and wicked, were shared by English tradition. In *Beowulf* (line 112) they are grouped with the monsters *eotenas* and *orcneas*, and they are also named with other evil beings. At the same time, an adjective *ælfsciene* (beautiful as an elf) is recorded several times in Old English texts.

It is an old and widespread belief that elves cause illnesses, and Old English terminology is rich in expressions which show this. *Ælfsiden* is said to mean 'a nightmare', and *ælfsogoða* 'hiccoughs'. *Ylfagescot* (elf-shot) is applied to certain diseases of men and beasts.[6] In Norwegian the term *alvskot* is given to various diseases and in Icelandic a form of skin disease in animals is called *álfabruni* (elf-burn).[7]

The *álfar* have survived into modern times as hidden beings, hardly to be distinguished from the *huldufólk*, the hidden people or fairies.[8]

The land-spirits or *landvættir* were even more closely attached to the soil than the elves; the welfare of the land, and thus of its inhabitants, depended largely upon them.

It is laid down in the first clause of the pagan law of Iceland, introduced about AD 930, that no one may approach the country in ships furnished with gaping heads and yawning snouts, i.e. dragon-heads. If they had them they must remove them before they came in sight of land, for otherwise the *landvættir* would take fright.

A similar conception of the *landvættir* appears in the *Egils Saga* (LVII), probably the work of Snorri (see Ch. I). The Icelandic poet, Egill, had been outlawed in Norway by Eirík Bloodaxe and his vicious Queen Gunnhild. Before he left Norway, Egill went up onto an island off the coast of Hörðaland. He fixed a horse's head on a hazel-pole and turned it towards land, saying: 'here I set up a pole of hatred (*niðstǫng*). I direct this hatred to King Eirík and Queen Gunnhild; I direct it to the *landvættir*[9] who inhabit this land, so that all of them shall lose their way, none of them find nor reach his home until they drive King Eirík and Gunnhild from the land'. The curse was inscribed in runes on the pole, and the gaping horse-head seems to fill the place of a dragon prow.

A more puzzling story is told in the *Landnámabók*.[10] As will be seen in Ch. XIV, a godless settler, Hjörleif, was murdered by Irish thralls on Hjörleifshöfði, a headland in the extreme south of Iceland. For some time afterwards no one dared to appropriate land in that region because of the *landvættir*. Perhaps they feared that the *landvættir* were angry because blood had been shed on their territory. They might also have feared that the *landvættir* had taken fright and that the land would not prosper.

The *landvættir* had their favourites. A certain Björn, nicknamed Goat-Björn, was short of livestock. He dreamed that a rock-dweller (*bergbúi*) came to him and offered his partnership. Soon afterwards a billy-goat joined Björn's goats; they multiplied and Björn grew rich. Second-sighted people used to see all the *landvættir* with Björn when they went to the assembly, and with his brothers when they were out fishing.[11]

Little is told of the appearance of the *landvættir* except in a rather apocryphal story given by Snorri.[12] Harald Gormsson, King of the Danes (died 986), having a grudge against the Icelanders, hired a wizard to go to their country in the form of a whale. When he reached the first fjord in Iceland, the whale saw that the mountains and hillocks were full of *landvættir*. In the first fjord he met a dragon, with other crawling monsters, who spewed poison on him. In the next fjord he met an enormous bird, whose wings brushed the mountains on both sides,[13] followed by other birds, large and small. In another fjord he faced a bull, which waded out to sea, bellowing terribly. Finally he met a rock-giant (*bergrisi*), standing higher than the hills, carrying an iron pole. A lot of other giants were with him. After this the whale made off.

This tale shows how the *landvættir* protected the land in which they dwelt. The symbols, however, appear to be largely Christian. It is told in a homily of the twelfth century, preserved both in Icelandic and Norwegian manuscripts, that the four evangelists were denoted by symbols of this kind. Matthew's symbol was a man, Luke's an ox, John's an eagle, while Mark's was a lion. These symbols, as the Norse homilist knew, derived from *Revelation* (IV) and ultimately from *Ezekiel* (X). The homily was intended to be read on the feast of St John the Evangelist, and Snorri probably heard it every year.[14]

In the next chapter I shall mention men in many parts of Scandinavia who venerated stones, waterfalls and trees and other natural objects. Many more examples could be given, and the sources seem to show that the objects were venerated, not for themselves, but for the protective beings, sometimes called *landvættir*, who lived in them.

Like the *álfar* and other minor deities, the *landvættir* survived the Conversion. Under a Norwegian law of the late thirteenth century, it was forbidden to believe that *landvættir* lived in groves, mounds and water-falls (see p. 237). A more detailed statement is found in the *Hauksbók*,[15] of the early fourteenth century. This is included in a homily traceable to Cæsarius of Arles, to which the Norse redactor has made an addition. He says that some women are so stupid as to take their food to stone-piles and into caves. They consecrate it to the *landvættir* and then eat it, believing that the *landvættir* will be friendly to them, and they will be more prosperous. The practice appears to be a debased form of communion.

The dwarfs (*dvergar*), as already seen, played some part in myth and a greater one in story, but there is little to suggest that they were venerated. They are remembered chiefly as craftsmen; they brewed the mead of poetry (see Ch. II, God of Poetry), and were renowned as forgers of costly treasures. These included the golden hair of Thór's wife, Sif, Óðinn's spear, Gungnir and, most wonderful of all, Thór's hammer,

Mjöllnir.[16] The *Grímnismál*[17] tells also how the dwarfs, sons of Ívaldi, built Freyr's ship, Skíðblaðnir. This ship could carry all the Æsir in full armour; she always had a following wind, and was made of so many pieces that she could be folded up and carried in a purse. Sometimes, when dwarfs were compelled to forge treasures, or surrender them, they laid a curse on them. The gold which Sigurð was to seize from the dragon, Fáfnir, had been taken by Loki from a dwarf, and the curse which it carried led to the tragedies of the Völsungar and Niflungar. A legendary king compelled two dwarfs to forge a magic sword, Tyrfing. It could never be drawn without bringing death, and three dastardly crimes were destined to be done with it.[18] Nearly the same was told of another sword, Dáinsleif, also made by dwarfs.[19]

Dwarfs were repositories of wisdom. The *Alvíssmál* (Words of the All-wise), a didactic poem like the *Vafþrúðnismál* (see Ch. I, Old Norse Poetry), tells how Thór held the dwarf, Alvíss, in conversation until daybreak, probing his secret wisdom. Dwarfs were also remembered as masters of runes and magic songs.[20]

Dwarfs were said to have strange origins. Snorri[21] told how they quickened as maggots in the flesh of the primeval giant, Ymir, and the gods had granted them the wits and shape of men.

A passage in the *Vǫluspá* (str. 9), which may be interpolated, gives another account of the origin of dwarfs. This is obscure and made no plainer by the numerous textual variants.[22] According to the best manuscript, they were fashioned from the blood of Brimir (the roarer?) and the limbs of Bláinn (the black one?). In this case, Brimir and Bláinn may be alternative names for Ymir. The reading of the four-teenth-century *Hauksbók* is also attractive. According to this, dwarfs were formed:

ór brimi blóðgu	from the bloody surf
ok ór Bláins leggjum	and the limbs of Bláinn.

When Ymir was killed, the sea was made of his blood.[23]

Four dwarfs, Austri, Vestri, Suðri, Norðri, were said to uphold the four corners of the sky, and several allusions to this myth are found in early poetry.[24]

Dwarfs lived in rocks or underground. In the *Vǫluspá* (str. 48) they are the 'wise ones of the wall-like rocks' (*veggbergs vísir*). The *Ynglinga Saga* (XII), following the *Ynglinga Tal*,[25] tells of a mythical king of the Swedes, who was enticed into a rock by a dwarf, hoping to meet Óðinn. The rock closed behind him and the king was never seen again. The place-name Dvergasteinn (Dwarf-stone), recorded both in Norway and

Iceland, seems to preserve the conception that dwarfs lived in rocks, as they were sometimes said to do in later folktale.[26]

Living as they do, dwarfs cannot face the sun. The dwarf Alvíss, whom Thór held in check until sunrise, was 'dayed up' (*uppi dagaðr*). This must mean that he was turned to stone by the sun's rays, as were giants, trolls and suchlike rock-dwellers. Probably in irony, Alvíss told Thór that, while men called the sun *sól* and gods called it *sunna*, dwarfs called it 'the plaything or playmate of the dwarf, Dvalinn' (*Dvalins leika*).[27]

If they are not of the same origin, the dwarfs are hard to distinguish from the dark or black elves. Snorri[28] seems to identify the two tribes, implying that the dwarfs lived in *Svartálfaheimr* (World of Black elves). The name Dáinn is several times applied to a dwarf and once, if the reading may be trusted, to an elf.[29] It perhaps means 'the dead one', and dwarfs were not far removed from the dead. The dwarf Alvíss had a pale nose and looked as if he had spent the night with a corpse.[30]

CHAPTER TWELVE

TEMPLES AND OBJECTS OF WORSHIP

THE ROMAN historian Tacitus stated that Germans did not confine their gods within walls, and did not make images of them, but rather consecrated forests and groves, calling by the names of gods that hidden power (*secretum*) which they beheld only with the reverence of their own eyes.[1] In another passage Tacitus speaks of the holy forest of the Semnones, believed to be the abode of the *regnator omnium deus* (see Ch. II, Woden-Wotan, above).

These passages show that, among the Germans, the belief in personal, but unseen gods was highly developed, and that worship was often conducted in the open air, without buildings or idols. Later sources also show that open-air worship was widespread.

It would not, however, be true to say that Germans of this time had no temples, for Tacitus himself speaks of the temple (*templum*) of the goddess Nerthus (see Ch. VII, Njörð, above). In his *Annals* (I,51) Tacitus also mentioned a famous temple, called *Tanfana*, in the land of the Marsi of western Germany, which was levelled by the Romans in AD 14.

The art of building was little developed among Germans of the first century, and buildings where large numbers could join in public worship were probably few. We may believe that worship was most often conducted in the open and especially in groves dedicated to one god or several.

It is noteworthy that words used in Germanic languages for 'place of worship' or 'temple' often had the meaning 'grove' as well. The O.H.G. *harug* is rendered in Latin as *fanum, lucus, nemus,* and the corresponding O.E. *hearg*, commonly used for 'temple' or 'idol', also had the meaning 'grove'. The O.E. *bearu* and words related to it alternate between such meanings as 'forest, holy grove, temple'. The Gothic *alhs* (temple) is said also to be related to words which mean 'holy grove'.[2]

The literary sources tell little of the holy places of the continental Germans and English in the Dark Ages, although some conception of their form may be gained. Penalties are prescribed in late O.E. laws against those who establish a *friðgeard* (or *friðsplott*) around a tree, stone well or other object of superstition. The word *friðgeard* evidently means a plot of ground, probably marked off by a hedge or fence, within which the divine peace must be observed. The ancient laws and history of Gotland also mention a *stafgarðr*, probably a sanctified enclosure.[3]

As the knowledge of building developed, temples grew more common, and they are frequently mentioned by Christian writers of the Middle Ages.[4] The Venerable Bede[5] shows that some of the heathen temples in England were sufficiently well built to be converted into Christian churches. Bede also describes how the Northumbrian high priest, Coifi, after adopting the Christian faith, ordered the temple to be destroyed and burnt down together with all its enclosures (*septis*).[6] This description, defective as it is, shows that the temple of Coifi was built of timber, and was evidently surrounded by fences or hedges, perhaps forming a *friðgeard*.

The history of Scandinavia comes to light later than that of England or Germany but, even in the last century of paganism, worship was conducted in the open, as well as in roofed temples.

It is told of one of the settlers of Iceland that he brought sacrifice to the foss (*hann blótaði forsinn*), and his home was called *at Forsi*. Another brought sacrifice to a grove (*hann blótaði lundinn*), and his home was called *at Lundi*,[7] Mention is made in the *Helgakviða Hundingsbana* II (str. 27) of a *Fjǫturlundr* or 'Fetter-grove', which is reminiscent of the sacred grove of the Semnones (see Ch. II, Woden-Wotan above). In the *Skírnismál* (str. 39), the fertility god, Freyr, is said to meet his bride in a *lundr lognfara* or 'windless grove' (see Ch. VII). The vikings in Ireland established a 'grove of Thór' (see Ch. III).

Sacrifice was also brought to rocks and stones. In the *Kristni Saga* (II) and the *Þorvalds þáttr Víðfǫrla* (II), which describe the first Christian mission to Iceland (*c.* 981–5), a chieftain and his family are said to bring sacrifice to a rock, which they believed was the home of their patron. The patron is designated in one text as *ármaðr*, the one who assures prosperity and good harvests; and in the other as *spámaðr* (prophet). According to a Norwegian law,[8] it was a pagan superstition to believe that elemental spirits (*landvættir*) dwelt in groves, mounds (*haugar*) and waterfalls.

The texts last quoted show that we have to do, not with nature-worship, or worship of natural objects themselves, but rather with the worship of gods or supernatural beings, who dwelt in the waterfall, the rock or grove, as the *regnator omnium deus* dwelt in the grove of the Semnones.

The place-names of Scandinavia[9] provide rich evidence of sanctuaries and holy places. They were often out of doors, and the words *vangr*, *vin*, *akr* (meadow, cornfield) were applied to them, as well as *haugr* (mound). The name *Forsetalundr*, in eastern Norway, may preserve memory of a grove dedicated to Forseti, son of Baldr.[10]

Vé was among the words commonly used for a sanctuary in early times.[11] It is found as an element in place-names, particularly in those of Sweden and Denmark, e.g. *Visby*, *Viborg*, and it is often compounded with names of gods, as in *Odense* (older *Óðinsvé*), *Härnevi*, *Ullavi*. *Vé* is also a common element in personal names. The *Landnámabók*[12] tells of a man of Sogn (West Norway), whose name was Geir, but he was known as *Végeirr* because he was particularly devout in religious practices. His sons and daughters all bore names beginning with *Vé-*.

The noun *vé* is related to the verb *vígja* (to consecrate),[13] and it seems often to be applied to a consecrated place separated from the profane world around it. It is thus comparable with the O.E. *friðgeard*. In the Gutnish text mentioned above, *vé* (*wi*) is named together with *stafgarðr* and *hult* (grove) among objects in which the islanders had placed their faith in days of old.

Sagas, poetry and laws of Iceland and Norway give clearer ideas of the way in which the word *vé* was used by heathen Scandinavians. In the lays of the *Edda* it is applied to dwellings of the holy gods, as in the phrases *vé goða*, *vé valtíva*. Such expressions probably reflect the oldest use of the word as a religious term; the divine beings were thought to be present in the sacred place, at least on ceremonial occasions. As Snorri[14] uses this word, it is synonymous with *griðastaðr*, a holy place in which no violence might be done. One who shed blood in the *vé* was deemed an outcast, a criminal, or a wolf in holy places (*vargr í véum*). Among the names of Thór is *Véurr*, which probably means 'servant or guardian of the holy place'.

Like the *friðgeard* or *stafgarðr*, the *vé* was probably enclosed by a fence or hedge, The sources also mention *vébǫnd*, evidently ropes which enclosed judicial courts while they were sitting. The following description is given in the *Egils Saga* (LVI) of a court in Norway in the tenth century:

In the place where the court was held there was a level field, and hazel poles were fixed in it forming a circle, and ropes were placed around them on the outside; these were called *vébǫnd*. Inside the circle sat the judges, twelve from Firðafylki, twelve from Sygnafylki and twelve from Hörðafylki. These three dozen men were to adjudicate in people's lawsuits.

Since the administration of law was partly a religious function, it is not rash to conclude that the 'holy ropes' (*vébǫnd*) marked off the sacred place from the profane. The duel (*hólmganga*), which also had a religious basis, was fought within an area marked out with poles (*hǫslur*) and, as it seems, ropes.[15]

Like other words which originally meant no more than a sacred place in the open, *vé* came later to mean a building in which sacrifice was offered, although passages in literature in which the word is used in this sense are few.[16]

The word *hǫrgr* (rarely fem. *hǫrg*) was also applied to places of worship, and it is found as an element in place-names over a fairly large area, although chiefly in Iceland and the west. As noted above, the O.E. and German equivalents of this word (O.E. *hearg*, O.H.G. *harug*, etc) were sometimes used for 'sacred grove', but the O.N. *hǫrgr* is not recorded with that meaning. It is sometimes applied to a pile of stones set up in the open as an altar. In the poem *Hyndluljóð* (str. 10), the goddess Freyja is made to say of her favourite, Óttar:

hǫrg hann mér gørði	he raised a *hǫrgr* for me,
hlaðinn steinum,	piled with stones;
nú er grjót þat	now all that rock
at gleri orðit;	has turned to glass;
rauð hann at nýju	he reddened it anew
nauta blóði;	with blood of oxen;
æ trúði Óttarr	always Óttar put faith
á ásynjur.	in goddesses (*ásynjur*).

The goddess implies that by smearing the plain rock with the blood of sacrifice, Óttar had turned it into precious glass. In a manuscript of the *Heiðreks Saga* (I). it is similarly told how the daughter of a legendary King Álf of Álfheimar reddened the *hǫrgr* (*rauð hǫrginn*) during a sacrifice to the guardian spirits (*dísablót*).

The *Landnámabók*[17] contains a story about a woman settler, Auð the Deep-minded, who came to Iceland from Ireland. Auð was a Christian and, beside her house, she set up crosses on some hillocks called *Kross-hólar*, where she performed her devotions. When Auð was dead, her relations, who were heathen, erected a *hǫrg* (fem.) by the hillocks, for they had great faith in them, and believed that they would go into them when they died.

If the *hǫrgr* was, at one time, a stone pile, the word came later to be applied to roofed temples. In some of the lays of the *Edda*, the *hǫrgr* is said to be constructed with lofty timbers (*hátimbraðr*) and sometimes it is said to burn.[18] Snorri[19] must think of a substantial building when he writes of the *hǫrgr*, *Vingólf*, set up for goddesses (*gyðjur*), describing it as a splendid house (*allfagrt hús*). Early Norwegian laws[20] also showed that the *hǫrgr* was a complete building, laying down that anyone who raised a building (*hús*) and called it a *horgr* should forfeit every penny he·had.

Excavations made in Iceland in recent times help to show the form of the *horgr* at the end of the pagan period. At Hörgsdal,[21] in the north of the island, a small rectangular building, *c.* 10 m × 6 m was uncovered and was evidently roofed and supported by pillars. Another structure, uncovered at Hörgsholt in the south-west, measured only about 5 m × 1½.

Passages already quoted from *Hyndluljóð*, *Heiðreks Saga* and Snorri's *Edda* have suggested to some that the *horgr* belonged especially to the cult of goddesses. This may well have been the case at the end of the pagan period, but it cannot have been so in earlier times. Place-names, such as *Óðinshargher*, *Thórshargher*, in Sweden, show that *horgar* were also dedicated to gods.

Nevertheless, excavations, place-names, even allusions in literature and law, suggest that in later times the *horgr* was a small temple or shrine, perhaps used chiefly for private or family worship. The cult of the *dísir* and of other female divinities was generally on a smaller scale and more private than that of the gods and it may, therefore, have been conducted in simple shrines, and in unpretentious buildings.

The word most commonly used for a temple or sacred building in the sagas is *hof*, and it is interesting to note that this word is rarely used by scalds, and never occurs with the meaning 'temple' in the poetry of the *Edda* except in such alliterative doublets as *horgr ok hof*.

The element *hof* occurs seldom in the place-names of Sweden and Denmark, but it is common in those of Iceland, where it appears both as a simplex and as the first element in compounds, e.g. *Hof*, *Hofstaðir*, *Hofteigr*. It is also common in many parts of Norway, and is often compounded with names of gods, e.g. *Þórshof*, *Freyshof*.

Both the use of *hof* in literature and its distribution in place-names suggest that it was not applied to temples until the last centuries of heathendom.

Literature and archaeology give only hazy ideas of the forms of places of worship designated by such terms as *vé*, *horgr*, but the *hof* is, in one passage, described in precise detail. It is told in the *Eyrbyggja Saga* how Thórólf Mostrarskegg, a chieftain of south-western Norway, emigrated to Iceland rather than submit to the tyranny of Harald Finehair. Thórólf was a devout man, placing his trust in Thór. Before he left his home, he took down the temple, shipping the timbers, as well as the soil beneath the altar, upon which the idol of Thór had stood. He sailed by the south coast of Iceland and, as he passed Reykjanes, he hurled overboard the main pillars (*ondvegissúlur*) of his temple, one of which carried the graven image of Thór. Thórólf resolved to settle at the place where these pillars should drift ashore, and he made land in a creek on Snæfellsnes, afterwards called *Hofsvágr* (Temple-creek). Soon afterwards he found his pillars on a headland nearby, which he called *Þórsnes* (Thór's ness). He set up a farm near the creek, which was called *Hofstaðir* (Temple-steads), and beside it he erected a temple (*hof*), which he dedicated to his patron, Thór. The temple is described in the saga (Ch. IV):

> He had a temple built, and it was a mighty building. There was a doorway in the side-wall, nearer to the one end, and inside stood the main pillars (*ǫndvegissúlur*) in which nails were set, called 'divine nails' (*reginnaglar*). Within there was a great sanctuary. Further in there was an apartment of the same form as the chancel in churches nowadays, and there was a pedestal in the middle of the floor there like an altar, and upon it lay an armring without joint, weighing twenty ounces, and all oaths must be sworn upon it. The temple-priest (*hofgoði*) must wear this ring on his arm at all public gatherings. The sacrificial bowl (*hlautbolli*) must stand on the pedestal, and there was a sacrificial twig in it, like an aspergillum (*stǫkkull*) and with it the blood, which was called *hlaut*, should be sprinkled from the bowl. This was blood of the kind shed when beasts were slaughtered as a sacrifice to the gods. The idols were arranged in this apartment around the pillar.

The authenticity of this description of the temple on Snæfellsnes has been questioned.[22] It seems probable, however, that it derives from a learned note written early in the twelfth century by Ari or one of his contemporaries. Snorri also described a temple in Thrándheim in the reign of Hákon the Good (died *c.* 960), and probably drew partly on the same source.[23]

The site of the temple described in the *Eyrbyggja Saga* was *Hofstaðir* (Temple-steads). This is not an unusual place-name in Iceland, and it is not necessary to suppose that every place to which it was applied was the site of a temple. Nevertheless, three of the four *Hofstaðir* named in the *Landnámabók* were remembered as sites of temples or places of worship. Not all the *Hofstaðir* are named in early documents, but among those whose names survive today is one close to lake Mývatn, in the north of Iceland. Tradition recorded in the nineteenth century had it that this was the site of a temple. It was excavated in 1908, and the remains of a ship-shaped building, *c.* 44 m × 8 m, were uncovered. This building was divided into two compartments, a large hall with benches running from end to end, capable of seating about 150 men, and a smaller compartment to the north, corresponding with the chancel (*sǫnghús*) mentioned in the *Eyrbyggja*.[24]

Some have doubted whether this building was really a temple.[25] Its

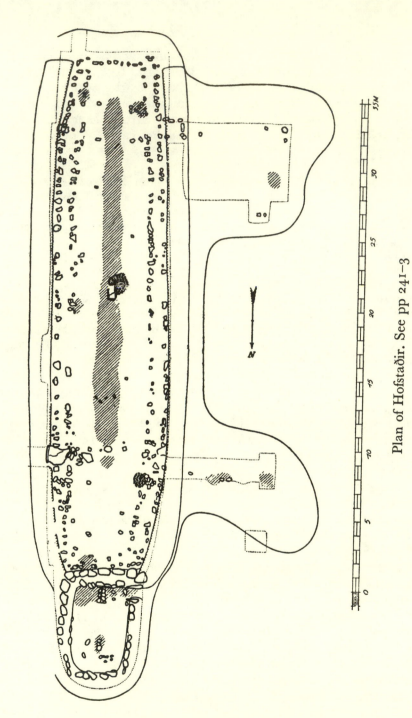

Plan of Hofstaðir. See pp 241-3

great size shows that it was used for public gatherings, although it might have been used for profane as well as religious purposes.

In form, the building at Hofstaðir was not unlike the houses of the *langhús* type.[26] This could imply that the religious architecture was based on the profane, or the profane on the religious. In fact, the description given in the *Eyrbyggja* and the ruins at Hofstðir suggest that, in the tenth century, the *hof* resembled a Christian church, and its form was probably modelled on that of western European churches of the period. The *hof*, in its turn, is believed by some to have influenced the form of stave churches of the Middle Ages, culminating in such fantastic beauty as the church of Borgund of the twelfth century.[27]

Historical literature sheds light on the place of the *hof* in the social and political organization of pagan Iceland. It is said in versions of the *Landnámabók*,[28] as well as in other sources, that, under the pagan law, an arm-ring weighing not less than two ounces (*aurar*) must be kept on an altar (*stalli*) in every main or public temple (*hǫfuðhof*), and the *goði* must wear it on his arm at legal assemblies. Those who had business to transact, prosecuting, defending, or bearing witness, must swear an oath on this ring.

At the end of this same passage in the *Landnámabók* a note is added on the distribution of public temples. When Iceland was divided into Quarters (*Fjórðungar*), about 963, there were to be three parishes (*þingsóknir*) in each Quarter, and three public temples in each parish. There were, in fact, four parishes in the northern Quarter, although three in each of the others, and perhaps there were twelve public temples there. There must, therefore, have been thirty-six or thirty-nine public temples in Iceland, besides private ones, or 'temples of ease'. Property owners were obliged to pay dues (*hoftollar*) to the temples, as they afterwards paid tithes to the Church.

It is evident from such records as these that temples filled an important place in the political and social, as well as in the religious life of heathen Iceland.

In Norway, during the Viking Age, the name *hof* perhaps replaced some of the older names for temples and holy places, such as *vé*, *hǫrgr*, *vin*, which survived as designations of places of worship of a more primitive kind. It has been shown in studies of the religious place-names of Norway that, at the end of the pagan period, the *hof* was a central place of worship,[29] as it was in Iceland. It is indeed remarkable how many Christian churches of Norway stood on or next to places called *Hof*. Either public temples were converted into churches, or else the temples were destroyed and churches built in their place.

Literary sources show that some of the temples were greater and more splendid than others. Snorri describes a particularly glorious one at Hlaðir, in Thrándheim, destroyed by King Ólaf Tryggvason, and another at Mærin (inner Thrándheim) destroyed by the same king.[30] Another famous temple was that of Guðbrand of Dalar, in central Norway.[31]

The most glorious of all Scandinavian temples, and perhaps the latest, was at Uppsala in Sweden. This was described by the German chronicler, Adam of Bremen (see Ch. I),[32] and some additional notes were appended to the description shortly after it was written, whether by Adam himself or another. Uppsala was the last bastion of northern heathendom, and the temple was evidently still in use when Adam wrote his magnificent description. His words may be summarized:

Ch. XXVI: this nation has a most splendid temple called Ubsola, standing not far from the city of Sictona (or Birka). In this temple, totally adorned with gold, the people worship statues of three gods; the most mighty of them, Thór, has his throne in the middle; Wodan and Fricco have their place on either side. Their significance is of this kind: 'Thór', they say, 'rules in the sky, and governs thunder, lightning, the winds, rain, fair weather and produce of the soil.' The second is Wodan, i.e. 'Rage' (*furor*); he makes wars and gives man bravery in face of enemies. The third is Fricco, distributing peace and pleasure among men, whose idol is fashioned with a gigantic 'priapus'. Wodan they depict armed, as our people depict Mars. Thór, with his sceptre, seems to resemble Jove. They also worship gods whom they have made from men and consign to immortality because of great deeds. In the Life of St Anskar, so it is recorded, they made Eirik (Hericus) a god.[33]

Ch. XXVIII: They have priests assigned to all these gods to perform the offerings of the people. If there is danger of pestilence or famine, sacrifice is offered to the idol Thór, if of war to Wodan; if marriage is to be celebrated they offer to Fricco.

It is the practice, every nine years, to hold a communal festival in Ubsola for all the provinces of Sueonia. No exemption from this festival is allowed. The kings and the people, communally and separately, send gifts and, most cruel of all, those who have embraced Christianity buy themselves off from these festivities.

The sacrifice is performed thus: nine head of every living male creature are offered, and it is the custom to placate the gods with the blood of these. The bodies are hung in a grove which stands beside the temple. This grove is so holy for the heathens that each of the separate trees is believed to be divine because of the death and gore of the objects sacrificed; there dogs and horses hang together with men. One of the Christians (*aliquis Christianorum*) told me that he had seen seventy-two bodies hanging together. For the rest, the incantations which they are accustomed to sing at this kind of sacrificial rite are manifold and disgraceful, and therefore it is better to be silent about them.

The marginal notes add some details to the description. According to the first of them (No. 138):

Beside this temple stands an enormous tree, spreading its branches far and wide; it is ever green, in winter as in summer. No one knows what kind of tree this is. There is also a well there, where heathen sacrifices are commonly performed, and a living man is plunged into it. If he is not found again, it is deemed that the will of the people will be fulfilled.

According to the second of these notes (No. 139):

A golden chain surrounds the temple, hanging over the gables (*fastigia*) of the building, glowing brilliantly towards those who approach, for the temple itself stands in a plain, with hills around it in the likeness of a theatre.

A third note (No. 141) may also be quoted:

For nine days the festivities with sacrifices of this kind are held. Every day they offer one man together with other animals, so that in nine days it makes seventy-two living things which are sacrificed.

This description is not that of an eye-witness. Parts of it, at least, must come from Adam's Christian informant, *aliquis Christianorum* among the Swedes, and parts may even be third or fourth hand.

The description, splendid as it is, is not clear in every detail, and archaeologists have not agreed about it. The most puzzling feature is the golden chain (*catena*), glowing above the gables. Some authorities suggest that, in this, Adam was inspired by the description of the temple of Solomon (II Chron. 3,15–16):

Also he made before the house two pillars of thirty and five cubits high, and the chapiter that was on the top of each of them was five cubits.
And he made chains, as in the oracle, and put them on the heads of the pillars; and he made an hundred pomegranates, and put them on the chains.

The description of Solomon's temple was frequently used as a text by medieval homilists,[34] and Adam must certainly have known it. But it is unlikely that he was inspired only by this text when he wrote of the temple of Uppsala. More probably he tried to equate what he had heard about the temple of Uppsala with what he had read about the temple of Solomon, and that is why he thought that the glowing decorations over the roof of the temple of Uppsala must have been a chain (*catena*).

S. Lindquist,[35] in a brilliant study, suggested that the description was that of one who had seen the temple from a distance, and mistook a gilded frieze, perhaps running between animal-headed pinnacles, for a chain. His argument is supported by comparison with stave-churches and early relic shrines of Sweden and Norway.

Archaeologists have not agreed on the form of this temple, but it is commonly believed that it was built of timbers and supported by two rows of pillars, standing on the site of the present church of Old Uppsala. Excavations made in 1927, when the church was restored, suggest that the temple was rectangular, and considerably longer than the present church.

Although we can know little about the appearance of the temple, except that it was large, timber-built, rectangular and garish, Adam's description contains many points of vital interest. It is as if centuries of heathen belief and practice had silted in this Swedish backwater.

The grove beside the building, sanctified by the blood of man and beast, was as holy as that in Germany, where the *regnator omnium deus* dwelt at the time of Tacitus, holy as, on a smaller scale, was the grove in the north of Iceland to which the settler used to bring his sacrifice. One tree was holier than all the others; it was evergreen like the ash Yggdrasill. In some ways it resembled the great column, Irminsul which, as the Saxons believed, upheld the universe. We may think also of Glasir,[36] the grove with golden foliage standing before the doors of Valhöll, and of the tree growing from unknown roots on which Óðinn swung in his death-agony. The temple itself, glowing with gold, is like Valhöll, whose roof glowed with gilded shields.

The sacred well is reminiscent of the mystical Urðarbrunnr (Well of Fate), in which Óðinn sacrificed his eye, and of that beside the temple of Fosite on the Frisian island.[37] The man drowning in the well may remind us of the slaves drowning after washing Nerthus, and of the *blótgrafar* and *blótkelda* mentioned in later Icelandic sagas.[38] We may even think of the settler in Iceland, who hurled sacrifice into the waterfall, evidently to please the deities who dwelt in it.

Adam, in his account of the temple, mentions three idols, representing Thór, Wodan and Fricco. The last name has caused some difficulty, but it is commonly agreed that it is a name for Freyr.[39] Although little is known about the form of idols, it is often stated, both in records of missionaries on the Continent and in Icelandic sagas that they stood three together.[40] Bede[41] speaks of idols of stone as well as of wood, while Icelandic writers suggest that those in the temples were mostly of wood, calling them *trégoð, skurðgoð*.

The *Eyrrbyggja Saga* relates that, in the temple on Snæfellsnes, the idols were placed around an altar (*stalli*) in the 'chancel', and idols kept in the temples of Iceland are mentioned in several other texts, which deserve to be quoted, although they must be treated with reserve. In the temple on Kjalarnes,[42] it is said, Thór stood in the middle with idols of other gods on each side, but the author of this text may well have been influenced by Adam's description of the temple at Uppsala. An even less trustworthy text[43] mentioned a temple in the south of Iceland dedicated to the goddess Thorgerð Hörgarbrúð, in which there were images of many gods.

The descriptions of idols in Norway are richer, although hardly more trustworthy, and many of them bear the stamp of clerical fantasy. An idol of Thór in central Norway is described by Snorri.[44] He was heavily decked with gold and silver, of enormous size, hollow and standing on a platform. Every day he was fed with four loaves of bread and meat. When, in an unguarded moment, one of St Ólaf's servants struck him with a club, he fell into fragments. Out of him jumped toads, snakes, and rats so well nourished that they were as big as cats. This description is found, in substantially similar words, in the Legendary Saga of the Saint. If apocryphal, it is at least old.

Another tale is told of an idol of Freyr in Thrándheim.[45] This one is described as a wooden man (tremaðr), made by human hands. Whatever the heathens may have thought, the idol was not Freyr himself. When the god-king Freyr died in Sweden, the Swedes had carved two wooden men, and put them into the howe to keep Freyr company. They were afterwards dug up and one of them was sent to Thrándheim where he was worshipped.

There is a more interesting tale about another idol of Freyr in Sweden, probably at Uppsala. This is found in the Story of Gunnar Helming,[46] already quoted (see Ch. VII, above). Gunnar, who had fled from Norway to Sweden, took refuge in the house or temple of Freyr, placing himself under the protection of Freyr's 'wife'. It was the fugitive's task to lead the horse, while the idol and his bride were carried in ceremonial procession through the provinces, assuring the fertility of the crops. When he grew tired of walking, Gunnar jumped into the chariot, where the animated idol fell upon him. After a hard struggle, Gunnar turned his mind to King Ólaf Tryggvason, and the mightier god whom he worshipped. Then the demon jumped out of the idol, and there was nothing left but a block of wood.

Foreign analogues of this story have been noticed,[47] but it preserves some genuine features of tradition, memories of the pre-eminence of the cult of Freyr in Sweden, of the wooden idol of the fertility god conveyed ceremonially in a chariot to promote the growth of the crops.[48] Not the least striking feature is the animated idol, severe and reticent, but well able to talk and wrestle.

Not all idols were kept in temples. Ólaf Tryggvason's favourite poet, Hallfreð,[49] was accused of keeping an ivory image of Thór in his purse, and worshipping it secretly. Ingimund the Old, who settled in northern Iceland, kept a silver image of Freyr.[50]

Amulets of this kind might be called *hlutir*. While all the great idols have perished, some of these are preserved. (See Plates 13-16.) Among them is the bronze image of a bearded man, sitting on a chair, and clasping an object like a hammer. This image, found in Iceland, probably dates from the tenth century, and may well represent Thór. Another, pronouncedly erotic figure, was found at Rällinge, in south-eastern Sweden, and may represent Freyr.[51] It could be regarded as a miniature of the great ithyphallic idol of Fricco (Freyr) in the temple of Uppsala. Among many bracteats of gold and silver, which appear to have religious significance, is one from Frøysland, in south-western Norway, which may represent the sacred marriage of Freyr with his wife Gerð.[52] Many metal images of Thór's hammer, suitable to wear on clothing or to carry in the purse, have also been found in Sweden, especially in the region of Birka.[53] (See Plates 17-18.)

The Oseberg and Gokstad finds provide ample evidence of artistry in wood, and many of the carved figures found in these tombs must have a religious meaning.[54] In the Great Saga of Ólaf Tryggvason, the image of Thór is said to be worn on the prow of a warship.[55] In the same way, images of gods were carved on the main pillars of a temple and probably of other buildings, as well as on chair-posts.[56] Pillars bearing such images were not lifeless, but animate. When Thórólf Mostrarskegg cast his pillars overboard, they sped quickly over the waves, guiding him to the place where he should make his home.

Scenes from the lives of gods provided favourite motives for wood-carvers and painters of the late pagan period. Although this is nowhere stated, we can hardly doubt that work of this kind adorned temples as well as dwelling-houses. Ólaf the Peacock, who built his house at Hjarðarholt in western Iceland late in the tenth century, had panels and rafters carved with pictures of mythical scenes.[57] A well-known poet described the pictures in a lay.[58] Among the scenes depicted was the cremation of Baldr; Freyr was seen riding on his boar, and Óðinn, mounted on his horse, was followed by valkyries and ravens. On another panel, Thór was seen struggling against the World Serpent. Fragments of verse dating from even earlier time are preserved, in which poets acknowledge the gift of an ornamental shield, and describe the mythical scenes, carved or painted, with which it is decorated.[59]

Mythical scenes were also carved on stone, and some of the finest examples belong to the end of the pagan period, or even to the time when Christianity blended with heathendom, as it must have done in the minds of artists of the early eleventh century in Cumberland and Man,[60] when they carved images of Thór and other pagan gods beside Christian symbols. Many carved stones of the pagan period found in Sweden and especially in Gotland also contain scenes from the lives of gods.[61]

Pictures, painted or carved in relief, may not be idols although, like Christian icons, they must have been objects of veneration, and they show that artists thought of gods in human form. But anthropomorphic figures were not the only ones venerated. Allusions in this chapter have shown that sacrifice was taken to wells, waterfalls, trees. Under the Christian law of Norway,[62] it was forbidden to keep a stick (*stafr*) in one's house and venerate it, a practice probably to be associated with the cult of the supporting pillar (*ǫndvegissúla*). The cult of stones and rocks is also prohibited under the law of Swedish Uppland.[63] In the Icelandic instance of this practice quoted above (p. 237), it could be seen that the rock was venerated, not for itself, but because it was the dwelling of a tutelary divinity.

Animals were also venerated. Flóki, who explored Iceland before it was settled, sacrificed to three ravens, who guided him on his way.[64] Hákon the Great (died 995), after he had been forcibly baptized, reverted to heathendom. He held a sacrifice and two ravens flew croaking over his head, showing that Óðinn had accepted the sacrifice.[65] Snorri[66] wrote of a king in Norway who offered sacrifice to a cow (*blét kú eina*) and took her wherever he went. Others were said to venerate magnificent boars (*sonargeltir*), swearing oaths on their bristles.[67] The beast most commonly venerated was the horse, or stallion, whose flesh provided the dish at sacrificial banquets. Brand, a man of northern Iceland, kept a horse called Faxi (the maned one), and had 'faith' (*átrúnaðr*) in him,[68] while Hrafnkell shared his favourite stallion with Freyr.[69] We read also of a stud of horses in Norway belonging to this god.[70]

Ravens, cattle, boars, horses are not worshipped for themselves, any more than the rock mentioned on p. 237 was worshipped for itself. The raven who guides the seafarer represents or embodies a god, whether Óðinn or another, and conveys his wisdom to man. Sacred horses among Germans described by Tacitus[71] were regarded as the mouthpiece of gods, and oracles were divined from their snorting and neighing. The divinity might even be transferred to the phallus of a dead horse which, venerated and called a god, embodies the force of a god of fertility.[72]

Stories of this kind, although known chiefly from Christian writers, help to show how pagans thought of idols and venerated objects. When the idol moved, benevolently or in anger, he was 'possessed', as heathens might say, by the god, but as Christians thought, by the demon, who is for them the heathen god.

It is partly because the idol is venerated and sacrifice brought to it, that it incorporates the god. A story told in the Great Saga of Ólaf Tryggvason illustrates this. An island off the coast of Norway was occupied by a certain Rauð, who kept a temple dedicated to Thór.[73] Rauð was most assiduous in his attentions to the idol (*hinn mesti blótmaðr*); he bestowed such sacrifice upon it that he gave it strength (*magnaði*). The demon talked out of the image (*líkneski, skurgoð*), and it used to walk with Rauð out of doors.

In the story quoted above (p. 237) from the *Kristni Saga* and the *Þorvalds Þáttr*, it was because sacrifice was taken to the rock that the 'demon' within it had power to assure prosperity and to tell the future. When respect was no longer paid to him and, instead of sacrifice, holy water was poured on the rock, the demon lost his power, and made off dressed in a miserable leather jerkin, instead of the fine clothes which he had worn before. In other words, when sacrifice is withdrawn, the rock is no longer the residence of the god, and he retires, dejected and impoverished.

CHAPTER THIRTEEN

SACRIFICE

PASSAGES CITED in the last chapter, and especially those from the *Eyrbyggja Saga* and from Adam's *Gesta* shed light on the modes of sacrifice and on the objects sacrificed. Some further details are given by Snorri in his life of Hákon the Good,[1] who also tells something of the purpose of sacrifice.

According to Snorri, all farmers of Thrándheim had to attend sacrifice in the temple (*hof*), taking such provisions as they needed while the sacrificial feast lasted, and all must join in the ceremonial beer-drinking. Cattle, horses and other domestic beasts were slaughtered, and their blood, called *hlaut*, was sprinkled on the altars and on the inner and outer walls of the temple, as well as upon the congregation. The meat was boiled, fires burned in the middle of the floor and cauldrons were suspended above them. The sacrificial cup was passed over the fire, and the chieftain would consecrate (*signa*) this as well as the sacrificial food. First of all the toast of Óðinn was drunk for victory and for the success (*ríkis*) of the King, and then the toasts of Njörð and Freyr were drunk for fruitful harvest and for peace (*til árs ok friðar*). After this the company drank the *bragafull*, and then toasts in memory (*minni*) of their kinsmen who lay buried in howes.[2]

The provenance of this passage has been much discussed,[3] but it is probable that Snorri was following a learned note like that which the author of the *Eyrbyggja Saga* followed when he described the temple of Thór on Snæfellsnes.[4]

A little later in this same saga (XV–XVIII), Snorri tells how the half-Christian king, Hákon, was compelled by his subjects to take part in the heathen feast. Reluctant as he was, he was forced to drink the toasts and to eat the horse-liver.

The meaning of the sacrificial feast, as Snorri saw it, is fairly plain. When blood was sprinkled over altars and men and the toasts were drunk, men were symbolically joined with gods of war and fertility, and with their dead ancestors, sharing their mystical powers. This is a form of communion.

But forms of sacrifice unlike these are described. Gifts are brought to gods in the hope that they will give a reward. A gift always looks for its return and, consequently, it is not wise to pester the gods with too much sacrifice.[5]

The purpose of a sacrifice of this kind may be deduced from the story quoted from the *Víga-Glúms Saga* (Ch. II, Cult of Óðinn). After Thorkell the Tall had been expelled from the region of Thverá (northern Iceland), he entered the temple of Freyr, leading an aged ox. ' "Freyr", said he, "you who have long been my patron, and accepted many gifts and repaid them well, now I give (*gef*) you this ox, so that Glúm may leave the land of Thverá no less compelled than I leave it now. Let some sign be seen whether you accept or reject it" '. The ox was so moved that he bellowed and dropped dead. Thorkell felt that it had turned out well, and he was now easier in mind, feeling that his prayer had been heard.

It is not told in this passage how the fugitive disposed of the carcass of the ox; he says only that he 'gives' him to the god. The same could be said of those who hurl sacrifice over a cliff or into a well or waterfall,[6] and no less positively in cases of human sacrifice.

It is improbable that human sacrifice was practised widely in the Viking Age, but classical authors frequently allude to it among continental Germans. Tacitus (*Germ.* IX) states that while Hercules and Mars were placated with animal sacrifice, human sacrifice was given to Mercury, who may be identified with Óðinn. The same author (*Germ.* XXXIX) tells how a man used to be sacrificed in the holy grove of the Semnones.

It is often told that prisoners of war were given to the gods, and this was probably regarded as thanksgiving for victory. After a battle the priestesses of the Cimbri would meet the prisoners in camp, crown them and conduct them to an enormous cauldron. The priestesses would then mount a ladder, and cut the throat of each prisoner as he was passed up, foretelling the future from the gushing blood.[7] A scene similar to this is depicted on the splendid Gundestrup bowl (see Plate 45). Although found in Denmark, this is commonly regarded as Celtic work,[8] and it is said that this form of sacrifice was Celtic rather than Germanic, but it should not be forgotten that Norsemen could also foretell the future from sacrificial blood.[9]

The Goths, according to Jordanes (*Getica* V), sacrificed prisoners of war to Mars, believing that the god of war was suitably placated with human blood. Procopius says of the men of Thule that they offered the first prisoner taken in battle to Ares. Not only was the sacrifice bloody, but the men of Thule would hang the victim on a tree, or cast him among thorns.[10]

Vernacular sources tell something about human sacrifice and its meaning in the north. It is said in the history of the Gotlanders,[11] a work of the thirteenth century, that the heathens of Gotland used to sacrifice their sons and daughters as well as cattle.

The significance of human sacrifice is often obscure. The supreme sacrifice was that of the King, and instances of this were cited in Ch. IX above. When the crops failed, the Swedes slaughtered their king, Dómaldi, and reddened the altars with his blood, or, as the *Historia Norvegiae*[12] has it, they hanged him as a sacrifice to Ceres, who was probably Freyja. Snorri tells later how the Swedes, in time of famine, burnt their king as a sacrifice to Óðinn (see Ch. IX, above).

As suggested in Ch. IX, the King is the representative of the god; it is not even extravagant to say that he incorporates the god, whether Freyr or another. The sacrifice takes place in autumn, the time when sacrifice was offered to the fertility-god Freyr and to the *dísir* (see Ch. XI above). Are we to suppose that the god, whether in the form of king, man, horse or boar, was slaughtered in the autumn in the hope that he would revive with the spring?[13]

Stories already quoted show that sacrificial victims were sometimes hanged. This is confirmed by the Arab scientist, Ibn Rustah, who wrote of practices of Scandinavians in Russia in the tenth century.[14] The wizards (or priests) decided what should be sacrificed, whether women, men or cattle. Once they had reached their decision it was irrevocable, and the wizard would take the victim, man or beast, tie a noose round its neck and hang it on a pole, saying: 'this is an offering to god'.

It might well be thought that sacrifice by hanging was a sacrifice to Óðinn, who was himself god of the hanged (*hanga-Týr*) and the 'gallows load' (*gálga farmr*), and often the recipient of human sacrifice. Such a conception might be confirmed by the story of King Víkar, who was hanged at the demand of Óðinn (see Ch. II, above). Ares and Mars, for whom the people of Thule and the Goths hanged men and armour might be identified with Óðinn, but Óðinn need not be the only god for whom victims were hanged. It was noted that a king of the Swedes was said to be hanged as a sacrifice to Ceres. According to a passage quoted from Adam of Bremen in the preceding chapter, men and victims of many kinds were to be seen hanging together in the holy grove of Uppsala. Óðinn was worshipped at Uppsala at the time at which Adam wrote, but it is doubtful whether he ever ranked high in the hierarchy of the agricultural Swedes.

It is by no means certain that all the victims who swung from trees were executed by the noose. The descriptions given by Adam and

Procopius might rather suggest that they were strung up after they were dead, and that the precious blood was sprinkled beforehand.[15]

Sacrifice, whether of man or beast, took many forms. At Uppsala, as already noted, victims were sunk in a well, and the slaves who washed the goddess Nerthus were drowned after the ceremony. In the preceding chapter I mentioned *blótkeldur* and *blótgrafar* recorded in Icelandic sagas and place-names. These were perhaps wells and morasses in which gifts, animate and inanimate, might be immersed.

In recent years a number of bodies in a good state of preservation have been dug up in the moors of Jutland. These are believed to date from about the beginning of our era, and some had, apparently, first been hanged and then sunk in the bog.[16]

Victims could be thrown over cliffs. The *Gautreks Saga* (I–II), which certainly incorporates some valid traditions, describes a form of ritual suicide. In times of famine, men and women of Gautland would hurl themselves over the Family Cliff (*Ætternisstapi*), believing that they would go to Valhöll. Remarkably strong support for this is found in later Swedish traditions.[17] In the *Hrafnkels Saga* (VI), the horse, Freyfaxi, was pushed over a cliff into a pool below. The slaughterer said: 'it is right that he who owns him should receive him.' This story, apocryphal as it must be, is supported by Norwegian traditions,[18] and might be regarded as a travesty of a sacrifice to Freyr.

Men could be sacrificed in the same way as the horse, Freyfaxi. When the acceptance of Christianity was debated at the Althingi (Great Assembly) in Iceland in the year AD 1000, adherents of the Christian party said: 'heathens sacrifice the worst men, hurling them over rocks or cliffs'.[19]

Statements like the last quoted might suggest that sacrificial victims were criminals, and that the death-penalty had a sacral meaning. This may be supported by the *Eyrbyggja Saga* (X) and the *Landnámabók*, where it is said that men were 'sentenced to sacrifice' (*dæmdir til blóts, skyldu til blóts dæma*), and their backs were broken on a stone, evidently to placate the god Thór. Criminals were certainly used for sacrifice, but it does not follow that the death-penalty was, in origin, sacrificial. It could well be that criminals and 'the worst men', rather than kings or priests, were used as victims in later times, when the significance of the sacrifice had faded.[20]

A peculiarly revolting form of human sacrifice was that of cutting the 'blood-eagle' (*blóðǫrn rísta*). The ribs were cut from the back and the lungs drawn out. Torf-Einar, Jarl of Orkney, defeated Hálfdan Highleg, son of Harald Fine-hair, and captured him; he cut the blood-eagle on his back and gave him to Óðinn (*gaf hann Óðni*).[21] In the *Reginsmál* (str. 26), the blood-eagle was said to be cut upon Lyngvi, after he had been captured by Sigurð. In the *Þáttr af Ragnars sonum* (III), it is told how the sons of Ragnar Loðbrók cut the eagle on the back of the Northumbrian King Ella (died 867) in order to avenge their father, whom the King had tortured in the serpent-pit. The *Þáttr* is late and untrustworthy, but allusion was made to this tradition already in the *Knútsdrápa* (str. 1) composed by Sighvat about 1038. Sighvat said:

Auk Ellu bak	Ívar, he who resided
at lét hinns sat,	in York,
Ívarr, ara,	had the eagle cut
Jórvík, skorit.	on the back of Ella.[22]

It has been noticed that, besides being associated with Óðinn, this form of torture was commonly used by men who avenged their fathers.[23] While it is plain that it was not prompted by brutality alone, the inner significance of the act remains obscure.[24]

Animal sacrifices were more common than human ones, and they often took the form of a sacrificial banquet. At the festival which Snorri described beasts of many kinds were slaughtered, and at least three gods as well as deified ancestors were revered.

Some gods were more suitably honoured by ·sacrifice of one beast than another. The boar was considered a suitable sacrifice for Freyr, as is told in various versions of the *Heiðreks Saga*.[25] The legendary king, Heiðrek the Wise used to sacrifice to the god Freyr. At Yule-tide, or in February, the sacrificial boar would be led before the king. He was called the *sonargǫltr* or 'leading boar',[26] and he was as big as an ox; he was deemed so holy that men laid hands upon him and swore binding oaths. A story closely resembling this one is told in a prose note appended to the *Helga kviða Hjǫrvarðssonar* (str. 30).

The association of the boar with Freyr and the Vanir is made plain in sources already quoted (see Ch. VII, Freyr). It is difficult to avoid the suspicion that the boar was one of the forms in which Freyr was conceived. This is confirmed by the word *vaningi* or 'son of the Vanir', which was applied, in poetry, both to the god Freyr and to the boar. Freyja, the sister of Freyr, was also called Sýr or 'Sow'.[27]

This implies that when the flesh of the boar was consumed at the sacrificial banquet, those who partook of it felt that they were consuming the god himself and absorbing his power.

The ox and the bull were also used as sacrifice for Freyr, as was shown in the passage quoted from *Víga-Glúms Saga* above. A more detailed story of a sacrifice of a bull to Freyr is given in the *Brandkrossa Þáttr* (I), a work of the late thirteenth century.[28] This passage in the

Þáttr was written under the influence of *Viga-Glúms Saga*, but adds something to it. Odd, like Thorkell the Tall, had been expelled from his estates and, before he left, he had a bull slaughtered and held a magnificent feast, saying that he gave (*gaf*) all of it to Freyr, so that the man who took his place should leave the estate in no less grief than he.

The fertility god, Freyr, and his sister Freyja, must have been thought of in the form of a bull and a cow. There are several tales which tell how cattle were revered and worshipped. Snorri[29] tells of a king in ancient days who used to sacrifice to a cow, drank her milk and took her wherever he went. After the cow died, she was placed in a howe, close to that of the king. It is told in the *Ragnars Saga Loðbrókar*, (Chs. IX–X) of a cow, called Síbilja, whom Eysteinn Beli, legendary king of the Swedes, used to worship and called a god (*goð*). Such great sacrifices were given to the cow that she grew fierce and raging. She would head the army in battle and, when she bellowed, the enemies would lose their heads and fight among each other! No one, not even their authors, would believe that such stories were true, but yet they cannot be made of nothing.

To these notes it may be added that 'Freyr' could also be used as a poetical word for ox.[30] In the 'Story of Thiðrandi', quoted in an earlier chapter (see Ch. XI), there was an ox called *Spámaðr* (Prophet), who was to be slaughtered for the feast of the Winter-nights. Horses were also much used for sacrifice, and their flesh, particularly the liver, was consumed.[31]

One of the strangest stories of a fertility sacrifice is given in the 'Story of Völsi' (*Vǫlsa Þáttr*) which is inserted in the Saga of St Ólaf in the *Flateyjarbók* (II, 331). As it stands, this story reads like a sophisticated author's burlesque of 'goings-on' among illiterate peasants living on a remote headland of northern Norway.

It is told that St Ólaf, well aware of the persistence of heathen practices in outlying parts of his kingdom, heard of an old man and wife, living on an isolated spot in the north. They had a son and daughter, as well as a thrall and serving-maid. One autumn a fat draught-horse died and, pagan as they were, the family cut him up and stewed him. When the horse was skinned, the farmer's son, full of boisterous humour, picked up the generative organ (*vingull*), ran into the house and shook it in front of the women, saying:

Hér meguð sjá	Here you can see
heldr rǫskligan	a good stout *vingull*
vingul skorinn	chopped off from
af viggs fǫður	the horse's father.

þér er, ambátt,	For you, serving-maid,
þessi Vǫlsi	this Völsi (phallus) will be
allódaufligr	lively enough
innan læra.	between the thighs.

The housewife grasped the *vingull*, saying that neither this nor anything else should go to waste. She dried it, and wrapped it in a linen cloth, with onions and herbs to preserve it, and put it into her chest. Every evening she brought it forth, uttering a formula, and she placed all her faith in it, holding it to be her god (*guð sinn*), and persuading all the household to do the same. The *vingull* was filled with such demoniacal power that it grew strong and great and could stand beside the housewife. Every evening she chanted a verse over it and passed it round the assembled company, each of whom contributed a verse.

Late one evening, St Ólaf arrived with his friends, Finn Arnason, and the Icelandic poet, Thormóð, all of them disguised. They sat down in the hall waiting for the people of the house to assemble. Last of all the housewife came in, bearing the *vingull*, which she addressed affectionately as *Vǫlsi*, while she clutched it to her bosom.[32] Völsi was passed from hand to hand, and everyone who received it uttered a verse, often obscene, and always accompanied with the puzzling refrain:

þiggi Mǫrnir (Maurnir, MS.)	May Mörnir
þetta blœti	receive this sacrifice.

If we could know what, or who, Mörnir was, we might understand the story better. The question is largely philological and has been much discussed, most ably by F. Ström,[33] some of whose arguments I shall use, while reaching a different conclusion. *Mǫrn* (fem. sing.) is used as a poetic word for 'troll-woman'[34] and, in at least one early scaldic passage[35] *Marnar faðir* (father of Mörn) seems to designate the giant Thjazi. This would suggest that Mörn was a name for the goddess Skaði, the 'goddess of snow-shoes', who became the wife of the fertility-god, Njörð (see Ch. VII, Njörð).

On such grounds it has been supposed that *Mǫrnir* is a fem. pl., and that the vingull, or phallus, was presented to fertility-goddesses, comparable with the *dísir*.

While this view is attractive, and has even been supported by comparison with an ancient Indian rite,[36] it is difficult to accept. A fem. pl., whether of the *o*, *i* or *u*-stem, in the form *Mǫrnir* would be exceptional, although forms such as *Marnar*, *Marnir*, even *Mernir* might well be possible.

Mǫrnir is recorded as a name for 'sword',[37] and it is most probably related to the verb *merja* (to crush), and is thus comparable with *beytill*

257

(cf *bauta* 'to hit, strike'), which also appears in verses of the 'Story of Völsi' with the meaning 'phallus'.

This implies that *vingull*, *beytill*, *Vǫlsi*, *Mǫrnir* are all one and the same. The phallus is not only the emblem, but even the embodiment of the god of fertility, *cum ingente priapo*. If it was right to suggest that the sacrificial boar (*sonargǫltr*) was the incarnation of Freyr, to whom he was sacrificed, it may be true that Völsi-Mörnir was both the sacrifice and the recipient of the sacrifice. On this basis we may better understand the sacrifice of the king-god, and the words of Óðinn: 'wounded with a spear and given to Óðinn, myself to myself'.

Other gods besides the Vanir were conceived in animal form. The attendant spirits of Óðinn were the wolves, Geri and Feki, and the ravens, Huginn and Muninn. Óðinn is the Raven-god (*Hrafnáss*), and when he escaped from the castle of the giant bearing the sacred mead of poetry he took the form of an eagle (see Ch. II). Flóki, offering sacrifice to his ravens (see Ch. XII above) probably thought of them as incarnations of Óðinn, and Hákon the Great, offering sacrifice to Óðinn, knew that the sacrifice had been accepted when two ravens flew croaking over his head.[38]

Poets who wished to say that a prince or warrior slew his enemies in battle would often say that he fed the wolf, the eagle or the raven, or else rejoiced them. Einar Skálaglamm said that 'the raven was filled with the sacrifice of the wolf',[39] and Gizur Gullbrárskáld, early in the eleventh century said:

Fylkir gleðr í fólki   The prince rejoices in
flagðs blakk ok svan Hlakkar   battle the troll-wife's
                            horse (wolf) and the
                            swan of Hlökk (raven).[40]

Expressions like these were part of the poet's stock-in-trade, but those who used them could not have dissociated them from the common conception that those who fell in battle were given to Óðinn, as the Swedish King Eirík the Victorious gave his enemies to Óðinn when he hurled a javelin over their heads, saying: 'you all belong to Óðinn'.[41] The association between Óðinn and the raven as the recipient of the dead was shown most plainly by the Icelander Helgi Trausti, who had killed his mother's lover, Thorgrím, son of Ásmóð. Helgi said:

Ásmóðar gafk Óðni   I have given to Óðinn
arfa þróttar djarfan;   the bold son of Ásmóð;
guldum galga valdi   I paid the lord of the gallows
Gauts tafn, en ná hrafni.   the sacrifice of Gaut (Óðinn),
                            and gave the corpse to the raven.[42]

In the description of the sacrificial feast which Snorri gave in his life of Hákon the Good, he laid emphasis on the toasts (*full*) drunk to the gods Óðinn, Njörð, Freyr. After this the company drank the *bragafull*, and then the *minni* or toast in memory of departed kinsmen.

The terms *bragafull* and *minni* are difficult to interpret. The first is found in the variant forms *bragafull* and *bragarfull*, and its basic meaning is probably 'the chieftain's toast'. Its significance is shown best in the *Ynglinga Saga* (XXXVII). After the death of a king or a jarl, his heir would hold a feast. He must sit on the step in front of the high seat until the cup, called *bragafull* (v.l. *bragarfull*), was brought forth. After that he was conducted to the high seat and was entitled to his inheritance.

In this passage, as elsewhere, the *bragarfull* was accompanied by oaths. In the prose note already quoted from the *Helgakviða Hjǫrvarðssonar* (str. 30) it is said:

The sacrificial boar (*sonargǫltr*) was led forward. Men placed their hands upon him, and swore oaths on the *bragarfull*.

When he wrote about the Jómsborg vikings,[43] Snorri used the word *minni* almost in the same way as he had used *bragafull* in the *Ynglinga Saga*. Before he stepped into his father's high seat, Sveinn Tjúguskegg drank his *minni*, swearing that before three years had passed, he would invade England, kill King Ethelred or drive him from the land. But in the same chapter, Snorri tells how the vikings drank Christ's *minni*, and the *minni* of the Archangel Michael.

As the passage quoted at the beginning of this chapter showed, the word *minni* could mean, for Snorri, 'toast in memory', e.g. of departed kinsmen. This, it appears is popular etymology. In Old Norse, the word *minni* means 'memory', but its application to 'toast in memory' must be influenced by the High German *minna* (later *minne*), which was used to mean little more than 'toast' (*amor*, e.g. *in amore sanctorum*).[44]

The author of the *Fagrskinna*,[45] a history of the Kings of Norway written rather earlier than the *Heimskringla*, was aware that the word *minni* had come to replace the older word *full*. He said that, in the old days, people poured out the *full* as they now did the *minni*, and they assigned the *full* to their mightiest kinsmen, or else to Thór or other gods. This text confirms Snorri's assertion that toasts of departed ancestors were drunk. Again the ceremony is a form of communion between men and gods, men and men.

Alcoholic liquor is a drug; it raises man into a higher world, where he is inspired by loftier thoughts. Its emotional affects are like those of poetry, and that is why, in the myth of the origin of poetry, poetry is

259

identified with the precious mead. The Germans described by Tacitus (*Germania* XXII) used to discuss vital questions, even those of peace and war, at banquets, for at no time was the mind more open to thought. Comparable beliefs are recorded among Indians and other Indo-European peoples, and even among the Aztecs of Mexico.[46]

The question may finally be asked, who conducted the sacrifices described in this chapter and the preceding one? It is plain that religious life was not sharply distinguished from the profane. In Iceland, where history is better preserved than in other northern lands, the organization of the pagan religion is fairly plain. It was seen in Ch. XII (p. 243) that the chief temples numbered thirty-six or thirty-nine. They were administered by the *goðar*, of whom there were probably thirty-six when the Constitution was established *c.* 930, and thirty-nine when it was reformed *c.* 963. The *goði* had to keep up the temple and conduct the sacrifice[47] and in return he received the temple-dues (*hoftollar*).

The word *goði* (pl. *goðar*) derives from *goð* (god), and its original meaning can be no other than 'the divine'. It may be compared with the Gothic *gudja* (priest). This implies that the office of *goði*, or *goðorð*, as it was called, was, in origin sacral.[48] On the other hand, historical sources show that, in Iceland, the religious ones were only a part of the *goði*'s rights and duties and that, by the end of the pagan period, the *goði* was little more than a secular chieftain. The *goðar* presided over local assemblies and were independent rulers, each over his own followers (*þingmenn*). They were united by contract when the General Assembly (*Alþingi*) was formed, *c.* 930, but they still maintained much of their independence. The *goðorð* was described in an early legal document as 'authority and not property'[49] and, therefore, in Christian times not subject to tithe, but it was normally inherited, and could be sold, lent, or even divided.[50]

The settlers of Iceland were predominantly of Norwegian culture and ancestry, and their constitutional law, introduced by Úlfljót *c.* 930, was based on the west Norwegian law of the *Gulaþing*.[51] One of the settlers, Thorhadd, had been a temple-*goði* (*hofgoði*) in Thrándheim, and brought much of his temple with him to Iceland.[52] We cannot, however, tell what was Thorhadd's social or political position in Norway.[53]

We hear little of *goðar* in other Scandinavian lands.[54] Two *goðar* are named in Danish inscriptions of the ninth and tenth centuries.[55] One of these, named twice, is designated *Nura kuþi*, perhaps implying that he was *goði* of a clan or local group, called *Nurir*.

In general it seems that in Scandinavia it was chiefly the prince or the king who presided over sacrifice. Sigurð, Jarl of Hlaðir, maintained the sacrifice on behalf of King Hákon the Good, who was then a nominal Christian.[56] It was seen in Ch. IX that kings were held responsible for the harvest and welfare of their subjects. When they sacrificed ardently, as did Hákon the Great, the people prospered, but when, like Ólaf the Wood-cutter and the sons of Eirík Bloodaxe, they neglected the sacrifice, the seasons went awry and there was famine.

While sacrifice was generally conducted by men, we hear also of priestesses and, in a passage already quoted (Ch. XII, p. 239), a woman was said to perform the sacrifice. It is also told in the *Kristni Saga* (II) how the missionary, Thorvald was preaching the faith in Iceland about the year 982, and meanwhile a woman was offering sacrifice in the temple.

Two women named in the *Landnámabók* are given the title *gyðja* or 'priestess'. In the *Vápnfirðinga Saga* (Ch. V), a certain Steinvör is said to be *hofgyðja* (temple-priestess), and to have charge of the temple, receiving the temple-dues. It is clear that such women did not wield political power, but it is possible that they could inherit the *goðorð* and exercise religious functions which went with it.[57]

It has been suggested that priestesses were associated particularly with the fertility-god, Freyr.[58] It is noteworthy that the *Landnámabók* names a Thuríð *hofgyðja*, dwelling in the extreme south of Iceland. This woman was half-sister of a Thórð *Freysgoði* (Freyr's priest), whose family were called *Freysgyðlingar* (priestlings of Freyr). In the region of their home is a Freysnes (Freyr's Headland).

The supposition that priestesses officiated particularly in the cult of Freyr may be supported by the tale of Gunnar Helming quoted above (Ch. XII), where the idol of Freyr in Sweden was said to be accompanied by a woman called his wife. The god and his priestess seem to form a divine pair, as did the goddess Nerthus and her priest.[59]

It was suggested above that there was no regular priesthood in Scandinavia. If there was, it probably developed late, and perhaps under the influence of Christianity. Adam of Bremen, in a passage quoted above (Ch. XII) mentioned priests (*sacerdotes*), who ministered to the idols of Thór, Wodan and Fricco at Uppsala.

In general, professional priests probably played little part in the religion of the English and continental Germans. Cæsar[60] said that Germans had no 'druids' (*druides*) to preside over sacrifice, perhaps implying that religious practices among Germans were less highly organized than were those of the Celts. Tacitus mentioned the priest of the goddess Nerthus, and the priests, *muliebri ornatu*, who ministered to the two Alcis (see Ch. X). He tells also of the *sacerdos civitatis*, who read the auguries from ships of wood, and of the priest, accompanied by a king or chieftain, who studied the neighing and snorting of sacred horses (*Germania* X). Bede[61] writes at some length of Coifi, chief priest of Northumbrians (*primus pontificum*), implying that, in that region, there was a fully developed pagan hierarchy by the time Christianity was introduced (see Ch. XII).

CHAPTER FOURTEEN

GODLESS MEN

IT HAS been noticed that the basis of Norse heathendom lay in the worship of gods or divine beings. This worship implied a cult, organized on a larger or smaller scale. In some instances, at least, the worship of the lesser divinities, such as the female tutelary spirits (*dísir*), or of the elves (*álfar*) or the deified priapus (*Vǫlsi*), was a family festival, over which the master of the house or his wife presided.[1]

The worship of major gods, on the other hand, was organized more elaborately, and the populations of districts, large or small, joined in sacrifice in public temples. Everyone was obliged to attend or contribute to the great festival at Uppsala, held every nine years. The temples in Guðbrandsdal and at Hlaðir were also centres of organized worship, over which kings or chieftains presided. On a smaller scale, a like organization can be observed in the religious cults of Iceland, where the *goði*, at once temporal and religious ruler, conducted the sacrifice, and property owners were obliged to pay dues (*hoftollar*) for the upkeep of the temple.[2]

The ninth and tenth centuries were an age of social and political upheaval, especially in Norway. The rise of the monarchy and the seizure of ancestral estates drove many from their homes. Some took refuge in other parts of Norway, while others tried their fortunes overseas. The most conservative people, the hereditary landowners, and especially those of western Norway, were those most radically affected by the social revolution of that era. Driven from their lands, they were obliged to seek a living elsewhere. Some of them carried their traditions, even took the pillars of their temples, to the newly discovered lands in the west, Iceland and the Faroe Islands. But others became homeless wanderers, divorced from the social organization and culture in which they had grown up. If they joined viking bands, they entered a new organization and they might then, like the Icelandic poet, Egill Skalla-Grímsson,[3] adopt the cult of a warrior god, such as Óðinn, of whom they had heard little in their childhood. But there were others who took up the beggar's staff, or fled to the forests to join outcasts, who had left society because of some crime, or because of persecution, gaining their bread by wits and strength.

Men like these, cut off from society, were also cut off from the religion of their ancestors and, for them, the cult of the gods had lost its meaning. Again and again, we read in the sources of 'godless men', who had rejected the belief in gods altogether.

Such godless men, the social misfits, must have lived at every period, but it is likely that Christian writers of the Middle Ages made more of them than history justified. In their eyes it was better to believe in no god than to bring sacrifice to stocks and stones, idols and demons. It is said of many idealized figures of the Heroic Age that they never sacrificed to the gods, and despised pagan practices. Among these unbelievers was the Danish Hrólf Kraki, 'most famous of all kings of ancient days'. Neither Hrólf nor his chosen champions ever sacrificed to gods, but believed only in their own might and main (á mátt sinn ok megin). Hrólf once exclaimed that it was not the wicked Óðinn who governed men's lives, but rather fate (auðna). Hrólf's champions spoke of Óðinn as that foul and faithless son of the devil. In contrast to Hrólf stands his archenemy, Aðils, the treacherous king of the Swedes, assiduous in the cult of gods and in the pursuit of magic.[4] Another hero, Ketill Hœngr, is made to say in verse:

Óðin blóta	I never gave sacrifice
gerða ek aldri,	to Óðinn,
hefik þó lengi lifat.	and yet I have lived long.[5]

No less famous was Örvar-Odd (Arrow-Odd), who lived for several centuries and travelled the world from Bjarmaland to Greece. Odd would never sacrifice, and thought it contemptible to crawl before stocks and stones.[6]

Sagas and other medieval works, which have a firmer basis in history, also describe godless men, both in Iceland and Norway and, as might be expected, their numbers grow as the Heathen Age approached its close. A number of men have the nickname 'godless' (goðlauss), and the Landnámabók[7] names a settler of Iceland, Hall the godless, adding that he was son of Helgi the godless, probably a man of western Norway. Neither Hall nor his father would ever sacrifice, but like Hrólf and his champions, they believed in their own might (á mátt sinn).

A more detailed story is told of Hjörleif, who came from Norway to settle in Iceland about 872. He was the foster-brother of Ingólf, remembered as the first permanent settler. These men had grown up in the west of Norway and, when young, they had raided and fought some battles together, and had once visited Iceland. But, while Ingólf stayed in Norway, Hjörleif lived as a viking in Ireland, where he met with memorable adventures and captured a number of thralls. When Hjörleif returned to Norway, his foster-brother held a sacrifice, and he learned from the omens that he should settle in Iceland. Hjörleif, on the other hand, refused to join in the sacrifice, for this was contrary to his practice. The two foster-brothers sailed for Iceland together. Ingólf was guided by the sacred pillars (*ǫndvegissúlur*) of his house, or temple; he threw them overboard, resolved to settle where they should drift ashore. It is not told that Hjörleif put trust in sacred objects or divine beings, and after he landed in Iceland he met with a miserable end, murdered by his Irish thralls. Ingólf, when he beheld the dead body of his foster-brother, exclaimed that such must be the fate of one who would not offer sacrifice to the gods.[8]

In some contexts, the words *máttr* and *megin*, in which godless men are said to believe, appear to have a magical or supernatural significance. But it is not necessary to believe that these men had reverted to an animist, pre-theistic form of religion, or that they worshipped a form of deity within themselves.[9] For the most part they believed only in themselves, in what they could do with their own strength and wits. Such sentiments were expressed most plainly by Finnbogi the Strong, a somewhat apocryphal hero of the tenth century. When the Emperor of Byzantium asked Finnbogi what he believed in, he answered: 'I believe in myself' (*ek trúi á sjálfan mik*).[10]

Two stories may be added to illustrate the outlook of such godless men. Even if these stories cannot be regarded as historical in every detail, they may show how some people thought of religion and its practices towards the end of the Heathen Age.

Snorri and other medieval historians describe the march of St Ólaf from Sweden into the eastern provinces of Norway to fight his last battle, at Stiklastaðir, in the year 1030.[11] Ólaf's army was a motley one and, as he marched through wastes and forest, adventurers and footpads flocked to his banner. Two of them are named, Afra-Fasti and Gauka-Thórir, who were said to be highwaymen and notorious robbers, leading a band of thirty men no better than themselves. When they heard that St Ólaf's army was passing through the region which they frequented, they resolved to join it. They were moved neither by religious fervour nor political ambition, but they craved experience. They had never taken part in a battle conducted by professional generals, deploying their men in formation, and they were anxious to see what tactics the King would adopt. When they offered their services, the King said that he would be glad to enlist such doughty men, but, said he: 'are you Christians?' Gauka-Thórir answered that they were neither Christian nor heathen; he and his men believed in nothing but their own strength and their luck in battle (*afl*, *sigrsæli*), and that had served them well enough. The King urged them to submit to baptism and adopt the true faith, but when they refused, he ordered them to leave his presence. The highwaymen felt this a disgrace, since no one had ever refused their support before. They resolved to follow the King's army at a distance, in company with the rest of the riff-raff.

When the King drew towards the battlefield, he mustered his men, and found that there were more than a thousand heathens among them. He ordered a mass baptism, but the greater number refused to submit, and turned back. Now Gauka-Thórir and Afra-Fasti came forward, but again refused baptism, and retired to take counsel together. One of them said: 'I shall join in the battle, giving support to one side or the other; it does not matter to me on which side I fight.' But the other said that he would prefer to fight at the side of the King, who had the greater need of support, and he added: 'if I have to believe in a god, why should it be worse for me to believe in the White Christ than any other?' These ruffians now submitted to baptism, and laid down their lives in the forefront of the King's army.

Arnljót, another of St Ólaf's followers, said that hitherto he had believed in nothing but his might and strength, but now he had come to believe in the King himself. When the King told him to believe in the White Christ, he said that he did not know where Christ lived or what he did, but he was ready to believe anything the King told him. Arnljót also laid down his life for the King.[12]

A third and equally significant story is told of the Christian King, Ólaf Tryggvason (995–1000). Bárð was the name of a powerful chieftain in Upplönd; he would not submit to the King, nor embrace the religion which he taught. The emissaries whom the King had sent to him failed to return. There was no temple on Bárð's estate, and the King had no reason to believe that he was devout in his worship of the gods. Wishing to make a final attempt to convert Bárð, Ólaf sent the Icelander, Thorvald Tasaldi to him. Declaring his religious beliefs, Bárð said: 'I believe neither in idols nor demons; I have travelled from land to land, and I have come across giants as well as black men, but they have not got the better of me. Therefore, I have believed in my might and strength . . .'[13]

In stories like these, to which many more could be added, we read of men whom society had rejected as outlaws, and especially of those who had travelled and seen much of the world and had, therefore, broken with the traditions of their homeland. Thus isolated, they could no longer practise the conventional religion which they had learnt in childhood, and they found nothing to replace the beliefs which this religion expressed except belief in themselves, and what they could do by their own courage, resolution and physical strength, all of which conceptions are covered by the words *máttr* and *megin*. It would be interesting if men who held such opinions in the Heathen Age could speak for themselves. It is possible that they do.

In earlier chapters I have mentioned the *Hávamál* (Words of the High One, Óðinn).[14] As already explained, this is not a single poem, but a collection of poems or fragments on various subjects and of diverse age and origin. Although the title *Hávamál* is given to the whole collection only two of the first seventy-nine strophes contain allusion to Óðinn. The rest tell hardly anything about religion or belief in gods. They read rather as the words of one who had travelled far and seen much (str. 18), and had come to despise tradition and all the comfort which traditional religion might bring with it. Yet the title *Hávamál* is not altogether inappropriate, even to this part of the collection. As I have attempted to explain, the cult of Óðinn, in some of its aspects, represents a breach with tradition and a rejection of traditional morality and social organization. In this way the cult of Óðinn draws near to atheism.

It is hardly necessary to emphasize that these first strophes of the *Hávamál* do not, in themselves, form a unit, but consist rather of verse sequences, often disordered and corrupt.[15] But most of these strophes show enough internal similarity for us to think that they stem from one period and one country and, for the present purpose, it is convenient to speak of their author or authors as one.

Few would deny that Norway was the land in which most of the strophes originated. The descriptions of nature apply more readily to Norway than to Iceland. The poet describes a withering pine-tree, and he speaks of tools and appliances better known in Norway than in Iceland, of piles of dried timber stored for winter, and of wooden tiles for roofing (str. 60), which could hardly have been used in Iceland. He speaks also of cremation, which was well known in Norway during the Viking Age, but never widespread in Iceland. He speaks of the son of a prince (str. 15), who filled no place in the social system of Iceland.

If these strophes were composed in Norway, we may wonder when and among what class of the people they originated. It has often been said that they express the cynical, individualist and selfish outlook of the peasant. It is true that some interest is shown in house and home, cattle and economy. But it would be hard to believe that the hereditary farmer, the *óðalsbóndi* of Norway, was so cynical and individualistic and had so little interest in his clan and traditions as the author of these verses. Indeed, it is well to beget a son, because he may put up a memorial stone (*bautasteinn*) for you (str. 72), but it is no use saving money for those you love; if you do, someone else will get it (str. 40).

Companions and friendship are valued highly, but this is not the selfless friendship and loyalty which so many saga-writers admired. It is a self-seeking friendship. 'When I was young, I went my way alone; I was rich and happy when I found a companion, for man is the joy (almost the plaything) of man' (str. 47). The poet tells how to make friends and how to keep them. A man should be washed and fed when he goes into the company of others (str. 61); he should not visit his friends when he is half starved, gaping at every morsel (str. 33). No one must try the patience of his friends too hard; he must move on, for by the third day the loved guest is hated (str. 35); when he comes another time they may tell him that the beer is finished, or else not brewed (str. 66).

You must win your friends, exchange presents with them and laugh when they laugh (strs. 41–2). If you trust them, be loyal to them, but if you do not trust them, pretend that you do, laugh with them just the same, but do not let them know what you think (strs. 44–6).

The sentiments expressed in these strophes are not those of men who tilled the soil under patriarchal guidance. They are rather those of men who have been uprooted, have travelled far and learnt much (str. 18). In other words they express the thoughts of men living in an age of social and political upheaval. This suggests the Viking Age, and especially the late ninth and tenth centuries, when Harald Finehair and his immediate followers were consolidating the authority of the central monarchy. Landowners were driven from hereditary estates and forced to take up the beggar's staff (str. 78), or to seek a livelihood other than that to which they were accustomed.

In these first strophes of the *Hávamál* moral virtues are ignored, except for bravery and decorum. Mystical beliefs, such as those in a future life, or even in the gods, play no part and are even scorned. A man must not attempt to keep out of battle, nor go in fear of his life, for death, whether by the spear or old age, is its inevitable conclusion (str. 16). But yet there is no disaster worse than death. Even a lame man can ride a horse, a deaf man can join in battle; it is better to be blind than burned on the funeral pyre, for a corpse is no use to anyone (str. 71). A man has nothing to hope for, but that his son will raise a cairn in his memory (str. 72), and that those who come after him will speak well of him (strs. 76–7).

CHAPTER FIFTEEN

DEATH

IN EARLIER CHAPTERS I have often mentioned Norse conceptions of death. Fallen warriors and heroes were said to go to Valhöll, or to be taken by Óðinn, and dead kings were sometimes raised to the status of elves, or even of gods.[1] It was seen also how intimately the cults of death were linked with those of fertility.[2]

It may now be helpful to summarize beliefs about death, and particularly those of the simpler people, whose lives are described so vividly in the Family Sagas.

At the outset, it must be recognized that we can look for no consistency. Different men held different beliefs, and a man might well hold views which were not logically consistent. Beliefs in the after-life were hazy but, in general, it may be said that life went on after death, at least for a time, and that there was communion, more or less intimate, between the living and the dead. The dead were trusted, venerated or feared. They could give advice and help the living, but also injure them.

It was widely believed that the after-life was inseparable from the body. The dead man lived on, but his life was in the grave, and he could still exercise his influence from there. This is shown in numerous stories about Icelandic peasants. It was said of one man that he was buried standing upright in the threshold of his house, and then he could control the household even better than before.[3] Another wished to be buried in a place where he could see the ships sailing the fjord;[4] and yet another asked to be placed on a hill from which he could watch the whole district.[5]

The benevolent dead may help their relatives and neighbours, but the wicked will grow even more dangerous and wicked than before. Such beliefs are best illustrated by the story of Thórólf Clubfoot,[6] which is so rich that it deserves to be retold in some detail.

Thórólf was a wicked man while he lived. He died sitting upright in his high seat, and all the servants were shocked at the sight of him. They sent for his virtuous son Arnkell, who warned the household not to step before the dead man's eyes before the obsequies (*nábjargir*)[7] had been performed and the eyes were closed. They must evidently be protected from the evil eye. Then Arnkell stepped behind his dead father and struggled hard before he could overcome him and lay him out. The dead man's head was wrapped in a cloth; the wall of the house was broken behind him, and he was dragged through the gap, probably in the hope that he would not find his way home through the door. The body was laid on a sledge drawn by oxen, and a heavy load it was. It was buried under huge stones, but as summer drew to its close and days grew short, people knew that Thórólf was not lying quiet in his grave. The oxen which had dragged the body were bewitched and went mad; every beast or bird which came near the grave dropped dead on the spot. The shepherd would often run home, saying that Thórólf had chased him, and one night he did not come home. His body was found black as coal, with every bone in it smashed. He was buried beside Thórólf.

Thórólf often visited his old home, persecuting the housewife who raved until she died. He plundered the neighbourhood, killing many on his way, and his victims were afterwards seen roaming with him. [8]

Thórólf's son, Arnkell, now resolved that the grave must be opened. The body was uncorrupt but had grown so heavy that the strongest oxen could hardly drag it. In the end they got the corpse to a headland above the sea, where they buried it again and fenced it off.

Seasons passed, and Thórólf gave no trouble, but when his son was dead he broke out and did such damage that the neighbours opened the grave again. He was still uncorrupt, but he looked more like a troll than a man, black as pitch and fat as an ox. The neighbours could drag Thórólf no further than the brink of the headland; they dropped him on to the beach, and kindled a fire and burned him up. Like others who walk after death, Thórólf had to be killed a second time, perhaps even a third, before he was really dead. [9] Even this was not the end of him. A miserable, lean cow went down to the beach where the corpse had been burned. She licked the stones on to which ashes had drifted, and was soon in calf. The calf was a bull, dapple-grey. [10] He was of abnormal size and strength. Long before he was full grown he gored his master to death, and then made off to sink in a marsh, and was never seen again.

This story contains two conceptions of death, which are not consistent. On the one hand there is the living corpse and, on the other, the wicked man reborn in the form of a bull.

I have mentioned some conceptions of death which were popular, at least in pagan Iceland, but there were others of which I have said nothing.

Some people believed that the dead did not stay in their graves; they went on a long journey. Their destination was the World of Death, or perhaps I should say the Worlds of Death, for there seems to be more than one. As Snorri has it,[11] wicked men go to Hel and thence to the Misty Hel (*Niflhel, Niflheimr*).[12] Snorri seems here to be drawing on a passage in the *Vafþrúðnismál* (str. 43), where it is said that men die from Hel into Niflhel. The way to these regions, as Snorri tells, lies downward and northward, passing through deep, dark valleys. The goddess who presides there is herself called Hel. Originally the conception of this goddess and her world was probably linked with that of the grave, for the name *Hel* may be related to the verb *hylja* (to cover).

A man who had to set out on this long journey needed supplies, tools and equipment. We read once of "death-shoes" (*helskór*) fastened to the feet of a corpse, for he had to walk to the Other World (*til Valhallar*).[13] In the same text it is told that a dead man was placed in a ship and the ship was placed in the burial mound. In fact, some five or six Icelanders of the pagan period were said in early sources to have been buried in ships or boats.[14] Here the work of archaeologists helps us. In recent years, three or four boat-graves dating from the tenth century have been excavated in Iceland.[15] Comparatively little excavation has yet been done in that country, and it may be expected that more finds of this kind will be made. It is not surprising that the boats in the Icelandic graves are only simple rowing boats, for grave-goods in Iceland are generally poor. But when we turn to Norway and Sweden the picture changes, for hundreds of boat-graves have been found in those countries, including such glorious ones as those of Gokstad and Oseberg, dating from the ninth century. These graves are accompanied by countless treasures, burned or buried with the chieftains who occupied them. (See Plate 46.)

It is probably right to assume that the burial ship was intended chiefly to carry the dead man to the Other World, although this may not have been its only object. In the *Gísla Saga* (XVII) it is told how such a great boulder was placed in the ship that all the timbers creaked. The hero said that he did not know how to fix a ship if the storm should carry this one away. Archaeologists have also pointed out that some of the burial ships are made immovable, or even laid upside-down.[16] The ship, which has taken its place in fertility ritual for many centuries[17] may well have been regarded as a symbol of rebirth as well as of death.

A man cannot set out on his long journey with nothing but a boat. He needs food and weapons, while a woman may need jewels and precious clothing, even needles and other equipment for her daily life.

It is told of a pagan Icelander that he was buried 'according to ancient custom' with his horse and his dog.[18] The bones of horses have often been found in graves, and particularly in those of Icelanders.[19] In the Oseberg grave, the bones of about thirteen horses have been counted. The horse might carry his master on the long journey, and his flesh might supplement his diet. It has appeared in earlier chapters[20] that the horse was a symbol both of death and fertility. Dogs, as the sagas sometimes show,[21] were the companions and friends of men, and many of their bones have been found in graves throughout the northern world.[22]

The dead might also need human company. It is told of one of the settlers of Iceland, Ásmund Atlason, that when he died his thrall would not live after him, and killed himself. Thrall and master were placed in a boat together and buried. But some time later, the voice of Ásmund was heard speaking in verse from the grave. He resented the company of the thrall and would rather be left alone. The howe was then opened and the thrall taken out.[23] It has been said that the basis of this story was that the thrall was sacrificed to his dead master.[24]

However that may be, it is plain that human sacrifices were given to the dead. The Oseberg grave contained the bones of two women, and it is believed that one was the Queen and the other her servant, slaughtered to accompany her.[25]

It might be expected that a man would want a wife or a mistress to go with him to the Other World. Norse literary sources tell little about this, although Odd Snorrason, who wrote his life of Ólaf Tryggvason late in the twelfth century, says that if a king of the Swedes died before his queen, she would be placed in the howe with him.[26] The archaeological researches of H. Shetelig[27] suggest that the custom of suttee, as it is called, was not introduced into Norway before the fourth century.

The most detailed accounts of practices of this kind come, not from Norse sources, but from the pens of two Arab travellers, who had visited the Rus or Scandinavians living on the Volga.[28] They could converse only through interpreters, and some of the remarks which they report may not be exact.

One of the Arabs, Ibn Rustah, says that when a chieftain among the Norsemen dies, his body is laid in a grave which looks like a large house. Meat, drink, money and jewels are placed with him and, besides this, his favourite wife is put alive in the cairn.

The other Arab, Ibn Fadlán, remarks that when a poor man among the Norsemen dies, they build a small boat, put his body in it and burn it up. But when a rich man dies, the procedure is different. Ibn Fadlán had himself attended the funeral of a Norse chief and left a lurid and horrifying description of it.

First of all the dead chief's property was divided into three parts, one for his family, one to buy drink for those attending the funeral, and one to pay for the equipment which the chief will take to the Other World. The chief's servants were then assembled and they were asked: 'which of you will die with him?' When one answered: 'I will'—and it was usually a woman—she was held to her word. From that time she was treated as a princess. Servants were appointed to wait on her (and, presumably, to prevent her escape).

Meanwhile a ship was procured for the dead chief and drawn up on posts on the shore. After some days the body was placed, splendidly dressed, in a tent on the ship, with every kind of food and drink. A dog was cut in half and thrown into the ship, as well as draught beasts, cows, a cock and a hen. Meanwhile, the girl who was to die passed from one man to another, who had intercourse with her, saying that he did it only for the love of the chief.

The girl was given a hen. She cut off its head and the body was thrown into the funeral ship. It is possible that birds of this kind symbolized rebirth. We may remember the story of Hadding's female companion who pulled off the head of a cock and threw it over the wall of death, where it came to life and crowed.[29] We may also think of the cock, Salgofnir, awakening the fallen warriors in Valhöll.[30]

The condemned girl was lifted from the ground three times. The first time she said: 'Behold I see my father and mother', and then: 'I see all my dead relations'. Finally she exclaimed: 'I see my master seated in Paradise, and Paradise is green and fair . . . He is calling me, send me to him.'

The girl was then taken on board the ship where she was cruelly slaughtered by an old woman called the 'angel of death'. Finally the ship was set alight and the flames consumed it speedily with all that was in it. Afterwards a kind of mound was built over the remains and inscriptions were written.

This Arab account shows that Norsemen had other conceptions of death than the sombre ones mentioned in this chapter. A Norseman who was present said that the Arabs were stupid men to place their beloved in the earth, where worms would eat them. Burned in a twinkling, the dead would go immediately to Paradise.

Some might hope for a brighter future than the half-life in the grave or the journey to distant sunless underworlds. This hope might be fulfilled in Valhöll, the warriors' Paradise, which has so frequently been mentioned in this book. It is, however, improbable that beliefs of that kind had deep roots, and it is plain that some despised them. Poets of the *Hávamál* (strs. 71 ff, cf str. 15) tell that death is the end and the worst evil that can befall. Ill health and injury are better; it is even better to be blind than burned on the funeral pyre, for a corpse is a useless object.[31]

Out of this negative background comes the noblest of northern thoughts of death. Death is the greatest evil known to man, but yet it can be overcome. Live well and die bravely and your repute will live after you. Fate will decide the moment and manner of your death, but fate will not decide how you will face it. A brave death will be rewarded, not with pork and mead as in Valhöll, but with the esteem of your friends, kinsmen and even of your enemies. They will tell how you lived and how you died. Your story will live, as has that of many a northern hero.

According to some religious doctrines, this life is not the end, but man, or his soul, is reborn to live in another body. We can see, although dimly, that Norsemen of the Viking Age knew of this belief. I have quoted the story of Thórólf Clubfoot, reborn as a bull. In another text we read of lovers who were reborn to continue their love in a second life. But that, says the early Icelandic writer, is now called an 'old wives' tale'.[32] It is improbable that many people of the Viking Age believed in metempsychosis, although several instances of the belief have been quoted in earlier chapters of this book, and particularly in the chapter on the Divine Kingship.

CHAPTER SIXTEEN

THE BEGINNING OF THE WORLD AND ITS END

THE STORY of the creation is given in detail only by Snorri[1], who combined several sources, not always consistent with each other, and added some deductions of his own. The most important of Snorri's sources are the *Vafþrúðnismál*, *Grímnismál* and *Vǫluspá* (see Ch. I), but he has added details from other sources not known to us.

Since the poems are often difficult to follow, it may be helpful first to recall the salient points in Snorri's story.

He begins by citing the *Vǫluspá* (str. 3) and, according to the form in which he quotes this poem, there was nothing at the beginning of time, but a great void, called *Ginnungagap*, a void charged with mighty, magic force.[2] Long before the earth was formed, *Niflheimr*, known later as the dark, misty world of death, existed. In it was a well, called Hvergelmir, from which flowed eleven rivers. In the south there was another world, blazing hot, and it was called *Múspell*; it was guarded by a giant, called *Surtr* (the Black).

The next stage is difficult to follow. The rivers from Niflheim froze, and frozen mist piled up into the Ginnungagap. The rime and ice met the sparks from the hot world, Múspell. They melted and the drops took the shape of a man, or giant, called Ymir or Augelmir.[3] All the terrible tribe of giants descend from this monster, for when he sweated a male and female grew under his arm, and one leg got a son with the other.

Snorri next gives an account of the origin of gods, for which no source can be found. Melting rime took the shape of a cow, Auðumbla,[4] who fed Ymir with her milk. The cow got her own nourishment from the salty blocks of rime, which she licked into the shape of a man. He was called Búri, and he had a son Bor. Bor married Bestla, daughter of a giant Bölthorn (Evil thorn), and their children were the gods, Óðinn, Vili, Vé.

These divine brothers killed Ymir, the giant, and such was the flow of blood that all the frost giants were drowned except one, who escaped mysteriously with his family to continue his evil race.

The three gods, Óðinn and his brothers, now built the earth. They carried the body of Ymir into the middle of the great void. They made sea and lakes of his blood, earth of his flesh and the sky of his skull, placing a dwarf under each of the four corners, as if to hold it up.

The clouds were made of Ymir's brains, and stars and heavenly bodies from sparks which flew from Múspell. The gods ordered their movements, and thus established days and years.

The earth was circular and on the outside was a mighty ocean. By its shores the gods established a dwelling place for the giants. Within, they built Miðgarð, the world of men, fortified, as it seems, with a fence made of Ymir's eyelashes.

The god's next task was to found the race of men. On the seashore they came upon two tree-trunks, and endowed them with breath, wit, hearing, vision and other qualities of life. The man was called *Askr* (Ash-tree) and the woman *Embla*, which may mean a creeper, or such-like, but has not yet been explained.[5] Finally the gods built Ásgarð, in the middle of the world, where they themselves were destined to live.

Much of this story derives from the *Vafþrúðnismál* and the *Grímnismál*, from which Snorri quotes a number of lines. It is told in them how the earth, sky and sea were made from Ymir's body and blood. A poet of the tenth century had also used the kenning 'wounds of the giant's neck' (*jǫtuns háls undir*) for 'sea'. The *Vafþrúðnismál* (31–3) tells of the origin of the first giant, Aurgelmir, whom Snorri identified with Ymir, and of how he propagated his race, although with fewer details than Snorri gives. The poem does not tell, as Snorri did, of the flood which drowned the giants in the blood of their own ancestor, except for one, who escaped with his family on a *lúðr*. The poem tells only that the giant was placed on a *lúðr*. This word has never been fully explained and interpretations of it vary between cradle, coffin, bier, ship,[6] but Snorri seems to think of it rather as an object which floats. It has often been said that there was no flood in the Norse creation myth, and that Snorri, knowing the story of Noah, felt the need of one. It must, however, be admitted that Snorri's story is altogether unlike the biblical one, and has closer affinities with some recorded among primitive peoples.

The most sophisticated and rational account of the creation known to Snorri was that of the *Vǫluspá*. Here, as elsewhere, the poet expresses individual rather than popular views. For him, the creation was little more than the first act in the drama leading to the Ragnarök.

At the beginning, according to Snorri's text of the poem, there was nothing but a void, although according to other texts, the giant Ymir existed already then. Considering how Ymir (Aurgelmir) was said to have taken shape, both by Snorri and in the *Vafþrúðnismál*, we may think that Snorri followed the better version of the *Vǫluspá*.[7]

The *Vǫluspá* tells next how the sons of Bur, who must be Óðinn and his brothers, lifted the world, evidently from the sea, and fashioned Miðgarð. When the sun shone from the south, the earth was overgrown with green herbage. Sun, moon and stars were set on their courses, day and night established, and man and woman were created out of the powerless, fateless *Askr* and *Embla*. Their creators were Óðinn, who was accompanied, not by his brothers Vili and Vé, but by the gods Hœnir and Lóður (see Ch. V).

The poet goes on to describe the Yggdrasill, tree of fate, upon which the welfare of the universe seems to depend (see Ch. II, Lord of the Gallows). Beneath it lay the well of fate (*Urðarbrunnr*), from which the fates, conceived in female form, proceeded to lay down the course of men's lives.

From these sketches of the poetic sources from which he chiefly drew, it is obvious that Snorri described several incidents which cannot be traced to them, at least in their extant forms.

One of the most striking is that about the cow, Auðumbla (Auðumla), who fed the giant Ymir and licked the blocks of ice into human form to form the first of gods. Auðumbla might thus be seen as mother, both of giants and gods. Some legends about the worship of cows were quoted in Ch. XII, while oxen or cattle were commonly offered as sacrifice. Even if such stories are doubted, it cannot be doubted that Snorri's tale of Auðumbla is, in essentials, age-old. Parallel myths have been cited from Persia and India, but there is none which resembles the story of Auðumbla more closely than that of the Egyptian sky-goddess, Hathor, described as mother-goddess, sky-goddess, fertility goddess, midwife, nurse of Horus and mother of all gods and goddesses. Like Auðumbla, Hathor is depicted in the form of a cow.[8]

Iranian tradition also has striking parallels with the Norse creation myth.

The creation, as Norse heathens saw it, was a natural evolutionary process, arising from the fusion of polarities, heat and cold, light and dark. Many variants of the Iranian creation myth are recorded, and they too contain such dualist explanations of the cosmos, the 'hot and moist, bright, sweet-smelling, and light' on the one hand, with the 'cold and dry, heavy, dark and stinking' on the other. The two are separated by a void, as it were a mighty gap.[9]

The first giant, Ymir, also finds his counterparts in Iranian and, to some extent, in Indian myth. Ymir, as was seen, was at once father and mother of the giants and was, in other words, bisexual. A myth like this one appears in variant forms in Iranian records. According to one of them, the god Zurvan existed before ages. He conceived twins, one 'light and fragrant', the other 'dark and stinking'. The fair one created heaven and earth, and everything beautiful and good, but the other created demons and everything evil.

The formation of the cosmos, as described in some Iranian sources, is also rather like that described in the Norse sources. It was made from the body of the first anthropomorphic figure. The sky was his head, the earth his feet, water his tears, plants his hair. This form of the creation myth is said to derive from India.[10]

Ymir, the name of the first anthropomorphic figure in Norse myth, could formally mean 'the roarer', which is not an unsuitable name for a giant, but it has often been associated with Iranian *Yima* (Sanscrit *Yama*), which means 'twin' and is the name given to the first man.[11]

As they are recorded, the Norse and oriental myths of creation are separated by many centuries and thousands of miles. They differ, even fundamentally, but details such as those about the cow and the hermaphrodite progenitor, as well as the cosmos created from the body of a primeval being, resemble each other in ways which makes it impossible to think of independent development. In other words, the Norse creation myth must be influenced by the eastern ones, but it is not yet possible to say when and how this influence was exerted. Some would suppose that the Goths and other Germanic peoples in south-eastern Europe in the first four centuries of our era fell under oriental influences. Myths, such as those last quoted, might then have been transmitted to Scandinavia, even through the medium of the Heruls, who returned to that region in the sixth century. It is, however, equally likely that such myths reached Europe at a much earlier period, even as early as the time when Indo-European language and culture were adopted. In this case the myths must have been adapted, finally formulated, and nearly fossilized in the north.

Norse creation myths are less sharply dualistic than some eastern ones. The first anthropomorphic figure was Ymir, progenitor of the evil giants, whose race will live to threaten the cosmos until the Ragnarök. They appear at once as demons of devouring death, of destructive fire and cold. But Ymir, according to Snorri's version of the myth, was also an ancestor of the gods, for Bestla, mother of Óðinn and his brothers, was daughter of a giant, Bölthorn. A myth of this kind seems to be present in the mind of the author of the *Hávamál* (str. 140), who makes Óðinn say: 'I learned nine mighty songs from the famous son of *Bǫlþórr* (sic), father of Bestla . . .' It seems that Óðinn had acquired some of his wisdom and magic from a giant, a maternal uncle.

Enough stories have been told in this book to show that gods and giants were not always on bad terms; the gods themselves were not wholly good, and they bear some of the marks of their giant ancestry.

The centre of the divine world must be the tree Yggdrasill (see Ch. II, Lord of the Gallows), where the gods sit in council every day.[12] The tree rises to the sky and its branches spread over the whole world. It is supported by three roots; one stretches to the world of death (Hel), another to the world of frost-giants, and the third to the world of men. It must be this tree on which Óðinn hanged himself in his quest for wisdom. The evergreen at Uppsala may be seen as its earthly replica. The Yggdrasill upholds the universe, even as the main pillars uphold a house.[13] The welfare of the universe must then depend on the Yggdrasill, just as the welfare of many peoples, even of families throughout the Indo-European world, depended on the welfare of one tree, regarded with awe and veneration.

The sibyl to whom the *Vǫluspá* is ascribed seems to remember the Yggdrasill before it had risen from the soil,[14] even before fate existed. When the mighty tree appears in its full stature, it has already begun to decay. It suffers greater torment than men can know; a hart is devouring its foliage, its trunk is rotting and the serpent, Níðhögg, is gnawing it from below. When the Ragnarök is at hand, the old tree will shiver and creak.

The Yggdrasill is also called *Mímameiðr*, the tree or post of Mími, who can be no other than Mímir (also called *Mímr*), wisest of the Æsir. It will be recalled how, when peace was concluded between the two tribes of gods, Mímir was sent as a hostage to the Vanir, who cut off his head and returned it to their erstwhile enemies.[15] Óðinn pickled the head and derived wisdom from it.

According to Snorri, three wells lay at the base of the Yggdrasill, one under each root. Under the root which reached to the world of frost-giants lay the well of Mímir (*Mímisbrunnr*), in which Óðinn had pledged his eye. Under another root was the well Hvergelmir (Roaring kettle?), and under the third was the well of fate (*Urðarbrunnr*).

In this passage, as in some others, Snorri may be too systematic, and probably the three names all apply to one well, which was basically the well of fate, and hence the source of wisdom. This well would thus correspond with the one beneath the holy tree at Uppsala, in which sacrifices were immersed and auguries were read. *Urðr*, the name for fate, is commonly identified with Old English *wyrd*, said ultimately to be related to Latin *vertere* (to turn), as if applied to a goddess spinning the threads of fate. In fact, *Urðr* is sometimes personified, but sometimes seems to be rather abstract, and her name is used as a word for death.

In the *Vǫluspá* (str. 20), the goddess of fate is seen with two others, *Verðandi* (Present?) and *Skuld* (Future), probably late additions, laying down the course of men's lives. Not only men, but also gods and giants are subject to the will of these hardly personal figures.

As the cosmos had a beginning, so it will have an end, which hangs over gods and men as a permanent threat. The end will be the *Ragnarǫk*, meaning 'fate of the gods'. In some sources, it is corruptly called *Ragnarøkkr*, 'twilight of the gods'. It was also called *aldar rǫk*, 'the fate of mankind'. The word *rǫk* is not uncommonly used in such senses as 'course of events', 'destiny,' 'fate'.

As we read the *Vǫluspá*, the only poem in which the whole course of the Ragnarök is traced, the elements of decay seem to be present almost since the beginning of time. In few lines the poet describes the Golden Age of the joyful, innocent, youthful gods; how they built shrines and temples, forged jewels and played at tables:

unz þrjár kvómu,	until three came,
þursa meyjar,	daughters of giants,
ámátkar mjǫk,	filled with cruel might
ór jǫtunheimum.	from the demon world.

It is as if the giant maidens had come to sow seeds of corruption. In the poem the world hastens on its course. We read of the witch Gullveig, pierced with spears and living yet (see Ch. VII, first section), of the war between the two tribes of gods and of the broken wall of Ásgarð. It is told next how Freyja had been promised, or given, to the giants, but the covenant was broken. The tempo increases. The innocent Baldr is pierced by the mistletoe and Loki is fettered, and one fearful scene succeeds another. The sibyl sees a river flowing from the giant world in the east, bearing swords and daggers. On the shore of corpses (*Nástrǫnd*) she sees a castle, bound or wattled with serpents' backs. Their poison drips through the skylight. Within she sees perjurers, murderers and seducers wading the swift, venomous streams, and the cruel serpent, Níðhǫgg, sucking the corpses of the dead.

In the east, the sibyl also sees the brood of the wolf, Fenrir, fed by an old giantess in the Iron Forest. One of these is destined to rob or swallow the sun. The sun grows dark and the storms tempestuous.

Two obscure strophes follow, in which three cocks are heard crowing in presage of doom. The one is crowing in the gallows tree, or gallows wood,[16] the second is awakening Óðinn's warriors in Valhöll, and the third, sooty-red, is crowing beneath the earth in the world of death.

The poet tells how the wolf (*freki*), Garm, chained before the cave,

Gnipahellir, will bay and break his bonds. This wolf can hardly be other than Fenrir, whom Týr had fettered at the cost of his arm.[17]

The world of men is described in few words. Moral values are rejected; brother slays brother and the bonds of kinship are neglected; it is an age of harlotry, a criminal, merciless age.

Heimdall, the watchman of the gods, sounds his horn, while the Yggdrasill shivers and groans. A giant (*jǫtunn*) breaks loose. This is probably Loki who, although counted among the gods, has close affinities with the giants.

Demons approach from various directions; the world serpent coils in a mighty wrath, and the rusty yellow eagle shrieks at the prospect of carrion, while Naglfar,[18] the ship of death, breaks her moorings.

Fire-demons, the sons of Múspell, board the ship, with Loki at the helm. Meanwhile, the whole of the giant world groans and the dwarfs sob before the doors of their rocky dwellings. The mountains crash and men tread the world of death. The sky is rent.

Surt, chief of the demons, arrives with a sword of fire, and the gods meet their fate. Freyr fights with Surt, and Óðinn falls before the wolf, to be avenged by his son Víðar, who pierces the monster to the heart. Thór fights with his old enemy the serpent and, as it seems, they kill each other.

The sun will turn black and stars vanish, while the earth sinks into the sea. Smoke and flames gush forth, playing against the firmament.

Even this is not the end of everything, for it is hardly possible to think of a state in which nothing is left at all, even though gods and men must die.

The earth, as we may believe, had been lifted by the gods from the sea (see p. 277). When they die it must sink back, but when the Ragnarök has passed it will rise again.

Some gods will survive, and once again they will meet and discuss the ancient wisdom of Óðinn. The gold pieces with which they had played tables at the beginning will be recovered; the Golden Age will return. Baldr and Höð, who innocently killed him, will come back and inhabit the divine sanctuaries. Worthy men will live in a hall called Gimlé,[19] roofed with gold, where they will enjoy delight throughout ages.

Now the mighty one who rules all will come to his godhead. Even yet the world is not purged of evil for the cruel, dark, glittering dragon is seen bearing corpses in his wings.

It must be emphasized that the *Vǫluspá* does not express popular views about the Ragnarök, any more than it did about the creation. The poet was pagan by upbringing, and his thoughts were grounded on pagan tradition. But he was eclectic; he adopted such pagan symbols as suited his taste and added others which he had learnt, perhaps at second hand, from Christian legend.

It is often difficult to know whether a motive is pagan or Christian, or whether it was common to both traditions.

Christian influences may be suspected in the decline of morals, when brothers will fight and the bonds of kindred will be ignored (cf Mark XIII, 2), as they may when the sun is darkened and the stars fall (cf Mark XIII, 24–5). Punishment for the wicked and reward for the good, clearly envisaged in the *Vǫluspá* (strs. 39 and 64) may also have more to do with Christian than with pagan belief.

In one strophe, the author of the *Vǫluspá* tells how the mighty one, who rules all, will come to his godhead (*regindómr*). Since this strophe is found only in one manuscript, some critics have believed it to be interpolated. But Sigurður Nordal, in his outstanding edition of the poem,[20] showed that it cannot easily be excluded from the text. In these lines, the poet showed that he had crossed the border-line which divides polytheism from monotheism. We could believe that he foresaw the decline and end of the pagan religion and hoped for a better one to take its place. He may also have been inspired by the widespread Christian apprehension that the world would come to an end in the year 1000 or 1033.

Even if the *Vǫluspá* expresses the views of a mystic and an exceptional poet, the apprehension that the end would come, and was even at hand, was not confined to him. Allusions to the impending catastrophe were made by several of the scalds. When Eirík Bloodaxe was killed in England (954), his widow commissioned a lay describing how the dead prince was received by Óðinn and fallen heroes in Valhöll. There was such a din as if Baldr were returning, as he will when the Ragnarök has passed. Why had Óðinn, god of war, stolen the victory from Eirík? It was because the grey wolf (Fenrir) was glaring at the dwellings of the gods, ready to spring; Óðinn needed the support of Eirík in the final battle.[21] Another thought was expressed by Eyvind in his lay in memory of Hákon the Good (died *c.* 960). Before Norway has so noble a king again, the wolf will pillage the dwellings of men.[22]

Kormák, praising his mistress, Steingerð, said that the mountains will fall into the sea, and the forces of nature be reversed, as they will at the time of the Ragnarök, before so beautiful a woman shall be born again.[23] Another Icelandic scald, in a lay in memory of the Orkney Jarl, Thorfinn (died 1064), said that the sun will turn black, the sky will fall and the waves will batter the mountain tops before a nobler prince is born in Orkney.[24]

Few details about the Ragnarök are described in sources other than the *Vǫluspá* except for the *Vafþrúðnismál* and by Snorri, who partly followed this poem. The beliefs expressed in the *Vafþrúðnismál* are cruder and more primitive than those of the *Vǫluspá*.

As in the *Vǫluspá*, Óðinn will be killed by the wolf, but according to the *Vafþrúðnismál* the wolf will swallow him. Óðinn's son, Víðar, will avenge him, not by stabbing the wolf to the heart, but by tearing his jaws.

The poet knows of several gods who will survive the Ragnarök. Víðar and Váli, the two sons of Óðinn, as well as Thór's sons, Móði and Magni, who will possess the hammer, Mjǫllnir. He knows also that the sun will be destroyed by Fenrir, but beforehand it will give birth to another sun, who will tread the path of her mother. The poet also tells about the scene of the final battle between gods and giants. It is a plain, or field, called *Vigríðr* (Battle-shaker?), a hundred leagues each way.[25] He speaks of the fire of Surt (*Surti*) and of the terrible winter, the *fimbulvetr*, which will form a part of the Ragnarök. Two men will survive it, hiding themselves in a forest, *Hoddmimisholt*. Their food will be the morning dew, and from them a new race of men will descend.

This *fimbulvetr* is one of the strangest motives in the story of the Ragnarök. The author of the *Vǫluspá* (str. 41) seems to make a cryptic allusion to it, but it is described in detail only by Snorri, who knew both this poem and the *Vafþrúðnismál*, but must have had access to other sources as well.

In the *fimbulvetr*, as Snorri tells, there will be frost and snow, and the sun will give neither light nor warmth. This winter will be the length of three winters with no summer between them. One wolf will swallow the sun and another the moon. Following the *Vafþrúðnismál*, Snorri also tells how two men will survive in the forest Hoddmimisholt.

A. Olrik[26] drew attention to a rather similar Persian myth, believed to be of great age. The wise lord had warned Yima of the approach of a winter more terrible than any before. It would rain, snow and hail for three years; Yima must build a *vara* (underground retreat). He must shelter the finest of men and women, as well as cattle, plants and sweet-smelling foods. After the winter had passed, Yima and the noble race he had reared would re-people the earth.

Possibly the Norse and Persian stories are related, as some of those about the creation must certainly have been. But such stories could also have developed independently among peoples who had reason to apprehend winters, bleaker, colder and darker than they had known before.

In his splendid analysis of the Ragnarök, A. Olrik showed that it had parallels both in Christian and in pagan legend. The wolf born to swallow the sun and the one who is to break loose in the Ragnarök had no parallels in Christian eschatology, but figures like them could be found in Asian legends and particularly in those of northern and western Asia. On the other hand, Loki, the god and demon, who is to break his bonds in the Ragnarök, had much in common with the fallen angel, who is to lie chained until the Last Day.

In the *Vǫluspá* (str. 51) some prominence is given to the people of Múspell (*Múspells . . . lýðir*), who will come over the sea in the ship Naglfar, with Loki at the helm. In the *Lokasenna* (str. 42), Loki taunts Freyr. He had given away his sword for his giant bride (see Ch. VII). He did not know how he would fight when the sons of Múspell rode over the dark forest (*Myrkviðr*).

These sons of Múspell are not named in any other poetic source, although Snorri had lucid ideas about them. They are demons of destruction and, in the Ragnarök, they appear to be led by the fire-giant Surt.

Snorri had other things to tell of Múspell and his tribe. Múspell owns the Naglfar, and the hot world in the south is called 'Múspell's World' (*Múspellsheimr*), or simply *Múspell*. It is guarded by Surt, with his sword of fire.

It is commonly agreed that the word Múspell is loaned from continental German. It is found in the Bavarian poem, *Muspilli* where it appears in the form *Muspelle* (dative). This poem was inserted into an older manuscript, probably in the late ninth century. The word occurs also in two passages of the Old Saxon *Heliand*, of the mid-ninth century, as *Mudspelles* (genitive) and *Mutspelli* (nominative).

In these Christian German texts, the word *Muspilli* can only be an abstract noun, meaning 'the end of the world', 'Day of Judgment'. Many attempts have been made to explain its origin. It is plainly a compound, and its second element is probably identical with O.N. *spell* (destruction), but no credible explanation of the first element has yet been offered.[27] Whatever its origin, the Norse pagans appear to have borrowed the word *Múspell* from their southern neighbours; they misunderstood it, believing not that it meant 'the end of the world', but was the name of a fire-demon, or father of fire-demons, who would destroy the world.

In the Ragnarök, the world is to be destroyed by fire, as in many Christian apocryphal works. It is also to be destroyed by water, for the earth will sink into the sea. Celts and other peoples of western Europe shared this natural fear; the sea must one day get the upper hand.

In short, the Ragnarök, as it is described in the *Vǫluspá* and by

Snorri, consists of motives drawn from many sources. Some of these were influenced by Christian legend, but others were inherent in pagan belief. For the latter we must look chiefly to the *Vafþrúðnismál* and to the allusions of the scalds.

ABBREVIATIONS

Finnur Jónsson, *ONOI.*—Finnur Jónsson, *Den oldnorske og oldislandske Litteraturs Historie*, ed. 2, I–III, 1920–1924.

Flb.—*Flateyjarbók*, ed. G. Vigfússon and C. R. Unger, I–III, 1860–1868.

Hkr.—*Heimskringla*, ed. Bjarni Aðalbjarnarson, I–III, 1941–1951.

J. de Vries, *Rel.²*—J. de Vries, *Altgermanische Religionsgeschichte*, ed. 2, I–II, 1956–1957.

SBVS.—*Saga-Book of the Viking Club* (later *Viking Society*), 1895 (in progress).

Skj.—*Den norsk-islandske Skjaldedigtning*, ed. Finnur Jónsson, A I–II, B I–II, 1912–1915.

SnE.—*Edda Snorra Sturlusonar*, ed. Finnur Jónsson, 1931.

SnE. Gylf.—*Gylfaginning* in *SnE.*, q.v.

SnE. Sk.—*Skáldskaparmál* in *SnE.*, q.v.

Yngl. S.—*Ynglinga Saga* in *Hkr.*, q.v.

NOTES

Introductory

1. Cf. Ólafur Lárusson, *Lög og Saga*, 1958, 60 ff; G. Turville-Petre, *Um Óðinsdýrkun á Íslandi*, 1958, 21 ff.
2. Cf. G. Turville-Petre, *The Heroic Age of Scandinavia*, 1951, 19 ff; further H. Arntz, *Handbuch der Runenkunde*, ed. 2, 1944; R. W. V. Elliott, *Runes*, 1959, 1 ff.
3. *Hávamál* 80; cf S. B. F. Jansson, *The Runes of Sweden*, 1962, 15 ff.
4. See M. Olsen, *Eggjum-Stenens Indskrift med de ældre Runer*, 1919; L. Jacobsen, *Eggjum-Stenen*, 1931; further Gerd Høst, *Norsk Tidsskrift for sprogvidenskap*, XIX, 1960, 489 ff.
5. See E. Wessén, *Runstenen vid Röks Kyrka*, 1958.
6. See Ch. III, Thór's Hammer and his Goats.
7. *Hedenske Kultminder i norske Stedsnavne*, I, 1915; *The Farms and Fanes of Ancient Norway*, 1928; besides numerous papers, some of which were reprinted in *Norrøne Studier*, 1938.
8. Especially by E. Wessén in various works, including *Studier till Sveriges hedna mythologi och fornhistoria*, 1924; *Schwedische Ortsnamen und altnordische Mythologie* in *Acta Philologica Scandinavica* IV, 1929, 97 ff; more critical views were expressed by J. Sahlgren, *Hednisk gudalära och nordiska ortnamn* in *Namn och Bygd*, XXXVIII, 1950, 1 ff.
9. See G. Knudsen in *Nordisk Kultur*, XXVI (*Religionshistorie*), 1942, 28 ff and refs.
10. See Ólafur Lárusson, *Nordisk Kultur*, XXVI, 74 ff; *idem*, *Nordisk Kultur*, V, (*Stedsnavn*), 1939, 71 ff.
11. See Ch. VIII, Ull.
12. See Ch. XII below.
13. A valuable introduction was provided by H. Shetelig and Hj. Falk (*Scandinavian Archaeology*, 1937), who gave useful notes on bibliography.
14. *The Gods of Prehistoric Man*, 1960, Ch. IV; cf Shetelig and Falk, *op. cit.*, 98 ff.
15. See Shetelig and Falk, *op. cit.*, 71 ff.
16. *Teutonic Mythology*, transl. J. S. Stallybrass, III, 1883, XXXIII.
17. See O. Almgren, *Hällristningar och Kultbruk*, 1927.
18. See Shetelig and Falk, *op. cit.*, 156 ff.
19. *Heimskringla*, Prologue; cf Arngrímur Jónsson, *Rerum Danicarum Fragmenta*, VII.
20. See *Osebergfundet* I-III, 1917-28, ed. A.W. Brøgger, Hj. Falk, H. Shetelig; further Bj. Hougen, *Osebergfunnets Billedvev* in *Viking* V, 1940, 85 ff. Further Plates 8-11, 32 etc.
21. See Kristján Eldjárn, *Kuml og Haugfé*, 1956.
22. See Ch. X, Ermanaric, Sigurð and the Burgundians.
23. *De Bello Gallico*, VI, 21-4.
24. See *Cornelii Taciti de origine et situ Germanorum*, ed. J. G. C. Anderson, 1938, Introduction, XIX ff.
25. Ed. Th. Mommsen, *Iordanis Romana et Getica* in *Monumenta Germaniae Historica*, 1882.
26. *Vita Anskarii*, ed. G. Waitz, *Scriptores rerum germanicarum*, 1884. See further S. U. Palme, *Kristendomens genombrott i Sverige*, 1959, 48 ff and refs.
27. *Gesta Hammaburgensis Ecclesiae Pontificum*, ed. B. Schmeidler (*Scriptores rerum Germanicarum*), 1917. See Ch. XII below.
28. See Ch. XV below.
29. For a survey of this subject see A. Olrik and H. Ellekilde, *Nordens Gudeverden*, I, 1926-51, 94 ff.

Old Norse Poetry

1. See Jón Helgason, *Norges og Islands Digtning* in *Nordisk Kultur*, VIII, B (*Litteraturhistoria*), 1952, 3 ff.
2. Facsimile editions: *Håndskriftet Nr. 2365, 4to., gl. Kgl. Samling*, ed. L. F. Wimmer and Finnur Jónsson, 1891, and *Codex Regius of the Elder Edda*, with introduction by A. Heusler, 1937.
3. See Jón Helgason, *op. cit.*, 26 ff.
4. See especially A. Heusler, *Deutsche Versgeschichte* I, 1925, 201 ff.
5. See G. Turville-Petre, *Origins of Icelandic Literature*, 1953, 55 ff and refs.
6. See S. Nordal, *Völuspá*, 1923, 117 ff.
7. *Norrøne Studier*, 1938, 130 ff.
8. The same motive is found in the *Saga Heiðreks Konungs* (ed. Ch. Tolkien, 1960, 44). Similarly in the *Baldrs Draumar* (str. 12), Óðinn gives himself away by asking an unanswerable and incomprehensible question.
9. See R. Höfler, *Edda, Skalden, Saga* (*Festschrift F. Genzmer*), 1952, 1 ff.
10. Facsimiles: *Håndskriftet Nr. 748, 4to, bl. 1–6*, ed. Finnur Jónsson, 1896; *Fragments of the Elder and Younger Edda, AM. 748 I and II, 4to.* with introduction by E. Wessén, 1945.
11. *Maal og Minne*, 1951, 1 ff and 1957, 81 ff.
12. See Jón Helgason, *op. cit.*, 173 ff and especially H. Kuhn, *Acta Philologica Scandinavica* XXII, 1952, 65 ff.
13. See Ch. II, and Ch. XIV.
14. See p. 14 below.
15. See H. Schneider, *Germanische Heldensage*, I, ed.2, 1962, 246 ff.
16. Cf Tacitus, *Germania* II.
17. For this view see especially S. Bugge, *The Home of the Eddic Poems*, 1899, and D. Hofmann, *Nordisch-Englische Lehnbeziehungen der Wikingerzeit*, 1955.
18. See P. Hallberg in *Arkiv för nordisk Filologi* LXIX, 1954, 51 ff.
19. See J. Young, *Arkiv för nordisk Filologi*, XLIX, 1933, 97 ff.; further K. von See, *Acta Philologica Scandinavica*, XXIV, 1957, 1 ff.
20. I refer particularly to the analytical methods employed by H. Kuhn in a number of works, e.g. *Das Füllwort of-um im altwestnordischen*, and in papers in *Beiträge zur Geschichte der deutschen Sprache und Literatur*, LVII, 1933, 1 ff.; LX, 1936, 431 ff; LXIII, 1939, 178 ff.
21. Originally the vowel was probably short. The etymology is not known.
22. See *Skj. B, I*, 22–5. It is not certain that all the strophes there collected belong to the *Haraldskvæði*.
23. Óðinn is called 'the one-eyed consort of Frigg'.
24. See Ch. II, God of War.
25. See Histories and Sagas, below.
26. See L. M. Hollander, *The Skalds*, 1945; G. Turville-Petre, *Origins of Icelandic Literature*, 1953, 26 ff, and references there given.
27. See G. Turville-Petre, *Skírnir*, 1954, 31 ff, for another view see J. de Vries, *Ogam* IX, 1, 1957, 13 ff.
28. See Ch. VIII, Gefjun.
29. See Ch. III, Thór and the Serpent.
30. See Ch. VIII, Bragi.
31. See Ch. VIII, Iðunn.
32. See Ch. III, Thór and the Giants.
33. *Ibid.*
34. See Ch. IV.
35. See Chs. V and VI.
36. Cf. S. Nordal, *Íslenzk Menning* I, 1942, 239.
37. See G. Turville-Petre, *Origins*, 45 ff.
38. *Kristni Saga* IX, cf. Ch. III, The Worship of Thór.
39. See Ch II, God of Poetry.
40. For this view see J. de Vries, *De Skaldenkenningen met mythologischen Inhoud*, 1934; further Jón Helgason, *op. cit.*, 95; H. Kuhn, *Zeitschrift für deutsches Altertum*, LXXIX, 1942, 133 ff.
41. Cf. *Heimskringla, Ól. Helg.* XLIII.
42. See G. Turville-Petre, *Origins*, 147.
43. Cf Kuhn, *op. cit.*
44. See Histories and Sagas, below.
45. See G. Turville-Petre, *Modern Language Review*, 1944, 374–91; I. L. Gordon, *Saga-Book of the Viking Society*, XIII, III, 1949–50, 183 ff.

Histories and Sagas

1. On Sæmund see G. Turville-Petre, *Origins of Icelandic Literature*, 1953, 81 ff; further Halldór Hermannsson, *Sæmund Sigfússon and the Oddaverjar*, 1932.

2. See Turville-Petre, *op. cit.*, 88 ff and refs.
3. The most reliable edition is that of Finnur Jónsson, 1900.
4. See especially Jón Jóhannesson, *Gerðir Landnámabókar*, 1941.
5. On the provenance of this passage see Jón Jóhannesson, *op. cit.*, 160 ff.
6. Cf Turville-Petre, *op. cit.*, 104, 107 and refs.
7. See *Eyrbyggja Saga*, ed. Einar Ól. Sveinsson, 1935, Introduction.
8. See *Austfirðinga Sǫgur*, ed. Jón Jóhannesson, 1950, Introduction, LXIV ff; *Borgfirðinga Sǫgur*, ed. S. Nordal and Guðni Jónsson, 1938, LXXXIII ff; further S. Nordal in *Nordisk Kultur* VIII, B (*Litteraturhistoria*), 1952, 190 ff.
9. Cf Turville-Petre, *op. cit.*, 169 ff.
10. On their ages see Einar Ól. Sveinsson, *Dating the Icelandic Sagas*, 1958.
11. For this view see especially W. Baetke, *Christliches Lehngut in der Sagareligion*, 1952.
12. *Tidrande och Diserna*, 1949; cf Turville-Petre in *Saga-Book of the Viking Society*, XIV, 1953–7, 137 ff.
13. Ari, *Libellus Islandorum*, VII.
14. Cf H. Kuhn, *Das nordgermanische Heidentum in den ersten christlichen Jahrhunderten* in *Zeitschrift für deutsches Altertum*, LXXIX. 1942, 33 ff.
15. See S. Nordal, *Hrafnkatla*, 1940 (also translated by R. G. Thomas as *Hrafnkels Saga Freysgoða*, 1958).
16. See Ch. VII, Freyr—Fróði—Nerthus —Ing.
17. Meaning 'Sagas of ancient time'. The term is modern.
18. See especially A. Heusler, *Die Lieder der Lücke im Codex Regius* in *Festschrift H. Paul*, 1902, 1–98.
19. See *The Saga of King Heidrek*, ed. Ch. Tolkien, 1960, Introduction.
20. The passage has been very widely discussed; see U. Brown, *Saga-Book of the Viking Society*, XIII, 1947–8, 51 ff; P. G. Foote, *ibid.* XIV, 1955–6, 226 ff; further Einar Ól. Sveinsson in *Kulturhistorisk Leksikon for nordisk Middelalder* IV, 1959, col. 503.
21. See U. Brown, *op. cit.*, 65 ff.

Snorri Sturluson

1. A select list is given in the bibliography, p. 322 below.
2. See Halldór Hermannsson, *Sæmund Sigfússon and the Oddaverjar*, 1932, 10 ff.
3. See Einar Ól. Sveinsson, *Sagnaritun Oddaverja* (*Studia Islandica I*), 1937.
4. See *Diplomatarium Islandicum* I, 1857–76, 289 ff.
5. The name is interpreted variously as 'Poetics' and the 'Book of Oddi'. An older interpretation was 'Great-grandmother'. See further Sigurður Nordal, *Snorri Sturluson*, 1920, 14.
6. See Nordal, *op. cit.*, 94 ff.
7. See E. Wessén, introduction to *Codex Regius of the Younger Edda* (*Corpus Codicum Islandicorum* XIV), 1940.
8. See Nordal, *op. cit.*, 116 ff.
9. See *Edda Snorra Sturlusonar*, ed. Finnur Jónsson, 1931, 16 note.
10. Cf W. Baetke, *Die Götterlehre der Snorra Edda*, 1950, p. 18 ff.
11. See A. Heusler, *Die gelehrte Urgeschichte im altisländischen Schriftum*, 1908, p. 26 ff.
12. Cf Heusler, *op. cit.*, 13ff.
13. Cf G. Turville-Petre in *Hommages à Georges Dumézil* (*Collection Latomus* XLV), 1960, 209 ff.
14. See E. Mogk, *Zur Bewertung der Snorra-Edda als religionsgeschichtliche Quelle*, 1932, 7 ff.
15. In many works. See especially *Loki*, ed. 2, 1959, 53 ff.
16. Cf J. de Vries, *Altgermanische Religionsgeschichte*, ed. 2, I, 1956, 43 ff.
17. See *Egils Saga Skalla-Grímsonar*, ed. S. Nordal, 1933, Introduction.
18. See *Heimskringla*, ed. Bjarni Aðalbjarnarson, I, 1941, 7; cf the Prologue to *Ólafs Saga Helga* in *Heimskringla* II, 1945, 421.
19. See Bjarni Aðalbjarnarson, Introduction to *Heimskringla*.
20. It has been supposed that the poem is a forgery of the eleventh or twelfth century, but this view has found little support. See Bjarni Aðalbjarnarson, *op. cit.*, I, XXXIV.
21. See especially B. Nerman, *Det Svenska Rikets Uppkomst*, 1925, 57 ff; R. W. Chambers, *Beowulf*, ed. 2, 1932, 4 ff.

22. Cf Bjarni Aðalbjarnarson, *op. cit.*, I, XXXV.
23. Cf E. Wessén, *Ynglingasaga*, 1952, IX ff.

24. See *Heimskringla*, edition cited, I, 58 and note.
25. *Getica*, Chs. 5 and 13.

Saxo

1. References apply to *Saxonis Grammatici Gesta Danorum*, ed. A. Holder, 1886; another edition is *Saxonis Gesta Danorum*, ed. J. Olrik and H. Ræder, 1931–2. See also *The First Nine Books of the Danish History of Saxo Grammaticus* translated by O. Elton with introductory material by F. York Powell, 1894.
2. Preface, p. 1.
3. See P. Herrmann, *Die Heldensagen des Saxo Grammaticus*, 1922, 1 ff and references there given.
4. *Kilderne til Sakses Oldhistorie* II, 286 ff.
5. *Skáldatal*, ed. Guðni Jónsson in *Edda Snorra Sturlusonar*, 1949, 352.
6. *Op. cit.*, II, 290.
7. *Skáldatal, loc. cit.*
8. Gizur is mentioned in many sources. See especially *Sturlunga Saga*, ed. Jón Jóhannesson and others 1, 1946, 60.
9. See *Veraldar Saga*, ed. Jakob Benediktsson, 1944, 72.
10. See G. Turville-Petre, *Origins of Icelandic Literature*, 1953, 195.
11. See *Flateyjarbók*, ed. G. Vigfússon and C. R. Unger, III, 1868, 464.
12. See *Islandske Annaler*, ed. G. Storm, 1888, 120 and 122.
13. *Op. cit.*, II, 280 ff.
14. *Viking Civilization*, revised by H. Ellekilde, 1930, 218.
15. See Herrmann, *op. cit.*, 15–16.
16. Published in *Sǫgur Danakonunga* ed. C. af Petersens and E. Olson, 1919–25, 3 ff.
17. The bibliography of this subject is very great. A useful list of works on it is given by D. A. Seip, *Kulturhistorisk Leksikon for nordisk Middelalder* II, 1957, Cols. 295–6.
18. See D. A. Seip, *Det norske grunnlag for Bråvallakvadet* in *Studier i norsk Språkhistorie*, 1934, 1 ff.
19. E.g. by a scholar so cautious as Jón Helgason, *Norges og Islands Digtning* in *Nordisk Kultur* VIII,B, 1952, 89.

20. Bjarni Guðnason, *Um Brávallaþulu* in *Skírnir* CXXXII, 1958, 82 ff.
21. Prologue, 3.
22. *Heimskringla, Ólafs Saga Helga*, Ch. CCVIII.
23. II, 67.
24. *SnE. Skáld*, Ch. 57.
25. *Danmarks Heltedigtning* I, 1903, 46 ff.
26. *The Heroic Legends of Denmark* translated and revised by L. M. Hollander, 1919, 90 ff.
27. *Ibid.*, 177 ff.
28. See *Arngrimi Jonae Opera Latine Conscripta*, ed. J. Benediktsson I, 1950, 347–8.
29. *Hrólfs Saga Kraka*, ed. D. Slay, 1960, Ch. 30.
30. See Ch. XIV.
31. VIII, 286.
32. VIII, 290.
33. VIII, 295.
34. *Gesta Hammaburgensis Ecclesiæ Pontificum*, ed. B. Schmeidler, 1917, IV, Ch. 40.
35. See Herrmann, *op. cit.*, 592 ff.
36. See *The Saga of King Heidrek the Wise*, ed. Ch. Tolkien, 1960, 66 and 84 ff.
37. On this debated point see W. Mohr, *Zeitschrift für deutsches Altertum* LXXV, 1938, 217–80.
38. See A. Heusler, *Die Anfänge der isländischen Saga*, 1914, 13 ff and refs.
39. Saxo, I, 25.
40. *Ibid.*, I, 23.
41. *Ibid.*, I, 32.
42. See Ch. II, God of War.
43. Saxo, I, 24.
44. Cf Olrik, *Kilderne*, I, 31.
45. Saxo, II, 44 and III, 73.
46. *Ibid.*, I, 30; III, 74–5; VI, 185.
47. *Ibid.*, IX, 301.
48. *Ibid.*, I, 25; III, 81.
49. *Ibid.*, I, 19–20.
50. *Ibid.*, III, 70.
51. *Ibid.*, III, 80.
52. See Ch. IV.

CHAPTER II: ÓÐINN

God of Poetry

1. While *Boðn* is probably related to Old English *byden*, M. Icel. *byðna* (vessel, vat), *Són* has not been convincingly explained. In some kennings it is used as a 'basic' word for 'blood' (e.g. *Sónar ófnir*, 'snake of blood', 'sword'), but this usage may derive from the name of *Són* as the vessel in which the blood was stored. See Alexander Jóhannesson, *Isländisches etymologisches Wörterbuch*, 1956, 764; J. de Vries, *Altnordisches Etymologisches Wörterbuch*, 1961, s.v. *Són*. Further Hj. Lindroth, *Maal og Minne*, 1915, 175.
2. Unless the order of the strophes is changed and made to conform with the sequence of Snorri's tale. Str. 106 must then be placed before str. 105.
2a. On the heron of oblivion see A. Holtsmark (in *Arv*, XIII, 1957, 21 ff.)
3. *Skj.* B, I, 38, 6 (Egill).
4. *Ibid.*, 123, 33 (Einar Skálaglamm).
5. *Ibid.*, 34, 1.
6. *Ibid.*, 80, 46 (Kormák).
7. *Ibid.*, 295, 2 (Hofgarða-Ref).
8. *Ibid.*, 128, 1 (Ulf Uggason).
9. *Ibid.*, 89, 2.
10. *Ibid.*, 387 (Steinthór).
11. *Ibid.*, 43, 4 (Egill).
12. *Ibid.*, 30, 1 (*Hǫfuðlausn*).
13. *Ibid.*, 42, 6 (Egill).
14. *Ibid.*, 464, 3.
15. *Ibid.*, 34, 2 (Egill, *Sonatorrek*).
16. *Ibid.*, 153, 15.
17. *Ibid.*, 45, 15.
18. *Ibid.*, 131, 1 (Eysteinn Valdason).
19. *Ibid.*, 385, 4.
20. *Ibid.*, 533, 31.
21. *Ibid.*, 104, 36.
22. *Ibid.*, 167, 1.
23. *Ibid.*, 100, 20.
24. *Ibid.*, 60, 1 (Eyvind).
25. *Ibid.*, 376, 5.
26. *Ibid.*, 173, III, 1.
27. *Ibid.*, 158, 5.
28. *SnE. Skáld*, Ch. 5.
29. *Skj.* B, I, 117, 1.
30. See especially E. Mogk, *Novellistische Darstellung mythologischer Stoffe Snorris und seiner Schule*, 1923, 23 ff.
31. See A. G. van Hamel, *The mastering of the mead* in *Studia Germanica till. E. A. Kock*, 1934, 76 ff.
32. See R. Stübe, *Kvasir und der magische Gebrauch des Speichels* in *Festchrift E. Mogk* 1924, 500 ff.
33. Ed. A. le Roy Andrews, 1909, Ch. I.
34. *Lagði fyrir dregg hráka sinn.*
35. See Stübe, *op. cit.*, especially 504 ff.
36. Cf Alexander Jóhannesson, *op. cit.*, 411; de Vries, *op. cit.*, s.v. *Kvasir* and refs. there given.
37. See *Loki*, ed. 2 (German), 1959, 70 ff and note 24.
38. Cf G. Sverdrup, *Rauschtrank und Labetrank im Glauben unserer Vorfahren*, 1941, esp. 3 ff.
39. See Sverdrup, *op. cit.*, 11 ff; A. Olrik, *Skjaldemjöden* in *Edda*, 1926, 236 ff.
40. See T. F. O'Rahilly, *Early Irish History and Mythology*, 1946, 326 ff; *Feis Tighe Chondín*, ed. M. Joynt, 1936, 40–1.
41. *Vedische Mythologie* I, 1891, 3 ff; *Kleine Ausgabe*, 1910, 67–79.
42. *Vedic Mythology*, 1897, 104 ff; cf J. Gonda, *Die Religionen Indiens* I, 1960, 62 ff.
43. See Macdonnell, *op. cit.*, 152.
44. *Op. cit.*, 239.

Lord of the Gallows

1. *Seldu* MS.
2. It is not altogether clear how *rúnar* should be interpreted here. It most probably means the runic letters and the magical force which went with them.
3. *Þatan* MS.
4. *Studier over de nordiske Gude- og Heltesagns Oprindelse*, 1889, 291 ff.
5. *Disputatio inter Mariam et Crucem*, ed. R. Morris, *Legends of the Holy Rood*, 1871, 200 and 134.
6. See Bugge, *op. cit.* 309.
7. Emended from *maet*. See Bugge, *op. cit.*, 309, footnote 2.
8. *Skj.* B, I, 37, 22.
9. *SnE. Skáld*, 44.
10. *Skj.* B, I, 4, 2. The interpretation has been questioned.

11. *Ibid.*, 94 (Helgi Trausti).
12. *Ibid.*, 114 and 182.
13. *Ibid.*, 136, 1.
14. *Ibid.*, 60, 1.
15. *Ibid.*, B, I, 199 (Thorbjörn Brúnason).
16. It has often been said that the expression *gefinn Óðni* (*Hávamál* 138) does not mean 'sacrificed' but rather 'dedicated to Óðinn'. The verb *gefa* is certainly used with the latter meaning in *Eyrbyggja Saga* VII, but as Snorri uses it (*Yngl. S.* XXV) it means 'sacrifice'.
17. *Yngl. S.* VII.
18. *Baldrs Draumar.*
19. Opinion on this point is divided. See S. Nordal, *Völuspá*, 1923, 20–1.
20. On the veneration of waterfalls see Ch. XII.
21. *Skj.* B., II, 1, 2.
22. *De Bell. Goth.* II, 15, 23.
23. *Getica*, V, 42.
24. *Yngl. S.* XLIII.
25. See A. Noreen, *Ynglingatal*, 1925, 245 ff and refs. there given.
26. *Yngl. S.* XV.
27. Ed G. Storm in *Monumenta Historica Norvegiæ*, 1880, 98; further G. Turville-Petre, *Origins of Icelandic Literature*, 1953, 174–5.
28. *Yngl. S.* XXV.
29. Cf H. M. Chadwick, *The Cult of Othin*, 1899, 15 ff.
30. *Flb.* II, 72.
31. *Vǫluspá* 24.
32. See *Kristni Saga* XII; *Eyrbyggja Saga* X.
33. See F. Ström, *On the Sacral Origin of the Germanic Death Penalties*, 1942, 118 ff. Ström (119) argues that the word *meiðr* does not mean 'tree', but rather 'pole, gallows' (cf R. Cleasby and G. Vigfússon, *Icelandic-English Dictionary*, 1874,

s.v.), but on p. 143 Ström translates *meiðr* in *Hávamál* 138 as 'tree'. In poetry the word is not infrequently used for a living tree.
34. See Chadwick, *op. cit.*, 73 ff; cf E. Magnússon, *Yggdrasill, Óðins Hestr*, 1895, 6 ff. For entirely different views see F. R. Schröder, *Ingunar-Freyr*, 1941, 9 ff.
35. *Hǫrva Sleipnir* (Rope Sleipnir), *Ynglingatal* 14 (*Skj.* B, I, 9, 14).
36. Book VII, 230 ff.
37. *Háleygjatal* 6 (*Skj.* B, I, 61, 6).
38. *Skj.* B, I, 239, 1.
39. See esp. G. Gjessing, *Hesten i førhistorisk kunst og kultus*, Viking VII, 1943, 5–143.
40. Cf *Hávamál* 145: *ey sér til gildis gjǫf.*
41. *SnE. Gylf.* 5.
42. Cf the proverb: *móðurbræðrum verði menn líkastir* (*Páls Saga* in *Biskupa Sögur* I, 1858, 134.
43. *Baldrs Draumar* 2.
44. E.g. *Vǫluspá* 2.
45. *Vafþrúðnismál*, 43.
46. On the significance of the number nine see esp. E. Mogk in *Reallexikon der germanischen Altertumskunde* (ed. J. Hoops) III, 1915–16, 312 ff.
47. See Ch. VI.
48. Cf S. Nordal, *Íslenzk Menning* I, 1942, 210 ff.
49. See A. G. van Hamel, *Óðinn Hanging on the Tree* in *Acta Philologica Scandinavica* VII, 1932, 260 ff.
50. On this view see especially R. Pipping, *Oden i galgen* in *Studier i nordisk Filologi*, XVIII, 2, 1928, 1 ff.
51. Evidence is summarized by J. de Vries, *Rel.* 2, 1, 333 ff. See further O. Höfler, *Kultische Geheimbünde der Germanen*, 1934, *passim.*
52. *The Dying God*, 1919, 43.

God of War

1. *SnE. Skáld* 6.
2. See especially A. Olrik, *Danmarks Heltedigtning* II, 1910, 257 and A. H. Krappe, *Études de Mythologie et de Folklore germaniques*, 1928, 70 ff.
3. See Hj. Falk, *Odensheite*, 1924, 18.
4. See Ch. X, Starkað.
5. Str. 24, prose; cf Ch. X, Starkað.
6. See Ch. X, Harald Wartooth.
7. See Ch. Tolkien, *The Saga of King Heidrek the Wise.* 1960, 50, footnote and Introduction XVII and refs.

8. *Skj.* B, I, 672.
9. *Ibid.*, B, II, 143.
10. *Ibid.*, 136.
11. See God of Poetry, above.
12. *Skj.* B, I, 59, 15.
13. See Ch. X, Harald Wartooth.
14. *Um útgarða færði frændr sína alla* (*Gísla Saga* II, Ch V).
15. *Hkr. Hák. Góð.* Ch. 14.
16. See Falk, *op. cit.*, 25.
17. *Lokasenna*, str. 22.
18. *Vǫlsunga Saga*, Chs. 11–12.

19. Saxo, *Gesta Danorum*, VII, 247.
20. *Sǫgubrot af fornkonungum* VIII.
21. *Skj.* B, I, 94; cf *Landnámabók*, ed. Finnur Jónsson, 1900, 117.
22. *Skj.* B, I, 132.
23. *Ibid.*, 118.
24. *Ibid.*, 24.
25. *Ibid.*, 23, 11.
26. *SnE. Gylf.* 24.
27. *Vafþrúðnismál* 41.
28. Reckoning on the decimal system, some scholars have concluded that the fallen warriors numbered 432,000 (not 614, 400), and have seen oriental influences in this number. (See F. R. Schröder, *Germanentum und Hellenismus*, 1924, 15 ff; cf O. Höfler, *Kultische Geheimbünde der Germanen*, 1934, 153). It is, however, improbable that the early Norsemen could think precisely in such high numbers as these. The author of the *Grímnismál*

probably meant only that the numbers of doors and of warriors were beyond comprehension. Cf M. Olsen, *Act Philologica Scandinavica* VI, 1931–2, 151–2. This paper was reprinted in *Norrøne Studier*, 1938, 109 ff.
29. *Teutonic Mythology* (transl. J. S. Stallybrass), II, 1883, 633–4.
30. Cf Olsen, *op. cit.*, 155 ff.
31. Especially by O. Höfler, *op. cit.*, 152–4 and J. de Vries, *Rel.²*, II, 378, note 3.
32. See Olsen, *op. cit.*, 164.
33. As in *valr lá þar á sandi* (the slain bodies lay on the sand), *Skj.* B, I, 24.
34. See A. Olrik and H. Ellekilde, *Nordens Gudeverden*, I, 1926–51, 472 ff and refs. given on p. 578.
35. Cf W. von Unwerth, *Untersuchungen über Totenkult und Óðinnverehrung bei Nordgermanen und Lappen*, 1911, 96 ff.

Father of Gods and Men

1. *SnE. Gylf.* 6; cf *Grímnismál* 48.
2. See Ch. VI.
3. See Oðinn's Eye and Woden-Wotan, below.
4. See above, Lord of the Gallows.
5. *SnE. Gylf.* 6.
6. *Ibid.*
7. *Askr* undoubtedly means 'Ash-tree'; *Embla* is of doubtful origin. See Ch. XVI. See S. Bugge, *The Home of the Eddic Poems* (transl. W. H. Schofield), 1899, XXVIII; further J. de Vries, *Altnordisches etymologisches Wörterbuch*, 1961, s.v. *embla*.

8. See Ch. V below.
9. *Vǫlsunga Saga*, ed. M. Olsen, 1906–8, Ch. 1.
10. *SnE.* Prologue Ch. 4; cf Arngrímur Jónsson, *Rerum Danicarum Fragmenta* (*Bibliotheca Arnamagnæana*, IX, ed. Jakob Benediktsson), 1950, 333.
11. *SnE.*, Prologue, Ch. 6.
12. See esp. A. Heusler, *Die gelehrte Urgeschichte im altisländischen Schriftum*, 1908, 10 ff.
13. *SnE.*, Prologue, 6; cf *Yngl. S.* VIII.

Óðinn's Animals

1. *SnE. Gylf.* 25; see Ch. V below.
2. *The Saga of King Heidrek the Wise*, ed. Ch. Tolkien, 1960, 44.
3. See Ch. VII, Freyr-Fróði.
4. See The Cult of Óðinn below; cf G. Gjessing in *Viking* VII, 1943, 88 ff.
5. Cf F. Ström, *Diser, Nornor, Valkyrjor*, 1954, 41 ff, but see J. de Vries, *Altnordisches etymologisches Wörterbuch*, 1961, s.v. *jódís*.
6. See Gjessing, *op. cit.*, 57 ff; K. Eldjárn, *Kuml og Haugfé*, 1956, 246 ff; further H. Schück, *Studier i nordisk Litteratur-och Religionshistoria*, II, 1904, 163 ff.

7. See Bj. Hougen, *Viking*, 1940, 94 ff.
8. *Skj.* B, I, 93, 13.
9. *Baldrs Draumar* 2; *SnE. Gylf.* 33.
10. *Gisla Saga Súrssonar*, XXX.
11. *Sturlunga Saga*, ed. Jón Jóhannesson and others, I, 1946, p. 98.
12. See Jón Árnason, *Íslenzkar Þjóðsögur og Æfintýri*, II, 1864, 98.
13. See Schück, *op. cit.*, 176 ff.
14. See O. Höfler, *Kultische Geheimbünde der Germanen*, I, 1934, 48 ff.
15. See Hj. Falk, *Odensheite*, 1924, esp. 30 ff; further J. de Vries, *Rel.²*, II, 65.
16. Cf Gjessing, *op. cit.*, 80 ff.

17. *SnE. Gylf.* 25.
18. See J. Grimm, *Teutonic Mythology* (transl. J. S. Stallybrass), I, 1900, 147. B. Sijmons and H. Gering (*Kommentar zu den Liedern der Edda* (1, 1927, 194) take *munr* as 'power of distinguishing' (*Unterscheidungsvermögen*). Finnur Jónsson (*Lexicon Poeticum antiquæ linguæ septentrionalis*, ed. 2, 1931, s.v. *muninn*) evidently associated *Muninn* with the verb *muna* (to remember). See further A. H. Krappe, *Études de Mythologie et de Folklore germaniques*, 1928, 30 ff.
19. Cf F. Ström, *Den döendes makt*, 1947, 56.
20. E.g. in *Hávarðar Saga Ísfirðings* (ed. Guðni Jónsson in *Vestfirðinga Sǫgur*, 1943), Ch. 20.
21. *Skj.* B, I, 48, 26; see also *Egils Saga Skalla-Grímssonar*, ed. S. Nordal, 1933, Ch. 61.
22. *Skj.* B, I, 302, 2.
23. *Ibid.*, 216, 2.
24. *Ibid.*, 430, 13.
25. *Ibid.*, 357, 2.
26. For examples see J. de Vries, *De Skaldenkenningen met mythologischen inhoud*, 1934, 17.
27. *Skj.* B, I, 15, 4 (Thjóðólf, *Haustlǫng*).
28. *Ibid.*, 129, 10 (Úlf Uggason).
29. *Ibid.*, 158, 8 (Hallfreð); cf A. Olrik and H. Ellekilde, *Nordens Gudeverden* I, 1926–51, 162.
30. *Ibid.*, 179, 3.
31. *Ibid.*, 463, 6.
32. *Ibid.*, 96, 2. For further examples of kennings of this type see J. de Vries, *op. cit.*, 15 ff, and especially W. von Unworth, *Untersuchungen über Totenkult und Odinnverehrung bei Nordgermanen und Lappen*, 1911, 103.
33. *Skj.* B, I, 107.
34. *Ibid.*, 90.
35. *Ibid.*, 22–5. The title is modern.
36. *Ibid.*, 88, 9.
37. *Ibid.*, 209, 11.
38. *Ibid.*, 43, 7 (Egill).
39. *Ibid.*, 150, 9.
40. *Ibid.*, 146.
41. *Ibid.*, 32, 11. For many more examples of kennings of this type, see R. Meissner, *Die Kenningar der Skalden*, 1921, 119 ff.
42. See Meissner, *op. cit.*, esp. 291 ff.
43. *Skj.* B, I, 45, 12 (Egill).
44. *Ibid.*, 325, 17.
45. *Ibid.*, 341, 10.
46. E.g. *Reginsmál* 20; *Njáls Saga*, Ch. 79.

47. See *Two Saxon Chronicles*, ed. C. Plummer and J. Earle, I, 1892, p. 77.
48. See *Asser's Life of King Alfred*, ed. W. H. Stevenson, 1904, 265–7.
49. Ed. A. Campbell, 1949, 24; cf my note to this edition, 96–7.
50. See C. E. Wright, *The Cultivation of Saga in Anglo-Saxon England*, 1939, 127 ff and 267 ff.
51. *Reginsmál*, 18.
52. Ed. S. Nordal, 1913–16, Chs. 11–12.
53. Ed. Jón Jóhannesson in *Austfirðinga Sǫgur*, 1950, Ch. 2.
54. Ch. 157.
55. On *Brjáns Saga* see Einar Ól. Sveinsson, *Um Njálu* I, 1933, 49 ff, and A. J. Goedheer, *Irish and Norse Traditions about the Battle of Clontarf*, 1938, 87 ff.
56. *Hkr. Ól. Trygg.*, Ch. 27.
57. See Ch. XIII below.
58. *SnE. Gylf.* 25.
59. *Helga Kviða Hundingsbana* I, 13.
60. *Skj.* B, I, 460, 11.
61. *Ibid.*, 43, 6 (Egill).
62. *Ibid.*, 307, 7 (Arnór). For more kennings of this type see Meissner, *op. cit.*, 291 ff.
63. Cf Krappe, *op. cit.*, 18 ff.
64. *Skj.* B, I, 165, 7 (*Eiríksmál*).
65. *SnE. Gylf.* 38; *Vafþrúðnismál* 53; cf *Vǫluspá* 53.
66. *SnE. Gylf.* 19. For kennings alluding to this see Meissner, *op. cit.*, 255.
67. *SnE. Gylf*, 6; according to the *Vafþrúðnismál* (45–7), Fenrir himself will swallow the sun. See further A. Olrik, *Ragnarök* (transl. W. Ranisch), 1922, 36 ff.
68. See B. S. Phillpotts, *The Elder Eddu and Ancient Scandinavian Drama*, 1920, esp. 115 ff.
69. *Skj.* B, I, 23, 8 and 25, 21 (*Hrafnsmál*); cf *Vatnsdæla Saga*, Ch. 9.
70. *Vǫlsunga Saga* (ed. M. Olsen, 1906–8), Ch. 8.
71. See O. Höfler, *op. cit.*, 56 ff.
72. *Ibid.*, 22 ff.
73. *Historia de gentibus septentrionalibus*, Book XVIII, Chs. XLV–VI.
74. Cf Höfler, *op. cit.*, esp. 36 ff and references; further A. Olrik and H. Ellekilde, *Nordens Gudeverden* II, 1951, 938 ff.
75. *Skj.* B, I, 142, 12 (*Þórsdrápa*).
76. *Ágrip af Nóregs Konunga Sǫgum*, ed. Finnur Jónsson, 1929, Ch. 1.

Óðinn's Names

1. *SnE. Gylf.* 11.
2. See Hj Falk, *Odensheite*, 1924.
3. See H. Gering and B. Sijmons, *Kommentar zu den Liedern der Edda*, I, 1927, 27 and refs.
4. See Ch. IX, below.
5. On Fjǫlnir see esp. W. von Unwerth, *Arkiv för nordisk Filologi*, 1917, 320 ff.
6. See G. Turville-Petre, 'Thurstable' in *English and Medieval Studies presented to J. R. R. Tolkien*, 1962, 241 ff.
7. See Falk, *op. cit.*, 23.
8. *Grímnismál* 34.
9. *Helgakviða Hjǫrvarðssonar.*
10. On this problem see S. Bugge, *The Home of the Eddic Poems* (transl. W. H. Schofield), 1899, 286; further O. Höfler in *Edda, Skalden, Saga (Festschrift Genzmer)*, 1952, esp. 67, footnote; also Falk, *op. cit.*, 26.
11. See Falk, *op. cit.*, 22.

Óðinn's Eye

1. *Skj.* B, I, 24, 12.
2. On Mímir see Ch. V, below.
3. *SnE. Gylf.* 8.
4. See Ch. VIII, Týr.
5. See Ch. VI, below.
6. *SnE. Gylf.*, 6, 9, 40, 68.
7. *Skj.* B, I, 158, 6 (Hallfreð); *ibid.*, 388.
8. See M. Olsen, *The Farms and Fanes of Ancient Norway*, 1928, 318 ff.
9. See A. H. Smith, *English Place-name Elements*, II, 1956, 104 ff and refs.; also E. Hellquist, *Svensk Etymologisk Ordbok*, ed. 3, II, 1957, s.v. *skälf*.
10. See further Woden-Wotan, below.
11. *Op. cit.*, 321 ff.
12. Snorri (*SnE. Gylf.* 9) seems to say that Óðinn is the owner of Válaskjálf, but the text is questionable.
13. *SnE. Gylf.*, 16.
14. See Ch. XVI, below.
15. The name *Skilfingar* is applied to a dynasty in the *Hyndluljóð* (11), and a genealogy preserved in the *Flb.* (I, 25), although it is not made clear which this dynasty is.
16. See esp. F. Läffler, *Arkiv för nordisk Filologi*, X, 1894, 166 ff; E. Björkman, *Namn och Bygd*, VII, 1919, 163 ff.

Cult of Óðinn

1. *Baldrs Draumar* 4; *Yngl. S.* VII.
2. *Hávamál*, 146 ff.
3. *Yng. S.* VI.
4. The most thorough study of *seiðr* is that of D. Strömbäck, *Sejd*, 1935.
5. The word *ergi* appears to cover many despicable and unmanly practices, e.g. homosexuality, witchcraft, cowardice. See Ólafur Lárusson, *Lög og Saga*, 1958, 144 ff.
6. *Yngl. S.* VII.
7. *Lokasenna* 24; cf Saxo, *Gesta*, III, 80 ff.
8. See G. Turville-Petre, *Um Óðinsdýrkun á Íslandi (Studia Islandica* XVII), 1958 and refs. there given.
9. See Ch. III, Worship of Thór, below.
10. *Hrafnkels Saga Freysgoða*, Ch. II; in the saga, Hrafnkell is said to be son of Hallfreð and is given the title *Freysgoði*. In the *Landnámabók* (ed. Finnur Jónsson, 1900), 90 and 205, he is son of Hrafn, and the title is not applied to him.
11. I am grateful to K. Hald for allowing me to read his paper on *The Cult of Odin in Danish Place-names*, to be published in *Saga-Book of the Viking Society.*
12. *Hedenske Kultminder i norske Stedsnavne*, I, 1915, 63 ff and *passim*; *Nordisk Kultur* XXVI (*Religionshistorie*), 1942, 60 ff.
13. Such views were discussed by H. M. Chadwick, *The Cult of Othin*, 1899, 49 ff; and by J. de Vries, *Tijdschrift voor nederlandse Taal en Letterkunde*, LII, 1933, 165 ff.
14. See A. Olrik and H. Ellekilde, *Nordens Gudeverden* I, 1926–51, 513.
15. See M. Olsen, *The Farms and Fanes of Ancient Norway*, 1928, 227 ff.
16. Cf A. Holtsmark, *Vitazgjafi* in *Studier i norrøn diktning*, 1956, 46 ff.
17. Ed. Finnur Jónsson, 1902–3, Ch. II, 19.
18. *Egils Saga* IV; cf *Hkr. Har. Hárf.* VI.
19. Cf Ólafur Lárusson, *Lög og Saga*, 1958, 55 ff.
20. Cf Jón Jóhannesson, *Íslendinga Saga* I,

1956, 27 ff. Entirely different and altogether eccentric views were expressed by Barði Guðmundsson, *Uppruni Íslendinga*, 1959, 109 ff.

21. *Flb.* I, 563–4; cf Bjarni Aðalbjarnarson in *Hkr.* I, 1941, Introduction.
22. *Skj.* B, I, 164 ff (*Eiríksmál*).
23. *Ibid.*, 22, 4.
24. *Ibid.*, 38, 3.
25. See G. Turville-Petre, *The Heroic Age of Scandinavia*, 1951, 92, 112.
26. Cf M. Olsen, *Nordisk Kultur*, XXVI, 66; *Hedenske Kultminder i norske Stedsnavne*, I, 205 ff.
27. *Hkr. Har. Hárf.*, XXI.
28. See Turville-Petre, *op. cit.*, 120–1.
29. See Lord of the Gallows, above, and Ch. X, Starkað.

30. *De Bello Gallico*, VI, 22; cf Turville-Petre, *Um Óðinsdýrkun á Íslandi*, 1958, 20–1.
31. Cf *Olrik and Ellekilde, op. cit.*, I, 533.
32. Cf Olsen, *The Farms and Fanes Of Ancient Norway*, 284; E. Wessén, *Acta Philologica Scandinavica* IV, 1929, 100 ff.
33. See Olrik and Ellekilde, *op. cit.*, I, 541–2, 544, 513, 517, 409, 474–5.
34. See God of War, above; further A. Mawer, *Acta Philologica Scandinavica*, VII, 15.
35. *Áfangar* II, 1944, 103 ff.
36. Cf Holtsmark, *op. cit.*, esp. 55 ff; cf M. Olsen in *Maal og Minne*, 1934, 92 ff.
37. See G. Turville-Petre, *Viga-Glúms Saga*, 61 ff.

Woden-Wotan

1. *Historia Ecclesiastica* I, 15.
2. See E. Hackenberg, *Die Stammtafeln der angelsächsischen Königreiche*, 1918.
3. See Ch. IV, below.
4. See Oðinn's Names, above.
5. Ed. A. Campbell, *The Chronicle of Æthelweard*, 1962, 7.
6. *Anglo-Saxon Magic*, 1948, 188.
7. Cf Storms, *op. cit.*, 195.
8. *Anglo-Saxon Dialogues of Salomon and Saturn*, ed. J. M. Kemble, II, 1847, 192.
9. Ed. B. Dickins, *Runic and Heroic Poems*, 1915, 12–13.
10. *Ibid.*, 28.
11. Useful collections are given by R. Jente, *Die mythologischen Ausdrücke im altenglischen Wortschatz*, 1921, 77 ff; E. A. Philippson, *Germanisches Heidentum bei den Angelsachsen*, 1929, 156 ff. See further B. Dickins, *English Names and Old English Heathenism* (*Essays and Studies by Members of the English Association*, XIX, 154 ff); F. M. Stenton, *Transactions of the Royal Historical Society*, XXIII, 1941, 1 ff.
12. See J. E. B. Gover, A. Mawer and F. M. Stenton, *The Place-names of Wiltshire*, 1939, pp. 318 and XIV.
13. On the alternation between the forms *Woden* and *Weden* see A. H. Smith, *English Place-name Elements*, II, 1956, 272.
14. See A. Olrik and H. Ellekilde, *Nordens*

Gudeverden I, 1926–51, 474 and 510.
15. Cf Philippson, *op. cit.*, 158–9.
16. See Gover, Mawer and Stenton, *op. cit.*, 17.
17. *Ibid.*, 15–16 and XIV; cf A. H. Smith, *op. cit.*, I, 1956, 210.
18. *Ælfric's Lives of Saints*, ed. W. Skeat, II, 1900, 264; *The Homilies of Wulfstan*, ed. D. Bethurum, 1957, 223 and notes p. 333 ff; *Anglo-Saxon Dialogues of Salomon and Saturn*, ed. J. M. Kemble, II, 1847, 122–3.
19. See Ch. III, Thór-Thunor, below.
20. See Ch. V, below.
21. See especially J. Grimm, *Teutonic Mythology* (transl. J. S. Stallybrass), I, 1900, 134 ff.
22. See Ch. IV, below.
23. See K. Helm, *Altgermanische Religionsgeschichte* I, 1913, 356 ff; further J. de Vries, *Rel.*², II, 28 ff.
24. *Bell. Gall.* VI, 17.
25. *Getica* V, 40–1.
26. E.g. S. Bugge, *The Home of the Eddic Poems* (transl. W. H. Schofield) 1899, 227.
27. See R. Much, *Die Germania des Tacitus*, ed. 2, 1959, 339 ff; further O. Höfler, *Edda, Skalden, Saga* (*Festschrift F. Genzmer*), 1952, 1 ff.
28. *Hávamál* 148; cf *Yngl. S.* VI.
29. Cf J. de Vries, *op. cit.*, I, 322.

CHAPTER III: THÓR

1. *Grímnismál* 4, 24; *SnE. Gylf.* 10.
2. *Hárbarðsljóð* 23.
3. Cf *Þrymskviða* 18 and the story of Hrungnir quoted in Thór and Giants below.
4. On the name *Jǫrmungandr* see J. de Vries, *La Valeur religieuse du mot germanique Irmin* in *Cahiers du Sud*, 1952, 18 ff; G. Turville-Petre, *Thurstable* in *English and Medieval Studies Presented to J. R. R. Tolkien*, 1962, 241 ff. One of the oldest scalds

called the serpent 'the belt of all lands' (*allra landa umbgjǫrð, Skj.* B, I, 6). The motive was often repeated.
5. Plate 22.
6. See Ch. I, Introductory.
7. *Ibid.*
8. See F. R. Schröder, *Arkiv för nordisk Filologi*, LXX, 1955, 1 ff.
9. *SnE. Gylf.* 32.
10. *Ibid.*, 38.

Thór and the Giants

1. *Hárbarðsljóð* 23; *Þrymskviða* 18.
2. *Skj.* B, I, 127.
3. *Ibid.*, B, I, 135.
4. See H. L. Ljungberg, *Tor* I, 1947, 179 ff.
5. *Ragnarsdrápa* 17 (*Skj.* B, I, 4, 17).
6. *Lokasenna* 63.
7. *Kormáks Saga*, V.
8. *Ragnarsdrápa* 1 (*Skj.* B, I, 1, 1).
9. Cf J. de Vries, *Rel.²*, II, 124.
10. *SnE. Skáld.* 25.
11. See *Blickling Homilies*, ed. R. Morris, 1874–80, 163, 30; *Exeter Book*, ed. G. P.

Krapp and E. van Kirk Dobbie, 1936, 6, 104.
12. See further F. R. Schröder, *Germanisch-Romanische Monatschrift*, XXVI, 1938, 81 ff.
13. Reconstructed text in *Skj.* B, I, 139 ff. The most detailed commentary is that of W. Kiil, *Arkiv för nordisk Filologi*, LXXI, 1956, 89 ff.
14. Str. 12; see Kiil, *op. cit.*
15. Cf Kill, *op. cit.*, 89.
16. On Gudmund see Ch. Tolkien, *The Saga of King Heidrek the Wise*, 1960, 84 ff.

Hammer and Goats

1. Saxo, III, 73.
2. See A. Jóhannesson, *Isländisches Etymologisches Wörterbuch*, 1956, 677; J. de Vries, *Altnordisches Etymologisches Wörterbuch*, 1961, s.v. *Mjǫlnir*; further T. F. O'Rahilly, *Early Irish History and Mythology*, 1946, 52 ff.
3. *Ragnarsdrápa* 15 (*Skj.* B, I, 3).
4. See previous section.
5. See F. von der Leyen, *Die Götter der Germanen*, 1938, 45 ff, and 233.
6. *Flb.* I, 319–21; cf *Hkr. Ól. Trygg.* LXIX; Oddr Snorrason, *Saga Ólafs Tryggvasonar*, ed. F. Jónsson, 1932, 163–4.
7. See J. de Vries, *Rel.²*, II, 113.
8. *SnE. Gylf.* 26–31.
9. See C. W. von Sydow, *Danske Studier*, 1910, 65 and 145 ff.
10. See S. Wikander, *Arv*, VI, 1950, 90 ff.
11. See especially W. Baetke, *Das Heilige im Germanischen*, 1942, 106 ff.
12. *SnE. Gylf.* 33.
13. See E. Wessén, *Runstenen vid Röks Kyrka*, 1958, 55–6 and refs.; further M. Olsen,

Arkiv för nordisk Filologi, XXXVII, 1921, 201 ff.
14. See M. Olsen, *op. cit.*, and *Nordisk Kultur* VI (Runorna), ed. O. von Friesen, 1933, 121 ff, 136 ff, 125 ff.
15. A list was given by R. Skovmand, *Aarbøger for nordisk Oldkyndighed og Historie*, 1942, 63–5. See further S.U. Palme, *Kristendomens genombrott i Sverige*, 1959, 99 ff.
16. See A. Bjørn and H. Shetelig, *Viking Antiquities in Great Britain and Ireland*, IV, 1940, 43.
17. See K. Eldjárn, *Kuml og Haugfé*, 1956, 325–7; Ól. Briem, *Heiðinn Siður á Íslandi*, 1945, 31.
18. See Eldjárn, *op. cit.*, 362–3.
19. *Hallfreðar Saga*, VI.
20. *Att helga land* in *Festskrift till. Axel Hagerström*, 1928, esp. 215 ff.
21. See *Diplomatarium Islandicum*, XII, 1932, 1 ff.
22. Ed. Finnur Jónsson, 1900, *Sturlubók* Ch. 257.

23. Cf Palme, *op. cit.*, 99 ff.
24. Cf Ch. II, God of War.
25. See Ch. XIII.
26. See E. Mogk in *Reallexikon der germ. Altertumskunde*, ed. J. Hoops, II, 1913–15, 363.
27. Cf Ljungberg, *op. cit.*, 134 ff.
28. See Jón Árnason, *Íslenzkar Þjóðsögur og Æfintýri*, I, 1862, 445; Jónas Jónasson, *Íslenzkir Þjóðhættir*, 1934, 401–2.

29. *Hkr.*, *Hák. Góð.* XVII.
30. *SnE. Skáld.* 44.
31. *SnE. Gylf.* 11.
32. Some further examples of magic belts are cited by H. Gering and B. Sijmons, *Kommentar zu den Liedern der Edda*, I, 1927, 429. See also J. de Vries, *Rel.²*, I, 291 ff.

The Worship of Thór

1. *SnE. Gylf.* 25, *Skáld.* 25.
2. *Ibid.*, *Skáld.* 12.
3. Text from *Skj.* B, I, 127.
4. *Ibid.*, 135.
5. F. R. Schröder, *Germanisch-Romanische Monatschrift*, XXVII, 1939, 339, remarks on interesting parallels, suggesting that Thór's hymns are relics of Indo-European heritage.
6. See Ch. I, Old Norse Poetry.
7. Hermann Pálsson, *Skírnir*, 1956, 187–92.
8. See J. de Vries, *Contributions to the Study of Othin* (*Folklore Fellows Communications*, XXXIII, 2, No. 94, 1931) esp. 46 ff.
9. See G. Turville-Petre, *Um Óðinsdýrkun á Íslandi* (*Studia Islandica* 17), 1958.
10. Some names compounded with *Frey*- are found, and a number of which the first element is *Ing*-. See Ch. VII, Freyr 3.
11. Examples in the *Eyrbyggja Saga* XI, VII; see further *Hauksbók*, ed. F. Jónsson, 1892, 503–4.
12. See Ól. Lárusson, *Nordisk Kultur* V (*Stedsnavn*), 1939, 72; Ól. Briem, *Heiðinn Siður á Íslandi*, 1945, 17 ff.
13. Ed. F. Jónsson, 1900, 217.
14. Chs. III-IV, IX-X.
15. See Ch. XII, below.
16. Thus Jón Jóhannesson, *Gerðir Landnámabókar*, 1941, 135–6. Einar Ól. Sveinsson, *Eyrbyggja Saga* (*Íslenzk Fornrit* IV) Introduction, assigns it to an earlier date.
17. See Einar Ól. Sveinsson, edition cited, Introduction 2.
18. Edition cited, 152–3.
19. *Ibid.*, 165.
20. *Ibid.*, 187.
21. *Ibid.*, 193.
22. *Ibid.*, 11.

23. *Eiríks Saga Rauða* VIII.
24. Interesting examples are found in *Laxdæla Saga* XL, and *Flóamanna Saga*, XX–XXI.
25. Among many stories illustrating this could be quoted that told by Rimbert in *Vita Anskarii* XXVI.
26. *Kristni Saga* IX.
27. Ch. CII.
28. *Hkr.*, *Hák. Góð.* XIV; *Flb.* I, 387, cf *Flb.* II, 72.
29. E.g. *Flb.* I, 387; II, 184.
30. Oddr Snorrason, *Saga Óláfs Tryggvasonar*, ed. F. Jónsson, 1932, 173; cf *Flb.* I, 397.
31. Edition cited, 163–4; cf *Hkr. Ól. Trygg.* LXIX.
32. Legendary Saga of St. Ólaf (*Óláfs Saga hins helga*, ed. O. A. Johnsen, 1922), XXXIV–VI; cf *Hkr. Ól. Heig.* CXII.
33. *Op. cit.*, 220–2; cf *Flb.* I, 488–9.
34. See Ch. XII, below.
35. See *Hedenske Kultminder i norske Stedsnavne* I, 1915, esp. 202 ff; the results of Olsen's researches were summarized in *Nordisk Kultur* XXVI (*Religionshistorie*, ed. N. Lid), 1942, 59 ff. See further Olsen's *Farms and Fanes of Ancient Norway*, 1928, *passim*.
36. See O. Lundberg in *Nordisk Kultur* XXVI, 50 ff; E. Wessén, *Studier til Sveriges hedna mythologi och Fornhistoria*, 1924, 129 ff and *passim*; idem *Schwedische Ortsnamen und altnordische Mythologie* in *Acta Philologica Scandinavica* X, 1929, 97 ff.
37. See G. Knudsen, *Nordisk Kultur*, XXVI, 33 ff and refs., also A. Olrik and H. Ellekilde, *Nordens Gudeverden*, I, 1926–51, 334 ff.

Thór in Viking Colonies

1. See C. Marstrander, *Bidrag til det norske sprogs Historie i Irland*, 1915, 66 and 155.
2. References and textual interpretations are given by J. Steenstrup, *Normannerne*, II, 1878, 356–62; and further by C. Marstrander, *Revue Celtique*, XXXVI, 1915, 244 ff.
3. *De moribus et actis primorum Normanniæ Ducum* I, ed. J. Lair, 1865, 126 ff.
4. *Two Saxon Chronicles*, ed. C. Plummer, I, 1892, 74–5.
5. *Sermo Lupi ad Anglos*, ed. D. Whitelock, 1939.
6. *Ælfric's Lives of Saints*, ed. W. W. Skeat, II, 1900, 264.
7. Text: F. Kluge, *Angelsächsisches Lesebuch*, ed. 4, 1915, 86–9; cf *Salomon and Saturn*, ed. J. F. Kemble, II, 1847, 120–5. An Icelandic version of this homily is preserved in *Hauksbók* (ed. Finnur Jónsson, 1892–6) 156 ff.
8. *The Homilies of Wulfstan*, ed. D. Bethurum, 1957, 220–4.
9. See E. A. Philippson, *Germanisches Heidentum bei den Angelsachsen*, 1929, 141 ff and R. Jente, *Die mythologischen Ausdrücke im altenglischen Wortschatz*, 1921, 83 ff; further H. Lindquist, *Middle-English Place-names of Scandinavian Origin*, I, 1912, 94 ff.
10. Cf B. Dickins, *English names and Old English Heathenism* in *Essays and Studies by Members of the English Association* XIX, 150. See also F. M. Stenton, *Transactions of the Royal Historical Society*, 4th Series, vol XXIII, 1941, 1–24.
11. See St. Rozniecki, *Perun und Thor* in *Archiv für slavische Philologie* 23, 1901, 473; G. Vernadsky, *Kievan Russia*, 1951, 54.
12. See Rozniecki, *op. cit.*, 493 and refs.
13. See N. K. Chadwick, *The Beginnings of Russian History*, 1946, 86 ff.
14. See Rozniecki, *op. cit.*, 514 ff; A. Brückner, *Archiv für slavische Philologie*, XL, 1926, 8.
15. On this passage see Rozniecki, *op. cit.*, 505.
16. *Gutalag och Guta Saga*, ed. H. Pipping, 1905–7, 63.
17. *Eyrbyggja Saga*, X.
18. Dudo of St. Quentin, *De moribus et actis primorum Normanniæ ducum*, I, ed. J. Lair, 1865, 129 ff.
19. See Brückner, *op. cit.*, 16 ff.
20. See J. Machal, *The Mythology of All Races*, III, 1918, 317 ff.
21. See A. Jóhannesson, *Isländisches etymologisches Wörterbuch*, 1956, 551; further J. de Vries, *Altnordisches etymologisches Wörterbuch*, 1961, 126.
22. See H. Ljungberg, *Tor*, I, 1947, 38.
23. *Op. cit.*, 79. Mrs Chadwick's interpretation of the story differs from that offered here.
24. Simon Grunau, *Preussische Chronik*, 1876, Tract. III, Ch. 4, 68 ff.
25. *SnE.*, *Gylf.* 6, *Skáld.* 28.
26. See F. R. Schroeder in *Festgabe für Karl Helm*, 1951, 32 ff; J. de Vries, *Rel.²*, II, 274 ff.
27. See J. A. Friis, *Lappisk Mythologi*, 1871, 65 ff; J. Fritzner, *Norsk Historisk Tidskrift*, IV, 1877, 145 ff.
28. *Danske Studier*, 1905, 39 ff; A. Olrik and H. Ellekilde, *Nordens Gudeverden*, I, 143.
29. See N. Lid, *Nordisk Kultur* XXVI (*Religionshistorie*), 1942, 126.
30. See Jón Árnason, *Íslenzkar Þjóðsögur og Æfintýri* I, 1862, 641 ff; Jónas Jónasson, *Íslenzkir Þjóðhættir*, 1934, 410.
31. See H. Ljungberg, *op. cit.*, 49ff.
32. See Olrik and Ellekilde, *op. cit.*, I, 96 ff; Friis, *op. cit.*, 70 ff.

Thór-Thunor

1. *Transactions of the Royal Historical Society*, 4th Series, XXIII, 1941, 17 ff. See further Bruce Dickins, *Essays and Studies*, XIX, 155 ff; E. A. Philippson, *Germanisches Heidentum bei den Angelsachsen*, 1929, 136 ff; R. Jente, *Die mythologischen Ausdrücke im altenglischen Wortschatz*, 1921, 81 ff.
2. See A. H. Smith, *English Place-name Elements*, II, 1956, 146, 217; further G. Turville-Petre, *Thurstable* in *English and Medieval Studies Presented to J. R. R. Tolkien*, 1962, 241 ff.
3. *Salomon and Saturn*, II ed. J. M. Kemble, 1847, 148.
4. See Stenton, *op. cit.*, 18; further C. Plummer, *Two Saxon Chronicles*, II, 1899, 21 ff.
5. See A. Campbell, *Old English Grammar*, 1959, 189 ff.

6. See W. Braune, *Althochdeutsches Lesebuch*, 1921, 166; J. Knight Bostock, *A Handbook on Old High German Literature*, 1955, 98.
7. The list begins with *Gesecg Seaxneting* (H. Sweet, *The Oldest English Texts*, 1885, 179). In a later version, Woden is added before Seaxnet.
8. Cf H. M. Chadwick, *The Origin of the English Nation*, 1907, 59; F. M. Stenton, *Anglo-Saxon England*, 1943, 53.
9. For details and bibliography of Saxnot see Jente, *op. cit.*, 96–7; Philippson, *op. cit.*, 117 ff; idem, *Die Genealogie der Götter*, 1953, 34. I am not able to accept all of Philippson's conclusions.
10. Reproduced by H. Arntz, *Handbuch der Runenkunde*, 1944, Tafel VIII.
11. W. Krogmann (*Acta Philologica Scandinavica*, XII, 1937–8, 62 ff) and Ljungberg (*op. cit.*, 209 ff) prefer to read *Wiguþonar*. To judge by reproductions they have some reason.
12. Cf W. Baetke, *Das Heilige im Germanischen*, 1942, 111–14 and especially 119.

13. See W. Krause, *Zeitschrift für deutsche Altertum*, LXIV, 1927, 269 ff.
14. The explanations of Krause (*op. cit.*) and Krogmann (*op. cit.*) are too intricate to be convincing.
15. Many of these were cited by J. Grimm, *Teutonic Mythology*, I, 170 ff and 185.
16. See above; further Ljungberg, *op. cit.*, 9 and 71 ff.
17. See M-L. Sjœstedt, *Dieux et Héros des Celtes*, 1940, 30–1; H. d'Arbois de Jubainville, *The Irish Mythological Cycle* (transl. R. I. Best), 1903, pp. XII, 213–19; further J. de Vries, *Keltische Religion*, 1961, 63 ff.
18. See J. Morris Jones, *A Welsh Grammar*, 1930, 160.
19. Cf M. Olsen, *Hedenske Kultminder* I, 203.
20. See T. G. E. Powell, *The Celts*, 1960, 128.
21. Cf H. M. Chadwick, *op. cit.*, 226 ff.
22. See K. Helm, *Altgermanische Religionsgeschichte* I, 1913, 363 ff; J. de Vries, *Rel.²*, II, 107 ff, Ljungberg, *op. cit.*, 71 and refs.

Conclusion

1. Following the translation of J. S. Stallybrass, *Teutonic Mythology*, III, 1883, XXXIII.
2. *Undersökningar i germansk mytologi*, esp. II, 1889, 100 ff. Rydberg's views were discussed by H. Ljungberg, *Tor*, I, 1947, 58 ff.
3. *Indra, Thór, Herakles* in *Zeitschrift für deutsche Philologie*, LXXVI, 1957, 1 ff.
4. Among many: *Les Dieux des Germains*, 1959, Chs. I and IV; *Les Dieux des Indo-Européens*, 1952, Ch. I; *L'Idéologie tripartie des Indo-Européens*, 1958, *passim*. See also J. de Vries, *Forschungsgeschichte der Mythologie*, 1961, 357–60.
5. See Ch. VII, below.

6. *Die Religionen Indiens* I, 1960, 53 ff.
7. E.g. Sigurð, Finn; on Marduk and Tiamat see E. O. James, *The Ancient Gods*, 1960, 208 ff.
8. See Gonda, *op. cit.*, 60.
9. *SnE. Skáld.* 44.
10. *Rigveda* IV, 17; VI, 70; VII, 53; VIII, 52; 59, 15, etc.
11. *Hymiskviða* 15; *Þrymskviða* 24.
12. *SnE. Gylf.* 31.
13. *Rigveda* V, 29, 7–9.
14. See Ch. II, God of Poetry.
15. See Gonda, *op. cit.*, 53.
16. See Gonda, *op. cit.*, 99 and 103; A. Hillebrandt, *Vedische Mythologie* (Kleine Ausgabe), 1910, 111 ff.

CHAPTER IV: BALDR
West Norse Sources

1. *SnE. Gylf.* 11.
2. In Iceland the name is given to matricary, and it is applied to various plants in other parts of Scandinavia and northern England. See esp. S. Bugge, *Studier over de nordiske Gude- og Heltesagns*

Oprindelse, I, 1881–9, 283 ff, and de Vries, *Rel.²*, II,2 31. The name is not likely to be of ancient origin.
3. *SnE. Gylf.* 18.
4. *Ibid.* 33–4.
5. G. Neckel, *Die Überlieferungen vom Gotte*

Balder, 1920, 35 ff, would interpret *feikn-stafir* in a more concrete sense, 'evil-bringing runes'.

6. Some would render *tivur* as 'sacrifice', believing it to be a loan from Old English *tifer, tiber*. See S. Bugge, *The Home of the Eddic Poems*, 1899, XL; further H. Gering and B. Sijmons, *Kommentar zu den Liedern der Edda*, I, 1927, 44.

7. *Zur Bewertung der Snorra Edda als religionsgeschichtliche und mythologische Quelle des nordgermanischen Heidentums*, 1932, 7 ff.

8. *SnE. Skáld.* 24.

9. *Skj.* B, I, 129–30. See Ch. I, Old Norse Poetry, above.

10. *Edda*, ed. G. Neckel, 1927, 273–5. Translated by Thomas Gray as *The Descent of Odin*, 1761.

11. The name *Váli* is not preserved in the text of the poem, but is known from other sources and demanded by the metrical form.

12. M. Olsen, *Arkiv för nordisk Filologi*, XL, 1924, 151, suggests that the death of Baldr and the journey of Hermóð could have been related in one poem. The strophe about Thökk, given by Snorri and cited above, would probably not be part of this, since it is in the measure *Ljóðaháttr*. S. Bugge (*Studier*, I, 48) attempted to reconstruct some of the lost lines in Snorri's source.

13. Óðinn uses the same device in the *Saga of King Heiðrek the Wise* (ed. Ch. Tolkien, 1960, 44). The saga is probably influenced by the poem.

14. *Skj.* B, I, 165.

15. Neckel, *op. cit.*, 147 ff.

16. The expression (*færði hǫfuð sitt*) implies that he offered his head to the chieftain to chop off if he liked.

17. In *Hrafns Saga*, ed. G. Vigfússon, *Sturlunga Saga* II, 1878, 283.

Saxo

1. *Saxonis Grammatici Gesta Danorum*, ed. A. Holder, 1886, Book III.

2. Cf P. Herrmann, *Die Heldensagen des Saxo Grammaticus*, 1922, 231.

3. Saxo mentions a variant, according to which the King gave his daughter to Óðinn.

4. G. Dumézil, *Loki*, 1959, 101, suggests that Gevar, directing Höð to the magic sword, takes the place of Loki.

5. See F. Klæber, *Beowulf and the Fight at Finnsburg*, 1950, pp. XLII ff.

6. See Herrmann, *op. cit.*, and references there given.

7. See G. Knudsen in *Festskrift til Finnur Jónsson*, 1928, 463 ff.

8. Poetical expressions such as *folkbaldr, liðbaldr, herbaldr, mannbaldr*, as D. Hofmann points out (*Nordisch-englische Lehnbeziehungen der Wikingerzeit*, 1955, 76), may not be associated immediately with the god Baldr. They may derive from Old English poetic expressions such as *beorna bealdor*. Cf E. A. Kock, *Notationes Norrænæ* V, 1925, § 787; H. Kuhn in *Festgabe für K. Helm*, 1951, 41.

9. Such as *brynju Hǫðr* (Höð of the corselet). See R. Meissner, *Die Kenningar der Skalden*, 1921, 261.

10. In the *Vǫluspá* (str. 20) the plural *Nǫnnur Herjans* (Óðinn's Nannas) means 'valkyries'.

11. A. Jóhannesson, *Isländisches Etymologisches Wörterbuch*, 1956, 685 suggests another etymology.

12. See further J. de Vries, *Arkiv för nordisk Filologi*, LXX, 1955, 41 ff. I am unable to follow de Vries in regarding the slaying of Baldr as a form of initiation.

13. This question is discussed most thoroughly by G. Dumézil, *op. cit.*, 94 ff.

14. Cf Neckel, *op. cit.*, 40–1.

15. See J. Frazer, *The Golden Bough* (abridged 1922), 658 ff.

16. See Hj. Falk, *Altnordische Waffenkunde*, 1914, 56.

The Character of Baldr and His Cult

1. See *Friðþjófs Saga ins Frækna*, ed. L. Larsson, 1901, 2, note.

2. *Arkiv för nordisk Filologi*, XL, 1924, 151 ff.

3. See Olsen, *op. cit.*, 169.

4. See G. Knudsen in *Nordisk Kultur* XXVI (*Religionshistorie*), 1942, 35.

5. See Olsen, *op. cit.*, 151 ff.

6. *Op. cit.*, 102 ff.

7. *Es gibt kein Balder 'Herr'* in *Erbe der Ver-gangenheit (Festgabe für K. Helm)*, 1951, 37 ff.
8. Views on the origin of the name *Baldr* are conveniently summarized by J. de Vries, *Altnordisches Etymologisches Wörter-buch*, 1958–61, s.v. *Baldr*.
9. *Op. cit.*, Ch. V.
10. On the seasonal festivals see E. O. James, *The Ancient Gods*, 1960, 134 ff.
11. *Germanisch-Romanische Monatschrift*, XXIV, 1953, 174 ff.
12. *Kalevala*, Runo XI–XV.
13. See J. de Vries, *Arkiv för nordisk Filologi*, LXX, 41 ff.
14. *Gautreks Saga*, VII.
15. *Styrbjarnar Þáttr* in *Flb.*, II, 70 ff.
16. *Vǫlsunga Saga*, ed. M. Olsen, 1906–8, XI.
17. Saxo, Book VIII; cf *Sǫgubrot af Forn-konungum* (ed. C. af Petersens and E. Olson in *Sǫgur Danakonunga*, 1919–25), IX.
18. *Studier* I, 32 ff.

19. See Bugge, *op. cit.*, 45 ff.
20. Ed. C. de Tischendorf, *Evangelia Apo-crypha*, ed. 2, 1876, 484.
21. Ed B. Dickins and A. S. C. Ross, 1934, 27–8.
22. *Op. cit.*, *loc. cit.*
23. The 'pathetic fallacy' is rare in O.N., although not so rare as commonly supposed. The poet Sighvat told how the cliffs of Norway had seemed to smile while St. Ólaf was alive, but now they did so no more (*Skj.* B, I, 252). Ari the Wise wrote how Iceland 'drooped' (*drúpði*) after the death of Bishop Gizur (*Biskupa Sögur* I, 1858, 145), and the settler Hallsteinn Thengilsson described, in a verse, how the neighbourhood 'drooped' on the death of his father (*Landnámabók*, 1900, 80).
24. See James, *op. cit.*, *loc. cit.*; Neckel, *op. cit.* 147 ff.
25. *Op. cit.*, 173 ff.

Continental and English Tradition

1. See Gísli Brynjúlfsson, *Antikvarisk Tids-krift*, 1852–4, 132.
2. See Neckel, *op. cit.*, 141 ff.
3. See B. Nerman, *Det svenska Rikets Upp-komst*, 1925, 90 ff.
4. *Op. cit.*, Introduction, XLI.
5. Cf Olsen, *op. cit.*, 153.
6. *Landnámabók* (1900), 101, names a *Vilbaldr*, evidently of Irish origin.
7. See K. Sisam, *Proceedings of the British Academy*, XXXIX, 1957, 301 ff.
8. *The Chronicle of Æthelweard*, ed. A. Camp-bell, 1962, 33 and XXIV, note.
9. See de Vries, *Rel.²*, II, 233 ff; further R. Jente, *Die mythologischen Ausdrücke im altenglischen Wortschatz*, 1921, 95 and refs.
10. See Jente, *op. cit.*, *loc. cit.*; E. A. Philipp-son, *Germanisches Heidentum bei den Angel-sachsen*, 1929, 169.
11. See *N.E.D.*, svv.
12. *Die germanischen Götternamen der antiken Inschriften*, 1936, 58 and 63 ff.
13. *Germanisch-Romanische Monatschrift*, XXXIV, 1953, 166.
14. *A Handbook on Old High German Literature*, 1955, 16 ff.

15. See G. Storms, *Anglo-Saxon Magic*, 1948, 107 ff; Bugge, *Studier*, I, 287; F. Genz-mer, *Arkiv för nordisk Filologi*, LXIII, 1948, 65 ff.
16. *Lebor Gabála Érenn*, ed. R. A. S. Maca-lister, IV, 1941, 114–15 and 148–9; cf Schröder, *op. cit.*, 179 and refs.
17. *Op. cit.*, 174 ff; further R. Th. Christian-sen, *Die finnischen und nordischen Varianten des zweiten Merseburger Spruches*, 1915.
18. *Kalevala*, Runo XV, 307 ff; translated by W. F. Kirby, Everyman's Library, 1923, I, 157.
19. See Storms, *op. cit.*, 110–13; Schröder, *op. cit.*, 179 and refs.
20. See Bostock, *op. cit.*, 23 ff.
21. *SnE. Gylf.* 22 and 34.
22. See Alexander Jóhannesson, *Isländisches Etymologisches Wörterbuch*, 1956, 560.
23. See Ch. VIII, Frigg.
24. See p. 117 above.
25. *Njáls Saga*, LXXV.
26. *SnE. Skáld.* 74.
27. *Ibid.*
28. The question is thoroughly discussed by Genzmer, *op. cit.*, 60 ff.

CHAPTER V: LOKI

1. See Chs. I, Old Norse Poetry and III, Thór's Hammer and Goats, above.
2. Reconstructed texts in *Skj.* B, I, 14 ff and *Den norsk-isländska skaldedigtningen*, ed. E. A. Kock, I, 1946, 9 ff; translation by L. M. Hollander, *The Skalds*, 1945,42 ff. The most detailed discussion of this part of the *Haustlǫng* is that of A. Holtsmark, *Arkiv för nordisk Filologi*, LXIV, 1949, 1–73.
3. F. Ström, *Loki*, 1956, 63 ff prefers to interpret the phrase as 'wife of Loki'.
4. Reconstructed texts in *Skj.* B, I, 139 ff, and by E. A. Kock, *op. cit.*, I, 76 ff. The most thorough discussion is that of V. Kiil, *Arkiv för nordisk Filologi*, LXXI, 1956, 89–167.
5. *SnE. Sk. Skáld* 27.
6. Kiil, *op. cit.*, 96–7, reads *gammleiði* and interprets as 'leader of the *gammr*' (a mythical bird), suggesting an allusion to the story of Loki as a falcon, pursued by the giant eagle.
7. Kiil, *op. cit.*, 100, applies the allusion to Thór.
8. Various interpretations are quoted by J. de Vries, *The Problem of Loki*, 1933, 126 ff. See also Ström, *op. cit.*, 131 ff.
9. On the *hafnýra* see B. Pering, *Heimdall*, 1941, 217 ff. Pering suggests that the 'sea-kidney' was the fruit of a West Indian plant, a kind of bean (*entada scandens*), which sometimes drifts to northern countries with the Gulf Stream, and is prized as an amulet, relieving women in childbirth.
10. De Vries, *op. cit.*, 127 ff, interprets *Singasteinn* in an entirely different way.
11. Text in *Edda*, ed. G. Neckel, 1927, 289–91.
12. *SnE. Gylf.* 5.
13. E.g. *Gísla Saga Súrssonar* II.
14. *Bjarnar Saga Hítdœlakappa* XVII.
15. *Grágás, Staðarhólsbók*, 1879, 392.
16. *Aldre Västgötalagen*, ed. E. Wessén, 1954, 29.
17. E.g. *Sneglu-Halla þáttr*, ed. Jónas Kristjánsson (*Íslenzk Fornrit* IX, 1956) 265 and 294.
18. Tacitus, *Germania* XLIII.
19. The form *Lævateinn* is emended from *Hævateinn*, but the emendation is demanded by alliteration.
20. *SnE. Gylf.* 19.
21. *SnE. Skáld.* 2–3.
22. *Ibid.*, 27.
23. *SnE. Gylf.* 25.
24. A summary of such stories was given by K. Krohn, *Übersicht über einige Resultate der Märchenforschung*, 1931, 114–122. For a fuller treatment see J. Sahlgren in *Saga och Sed*, 1940, 1–50 and 1941, 115–51.
25. *SnE. Skáld.* 44.
26. *SnE. Gylf.* 25.
27. *SnE. Skáld.* 47.
28. See especially de Vries, *op. cit.*, 155–61.
29. On this strophe see S. Nordal, *Völuspá*, 1923, 75–7.
30. See de Vries, *op. cit.*, 180 ff.; K. Krohn, *Skandinavisk Mytologi*, 1922, 153.
31. *Flb.* I, 275–83.
32. Important discussions are those of H. Celander, *Lokes mytiska Ursprung*, 1911; de Vries, *op. cit.*, 225–50; A. Olrik, *Danske Studier*, 1908, 193–207 and 1909, 69–84; idem, *Myterne om Loke* in *Festskrift til H. F. Feilberg*, 1911, 548–93; A. B. Rooth, *Loki in Scandinavian Mythology*, 1961.
33. *Yngl. S.* IV.
34. *SnE. Skáld.* 23.
35. See Ström, *op. cit.*, 56; Holtsmark, *op. cit.*, 52 ff; further W. Krogmann, *Acta Philologica Scandinavica*, VI, 1931–2, 311 and 321 ff.
36. *Sǫgur Danakonunga*, ed. C. af Petersens and E. Olson, 1925, 11.
37. *SnE. Gylf.* 4.
38. See Ström, *op. cit.*, 57; Holtsmark, *op. cit.*, 48 ff; Krogmann, *op. cit., loc. cit.*
39. See H. Gering and B. Sijmons, *Kommentar zu den Liedern der Edda*, I, 1927, 21–2.
40. Cf *Sæmundar Edda*, ed. F. Detter and R. Heinzel, II, 1903, 27.
41. Various interpretations of this inscription are cited by Krogmann, *op. cit.*, 62 ff. See also F. von der Leyen, *Die Götter der Germanen*, 1938, 137 ff.
42. *Teutonic Mythology* (transl. J. S. Stallybrass), I, 1900, 241 ff; Olrik in *Festskrift til H. F. Feilberg*, 587 ff discusses the etymology of *Loki* (*Lokki*).
43. See J. Sahlgren, *Namn och Bygd*, VI, 1918, 33 ff.
44. Hauk Valdísarson, *Íslendinga Drápa*, str. 1 (*Skj.* B, I, 539).
45. *Skj.* B, I, 61 and 539.
46. Cf Kiil, *op. cit.*, 95–6.
47. See O. Schoning, *Dødsriger i nordisk*

hedentro, 1903, 27 ff; further H. Schneider, *Archiv für Religionswissenschaft*, XXXV, 1938, 25 ff.

48. See de Vries, *op. cit.*, esp. Ch. XII.
49. See Holtsmark, *op. cit.*, 54 ff.
50. *Ragnarök*, revised edition, translated into German by W. Ranisch, 1922, Ch. V and *passim*.
51. See Olrik, *Myterne*, 560 ff and *Ragnarök passim*; further G. Vernadsky, *Sæculum* II, 1951, 364 ff.
52. See G. Dumézil, *Loki*, ed. 2, 1959, 210 ff.
53. *Fled Bricrend*, ed. G. Henderson, 1899, V–VI.

54. *Táin Bó Cúalgne*, ed. E. Windisch, 1905, 897.
55. *Helga Kviða Hundingsbana* II, 34.
56. *Hárbarðslióð*, 24.
57. *Loki*, ed. 1, 1948; ed. 2, 1959.
58. A lucid survey was given by G. Dumézil, *Légendes sur les Nartes*, 1930.
59. Ed. 1, 247.
60. Ed. 2, 201.
61. *Les Dieux des Germains*, 1959, 98, 103–4.
62. *Op. cit.*, 98.
63. *SnE. Gylf.* 25.

CHAPTER VI: HEIMDALL

1. *Skj.* B, I, 523.
2. Finnur Jónsson, *ONOI*, II, 76; B. Pering, *Heimdall*, 1941, 13–14.
3. *Landnámabók*, ed. Finnur Jónsson, 1900, 84. Finnur Jónsson and others following him reject the reading *Heimdala* and emend *Heimdalar*.
4. *Lokasenna* 48.
5. Older interpretations of the phrase *Heimdallar hljóð* are quoted by B. Sijmons and H. Gering, *Kommentar zu den Liedern der Edda*, I, 1927, 36; see further Pering, *op. cit.*, 241 ff. Other views were expressed by Å. Ohlmarks (*Heimdallr und das Horn*, 1937, 315 ff, and especially 272 ff), who believed that the horn was the moon.
6. *SnE. Gylf.* 8.
7. Cf S. Nordal, *Völuspá*, 1923, 67–8.
8. See Sijmons and Gering, *op. cit.*, I, 3; Nordal, *op. cit.*, 35.
9. See Finnur Jónsson, *ONOI*, I, 194–5; Jean Young, *Arkiv för nordisk Filologi* XLIX, 1933, 106.
10. See A. Heusler, *Archiv für das Studium der neueren Sprachen*, CXVI, 1906, 270 ff; G. Neckel, *Beiträge zur Eddaforschung*, 1908, 104 ff; further K. von See, *Acta Philologica Scandinavica*, XXIV, 1957, 1 ff.
11. See Pering, *op. cit.*, 41–2.
12. See Jakob Benediktsson, *Bibliotheca Arnamagnæana*, XII, 1957, 229 ff.
13. It is difficult to accept von See's suggestion (*op. cit.*, 6–7) that the Gaelic word or noun, *Rígr*, was introduced into Iceland from the British Isles *c.* 1200. The Latin work of the Welshman, Geoffrey of Monmouth, was known to Icelanders at that time, but there is little

evidence of literary contact with the Gaelic world then.

14. See G. Vigfússon, *Sturlunga Saga* I, 1878, CLXXXVI; *Corpus Poeticum Boreale* I, 1883, LXX; further Young, *op. cit.*, esp. 98 and 105–6 and refs. there given.
15. See J. de Vries, *Études Germaniques*, 1955, 264: further R. Much, *Deutsche Islandforschung* I, 1930, 63 ff.
16. *Skj.* B, I, 68.
17. *Skj.* B, I, 670.
18. Cf I. Lindquist, *Vetenskaps-Societeten i Lund, Årsbok*, 1937, 89, 97–8.
19. See Bruce Dickins, *Place-names of Surrey*, 1934, 403–6; J. Grimm, *Teutonic Mythology* (transl. J. Stallybrass), I, 1900, 52.
20. *SnE. Gylf.* 15.
21. Cf Lindquist, *op. cit.*, 68.
22. See Ohlmarks, *op. cit.*, 272 ff. and references.
23. *Études Celtiques*, VIII, 1959, 280.
24. Cf Ohlmarks, *op. cit.*, 276.
25. *Skj.* B, I, 657; *SnE. Skáld.* 34, LXXVII.
26. See esp. Young, *op. cit.*, 103 ff.
27. *Death Tales of the Ulster Heroes*, ed. K. Meyer, 1906, 5 ff; further R. Thurneysen, *die irische Helden- und Königsage*, 1921, 534 ff.
28. *The Feast of Bricriu*, ed. G. Henderson, 1899, 24–5.
29. Ed. W. Stokes, *Revue Celtique*, VIII, 47 ff; translation in *The Cuchullin Saga*, ed. E. Hull, 1898 ff; further R. Thurneysen, *op. cit.*, 505 ff.
30. *Scéla Mucce Meic Dathó*, ed. R. Thurneysen, 1951, 17; cf N. K. Chadwick, *An Early Irish Reader*, 48–9, note.
31. Cf J. de Vries, *Betrachtungen zum Märchen*, 1954, 98 ff.

32. See Pering, *op. cit.*, 247 ff.
33. Pering, *op. cit.*, 64 and 274 ff, discusses this form and gives useful references.
34. *SnE. Gylf.* 22.
35. See J. de Vries, *Études Germaniques*, 1955, 265 and refs.; and esp. M. Olsen, *Maal og Minne*, 1909, 25; also O. von Friesen, *Festskrift til Finnur Jónsson*, 1928, 260 ff.
36. *Lexicon Islandico-Latino-Danicum*, I, 1814, 137.
37. See esp. H. Pipping, *Eddastudier* I–II (*Studier i nordisk Filologi* 16–17), 1925–6.
38. *Þrymskviða* 14.
39. *Grímnismál* XIII; *SnE. Gylf.* 15.
40. *SnE. Gylf.* 38.
41. See F. Paasche, *Hedenskap og Kristendom*,

1948, 62 ff.; *Edda* I, 1914, 33–74; Ohlmarks, *op. cit.*
42. See K. Liestøl, *Draumkvæde*, 1946.
43. See *SnE. Gylf.* 34; cf *Húsdrápa* (*Skj.* B, I, 129) Str. 10.
44. Cf Liestøl, *op. cit.*, 70–1.
45. St. Michael was the *fylgjuengill* of Hall af Síðu (*Njáls Saga* C).
46. *Études Germaniques*, 1955, 266 ff.
47. *Les Dieux des Indo-Européens*, 1952, 104–5; cf *Études Celtiques*, cited above.
48. See p. 150 above.
49. *SnE. Skáld* 16.
50. In many works, and especially in *Loki* (ed. 2, 1959), 53 ff).

CHAPTER VII: VANIR

1. See A. Jóhannesson, *Isländisches Etymologisches Wörterbuch*, 1956, pp. 25, 114, 132; J. de Vries, *Altnordisches Etymologisches Wörterbuch*, 1961, svv. *áss* and *vanr*.

War of Æsir and Vanir

1. See Bjarni Aðalbjarnarson, *Heimskringla* I, 1941, pp. XXII ff; further A. Heusler, *Die gelehrte Urgeschichte im altisländischen Schriftum*, 1908, pp. 43 ff.
2. See Aðalbjarnarson, *op. cit.*, I, p. 10, note 3.
3. See Ch. V.
4. See Ch. II, God of Poetry.
5. *Vafþrúðnismál* 39; *Lokasenna* 34.
6. See E. Mogk, *Novellistische Darstellung mythologischer Stoffe Snorris und seiner Schule*, 1923, 1 ff; idem, *Zur Gigantomachie der Vǫluspá*, 1924, 1–10.
7. *Folkvíg* is usually translated 'battle' (cf *folkorrusta*). The word is rare.
8. The phrase *geirum studdu* means more precisely 'they supported her, held her up with spears', i.e. they pierced her from all sides so that she could not fall. The expression is several times recorded. Cf S. Nordal, *Vǫluspá*, 1923, p. 58.
9. *Heiðr* probably 'Bright' see below.
10. In lines 5–6 of this strophe I have adopted the reading of *Hauksbók*. See Nordal, *op. cit.*, 58–9 and especially D. Strömbäck, *Sejd*, 1935, 17–21.
11. The interpretation of lines 4–8 of this strophe is difficult and has been widely

discussed. See particularly G. Dumézil, *Tarpeia*, 1947, 259–60.
12. *Vígspá*, the reading of both manuscripts, is adopted and construed as instrumental dative. Many editors emend to *vígská* (warlike).
13. *Knáttu . . . vǫllu sporna* more literally 'trod (could tread) the fields', cf the common Old English expression: *ahton wælstowe gewald; hæfde wigsigor . . . weold wælstowe* (*Genesis* 2003–5).
14. Mogk, in works cited above, and more recently E. A. Philippson, *Die Genealogie der Götter*, 1953, 81, interpret it as a battle between gods and giants.
15. See Ch. II, God of War, above.
16. See J. de Vries, *Altnordisches Etymologisches Wörterbuch*, 1961, 651.
17. *Lexicon Islandico-Latino-Danicum* II, 1814, 419.
18. See Hj. Falk, *Altwestnordische Kleiderkunde*, 1919, 28–9.
19. Cf Dumézil, *op cit.*, 256, 267, 270 ff.
20. E.g. *Heiðr vǫlva* (*Landnámabók*, ed. Finnur Jónsson, 1900, p. 59); cf *Hrólfs Saga Kraka* (ed. D. Slay, 1960) Ch. 3.
21. *SnE. Gylf.* 22; cf R. Meissner, *De Kenningar der Skalden*, 1921, 227.
22. *SnE. loc. sit.*; cf *Þrymskviða* str. 13.

23. *Lokasenna* str. 32.
24. *Ynglinga Saga* IV and VII.
25. See especially B. Salin in *Studier tillägn. O. Montelius*, 1903, 133–41; H. Schück, *Studier i nordisk Litteratur- och Religionshistoria* I, 1904, 60 ff; N. Odeen in *Studier till. A. Kock*, 1928, 294 ff; E. Mogk in works cited in Note 6 above; Philippson, *op. cit.*, 19 and 81. Cf Ch. II, Woden-Wotan, above.
26. See W. Stokes, *Revue Celtique* XII, 1891, 52 ff; J. Frazer, *Ériu* VIII, 1916, 1 ff; H. d'Arbois de Jubainville, *Cours de Littérature Celtique* V, 1892, 393 ff.
27. See T. F. O'Rahilly, *Early Irish History*

and Mythology, 1946, 141 and 388 ff.
28. See d'Arbois, *The Irish Mythological Cycle* (transl. R. I. Best), 1903, 96.
29. Cf O'Rahilly, *op. cit.*, 313.
30. See Ch. VIII, Týr.
31. See d'Arbois, *Cours* V, 438.
32. See *Hávamál* 148; *Ynglinga Saga* VII.
33. See J. de Vries, *Keltische Religion*, 1961, p. 54.
34. See Ch. II, Lord of the Gallows.
35. Cf de Vries, *op. cit.*, 153.
36. *Skírnir Frey* (*Grímnismál* 43).
37. *Tarpeia*, 1947, 249 ff; *Les Dieux des Indo-Européens*, 1952, 25 ff; *Loki* (ed. 2), 1959, 69 ff; *Mitra-Varuna*, 1948, 163 ff.

Njörð

1. *Ynglinga Saga* IV.
2. According to *SnE. Gylf.* 13, Freyr and Freyja were apparently born to Njörð by a nameless woman after Skaði had left him. In the *Skírnismál* (1–2) Freyr is called *mǫgr* and *sonr* of Njörð and Skaði. This may reflect a later tradition, or perhaps the words are used loosely. Randvér, in the *Hamðismál* (17) is called *sonr* of Svanhild, but was really stepson.
3. See Ch. III, The Worship of Thór.
4. *Hák. Góða* 14; cf Ch. XIII.
5. *Egils Saga* 56.
6. *Vafþrúðnismál* 38.
7. *Grímnismál* 16.
8. See especially *Nordisk Kultur* XXVI, *Religionshistorie* (ed. N. Lid), 1942, pp. 60 ff.
9. See A. Olrik and H. Ellekilde, *Nordens Gudeverden*, 1926–51, I, 410 and 533 and references, pp. 572 and 585 ff.
10. An interesting map, illustrating the place-names compounded with *Njǫrð-* (*Njarð-*) was given by J. de Vries, *Altgermanische Religionsgeschichte*, ed. 2, II, 1957, 194.
11. See A. Bugge, *Vesterlandenes Indflydelse paa Nordboernes . . . i Vikingetiden*, 1905, 144 ff.
12. *Vafþrúðnismál* 39; cf *Lokasenna* 34.
13. *Grímnismál* 16.
14. *SnE. Gylf.* 11.
15. *Vatnsdæla Saga* XLVII.
16. See A. Heusler, *Die gelehrte Urgeschichte*, 1908, 37 ff.
17. *Historia Norvegiæ* in *Monumenta Historica Norvegiæ*, ed. G. Storm, 1880, 97.
18. See *SnE. Prol.* 4–5 footnote to l. 21; cf Arngrímur Jónsson, *Supplementum His-*

toriæ Norvegicæ, ed. Jakob Benediktsson, *Bibliotheca Arnamagnæana* IX, 1950, 148.
19. *Ynglinga Saga* V.
20. *Ibid.*, IX.
21. See Ch. X, Hadding.
22. See Ch. V.
23. *SnE. Skáld.* 3.
24. 'World of din'; a variant is *Þrúðheimr* (World of Strength).
25. *SnE. Gylf.* 12.
26. See Ch. II, Father of Gods and Men.
27. Þórðr Sjáreksson: *nama snotr una . . . goðbrúðr Vani* (the wise bride of gods did not love the Vanr); See *SnE. Skáld.* 14.
28. *Ǫndurdís* (Bragi, *Ragnarsdrápa* 20), *ǫndurgoð* (Thjóðolf, *Haustlǫng* 7; cf Eyvind, *Háleygjatal* 3).
29. *SnE. Gylf.* 12.
30. *Lokasenna* 52.
31. *Ibid.*, 51.
32. *Ibid.*, 50.
33. *Ibid.*, 65, prose; cf *SnE. Gylf.* 36.
34. *SnE. Skáld.* 22.
35. See J. de Vries, *Altnordisches Etymologisches Wörterbuch*, 1961 s.v. *Skaði* and references.
36. See H. Schück, *Studier i nordisk Litteratur- och Religionshistoria* II, 1904, pp. 224 ff. On Skaði see further F. R. Schröder, *Skaði und die Götter Skandinaviens*, 1941.
37. *Skír brúðr goða* (*Grímnismál* 11).
38. *Lokasenna* 51.
39. See Olrik and Ellerkilde, *op. cit.* I, 535 and references.
40. A particularly instructive, if speculative study of Skaði is that of F. R. Schröder, *Skaði und die Götter Skandinaviens*, 1941.

Freyr-Fróði-Nerthus-Ing

1. See Einar Ól. Sveinsson, *Dating the Ice-landic Sagas*, 1958, 85 ff; cf *Víga-Glúms Saga*, ed. G. Turville-Petre, 1960, XXI–II.
2. See Ch. II, The Cult of Óðinn.
3. See Turville-Petre, *op. cit.*, 61–2 and references.
4. *Ketils Saga Hœings*, Ch. II (v.l. *Vitaskrapi*).
5. See A. Holtsmark, *Maal og Minne* 1933, 120.
6. See A. Olrik and H. Ellekilde, *Nordens Gudeverden*, 1926–51, I, 517.
7. See Ch. III, The Worship of Thór.
8. *Landnámabók*, ed. Finnur Jónsson 1900, 72 ff and 193 ff.
9. See Ch. III, The Worship of Thór, and Ch. XII.
10. See p. 169 ff, below.
11. *Landnámabók*, edition cited, 73.
12. *Ibid.*, 72.
13. *Ibid.*, 71.
14. *Ibid.*, 125; cf Einar Ól. Sveinsson, *Land-nám í Skaftafells Þingi*, 1948, 139 ff.
15. *Gísla Saga* (longer version), ed. K. Gíslason, 1849, 101.
16. See S. Nordal, *Hrafnkatla*, 1940.
17. Cf Ól. Briem, *Heiðinn Siður á Íslandi*, 1945, 38.
18. E.g. *Laxdœla Saga*, Chs. 37–8; *Eyrbyggja Saga* 20.
19. *Flb.* I, 401.
20. Cf A. Liestøl, *Maal og Minne* XXXVII, 1945, 59–66; K. Liestøl, *Arv* II, 1946, 94 ff.
21. *SnE. Skáld.* 44.
22. *Húsdrápa* 7 in *Skj.* B, I, 129.
23. *Heiðreks Saga*, ed. Jón Helgason, 1924, 54 and 129; cf H. Rosén, *Freykult och Djurkult* in *Fornvännen*, 8, 1913, 213 ff; G. Turville-Petre in *Proceedings of the Leeds Philosophical and Literary Society*, III, 1935, 330.
24. *Brandkrossa Þáttr*, Ch. I.
25. See Ól. Briem, *op. cit.*, 38 and 47; Ól. Lárusson, *Nordisk Kultur* XXVI, *Religionshistorie*, 1942, 79.
26. See M. Olsen, *Nordisk Kultur* XXVI, 60 ff.
27. Cf M. Olsen, *The Farms and Fanes of Ancient Norway*, 1928, 263 ff. See also Ch. XII below.
28. A map showing the distribution of place-names compounded with *Freyr* was given by J. de Vries, *Altgermanische Re-ligionsgeschichte* ed. 2, II, 1957, 195; see further E. Wessén, *Studier i nordisk Filologi* XIV, 1923 and *idem*, *Acta Philologica Scandinavica* IV, 1929, 97 ff.
29. *Flb.* III, 246.
30. *Hallfreðar Saga* Ch. V.
31. Adam of Bremen IV, 26; cf Ch. XII, below.
32. See Ch. XII, below.
33. See Ch. IX, below.
34. *Ynglinga Saga* X.
35. *Flb.* I, 404.
36. *Vellekla* 18 (*Skj.* B, I, 120).
37. *Ynglinga Saga* X.
38. *Gesta Danorum* (ed. A. Holder, 1886) V, 170–1.
39. *Opera Latine Conscripta*, ed. J. Benediktsson, I, 1950, 339.
40. *SnE. Gylf.* 23. See further G. Neckel, *Die Überlieferungen vom Gotte Balder*, 1920, 118.
41. See Ch. XII, below.
42. *Skírnismál* 2.
43. Cf Swedish *frodas*, etc. See E. Hellquist, *Svensk Etymologisk Ordbok*, 1957, s.v.
44. See Ch. IX.
45. It may be added that the name *Ingui* appears in a legendary genealogy of Bernicia. See M. Redin, *Studies in un-compounded Personal Names in Old English*, 1919, 127.
46. *Saga Ólafs Konungs hins Helga*, ed. O. A. Johnsen and J. Helgason, I, 1941, 3–4.
47. See Turville-Petre, *op. cit.*, 325 ff.
48. Cf F. Klæber, *Beowulf* ed. 3, 1936, XXXVII.
49. *Runic and Heroic Poems* ed. Bruce Dickins, 1915, 20.
50. Opinions about the origin of this name were summarized by J. de Vries, *Alt-nordisches Etymologisches Wörterbuch*, 1961, s.v. *Yngvi*.
51. Cf A. Bugge, *Saga-Book of the Viking Society* IX, 1920–5, 368.
52. *Þórsdrápa* 7 (*Skj.* B, I, 141); E. A. Kock, *Notationes Norrœnæ*, 1923–1944 (§ 449) avoids tmesis and construes *njarðráð* (mighty counsel, plan).
53. *Flb.* I, 332 ff. Cf Ch. XII.
54. See M. Olsen, *Farms and Fanes of Ancient Norway*, 1928, 287 ff; Einar Ól. Sveinsson, *op. cit.*, 139 ff; Ól. Briem *op. cit.*, 47 ff; also *Kristni Saga* II, and *Þorvalds Þáttr Víðfǫrla* IV.

55. See p. 116 above.
56. See esp. E. Wessén, *Studier till Sveriges hedna mytologi och fornhistoria*, 1924, 79 ff; further M. Olsen, *Hedenske Kultminder i norske stedsnavne* I, 1915, 68 ff.
57. See E. Wessén, *Acta Philologica Scandinavica* IV, 1929, 109.
58. See H. Shetelig and Hj. Falk, *Scandinavian Archaeology*, 1937, 187.
59. *Ibid.*, 156 ff.
60. See Bjørn Hougen, *Viking*, 1940, 85 ff.
61. *Lokasenna* 37.
62. See F. Genzmer, *Arkiv för nordisk Filologi*, 63, 1948, 64 ff.
63. *Grímnismál* 43–4.
64. *SnE. Gylf.* 26; cf *SnE. Skáld.* 44.
65. See J. de Vries, *Altgermanische Religionsgeschichte* I, 1956, 108 ff; further O. Almgren, *Hällristningar och Kultbruk*, 1926.
66. See Kristján Eldjárn, *Kuml og Haugfé*, 1956, 212 ff.
67. E.g. *Gísla Saga* Ch. 17. It may be noted that the grave there described was that of Thorgrím Freyr's Priest.
68. *Flb.* I, 339.
69. Saxo (ed. Holder) III, 74–5.
70. *Ibid.*, I, 30; cf Ch. X, Hadding, below.
71. Adam of Bremen, IV, 26; cf Ch. XII, below.

72. See *Opuscula archæologica Oscari Montelio . . . dicata*, 1913, 406.
73. Book VI, 185.
74. *Hyndluljóð* 30; *Lokasenna* 42; *SnE. Gylf.* 23; *Ynglinga Saga* 10.
75. See Ch. II, Óðinn's Eye.
76. In *Maal og Minne*, 1909, 17–36. A very different opinion was expressed by J. Sahlgren, *Eddica et Scaldica*, 1927–8, 211–310.
77. Thus Finnur Jónsson, *Goðafræði Norðmanna og Íslendinga*, 1913. For other etymologies see J. de Vries, *Altnordisches Etymologiisches Wörterbuch*, s.v. *Beyla*.
78. See Olsen, *op. cit.*, 29; Sahlgren (*op. cit.*, 256 ff) derives from *barr* (pine-needle).
79. Cf B. Phillpotts, *The Elder Edda and Ancient Scandinavian Drama*, 1920, 13 ff.
80. See de Vries, *op. cit.*, s.v. *kalekr*.
81. See Sahlgren, *op. cit.*, 261 ff.
82. See S. Bugge, *Arkiv för Nordisk Filologi* V, 1889, 1 ff.
83. See Bugge, *op. cit.*, 20 ff.
84. See Sahlgren, *op. cit.*, 284.
85. *Lokasenna* 35; see Sahlgren, *op. cit.*, 225.
86. Str. 7; see Sahlgren, *op. cit.*, 224 ff.
87. *Þorgrímspula* 3 (*Skj.* B, I, 656).
88. Thorbjörn Hornklofi in *Heimskringla*, *Haralds Saga Hárf.* XV; cf Sahlgren, *op. cit.*, 304–5.

Freyja

1. *SnE. Gylf.* 13; *Grágás* II, ed. V. Finsen, 1852, 184.
2. See F. Holthausen, *Wörterbuch des Altwestnordischen*, 1948, 296; further H. Kuhn, *Anzeiger für deutsches Altertum*, 56, 1937, 156. The gen. form *Sýrar* (instead of *Sýr*) is surprising, but appears also in other instances where the word is used as a nickname. See E. H. Lind, *Norskisländska Personbinamn*, 1920–1, s.v. *sýr*.
3. See J. de Vries, *Altnordische Literaturgeschichte* II, 1942, 126 and refs.
4. Cf B. Sijmons and H. Gering, *Kommentar zu den Liedern der Edda* I, 1927, 397.
5. *Hyndluljóð* 46–7.
6. Ari, *Íslendingabók* VII.
7. *SnE. Gylf.* 13 and 34; cf *Skáld.* 29.
8. See F. R. Schröder, *Germanisch-Romanische Monatschrift* 17, 1929, 414 ff; G. Neckel, *Die Überlieferungen vom Gotte Balder*, 1920, 51 ff.
9. *SnE. Gylf.* 22; *Ynglinga Saga* X.

10. E. A. Philippson, *Die Genealogie der Götter*, 1953, 27 ff, attempts to distinguish Óð from Óðinn.
11. See Ch. VIII, Ull.
12. *SnE. Gylf.* 22.
13. See Ch. V.
14. *Sǫrla Þáttr* in *Flb.* I, 275 ff.
15. *Íslenzk Fornrit* VIII, ed. Einar Ól. Sveinsson, 1939, *Hallfreðar Saga*, Ch. 6.
16. See Ch. III, Thór and the Giants.
17. This was strongly emphasized by J. Sahlgren (*Eddica et scaldica*, 1927–8, 225–39), who interpreted the name *Gerðr* as 'protectress, defender'. He compared words for 'prince', such as *jaðarr* (O.E. *eodor*) in which the meaning seems to develop from 'edge, protective boundary, fence'. He saw *Gerðr* as the second element in a compound and compared names for women such as *Ásgerðr*, *Freygerðr*.
18. See Sahlgren, *op. cit.*, 239 and Finnur

Jónsson, *Lexicon Poeticum* ed. 2, 1931, s.v. *Aurboða*. For other views see A. Jóhannesson, *Isländisches Etymologisches Wörterbuch*, 1956, 607.

19. *SnE. Gylf.* 3.
20. *Ynglinga Saga* IV and VII.
21. *Sǫrla Þáttr loc. cit.*
22. *SnE. Gylf.* 22.
23. See E. Hellquist, *Svensk Etymologisk Ordbok*, I, 1952, s.v. *hör*.
24. See A. Olrik and H. Ellekilde, *Nordens Gudeverden* I, 1926–51, 535.
25. See G. Knudsen, *Nordisk Kultur XXVI, Religionshistorie*, 1942, 34–5.
26. For further examples see R. Meissner, *Die Kenningar der Skalden*, 1921, 227.

27. See A. Jóhannesson, *op. cit.*, 522.
28. Cf Meissner, *op. cit.*, 406.
29. Cf J. de Vries, *Altgermanische Religionsgeschichte*, ed. 2, II, 1957, 293 and 329.
30. F. Ström, *Nordisk Hedendom*, 1961, 104, identifies Gefjun with Freyja and gives a myth of Gefjun to Freyja.
31. *Nordisk Kultur* XXVI, *Religionshistorie*, 60.
32. See Olrik and Ellekilde, *op. cit.*, 533 and 410.
33. *Ibid.*, 540; further J. de Vries, *Altnord. etymologisches Wörterbuch*, s.v. *áll*, 5 and refs.
34. De Vries, *Religionsgeschichte* II, 309, supplies a map giving a useful survey of such names.

CHAPTER VIII: MINOR DEITIES

Týr

1. Cf Bruce Dickins, *Runic and Heroic Poems*, 1915, pp. 18, 26, 30; H. Arntz, *Handbuch der Runenkunde*, ed. 2, 1944, 216–19.
2. *SnE. Skáld.* 17.
3. *Lokasenna* 38.
4. *SnE. Gylf.* 21.
5. See Ch. V.
6. See G. Dumézil, *Mitra-Varuna*, 1948, 133 ff, and *Les Dieux des Germains*, 1959, 40 ff.
7. *SnE. Gylf.* 13.
8. See Olrik and Ellekilde, *Nordens Gudeverden* I, 1926–51, 411, 425; G. Knudsen, *Nordisk Kultur* XXVI, *Religionshistorie*, 1942, 34.
9. See M. Olsen, *Norrøne Studier*, 1938, 63 ff, and *Farms and Fanes of Ancient Norway*, 1928, 297; further F. R. Schröder, *Ingun-*

ar-*Freyr*, 1941, 58 ff.
10. Jordanes, *Getica* V.
11. Tacitus, *Annals* XIII, 57.
12. *Idem, History* IV, 64.
13. See E. Mogk in *Reallexikon der germanischen Altertumskunde*, ed. J. Hoops, III, 1915–16, 198; further Dumézil, *Mitra-Varuna*, 149.
14. See R. Jente, *Die mythologischen Ausdrücke im altenglischen Wortschatz*, 1921, 86 ff.
15. See Bruce Dickins, *Essays and Studies by members of the English Association* XIX, 154 ff; F. M. Stenton, *Trans. Roy. Hist. Soc.* 4th series, XXIII, 1941, 15 ff; A. H. Smith, *English Place-name elements* II, 1956, 180.
16. See J. de Vries, *Altgermanische Religionsgeschichte* II, 1957, 25–6.

Ull

1. *SnE. Gylf.* 17; *Skáld.* 22.
2. *Egils Saga* LXXI; further R. Meissner, *Die Kenningar der Skalden*, 1921, 363 ff and 262 ff.
3. *Haustlǫng* 15 (*Skj.* B, I, 17).
4. Explanations are offered by Meissner, *op. cit.*, 166 and by F. Jónsson, *Lexicon Poeticum Antiquæ Linguæ Septentrionalis*, ed. 2, 1931, s.v. *Ullr*.
5. See Ch. III, Thór and the Giants.
6. See Ch. VII, Njörð.
7. On the relationship of Skaði, Ull, Njörð see esp. H. Schück, *Studier i nordisk Literatur- och Religionshistoria*, II, 1904, 222 ff; further F. R. Schröder, *Skaði und die Götter Skandinaviens*, 1941,

1 ff and 74 ff.
8. See F. R. Schröder, *Ingunar-Freyr*, 1941, 1–15; cf Chs. II, Lord of the Gallows, and XII.
9. Cf Hj. Falk, *Altnordische Waffenkunde*, 1914, 92.
10. See G. Knudsen, *Nordisk Kultur* XXVI (*Religionshistorie*), 1942, 36; A. Olrik and H. Ellekilde, *Nordens Gudeverden* I, 1926–51, 477–8 and *passim*.
11. See Ch. VII, Freyja, above; further M. Olsen, *Hedenske Kultminder* I, 1915, 90 ff; J. de Vries, *Tijdschrift voor nederlandse Taal en Letterkunde*, LIII, 1934, 192 ff.
12. See M. Olsen, *Nordisk Kultur* XXVI (*Religionshistorie*) 60 ff.

13. Cf E. Wessén, *Studier till Sveriges hedna mytologi och fornhistoria*, 1924, 129 ff.
14. See Ch. XII below; further M. Olsen, *Farms and Fanes of Ancient Norway*, 1928, 263 ff.
15. *Nordisk Kultur* XXVI (*Religionshistorie*), 79.
16. See Ch. XII, below.
17. *Gesta Danorum* III, 81-2.
18. See Ch. IV, Saxo, above.
19. See Meissner, *op. cit.*, 166.
20. *Gesta* I, 25.
21. It has been widely discussed; see P.

Herrmann, *Dänische Geschichte des Saxo Grammaticus* II, 1922, 110; G. Dumézil, *La Saga de Hadingus*, 1953, 111 footnote 3; further Dumézil, *Mitra-Varuna*, 1948, 152 ff.
22. *Ynglinga Saga* III.
23. See Ch. II, Father of Gods and Men, above.
24. See J. Palmér, *Acta Philologica Scandinavica* V, 1930-1, 290 ff.
25. Cf O. von Friesen, *Nordisk Kultur* VI, *Runorna*, 1923, 18.
26. *Rel.*[2], II, 1957, 162.

Bragi

1. See Ch. II, God of Poetry.
2. See next section.
3. Cf G. Vigfússon and F. York Powell, *Corpus Poeticum Boreale* II, 1883, 2 ff; Jón Jóhannesson, *Afmælisrit Dr. Einars Arnórssonar*, n.d., 1 ff; G. Turville-Petre, *Origins of Icelandic Literature*, 1953,36, and *Skírnir*, 1954, 47 ff.
4. *Skj.* B, I, 164-6.
5. *Ibid.*, 59.

6. See Ch. IV, The West Norse Sources.
7. Cf S. Nordal, *Íslenzk Menning* I, 1942, 236-7.
8. E.g. in *bragarmál, bragarháttr*.
9. *SnE. Gylf.* 14.
10. See S. Blöndal, *Íslensk-dönsk orðabók*, 1920-4, s.v. *bragr*.
11. As in *Ásabragr* (*Skírnismál* 33).
12. For a full discussion see H. Kuhn, *Festgabe für K. Helm*, 1951, 41 ff.

Iðunn

1. Ch. V.
2. *SnE. Skáld.* 2-3.
3. See E. H. Lind, *Norsk-isländska Dopnamn*, 1915, s.v. *Iðunnr*.
4. G. Knudsen (*Nordisk Kultur* XXVI, *Religionshistorie*, 1942, 36) considers that the Danish place-name *Enø* (older *Ithænø*) contains the name of Iðunn. It could be a personal name.
5. See Ch. I, Old Norse Poetry.
6. See S. Bugge, *Arkiv för nordisk filologi*, V, 1889, 1 ff.
7. See *Saga Heiðreks Konungs*, ed. Ch. Tolkien, 1960, VII.
8. Translation by P. W. Joyce, *Old Celtic Romances*, 1920, 58 and 63 ff.
9. See Ch. II, God of Poetry.

10. A text was edited by J. Pokorny, *Zeitschrift für Celtische Philologie*, XVII, 1928, 193 ff (with translation into German). Translation into French by H. d'Arbois de Jubainville, *L'Épopée Celtique en Irlande*, I, 1892, 385 ff. See also J. Seymour, *Irish Visions of the Other World*, 1930, 66 ff. Valuable observations were also made by H. R. Patch, *The Other World*, 1950, especially 27 ff.
11. See *Osebergfundet*, ed. A. W. Brøgger, Hj. Falk, H. Schetelig, 1917 ff, especially I, 35, 70, 73; II, 72.
12. See Ch. VII, Freyr-Fróði-Nerthus-Ing.
13. *Lokasenna*, 17.
14. See H. Gering and B. Sijmons, *Kommentar zu den Liedern der Edda*, I, 1927, 224-5.

Gefjun

1. The names *Gefn* and *Gefjun* are probably related to the verb *gefa* (to give). See Alexander Jóhannesson, *Isländisches Etymologisches Wörterbuch*, 1958, 188.
2. *SnE. Gylf.* 1.
3. Cf A. Holtsmark, *Maal og Minne*, 1944, 169 ff.

4. See A. Olrik and H. Ellekilde, *Nordens Gudeverden* II, 1951, 712 ff; G. Storms, *Anglo-Saxon Magic*, 1948, 172 ff.
5. See Ch. VII, Freyja.
6. *SnE. Gylf.* 23.
7. See Olrik and Ellekilde, *op. cit.* I, 521, cf 509.

Frigg and Some Others

1. See Ch. IV, The West Norse Sources.
2. See Ch. II, Woden-Wotan.
3. See Ch. IV, Continental and English Tradition.
4. *SnE. Gylf.* 22.
5. See Alexander Jóhannesson, *Isländisches Etymologisches Wörterbuch*, 1956, 1003.
6. *Lokasenna* 26.
7. See Ull, above.
8. *Gesta Danorum* I, 25.
9. *Lokasenna* 29; cf Ch. II, Woden-Wotan, above.
10. See F. Ström, *Nordisk Hedendom*, 1961, 130.
11. *SnE. Gylf.* 6; *Skáld.* 28.
12. See B. Sijmons and H. Gering, *Kommentar zu den Liedern der Edda*, I, 1927, 290.
13. See below.
14. See Olrik and Ellekilde, *op. cit.*, I, 518.
15. *Salomon and Saturn*, ed. J. M. Kemble II, 1847, 124; R. Jente, *Die mythologischen Ausdrücke im altenglischen Wortschatz*, 1921, 107 ff.
16. *SnE. Gylf.* 22.
17. See R. Meissner, *Die Kenningar der Skalden*, 1921, 405 ff.
18. See Ch. III, Thór in the Viking Colonies.

CHAPTER IX: THE DIVINE KINGSHIP

1. In *The Sacral Kingship* (Contributions to the Central Theme of the VIIIth International Congress for the History of Religions), 1959, conceptions of the sacral kingship in many lands and ages are described. See further E. O. James, *The Ancient Gods*, 1960, 107 ff.
2. *Getica* XIII.
3. See J. de Vries, *Altnordisches Etymologisches Wörterbuch*, 1961, s.v. *áss*.
4. Cf Arngrímur Jónsson, *Rerum Danicarum Fragmenta*, I.
5. *Ynglinga Saga* XI and XIV–XV.
6. On suchlike conceptions see W. Baetke, *Das Heilige im Germanischen*, 1942, 147 ff.
7. *Ynglinga Saga* XLII; see B. Aðalbjarnarson, note *ad loc.*
8. *Fagrskinna*, ed. F. Jónsson, 1902–3, 383.
9. *Hkr. Háfd. Sv.* IX.
10. *Ágrip* I.
11. *The Saga Library*, *The Stories of the Kings of Norway*, I, 1893, 242 (=*Hkr., Ól. Trygg.* XVI).
12. *Ólafs Saga hins Helga* (The Legendary Saga), ed. O. A. Johnsen, 1922, I–II; cf *Flb.* II, 6–9.
13. *Flb.* II, 135.
14. *Landnámabók*, ed. Finnur Jónsson, 1900, 12.

CHAPTER X: THE DIVINE HEROES

Ermanaric, Sigurð and the Burgundians

1. Detailed bibliography was given by H. Schneider, *Germanische Heldensage* I–II, 1933. Second edition with additional bibliography by R. Wisniewski, 1962.
2. See C. Brady, *The Legends of Ermanaric*, 1943; G. Zink, *Les Légendes héroiques de Dietrich et d'Ermrich*, 1950.
3. *Skj.* B, I, 1 ff.
4. Cf E. A. Thompson, *A History of Attila and the Huns*, 1948, 65 ff.
5. *SnE. Skáld.* 48–9.
6. Ed M. Olsen, 1908, XXI. In this saga as in some other sources, difficulty is overcome by identifying the valkyrie with Brynhild.
7. See especially A. Heusler, *Die Lieder der Lücke im Codex Regius* in *Germanistische Abhandlungen H. Paul dargebracht*, 1902, 1 ff.
8. See G. Vigfússon and F. York Powell, *Sigfrid-Arminius*, 1886; further O. Höfler in *Festschrift für F. R. Schröder*, 1959, 11 ff, re-issued with some additions as *Siegfried, Arminius and die Symbolik*, 1961. Full bibliography is given in these works.
9. Some suggestions are mentioned by Höfler, *op. cit.*, 22 ff.
10. *Op. cit.*, 27 ff.
11. See R. Much, *Die Germania des Tacitus*, ed.2, 1959, 318.
12. See Höfler, *op. cit.*, 96 ff.
13. *Reginsmál*; *SnE. Skáld.* 47–8.
14. *Volsunga Saga* XVIII.
15. *Fáfnismál* Strs. 12 ff; cf *Volsunga Saga*, *loc. cit.*
16. *Fáfnismál* Strs. 31 ff; *SnE. Skáld.* 48; *Volsunga Saga* XIX.

17. *Fáfnismál* Strs. 2–4.
18. Chs. I ff.
19. *Vǫlsunga Saga* XI–XII.
20. *Ibid.*, VIII.
21. *Frá Dauða Sinfjǫtla*; cf *Vǫlsunga Saga* X.
22. Attempts to attribute the exploit in *Beowulf* to Sigemund's son, Sigfrit-Sigurð, are forced. See J. Hoops, *Kommentar zum Beowulf*, 1932, 110 ff; F. Klæber, *Beowulf*, 1950, 160 ff.
23. *The Origin of the English Nation*, 1907, 148 ff.
24. Sigmund has been identified in history as Sigimundus, a king of the Burgundians, who, according to Gregory of Tours (III, 5), murdered his son Sigiricus at the instigation of a stepmother in A.D. 522. See G. Schütte, *Sigfrid und Brünhild*, 1935, 50–4.
25. See Hj. Falk, *Odinsheite*, 1924, svv.
26. V. Jansson, *Niflheim (Språkvetenskapliga Sällskapets i Uppsala Förhandlingar*, 1934–6, 75 ff) shows reason to doubt that there was a Norse word *nifl* meaning 'darkness', but the existence of such a word in continental German cannot be questioned. The Norse *Niflungar* is borrowed from the Continent.
27. Bragi, *Ragnarsdrápa* 3 (*Skj.* B, I, 1); cf *SnE. Skáld.* 51.
28. *Nibelungensage und Nibelungenlied*, 1922, 53 ff.
29. *Nibelungenlied, Âv.* III.

30. Cf *Heiðreks Saga*, ed. Ch. Tolkien, 1960, 68.
31. *Reginsmál* 31 (prose) etc.
32. *Early Irish History and Mythology*, 1946, 318 ff.
33. Ed. K. Meyer, *Revue Celtique* V, 195 ff; cf G. Murphy, *Duanaire Finn* III, 1953, pp. L ff.
34. *Nibelungenlied, Âv.* XV.
35. See *Death-tales of the Ulster Heroes*, ed. K. Meyer, 1906, 27.
36. *Þiðreks Saga*, ed. H. Bertelsen, 1905–11, CVI.
37. See A. Heiermeier, *Zeitschrift für Celtische Philologie* XXII, 1940, 58 ff.
38. See G. Murphy, *op. cit.*, p. XXI and references there given.
39. *Guðrúnarkviða* II, Str.2; *Vǫlsunga Saga* XXVII; further O. Höfler, *op. cit.*, 49 ff.
40. See H. Zimmer, *Keltische Beiträge* III, in *Zeitschrift für deutsches Altertum* XXXV, 1891. Contrast K. Meyer, *Sitz. Ber. der preuss. Akad. der Wissenschaften*, 1918, 1042 ff; further A. Nutt, *Waifs and Strays of Celtic Tradition* IV, 1891, pp. XXII ff.
41. See especially S. Bugge, *The Home of the Eddic Poems*, 1899, 107 ff, and Heiermeier, *op. cit.* 558 ff.
42. On this point see especially J. de Vries, *Betrachtungen zum Märchen*, 1954, 98 ff; *Kelten und Germanen*, 1960, 130 ff and *passim*.

Starkað

1. For the latter view see especially G. Dumézil, *Aspects de la Fonction Guerrière*, 1956, 80 and 107 ff.
2. Cf *Heiðreks Saga*, ed. Ch. Tolkien, 1960, 66–7.
3. *Heiðreks Saga, loc. cit.* See further P. Herrmann, *Die Heldensage des Saxo Grammaticus*, 1922, 422; H. Schneider, *Germanische Heldensage* II, 1933, 166–7 and references.
4. Cf J. de Vries, *Germanisch-Romanische Monatschrift* XXXVI, 1955, 290 ff.
5. See E. A. Kock, *Fornjermansk Forskning*, 1922, § 29.
6. *Gautreks Saga* VII (= *Vikarsbálkr*, Str. 25).
7. *Egils Saga ok Ásmundar*, XVIII.
8. Including *Ynglinga Saga* XII and XXV. Arngrímur Jónsson, *Rerum Danicarum Fragmenta* VIII–X; *Norna-Gests Þáttr* VII–VIII.

9. Saxo VIII, 265 ff.
10. *Heiðreks Saga* (ed. Tolkien) 67.
11. See Ch. III, Worship of Thór.
12. Dumézil (*op. cit.*, 111) gives an interpretation of this line which can hardly be intended seriously. The god prostrated Starkað in order to amputate his superfluous arms: '*le chirurgien a d'abord "terrassé" son patient.*'
13. On the provenance of this passage see Jakob Benediktsson, *Arngrími Jonae, Opera Latine conscripta*, IV, 1957, 232–3.
14. *SnE. Skáld.* 25.
15. *Hávamál* Strs. 104–5; cf *SnE. Skáld.* 6.
16. *SnE. Gylf.* 5.
17. *Op. cit.*, 82 ff.
18. Saxo VII, 227.
19. *Op. cit.*, 389 ff.
20. *Helgakviða Hundingsbana* II, 27.

21. See S. Bugge, *The Home of the Eddic Poems*, 1899, 166 ff.
22. *Studier over de nordiske Gude- og Heltesagns oprindelse*, 1881–9, 383.
23. *Ynglinga Saga* IX.
24. *Ibid.*, *loc. cit.*
25. *Hárbarðsljóð*, str. 24.

Harald Wartooth

1. In *Edda Snorra Sturlusonar*, ed. Guðni Jónsson, 1949, 339.
2. *Sǫgur Danakonunga*, ed. C. af Petersens and E. Olson, 1919–25, 3 ff.
3. On *Skjǫldunga Saga* see Jakob Benediktsson, *Bibliotheca Arnamagnæana* xii, 1957, 107 ff.
4. *Skj.* B, I, 117.
5. *Vǫlsunga Saga* II.
6. Saxo vii, 247.
7. *Ibid.*, 248.
8. See P. Herrmann, *Die Heldensagen des Saxo Grammaticus*, 1922, 524 ff.
9. Saxo vii, 255.
10. See especially Bjarni Guðnason, *Um Brávallaþulu* in *Skírnir* cxxxii, 1958, 82 ff, where full bibliographical notes are given.
11. See A. Heusler in *Reallexikon der germanischen Altertumskunde* (ed. J. Hoops) II, 1913–15, 449.
12. *Skj.* B, I, 164 ff.
13. *Ibid.*, 57 ff.

Hadding

1. Cf A. Olrik, *Kilderne til Sakses Old-historie* II, 1894, 1 ff.
2. Cf *Brot af Sigurðarkviðu* Str. 17.
3. *Ibid.*, Str. 4, cf *Vǫlsunga Saga* XXXII.
4. Cf *Brennu-Njáls Saga*, ed. Einar Ól. Sveinsson, 1954, 303, note.
5. *Furuis hostiis*.
6. *SnE. Gylf.* 34.
7. See Ch. III, Thór and the Giants, above.
8. Cf Olrik, *op. cit.*, 8.
9. *Helgakviða Hundingsbana* II, Str. 49.
10. *Reginsmál* Strs. 16 ff.
11. *SnE. Gylf.* 12.
12. Also called *Alstignus, Alstagnus, Haustuin*. On the identification of this Viking with Hadding see Olrik, *op. cit.*, 5; P. Herrmann, *Die Heldensagen des Saxo Grammaticus* 1922, 91 ff; and especially the criticism of G. Dumézil, *La Saga de Hadingus*, 1953, 17–18.
13. On Hasting's career see esp. J. Steenstrup, *Normannerne* II, 1878, *passim*.
14. *SnE. Gylf.* 12.
15. On this point see Dumézil, *op. cit.*, 28 ff.
16. *Yngl. S.* IX.
17. O. Elton's translation, 40.
18. Haldórr Skvaldri: *harðél Haddings* (the violent storm of Hadding, i.e. battle). See *Skj.* B, I, 460.
19. *Yngl. S.*, IV; cf *Lokasenna* Str. 36.
20. *Lokasenna* Str. 32.
21. Cf Dumézil, *op. cit.*, 118.
22. See *Ǫrvar-Odds Saga*, ed. R. C. Boer, 1888, 97, 100, 101, further 105; *Heiðreks Saga* ed. Jón Helgason, 1924, 4 and 99.
23. E.g. *Flateyjarbók* ed. G. Vigfússon and C. R. Unger, I, 1860, 24.
24. Some critics have deduced that there was a singular *Haddingi* from the obscure lines of *Guðrúnarkviða* II, Str. 22:
    lyngfiskr langr (v.l. lagar)
    lands Haddingja
    ax óskorit.
    See B. Sijmons and H. Gering, *Kommentar zu den Liedern der Edda* II, 1931, 303. The form *Haddingja* in this passage is more likely to be gen. pl.
25. *Heiðreks Saga*, 4.
26. Vol. I, 24.
27. *Historia Norwegiæ* in *Monumenta Historica Norvegiæ*, ed. G. Storm, 1880, 82.
28. In fact, the text of the *Edda* reads *Haddingjaskaði*, but the form *Haddingjaskati* is found in the *Flateyjarbók*, *loc. cit.*
29. See *Fernir Forníslenkir Rímnaflokkar*, ed. Finnur Jónsson, 1896, 17 ff. The underlying traditions were carefully studied by U. Brown, *SBVS.* XIII, ii, 1947–8, 51 ff.
30. In the *Hrómundar Saga Gripssonar*, derived from the *Griplur*, the name appears as *Haldingr* (pl. *Haldingjar*). See *Fornaldar Sögur Norðurlanda* ed. Guðni Jónsson, II, 1950, 415 ff.
31. Called *Lára* in *Hrómundar Saga*, 416–17.
32. See *Runic and Heroic Poems*, ed. B. Dickins, 1915, 20.

33. See R. Much in *Reallexikon der germanischen Altertumskunde* II, 1913–15, 452.
34. *Hkr., Yngl. S.* XVII.
35. *Germania* xliii.
36. See R. Much, *Die Germania des Tacitus*, ed. 2, 1959, 380.
37. See N. Lid, *Nordisk Kultur* xxvi (*Religionshistorie*), 1942, 118–19; further M. Olsen, *Hedenske Kultminder i norske stedsnavne* I, 1915, 248 ff.
38. Cf Old English *heord*. See J. de Vries, *Altnordisches Etymologisches Wörterbuch*, 1961, s.v. *haddr*.

39. For examples see Finnur Jónsson, *Lexicon Poeticum Antiquae Linguae Septentrionalis*, ed. 2. 1931, s.v. *haddr*.
40. Saxo, vi, 185.
41. *Yngl. S.* VII.
42. Cf Ólafur Lárusson, *Lög og Saga*, 1958, 145.
43. *Op. cit.*, 127–8.
44. Edition cited, 38.
45. See J. E. Turville-Petre, *Hengest and Horsa* in *SBVS*. xiv, 4, 1956–7, 273 ff.
46. Ed. Finnur Jónsson, 1892–6, 503–4.

CHAPTER XI: GUARDIAN SPIRITS

The Dísir

1. *Viga-Glúms Saga*, V; *Heiðreks Saga*, ed. J. Helgason, 1924, 91. The 'winter-nights' are the three days when winter begins, falling about mid-October.
2. *Egils Saga* XLIV.
3. *Viga-Glúms Saga* V.
4. *Heiðreks Saga* (ed. Ch. Tolkien, 1960), VII; *Ynglinga Saga* XXIX.
5. Ed. J. Helgason, 91.
6. For a rather different view see J. de Vries, *Acta Philologica Scandinavica*, VII, 1931–2, 175.
7. *Hálfs Saga ok Hálfsrekka*, XV.
8. *Vǫlsunga Saga* XXXVII; cf. *Atlamál*, 28.
9. *Hvǫttumk at dísir* (*Hamðismál*, 28).
10. In the *Krákumál* 29 (*Skj.* B, I, 656) the dying hero says: *heim bjóða mér dísir* (the dísir invite me home). The *dísir* appear in this context to be valkyries.
11. *Sigrdrífumál*, 9.
12. E.g. *Ímundís*, 'battle-goddess', 'valkyrie', *Haustlǫng* 17 (*Skj.* B, I, 17).
13. See D. Hofmann, *Nordisch-englische Lehnbeziehungen der Wikingerzeit*, 1955, 140 ff and references.
14. See esp. K. F. Johansson, *Skrifter utg. av. Kungl. hum. vetenskapssamfundet i Uppsala*, XX, 1, 1918, 103 ff.
15. *Þiðranda Þáttr* in *Flb.* I, 418–21, and *Fornmanna Sögur* II, 1826, 192–7. The latter text is followed here.
16. *Njáls Saga* XCVI.
17. This motive is far from clear. Thorhall the Prophet survived the feast, and the man who was to die was not a prophet.
18. See D. Strömbäck, *Tidrande och Diserna*, 1949, 14 ff and references; cf G. Turville-Petre, *Saga-Book of the Viking Society* XIV, 1–2, 19535–, 137 ff.
19. *Op. cit., passim.*

20. *Kristni Saga* VII.
21. See F. Ström, *Arv*, VIII, 1952, 80 ff.
22. For further examples of autumn festivals see A. Olrik and E. Ellekilde, *Nordens Gudeveden* II, 1951, 861 ff.
23. See Ch. XII.
24. *SnE. Gylf* 22.
25. *Heiðreks Saga* (ed.Tolkien), VII.
26. *Úfar ro dísir* (*Grímnismál* 53).
27. *Yðr munu dauðar/dísir allar* (*Hálfs Saga ok Hálfsrekka* XV).
28. *Atlamál* 28 (*væri, værit* MS.).
29. *Viga-Glums Saga* XIX.
30. *Bjarnar Saga Hítdœlakappa*, XXXII.
31. Cf. My paper in *Early English and Norse Studies Presented to Hugh Smith*, 1963, 196 ff.
32. See M. Olsen in *Nordisk Kultur*, XXVI, 1942, 60 ff.
33. See Ch. VIII, Ull.
34. See M. Olsen, *Hedenske Kultminder i norske stedsnavne*, I, 1915, 70, 178, 181 ff; Strömbäck, *op. cit.*, 48.
35. Ed. Tolkien, 67.
36. Ed. G. Storm, *Monumenta Historica Norvegiæ*, 1880, 101; see note *ad loc.* on a textual difficulty.
37. See F. Ström, *Diser, Nornor, Valkyrjor*, 1954, 42 ff.
38. See Ström, *op. cit.*, 41. This interpretation is doubtful because of the syntax of the *Ynglinga Tal.* Snorri (*SnE. Skáld.* 86) cites a form *ioðdís* (sic), meaning 'sister'. The sister of Úlf and Nari is, of course, Hel.
39. See G. Gjessing in *Viking*, VII, 1943, 5 ff.
40. See J. K. Bostock, *Old High German Literature*, 1955, 17.
41. See J. de Vries, *Rel.*[2] II, 288 ff, where useful references are given.
42. *De Temporum Ratione*, XV.

Fylgja and Hamingja

1. 'Wraith', 'double-ganger' might be possible in some dialects.
2. See G. Turville-Petre, *Saga-Book of the Viking Society*, XII, Part II, 1940, 119 ff; further A. Jóhannesson, *Isländisches Etymologisches Wörterbuch*, 1956, 558.
3. See Jónas Jónasson, *Íslenzkir Þjóðhættir*, 1934, 261 ff.
4. Cf E. O. James in *Encyclopædia of Religion and Ethics*, 1908–26, s.v. *Tutelary gods and spirits*; also A. C. Krujt in the same publication under *Indonesians*.
5. See G. Turville-Petre, *Dreams in Icelandic Tradition*, Folklore LXIX, 1958, 93 ff, and another article at press.
6. *Njáls Saga* XLI.
7. *Ljósvetninga Saga* XI.
8. *Vápnfirðinga Saga* XIII; cf *Ljósvetninga Saga* XVI.
9. *Njáls Saga* XXXIII; *Qrvar-Odds Saga* (ed. R. C. Boer, 1888), 22–3.
10. *Hávarðar Saga Ísfirðings* XX; *Njáls Saga* LXII.
11. *Vatnsdœla Saga* XLII.
12. Cf W. Henzen, *Über die Träume in der altnord. Saga-Litteratur*, 1890, 38; further R. Mentz, *Die Träume in den altfranzösschen Karls- und Artus Epen*, 1888.
13. The Icelandic *sál* is believed to be borrowed from the Old English *sawl, sawol*. See Alexander Jóhannesson, *op. cit.*, 1146.
14. *Hávarðar Saga* XX.
15. See Ch. II, Óðinn and his Animals.
16. *Vatnsdœla Saga* XXX; cf W. H. Vogt's introduction to this saga (1921), p. LXXIV.
17. See my paper in *Saga-Book* cited above, esp. 125 and note 3 *ad loc*.
18. *Atlamál*, 19.
19. On the formation of the compound *hamingja* see Jóhannesson, *op. cit.*, 210.
20. *Viga-Glúms Saga* IX.

Elves, earth-spirits, dwarfs

1. *Kormáks Saga* XXII (*Íslenzk Fornrit* VIII, 1939); see Einar Ól. Sveinsson, note *ad loc*.
2. *Hkr. Ól. Helg.* XCI.
3. See A. Olrik and H. Ellekilde, *Nordens Gudeverden*, I, 1926–51, 169 ff; Ellekilde in *Acta Philologica Scandinavica* VIII, 1933–4, 182 ff. For another view see J. de Vries, *Acta Phil. Scand.* VII, 1932–3, 169 ff. See also Ch. XIII below.
4. *Heiðreks Saga*, ed. J. Helgason, 1924, 91.
5. *SnE. Gylf.* 9.
6. See R. Jente, *Die mythologischen Ausdrücke im altenglischen Wortschatz*, 1921, 167 ff; also G. Storms, *Anglo-Saxon Magic*, 1948, 140 ff and 248 ff.
7. Biørn Haldorsen, *Lexicon* I, 1814, 23; further N. Lid, *Maal og Minne*, 1921, 37 ff.
8. See Jónas Jónasson, *Íslenzkir Þjóðhættir* 1934, 406 ff.
9. As used in the saga the word *landvættir* seems to correspond with *landálfr* (land-elf), used by Egill in str. 29.
10. Ed. F. Jónsson, 1900, 215, 102.
11. *Ibid.* 101, 214.
12. *Hkr., Ól. Trygg.* XXXIII.
13. On the origin of this motive see Einar Ól Sveinsson, *Dating the Icelandic Sagas*, 1958, 85–6.
14. Cf Matthías Þórðarson, *Þjóðminjasafn Íslands*, 1914,8; Ól. Briem, *Heiðinn Siður á Íslandi*, 1945, 75, note 1.
15. Ed. F. Jónsson, 1892–6, 167. The homily is traceable, not to Augustin, as is said in the *Hauksbók* and elsewhere, but to Cæsarius of Arles. I am indebted to Joan Turville-Petre for this information. A version of this homily was also given by Ælfric, *Lives of Saints*, ed. W. W. Skeat, I, 1881, 368 ff.
16. See Ch. III, Thor's Hammer.
17. Str. 43; cf *SnE., Gylf.* 26.
18. *Saga Heiðreks Konungs*, ed. Ch. Tolkien, 1960, 68.
19. *SnE. Skáld.* 63.
20. *Hávamál* 143 and 160.
21. *SnE. Gylf.* 7.
22. See S. Gutenbrunner, *Arkiv för nordisk Filologi*, LXX. 1955, 61 ff.
23. *Vafþrúðnismál* 21.
24. *Skj* B, I, 156 (Hallfreðr) and 321 (Arnór).
25. Cf *Historia Norvegiæ* (ed. G. Storm in *Monumenta Historica Norvegiæ*, 1880) 97.
26. See A. Olrik and H. Ellekilde, *Nordens Gudeverden* I, 1926–51, 351 and refs.
27. *Alvíssmál* 16.
28. *SnE. Gylf.* 21; *Skáld.* 47.
29. *Hávamál* 143.
30. *Alvíssmál* 2.

CHAPTER XII: TEMPLES AND OBJECTS OF WORSHIP

1. *Germania* IX.
2. See esp. R. Jente, *Die mythologischen Ausdrücke im altenglischen Wortschatz*, 1921, 7 ff; further S. Feist, *Etym. Wörterbuch der gotischen Sprache*, 1923, s.v. *alhs.*
3. *Gutalag och Guta Saga*, ed. H. Pipping, 1905–7, 7, 63.
4. See J. Grimm, *Teutonic Mythology* (transl. J. S. Stallybrass), I, 1900, 79 ff.
5. *Historia Ecclesiastica* I, 30; II, 15.
6. *Ibid.*, II, 13.
7. *Landnámabók*, ed. Finnur Jónsson, 1900, 221, 197.
8. *Norges gamle Love*, ed. R. Keyser and P. A. Munch, etc., 1846–95, II, 308.
9. See General Bibliography.
10. See M. Olsen, *Farms and Fanes of Ancient Norway*, 1928, 280.
11. A summary is given by A. Olrik and H. Ellekilde, *Nordens Gudeverden*, I, 1926–51, 528 ff.
12. Edition cited, 172.
13. See further W. Baetke, *Das Heilige im Germanischen*, 1942, esp. 80 ff.
14. *SnE. Gylf.* 22.
15. *Kormáks Saga*, X; see Einar Ól. Sveinsson, *Íslenzk Fornrit* VIII, 1939, 237 note.
16. It seems to be used in that sense by the Icelandic scald, Einar Skálaglamm (died *c.* 995) in *Vellekla* 15 and *Hákonar Drápa* 1 (*Skj.* B, I, 119, 116)
17. Edition cited, 158.
18. *Skj.* B, II, 322, 1; B, I, 527, 9.
19. *SnE. Gylf.* VII.
20. See Olsen, *op. cit.*, 283; *Norges gamle love* I, 430.
21. See D. Bruun, *Fortidsminder og Nutidshjem paa Island*, 1928, 48 ff; further Bruun and F. Jónsson, *Aarbøger for nordisk Oldkyndighed og Historie*, 1909, 245 ff.
22. See Aa. Roussell, *Forntida Gårdar i Island*, 1943, 217.
23. Cf Einar Ól. Sveinsson, *Íslenzk Fornrit*, IV, 1935, Introduction, § 2.
24. Described in many works. See Ól. Briem, *Heiðinn Siður á Íslandi*, 1945, 137 ff. See also plan.
25. See Rousell, *op cit.*, 219.
26. *Ibid.*, 201 ff.
27. See Plate 6.
28. Edition cited, 96.
29. See especially Olsen, *op. cit.*, 263 ff.
30. *Hkr.*, *Hák. Góða* XIV; *Ól. Trygg.* LIX and LXVIII–IX.
31. *Njáls Saga*, LXXXVIII.
32. *Gesta Hammaburgensis Ecclesiæ Pontificum*, ed. B. Schmeidler, 1917, Book IV, XXVI ff.
33. See Ch. IX, above.
34. For Norwegian and Icelandic examples see G. Turville-Petre, *Medieval Studies*, XI, 1949, 206 ff.
35. In *Fornvännen*, XVIII, 1949, 206 ff.
36. *SnE. Skáld.*, 43.
37. See Grimm, *op. cit.*, 1, 84.
38. *Vatnsdœla Saga*, XXX; *Kjalnesinga Saga*, II.
39. See E. Wessén, *Studier till Sveriges hedna mytologi*, 1924, 183 ff.
40. See Grimm, *op. cit.*, 113.
41. *Hist. Eccl.* III, 22.
42. *Kjalnesinga Saga*, II.
43. *Harðar Saga ok Hólmverja*, XIX. On Thorgerð see F. R. Schröder, *Ingunar-Freyr*, 1941, 48 ff.
44. *Hkr.*, *Ól. Helg.* CXII; cf *Ólafs Saga hins Helga* (The Legendary Saga), ed. O. A. Johnsen, 1922, XXXIV ff.
45. *Flb.* I, 400.
46. *Íslenzk Fornrit* IX, ed. J. Kristjánsson, 1956, 109 ff.
47. See J. Kristjánsson, *op. cit.*, Introduction, LXI; A. H. Krappe, *Acta Philologica Scandinavica*, III, 1928–9, 226 ff.
48. For further examples see Grimm, *op. cit.*, I, 213, 251 ff.
49. *Hallfreðar Saga*, VI.
50. *Vatnsdœla Saga*, X; cf *Landnámabók*, edition cited, 182.
51. See Plate 13.
52. Cf Plate 44.
53. See Plates 17–18. Further S. U. Palme, *Kristendomens genombrott i Sverige*, 1959, 97 ff.
54. See Plates 7–11.
55. Cf *Fornmanna Sögur*, II, 1826, 324 ff; *Saga Ólafs Tryggvasonar af Oddr Snorrason*, ed. F. Jónsson, 1932, 221–2.
56. *Fóstbrœðra Saga*, XXIII.
57. *Laxdœla Saga*, XXIX.
58. The *Húsdrápa* of Úlf Uggason, (*Skj.*, B, I, 128 ff). See Ch. I, Old Norse Poetry.
59. Ibid.
60. See Plate 39.
61. Plates 22–3.
62. *Norges gamle love*, I, 383; cf E. Mogk in *Reallexikon der germanischen Altertumskunde*, II, 1913–15, 311 ff.

63. Cf F. Ström, *Arv*, VII, 1951, 23 ff.
64. *Landnámabók*, edition cited, 5.
65. *Hkr. Ól.Trygg.*, XXVII.
66. *Hkr.*, *Ól.Trygg.*, LXIV; cf *Ragnars Saga Loðbrókar*, IX. The ox in the story of Thidðrandi (see Ch. XI) was called *Spámaðr* (Prophet).
67. *Helga Kviða Hj.* 30, prose; cf *The Saga of King Heiðrek the Wise*, ed. Ch. Tolkien,

1960, VIII.
68. *Vatnsdæla Saga*, XXXIV.
69. See A. Liestøl, *Maal og Minne*, 1945, 59 ff; K. Liestøl, *Arv*, II, 1946, 94 ff.
70. *Flb.* I, 401.
71. *Germania*, X.
72. See Ch. XIII, below.
73. *Flb.* I, 291 ff.

CHAPTER XIII: SACRIFICE

1. *Hkr.*, *Hák. Góða*, XIV.
2. See p. 259 below.
3. See Einar Ól. Sveinsson, *Íslenzk Fornrit* IV, 1935, XIII ff; Bjarni Aðalbjarnarson, *Íslenzk Fornrit* XXVI, 1941, p. LXXXVIII; Jóhannes Halldórsson, *Íslenzk Fornrit* XIV, 1959, pp. VIII ff.
4. See Ch. XII, p. 241 above.
5. Betra er óbeðit   en sé   of blótit
   ey sér til gildis gjǫf,
   betra er ósent en sé ofsóit (*Hávamál*, 145).
6. See Ch. XII, p. 237 above.
7. See J. Grimm, *Teutonic Mythology* (transl. J. S. Stallybrass), I, 1900, 56.
8. See H. Shetelig and Hj. Falk, *Scandinavian Archaeology*, 1937, 187 ff.
9. *Hymiskviða*, str. 1.
10. *De Bello Gothico* II, 14, 15; cf F. Nansen, *In Northern Mists*, I, 1911, 139 ff.
11. *Guta Lag och Guta Saga*, ed. H. Pipping, 1907, 63.
12. *Monumenta Historica Norvegiæ*, ed. G. Storm, 1880, 98.
13. Illuminating observations on this problem were made by K. Johansson, *Skrifter utgifna af kungl. humanistiska vetenskapssamfundet i Uppsala* XX, 1919, esp. 94 ff.
14. See H. Birkeland, *Nordens Historie i Middelalderen etter arabiske kilder*, 1954, 14 ff.
15. Cf F. Ström, *On the Sacral Origin of the Germanic Death Penalties*, 1942, 144 ff.
16. See F. Ström, *Nordisk Hedendom*, 1961, 32.
17. A summary was given by A. Olrik and H. Ellekilde, *Nordens Gudeverden*, I, 1926–51, 470 ff.
18. See A. Liestøl, *Maal og Minne*, XXXVII, 1945, 59–66; K. Liestøl, *Arv*, II, 1946, 94–110.
19. *Kristni Saga* XII; cf *Hkr. Ól. Trygg.* LXVII.
20. The question has been discussed most thoroughly by F. Ström, *On the Sacral Origin*; and in *Saga och Sed*, 1952, 51 ff. Another view was expressed by D. Strömbäck, *Saga och Sed*, 1942, 51 ff.

21. *Orkneyinga Saga*, ed. S. Nordal, 1916, 12.
22. *Skj.* B, I, 232; cf E. A. Kock, *Notationes Norrænæ*, 1923–44, § 3224.
23. For further examples see B. Sijmons and H. Gering, *Kommentar zu den Liedern der Edda* II, 1931, 182.
24. Cf J. de Vries, *Rel.*[2] I, 411.
25. *Heiðreks Saga*, ed. Jón Helgason, 1924, 54 and 129.
26. On the origin of this word see Sijmons and Gering, *op. cit.*, II, 60 and references.
27. *Skj.* B, I, 661.
28. Ed. Jón Jóhannesson, *Íslenzk Fornrit* XI, 1950, 185 ff.
29. *Hkr. Ól. Trygg.* LXIV.
30. *Skj.* B, I, 669.
31. *Hkr. Hák. Góða* XVIII.
32. The name *Vǫlsi* is probably derived from *vǫlr* (staff).
33. *Diser, Nornor Valkyrjor*, 1954, 22 ff.
34. *Skj.* B, I, 659.
35. *Haustlǫng*, Str.12 (*Skj.* B, I, 16).
36. See F. Ström, *Diser*, 22 ff, partly following K. F. Johansson, *op. cit.*
37. See Hj. Falk, *Altnordische Waffenkunde*, 1914, 56.
38. *Hkr. Ól.Trygg.* XXVII.
39. *Vellekla* 36 (*Skj.* B, I, 124).
40. *Skj.* B, I, 292.
41. *Flb.* II, 72.
42. *Skj.* B, I, 94.
43. *Hkr. Ól. Trygg.* XXXV.
44. Cf M. Cahen, *Études sur le vocabulaire religieux du vieux Scandinave*, 1921, 172 ff; also R. Meissner in *Deutsche Islandforschung* I, 1930, 232 ff.
45. Ed. Finnur Jónsson, 1903, 85.
46. Cf G. Sverdrup, *Rauschtrank und Labetrank*, 1941, 3 ff.
47. *Eyrbyggja Saga*, IV; *Landnámabók*, ed. Finnur Jónsson, 1900, 96.
48. This has been questioned. See Ól. Lárusson in *Kulturhistorisk Leksikon for nordisk Middelalder*, V, 1960, 363 ff and

refs.; *idem. Lög og Saga*, 1958, esp. 63 ff
and 91 ff.

49. *Grágás*, I, B, ed. V. Finsen, 1852, 206.

50. See Jón Jóhannesson, *Íslendinga Saga*,
I, 1956, 81 ff.

51. Ari, *Íslendingabók*, II.

52. *Landnámabók*, edition cited, 208, 94.

53. Cf Jón Jóhannesson, *op. cit.*, 72 ff. It is
-questionable whether the term *hofgoði*
necessarily implied political as well as
religious functions. Cf Björn Sigfússon,
Íslenzk Fornrit, X, 1940, 169 note.

54. J. de Vries (*Rel.²* I, 401; following W.

Krause) cites an example from a Nor.
wegian inscription of *c.* 400, but the
reading is doubtful.

55. See *Nordisk Kultur*, VI, *Runorna*, ed. O.
von Friesen, 1933, 120 ff.

56. *Hkr., Hák. Góða*, XIV.

57. Cf Jón Jóhannesson, *op. cit.*, 79.

58. See M. Olsen, *The Farms and Fanes of
Ancient Norway*, 1928, 287 ff.

59. Cf Ch. VII, Freyr-Froði-Nerthus-Ing,
above.

60. *De Bello Gallico*, VI, 21.

61. *Historia Ecclesiastica*, II, 13.

CHAPTER XIV: GODLESS MEN

1. See Chs. XI and XIII.

2. See Ch. XII.

3. See S. Nordal, *Átrúnaður Egils Skalla-
grímssonar*, in *Áfangar* II, 1944, 103 ff.

4. *Hrólfs Saga Kraka*, ed. D. Slay, 1960,
Chs. XXXII, XXX, XXXIII, XIII.

5. *Ketils Saga Hœngs*, V.

6. *Qrvar-Odds Saga*, ed. R. C. Boer, 1888,
8–9.

7. Ed. Finnur Jónsson, 1900, 134.

8. *Ibid.*, 132.

9. For this view see A. G. van Hamel,
Acta Philologica Scandinavica, VII,1932,
260 ff.

10. *Finnboga Saga hins Ramma*, ed. H. Gering,
1879, XIX.

11. *Hkr., Ól. Helg.*, CCI ff; *Ólafs Saga hins
Helga*, ed. O. A. Johnsen (The Legendary Saga), LXXII ff.

12. *Hkr., Ól. Helg.* CCXV.

13. *Þorvalds Þáttr Tasalda*, ed. Jónas Kristjánsson in *Íslenzk Fornrit*, IX, 1956,
123 ff.

14. See Ch. I, Old Norse Poetry.

15. For an attempt to restore the sequences
see J. de Vries, *Arkiv för nordisk Filologi*,
LX, 1934, 21 ff.

CHAPTER XV: DEATH

1. See Chs. I, Histories and Sagas; IX
and X.

2. See Ch. VII, Freyja, etc.

3. *Laxdæla Saga* XVII.

4. *Svarfdæla Saga* XXII.

5. *Hœnsa-Þóris Saga* XVII; see further
Jónas Jónasson, *Íslenzkir Þjóðhættir*, 1934,
420.

6. *Eyrbyggja Saga* XXXIII ff; closely similar stories are given in *Egils Saga*
LVIII and in *Grettis Saga* XXII ff. See
further Matthías Þórðarson in *Festskrift
til Finnur Jónsson*, 1928, 95 ff.

7. On the *nábjargir* see Matthías Þórðarson,
op. cit., 99 ff and references.

8. The same motives appear in the story
of the ghosts at Fróðá (*Eyrbyggja Saga*
LIII ff.)

9. Glám also had to be killed a second
time (*Grettis Saga* XXXV).

10. A mysterious ox named Harri (Lord)
was also a dapple grey (*apalgrár*). See
Laxdæla Saga XXXI.

11. *SnE. Gylf*, 4.

12. The names *Niflhel, Niflheimr* are generally
interpreted in this way, although V.
Jansson has shown that there are some
reasons to doubt whether this interpretation is correct. See Ch. X, Ermanaric,
Footnote 26 above.

13. *Gísla Saga* XIV.

14. See Ól. Briem, *Heiðinn Siður á Íslandi*,
1945,96.

15. See Kristján Eldjárn, *Kuml og Haugfé*,
1956, 215–18.

16. Cf J. Brøndsted, *The Vikings*, 1960, 272.

17. See de Vries, *Rel.²*, I,105 and 471 ff.

18. *Flb.* I, 436.

19. See Eldjárn, *op. cit.*, 246–9.

20. See Chs. VII, Freyr-Fróði-Nerthus-Ing;
XI, XIII.

21. Gunnar's faithful dog, Sám, is particularly famous. See *Njáls Saga* LXX,
LXXV–VI.

22. See Eldjárn, *op. cit.*, 249 ff.

23. *Landnámabók*, ed. Finnur Jónsson, 1900,
24–5.

24. See Ól. Briem, *op. cit.*, 100.

25. J. Brøndsted, *The Vikings*, 1960, 134.
26. *Saga Óláfs Tryggvasonar*, ed. Finnur Jónsson, 1932, 14–15.
27. See *Saga-Book of the Viking Society* VI, Part II, 1910, 180 ff.
28. See H. Birkeland, *Nordens historie i middelalderen etter arabiske kilder*, 1955. A translation of Ibn Fadlán's description of the cremation was published by C.

Waddy in *Antiquity*, 1934, 58 ff. Some of the phrases used here are taken from that translation.

29. Saxo, *Gesta*, I, 31; cf Ch. X, Hadding, above.
30. *Helga Kviða Hundingsbana* II, 49.
31. See Ch. XIV, above.
32. *Helga Kviða Hundingsbana* II, 51 (prose).

CHAPTER XVI: THE BEGINNING OF THE WORLD AND ITS END

1. *Sne. Gylf.* 4–9.
2. See J. de Vries, *Acta Philologica Scandinavica* V, 1929, 41 ff.
3. Snorri identifies Ymir and Aurgelmir. In the *Vafþrúðnismál* (strs. 21 and 30) they seem to be distinguished.
4. Also *Auðumla*. The first element in the cow's name must be *auðr* (riches); the second element has been associated with English dialect *hummel*, *humble* and related words meaning 'hornless cow'.
5. The name *Embla* has been related to Greek ἄμπελος (vine), and supposed to mean some kind of creeper. See S. Nordal, *Völuspá*, 1923, 51–2.
6. I have discussed the word *lúðr* briefly in *Collection Latomus* XLV (Hommages à Georges Dumézil), 1960, 209 ff, where references will be found.
7. Cf Nordal, *op. cit.*, 38.
8. On Hathor see E. O. James, *The Ancient Gods*, 1960, 82 ff.
9. On Iranian creation myths, see R. C. Zaehner, *The Dawn and Twilight of Zoroastrianism*, 1961, especially 203, 248–50.
10. *Ibid.*, 207–8.
11. See J. de Vries, *Altnordisches Etymologisches Wörterbuch*, 1961, s.v. *Ymir*. The name of *Tuisto* (or *Tuisco*?), said by Tacitus to be the first ancestor of the Germans (*Germania* II), is believed to mean either 'twin' or 'hermaphrodite'. See R. Much, *Die Germania des Tacitus*, ed. 2, 1959, 22; further F. R. Schroeder, *Germanisch-Romanische Monatschrift*, XIX, 1931, 8 ff.
12. *SnE. Gylf.* 8; cf *Grímnismál* str. 29.

13. See my paper in *English and Medieval Studies presented to J. R. R. Tolkien*, 1962, 241 ff.
14. Cf Nordal, *op. cit.*, 37.
15. See Ch. V, above.
16. Reading *galgviðr* with the *Hauksbók*; the *Codex Regius* has *gaglviðr*. See Nordal, *op. cit.*, 83.
17. See Ch. VIII, Týr.
18. The ship, bearing Loki and the demon sons of Múspell, may reasonably be called the 'ship of death'. It is not, however, necessary to associate its name, *Naglfar*, with Latin *necare* (to kill) and Greek νεκρος (corpse), as has often been done. Snorri (*Gylf.* 37) explains that the ship was built of the uncut nails of the dead, apparently reflecting a widespread belief. For a discussion of this problem see H. Lie, *Maal og Minne*, 1954, 152 ff.
19. Probably from *Gim+hlé* meaning 'fire-shelter'. Gimlé escapes the fire of Ragnarök.
20. *Op. cit.*, 106 ff.
21. *Skj.* B, I, 164 ff.
22. *Ibid.*, 60.
23. *Kormáks Saga* XIX.
24. *Skj.* B, I, 321.
25. In the *Fáfnismál* (str. 15) the field is called *Óskópnir*, a name not yet explained.
26. *Ragnarök* (transl. W. Ranisch), 1922, 19 ff and 331 ff. See further Zaehner, *op. cit.*, 135.
27. For various suggestions see J. K. Bostock, *A Handbook on Old High German Literature*, 1955, 122 ff.

BIBLIOGRAPHY

The following bibliographical notes are intended for the general reader who may wish to read further on one subject or another. In order to help those who are less experienced the languages in which works are written are indicated in cases where there could be any doubt. The following abbreviations are used:

D	Danish
Du	Dutch
E	English
F	French
G	German
I	Icelandic
N	Norwegian
S	Swedish

GENERAL

J. Grimm, *Deutsche Mythologie* (1835 and subsequently) was translated into English with some additions by J. S. Stallybrass (*Teutonic Mythology*, 4 vols 1883–1900). It covers the pagan religion of all Germanic peoples and is a mine of valuable information. J. de Vries, *Altgermanische Religionsgeschichte* (I–II, first edition 1935–7; second edition greatly altered 1956–7, *G*) is a splendid handbook, containing nearly exhaustive bibliography. J. A. MacCulloch (*The Mythology of all Races*, II, *Eddic*, 1930, *E*) gave a sound if rather old-fashioned account. In *Les Dieux des Germains* (ed. 2, 1959, *F*), G. Dumézil presented an interesting personal interpretation of many Norse myths, which he saw as part of an Indo-European heritage. A particularly well-balanced sketch is that of Ólafur Briem, *Heiðinn Siður á Íslandi* (1945, *I*). F. Ström (*Nordisk Hedendom*, 1961, *S*) gave a lively study in popular form. *Nordisk Kultur* XXVI, *Religionshistorie* (ed. N. Lid, 1942) contains authoritative essays in various languages by many scholars. The evidence is there drawn largely from place-names. A. Olrik and H. Ellekilde (*Nordens Gudeverden* I–II, 1926–51, *D*) have drawn much useful information from Scandinavian traditions of later times.

CHAPTER I

THE SOURCES. Introductory

The early history of Iceland was described by K. Gjerset (*History of Iceland*, 1925, *E*) and with greater acumen by Jón Jóhannesson (*Íslendinga Saga*, I, 1956, *I*). On the history of Norway see especially H. Shetelig: *Det norske folks liv og historie* (I, 1929, *N*), and of Denmark, E. Arup (*Danmarks Historie* I, 1925, *D*). See further L. Musset, *Les Peuples Scandinaves au moyen Age* (1951, *F*, good bibliography); G. Turville-Petre, *The Heroic Age of Scandinavia* (1951, *E*).

An excellent introduction to Celtic heathendom, with extensive bibliography, is that of J. de Vries, *Keltische Religion* (1961, *G*).

Among many books on runes, the following may be recommended: H. Arntz, *Handbuch der Runenkunde* (ed. 2, 1944, *G*); R..W. V. Elliott, *Runes* (1959, *E*); S. B. F. Jansson, *The Runes of Sweden* (1962, *E*).

An introduction to Scandinavian place-names will be found in *Nordisk Kultur*, V, *Stedsnavn* (ed. M. Olsen, 1939, in various languages). M. Olsen, *Farms and Fanes of Ancient Norway* (translated into English by Th. Gleditsch, 1928) is a humane and lucid discussion of many place-name problems. The same author's *Hedenske Kultminder i norske Stedsnavne* (I, 1915, *N*) is a monumental work.

H. Shetelig and Hj. Falk (*Scandinavian Archaeology*, 1937, *E*) gave an enjoyable general introduction to Scandinavian archaeology. M. Stenberger's *Sweden* (no date, probably 1962, *E*) is comprehensive, but the terminology is unusual. On the rock carvings of the Bronze Age see O. Almgren, *Hällristningar och Kultbruk* (1927, *S*).

The Old Norse Poetry

Among the most authoritative and appreciative works on Old Norse poetry is that of Einar Ól. Sveinsson (*Íslenzkar Bókmenntir í Fornöld*, I, 1962, *I*). A. Heusler, *Die altgermanische Dichtung* (ed. 2, 1941, *G*) is solid and reliable. J. de Vries, *Altnordische Literaturgeschichte* (I–II, 1941–2 *G*) is useful especially for the older period. Finnur Jónsson, *Den oldnorske og oldislandske Litteraturs Historie* (ed.2,1920–4, *D*) is of lasting value although often marred by prejudice. Jón Helgason, *Norges og Islands Digtning* (in *Nordisk Kultur*, VIII, B, 1952, *D*) is an admirably well-balanced survey. B. S. Phillpotts, *The Elder Edda and Ancient Scandinavian Drama* (1920, *E*) is persuasive, although the views expressed are somewhat extreme.

There are many editions of the Poetic Edda of varying merit. Among the best may be mentioned *Edda, die Lieder des Codex Regius*, ed. G. Neckel (ed. 4, revised by H. Kuhn, 1962); *Eddadigte*, ed. Jón Helgason (I–III, 1951–2, not complete).

Translations include those of H. A. Bellows (*The Poetic Edda*, 1923 and subsequently), and of L. M. Hollander (*The Poetic Edda*, ed. 2, 1962), which is in a highly artificial style.

The whole corpus of scaldic poetry was published by Finnur, Jónsson *Den norsk-islandske Skjaldedigtning* (4 vols 1908–15). Many will prefer the readings of E. A. Kock, *Den norsk-isländska Skaldedigtningen* (I–II, 1946–50).

L. M. Hollander (*The Skalds*, 1945) described scaldic poetry and translated some of it into English.

Histories and Sagas

These are studied in the works of Finnur Jónsson and J. de Vries mentioned under Old Norse Poetry above. Other valuable works include those of W. P. Ker (*The Dark Ages*, 1904 and subsequently, *E*), and of H. Koht (*The Old Norse Sagas* 1931, *E*). K. Liestøl, *The Origin of the Icelandic Family Sagas* (1930, *E*) is splendidly compiled but one-sided. Einar Ól. Sveinsson, *The Age of the Sturlungs* (1953, *E*) is an enjoyable description of the age in which most of the historical literature was written. An excellent survey, although rather too short, is that of Sigurður Nordal, *Sagalitteraturen* in *Nordisk Kultur* (VIII, B, 1952 D). See also Stefán Einarsson, *A History of Icelandic Literature* (1957, *E*); G. Turville-Petre, *Origins of Icelandic Literature* (1953, *E*).

Snorri Sturluson

Sigurður Nordal (*Snorri Sturluson*, 1920, *I*) deals lucidly with Snorri's life, ambitions and literary achievements. Very sceptical views on the value of Snorri's mythological work were expressed by E. Mogk in several works, including *Lokis Anteil an Baldrs Tode* (1925, *G*) and *Zur Bewertung der Snorra Edda als religionsgeschichtliche und mythologische Quelle* (1932, *G*). W. Baetke's *Die Götterlehre der Snorra Edda* (1950, *G*) is clear and well reasoned.

Snorri's *Edda* has been edited many times. A convenient critical edition is that of Finnur Jónsson, *Edda Snorra Sturlusonar* (1931 D).

The best edition of the *Heimskringla* is that of Bjarni Aðalbjarnarson, *Heimskringla* (I–III, 1941–51), which includes a full commentary in Icelandic.

A good translation of Snorri's *Edda* is that of A. G. Brodeur, *The Prose Edda* (1920 and subsequently). An incomplete translation is that of J. I. Young, *The Prose Edda* (1954). The latter contains a short introduction by S. Nordal.

The *Heimskringla* was translated into strange English by William Morris and Eiríkr Magnússon, *Stories of the Kings of Norway* (I–IV, 1893–1905). The series includes excellent notes and introductory material.

Saxo

A. Olrik, *Kilderne til Sakses Oldhistorie* (I–II, 1892–4, *D*) remains a standard work. The same author's *Danmarks Heltedigtning* (I–II, 1903–10, *D*) was translated into English and revised by L. M. Hollander, as *The Heroic Legends of Denmark* (1919). Useful commentary was supplied by P. Herrmann (*Die Heldensagen des Saxo Grammaticus* 1922, *G*).

Good texts were published by A. Holder (1886) and by J. Olrik and H. Ræder (1931).

Translation: *The First nine books of the Danish History of Saxo Grammaticus*, translated by O. Elton (1894).

CHAPTER II

ÓÐINN

General: H. M. Chadwick (*The Cult of Othin*, 1899, *E*) provides a readable, factual introduction; G. Dumézil (*Mitra-Varuna*, 1948, *F*) studies Óðinn against the background of Indo-European myth. See also J. de Vries, *Contributions to the Study of Othinn* (1931, *E*); W. von Unwerth, *Untersuchungen über Totenkult und Óðinnverehrung bei Nordgermanen und Lappen* (1911, *G*); O. Höfler, *Kultische Geheimbünde der Germanen* (I, 1934, *G*, stimulating); G. Turville-Petre, *Um Óðinsdýrkun á Íslandi* (*Studia Islandica* 17, 1958, *I*).

Óðinn was studied as god of poetry and the sacred mead by A. Olrik, *Skjaldemjøden* (in *Edda* XXIV, 1926, 236 ff, *D*). Olrik quoted parallels from many other lands. A. G. van Hamel (*The Mastering of the Mead* in *Studier till. E. A. Kock*, 1934, *E*) analysed the Norse sources of the myth; J. de Vries (*Die Skaldenkenningen met mythologischen Inhoud*, 1943, 5 ff, *Du*) assembled poetic allusions to this myth.

The hanging Óðinn has been the subject of many works. A. G. van Hamel (*Óðinn hanging on the Tree* in *Acta Philologica Scandinavica*, VII, 1932, 260 ff, *E*) offered an animistic explanation, comparing Irish parallels. S. Bugge (*Studier over de nordiske Gude- og Heltesagns Oprindelse*, 1881–9, *N*) emphasized Christian influences; and R. Pipping (*Oden i Galgen* in *Studier i nordisk Filologi*, XVIII, 2, 1928, 1 ff, *S*) compared the practices of shamans. F. Ström (*Den Döendes Makt och Odin i Trädet*, 1947, *S*), in an illuminating work, sees the god acquiring wisdom from the world of death.

Outstanding works on Valhöll are those of G. Neckel (*Walhall*, 1931, *G*), and of M. Olsen (*Valhall med de mange dører* in *Norrøne Studier*, 1938, *N*). Olsen considers the possibility of Roman influences on the Norse concept.

Óðinn's relations with the horse were discussed thoroughly by H. Gjessing (*Hesten i før-historisk kunst og kultus* in *Viking*, VII, 1943, 51 ff, *N*). On his ravens see A. H. Krappe, *Etudes de Mythologie et de Folklore germaniques* (1928, 29 ff, *F*).

Óðinn's names were collected and explained by Hj. Falk (*Odensheite*, 1924, *N*).

CHAPTER III

THÓR

In *Tor* (I, 1947, *S*, not complete) H. Ljungberg assembled the Norse material and compared Thór with other Indo-European gods. He also reviewed the opinions of many former scholars.

Among outstanding papers on Thór may be mentioned those of F. R. Schröder, *Thór, Indra, Herakles* (*Zeitschrift für deutsche Philologie*, LXXVI, 1957, 1 ff, *G*) and *Das Hymirlied* (*Arkiv för nordisk Filologi* LXX, 1935, 1 ff, *G*). The intricate *Þórsdrápa* was discussed in close detail by V. Kiil in *Arkiv för nordisk Filologi* (LXXI, 1958, 89 ff *N*). The miniature 'Thór's hammers' were listed and partially described by R. Skovmand in *Aarbøger for nordisk Oldkyndighed og Historie* (1942, 63 ff *D*).

Evidence of the cult of Thór in England was given by R. Jente, *Die mythologischen Ausdrücke im altenglischen Wortschatz* (1921, 81 ff *G*), by E. A. Philippson, *Germanisches Heidentum bei den Angelsachsen* (1929, 136 ff *G*), by F. M. Stenton, *Transactions of the Royal Historical Society*,

(Ser. IV, XXIII, 1941, 244 ff *E*) and by G. Turville-Petre, *Thurstable* in *English and Medieval Studies Presented to J. R. R. Tolkien*, 1962, 241 ff (*E*).

Although much criticized by scholars in other disciplines, the tripartite division of Norse and other Indo-European gods proposed by G. Dumézil (see pp. 103 ff above) has won considerable approval among Germanic specialists; see J. de Vries, *Forschungsgeschichte der Mythologie* (1961, 357 ff *G*); H. Ringgren and Å. V. Ström (*Religionerna*, ed. 2, 1959, 175 ff *S*). Thór's place in this system is explained by Dumézil in numerous works, most clearly in the following: *L'idéologie tripartiedes Indo-Européens* (1958, 54 ff); *Les Dieux des Germains* (ed. 2, 1958, 106 ff); (*Aspects de la Fonction Guerrière chez les Indo-Européens* (1956, 69 ff.) Dumézil meets some of his critics in *Revue de l'Histoire des Religions* (CLII, 1957, 8 ff *F*).

CHAPTER IV

BALDR

The figure of Baldr has been judged variously. As the passive, suffering god, some have compared him with Christ and seen influences of Christian legend in the myths about him (S. Bugge, *Studier over de nordiske Gude- og Heltesagns Oprindelse*, 1881–1889, 32 ff, *N*; M. Olsen; *Arkiv för nordisk Filologi*, XL, 1924, 148 ff, *N*). G. Neckel (*Die Überlieferungen vom Gotte Balder*, 1920, *G*) on the other hand, compared Baldr especially with near-eastern gods of the type Attis, Adonis, and believed that Baldr was of near-eastern origin. In this case Baldr would be a god of fertility like Freyr. J. de Vries (*Arkiv för nordisk Filologi*, LXX, 1955, 41 ff, *G*) regarded the slaughter of Baldr as a form of initiation ritual.

The place of Baldr in the Merseburg Charm and continental tradition was discussed most ably by F. R. Schröder, *Balder und der zweite Merseburger Spruch* (*Germanisch-Romanische Monatschrift*, XXXIV, 1953, 161 ff, *G*).

CHAPTER V

LOKI

More ink has been spilt on Loki than on any other figure in Norse myth. This, in itself, is enough to show how little scholars agree, and how far we are from understanding him.

A. Olrik published a number of works, of which the most illuminating was *Myterne om Loke* (in *Festskrift til* H. F. Feilberg, 1911, *D*). Olrik analysed the different traits in Loki's character, and explained them partly in the light of Estonian and Finnish folklore, which he seemed to rate as high as the oldest Norse poetry. He traced many elements in the Loki myth to near eastern or Caucasian influences, transmitted to Scandinavia by the Goths.

H. Celander (*Lokes mytiska ursprung*, 1911, *S*) was interested largely in modern Swedish folklore. He drew attention to the Swedish dialect word *locke*, meaning 'spider', and saw Loki essentially as a dwarf or gnome. Recently A. B. Rooth (*Loki in Scandinavian Mythology*, 1961, *E*) has followed a similar line, but her methods are different. By a process of elimination she attempts to find the 'authentic' Loki figure. Motives which are also found outside Scandinavia are said to be borrowed. Much is ascribed to Irish influences, even though some of the Irish stories quoted, such as the *Táin Bó Fraich*, are quite unlike the Norse stories of Loki. The fundamental Scandinavian Loki appears to be a spider (*locke*).

In *The Problem of Loki* (1933, *E*), J. de Vries gave prime importance to the Old Norse sources, considering their age and reliability. He saw Loki as a 'trickster'. A. Holtsmark (*Arkiv för nordisk Filologi*, LXIV, 1949, 1 ff, *N*) compared him with the fool in medieval drama.

F. Ström (*Loki*, 1956, *G*) again studied Loki primarily from ancient literature, and found him an hypostatis of Óðinn, his foster-brother. This view has been much criticized, but cannot be lightly rejected.

Entirely different methods were employed by G. Dumézil (*Loki*, ed. 1, 1948, *F*; ed. 2, considerably altered, 1959, *G*) who compared the myth of Loki with the Caucasian legend of

Syrdon. Dumézil, as he showed in another work (*Les Dieux des Germains*, 1959, 98, 103–4, F), saw the Caucasian legend and the Norse myth as relics of Indo-European culture.

A careful survey of recent studies of Loki has been published by A. Holtsmark (*Mål og Minne*, 1962, 81 ff, N).

CHAPTER VI

HEIMDALL

The most thorough study of Heimdall is that of H. Pipping (*Eddastudier* I–II in *Studier i nordisk Filologi*, XVI–XVII,1925–6, S). The sources were carefully surveyed by B. Pering (*Heimdall*, 1941, G); the conclusions there drawn cannot be accepted. Å. Ohlmarks, in a very learned and detailed study (*Heimdall und das Horn*, 1937) favours a naturalistic interpretation of the myth, seeing Heimdall as the sun and his horn as the moon. A particularly useful paper was that of I. Lindquist (in *Vetenskaps-Societeten i Lund, Årsbok*, 1937, 55 ff, S). J. de Vries published a carefully balanced survey in *Études Germaniques* (1955, 257 ff, F).

CHAPTER VII

THE VANIR

As well as in general works mentioned above, G. Dumézil has studied the Vanir, gods of his third estate, in *Tarpeia* (1947, F), where he analyses the story of the war of the Vanir as it is told in the obscure lines of the *Vǫluspá*. He deals extensively with the myth of Njörð and his giantess bride in *La Saga de Hadingus* (1953, F).

Two works by F. R. Schröder (*Ingunar-Freyr*, 1941 and *Skaði und die Götter Skandinaviens*, 1941, G) are stimulating, if somewhat adventurous for the beginner.

An important work touching on Freyr as god of the cornfield was that of A. Holtsmark (*Vitazgjafi* in *Maal og Minne*, 1933,120 ff, N).

H. Rosén gathered material about Freyr and his sacred animals, the boar, horse, ox and perhaps dog in *Freykult och Djurkult* (in *Fornvännen*, VIII, 1913, 213 ff, S). This remains a standard work. The cult of the horse has been further studied by A. Liestøl (*Maal og Minne*, XXXVIII, 1945, 59–66, N) and by K. Liestøl (*Arv*, II, 1946, 94 ff, N).

The *Skírnismál* and the myth told in it have been widely discussed. M. Olsen's explanation of this myth as a seasonal, fertility one (*Maal og Minne*, 1909, 17 ff, N) has been widely accepted. J. Sahlgren (*Eddica et Scaldica*, 1927–8, 211 ff, S) explained the myth in entirely different and more martial terms. An important contribution to the study of the *Skírnismál* has lately been made by Ursula Dronke in *English and Medieval Studies presented to J. R. R. Tolkien* (1962, 250 ff, E).

A well-balanced survey of the Vanir, their significance and origins, is that of Ólafur Briem, *Studia Islandica* (XXI, 1963, I).

CHAPTER VIII

MINOR DEITIES

Týr and Ull have been studied in relation to figures in other Indo-European myth by G. Dumézil (*Mitra-Varuna*, 1948, F). Whether accepted or not, Dumézil's views are there presented with admirable clarity. On Ull see also P. Herrmann, *Die Heldensagen des Saxo Grammaticus* (1922, 241 ff, G). Theories about the etymology of Ull's name were discussed by F. R. Schröder, *Skadi und die Götter Skandinaviens* (1941, 74 ff, G).

Evidence from place-names commemorating Ull has been collected and sifted by several scholars, including M. Olsen (*Hedenske Kultminder i norske Stedsnavne*, I, 1915, esp. 90 ff, *N*) and E. Wessén (*Studier till Sveriges hedna mytologi och fornhistoria*, 1924, esp. 129 ff, *S*).

M. Olsen wrote on place-names containing the element *Týr* in *Norrøne Studier* (1938, 80 ff *N*, reprinted from an article published in 1905). Many of these place-names are also cited by A. Olrik and H. Ellekilde in *Nordens Gudeverden* (I, 1926–51, *passim D*).

S. Nordal (*Íslenzk Menning*, I, 1942, 235 ff, *I*) discussed Bragi as god of poetry, as did E. Mogk (*Beiträge zur Geschichte der deutschen Sprache und Literatur*, XII, 1887, 383 ff, *G*).

On the myth of Iðunn see A. Holtsmark, *Arkiv för nordisk Filologi* (LXIV, 1949, 28 ff *N*). Gefjun and her plough were discussed by the same scholar in *Maal og Minne* (1944, 169 ff, *N*), and further by F. R. Schröder in *Arkiv för nordisk Filologi* (LXVII, 1952, 1 ff, *G*); see also Olrik and Ellekilde, *op. cit.* II, 713 ff, *D*).

On Frigg see especially H. Jungner, *Namn och Bygd* XII, 1924, 1 ff, *S*.

CHAPTER IX

THE DIVINE KINGSHIP

Much has been written about the divine kingship in Scandinavia in recent years. The most ambitious work was that of O. Höfler (*Germanisches Sakralkönigtum*, I, 1952, *G*). This is suggestive but not reliable. Valuable observations were made by A. Holtsmark in her review of Höfler (*Maal og Minne*, 1953, 142 ff, *N*). Höfler's book was also reviewed at length by J. de Vries (*Germanisch-Romanische Monatschrift*, XXXIV, 1953, 183 ff, *G*). Höfler later gave an outline of his views on divine kingship in *La Regalità Sacra* (*The Sacral Kingship*, 1959, 664 ff, *G*). The same volume contains a paper by Å. V. Ström, *The King God and his Connection with Sacrifice* (702 ff, *E*).

O. von Friesen (*Saga och Sed*, 1932–4, 15 ff, *S*) discussed the etymology of the word *konungr* (king), and believed it to be related to *kona* (woman). The king could thus be seen as the mate of the fertility god in a matriarchal system. This theory has won few adherents and was criticized by J. de Vries (*Sæculum*, VII, 1956, 289 ff, *G*) in a valuable contribution.

CHAPTER X

THE DIVINE HEROES

The heroic legends have been described by many scholars. The fullest treatment is that of H. Schneider (*Germanische Heldensage*, I–II, 1, 2, 1928–34, *G*). The first volume of this work has lately been reprinted (1962) with some additions and a bibliography by R. Wisniewski, brought up to date.

A. Olrik, *Kilderne til Sakses Oldhistorie* (I–II, 1892–4, *D*) is a fundamental study of the legends preserved by Saxo Grammaticus. The same author's *Danmarks Heltedigtning* (I–II, 1903–10, *D*) was translated with some revision into English by L. M. Hollander as *The Heroic Legends of Denmark* (1919).

The legends of Ermanaric were conveniently assembled by C. Brady (*The Legends of Ermanaric*, 1943, *E*) and carefully analysed by G. Zink (*Les Légendes héroiques de Dietrich et d'Ermrich*, 1950, *F*).

Among notable works touching particularly on Sigurð may be mentioned that of J. de Vries, *Betrachtungen zum Märchen* (1954, *G*). In *Siegfried Arminius und die Symbolik* (1961, *G*), O. Höfler saw the Cheruscan hero, Arminius, as the prototype of Sigurð, as had others before him. G. Schütte (*Sigfrid und Brünhild*, 1935, *G*) found the basis for the legends of Sigurð and the Niflungar chiefly in the history of the Merovingian Franks. Schütte's extreme views are not adopted in this book.

Starkað was discussed in the general works mentioned above. A useful contribution was that of G. Dumézil (*Aspects de la Fonction Guerrière*, 1956, *F*), who saw Starkað as a Thór hero. J. de Vries (*Germanisch-Romanische Monatschrift*, XXXVI, 1955, 28 ff, *G*) draws Starkað closer to Óðinn, as I have done in this chapter.

An important work on Hadding and his place in religious history is that of G. Dumézil, *La Saga de Hadingus* (1953, *F*).

CHAPTER XI

GUARDIAN SPIRITS

An important study of the *dísir* in a wide European context was that of K. F. Johansson, *Über die altindische Disana und verwandtes* (1918, *G*). H. Celander (in *Saga och Sed*, 1943, 71 ff, *S*) assembled traditions from early literature and modern sources about *dísir* and suchlike beings.

D. Strömbäck, *Tidrande och Diserna* (1949, *S*) is a perceptive examination of the story of Thiðrandi whom the *dísir* killed. Strömbäck strongly emphasized the Christian elements in this story (cf my review in *Saga-Book of the Viking Society*, XIV, 1953-5, 137 ff, *E*). The motives of the *dísir* in slaying Thiðrandi were studied from a more pagan point of view by F. Ström (*Arv*, VIII, 1952, 77 ff, *S*). The same scholar further developed his views on the *dísir* in *Diser, Nornor, Valkyrjor* (1954, *S*).

The *fylgjur* and *hamingjur* have also been discussed widely. M. Rieger, *Über den nordischen Fylgjenglauben* (*Zeitschrift für deutsches Altertum*, XLII, 1898, 277 ff, *G*) is still useful. The conception is also explained lucidly by D. Strömbäck (*Sejd*, 1935, 152 ff, *S*). Other works include that of P. C. M. Sluijter (*Ijslands Volksgeloof*, 1936, 84 ff, *Du*) and my short paper in *Saga-Book of the Viking Society*, XII, 1940, 119 ff, *E*).

The *álfar* and their sacrifice were discussed especially by J. de Vries (*Acta Philologica Scandinavica*, VII, 1932-3, 169 ff, *G*) and by H. Ellekilde in the same journal (VIII, 1933-4, 182 ff, *D*).

CHAPTER XII

TEMPLES AND OBJECTS OF WORSHIP

In *Farms and Fanes of Ancient Norway* (1928, *E*), M. Olsen studied the distribution of temples in early Norway, explaining their organization, significance and the terms applied to them. The same scholar summarized many of his earlier findings in *Nordisk Kultur* XXVI (*Religionshistorie*, ed. N. Lid, 1942, 59 ff). Both of these works provide serviceable introductions.

The conceptions underlying such words as *helgi* (*helga*), *vé* (*vígja*) were analysed from a philosophical and philological point of view by W. Baetke (*Das Heilige in Germanischen*, 1942). This is a brilliant, if rather difficult book.

In *Hednatemplet i Uppsala* (*Fornvännen*, XVIII, 1923, 85 ff, *S*) S. Lindquist examined many details in Adam of Bremen's description of the temple at Uppsala and in the notes appended to it. Another important study of the Uppsala temple and grove around it, in a wider setting was that of Th. Palm, *Uppsalalunden och Uppsalatemplet* (in *Årsbok Vetenskaps. Soc. i Lund*, 1941, 79 ff, *S*).

The remains of the supposed temple at Hofstaðir in northern Iceland were described by D. Bruun and Finnur Jónsson (*Aarbøger for nordisk Oldkyndighed og Historie*, 1909, 245 ff, *D*) and briefly by D. Bruun, *Fortidsminder og Nutidshjem paa Island* (1928, 33 ff, *D*). Aa. Roussell (in *Forntida Gårdar i Island*, ed. M. Stenberger, 1943, 215 ff, *D*) considered such remains found in Iceland. He was perhaps unwarrantably sceptical about some of them.

CHAPTER XIII

SACRIFICE

The forms and meaning of sacrifice have been studied by many. J. de Vries's chapter in his *Altgermanische Religionsgeschichte* (ed. 2, I, 1956, 406 ff, *G*) is detailed and thorough. An interesting, if slighter introduction was provided by V. Grönbech in *The Culture of the Teutons* (transl. into English by W. Worster, II, 1931, 201 ff). Among recent studies should be mentioned that of F. Ström, *Tro och Blot* (in *Arv*, 1951, 23 ff, *S*). A. G. van Hamel (*Ijslands Odinsgeloof*, 1936, *Du*) sees sacrifice chiefly as a form of magic.

A useful survey of human sacrifice among Scandinavians and other Germanic peoples is that of E. Mogk, *Die Menschenopfer der Germanen (Abhandlungen der k. sächs. Gesellschaft der Wissenschaften*, XXVII, 1909, *G*).

The question how far the death-penalty originated in human sacrifice has been much discussed in recent years. F. Ström (*On the Sacral Origin of the Germanic Death Penalties*, 1942, *E*) denied that there was any connexion between the sacrifice and the penalties. This book covers an immense amount of material and includes a thorough bibliography. The same scholar made further observations in a paper published in *Saga och Sed* (1952, 5 ff, *S*). D. Ström- bäck (*Saga och Sed*, 1942, 51 ff, *S*) criticized Ström's views, citing a number of texts which suggested that the purpose of the death penalty was to appease the gods. This implies that the law was in itself divine.

The strange tale of Völsi (see pp. 256 ff above) has attracted much attention. Older critical studies are those of A. Heusler (*Zeitschrift des Vereins für Volkskunde*, XIII, 1903, 24 ff, *G*) and of W. von Unwerth (*Wörter und Sachen*, II, 1910, 161 ff, *G*). F. Ström also studied details in this tale in *Diser, Nornor, Valkyrjor* (1954, 22 ff, *S*).

CHAPTER XIV

GODLESS MEN

A great many stories of godless men were collected by K. Maurer (*Die Bekehrung des nor- wegischen Stammes zum Christenthume* II, 1855, 247 ff, *G*). In *Óðinn Hanging on the Tree* (*Acta Philologica Scandinavica*, VII, 1932, 260 ff, *E*) A. G. van Hamel suggests that those who believed only in their might (*á mátt sinn ok megin*) had reverted to a pretheistic form of belief in magic. This accords with van Hamel's view that 'the gods were not a necessary element of ancient Germanic belief and where they are worshipped, they form the superstructure, not the foundation of the religious system' (*Saga-Book of the Viking Society*, XI, 1928–36, 142 ff). Views like these would find few adherents today.

F. Ström (*Den egna kraftens män*, 1948, 141 ff, *S*) studied the godless men against their social background. He also analysed the meanings of terms such as *máttr, megin* and others in the light of contexts in which they occur. H. Ljungberg (*Den nordiska religionen och kristendomen*, 1938, *S*) devoted a section to the godless men.

CHAPTER XV

DEATH

W. von Unwerth (*Untersuchungen über Totenkult und Óðinnverehrung bei Nordgermanen und Lappen* 1911, *G*) critically examined many of the Old Norse sources and considered the particular relations of the dead with Óðinn. He compared similar beliefs recorded among Lapps of later times. G. Neckel, *Walhall* (1931, *G*) is a sound and thorough study. A rather striking work was that of H. J. Klare (*Die Toten in der altnordischen Literatur* in *Acta Philologica Scandi- navica*, VIII, 1933–4, *G*). Klare's conclusions were slightly extreme because he saw the dead as little more than 'living corpses'. Although this conception was widespread, it seems that there were others as well. H. R. Ellis (*The Road to Hel*, 1943, *E*) is sadly unreliable. R. Th. Christiansen (*The Dead and the Living*, 1946, *E*) worked partly from the later traditions of Scandinavia and attempted to distinguish pagan survivals from beliefs arising under later influences, Christian and European. S. Lindquist (*Fornvännen*, 1920, 56 ff, *S*), who is primarily an archaeologist, used his great knowledge of graves and grave-goods to throw light on the descriptions in Old Norse literary sources. The works of many other archaeologists are of great value for the study of Norse conceptions of death. These are too numerous to be cited here, but among the most valuable is *Osebergfunnet* (I–IV, 1917–28, *N*) by A. W. Brögger and other scholars. K. Eldjárn (*Kuml og Haugfé*, 1956, *I*) thoroughly examined the graves and grave-goods of ancient Iceland, thus demonstrating pagan conceptions of death in that country.

CHAPTER XVI

THE BEGINNING OF THE WORLD AND ITS END

Although much criticized in recent years, the most thorough study of all the incidents in the Ragnarök is that of A. Olrik. This was first published (in Danish) in two parts (in *Aarbøger for nordisk Oldkyndighed og Historie*, 1902, and in *Danske Studier*, 1913, *D*), and appeared later, with some revision, in the German translation of W. Ranisch (*Ragnarök*, 1922). Olrik compared numerous parallels, especially from Ireland, Persia and the Caucasus, and in Christian legends of the end of the world. He inclined to think that eastern beliefs had influenced the Norsemen during the Migration and Viking Ages, and that other foreign elements had been introduced at later times. The Norse Ragnarök would thus be a conglomeration of various elements of different origins and ages. R. Reitsenstein (in *Kyrkohistorisk Årsskrift*, 1924, 120 ff, *G*) concentrated on Persian parallels and traced the Norse conceptions of the Ragnarök largely to Manichaean missionaries. At the present time, many would see inherited Indo-European tradition rather than a mosaic in the Ragnarök, although it is difficult to avoid the suspicion that Christian eschatology exerted some influence.

S. Nordal's edition of the *Vǫluspá* (1923 and subsequently, *I*) is particularly important for the study of the Ragnarök.

INDEX

Absalon, Bishop of Roskilde and Arch-bishop of Lund, 27–8
Adam of Bremen, 7, 32, 49, 52, 73, 93, 101, 244-7, 251, 253, 261
Alcis, 219–20, 261
Álfheimr (Elf-world), 231
Álfhild (of Álfheimar), 205, 208, 239
Álfr (King of Álfheimar), 231, 239
Áli inn frœkni (also called *Armóðr*), 207, 209
Althingi (*Alþingi*), 254, 260
Alvíss (dwarf), 234–5
Álvíssmál (Words of All-wise), 159, 234
Ammianus Marcellinus, 197
Annals of St Neots, 59
Andvari (dwarf), 138
Angantýr, King of Goths, 51
Angrboða (Distress-bringer), 60, 129, 133, 180
Ansis, 190
Anskar, St, 7, 195
Ari Thorgilsson, the Wise, 17, 26, 163
Arnhall Thorvaldsson (Icelandic poet), 28
Arminius, 102, 199–200, 204–5
Arngrímur Jónsson (Icelandic historian), 31, 170, 209, 217
Arnoldus Tylensis, see Arnhall Thorvaldsson
Ásaland (*Ásaheimr*), 156
Ásgarð, 23, 36, 38, 63, 76–8, 81, 89–90, 94, 107, 112, 127, 134, 136, 138, 141, 158–9, 164, 176, 276, 280
Askr (Ash-tree), 55, 276–7
Atlakviða, 182–3
Atlamál, 226
Atli (Attila), 182, 197, 210, 224
Aðils, King, 114, 226, 264
Aurgelmir (giant), 275–6
Aun the Old, King, 47
Aurboða (or *Orboða*), 177
Austri (dwarf), 39, 234
Auðumbla (or Auðumla), 55, 275, 277

Ægir, 10, 111, 130, 152
Ælfric (homilist), 95
Æsir, 23–4, 34, 40, 47, 55, 65, 106–9, 136, 142, 156–64, 173, 175, 177, 186–7, 190
Æthelweard (English chronicler), 70, 121
Ætternisstapi (Family cliff), 254

Baldr, 10, 15, 24, 32–3, 44, 55, 63–4, 70, 82, 90, 106–22, 124–6, 130, 132–4, 138–40, 144, 146, 154, 164, 168, 184, 188–9, 202, 204, 215, 238, 248, 280–2
Baldrs Draumar (Dreams of Baldr), 45, 109–11, 113–14, 119, 132, 140
Balor, 160
Baugi (giant), 36, 39, 51
Bældæg Wodening (Bældæg son of Woden), 70, 121–2
Bec mac Buain of the Tuatha Dé Danann, 40–1
Bede (the Venerable), 70, 227, 237, 262
Beowulf, 26, 31, 64, 68, 120–1, 170, 200, 210, 231, 262
Bestla, 38, 49, 55, 209, 275, 278
Bifrǫst (*Bilfrǫst*), 147, 154
Bilskírnir, 75
Bjarnar Saga Hítdœlakappa, 18
Bjarkamál, 30–1
Bjarni Kolbeinsson, Bishop, 46
Björn Halldórsson (Icelandic lexico-grapher), 153, 158
Björn Hítdœlakappi, 225
Blóðughófi (Bloody-hoofed), 124–5, 173
Bölthór (Bölthorn, *Bǫlþórr*), 49, 55, 64, 209, 275, 278
Bölverk (*Bǫlverkr*, Evil-doer), 36, 50, 52, 62
Bor, 275
Bostock, J. K., 122
Bous, 33, 113–14
Bragi Boddason, the Old, 15, 43, 75–7, 81, 180, 185–6, 197–8
Brandkrossa Þáttr, 255–6
Brávallaþula, 29–30

Brávellir, 212
Breiðablik, 106, 108, 116
Bress (Irish King), 160–1
Bricriu of the Evil Tongue, 145
Brísing (belt or necklace, Brísinga men),
    127, 129, 133, 140, 147, 159, 176
Brjáns Saga, 60
Brún (Brúni, i.e. Óðinn), 212–3
Brunehilda, 199
Bugge, S., 42, 119, 211
Bur (Bor), 55, 277
Buri (Búri), 55
Brynhild, 198

Cæsarius of Arles, 233
Cet (Irish hero), 152
Chadwick, H. M., 201
Chadwick, Mrs., 97
Charles the Great, 54
Cherusci, 199, 205
Cimbri, 252
Codex Regius of the Elder Edda, 11–12,
    97, 130, 139
Coifi, 237, 262
Coill Tomair (Grove of Thor), 94, 102
Columba, St, 88
Conall the Victorious (Irish hero), 152–3
Conchobar, King, 152
Conganchnes (Horny-skin), 204
Conle (Connla), 187

Dag, 47, 73–4
Dáinn (dwarf), 235
Dáinsleif (sword), 234
Danpr, 150
Danr, 150
Dian Cecht (Irish hero), 123
Dickins, B., 119
Diermes (or Tiermes), 98
dísablót (sacrifice of the dísir), 225, 227,
    231, 239
dísir, 221–8, 231, 240, 253, 257, 263
døkkálfar, 231
Dómaldi, King, 46, 191, 253
Draumkvæde, 154
Draupnir (arm-ring), 107, 137
Dream of the Rood, 119
Droplaugarsona Saga, 18
Dróttkvætt (Court-measure), 14, 85
Dudo of St Quentin, 94

Dumézil, G., 24, 40, 209, 252, 254
Dvalinn (dwarf), 39, 235
dvergar (dwarfs), 230, 233–4
Dyggvi, King, 226

Earth-spirits, 230 ff.
Edda (Poetic) 8–9, 11, 13–14, 20–1, 32,
    54, 76, 238–9. See also under in-
    dividual lays.
Edda (Prose, Snorri's Edda), 22–6, 30–1,
    81, 119, 121, 129, 150, 187, 191, 197,
    240
Egill Skalla-Grímsson, 15, 37–8, 43, 58,
    69, 162, 232, 263
Egils Saga, 25, 232, 238
Eilíf Goðrúnarson (poet), 15, 78–9, 81,
    85, 128, 134
Einar Skálaglamm (poet), 15–16, 39–40,
    169, 193, 212, 258
Eir (goddess), 189
Eirík (a king of the Swedes), 195, 244
Eikík Bloodaxe, 14–15, 31, 52, 67–8, 111,
    115, 162, 193, 213, 232, 261, 282
Eiríksmál (Lay of Eirík Bloodaxe), 14,
    53–4, 184
Eirík the Victorious, King, 47, 118, 258
Ella (King of Northumbria), 255
Elves (álfar), 230 ff.
Embla, 55, 276–7
Encomium Emmae Reginae, 59
Erce, eorþan modor (Erce, mother of
    earth), 188
Ermanaric, 9, 20, 197–8
Erminaz, 191
Exeter Book, 78
Eyrbyggja Saga, 18–19, 47, 87, 220, 240–3,
    246, 251, 254
Eysteinn, Archbishop of Niðaróss, 18
Eysteinn Beli, King, 256
Eyvind the Plagiarist (poet), 12, 14–15,
    44, 56, 144, 166, 185, 193, 282

Fáfnir (dragon), 200, 202, 234
Fagrskinna, 67, 259
Fárbauti (giant), 55, 127, 129, 133, 141,
    144, 147
Faxi (the maned one), 249
Fenrir (wolf), 60, 64, 127, 133, 160, 180,
    280–3
Fensalir, 189

Finn (Irish hero), 40–1, 76, 203–4
Finnbogi the Strong, 265
Fir Bolg, 160
Fitela (Sinfjötli), 201
Fjalar (dwarf), 36–8
Fjölnir, 62, 191, 216
Fjǫlsvinnsmál, 132, 136
Fjörgyn (Jörð), 97, 189
Fjörgynn (god), 97, 189
Fjǫturlundr (Fetter-grove), 74
Flateyjarbók, 67, 82, 129, 140, 217, 256
Flóki, 60, 249, 258
Flosi, 131
Folkvangr (home of Freyja), 177
Fomorians, 160–1
Fornaldar Sögur, 20, 53
Forseti, 106, 238
'Fragmentary History of Ancient Kings,'
    212–13
Frazer, J. G., 50
Freki (wolf), 54, 60, 258
Freyfaxi, 167, 254
Freyja, 3, 10–11, 40, 46, 55, 65–6, 77, 81,
    120, 130, 134–6, 141, 156, 159, 162,
    168, 170, 172, 175–9, 183, 187–9, 217,
    225–6, 239, 280
Freyr, 18–19, 26, 33, 52, 55–6, 62, 65–6,
    69–70, 82, 86, 90, 93, 95–6, 100, 107,
    109, 117, 124–5, 137, 152, 156, 159,
    162–3, 165–70, 172–8, 183–4, 187,
    191, 193, 212, 214, 216–19, 224, 226,
    231, 234, 237, 246–9, 251–6, 258–9,
    261, 281, 284
Freysfaxi, 167
Freysgoði (Freyr's priest), 65, 166, 172,
    261
Freysgyðlingar, 166, 172, 261
Fricco, see Freyr
Fricg (Frycg), see Frigg
Frigg, 33, 53, 55, 63, 67, 72–3, 106–9,
    111, 118, 124, 130, 134, 180, 184,
    188–9, 209
Frija, see Frigg
friðgeard (or *friðsplott*), 236–8
Friðþjófs Saga, 116
Frøblod or Frøblot (Freyr's sacrifice), 173
    214, 217
Fróði (the name of several kings of the
    Danes), 166, 169–70, 172–3, 209
Fróða friðr (Peace of Fróði), 169

Fulla (Fyllr, Fylla), 124
fylgja (pl. *fylgjur*), 221, 223–4, 227–30

Galar (dwarf), 36, 38
Gangleri, 61–2
Gapt, 190
Garm, 181, 280
Gauka-Thórir, 265–6
Gautr (Geat, Geata), 62, 70, 190–1
Gautreks Saga, 44, 46, 205–8, 254
Gefjun, 15, 178, 180, 187–8
Gefn, see Freyja
Geirröð (*Geirrøðr*), 15, 31–2, 76, 78–81,
    85, 98, 128, 134, 224
Geirstaðaálfr (Elf of Geirstaðir), 193, 231
Geri (wolf), 54, 60, 258
Gersemi (daughter of Freyja), 159, 176
Gerð (Freyr's wife), 165, 170, 174, 177,
    187, 216, 247
Gilling (giant), 36, 39
Gimlé, 281
Ginnungagap, 275
Gísla Saga, 166, 224, 271
Gísli Súrsson, 17, 38, 57
Gizur Grýtingaliði, 51, 53
Gizur Gullbrárskáld, 16, 258
Gizur Hallson, 28
Gjallarhorn (the ringing horn), 149, 154
Gjálp (*Gjǫlp*), 85
Gjöll (river), 107, 215
Gjúki (Gibica), 197, 199, 209
Glasir (tree), 246
Glaðsheimr (World of Joy), 54
Glúm (*Víga-Glúmr*), 69–70, 165–6, 230,
    251
Godan, see Wotan
Gonda, J., 104
goði (pl. *goðar*), 260, 263
Grettir Ásmundarson, 16, 148, 151
Grím Kamban, 195
Grimm, J., 4, 54, 103, 143
Grímismál (Words of Grímnir, Óðinn),
    10, 13, 52, 54, 56, 58, 61, 63–4, 108,
    125, 148, 173, 177, 182, 185, 231–4,
    275–6
Gríplur, 218–19
Gríð (giantess), 79, 85
Gróa (witch), 78
Grottasǫngr, 169
Grutte Grey-beard, 154

Gulaþing (Law of), 260
Gullinbursti (Golden-bristled), 107, 168
Gullinkambi (Golden-combed), 215
Gullintanni (Golden-toothed), 151
Gullveig, 158–9, 280
Gundestrup Bowl, 252
Gundicarius (Gunnar), 197
Gungnir (spear), 43, 137, 233
Gunnar (legendary hero), 197, 202, 224
Gunnar Helming, 169–70, 211, 247
Gunnar of Hlíðarendi, 120, 229
Gunnars Þáttr, 172
Gunnhild (Queen), 52, 213, 232
Gunnlaug Leifsson, 90, 223
Gunnlöð (giantess), 36–7
Guðmund of Glæsisvellir (the Shining Fields), 32, 80
Gutenbrunner, S., 122
Guðbrand of Dalar, 244
Guðmund the Mighty, 229
Guðrún (Gjúkadóttir), 57, 182, 197–8, 202
Guðrúnarhvǫt, 197
Guðrúnarkviða II, 199
Gylfaginning (Deceiving of Gylfi), 13, 23–4, 54, 108, 147, 149
Gylfi (King of the Swedes), 23–4, 187
Gymir (giant), 174

Hadding (Hadingus, pl. Haddingjar), 30, 173, 212–17, 219, 273
Hákon the Good, 12, 14, 52, 55, 84, 185, 213, 241, 251, 259, 261, 282
Hákon the Great, 15, 53, 60, 91, 128
Hákon Hákonarson, 23
Hákonarmál (Lay of Hákon), 14, 52–4, 185, 213
Háleygjatal, 56, 191
Hálfan the Black, 192
Hálfdan Highleg, 254
Hálfs Saga ok Hálfsrekka, 40
Hall (of Síða), 222
Hall (the godless), 264
Hallfreð (poet), 16, 38–9, 83, 169, 176, 228, 247
Hallfreðar Saga, 228
hamingja, 227, 230
Hamel, A. G. van, 50
Hamðir, 197, 202, 221
Hamðismál, 12, 197

Harald Bluetooth, 27
Harald Finehair, 1, 14, 53–4, 59, 67–8, 126, 192–3, 240, 268
Harald Gormsson, King of the Danes, 233
Harald Greycloak, 193
Harald Wartooth, 29, 31, 51, 53, 115, 119, 206, 210–13, 215, 220
Haraldskvæði (Lay of Harald), 14, 67
Hárbarðsljóð, 11, 51, 78, 97, 210–11
Harðgreip (Harthgrepa), 213
Hasdingi, 218
Hasting (Hæsten), 216
Hatherus, 207
Háttatal (List of verse-forms), 22
Haðar Saga (Saga of Höð), 114
Hauk Erlendsson, 17
Hauk Valdísarson, 144
Hauksbók, 139, 220, 233–4
Haustlǫng, 76–8, 81, 126–8, 132–4, 139, 141, 186
Hávamál (Words of the High one, Óðinn), 11–13, 36–7, 39, 42–4, 48–9, 52, 72, 74, 209, 214, 267–8, 273, 278
Hæðcyn, 120–1
Heardingas, 171, 218–9
Heaðobards, 210–11
Heimdalargaldr (the Magic Song of Heimdall), 147–8
Heimdall (Heimdalr, Heimdallr), 15, 49, 55, 82, 107, 109, 129, 133, 140, 147–54, 281
Heimskringla, 25–6, 30, 259, 262
Heið (Heiðr), 158–9
Heiðrek the Wise, King, 255
Heiðreks Saga, 20, 51, 53, 221–5, 239–40, 255
Heiðrún (goat), 54, 176
Hel, 49, 60, 107, 109, 120, 128, 133, 140, 215, 271, 279
Helgakviða Hjǫrvarðssonar, 259
Helgakviða Hundingsbana II, 47, 51, 58, 73–4, 207–8, 237
Helgi the Lean, 84, 88, 166
Helgi Hjǫrvarðsson, 11
Helgi Hundingsbani, 9, 11, 21 47, 51, 73–4, 199, 206, 208, 217, 219
Helgi Trausti, 258
Heliand, 284
Hemra (mythical river), 80

Hengest (Hengist), 70, 220
Hercules (Barbatus, Magusanus, Saxanus), 103
Herebeald, 120–1
Heremod, 185
Hermóð, 57, 80, 107, 110, 185, 189, 215
Heroic Sagas, see *Fornaldar Sögur*
Heusler, A., 33, 202
Hillebrandt, A., 41
Historia de antiquitate regum norwagensium, 18
Historia Langobardorum, 72
Historia Norvegiae, 46, 226, 253
History of the Bishops of Hamburg, see Adam of Bremen
Hjalti (Danish hero), 30
Hjörleif, 232, 264–5
Hlaðir, Jarls of (*Hlaða Jarlar*), 56, 164
Hliðskjálf, 55, 63–4, 73, 149
Hlöð, King of the Huns, 51
Hnitbjörg (mythical rock), 36–7
Hnoss (daughter of Freyja), 159, 176
Hoddmímisholt (mythical forest), 283
Hœnir, 56, 127–8, 132, 138–9, 141–2, 156, 277
hof (temple), 240, 241, 243, 251
hofgyðja (temple-priestess), 172, 261
Höfler, O., 60, 199
Hofstaðir (Temple-steads), 240–1, 243
Hofuðlausn (Head-ransom), 37
Högni (Hagen), 202–3
Hollander, L. M., 31
Hora galles, 98
hörgr (shrine), 178, 239–41
Hörn (*Horn*, goddess), 3, 178
Horsa, 70, 220
Höð (*Hoðr*), 32–3, 106, 108–11, 112–15, 118–19, 121, 124, 133, 140, 143, 146, 202, 211, 281
Hrafnkell Freysgoði, 19, 65, 167, 249
Hrafnkels Saga, 19–20, 167, 254
Hrafnsmál (Words of the Raven), 14, 59
Hreiðmar, 138, 200
Hrímfaxi (Frost-maned), 5
Hrímgrímnir (Frost-masked), 174
hrímþursar (frost-giants), 170, 177
Hring, 51, 212
Hringhorni (ship), 107
Hrólf Kraki, 20, 30, 31, 87, 220, 264
Hrólfs Saga Kraka, 31

Hrólf of Skálmarnes, 21
Hrómund Gripsson, 21, 219
Hröngvið (viking), 21
Hrungnir (giant), 15, 76–7, 176
Hrym (giant), 140
Huginn (raven), 54, 57–8, 142, 229, 258
Hunding, King of the Swedes, 215–16
Húsdrápa (House-lay), 15, 82, 109, 128–9, 175
Húskarlahvöt (Incitement of Housecarles), 30
Hvergelmir (mythical well), 275, 279
Hymir (giant), 181
Hymiskviða, 76, 81–2, 101, 132, 137, 181
Hyndluljóð, 52, 56, 129, 176, 178, 185, 220, 239–40

Ibn Fadlán (Fozlan), 8, 215, 272
Ibn Rustah, 253, 272
Ibor (Lombard), 72
Indra, 41, 76, 103–4, 200, 204
Ing, 156, 165, 170–3, 218
Ingel, 210
Ingimund the Old, 248
Ingjald (Ingellus), 166, 209–10
Ingólf (settler of Iceland), 264–5
Ingvaz, 191
Irmin, 62, 102
Irminsul, 102, 246
Istraz, 191
Ívaldi (black elf, dwarf), 137, 234
Iðunn, 15, 127–8, 132–4, 164, 175, 180, 185–7

Járnsaxa (giantess), 77, 144
Jól (Yule), 61
Jómsborg vikings, 259
Jón Loptsson, 21, 22
Jordanes, 7, 26, 46, 73, 190, 197, 252
Jörmunrekk, 197–8
Jörð (Earth), 55, 97, 104, 189

Kalevala, 124
Kálfsvísa, 124
Kára (heroine), 217–18
Kárulkjóð, 21, 217
Ketill Hœngr, 264
Kirby, W. F., 123
Klæber, F., 121
Knútsdrápa, 255

Kormák (Icelandic poet), 77, 111, 282
Kristni Saga, 89, 237, 250, 261
Kuhn, H., 117
Kvasir, 35, 39–40, 139, 156–7, 160

Landdísasteinar (Stones of the land dísir), 225
Landnámabók, 17, 84, 86–8, 232, 238–9, 241, 243, 254, 261, 264
landvættir, 225, 232–3, 237
Lárusson, Ólafur, 183
Laxdœla Saga, 109
Lay of Eirík, see Eiríksmál
Lay of Hákon see Hákonarmál
Lay of Hildebrand, 9
Lævateinn (the guileful twig), 132, 136
Legendary Saga of St Ólaf, 247
Lemminkäinen (Finnish hero), 118, 122
Lenno (Hlenni), 207
Libellus Islandorum (Íslendingabók), 17, 163
Lindquist, S., 245
Liser (viking), 214, 216
Litr (dwarf), 107
ljósálfar, 231
Ljóðaháttr, 30
Ljósvetninga Saga, 151
Ljóðatal (list of songs), 11
Lofn (goddess), 189
Logaþore, 100
Lokasenna (Flyting of Loki), 10, 13, 97, 109, 130–2, 139–40, 159, 162, 170, 174, 185, 188–9, 284
Loka-táttur, 141
Loker, 214
Loki, 10–11, 15, 23, 38, 55–6, 60, 79, 82, 106, 108–14, 126–48, 154, 162, 164, 180, 185–6, 226, 234, 280–1, 284
Lóður, 56, 142–4, 277
Lug (Irish hero), 160–1, 181

Macdonell, A. A., 41
Mac Datho's Pig, Story of, 153
Macgnimartha Finn, 203
Magni (son of Thór), 77, 283
Magnús Bareleg, King, 22
Magnús the Blind, King, 148
Magnús, Bishop of Skálaholt, 29
Magnus, Olaus, 61
Magnússon, E., 193

Málaháttr, 85
Málsháttakvæði, 51
Mannus, 191
Mardöll (or Marþöll), 153, 178
Marduk, 76, 200
Maringer, J., 3
Martin, St, Life of, 95
megingjarðar (belt of Thór), 85
Melabók, 17
Meldos (Celtic god?), 102
Mes-Gegra, King, 152–3
Mímameið (Mímameiðr) see Yggdrasill
Mímir, 63, 142–3, 149–50, 156, 279
Mímung (sword), 204
Mistilteinn (sword), 116
Mithotyn (magician), 184
Miðgarð, 13, 75, 135, 275
Miðgarðsorm, 75, 128
Mjöllnir (Thór's hammer), 75, 79, 81–2, 137, 233, 283
Mogk, E., 109
Morris, William, 193
Móði (son of Thór), 283
Muninn (Óðinn's raven), 54, 57–8, 142, 230, 258
Murphy, G., 203
Múspell, 132, 140, 275–6, 281, 284

Naglfar (ship), 281, 284
Nanna Nepsdóttir, 106–7, 112–15
Nari (Narfi), 133, 140, 226
Narts, 146
Násheimr (World of Death), 57
Náströnd (Shore of corpses), 280
Neckel, G., 117
Nerthus, 7, 156, 165, 167, 173–4, 177, 236, 246, 254, 262
Nestorian Chronicle, 7
Nibelunc, 202
Nibelungenlied, 198, 203–4
Niflhel (Niflheimr), 49, 109, 135, 271, 275
Niflungar, 201–3, 234
Nine Herbs Charm, 70
Níðhögg, 279–80
Najáll, 131, 229
Njáls Saga, 60, 89, 131, 222
Njörð, 11, 18, 26, 30, 43, 52, 55, 56, 65–77, 86–90, 100, 134, 156–7, 162–5, 172, 174–5, 182, 184, 211, 215–7, 236, 251, 257, 259

Nóatún (Place of ships, harbour), 163–5
Nordal, S., 69, 282
Nóregs Konunga Tal (List of the Kings of Norway), 22
Norna-Gests Þáttr, 209
Norðri (dwarf), 234
Nuadu (Irish hero), 123, 160, 181

Ódáinsakr (field of eternal life), 32
Odd Snorrason, 90–1, 272
Oddaverjar, 22
Oisín (Irish hero), 204
Ólaf the Elf, 194, 231
Ólaf the Peacock, 109, 248
Ólaf, St, 16, 18, 30, 48, 90–1, 193–4, 230, 247, 256–7, 265–6
Ólaf the Stout (Digri), 194
Ólaf Trételgja (Wood-cutter), 46, 192, 261
Ólaf Tryggvason, 16, 18, 28, 32, 38, 80, 82–3, 90–1, 147–9, 194, 223, 228, 244, 247–8, 266, 272
Old English Chronicle, 59
Old English Runic Poem, 170–1
Olo, 207, 209
Ollerus (Ull), 184
Olrik, A., 27–30, 40, 98, 144–5, 283
Olsen, M., 2, 10, 54, 64, 66, 92, 116, 120, 174, 178
O'Rahilly, T. F., 203
Qrboða see *Aurboða*
Origo gentis Langobardorum, 72
Orkneyinga Saga, 22, 53, 60
Örlyg (settler of Iceland), 88
Örvar-Odd (Arrow-Odd), 229, 264
Óð (*Óðr*), 176, 183
Óðinn, 2, 9–13, 16, 25–6, 31, 33, 38–74, 77, 84–5, 90, 93, 95, 100, 103–5, 107–111, 113–15, 118–19, 121–2, 125, 127–134, 137–46, 149–56, 158–9, 161–4, 166, 168–9, 176–7, 181–5, 187–8, 190–2, 198, 201–2, 204–17, 224, 229–30, 233–4, 236–7, 246, 248–9, 251–5, 258–259, 261, 263–4, 267, 269, 275, 277–83
Óðrœrir (heart-stirrer), 36–7
Óðinsdagr (Wednesday),73
Oþon (Óðinn), 95

Passio et Vita Waldevi, 59

Patrick, Bishop, 87
Patrick's Fjord (*Patreksfjörðr*), 87
Paulus Diaconus, 72–3
Perkunas, 96–7
Perun, 96–7
Phol, 124–5
Pliny, the Elder, 7
Procopius, 46, 252, 254
Pytheas, 7

Ragnar Loðbrók, 15, 20, 59, 255
Ragnarök (Doom of the gods), 9–10, 23, 53–4, 60, 64, 76, 110–11, 118, 127, 132, 140, 142, 144, 145, 147–9, 152, 181
Ragnarsdrápa (Lay of Ragnar), 15, 75–6, 185, 188, 197
Ragnars Saga Loðbrókar, 256
Ragnhild (Regnilda), 214–6
Raos, 218
Raptos, 218
Rati (gimlet?), 36–7
Reginn, 203–4
Reginsmál, 132, 138, 204, 254
Regnaldus, 209
Rerum Danicarum Fragmenta, 209
Revelation, 223, 231
Ríg (*Rígr*), 150–2
Rígsþula, 13, 150–1
Rimbert, 7, 195
Rind (*Rindr, Rinda*), 33, 55, 110, 113
Rosomoni, 197
Ross, A. S. C., 119
Rúnatals Þáttr, 37, 42, 49
Runic Poem (Icelandic), 71
Rydberg, V., 103

Salgofnir (cock), 215, 273
Salomon and Saturn, 71, 99
Saxnot, 100
Saxo Grammaticus, 21, 27–34, 51, 53, 78, 80, 82, 106, 112–16, 138, 169, 170, 173, 182, 184, 188, 191, 206, 209–10, 212–19
Sæming, 56, 164, 191
Sæmund Sigfússon, 17, 22
Schröder, F. R., 117–18, 122–3
Scylfingas, 62, 64
Seaxnet, see Saxnot

Second Lay of Helgi Hundingsbani see *Helga Kviða Hundingsbana* II
Second Merseburg Charm, 73, 122–5, 188
Segimerus (*Sigmarr*), 199
Seip. D. A., 12
seiðr (witchcraft), 65, 159–60, 175, 177
Shetelig, H., 272
Síbilja (cow), 256
Sif (wife of Thór), 77, 98, 133, 137, 170, 177, 182, 233
Sigeberht, 199–201, 204
Sigfrid, 199, 201
Sighvat (Sigvat, Icelandic poet), 48, 230–1, 255
Sigmund Völsung hero), 52–3, 61, 115, 118, 185, 200–1
Signý (mother of Sinfjötli), 201
Sigrdrífa (Victory-giver), 198
Sigrdrjfumál (Words of Sigrdrífa), 12, 56, 142, 180, 185, 198
Sigrún (mistress of Helgi), 217
Sigurð (the Dragon-slayer), 6, 9, 12, 41, 59–60, 76, 102, 111, 120, 150, 153, 197
Sigurð (*Hjǫrtr*, Hart), 199
Sigurð Hlöðvésson, Jarl of Orkney, 60
Sigurð, Jarl of Hlaðir, 260
Sigyn (wife of Loki), 108, 127–8, 133, 140
Sinfjötli (Fitela), 52, 60, 185, 200–1
Siward of Northumbria, 59–60
Sjöfn (goddess), 189
Skáldatal (List of Poets), 212
Skáldskaparmál (Speech of Poetry), 22, 25, 35, 109, 133, 148, 156, 160, 169
Skarpheðinn (Icelandic hero), 131
Skaði (daughter of Thjazi), 30, 56, 130, 134, 139–40, 144, 164–5, 174, 182, 215–6, 257
Skinfaxi (Shining maned), 5
Skírnir, 174–5, 187
Skírnismál, 9, 13, 110, 174–5, 187, 237
Skíðblaðnir (ship), 137, 173, 234
Skjöld, 56, 191
Skjöldungar, 22, 56, 191
Skjǫldunga Saga, 20, 22, 24, 31, 212
Skuld (goddess of fate), 280
Sleipnir (Óðinn's horse), 33, 48, 56–7, 129, 134–5
Slíðrugtanni (Cutting-tusked, boar), 107, 168

Snorri Goði, 18
Snorri Sturluson, 3, 6, 8, 13, 15–18, 21–26, 30–1, 33, 35–7, 39–40, 43–4, 46, 49–52, 54–58, 61–3, 76–9, 81, 84, 85–6, 98, 104, 106–15, 118–19, 121, 127–38, 140–3, 146–50, 153–6, 162–4, 169–70, 173, 176–7, 180–2, 185, 187–9, 191–3, 197–8, 209, 226, 231–5, 238–41, 247, 249, 251, 253, 255–6, 259, 265, 271, 275–9, 283–6
Sǫgubrot (Fragmentary History of Kings of Denmark), 29, 142
Sǫrla Þáttr, 140
Sörli, 197, 202, 221
Soslan (or Sosryko), 146
stafgarðr, 237–8
Starkað, 29, 35, 44–5, 68, 174, 205–11
Starkað Aludreng, 208
Steingerð (mistress of Kormák), 282
Steinunn (poetess), 16, 89
Steinvör (priestess), 261
Storms, G., 70
Stórvirkr (Man of Great Deeds), 205
Ström, F., 257
Strömbäck, D., 19, 83–4, 223
Sturla Thórðarson, 17, 52
Styrbjarnar Þáttr, 47
Styrmir Kárason, 168
Surt (*Surtr*, fire giant), 38, 275, 281, 284
Suttung (giant), 36–7, 39
Suðri (dwarf), 234
Svanhild (Swan-Hild), 197–8
Svartálfaheimr (World of Black Elves), 235
Svaðilfari (stallion), 56, 134–5
Sváva (heroine), 74
Sveinn Tjúguskegg, 259
Sverrir (King of Norway), 29
Syrdon, 146

Tacitus, 7, 27, 73, 102, 199, 219, 236, 246, 249, 252, 260–1, 271–2
Tanais (river), 156
Tanfana, 236
Taranis (Celtic god?), 102
Thangbrand (missionary), 16, 89–90
Theodoric (King of Goths), 190
Theodricus (Theodoricus, Norwegian historian), 18
Thiðrandi, 221–7, 256
Thjálfi, 77–8, 82, 132, 137

Thjazi (giant), 127, 130, 133–4, 139, 257
Thjóðólf of Hvin, 14–15, 26, 68, 76, 126–129, 142, 186
Thökk (giantess), 107, 111, 120
Thór, 2, 5, 10–11, 13, 15–16, 20, 25, 32–33, 41, 44–5, 50, 55, 67, 69, 73, 75–99, 101, 104–5, 107, 113, 128, 130–2, 134–5, 137–9, 144, 151, 153–4, 166, 168–9, 181, 183, 189–90, 200, 204–7, 209–11, 215, 220, 233–5, 237–8, 240–1, 246–51, 261–2, 281
Thorbjörn Dísarskáld (Poet of the Dís), 76, 85, 89
Thorbjörn Hornklofi, 14, 59, 63, 67, 175
Thorfinn Karlsefni, 89
Thorfinn, Jarl of Orkney, 282
Thorgerð Hörgarbrúð, 247
Thorgrím Freysgoði (Priest of Freyr), 166–7, 224
Thorhadd (settler of Iceland), 260
Thorhall, 89, 120, 222–3
Thorkell the Tall, 252, 256
Thorkillus (see Thurkillus)
Thorleif (poet), 53
Thormóð (Icelandic poet), 30, 111, 257
Thórólf Clubfoot, 269–70
Thórólf Mostrarskegg (settler of Iceland), 87, 220, 240, 248
Thorsteinn Bœjarmagn, see Þorsteins Þáttr
Thorvald (Icelandic missionary), 261
Thorvald Tasaldi, 266
Thórð Freysgoði (Freyr's priest), 166, 172
Thrúð (daughter of Thór), 77
Thrúðheim (World of Might), 75
Thrúðvangar (Fields of Might), 75, 78
Thrym (giant), 10, 177
Thrymheim, 164
Thunaer (Thór), 100
Thund (Þundr, Óðinn), 49
Thunor (Þunor), 98, 100
Thuríð (priestess), 172
Thurkillus, 31–2, 80, 138
Tiermes, see Diermes
Tiw (Tig), 182
Tomar, 94
Torf-Einar, Jarl of Orkney, 53, 254
Tuatha Dé Danann, 160–1
Tuirenn (children of), 175, 186

Tuisto, 27, 191
Tuonela (swan of), 118
Tvastr, 104
Tylenses (men of Iceland), 28
Týr, 28, 63, 73, 100, 103, 161, 180–4, 190
Tyrfing (sword), 234

Þáttr af Ragnars sonum, 255
Þiðreks Saga, 198–200, 202–4
Þorbjörn Hornklofi, 54 (see Thorbjörn Hornklofi)
Þorgils Saga ok Hafliða, 21
Þorgrímsþula, 124
Þórsdrápa (Lay of Thór), 15, 31, 78–9, 85, 98, 128, 134
Þorsteins Þáttr. Bœjarmagns, 31–2, 80
Þorvalds Þáttr Víðforla, 237, 250
Þrymskviða, 9, 13, 81, 132, 137, 144, 154, 170, 177

Ukko, 98
Úlfljót, 260
Úlf Uggason, 76, 109, 128, 147
Ull (Ullr, Ullinn), 3, 66, 164, 176, 182–4, 225
Urðarbrunnr (Well of Fate), 246, 277, 279
Útgarðaloki (Utgardilocus), 82, 137–8
Útgarð, 138

Vafthrúðnir (Vafþrúðnir), giant, 10, 49, 110
Vafþrúðnismál (Words of Vafthrúðnir), 5, 10, 13, 49, 110, 234, 271, 275–7, 283, 285
Valdemar the Great, King, 27–8
Valgrind (Grill of the Fallen), 54
Valhöll (Valhǫll), 10, 14, 33, 52, 54–5, 57, 67, 75, 77, 84, 101, 115, 135, 176, 184
Váli (son of Óðinn), 55, 64, 110, 114, 139–40, 283
Vanadís (Goddess of the Vanir, Freyja), 136, 159, 175, 225–6, 231
Vanaheimr or Vanaland, 156–7
Vanir, 26, 35, 40, 47, 55, 103, 136, 141–2, 154, 156–63, 165, 168, 170–2, 175–6
Vápnfirðinga Saga, 261

Vár (goddess), 189
Varuna, 103
Varus, 199
Vatnsdæla Saga, 167, 229
Vé (brother of Óðinn), 55–6, 184, 188, 275, 277
Végeirr, 238
Vellekla (Gold Dearth), 15, 53, 60
Vercelli Codex, 119
Verðandi (Fate goddess), 280
Vestri (dwarf), 234
Vetrliði Sumarliðason, 75 85, 89, 211
Víga-Glúm, 69
Víga-Glúms Saga, 165–6, 168, 221, 252, 255–6
Vigfúss of Vörs, 69–70
Víkar, King, 44–6, 48, 118, 206–7, 211, 253
Vili (brother of Óðinn), 55–6, 184, 188, 275, 277
Vimur (mythical river), 79–80
Vitazgjafi (the certain giver), 69–70, 165–6
Vita Anskarii, 7
Viðar (son of Óðinn), 64, 281, 283
Víðófnir (cock), 132
Volla (Folla), 124, 188
Volos, 96
Vǫlsa Þáttr (Story of Völsi), 256
Völsi (*Vǫlsi*), 96, 201, 231, 257–8, 263
Völsungar, 53, 56, 61, 200–1, 212, 234
Vǫlsunga Saga, 20, 197–8, 200–2, 204

Vǫluspá (Sibyl's Prophecy), 9, 12–13, 23, 45, 49, 63, 76, 97, 101–2, 108–11, 115, 119, 129, 131–2, 135–40, 143, 150, 154–5, 157, 159, 170, 176–7, 215, 234, 275–7, 280–4
Völuspá (Short), 129, 133–4, 137, 147, 152
Vries, J. de, 154, 184, 209

Wæls (*Wælses eafera*), 201
Wælsing (*Vǫlsungr*), 201
Widsith, 31
Wilfred (missionary), 93
Winnili, 72
Wodan, Woden, see Óðinn
Wulfstan (homilist), 95

Ýdalir (Yew-dales), 182
Yggdrasill (tree of fate), 65, 75, 116, 124, 132, 148–9, 183, 246, 277, 279, 281
Ylfagescot, 232
Ymir (giant), 10, 234, 275–8
Ynglinga Saga, 26, 35, 40, 43–4, 46, 61–2, 142, 156, 158, 163, 169, 187
Ynglinga Tal (List of the Ynglingar), 14, 20, 26, 46, 56, 128, 192, 226, 234
Ynglingar, 56, 62, 68, 91–2, 94, 100, 170, 174
Yngvi (Freyr), 26, 169
Yngvi, King of the Turks, 56, 163

Zurvan, 278